Child Psychology
A Contemporary Viewpoint

McGRAW-HILL SERIES IN PSYCHOLOGY
CONSULTING EDITORS
Norman Garmezy

Adams Human Memory
Berlyne Conflict, Arousal, and Curiosity
Blum Psychoanalytic Theories of Personality
Bock Multivariate Statistical Methods in Behavioral Research
Brown The Motivation of Behavior
Campbell, Dunnette, Lawler, and Weick Managerial Behavior, Performance, and Effectiveness
Crites Vocational Psychology
D'Amato Experimental Psychology: Methodology, Psychophysics, and Learning
Dollard and Miller Personality and Psychotherapy
Ferguson Statistical Analysis in Psychology and Education
Fedor, Bever, and Garrett The Psychology of Language: An Introduction to Psycholinguistics and Generative Grammar
Forgus and Melamed Perception: A Cognitive-Stage Approach
Franks Behavior Therapy: Appraisal and Status
Gilmer and Deci Industrial and Organizational Psychology
Guilford Psychometric Methods
Guilford The Nature of Human Intelligence
Guilford and Fruchter Fundamental Statistics in Psychology and Education
Guilford and Hoepfner The Analysis of Intelligence
Guion Personnel Testing
Hetherington and Parke Child Psychology: A Contemporary Viewpoint
Hirsh The Measurement of Hearing
Hjelle and Ziegler Personality Theories: Basic Assumptions, Research, and Applications
Horowitz Elements of Statistics for Psychology and Education
Hulse, Deese, and Egeth The Psychology of Learning
Hurlock Adolescent Development
Hurlock Child Development
Hurlock Developmental Psychology
Krech, Crutchfield, and Ballachey Individual in Society
Lakin Interpersonal Encounter: Theory and Practice in Sensitivity Training

Child Psychology
A Contemporary Viewpoint
Second Edition

E. Mavis Hetherington
University of Virginia

Ross D. Parke
University of Illinois
at Champaign-Urbana

McGraw-Hill Book Company

New York St. Louis San Francisco Auckland Bogotá Düsseldorf
Johannesburg London Madrid Mexico Montreal New Delhi
Panama Paris São Paulo Singapore Sydney Tokyo Toronto

CHILD PSYCHOLOGY
A Contemporary Viewpoint

567890VHVH 83210

This book was set in Souvenir Light by Black Dot, Inc. The editors were Janis M. Yates and James R. Belser; the designer was Joseph Gillians; the production supervisor was Dennis J. Conroy. New drawings were done by J & R Services, Inc.
Von Hoffmann Press, Inc., was printer and binder.

Library of Congress Cataloging in Publication Data

Hetherington, Eileen Mavis, date
  Child psychology.

  (McGraw-Hill series in psychology)
  Includes bibliographical references and index.
  1. Child psychology. I. Parke, Ross D., joint author. II. Title.
BF721.H418 1979   155.4   78-27624
ISBN 0-07-028431-8

To John and Sue
and our children:
Grant, Eric, and Jason
Gillian, Timothy, and Megan

Contents

Amount of Stimulation and Organization of the Environment. The
Effects of Television on Family Interaction.

Preface

Our goals in this second edition of *Child Psychology: A Contemporary Viewpoint* remain the same as in our first edition. Our primary aim is to present the best contemporary ideas and issues in child psychology in a way that students at all levels can understand and appreciate. To attain our goal we have used a number of distinctive features in this edition.

1 *Topic orientation:* This book is oriented around such topics as: cognition, intelligence, language, early experience, genetics, sex typing, and moral development rather than chronologically organized. Within each specific topic area, the significant developmental changes that occur are discussed.

2 *Multiple theoretical viewpoints:* Topical organization permits a more adequate and sophisticated presentation of the theories that guide research in each area and recognizes that there are few universal theories of child behavior, but rather that there are smaller theories to guide research in specific topic areas.

   Books often have special theoretical viewpoints such as a behavioral bent, a social stance, a biological bias, or a cognitive cast. This volume is a theoretically eclectic. Each orientation is represented but in varying degrees in different topics. Naturally, biological factors predominate in our discussions of genetics and of early development, but these same factors receive their due in our discussions of other topics as well, such as sex typing. Similarly, social factors predominate in our discussions of the family and peers, but cognitive, behavioral, and biological factors are interwoven in these discussions as well. Cognitive factors get special treatment in our discussion of intellectual and language development, but again other factors, such as social dimensions, play a significant role. This orientation reflects the increasing recognition of the interplay among biological, cognitive, and social factors in children.

3 *Process orientation:* There is an emphasis on the processes of development. In each topic area the processes that are responsible for changes in the child's development are stressed. As a result, the student not only knows the content of development, but understands the processes underlying development. This process focus is the distinguishing feature of child psychology in the last fifteen years.

4 *Research orientation:* In line with our emphasis on child psychology as a scientific discipline are the illustration and discussion of the research methods used by workers in the field in order to ensure that the student gains an understanding of the methodological approaches unique to child psychology. To reflect recent methodological advances, naturalistic field studies as well as laboratory studies are emphasized.

5 *The applied-basic relationship:* Some instructors like a "basic" text while others prefer an applied orientation. We think that this is an unnecessary and artifical distinction. We have tried instead to show how "basic" information about the processes of development can have implications for understanding a wide range of real-life problems. For example, our discussion of the role of imitation in learning focuses on the effects of television on children's cognitive and social development. Studies of the effects of distractors, such as roadway noise, can help us understand the development of reading. Theories of early mother-infant attachment have clear implications for understanding the effects of day care. Child abuse, desegregation, and mainstreaming are other examples of applied topics that are highlighted in this revision. Field studies are given greater emphasis in this revision in other to illustrate the application of laboratory findings to real-life situations. Throughout the book, we have consistently tried to illustrate the interplay between applied and basic research.

Some Highlights of the Revised Research

In this revised edition, we have rewritten all the chapters to reflect recent advances in the field. Our coverage of cognitive development has been expanded by the addition of a new chapter that treats cognitive development from an information-processing viewpoint. Recent studies of attention, meta-memory, and problem solving are included. Social cognition receives more space in this edition. The language chapter reflects recent interest in the development of meaning and children's understanding of the social rules of language, or pragmatics. Our treatment of infancy and early development includes recent studies of the effects of prematurity and low birthweight, crib death or the Sudden Infant Death Syndrome, the role of the father in early infancy, and the development of imitation in the first two years of life. New information on social development is reflected in new investigations of play and peers as well as in the effects of divorce, single-parent families, and working mothers on children's social and cognitive development. Recent investigations of hormones and sex-role development are features. Recent work on alturism, including the early development of helping and sharing, received expanded treatment. New findings on agression also receive separate and more intensive coverage in this edition. Together these changes result in a current view of basic research on the principal topics of child psychology as well as an up-to-date review of recent trends in socially relevant problem areas.

Special Features

We have included a number of features that will make the book more interesting and more helpful for students.

1 *Boxes:* One of our special features is the use of "boxes" throughout the text. The aim of these boxes, which contain a detailed discussion of a particular study or a special issue, is to give students some of the flavor of research in child psychology and to permit an in-depth look at certain topics. Each chapter in the book contains a number of boxes. Some of the boxes focus on the effects of father absence, special ways of improving memory capacity, or alternative treatment strategies for hyperactive children. Others focus on communication development, androgyny in the school, or hormones and behavior.

2 *Glossary:* A glossary of the specialized terms that have been used in the book is provided at the end of the book to serve as a useful study aid for students.

3 *Chapter summaries:* At the end of each chapter, we have provided a summary of the main points in the chapter. This also should be a useful study aid for students.

4 *References:* Many books include the references at the end of the book; instead, we have included the references at the end of each chapter. This makes it easier to follow up a topic or point of interest.

5 *Separate author and subject index:* A separate index for the authors cited in the book and a separate index for different topics are included. The subject or topic index will aid the student in finding related material in different parts of the book.

Supplementary Aids

1 *A Study Guide,* which summarizes the main points in each chapter and provides review questions plus a chapter-by-chapter glossary, is available. This will be a particularly helpful aid for students and will ensure that they understand the material presented in the text.

2 *A Teacher's Manual,* which summarizes the main points in each chapter and provides and extensive list of test questions as well as class and field exercises, is available to all instructors who adopt *Child Psychology.*

3 *A Book of Readings, Contemporary Readings in Child Psychology,* edited

by Professors Hetherington and Parke is available as a companion volume for the text. The book of readings is organized topically in order to complement the organization of the text. Brief introductions highlight the main features of the papers included in the reader. Both original research papers and recent reviews of major topics are included. The softback format is designed to keep reasonable the total cost of the text-reader combination.

A Comment on the Use of the Text: The Short versus the Long Course

The volume is organized around the one-semester or quarter course. However, there are ways in which the book can be used for shorter courses; for example, a brief course might emphasize early development, which would involve concentration on chapters 1, 2, 3, 4, 5, and 7. Alternatively, a short, cognitively oriented course could use chapters 1, 6, 8, 9, 10, and 11. An instructor with a social orientation might focus on chapters 1, 12, 13, 14, 15, and 16.

Special acknowledgement: Chapter 8–Language and communication of this edition draws substantially from the language chapter of the first edition which was written by Diana Arezzo Slaby.

A number of individuals have reviewed various chapters of our first edition in preparation for this revision, and others have provided helpful reviews of our manuscripts for this second edition. Thanks are extended for their constructive comments and suggestions: Dr. Tony Antonucci, Syracuse University; Dr. Raymond Baird, University of Texas, San Antonio; Dr. Lois Bloom, Teachers College–Columbia University; Dr. Rachel Clifton, University of Massachusetts; Dr. Walter Duryea, Montclair State College; Dr. Carol Eckerman, Duke University; Dr. Edward Fahrmeier, University of Maryland; Dr. Terrence Faw, Lewis and Clark College; Dr. Donna Gelfand, University of Utah; Dr. Rochel Gelman, University of Pennsylvania; Dr. Joseph Glick, City College of New York–Graduate Center; Dr. John Hagan, University of Michigan; Dr. Willard W. Hartup, University of Minnesota; Dr. Robert McCall, Boys Town, Nebraska; Dr. Ruth Montague, Murray State University; Dr. Kathryn Nelson, Yale University; Dr. Sandra Scarr-Salapatek, Yale University; Dr. Alexander Siegel, University of Pittsburgh; Dr. Joseph Smith, Shippenburg State College; Dr. Alan Sroufe, University of Minnesota; Dr. James Strazec, SUNY at Cortland.

Special thanks to Brenda Congdon and Carolyn O'Brien for their patient and professional assistance in preparing the manuscript.

E. Mavis Hetherington
Ross D. Parke

Child Psychology
A Contemporary Viewpoint

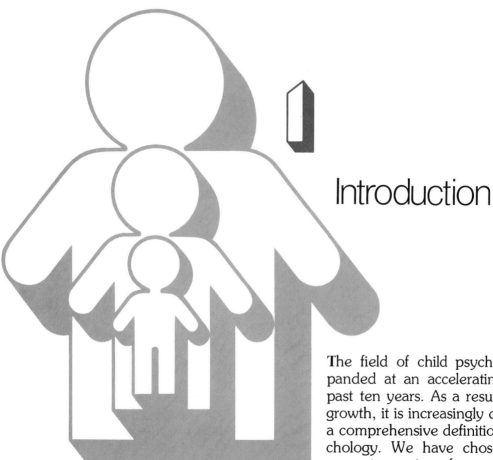

Introduction

The field of child psychology has expanded at an accelerating pace in the past ten years. As a result of this rapid growth, it is increasingly difficult to offer a comprehensive definition of child psychology. We have chosen instead to present a series of examples from the wide range of research activities that are subsumed under the child psychology label. From these examples you should gain a good idea of the content as well as the methods of child psychology today.

Two central issues concern the child psychologist: how do children change as they develop, and what are the determinants of these developmental changes? One can employ a variety of approaches in investigating these issues, but certain characteristics are common to all approaches to modern child psychology.

1

Unlike earlier approaches, contemporary child psychology is no longer only a description of age-related changes; rather, it is concerned with the processes that produce and account for these changes. It is this emphasis on the processes of development that best characterizes the current field. This volume is organized around these processes of development. In the later sections of the book we have tried to illustrate how these processes may account for specific aspects of the child's development. Within each of the topics developmental and age-related changes are recognized, but the focus is on the manner in which change takes place. This organization around specific topics and processes reflects the way that scientific information about children is generated. The field is highly specialized, with various viewpoints predominating in each topic area. Some theories are more appropriate for explaining language, while other theories provide a better framework for understanding socialization. Our central assumption is that child psychology is a science; therefore, in this volume, the emphasis is on our current understanding of the child as derived from scientific theory and investigation. As you will see shortly, a variety of methodologies and research strategies are employed to understand children, ranging from the laboratory experiment to observational studies of children in natural settings. In this chapter we will examine some of the primary approaches used to generate the building blocks of this volume, empirical data about children. Our emphasis on a scientific approach to child psychology does not mean that the information does not have applied implications and relevance to real-life events and problems. Throughout this book we will try to illustrate the implications and applications that child psychology can have for applied problems and real-life events.

In the next section, we present a sampling of the topics, trends, and methods that characterize the field of child psychology. Then we will discuss in detail some of the methods used in this field.

A Sample of Recent Research in Child Psychology

Now we turn to contemporary child psychology and a sample of recent research in the field. These examples will not only introduce you to the wide diversity of issues, topics, and questions studied by developmental psychologists, but also provide some examples of different methodological approaches employed in child psychology. After this sampling of investigations we will turn our attention to a detailed examination of the methods of this field.

Learning by Television: "Sesame Street"

Can children learn new intellectual skills from watching television? To answer this question, "Sesame Street" was introduced to millions of American children in 1969. The show aimed toward improving the cognitive skills of preschoolers so that they would be better prepared for elementary school education. By using TV as a medium, the Children's Television Workshop hoped to bring the educational message to a large portion of children who normally have no preschool education. Only 2 in every 5 three- and four-year-olds attend

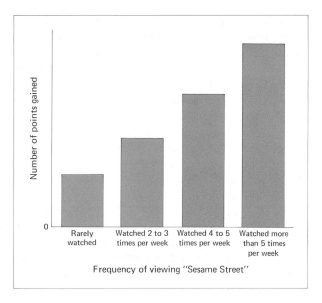

FIGURE 1-1 Improvement in total test scores for children with different amounts of viewing experience. *(Based on Ball & Bogatz, 1972.)*

preschool programs. The show introduced Cookie Monster, Bert, Ernie, and their zany companions. However, it was not merely puppets and a host of clever attention-holding tactics, but a well-defined set of educational goals that made "Sesame Street" so successful. And it has worked, as demonstrated in evaluations conducted by Ball and Bogatz (1972). Children were tested on a variety of items such as identifying body parts, letters, numbers, geometric forms, sorting, and classification before and after a six-month viewing period.

Although there was an initial concern that not enough children would watch to permit an evaluation, nearly everyone watched occasionally. Therefore, children were divided into four groups based on their frequency of watching the program: Group 1 watched "Sesame Street" rarely, group 2 watched two or three times a week, children in group 3 viewed four or five times a week, and group 4 viewers saw the program more than five times a week. Children who watched "Sesame Street" showed a marked improvement in a variety of cognitive skills; more importantly, as Figure 1-1 clearly shows, as viewing became heavier, the amount of improvement increased. The more one watched, the more one learned. Nor was the viewing context important; children who watched at home and those who watched the program in a preschool setting both gained. Finally, the results were not restricted to middle-class children; disadvantaged children who watched showed marked improvements as well. Perhaps one of the most interesting outcomes is that reading skill improved, even though this was not specifically taught on "Sesame Street." These results leave little doubt that children learn by observation and that TV can be an important educational tool.

Observational learning, such as that on *Sesame Street,* has been found to be effective in teaching children. (Children's Television Workshop.)

Early Stimulation and Development: Waterbeds for Premature Infants

Waterbeds not only have found their way into many homes, but also have found a place in hospital nurseries as well. Infants who are born before the full nine months of pregnancy have a greater chance than full-term babies of developing later disorders, especially respiratory and breathing problems. By duplicating the environment of the womb, perhaps these premature infants would adjust better to the external environment. To test this proposition, Korner and her colleagues (Korner, Kraemer, Huffner, & Cosper, 1975) at Stanford University designed an infant waterbed. The waterbed is highly responsive to the infant's own movement and can be adjusted to provide slight head to foot movement. The pattern of rhythm is very similar to the womb that the premature infant has just left. To determine the effects of the waterbed on the infant's breathing patterns, one group of babies were placed on gently moving waterbeds for a seven-day period, while a control group of equally premature infants were left on regular infant mattresses. The stimulation provided by the waterbeds reduced the frequency of episodes of apnea, a condition which involves short interruptions in the infant's breathing patterns. Infants who experience extended or frequent apnea episodes may, in fact, suffer later brain damage. As Figure 1-2 shows, breathing irregularities were reduced significantly for the waterbed babies. Nor were there any serious side effects such as weight loss or "seasickness." This ingenious experiment underlines the important role of stimulation in early development and suggests that premature infants may adapt more successfully to their external environment with the aid of a waterbed.

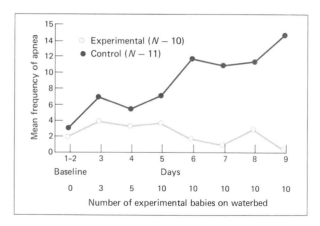

FIGURE 1-2 The effects of waterbed stimulation on premature infants. *(From Korner, Kraemer, Huffner, & Cosper, 1975, by permission of the senior author and the publisher.)*

Noise and Children's Auditory and Verbal Skills

In recent years, interest has developed in the impact of influences in the child's daily environment on his or her development. This subfield of child development is often called *environmental* or *ecological psychology.* The following study of the effects of roadway traffic noise on children's development is an example of ecological research.

Although it is assumed that traffic noise is annoying and undesirable, until recently little was known about the detrimental impact that noise may have on children's cognitive development. Cohen, Glass, and Singer (1973) studied children who lived in thirty-two-floor apartment buildings located close to a heavily traveled expressway to determine if there was any relationship between the noise level in their apartment and the children's auditory discrimination skills and their reading ability.

Since noise level decreased in higher floors of the building, these investigators asked if the cognitive skills of children in the lower floors were more impaired than those of their neighbors in the higher parts of the building. The children (second through fifth graders) were given an auditory discrimination test which involved listening to pairs of words, some of which differed from each other in either initial or final sound (for example, gear-beer or cope-coke); children were simply asked to determine which pairs were different. In addition, standardized reading test scores were available from school records.

For the children living in these apartments for four years or more, the lower the floor level of the apartment, the poorer their auditory discrimination. A similar relationship between floor level and reading test scores was obtained; that is, those children who lived on lower floors showed more reading defects. Moreover, these investigators demonstrated that auditory discrimination skills and reading are related, which suggests that impairments in auditory skills may, in part, be mediating the poorer reading scores.

Of course, there could be numerous alternative explanations, besides noise, for these effects. Perhaps poorer children who obtained less adequate physical care and whose parents were less educated lived on lower floors. However, the socioeconomic range was very restricted and the prices of apartments varied

Children who live on the lower floors of apartment buildings near noisy streets show greater disruptions in cognitive development than children living on higher floors. (Top photo: Katrina Thomas, Photo Researchers, Inc.; bottom photo: Inger McAbe, Rapho/Photo Researchers, Inc.)

minimally across floors. More importantly, the relationships between floor level and auditory discrimination are still present even when parental educational level is controlled.

What is the explanation? The authors suggest that the children who live under prolonged exposure to unwanted noise learn to "tune out" auditory cues. This problem results from overcompensating; that is, children fail to attend between relevant parts of their auditory world, such as speech, and the irrelevant aspects, such as the traffic sounds. They appear to ignore all auditory cues in their efforts to cope with the annoying and undesirable parts of their auditory environment. The ability to distinguish speech sounds is not learned as well in this type of home, as the auditory test results clearly show. As a result of this problem, learning to read becomes more difficult. In summary, children who live in a noisy environment tend to show auditory discrimination defects. Adapting to urban noise may be a reasonable way of coping, but there seems to be a price in cognitive skills. As this investigation clearly illustrates, research in child psychology can have clear implications for social issues and, in this case, for environmental design and planning.

The Infant as Shaper of Adult Socializing Agents

Socialization research has undergone an important theoretical shift in recent years. Instead of assuming that adults influence children—a unidirectional viewpoint—we have finally recognized that children also influence adults. The influence process, in short, is bidirectional, with both adults and children exerting control over each other. Anyone who has heard an infant crying at 3 A.M. clearly knows that even infants exert an enormous impact on parents!

Interest in this general approach has led to the emergence of new research strategies designed to illustrate children's control over adult behavior. A recent study by Gewirtz and Boyd (1977) is an excellent example. Instead of examining the way in which the behavior of infants is modified by adults, these investigators turned the tables on the adult and examined the impact of 3-month-old infants' vocalizations on the social responsiveness of their mothers. Mother and infant interacted with one another through a glass barrier. Each time that the mother smiled and vocalized to her infant, she immediately heard an infant vocalization. Although the mothers assumed that they were hearing their own infants, they were, in actuality, listening to tape-recorded infant vocalizations. In this way, the simulated infant vocalizations could be presented as soon as the mother smiled or spoke. Over the trials, the frequency at which the mothers smiled and vocalized increased as a result of the feedback from "their" infants. When the feedback was discontinued and the mothers thought their babies were no longer responding to them, the mothers' smiling and verbal behavior dropped. Infants can modify their mother's behavior, which suggests that infants can play an active role in modifying their social world.

When All Else Fails: Shock as a Therapeutic Technique for Modifying Children's Behavior

Is the use of electric shock in modifying harmful or undesirable behavior ever justified? Read the following study and make your own judgment.

In this case, Lang and Melamed (1969) used electricity to suppress the chronic and life-endangering vomiting behavior of a 9 month-old infant. When these investigators first encountered their patient, he was in critical condition. From a 6 month weight of 17 pounds the infant had dropped to a skinny 12 pounds, and even though he was being fed through a naso-gastric pump, he was continuing to deteriorate. The reason was obvious: he reliably regurgitated most of his food intake within ten minutes of each feeding and continued to bring up small amounts throughout the day. Before initiating treatment, Lang and Melamed did a careful evaluation of the pattern of the vomiting behavior. They reasoned that if they could detect some early signs that the child was beginning to regurgitate, they could arrange for a maximally effective presentation of the aversive event, electric shock. One of the principles derived from punishment research is that the earlier the punishment is administered, the more effective is the suppression of the undesired behavior. By the use of electromyographic recordings which detect changes in the muscle activity, they were able to determine when the child was about to vomit. At the first sign that the child was about to vomit, he received a one-second electric shock on the calf of his leg. The unpleasant shock continued at one-second intervals until vomiting was terminated. The treatment was relatively short and very effective; each session lasted less than one hour, and after two sessions shock was rarely required. By the sixth session the infant no longer vomited during the testing procedures. The number of shocks actually used was, in fact, quite low. After eight sessions, or three periods in which there was no evidence of the undesirable behavior, therapy was discontinued. A few days later there was a brief setback, but three additional sessions eliminated any further vomiting.

On the day of discharge from the hospital, the child had gained weight and was, in general, a healthy, smiling contrast to the anemic child who had entered the hospital thirteen days before (see photos, page 9). After one year the infant continued to develop normally and no additional treatment was required. The remarkable success of this well-timed punishment procedure is highlighted further by the failure of all other therapeutic approaches to correct this illness.

In our view, the technique was justified since all else had failed and through this approach the infant's life was saved. Nevertheless, the use of potentially harmful procedures raises important ethical questions that we will address later in the chapter. Finally, this study clearly indicates that principles derived from laboratory studies can have important and practical application.

The Methods of Child Psychology

In this section we will examine some of the designs and methods that are used to understand the developing child. Two principal designs are used to investigate children's development: a cross-sectional method and a longitudinal method. In the cross-sectional approach, different children at different ages are selected and studied, while in the case of the longitudinal approach, the investigator studies the same children at a variety of ages as they develop. These approaches represent plans or designs for gathering information about children of different developmental levels. In addition, the investigator has to decide on the type of method to employ. Two methodological approaches will be considered: correlational and experimental strategies.

Now we turn to a detailed look at an example of each approach.

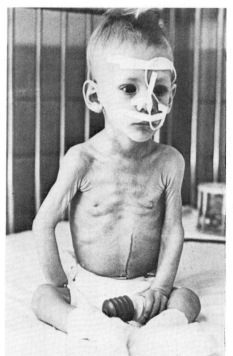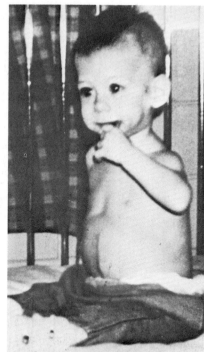

A 9-month-old infant before and after shock treatment. (From Lang and Melamed, 1969; courtesy of Peter Lang.)

Designs for Development: Cross-Sectional and Longitudinal

The Cross-Sectional Design   Children not only learn to love their mothers, but learn to leave them as well. To demonstrate how children's independence changes across development, you can use a cross-sectional design. This design involves selecting *different groups* of children at *different age levels*. Rheingold and Eckerman (1970) used a cross-sectional design in their recent investigation of this issue and recruited children at nine different ages. There were three boys and three girls at each half year of age between 12 and 60 months and, of course, their mothers. For their study, a seminaturalistic setting, a large unfenced lawn, was chosen. Mother and child were placed at one end of the lawn with the mother sitting in a chair and the child free to leave. Observers were stationed in nearby windows to track the path of the child's excursions. A clear relationship between age and distance traveled emerged. The average farthest distance for 1-year-olds was 6.9 meters; by 2 years of age children ventured 15.1 meters; 3-year-olds went 17.3 meters; and 4-year-olds ventured 20.6 meters. Stating the relationship differently, there was a linear increase in the distance traveled with increasing age. For each month of age the children went about a third of a meter farther.

The important feature of this cross-sectional design is that Rheingold and Eckerman were able to determine how independence develops over age by comparing the behavior of groups of different children at different ages in the same situation. One unique feature of this approach is they collected their data across a wide age range in a very short time—a couple of months. They did not have to wait until the 12-month-old infant became a 4-year-old toddler to evaluate developmental advances. This advantage, of course, becomes very clear when the comparisons involve even wider age ranges. With only a little more time, they could easily have included 8-, 12-, and 16-year-olds and tracked how independence changes in adolescence.

However, the distinctive characteristic of this approach, namely, the examination of different children at each age level, has disadvantages. This approach yields no information about the possible historical or past determinants of the age-related changes that are observed because it is impossible to know what these children were like at earlier ages. Nor is there any information about the ways in which individual children develop. How stable is independence? Is the independent child at 1 year likely to be more independent at 5 years than a peer who exhibited little independence until 2 years of age? A cross-sectional approach cannot answer this question, but the longitudinal method is designed to tackle this kind of issue. In the next section, this alternative research method will be explored.

The Longitudinal Design: The Fels Research Institute Study In 1929, a most ambitious project began: the Fels Longitudinal Study. By describing this undertaking, we can illustrate one of the strategies employed by child psychologists in their efforts to unravel some of the mysteries of development. When a parent enrolled a child in the study, there was a catch: the parent had to agree to have the child weighed, measured, observed, and tested for the next eighteen years. Such is the nature of longitudinal research; the subject is assessed repeatedly in order to determine the stability of the patterns of behavior of a particular individual over time.

Age-related changes in independence, for example, could be assessed just as they were in Rheingold and Eckerman's cross-sectional study that we reviewed above. In the case of the longitudinal study, however, the *same—not different*—individuals would be evaluated at each time point. For the longitudinal approach, patience is a key since one has to wait until the infants mature in order to understand adolescence. However, a question of interest to child psychologists concerns the effects of early experience on later behavior; although there are a variety of ways to answer this question, the longitudinal method offers a particularly powerful technique. By tracking children over time, the impact of early events on later behavior can be determined.

Let us take a famous illustration, the Kagan and Moss Birth to Maturity Study (1962), to show how dependence and independence can be studied longitudinally.

Kagan and Moss brought back seventy-one of the Fels longitudinal subjects, who were then between 20 and 29 years old. A number of interviews and test procedures were employed in order to assess how dependent or independent these Fels subjects were as adults. Of course, these same individuals had been

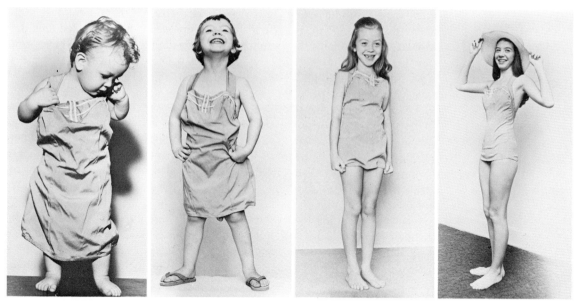

A girl wearing the same bathing suit at evenly spaced intervals for sixteen years. (Photos by Bob Williams.)

observed, measured, and tested throughout the first eighteen years. Kagan and Moss were able to use these early records as predictors of the adult behavior. Typically, a Fels child and mother were observed every six months in the home until the child was 12 years old. In order to assess interaction with peers, children ages 3 to 5 were observed twice a year at the Fels Institute nursery school. From ages 6 to 12, these same children were observed at a summer day camp. In all these situations—home, school, and camp—ratings of each child's dependence were made. It was this vast array of information about the children's behavior at different ages that Kagan and Moss used in their search for the patterns of behavior stability and change over time.

Kagan and Moss divided the childhood data into four age periods: birth to 3 years; 3 to 6 years; 6 to 10 years; and 10 to 14 years. For each age period the child's own behavior as well as the mother's behavior was rated. By relating these findings to the special adulthood assessments, these investigators sought to determine how early behavior patterns become established and the nature of the parental behaviors associated with later adult patterns. First, is behavior stable, or does it merely fluctuate randomly over time? While the first three years bear little clear relationship to adult behaviors, by the preschool years, some behaviors began to stabilize. By the time that children were 6 to 10 years of age, you could predict how dependent the children would be as young adults. Children who were dependent at age 6 were likely to be passive and dependent in adulthood. However, the extent to which dependent behavior is stable between childhood and adulthood varies with the sex of the child. Girls show greater stability of passive-dependent behaviors than males, while boys show greater stability of independent assertive behaviors. Kagan and Moss argue that the sex-role appropriateness of the behavior determined the extent of stability; boys are expected and encouraged to behave in an independent assertive fashion, while dependent behavior is more common for girls—or at least was more common when these children were growing up in the 1930s and 1940s!

What are the advantages and disadvantages of the longitudinal design? Some of the strengths are clear: the impact of earlier events on later behavior can be determined. Differences in behavior at different points in development can also be determined, just as in the case of a cross-sectional approach. The clear advantage over the cross-sectional approach, however, is that the same children are observed at each age point and so the stability of a behavior for an individual can be noted.

But there are disadvantages to the longitudinal approach, aside from the cost and expense. There is a problem of subject loss: individuals move, become ill, or simply lose interest in being tested. The result is a shrinking sample, which not only reduces the reliability of the results, but may bias the results. Can we assume that the sample dropouts are similar to those who continue in the study? If not, the conclusions may be restricted to individuals who possess certain traits, such as immobility, scientific interest, and patience.

Another problem plagues the longitudinal approach: cross-generational change. Is the 4-year-old today similar to the 4-year-old of the 1930s? Times have changed: the family structure has shifted, more women work, and more children attend nursery school and day-care centers. As a result, the experiences of the 4-year-old of forty years ago and the typical experience of a modern 4-year-old will be quite different. Therefore, it is difficult to conclude that the long-term effects of the experiences of our 1930s 4-year-old on later behavior can apply to our present 4-year-old. These changes in culture always date and limit the conclusions of longitudinal studies, particularly those which set out with a large sample and track them over time. In the Fels study, which we discussed, this problem is less serious since it is a continuing study and a small sample of new children are enrolled each year. Therefore, it is possible to directly check on the differences between a 1930 4-year-old and a 1970 4-year-old to determine if, in fact, cultural shifts have produced changes in child behavior.

A final problem is inflexibility. It requires a rare wisdom and foresight to choose the measures that are likely to be important over a twenty-year period. Unlike a cross-sectional study, where you can test your hunches and hypotheses until you find an appropriate measure to work with, in the longitudinal project you choose and hope. If you choose incorrectly, few interesting relationships may emerge. Moreover, the theory and research that are the source of hypotheses are constantly shifting, but in longitudinal research it is often not possible to take advantage of new insights and new methods. For example, in a longitudinal study of IQ, if a new test is discovered ten years after a study has begun, what can the longitudinal investigators do? Several options are available: they can start over with a new sample and the new test, or alternatively, they can begin to give the test to their 10-year-olds. But then you lose the possibility of comparing the earlier results with the later findings since the test instruments are not comparable.

The Short-Term Longitudinal Project As an alternative to extended longitudinal projects, more recently investigators have chosen a new strategy: the short-term longitudinal project. This strategy involves the tracking of a group of individuals for a short time span of a few months to a few years. Unlike older approaches, the focus is usually more limited and restricted to a few key issues and questions which are more theoretically tied. For example, Roger Brown and his colleagues at Harvard University tracked the language development of three children over a two- to five-year period. This project has yielded a wealth of detailed information concerning the natural development of language and grammar, and we will be discussing some of these findings in a later chapter. What are the advantages of this approach?

The shorter the elapsed time of data collection the less will be the attrition of the sample, and the greater the ease of maintaining the same staff and measuring instruments and procedures. Annual increments can still be studied, and the effects of different life experiences can be cancelled out or measured and statistically controlled. (Bayley, 1965, p. 189)

Another advantage of this short-term approach is that the insights gained from this first project can now be utilized in designing another project. The interaction between knowledge gained from data and design can be more closely interwoven.

The Cross-Sectional/Short-term Longitudinal Design Both cross-sectional and longitudinal designs have features that are helpful in answering developmental questions. A design that combines these two approaches is the cross-sectional/short-term longitudinal design.

Consider how you might answer the question of how dependence and independence change between ages 6 and 14 years of age. However, you have neither the time nor the money to run a longitudinal study in which you test the same children at different ages across childhood. You could use a cross-sectional design, but you are interested in the stability of the behavior of individual children. Since a cross-sectional study involves different children at each age, this type of study would not be satisfactory. A compromise approach—the cross-sectional/short-term longitudinal design—would be the most suitable alternative. According to this approach one group would be tested at 6 years of age and again at 10 years of age, while a second sample of children would be tested for the first time at 10 years of age and later at age 14 years. Table 1-1 summarizes the design and contrasts this approach with the cross-sectional and longitudinal designs. There are distinct advantages to this combined cross-sectional/short-term longitudinal design. Information concerning the patterns of interaction at the three age points can be determined just as in a usual cross-sectional study. In addition, data concerning the developmental changes

TABLE 1-1 COMPARISON OF THREE DEVELOPMENTAL DESIGNS

	Longitudinal	Cross-sectional	Cross-sectional/longitudinal
Main feature	Same group of children tested (Group A) at several age points Age Group 6 A 10 A 14 A	Different groups of children tested (Groups A, B, C) at each age point Age Group 6 A 10 B 14 C	Different groups of children (A, B) each tested at two points Age Group 6 A 10 A B 14 B
Approximate time for data collection	8 years	Time required to test each child once (typically less than 1 year)	4 years

that occur for individual children between 6 and 10 and between 10 and 14 years can also be determined. By testing both groups of children at age 10, one group for the second time and another group for the first time, the effects of repeated testing can be determined. Does testing the child at 6 years affect the child's response at 10 years? By testing another group for the first time at 10 years, it is possible to determine this effect. A final advantage of this approach is time: approximately half the time would be required to execute this design in comparison with the complete longitudinal study.

It is clear that both cross-sectional and longitudinal studies are useful, and the choice of design will depend on the type of issue under investigation. Whether a longitudinal or cross-sectional design is used, the investigator also has a choice of different research strategies. In the next section we will discuss two alternative research approaches: correlational and experimental strategies.

Correlational versus Experimental Strategies

To illustrate these two strategies consider how we could answer a question that has concerned parents, public, and psychologists alike: Does viewing TV violence affect children's behavior? Over the last fifteen years this question has frequently been posed, and child psychologists have used a variety of techniques to try to settle this issue. By using this issue as an example, we can illustrate the differences between correlational and experimental approaches to answer questions about children. First, let us examine the correlational approach.

Correlational Strategy To illustrate the correlational approach consider the study of TV viewing habits and aggression reported by Eron (1963). Parents were asked about the TV habits of their sons and daughters. Specifically, information about the length of time that children watched TV and the extent to which violence characterized favorite programs was obtained from these parental interviews. To determine whether variations in TV viewing were related to aggression, their classmates rated these third-grade children in terms of aggressive behaviors. The results were interesting: boys who were rated as aggressive by their peers preferred violent TV programs. In other words, as the amount of violence in favorite programs increased, the rate of peer aggression increased. However, as total amount of time watched increases, aggression scores decrease. Clearly, the type of program rather than simply viewing time is a critical factor. For girls, on the other hand, there were no differences.

Now that we have seen an example of the correlational approach, a more formal definition will be helpful. Correlation is an index or estimate of how two factors or measures vary together; it is expressed in terms of the direction and size of the relationship. Correlations can range from +1.00, which indicates that as one measure increases the other shows a fixed predictable increase, to 0, which shows only a chance relationship between the two variables, to −1.00, which shows that as one measure increases the other shows a fixed predictable decrease. Thus the plus and minus signs show the direction of the relationship, and the size of the correlation shows the extent to which two variables are related. A positive correlation exists when increases in one variable are associated with increases in a second variable. In our TV-aggression example, increases in peer ratings of aggression are positively correlated with the amount of violence in the boys' favorite programs. To take another example, height and weight are positively correlated since increased height is typically associated with increases in weight. A negative correlation implies that increases in one variable are associated with decreases in the second variable. For example, the more cigarettes an individual smokes, the shorter is his or her life expectancy. Finally, if changes in one variable are not related in any systematic way to changes in another variable, we speak of a zero correlation. Height, for example, has a zero correlation with intelligence. Knowledge of how tall a person is gives us no information about the person's intelligence level. A word of caution is necessary. The fact that two factors are correlated does not *mean* that one factor *caused* the other. It only means that the two factors are related in some systematic way to each other. To return to our TV example, can we conclude that watching violent TV causes increases in aggressive behavior? Absolutely not! The results of this study merely tell us that there is a relationship between preference for violent fare and aggressive behavior. The direction of the relationship is not clear. An equally plausible explanation could be that children who prefer violent programs are already aggressive and their TV viewing may have had little effect on their level of aggressiveness. Correlational findings cannot establish causal relationships! Similarly, consider the finding that boys who watch TV are not as aggressive as boys who watch it less. "Is it because they are by temperament less active; is it because they discharge their aggressive impulses in this fantasylike way, and, thus, do not have to act them out in real life; or is it because their time is taken up in watching TV and they have less opportunity to act out aggression?" (Eron, 1963, pp. 195–196). There are other problems with correlational research as well. In this study the characteristics of the TV shows are often difficult to define in a clear and unambiguous fashion. Although programs may be defined as aggressive, there are a variety of other behaviors displayed as well. Even Batman and Superman and Elliott Ness in "The Untouchables" show helpfulness and cooperation between their bouts of violence. Similarly, the usual TV films provide few female aggressive models, which may account for the failure of the Eron study to find any relationships between TV viewing and aggression for girls. It is due to the ambiguities in interpretation that this type of correlational study is only one step in the course of establishing a full understanding of the causal factors in the TV violence–aggressive behavior puzzle. To clarify the causal links, we need to turn to another approach, namely, the *experiment.*

Experimental Strategy   In contrast to the correlational method the experimental strategy involves introducing some type of change in the child's environment and then measuring the effects of this change on the child's subsequent behavior. Experiments vary in terms of both the degree of control that is exercised over important variables and the location or setting in which the experiment is conducted. The most common type of experiment and the one that permits the greatest degree of control is the laboratory experiment. We will examine this type of experiment first and then discuss two alternative experimental strategies—field and natural experiments.

The laboratory experiment   To illustrate the laboratory experiment as a method for investigating the TV-aggression question, consider a recent investigation by Liebert and Baron (1972).One-hundred thirty-six boys and girls participated in this study; half of the children were 5 to 6 years old, and the remaining children were 8 to 9 years of age. Let us follow the course of events experienced by the child. In this study, the parent and child came to a laboratory where the experiment was being conducted. The parents were informed about the details of the study, and a written consent for the child's participation was obtained. A common practice is to test children during school hours, and in this case, parents are informed about projects by letter; according to current ethical standards, only if the parent grants written consent can a child participate in a psychological study. The next step in the Liebert-Baron study was to randomly assign children to various experimental treatment conditions. In other words, some children were designated the experimental subjects, while others were assigned to the control condition—on a purely chance basis. By this procedure, children in the two conditions should not differ in any systematic fashion; therefore, the results should be due to effects of the experimental conditions, not to initial differences in the children. Next the experimenter, a 28-year-old female, escorted each child individually to a room containing children's furniture and a television videotape monitor. The experimenter turned on the TV and suggested that the children watch TV for a few minutes until they were ready to begin. All children watched two brief commercials selected for their humor and attention-getting value. Then the critical part of the procedure began. Half of the children, the experimental group, observed $3^{1}/_{2}$ minutes of a program from the TV series "The Untouchables." The sequence contained a chase, two fistfighting scenes, two shootings, and a knifing. The children in the control group watched a highly active $3^{1}/_{2}$-minute videotaped sports sequence in which athletes competed in hurdle races and high jumps. Then all the children watched another 60 seconds of a tire commercial. Two aspects of the procedure so far merit comment. First, the *single* difference in treatment between the children in the experimental and control conditions involved the particular type of program that they were exposed to. In all other ways their experience was similar. By carefully equating the treatments, one is reasonably certain that any subsequent differences in behavior are, in fact, *caused* by the type of TV program that the children watched. There is another important aspect of the procedure: the TV viewing was presented as part of the waiting period prior to the onset of the "real" part of the experiment. In this way, the subject's suspicions about the purpose of the experiment were reduced, and it is unlikely that the effects are attributable to the subject's prior knowledge of the experimenter's true purpose.

In the next phase, the impact of this viewing experience was assessed. The subject was seated before a panel arrayed with two buttons labeled "hurt" and "help," which was connected to another child's panel in the adjoining room. The second child was playing a game which required turning a handle. The subject was informed that if he wanted to make the handle turning easier for the other boy, he could depress the "help" button. On the other hand, by pushing the "hurt" button, the handle in the other room will feel hot and hurt the child. In fact, the "other" child was an accomplice of the experimenter and was not affected by the help-hurt buttons. The amount of time that children in the two viewing conditions depressed the hurt button was employed as the main measure of aggression. In this experiment, the time spent in depressing the hurt button is the *dependent variable.* In an experiment the dependent variable is the measure that is altered or affected by the treatment, or the *independent variable.* In our example, the independent variable was the type of TV program that the children watched. The results were clear. Children who viewed "The Untouchables" program showed reliably greater willingness to engage in interpersonal aggression than those who had observed the neutral program.

Exposure to TV violence does, in fact, *cause* increased interpersonal aggression. However, there are limitations to the study which make it difficult to generalize from this situation to the naturalistic environment. The test setting and the aggression index were artificially contrived and the TV program was edited; while it permits experimental control over the relevant variables, the legitimacy of generalization from this type of laboratory study to the field is highly questionable. As one observer once noted, much of American developmental psychology is "the science of the strange behavior of a child in a strange situation with a strange adult" (Bronfenbrenner, 1977, pp. 277–278).

In the next section, we examine two alternative experimental strategies that overcome some of the limitations of the laboratory experiment.

Other Experimental Strategies: Natural and Field Experiments   Experiments can sometimes be conducted outside the laboratory in the child's natural environment, and therefore some of the problems associated with the laboratory experiment, such as the artificiality of the setting, can be avoided. The clever investigator can arrange to introduce a change in the child's normal environment or even take advantage of a naturally occurring change in the child's everyday world. Let us examine each of these types of experiments.

The field experiment   In the field experiment, the investigator *deliberately* introduces a change in a naturalistic setting. An excellent example is the recent study by Friedrich and Stein (1973), who were interested in the impact of viewing violent TV on children's aggressive behavior. A field experiment differs from a laboratory experiment in a variety of ways. Unlike the lab studies, where the child enters into a specially created world of the experimenter, the hallmark of the field experiment is the fact that the experimenter enters the child's world. In this case, the investigators moved into the nursery school and controlled the types of TV programs that the children watched. The observations of the impact of TV viewing were made during the daily play sessions at the nursery school; adult observers recorded the frequency of aggressive and prosocial behavior. The study was conducted during a nine-week summer nursery school session. For the first three weeks, the investigators observed the children in order to achieve a baseline measure of their interaction patterns. For the next four weeks, the children watched a half-hour TV program each day. Some children always saw aggressive programs, such as Batman and Superman cartoons; other children watched a prosocial program, "Mister Rogers' Neighborhood"; the remaining children were put on a neutral TV fare of farm films, nature shows, and circus movies. In the last two weeks the long-term effects of the TV diets were assessed. To minimize bias, the adults did not know the type of programs that different children had been watching. The impact of the programs was determined by comparing the children's behavior during the first three weeks, or the baseline period, with their behavior during the period of TV viewing. Exposure to aggressive cartoons did affect the children's behavior, but the amount of aggression exhibited in the pre-TV sessions was an important factor. Children who were initially high in aggression were more aggressive following exposure to the aggressive cartoons in comparison to subjects exposed to neutral or prosocial programs. However, the behavior of children who were less aggressive during this initial period did not differ across the TV diets. Exposure to TV violence does affect interpersonal aggressive behavior if a child is already likely to behave aggressively!

One advantage of the field experimental approach over the laboratory experiment is that the results can be generalized more readily to natural environments. The TV programs were unedited and typical of the kind of fare that children are exposed to in their home environment. Moreover, the children's behavior was measured in a naturalistic setting. Any conclusion drawn from this type of study can be much more readily applied to children's daily behavior than studies conducted under more artificial circumstances. The study still retained the important feature of an *experiment*. The independent variable, namely, the type of TV program, was under the control of the experimenter. Hence, it is still possible to make causal statements; the TV diet, it appears, was the *cause* of the changes in aggressive behavior. If the children themselves had chosen the type of TV diet, we would never be sure that any changes were merely due to the possible fact that aggressive children seek out aggressive programs! That may be the case, but through experimental control, this possibility was eliminated.

However, the field experiment is not always feasible since changes cannot always be introduced by the experimenter for ethical, practical reasons. In the next section, we examine another alternative—the natural experiment.

The natural experiment In this case, the investigator capitalizes upon a change in the child's world that occurred naturally and was not due to the investigator's intervention. Social policy may produce changes in school integration; or children may be adopted, or hospitalized, or sent to camp. The investigator may take advantage of these "happenings" and measure their effect on the child's behavior. For example, Williams and Handford (1977) took advantage of a naturally occurring event, namely, the introduction of TV into a small town in Canada which previously did not have any TV reception. By measuring the children's aggressive play behavior in school and in the laboratory *before* and *after* the children's exposure to TV, these investigators were able to demonstrate that aggression increased after TV arrived in town. Both the advantage and limitation of this type of design flow from the uniqueness of the independent variable, the introduction of TV to the town. To the extent that it has not been arbitrarily introduced by the experimenter, the event may be more ecologically valid. In other words, it is part of the child's natural environment and therefore it is easier to make statements that readily can apply to children's real-life behavior. However, the specification of the exact nature and boundaries of the independent variable is often difficult. Children watch a variety of programs, and it is difficult to determine precisely whether violent TV programs are the "cause" of the increased aggressive behavior or if some other aspect of TV viewing is.

No research strategy is without its limitations. In our comparison of laboratory, field, and natural experiments, we see that there is often a trade-off between experimental control and generalizability of findings. Control is greatest in the laboratory experiment, but the extent to which the results can be applied to children in their natural environment is often limited. On the other hand, the results of field and natural experiments can be more readily generalized to real-life settings, but the clarity of the results may be less precise since the amount of control that the investigator can gain over important variables is less in field settings. No strategy is always "best." It is important to remember that each method has a role in helping the investigator understand children's behavior. Often an investigator may start off in an unexplored area by using a correlational approach in order to establish some possible relationships. Finally, experiments may follow to more clearly isolate the causal links between the variables indicated by the earlier methods. Multiple methodological strategies are increasingly the preferred approach in studying children's development.

The Ethics of Research with Children

In the final analysis, the most important consideration in deciding upon a particular research strategy is the effects of the procedure on the child. In recent years there has been an increasing awareness of the ethical issues involved in research with children. Various government review boards have suggested guidelines for child research projects. These guidelines have been developed to protect children from harmful and dangerous procedures. Box 1-1 outlines a children's bill of research rights to illustrate the kinds of protections that are necessary for child research participants. In reading this list of children's rights, remember that very often children are too young to fully appreciate the complex issues that are involved in making informed decisions. Therefore, it is often parents who have to make decisions about their children's participation in research projects.

As a consequence of the increasing awareness of children's research rights, some types of investigations are becoming less frequent. Fewer child psychologists can be found looking out of waiting-room windows, watching behind one-way mirrors, or observing through the lens of a hidden camera. For example, laboratory research involving deception, in which the child is misled about the true purpose of the study, is becoming less frequent. Many investigators are increasingly accepting the view that this type of procedure is no longer acceptable. Of course, it should be stressed that most research has always been executed safely and without deception of the children.

Before leaving our discussion of ethical issues in research, some of the types of difficulties that are occasionally encountered should be recognized. Sometimes the ethical course of action is not clear. Consider these dilemmas: you be the judge.

Is it unethical to study the long-term effects of being a premature or a full-term infant and not inform the families that they were selected because their infant was premature? Will informing these parents sensitize them to expect their premature offspring to be different and make them more anxious? Is deception or full disclosure of the aims of the study likely to have the most positive outcome?

Let us look at another study. In order to study children's persistence in the face of failure, children are given a very difficult task that guarantees that they will not be able to master the task. An attempt to eliminate any negative effects of the failure experience was made by giving all children another task in which they succeeded before they finished the session. Since failure is a common experience in school, is its use justified in this case? Or perhaps the long-term goal of the study—to teach children to continue to work even after a failure experience—justified this experiment.

BOX 1-1
A CHILDREN'S BILL OF RESEARCH RIGHTS

1 *The right to be fully informed:* Each child participant has the right to full and truthful information about the purposes of the study and the procedures to be employed.

2 *The right to informed and voluntary consent of participation:* Each child participant has the right to either verbally or in written form agree to participate in a research project. In the case of children who are too young to understand the aims and procedures and to make an informed decision about partici-pation, parental consent should always be secured.

3 *The right to voluntary withdrawal:* Each child participant has the right to withdraw at any time from continued participation in any re-search project.

4 *The right to full compensation:* Each child participant has the right to be fully compensat-ed for his or her time and effort as a research

subject, even if he or she withdraws and does not complete participation in the project.

5 *The right to nonharmful treatment:* Each child participant has the right to expect that he or she will not experience any harm or damage-producing events during the course of the research procedure.

6 *The right to knowledge of results:* Each child participant has the right to new information concerning the results of the research project. In the case of young children, their parents have the right to be provided this information. Often, this information will take the form of the group scores on a task, rather than the individ-ual participant's own score.

7 *The right to confidentiality of their research data:* Each child participant has the right to expect that personal information gathered as part of the research project will remain private and confidential. Nor will any in-formation about individual research partici-pants be available to any other individuals or agencies. ■

Or consider this situation. You are an observer in a nursery school, and you are interested in the development of aggression and other forms of antisocial behavior in young children. When the teacher is out of the room, a child takes an expensive truck from the toy closet and puts it in his school bag. Do you score it and tell the teacher or just score it as an antisocial behavior and forget it?

Finally, what about the study that we discussed earlier, in which the infant was treated for his vomiting problem with electric shock? Do you think it was justified?

In the final analysis, a cost-benefit ratio is usually the guiding principle. Is the cost in terms of the child's time and effort warranted by the increase in information and understanding about children that will result from the research project? Research is a tool for increasing our knowledge about children, and through this knowledge, children, in the long run, will, it is hoped, benefit. The ethics of research in child psychology is a continuing debate, and the last word is yet to be heard. As you read research reports throughout the remainder of the book, think about these ethical issues.

Summary

In this chapter, we have introduced the field of child psychology and provided an overview of the volume. Two principal questions concern the child psychologist: How do children change as they develop, and what are the determinants of these developmental changes? The emphasis of modern child psychology is on the processes that produce and account for these changes. A number of methodological tactics were discussed, including the cross-sectional and longitudinal approaches. The cross-sectional approach involves studying different children at various age levels in order to assess developmental differences. The longitudinal approach involves the examination of the same children at different age levels. Each approach has advantages and limitations. The cross-sectional approach is more economical and less time-consuming than the longitudinal design. On the other hand, the longitudinal approach permits an examination of changes in the development of individual children and is better suited to answering questions concerning stability of behavior over time.

Two research strategies were discussed: correlational and experimental. The correlational approach involves the examination of the relationship between two events; for example, peer ratings of a child's aggressiveness were related to the child's preferences for violent TV programs, and as the preference for TV violence increased, the peer ratings of this behavior increased. However, it is impossible to determine if there is a cause-effect relationship. An alternative approach which permits the establishment of causal links is the laboratory experiment; in this approach children receive a particular treatment and then their behavior is assessed in a controlled setting. For example, by exposing children to aggressive and nonaggressive TV and then measuring their reactions, the causal link between TV watching and viewer behavior can be established. Two alternatives to the laboratory experiment were described: the natural and the field experiment. Both involve measurement of the impact of some experimental manipulation in a naturalistic setting. In the natural experiment, the investigator measures the impact of a naturally occurring change, such as the introduction of TV, on the child's behavior in a field setting. The unique feature of this approach is that the investigator is not responsible for the alteration in the child's environment. In the field experiment, the investigator deliberately produces a change and then measures the outcome in a real-life context. The advantage of these field-based experiments over the laboratory study is the greater degree to which the results can be generalized to real-life settings. Finally the issue of research ethics was discussed and a series of children's research rights were outlined.

References

Ball, S., & Bogatz, J. Summative research of Sesame Street: Implications for the study of preschool children. In A.D. Pick (ED.), *Minnesota symposia on child psychology* (Vol. 6). Minneapolis: University of Minnesota Press, 1972.

Bayley, N. Research in child development: A longitudinal perspective. *Merrill-Palmer Quarterly*, 1965, **11**, 184–190.

Bronfenbrenner, U. Ecological factors in human development in retrospect and prospect. In H. McGurk (Ed.), *Ecological factors in human development.* Amsterdam: North-Holland Publishing, 1977.

Cohen, S., Glass, D.C., & Singer, J.E. Apartment noise, auditory discrimination and reading ability in children. *Journal of Experimental Social Psychology*, 1973, **9**, 407–422.

Eron, L.P. Relationship of T.V. viewing habits and aggressive behavior in children. *Journal of Abnormal and Social Psychology*, 1963, **67**, 193–196.

Friedrich, L.K., & Stein, A.H. Aggressive and prosocial television programs and the natural behavior of preschool children. *Monographs of the Society for Research in Child Development*, 1973, **38** (Serial No. 151).

Gewirtz, J.L., & Boyd, E.F. Experiments on mother-infant interaction underlying mutual attachment acquisition: The infant conditions the mother. In T. Alloway, P. Pliner, & L. Krames (Eds.), *Attachment Behavior.* New York: Plenum, 1977.

Kagan, J., & Moss, H. *Birth to Maturity.* New York: Wiley, 1962.

Korner, A.F., Kraemer, H.C., Huffner, M.E., & Cosper, L.M. Effects of waterbed flotation on premature infants: A pilot study. *Pediatrics*, 1975, **56**, 361–367.

Lang, P.J., & Melamed, B.B. Case report: Avoidance conditioning therapy of an infant with chronic ruminative vomiting. *Journal of Abnormal Psychology*, 1969, **74**, 1–8.

Liebert, R.M., & Baron, R.A. Some immediate effects of televised violence on children's behavior. *Developmental Psychology*, 1972, **6**, 469–475.

Rheingold, H., & Eckerman, C. The infant separates himself from his mother. *Science*, 1970, **168**, 78–83.

Williams, T., & Handford, G. Television in community life. Unpublished manuscript, University of British Columbia, 1977.

2

The Biological
Bases of
Development

If you look at newborn infants in the nursery of a maternity ward, one of the things that is most striking is their diversity. This diversity is found not only in their physical characteristics but also in their behavior. One infant may sleep most of the time, another may be squalling and irritable, and still another may be wakeful but contented and seem to scan and visually explore the room. What contributes to this individuality in such young children? Before birth, in fact it could be argued that even before conception, the transactions between a vast array of genetic factors and environmental factors begin which make the individual unique. These genetic-environmental transactions continue to shape development through-

24

out the entire life span, from conception until death. One might say from sperm to worm. The infant may enter the world impaired by lack of oxygen because a genetic predisposition to be of large body size resulted in a difficult labor. The adult may exit from the world early because of a lifetime of gluttony and an inherited proclivity for heart disease.

Human development is the process by which the genotype comes to be expressed as a phenotype (Scarr-Salapatek, 1975). An individual's *genotype* is the material inherited from ancestors which makes the individual genetically unique. With the exception of identical twins, no two individuals have the same genotype. An individual's *phenotype* is the way the genotype is expressed in observable or measurable characteristics.

The expression of the genotype is modified by a variety of experiences. Whether or not a child's genotype for high intellectual ability is manifested in school performance will depend in part upon whether or not the child's parents stimulate and encourage the child in intellectual pursuits. A child reared in a deprived slum environment may manifest a genotype for high intelligence by being a school dropout and becoming the most devious, skillful con artist in the neighborhood. Similarly, although a child may appear to have his grandfather's temper, any inherited predisposition for impulsive and uncontrolled behavior will be considerably modified by how "cute" his parents think his rages are and whether he eventually gets his own way and finds it rewarding to have tantrums.

Some genotypes such as eye or hair color may be directly expressed in phenotypes, although as many people know, a visit to a skillful hairdresser can modify the direct phenotypical expression of hair color. However, most of the phenotypical intellectual, social, emotional, and personality characteristics in which psychologists are interested are the result of extremely complex transactions between genetic and environmental factors during the course of development. In this chapter some of the principles and processes which guide these transactions will be reviewed. The effects of transactions among genes and between genetic and environmental factors, and the importance of the timing of such transactions, on the development of the child will be explored. In addition, a discussion of the biochemical bases of heredity will be presented. Finally, two approaches to the study of the role of genetic and environmental factors in development will be examined. The first approach involves the study of individuals having different degrees of biological relatedness. These are called kinship studies. In such studies a comparison is made of the similarity of a characteristic such as intelligence test performance of unrelated strangers versus that of distantly related relatives such as a child to his or her grandparents, cousins, aunts, and uncles, or of members of the immediate family such as parents, children, and siblings. If the score on an intelligence test is strongly influenced by inheritance, it would be expected that there would be an increase in resemblance from strangers to distant relatives to immediate relatives. However, it could also be argued that immediate relatives are more likely to be exposed to the same environment and that it will be impossible to separate the effects of heredity and environment in these studies. Adoption studies and studies of twins, which will be discussed later in the chapter, are special types of kinship studies which attempt to separate these effects. The second approach to the study of the contributions of environmental and inherited factors to development involves an examination of the stability of individual attributes over time. If the squalling, irritable infant evolves into an irascible, bad-tempered, petulant adult, one possible explanation would be that the individual has an inherited predisposition to be irritable which is manifested throughout his life span.

The Range of Reaction and Canalization

At one time scientists were preoccupied with the question of the relative amounts contributed by genetic or environmental factors to different characteristics such as intelligence, motor skills, and personality. This resulted in what was called the nature-nurture controversy, with many psychologists assuming extreme positions on the issue. Those who were more biologically oriented emphasized the exclusive role of heredity and maturational factors in shaping development, while those who were more environmentally oriented often took an equally extreme and invalid position by denying any contribution of innate predispositions or capacities and emphasizing the exclusive role of learning and experience.

In the United States with its political and social philosophy based on a belief in the equality of people and the importance of opportunity, education, and initiative, theories of biological determination fell on fallow ground. In contrast the environmentalist position of John B. Watson and the behaviorists flourished. In 1926 in the heat of the nature-nurture controversy Watson expounded:

Give me a dozen healthy infants, well-formed and my own specific world to bring them up in and I'll guarantee to take any one at random and train him to become any type of specialist I might select—a doctor, lawyer, artist, merchant-chief and, yes, even into beggar-man and thief, regardless of his talents, penchants, tendencies, abilities, vocations and race of his ancestors. (Watson, 1926, p. 10)

"Very interesting, Dr. Watson!" This expansively optimistic view of the total malleability of human behavior is not held by contemporary psychologists. However, as the student will soon see, particularly in the area of intellectual development, the nature-nurture controversy is alive in new guises. People are still asking the question: How much do environmental and genetic factors contribute to development? However, they also want to know how and when the transactions between these factors affect development. The concepts of the *range of reaction* and of *canalization* help to explain some of the variations in the complex transactions which occur between inherited factors and environmental factors.

Heredity does not rigidly fix behavior, but instead establishes a range of possible responses that the individual may make to different environments. Different children will vary in the array of possible responses they will make under different life experiences. These genetically based variations of individuals' responsiveness to environments is called the *range of reaction* (Gottesman, 1963). The genotype thus sets boundaries on the range of possible phenotypes within which individual characteristics may be expressed.

Let us take the example of the effect on intelligence test performance of the range of reaction as it interacts with environments with different degrees of stimulation or enrichment. Figure 2-1 presents the effects of varying degrees of environmental enrichment on the test performances of three children with different intellectual reaction ranges. It can be seen that under similar conditions of enrichment child C always performs better than the other two children. However, it is also apparent that child C has the widest range of reaction. The difference in child C's performance when raised in a stimulating versus a restricted environment is greater than that of the other two children. Child A has a lower and more limited range of reaction. She not only scores below average in intelligence whether she is in an enriched or restricted habitat, but also shows less variation in response to favorableness of the environment.

Some kinds of genotypes are more difficult to deflect from their genetically programmed path of growth than others. These seem to have fewer possible alternative paths from genotype to phenotype, and it takes intense or more specific environmental pushes to deflect them. The term *canalization* is used to describe the limiting of phenotypes to one or few developmental outcomes (Waddington, 1962, 1966). A characteristic which is strongly canalized is relatively difficult to modify even by what might be viewed as widely divergent or extreme experiences. For example, infant babbling is strongly canalized since babbling occurs even in infants who are born deaf and have never heard their own voices or the speech of others (Lenneberg, 1967). In contrast, intelligence is less highly canalized since it can be modified by a variety of physical, social, and educational experiences and will be manifested in a wide range of problem-solving and adaptive behaviors.

In addition to the effects of range of reactivity and canalization, the extent to which an individual's genotype is expressed in his phenotype depends on the timing, kind, and amount of environmental pressures, or pushes, to which he is

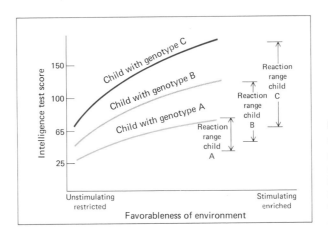

FIGURE 2-1 Hypothetical intellectual reaction ranges of children with three genotypes in stimulating and unstimulating environments. *(Adapted from Gottesman, 1963.)*

exposed. Different experiences at different points in the course of development have different effects on the developing child. If a pregnant woman contracts German measles in the first three months of pregnancy, the child she is carrying, who may be genotypically predisposed to be of normal intelligence, may be born severely mentally retarded. However, if the mother contracts the disease later in pregnancy, it is unlikely to have an effect in modifying the expression of the child's intellectual genotype (Waddington, 1962, 1966).

The critical task in contemporary developmental behavior genetics is to identify the processes that initiate, influence, and shape development, as well as the timing of these processes. Let us examine some findings in genetics and prenatal development keeping this issue in mind.

Conception and the Beginnings of Life

At the time of conception, a *sperm* cell from the father penetrates and unites with the *ovum* (the egg cell) from the mother to form the *zygote*, or fertilized ovum. The cells of the zygote multiply rapidly by cell division and develop into the future child.

The human body is composed of two structurally and functionally different types of cells. The first type of cells is the gametes, or germ cells, composed of the female ovum and the male sperm cell. All other cells in the body are somatic, or body cells, which compose such things as the bones, muscles, organs, and digestive, respiratory, and nervous systems. Gametes and body cells contain a

A fertilized ovum at the moment of conception. (Courtesy of the American Museum of Natural History)

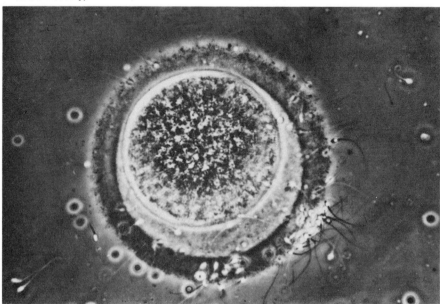

different number of chromosomes and divide in a different manner. The gametes, which contain all the hereditary material of the child, differ markedly in size. The ovum is the largest cell in the body and the sperm the smallest. The relative size of these cells can be understood if it is noted that an ovum is about 90,000 times as heavy as a sperm. Although an ovum is much larger than a sperm, it is still smaller than the periods printed on this page. The number of sperm cells that could be contained in a teaspoon is sufficient to father all of the people alive today (Scheinfeld, 1965). Although the ovum is much larger than the sperm, both cells contribute almost equally to the inheritance of the offspring. Within each cell nucleus are threadlike entities known as *chromosomes*. Beaded along the length of the chromosomes are the *genes*, which contain the genetic code that will participate in directing an individual's development.

Each gamete contains 23 chromosomes. Each body cell of most normal men and women and the nucleus of the fertilized ovum (the zygote) contain 46 chromosomes (two sets of 23 chromosomes, 1 chromosome in each pair coming from the mother and 1 from the father).

Cell division in body cells occurs by *mitosis*, a process in which each of the 46 chromosomes in the nucleus of the parent cell duplicates itself. The resulting identical two sets of 46 chromosomes move to opposite sides of the parent cell. The parent cell then separates between the two clusters of 46 identical chromosomes and becomes two new cells, or daughter cells. These daughter cells and all the body cells formed by mitosis in the course of human development contain 46 chromosomes which are identical to those in the zygote. The process of mitosis is shown in Figure 2-2.

Reproductive, or germ cells divide by a different process called *meiosis*, which is essentially a process of reduction division. In the testes and ovaries a cell with 23 pairs of chromosomes divides in such a way that the daughter cells include only one member of each pair of chromosomes. This process is presented in Figure 2-3. Thus, mature sperm and egg cells contain only 23 single chromosomes rather than 23 chromosome pairs. When the sperm and egg cells with their 23 chromosomes unite, the zygote contains the 46 chromosomes, half contributed by each parent.

Since, at conception, any possible combination of chromosomes from the sperm and ovum may occur, the number of possible combinations in a zygote is immense. There are about 3.8 billion people alive today, but there are about 70 trillion potential human genotypes.

In addition, increasing this genetic variability is a phenomenon called *crossing-over*, which occurs during meiosis. In this process genetic material is exchanged between pairs of chromsomes. At the beginning of meiosis two chromosomes form pairs with their lengths stretched like parallel threads, and then equivalent sections of each chromosome break away and attach themselves to the adjacent chromosome. Thus the chromosomes are actually altered because genes are exchanged between pairs of chromosomes and the genetic characteristics associated with those genes are now carried on different chromosomes. This process of crossing-over enlarges the already broad genetic array of

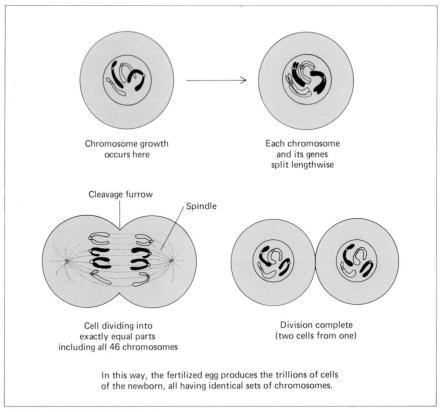

Chromosome growth
occurs here

Each chromosome
and its genes
split lengthwise

Cleavage furrow

Spindle

Cell dividing into
exactly equal parts
including all 46 chromosomes

Division complete
(two cells from one)

In this way, the fertilized egg produces the trillions of cells
of the newborn, all having identical sets of chromosomes.

FIGURE 2-2   Mitosis: a process of cell replication in the zygote and body cells in which both pairs of each chromosome are reproduced. After cell division in humans, each cell contains the identical set of 46 chromosomes (that is, 23 pairs); only 4 chromosomes (2 pairs) are shown here for the sake of simplification. *(Adapted from Rugh & Shettles, 1974, with permission of the publisher and the senior author.)*

possible combinations of characteristics that take place in reproduction and ensures the genetic uniqueness of individuals.

Chromosomes and Genes

Arranged along the length of a chromosome and occupying a specific location on it are thousands of segments called genes which are the basic units of hereditary transmission and which specify the protein and enzyme reactions to be activated during development. In the past few decades great advances have been made in understanding the structure and processes associated with genetic transmission.

The gene is composed of *deoxyribonucleic acid,* or DNA, which contains the genetic code that directs the functioning of *riboncucleic acid,* or RNA. RNA

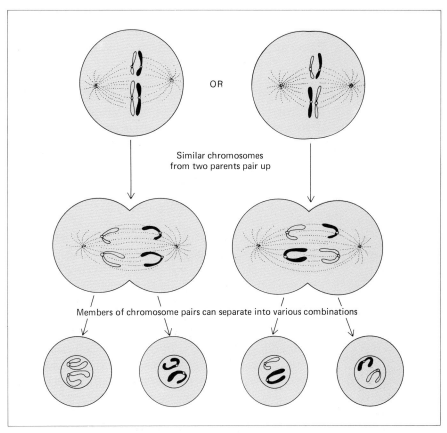

FIGURE 2-3   Meiosis: a process of reduction division in the germ cell (ovum and sperm). Following meiosis only one member of each pair of chromosomes, 23 chromosomes rather than 23 pairs of chromosomes, is present in each of the new germ cells. *(Adapted from Rugh & Shettles, 1974, with permission of the publisher and the senior author.)*

serves as a messenger in carrying the DNA-originated directions from the nucleus of a cell to its *cytoplasm*, which composes the rest of the cell, where the instructions are carried out. These directions lead to the synthesis of proteins from the amino acids in the cytoplasm. Since the body is composed of protein, instructions are being relayed as to how the newly formed organism is to develop. The DNA in each gene contains instructions for a specific type of protein chain. It has been found that genes of different types direct structural development and regulate cellular, chemical, and metabolic processes. Some of these protein chains control body processes, some are structural and form new tissues, and some regulate the functioning and turning off and on of structural genes. When even one of these genes is defective, marked developmental deviations may occur in the child.

The Double Helix James Watson and Francis Crick (1953) have proposed their now famous double-helix model of the structure and function of DNA, which helps to explain how genes replicate themselves during cell division. They suggest that a molecule of DNA is like a spiral staircase, or a double helix or coil, with the side strips being composed of molecules of phosphate and sugar and the steps being composed of pairs of four chemical bases. Genetic information is coded by the ordering, or arrangement, of these chemical steps at different locations on the chromosome. Only bases that are compatible with each other form pairs to make the steps (thus cytosine and guanine are paired and thymine and adenine appear together), but these pairs can follow each other in any order. A single gene might be a chunk of DNA stairways perhaps 2,000 steps long—and geneticists now think that it is the order of these steps that gives every gene its special character (Pfeiffer, 1964, p. 61). This creates a kind of alphabet of life.

We have described the process of cell division, but what happens to our DNA molecules while cells are duplicating themselves? Watson and Crick speculate that during cell division this DNA ladder duplicates itself first by separating, or unzipping, down the middle of the structure—the bases separate from their mates, cytosine from guanine, and thymine from adenine. Think of the staircase being cut in half. Then each half of the DNA molecule serves as the framework to evolve a copy of the missing half from the materials of the surrounding cell and constructs a compatible half identical to the one from which it just separated. Thus, as a result of this unzipping and reconstruction of genes,

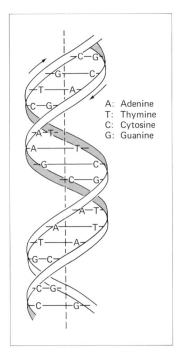

A: Adenine
T: Thymine
C: Cytosine
G: Guanine

FIGURE 2-4 The alphabet of life: a model of DNA, *(From Watson & Crick, 1953, with permission of the publisher and the senior author.)*

every cell in the body carries the same genetic code or pattern as the original one.

Homozygotes and Heterozygotes

Much of the original work which served as the basis for modern genetics was done at the end of the nineteenth century by Gregor Mendel, who worked with rather simple hereditary characteristics such as blossom color in hybridized plants. Many of the attributes he studied were ones in which a single pair of genes seemed largely responsible for the phenotypical appearance of the characteristic of the plant. It is now recognized that most phenotypical characteristics are determined by more than one gene. Although contemporary geneticists take a more complex approach in studying the transactions among a number of genetic factors and an array of environmental effects, some of Mendel's principles dealing with *dominant* and *recessive* genes are still accepted.

At each gene *locus*, or position on the chromosome, there may be two or more alternative forms of the gene called *alleles*. Recall that a child has two alleles of every gene in her body, one from her mother and one from her father. If the alleles from both parents are the same, a child is said to be *homozygous* at that locus; if they differ, she is said to be *heterozygous*. For example, if a child has alleles to be curly-haired from both parents, she is homozygous; but if she has a curly-haired allele from one parent and a straight-haired allele from the other, she is heterozygous. Using the code "A" to represent one allele and "a" another, and considering that each of a child's two genes may exist in either allelic state, it can be seen that three types of allelic combinations may result: AA, aa, or Aa (aA), depending on the parents' alleles. In our example of hair curliness, if "A" represents curly hair and "a" straight hair, the child with an AA combination will be curly-haired and the child with aa alleles will be straight-haired. But what happens with the heterozygous Aa child with different alleles from each parent? If a trait is determined by a single allelic pair, there are three main ways in which a heterozygous combination of alleles can be expressed in the phenotype. In the first case the heterozygous combination of alleles may be expressed in a phenotype intermediate between those carried by the individual alleles. For example, a very tall and a very short parent may produce a child of average height. A second possible form in which the heterozygous combination of alleles may be expressed is by showing codominant or combined attributes carried by two alleles. In relation to some alleles which control chemical substances in the blood, the blood of the heterozygotic child will contain both the blood substances which are contained singly in the blood of each parent. Finally, the characteristic associated with only one of the alleles may be expressed. One allele will be *dominant* over the other, that is, it would be more likely to be expressed phenotypically than the less powerful *recessive* gene.

If the phenotype Aa is the same as the phenotype AA, the allele A is said to be dominant and the allele a is said to be recessive. It can be seen by looking at the list of some well-known dominant and recessive characteristics presented in Table 2-1 that most of the serious deleterious genes are recessive. This is fortunate since otherwise we would be confronted with an exploding rate of genetic abnormalities. One of the reasons that there historically have been prohibitions on close blood relatives marrying is that in the offspring of such unions there is a greater chance of the same harmful recessive allele being contributed by each parent.

Let us examine the development of phenylketonuria (PKU) as an example of the action of dominant and recessive genes. This example is important not only in order to illustrate the development of a recessive disorder but also to emphasize again the fact that "genetic" does not mean "unchangeable." The adverse outcome of this genetically based metabolic disorder can be effectively countered by dietetic intervention procedures. As was emphasized earlier, the timing of this environmental intervention is critical.

Phenylketonuria is a disorder caused by a recessive gene which leads to the absence of an enzyme necessary to metabolize certain types of proteins, some of which are found in milk, the basic diet for infants. Thus, an infant with two recessive genes for phenylketonuria is unable to convert the protein phenylalanine into tyrosine, which results in an accumulation of phenylpyruvic acid in the body. This has damaging effects on the developing nervous system of the child, and usually results in mental retardation. The infant appears normal at birth, but with the gradual buildup of phenylpyruvic acid, increasing signs of mental retardation are shown. In addition to mental deficits, phenylketonuric children frequently have other characteristics, such as fair hair, irritability, poor coordination and awkwardness, hyperactivity, and convulsions.

The genetic transmission patterns for PKU are presented in Figure 2-5. Approximately 1 out of every 20 persons carries the recessive allele for

TABLE 2-1 SOME COMMON DOMINANT AND RECESSIVE CHARACTERISTICS

Dominant traits	Recessive traits
Brown eyes	Grey, green, blue hazel eyes
Curly hair	Straight hair
Normal hair	Baldness
Dark hair	Light or blonde hair
Nonred hair (blonde, brunette)	Red hair
Normal coloring	Albinism (lack of pigment)
Thick lips	Thin lips
Roman nose	Straight nose
Cheek dimples	No dimples
Extra, fused, or short digits	Normal digits
Double-jointedness	Normal joints
Normal color vision	Color blindness, red-green
Normal vision	Myopia, nearsightedness
Farsightedness	Normal vision
Immunity to poison ivy	Susceptibility to poison ivy
Normal hearing	Congenital deafness
Normal blood clotting	Hemophilia
Normal metabolism	Phenylketonuria
Normal blood cells	Sickle-cell anemia

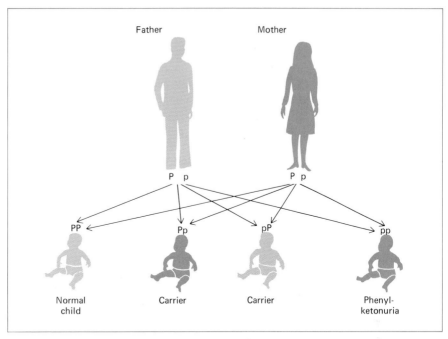

FIGURE 2-5   The genetic transmission of phenylketonuria in the children of two heterozygous parents carrying the recessive allele for phenylketonuria. (P is the dominant gene; p is the recessive gene.)

phenylketonuria (p). If a heterozygote (Pp) marries an individual who carries two dominant alleles (PP) for normal metabolizing of phenylalanine, their children will be intellectually unaffected by phenylalanine. However, if two of these heterozygotes (Pp) marry, they will have 1 chance in 4 of producing a phenylketonuric child (pp).

A method has been developed for testing parents who may carry the recessive gene for PKU (Hsia, Driscoll, Troll & Knox, 1956). The parent swallows a doze of l-phenylalanine, and subsequent tests may reveal an abnormally high level of phenylpyruvic acid in the blood. When parents have such information, they are aware of their potential risks in reproduction and can prepare for the immediate testing of their child for PKU in order to plan for dietary therapy at birth. Many hospitals also routinely test infants for PKU in the first week of life by assessing the level of phenylpyruvic acid in the blood after the infant has eaten protein. This test is sometimes inaccurate since phenyplyruvic acid has not yet had time to accumulate; therefore, in many states a urine test is required about six weeks after birth.

The damage caused by PKU can be restricted if infants are fed an early diet of milk substitutes, which limits their intake of phenylalanine. Children can be kept on this diet until about middle childhood, when the brain has developed to the point where it cannot be injured by the accumulation of phenylpyruvic acid. The importance of early dietary therapy is demonstrated graphically in Figure 2-5, which shows the relation between the start of treatment and eventual IQ of

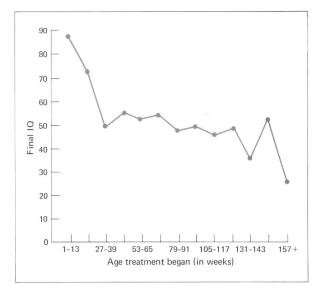

FIGURE 2-6 The relationship between age of starting dietary control and intelligence in phenylketonuria. *(Adapted from Baumeister, 1947, **71**, 840-847 with permission of the publisher and the author.)*

PKU patients. It can be seen that the effects of starting treatment decrease rapidly after the first few months of life, and that starting dietary remedies as early as 7 months can do little to reverse the destructive course of the disorder. This is an example of the point we emphasized earlier, that the timing of intervention is critical.

Homozygotic phenylketonurics seldom reproduce, but when they do, the results are disastrous. Male phenylketonurics pass on only one recessive gene for the disorder to their offspring, which may be counteracted by a normal gene in the women they marry. However, female phenylketonurics seem to present their children with a damaging prenatal intrauterine environment as well as a defective gene. Howell and Stevenson (1971) reported that of 121 babies born to 33 PKU women, only 16 were normal; the others died young, had PKU, or were mentally retarded, often with microencephaly (a disorder characterized by an extremely small skull and brain). The most common attribute of these infants was retarded prenatal growth, often manifested in deviant development of the nervous system and accompanying mental retardation. These investigators suggest that although pregnant phenylketonuric women are put on diets to limit their intake of phenylalanine, the harm to the fetus may have occurred in the first month of pregnancy before pregnancy and PKU have been diagnosed and treatment begun.

Complex Gene Interaction

What has been presented thus far is a rather simple genetic model of one gene determining one characteristic. It is now recognized that many characteristics are determined by a constellation of genes that act together (polygenic inheritance) and that a single pair of genes may influence more than one characteristic (pleiotropism).

Some genes, called *modifier genes*, influence the action or phenotypical expression of other genes. The action of a modifer gene is clearly demonstrated in the inheritance of early cataracts. The occurrence of cataracts is determined by a dominant gene; however, the type of opacity and the location on the lens of the cataract seem to be determined by modifier genes.

Similarly, children with phenylketonuria have differing phenylalanine levels in spite of the fact that they have identical genes at the critical locus. This is because modifier genes at other loci determine the variation in phenylalanine levels and in intelligence levels in untreated cases.

In attempting to understand the impact of genetic factors on development, in addition to the complexities introduced by such multiple gene interactions, it must be recognized that the effects of many genes are not displayed at birth but are manifested with time. For example, sexual maturing, baldness, longevity, and the occurrence of a degenerative disorder of the nervous system called Huntington's chorea are only a few genetically influenced attributes that emerge later in life.

Sex Chromosomes and Sex-linked Characteristics

Of the 23 pairs of chromosomes, 22 pairs are *autosomes*, that is, they are possessed equally by males and females. In contrast, the twenty-third pair, the *sex chromosomes*, differs in males and females. The female has two X chromosomes (XX), and the male has an X and a Y (XY) chromosome. The X chromosome is about five times as long as the Y chromosome and carries more genes on it. Since the mother is XX, her ovum always contains an X chromosome. However, sperms may carry either an X or a Y chromosome. If a sperm with an X chromosome fertilizes the egg, the offspring will be female (XX); if the sperm carries a Y chromosome, the offspring will be male (XY). The sex of the child is thus determined by the father.

The fact that some genes on the X chromosome have no equivalent genes on the Y chromosome results in the appearance of sex-linked, recessive characteristics in males. Since a male has only one X chromosome, if the recessive allele for a defect is present on the X chromosome, the disorder will be manifested since there is no equivalent allele on the Y chromosome to counteract its effect. In women the phenotypical expression of a recessive allele for a defect will be determined by its interaction with the matching allele on the other X chromosome. If the matching allele is a dominant one for normal development, it will overrule the effects of a damaging recessive allele.

For example, hemophilia, a disease in which the blood does not clot, is a sex-linked recessive trait carried on the X chromosome. Since it is recessive, if a female receives the deleterious recessive gene from one parent, unless the matching gene from the other is also for hemophilia, she will have blood which clots normally. Only if she is homozygous for the recessive gene will her blood clotting be impaired. In contrast, if a male receives the gene from the mother on the X chromosome, there can be no counteracting gene from the father and the son will be afflicted.

There are many X-linked characteristics in addition to hemophilia. These

This Down's syndrome baby has folds on the corner of the eyes and a flat profile typical of such children. (From Smith & Wilson, 1973, p. 51)

include color blindness, certain types of night blindness, one form of muscular dystrophy, diabetes, atrophy of the optic nerve, and a disorder resulting in an inability to produce antibodies to cope with certain bacterial infections. Also, the high rate of miscarriage, infant mortality, and childhood deaths in males is partly attributable to their greater vulnerability to sex-linked disorders. Even resistance to certain childhood diseases appears to be sex-linked. Thus, although a ratio of 106 males to 100 females are born, this numerical imbalance is rapidly eliminated in the early years of development. Even before birth, it has been estimated that 50 percent more male than female fetuses die or are miscarried. This higher mortality rate of males continues throughout development. In the first month of life, deaths of male infants exceed female deaths by 40 percent; in

TABLE 2-2   RISK OF DOWN'S SYNDROME BY MATERNAL AGE

Age of mother	Risk of Down's syndrome in child	
	At any pregnancy	After the birth of a Down's syndrome child
-29	1 in 3,000	1 in 1,000
30-34	1 in 600	1 in 200
35-39	1 in 280	1 in 100
40-44	1 in 70	1 in 25
45-49	1 in 40	1 in 15
All mothers	1 in 665	1 in 200

Source: Reprinted from C. O. Carter and D. MacCarthy, Incidence of mongolism and its diagnosis in the newborn, *British Journal of Social Medicine*, 1951, **5**, 83-90.

the first year, by 33 percent; between 5 and 9, by 44 percent; between 10 and 14, by 70 percent; and between 15 and 19, by 145 percent (Montague, 1959). The high rate of mortality for males in later years may not be entirely due to their greater genetic vulnerability. Partially it may be attributable to the more adventurous risk-taking activities of males and to such things as their participation in war. In any event, the presence of only a single X chromosome is a genetic liability for males.

Chromosome Abnormalities

Developmental disorders sometimes appear because of defects or variations in chromosomes, or chromosome matching. Some of these deviations occur in the autosomes; others occur in the sex chromosomes. Almost 1 percent of all neonates have diagnosable chromosomal abnormalities in their cells. In addition it is estimated that 25 to 30 percent of spontaneous abortions are attributable to chromosomal aberrations.

Down's syndrome will be discussed as one example out of the many identifiable autosomal disorders, followed by a presentation of several of the more common disorders based on deviations in the sex chromosomes.

Down's Syndrome   A disorder known as *trisomy 21*, or *Down's syndrome*, was for some time regarded as a nongenetic disorder attributable to the effects on the infant in utero of physiological and biological factors in aging of the mother. As can be seen from Table 2-2, the incidence of Down's syndrome does increase dramatically with maternal age.

The disorder is characterized by physical and mental retardation and a rather unique appearance. Children with Down's syndrome have almond eyes with eyelid folds that many early observers found to be similar to those of Orientals, round heads often flattened on the back, short necks, protruding tongues, and small noses. In addition, they frequently have other unusual characteristics such as webbed fingers or toes, a rare long simian crease which extends across the hand, dental anomalies, and an awkward flat-footed walk.

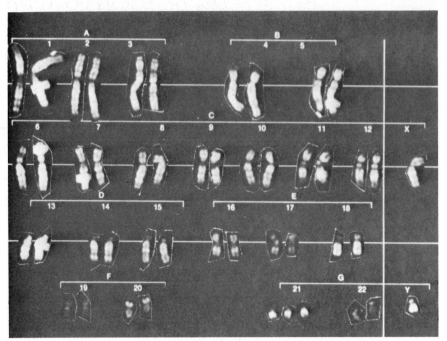

The autosomes of a male who has Down's syndrome. (Courtesy of the University of Virginia Hospital Chromosome Laboratory)

Their greater susceptibility to leukemia, heart disorders, and particularly to respiratory infections normally resulted in extremely early deaths. At one time it was unusual to see these individuals as adolescents or postadolescents; however, since advances have been made in the treatment of these disorders (such as the use of antibiotics for pneumonia), their life span has greatly increased. Most children with Down's syndrome have affectionate, placid, cheerful temperaments and are therefore more likely to be kept in the home for a longer period of time than are children with other forms of mental retardation associated with hyperactive, wild, uncontrollable behavior. In spite of this fact, over 10 percent of institutionalized retardates are persons with Down's syndrome.

In 1959 it was demonstrated that Down's syndrome is related to a deviation in the twenty-first set of autosomes. This was an important genetic breakthrough since it was the first identification of a chromosomal aberration as a cause of human disease. Down's syndrome is attributable to either *translocation* or *nondisjunction* of chromosome 21. Afflicted individuals may have one of their twenty-first chromosomes translocated to another chromsome. In translocation part of chromosome 21 becomes attached to another chromosome, usually to chromosome 13, 14, 15, or 22. Thus, the right number of chromosomes (46) are present, but they are misarranged. However, more commonly, Down's syndrome is based on nondisjunction of a chromosome where the afflicted individual has an extra chromosome or part of a third chromosome on the twenty-first set of autosomes. This is thought to be a result of failure of the chromosomes to separate at meiosis in the egg, and consequently, as can be seen in the photograph on this page, the individual has 47 rather than the usual 46 chromosomes. Why this occurs more frequently in older mothers is not known. It has been speculated that some deterioration of the ova produced by older women may occur or that such women may have been exposed to more radiation during the course of their lifetime which could lead to increased chromosomal abnormalities.

The role of genetic factors in this disorder is supported by comparative studies of identical, or *monzygotic* (MZ) twins and fraternal, or *dizygotic* (DZ) twins. Monozygotic twins are created by the separation of the zygote following fertilization of a single egg by a single sperm. Following the separation of the zygote, two fetuses develop instead of one. In contrast, dizygotic twins develop from two eggs that have been fertilized by two different sperms, also producing two fetuses. It can be seen that the genetic endowment, or genotypes, of the monozygotic twins is identical, whereas the genotypes of the fraternal twins are no more alike than those of separately born siblings. If a characteristic is genetically determined, the *concordance rate*, or agreement between presence or absence of a trait, is higher in identical than in fraternal twins. In all pairs of identical twins, if one infant has Down's syndrome, so does the other; whereas the occurrence of the disorder in both fraternal twins is relatively rare. In addition, non-mentally retarded relatives of Down's syndrome patients often show a few or muted symptoms of the disorder, as can be seen in Box 2-1. Although these relatives do not have Down's syndrome, the presence of these symptoms is associated with an increased incidence of behavior disorders.

Down's syndrome is one of the genetic disorders which can be detected before birth through *amniocentesis*. In amniocentesis a needle is inserted into the amniotic sac, which surrounds the fetus, and fluid is removed. This fluid contains cells which have been sloughed off by the fetus. Since each cell contains the genetic blueprint of the individual, these cells can be examined for the presence of certain chromosomal and metabolic disorders. However, only about sixty disorders out of the extremely large number of genetic anomalies can be detected in this manner. The sixteenth week of pregnancy seems to be the best time to perform amniocentesis. At that time there are sufficient fetal cells in the amniotic fluid and the fetus is still small and unlikely to be injured. In addition it is still early enough in the pregnancy to permit safe abortion. Unlike phenylketonuria, there is no way of treating Down's syndrome. If amniocentesis is performed and the presence of the syndrome is detected, the only option that can be offered to the parents is whether or not they wish to abort the defective fetus.

Sex Chromosome Abnormalities   In additon to abnormalities in the autosomes, such as those found in Down's syndrome, problems in sexual differentiation sometimes occur based on deviations in the number of sex chromosomes. Diagnosis of such individuals can be made on the basis of chromsome counts from cells drawn from samples of skin or mouth tissue and prenatally through amniocentesis.

BOX 2-1
MINOR PHYSICAL ANOMALIES AND BEHAVIOR

 A set of minor physical anomalies has been associated with Down's syndrome. These include fine electric hair, two or more hair whorls, head circumference out of normal range, epicanthus (skin fold covering part of the eye), unusually wide set eyes, malformed ears, asymmetrical ears, soft pliable ears, low-seated ears, no ear lobes, high-steepled palate, furrowed tongue, tongue with smooth and rough spots, single crease across the palm of the hand, curved fifth finger, third toe longer than second, partial webbing of the two middle toes, and a large gap between the first and second toes (Waldrop & Halverson, 1971). Now don't start to worry if you possess some of these characteristics since most people possess two or more of these attributes. However, what is the significance of a relatively large number of these anomalies being found in individuals who are apparently ''normal''? It is the number of anomalies, the cumulative incidence, not the presence of any particular anomaly that has been associated with certain clusters of deviant behavior. For boys the association between multiple physical anomalies and behavior is clearer and more consistent than it is for girls. For boys multiple physical anomalies and hyperactive, disruptive, acting-out behavior, low achievement, and an enjoyment of fast-moving impulsive play are related. In contrast, although girls with many of these anomalies sometimes show a pattern of extreme impulsivity and activity where they are regarded as mean and noisy by their peers, more often they are described as inhibited, fearful, socially ill at ease, uncoordinated, and inattentive.

It is thought that the same genetic factors or prenatal factors operating in the first few weeks of pregnancy which are associated with the physical anomalies also produce abnormalities in the central nervous system that may contribute to behavioral problems (Quinn & Rapaport, 1974). The fact that the anomalies are present at birth permits early detection of infants who are at high risk for developing related problem behaviors. Particularly in boys, where there is only a small percentage of errors made in predicting impulsive hyperactive behavior from the presence of a large number of these anomalies, there would seem to be considerable promise in setting up early intervention programs to help develop increased self-control in these children. ■

Source: Halverson, C. F., & Victor, J. B. Minor physical anomalies and problem behavior in elementary school children. *Child Development,* 1976, **47**, 281–285. Waldrop, M. F., & Halverson, C. F. Minor physical anomalies and hyperactive behavior in young children. In J. Hellmuth (Ed.), *Exceptional infant: Studies in abnormalities* (Vol. 2). Brunner/Mazel, New York, 1971. Waldrop, M. F., Bell, R. Q., & Goering, J. D. Minor physical anomalies and inhibited behavior in elementary school girls. *Journal of Child Psychology and Psychiatry,* 1976, **17**, 113–122.

Turner's syndrome One type of sex chromosome abnormality is *Turner's syndrome.* Females having Turner's syndrome, instead of having the customary XX combination of sex chromosomes, are missing the second X chromosome and are XO. They have only 45 chromosomes. These girls remain small in stature, are usually of normal intelligence, and often have short fingers and webbed necks and unusually shaped mouths and ears. In personality they tend to be relaxed, docile, pleasant, and not easily upset. At puberty they remain infantile in the development of the mammary glands and other secondary sex characteristics because of the lack of female hormones. However, successful treatment is possible through the administration of estrogens (female hormones), which at puberty will lead to normal sexual development although the girls will remain sterile. It should be noted that even when treated they are still short and have an eternally pubescent or little girlish appearance. Girls with Turner's syndrome show feminine personality characteristics and interests even without hormone treatment, and it has been concluded that the normal female XX genetic pattern is not essential for the development of a feminine identity and behaviors.

Sex chromosome deviations in males   Two types of abnormal sex chromosomal patterns in males have been extensively studied. The first, known as Klinefelter's syndrome, involves an additional X chromosome, an XXY rather than the normal XY male chromosomal array. The second pattern involves an extra Y chromosome, yielding an XYY array.

Males afflicted with Klinefelter's syndrome (XXY) have testes although they are sterile, and they have many female characteristics such as breast development and a rounded broad-hipped female figure. They share in common with XYY males a tendency to be significantly taller than normal XY males.

The psychological characteristics of males with these two types of chromosomal deviations have been a topic of considerable interest and controversy. It has been reported that both XXY and XYY males are impulsive and antisocial and are overrepresented in institutions for the mentally retarded and in prisons, particularly in men charged with violent crimes (Forssman & Hambert, 1966; Hook, 1973).

It has even been suggested that intervention procedures be taken to restrain people identified as having these hormonal patterns. In some hospitals, screening programs testing infants for the presence of chromosomal anomalies were undertaken. These programs have been severely criticized because of the adverse effects of labeling and particularly of reporting to parents that a child has chromosomal deviations and because of the poor quality of much of the research from which these conclusions were drawn.

Many of the generalizations about violent behavior and XYY or XXY patterns in males were based on small samples, often even on single cases, and the subjects were usually selected only from deviant groups such as institutional populations. Recently a carefully conducted study was done in Denmark to determine if XYY and XXY males have an elevated crime rate and what the role of aggressiveness and intelligence might be in any increased rate of antisocial behavior. This study is notable because it did not use an institutionalized population but sampled from a more representative population of Danes. Many American psychologists are now studying the incidence and development of psychological disorders in Denmark because excellent records are kept in that country. These records usually yield detailed information about the social, educational, health and family histories of individuals which are not available in the United States.

BOX 2-2
CRIMINALITY IN XYY AND XXY MALES

 Are XYY and XXY males more predisposed to become involved in criminal activities and to commit violent crimes? If they are more antisocial and violent, what factors might mediate the development of such behavior? A study was undertaken of male children born to Danish women who were residents of Copenhagen between January 1, 1944, and December 31, 1947. Since the chromosomal patterns in which the investigators were interested are rare and since males having these patterns have been demonstrated to be taller than the general population, only males in the tallest 15.9 percent of the population were included in the study to maximize the likelihood of obtaining an adequate sample. Chromosome determinations from blood samples and smear cells from the mouth and cheeks were made on 4,139 men. Twelve XYYs and sixteen XXYs were identified, and the remainder of the group of normal XY males composed the control group. It can be seen how rare these disorders are when it is remembered that this population had already been preselected for height. Measures were obtained of height, convictions for criminal offenses, level of intellectual functioning as indicated by scores on an army selection test and by educational attainment, and parents' social class at the time of the subject's birth. Both the XXY and XYY males showed poorer intellectual functioning than the XY males. However, only XYY males had a higher rate of criminal convictions than did normals. In addition within the groups, even within the normal XY group, there was a relation between having been convicted of a crime and low intelligence. This of course could be attributable to the fact that brighter criminals may be more adept at escaping detection. The investigators concluded that intellectual functioning is clearly an important mediating variable in the development of criminality but that it cannot be said to be the only factor involved.

They then moved on to answer the critical question of whether the chromosomally deviant groups were more violent in the types of crimes they commit. This did not prove to be the case. The elevated crime rate in the XYY sample reflected a high rate of property offenses, not crimes against people. There was only a single instance of a mild form of violence against an unoffending person by an XYY male who was a chronic criminal with nearly fifty offenses against property on his record.

What can we conclude from this carefully executed study? The image of the XYY and XXY male as a violent, assaultive individual is clearly not valid. However, XYY males are more likely to be involved in crimes against property than are males with a normal complement of sex hormones, and low intelligence contributes to criminality to some extent. ■

Source: Witkin, H. A., Mednick, S. A., Schulsinger, F., Bakkestrom, E., Christiansen, K. O., Goodenough, D. R., Hirchhorn, K., Lunsteen, C., Owen, D. R., Philip, J., Ruben, D. B., & Stocking, M. Criminality in XYY and XXY men. *Science*, 1976, **193**, 547–555.

Intersexuality The precise relation of deviations in the sex chromosomes to the development of *intersexuality*, or *hermaphroditism*, that is, the presence of some of the sexual characteristics or reproductive systems of both males and females, is open to question. Although some intersexual individuals may be developmental accidents, or mutations, it is also believed that rare recessive or sex-linked genes may also cause these conditions. There are great variations in intersexuality. Some individuals have both ovaries and testes; others possess the internal reproductive system of one sex and the external genitalia of the other. However, intersexes never have both a complete male and female sexual system, and in most cases they are sterile.

Mutation and Selection

Genetic variability results not only from the vast number of genetic combinations possible from the chromosomes in the gametes and the exchange of genetic material in the process of crossing-over during meiosis, but also from the development of *mutations*. Mutations are changes in the genes which may produce new phenotypes. In some cases a mutation occurs because of transformations in the gene; in other cases it may be the result of alternations in the arrangement of genes or the quantity of chromosomal material. Down's syndrome, which was discussed earlier, is one of the most frequently cited examples of a mutation developing from the addition of chromosomal material to the twenty-first pair of chromosomes.

The survival of a mutation depends upon a variety of factors; primarily its survival depends upon its adaptability in relation to the environment in which it must develop. The vast majority of mutations are deleterious, or lethal, and do not survive. Theories of evolution are based on the notion of the interaction of mutations with physical and environmental factors in the selective survival of individuals having certain characteristics. Some characteristics such as sicklemia, which will be discussed later, may be advantageous in one environment but detrimental in another.

Causes of Mutation   The reasons for spontaneous mutations in genes are not well understood and are of great concern to contemporary geneticists. Some mutations are controlled by special genes called *mutator genes*, which increase the rate of mutations in individuals who carry them. Other mutations occur because of external agents, or factors, the best known of which are *high temperatures* and *radiation*.

High temperatures   High temperatures can contribute to increased rates of mutation in animals. The following provocative speculation about the transactions between clothing, temperature, and mutations in human beings has been offered.

Most mammals have a temperature-regulating device that keeps the body warmer than the scrotum. Swedish investigators found that wearing tight trousers can raise scrotal temperatures from 30.7°C to 34°C. This, on the basis of crude estimates of known mutation rates and the temperature effect, could increase the incidence of mutation by 85 percent, that is, nearly double. It is an amusing possibility that perhaps half of what is considered to be spontaneous mutation originating in males is in reality contributed by current sexual taboos, and that the Scottish kilt may have more merits than its wearers suspect. (Lerner & Libby, 1976, p. 294)

Radiation Radiation is the most extensively studied and controversial external source of mutations. In some cases radiation occurs naturally through variations in cosmic radiation, in the amount of radioactive material in the soil in different parts of the world, or through eating radioactive foods (Gentry, Parkhurst, & Bulin, 1959). In other cases, developmental deviations occur through radiation produced by humans, such as x-rays or radiation from atomic fallout.

In both cases, radiation of pregnant women is associated with a high rate of abnormalities such as mental retardation, microcephaly (small heads), decrements in height and weight, and leukemia (cancer of the blood) in their offspring, and with chromosomal abnormalities in adults. However, the genetic evidence of transmission of radiation effects has not been demonstrated conclusively in humans. Careful studies of children of radiologists (Crow, 1955) and of Japanese populations exposed to radiation from atomic attacks (Neel & Schull, 1956; Schull & Neel, 1958) found no difference from those in nonexposed populations in the incidence of abnormal characteristics in their offspring if the parents were not pregnant with the child at the time of exposure. Although much concern has been expressed about the continued accumulation of atomic fallout effects through nuclear testing, at the present time these are minimal when compared with those resulting from the use of x-rays or from natural radiation (Lerner, 1968).

Sickle-Cell Anemia: An Example of Selective Survival of a Mutation One of the most dramatic examples of the interaction of genetic factors and environment in selective survival is found in the history of a blood disease called sickle-cell anemia. A mutation appearing in the red blood cells proved adaptive in one environment and destructive in another. The history of the investigation of this disorder reads like a contemporary genetic detective story.

A blood test of a random sample of American blacks would reveal that in about 8 percent of these people under conditions of low oxygen, 40 percent of their red blood cells would assume unusual crescent, sickle, or holly-leaf shapes. In most of these individuals the tendency of the blood to sickle is not associated with any deleterious symptoms, and these individuals are said to have the *sickle-cell trait,* or *sicklemia.* However, 1 in 40 of these persons will be afflicted with a severe, chronic, often fatal form of anemia called *sickle-cell anemia.*

Two questions puzzled geneticists: What was the underlying genetic basis for the sickle-cell trait and for sickle-cell anemia? And why was the incidence of sickling relatively prevalent in blacks but rare in Caucasians? It was found (Neel, 1949) that a recessive sickling gene exists which results in the sickle-cell trait in a heterozygous state and leads to sickle-cell anemia in a homozygous state. Thus both parents of a child having sickle-cell anemia will themselves have the sickle-cell trait. In its homozygous state in the child this sickling gene causes chemical changes in the hemoglobin molecule, but only rarely do overt adverse symptoms appear in the heterozygotic parents.

The high incidence of the sickle-cell trait in blacks and particularly in some African tribes, such as the Baamba where 39 percent of the population have this trait, was baffling to geneticists. Since sickle-cell anemia sufferers die early and

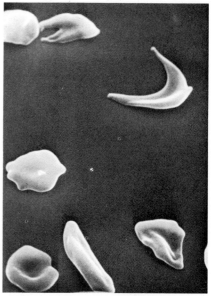

Normal blood cells on the left contrast with the sickle-shaped red blood cells of a person with sickle-cell anemia. (Dr. Marion I. Barnhart, Wayne State University)

only a small percentage have children, how could this high frequency of a recessive characteristic be maintained? It was noted that the unusually high rates of the sickle-cell trait often occurred in areas with a high incidence of malaria. Investigators found a much lower rate of presence of the malarial parasite in sicklers than in nonsicklers, particularly if the subjects were children who had not yet had the opportunity to acquire immunity to malaria (Allison, 1954). The incidences of malarial parasites in 290 Ganda children, aged 5 months to 5 years, are presented in Table 2-3. The sickle-cell trait was found to be associated with a resistance to malarial infection. Thus, in malarial regions the heterozygous presence of the sickling gene actually has a selective advantage in survival. Heterozygotes, having a higher rate of survival, reproduce more frequently than noncarriers and maintain the frequency of the gene in the population. This is not the case in nonmalarial areas where there is no positive adaptive function served by the sickle-cell gene.

TABLE 2-3 INCIDENCE OF MALARIAL PARASITES IN GANDA CHILDREN

	With parasitaemia	Without parasitaemia	Total
Sicklers	12 (27.9%)	31 (72.1%)	43
Nonsicklers	113 (45.7%)	134 (54.3%)	247

Source: From Allison, A. C. Protection afforded by sickle-cell trait against subtertian malarial infection. *British Medical Journal*, 1954, **1**, 290–294.

Although sickle-cell carriers have few adverse symptoms, under certain environmental circumstances they, too, can suffer from their genetic endowment. The Air Force Academy at Colorado Springs recently announced that it would not admit any heterozygotic sickle-cell trait carriers because a combination of exercise and the high altitude at the mountain school had resulted in three deaths of sickle-cell carriers in the last few years. At high altitudes, severe oxygen deprivation resulting from extreme physical exertion can cause a sickle-cell crisis in heterozygotes. Under oxygen deprivation these heterozygotes have 30 to 40 percent sickled cells, which clog blood vessels and can cause not only severe pain and tissue damage but death by blocking critical vessels in the brain and lungs.

The effects of the sickle-cell gene thus vary from an adaptive effect in high malarial areas, which increases the selective survival of the mutation, to a destructive effect in nonmalarial areas, particularly those areas with high altitudes, which leads to increased mortality rates.

Evolution Sickle-cell anemia is only one example of the selective survival of a mutation. Both animals and environments change. There is a constant process of natural selection and survival of organisms that have characteristics that help them adapt constructively to their surroundings. Those individuals who have a fortuitous combination of genes are more likely to survive and reproduce. Their adaptive attributes will be transmitted. The less adaptive organism will eventually be wiped out. Most of the evolutionary changes that have been traditionally discussed have involved physical changes. For example, it seems likely that certain body types may be the result of adaptation to their environment and natural selection. A short squat body such as is found in Eskimos tends to conserve heat and would be adaptive in the bitterly cold conditions of the arctic. In contrast, the tall slender body found frequently in northeast Africa would dissipate heat more rapidly and be advantageous in the excessively hot African climate.

One of the most intense controversies in contemporary genetics is whether social behavior in both humans and animals might also be based on biological and genetic factors which are a product of selective adaptation and evolution.

Edward O. Wilson (1975) has proposed that many characteristics we tend to think of as exclusively human characteristics such as morality, altruism, slavery, or despotism are also found in animals, and that in both humans and animals the characteristics have evolved because of their survival value. He views the evolution of altruism—giving up personal satisfactions for the gains of the others, or the larger social group—as a critical adaptive evolutionary development. In fact, the title of his first chapter in his provocative book, *Sociobiology*, is "The Morality of the Gene." Wilson's strong emphasis on the genetic basis of social behavior has little experimental support. If a genetic foundation exists for social behavior, evidence suggests that its expression may be indirect and that it is greatly modified by cultural factors.

Chimpanzees show altruistic behavior by picking lice out of each other's fur. (Dr. H. Albrecht, Bruce Coleman, Inc.)

Genetic Counseling and Genetic Engineering

Advances in biology and genetics have opened new opportunities for shaping and controlling some aspects of development. Through amniocentesis and chromosomal analysis in early pregnancy we can detect not only the sex of the child but whether the child in utero has disorders such as sex chromosome abnormalities, Down's syndrome, sickle-cell anemia, or Tay Sachs syndrome, a lethal genetic disorder leading to mental deficiency, blindness, and paralysis. Parents then have the option to abort and avoid the distress associated with having an abnormal child. But what kinds of ethical issues may arise from our growing genetic sophistication? Although XYY males are more likely to become involved in crimes, not all males with the extra Y chromosome do so. Some hospital programs have done routine chromsomal screening of newborn infants and reported to the parents the presence of chromosomal deviations. Are children unfairly stigmatized by being labeled as XYY children? What does knowing this do to the parents' attitudes and relationship with the child? Research shows that parents frequently respond in terms of expectations, even false expectations, about their children. Such knowledge could initiate a destructive self-fulfilling prophecy.

If a fetus has no detectable genetic abnormalities, is sex of a child sufficient reason to abort? In this country almost all surveys show that on the average male children are preferred over female by expectant parents. In some other countries this preference is even more extreme. A recent report about 100 pregnant women in China who were screened to determine the sex of their unborn child stated that over 60 percent of the mothers carrying girls wished to abort where only 1 of the 53 women carrying a male child chose to abort (*China Medical Journal*, 1975).

Biologists have been able to transplant animal embryos from one uterus to another, to remove and transfer genes from one organism to another, and to artificially synthesize a gene in a test tube. The process which appears to have captured the public's imagination is one called cloning, in which body cells are artificially induced to reproduce themselves. Through cloning it would be possible to reproduce a series of identical individuals from a single body cell. A recent novel presented the terrifying picture of cloned cells from Hitler being implanted in dozens of women by rabid Nazis hoping to develop another Fuhrer. Some people might not regard all cloning as quite so undesirable. A basketball team of cloned Julius Ervings (Dr. J's) would warm the cockles of many a coach's heart, and a university president might be delighted at the thought of the university's laboratories being filled with industrious clones from Nobel Prize winners.

Most of the genetic engineering research has been done on animals because of ethical constraints on transplanting embryos from one woman to another or transferring or removing human genes. However, the specter of engineering superbeings, the destruction of genetic uniqueness, and even the possibility of artifically producing a new bacteria or species destructive to human beings are now concerning not only the popular press and the public but the scientists themselves. Over the past four years groups of scientists have met and attempted to work out safety guidelines and restrictions for research with hybrid cells. The key issue is as greater genetic control becomes possible, how should it be used and how should it be limited for the good of human beings?

Heredity and Behavior

Biologists and geneticists have made great advances in understanding some of the processes and mechanisms related to development. However, their main contributions have been in the area of physical development or gross developmental deviations such as Down's syndrome. In spite of Edward Wilson's position, we find that we have little knowledge of possible genetic processes involved in most of the important human attributes with which psychologists are concerned. Although biologists can point to the twenty-first chromosome as the basis of mental retardation in Down's syndrome, they can't tell us why one child has an IQ of 90 and his sibling has an IQ of 150. They can't show what genetic material is transmitted or what biochemical or metabolic factors are involved in the development of aggression, altruism, sociability, intelligence, or different forms of psychopathology. Most of the advances in understanding the possible role of genetic factors in human behavior have come from behavior geneticists.

It will become apparent that in the questions they ask, in their research methods, and in their focus on genetic contributions to *behavior*, behavior geneticists differ greatly from biologists interested in the study of heredity. Studies of behavior genetics can be conducted without mentioning chromosomes, genes, and DNA. In fact, behavior genetics was well underway before modern gene theory was developed.

Some behavior geneticists are mainly concerned with investigating behavior differences between species. What genetic, biological, and evolutionary processes have led to patterns of such things as mating, aggression, or fear responses that differ markedly between species?

Other behavior geneticists are more interested in understanding genetic contributions to individual differences within a species, and this is where their concerns overlap most with those of child psychologists. We are all aware of the diversity in human behavior. Some children find it easier to solve problems than others; some are gregarious, and others introspective and socially isolated; some are emotionally unstable, and others cope easily with adversity. How do genetic factors contribute to the wide range of individual differences observed in human behavior throughout the entire life span?

The study of similarities in characteristics of family members is one of the most frequently used procedures in investigating this issue. Studies of twins are most often used. However, the study of the similarity between the attributes of adopted children and their natural and adoptive parents has also proved fruitful. Because of the unique genetic patterns in twins, many of these studies involve comparing the similarities in certain attributes of identical, or monozygotic twins, and of fraternal, or dizygotic twins. Monozygotic twins are more similar than dizygotic twins in genetic endowment, since they developed from a single zygote. In twin studies the implicit assumption is also made that environmental influences are equally similar for both types of twins. If identical twins show more resemblance on a particular trait than do fraternal twins, who have different genotypes, it is assumed that the appearance of the trait is strongly influenced by genetic factors. If sets of identical and fraternal twins who have shared the same home resemble each other almost equally on a characteristic, it is assumed that this characteristic is more strongly influenced by environmental than genetic factors.

The assumption of similar environmental influences for both types of twins has been questioned by some investigators, for it seems possible that because identical twins are more similar in appearance and other attributes, they elicit more similar social responses, especially in treatment by parents. On the other hand, if parents believe their twins are monozygotic, they may have some preconceived notion that since the twins are more alike they should be treated more similarly. The critical question, then, is: Do parents create or respond to similarities in identical twins? Some evidence which may help us answer this question is found in studies in which the parents have incorrectly classified the zygosity of their twins. These misclassifications are surprisingly high, ranging from 12 percent in some monozygotic (identical) pairs to 35 percent in dizygotic (fraternal) pairs (Smith, 1965). The similarity of parental treatment seems to be determined by genetic rather than believed similarity. That is, mothers of monozygotic twins, whom they wrongly believe to be dizygotic, treat them more like correctly identified monozygotic twins; and mothers of dizygotic twins, whom they wrongly believe to be monozygotic, treat them more like correctly classified dizygotic pairs. Despite the mothers' erroneous beliefs the twins are recognized as having similarities and differences appropriate to their degree of genetic relatedness (Scarr, 1968).

In a study (Lytton, 1976) involving direct observations of mothers interacting with $2^1/_2$-year-old identical or fraternal twins, it was found that the greater similarity which mothers show in responding to identical rather than fraternal twins is based on the more similar behaviors of the identical twins. Some behaviors seem to be spontaneously performed by mothers, apparently not in response to signals from their children. For example, a mother may begin to play with an infant who is making no demands for attention. Other maternal behaviors are clearly triggered by the child's behavior. The infant cries and she picks the child up. In the spontaneously initiated maternal behaviors, identical twins were not treated more similarly than fraternal twins by their mothers. However, in the maternal behaviors made in response to a child's signal, maternal responses were more similar with identical than fraternal twins. Monozygotic twins are biologically predisposed to be more temperamentally similar in ways that will elicit more similar responses from their parents. They are more likely to be similarly fearful, sociable, active, or irritable. These are all characteristics that shape the kind of responses likely to be made by their caretakers. In answer to our earlier question, it seems that parents do not initially create but instead respond to present similarities in identical twins. However, even if the similarity of response in the parents is induced by the phenotypical similarity of the identical twins, it still results in monozygotic twins having more similar environments.

Other investigators have argued that prenatal as well as postnatal factors must be considered in evaluating experiential similarities of twins (Allen, 1965; Corney & Aherne, 1965; Price, 1950; Strong & Corney, 1967). Infants in utero are carried in a sac called the chorion. About 30 percent of monozygotic twins share the same chorion in utero; the remaining 70 percent are in separate chorions, as are dizygotic twins. When monozygotic twins share the same chorion, there is a high probability that fetal crowding will occur and that one twin will obtain a significantly larger share of the maternal blood supply and nourishment than the other. This leads to functional and physical differences in monozygotic twins, and they may often show greater differences in birthweights than do dizygotic twins. Thus, in some cases twins who are genotypically identical may be less overtly similar at birth than fraternal twins but will become increasingly similar with age.

Physical and Physiological Characterictics

Monozygotic twins are more similar than dizygotic twins in a variety of traits associated with physical measures and measures of biological functioning. In height, weight, shoulder width, hand length, and hand width, identical twins are more alike than fraternal twins (Huntley, 1966; Mittler, 1969; Newman et al., 1937). They are also more similar in facial and dental characteristics and in body build.

Studies of twins indicate that heredity is an important factor in rate of physical maturing as measured by such things as age of first menstruation, ossification of the bones in the hand (which is used as a measure of maturity), and longevity. Even in old age, after exposure to a wide range of environmental influences, identical twins are more similar than fraternal twins in pattern and timing of the formation of wrinkles, loss of teeth, and graying and thinning of hair (Kallman & Sander, 1949).

Of interest to psychologists is the similarity in identical twins in functioning of the brain and of the *autonomic nervous system*, that system that is so closely related to emotional arousal and responsiveness. Variations in responses in the autonomic nervous system have been related to the way individuals adapt to

The similarity in the pattern of aging can be seen in these pictures of identical twins taken over the course of their lifetime. (From Kallmann and Jarvik, 1959)

stress and anxiety-arousing situations, control their impulses, and deal with emotional conflicts. In recordings of electrical brain-wave patterns, it has been found that young adult monozygotic twins have recordings as similar as two recordings from the same person on two different occasions. Thus, it is possible to predict the pattern of electrical impulses in the brain of one identical twin from the recordings of the brain of the other as accurately as it is to predict the patterns of impulses of the same individual from one recording to another. In contrast, there is only a modest relationship between the brain-wave recordings of fraternal twins.

Jost and Sontag (1944) found great similarity in monozygotic twins on a composite measure of autonomic functioning, the *index of autonomic stability,* which included blood pressure, respiration rate, galvanic skin response (electrical conductance rates on the skin), salivation, and heart rate. In a more recent study Lader and Wing (1966) compared changes in electrical skin-conductance rates of identical and fraternal twins during the presentation of twenty tones. When the size of the initial galvanic skin response was controlled for, the *habituation,* or change, in the response over the series of tones was much more similar for identical twins than for fraternal twins. The frequency of spontaneous fluctuations or *lability* in galvanic skin responses (that is, changes that are not induced by external stimuli but seem to be internally generated) was also highly correlated in identical twins but not significantly related in fraternal twins. In addition to resemblance on these measures of skin conductance, near the end of the series of tones heart rates were highly correlated for identical but not fraternal twins.

In earlier studies the same experimenters found that similar measures of autonomic habituation and lability differ in patients having severe anxiety and in normal subjects with no known emotional disorders. Other investigators have found that lability in autonomic measures, even in infants, is associated with later behavioral impulsivity (that is, a tendency to respond quickly, make errors, and have a short span of attention). Therefore it may be possible that impulsivity is partially genetically based and associated with inherited differences in the functioning of the nervous system. Since the autonomic nervous system plays a key role in anxiety reactions and in psychosomatic disorders in which emotional conflicts result in physical symptoms such as ulcers, high blood pressure, and asthma, it also may be that there is a strong hereditary component in predisposition to these disorders.

Intellectual
Characteristics

The results of studies on similarities in intelligence test scores (IQ) of twins have been remarkably consistent. Performance on intelligence tests is heavily weighted by genetic factors. The closer the genetic kinship bonds, the more similar the IQ.

The results of an ambitious summary of fifty-two different investigations from four continents and eight countries are presented in Table 2-4. In interpreting the correlations it should be remembered that a *correlation coefficient* is an estimate of how two measures vary together. As might be expected, the correlations of IQs for unrelated persons are extremely small; we cannot predict the IQ of one unrelated person from another effectively even if they are reared together. However, as genetic similarity increases, so does similarity in intelligence scores. It can be seen that a marked drop in the correlation of intelligence test scores occurs as kinship bonds become further removed. Also, the correlation is lower in dizygotic twins than in monozygotic twins. Even monozygotic twins reared apart, and thus exposed to different home environments, have intelligence test scores more similar than those of dizygotic twins raised in the same home.

Recent studies of intelligence test scores of infants in the first year of life, as early as 3 months of age, show about the same sized correlations between scores of identical and fraternal twins as those found with older people (Nichols & Bromon, 1974; Matheny, 1975). This is remarkable since infant intelligence tests are heavily weighted with items involving perceptual and sensorimotor skills, whereas tests for older children have more verbal and abstract reasoning items. Both types of ability appear to be strongly influenced by genetic factors. Children show different patterns of mental abilities. One child may be good in abstract reasoning and working with geometric designs; another may excel in information

TABLE 2-4 CORRELATION COEFFICIENTS FOR INTELLIGENCE TEST SCORES FROM FIFTY-TWO STUDIES INVOLVING FAMILY RELATIONSHIPS WITH DIFFERENT AMOUNTS OF GENETIC SIMILARITY

Relationship		Median correlation	Approximate range of correlations	Number of groups
Unrelated persons	Reared apart	-0.01	-0.03-0.03	4
	Reared together	0.23	0.15-0.32	5
Foster-parent–child		0.20	0.18-0.38	3
Parent-child		0.50	0.23-0.80	12
Siblings	Reared apart	0.40	0.35-0.46	2
	Reared together	0.49	0.32-0.78	35
Twins				
Dizygotic	Opposite sex	0.53	0.40-0.65	9
	Like sex	0.53	0.45-0.88	11
Monozygotic	Reared apart	0.75	0.63-0.85	4
	Reared together	0.87	0.76-0.95	14

Source: From Erlenmeyer-Kimling, L., & Jarvik, L. F. Genetics and intelligence. *Science*, 1963, **142**, 1477–1479.

and vocabulary. In addition, mental development proceeds at different rates in different children. Just as children show spurts and plateaus in physical growth at different times, they show variations in the rate and timing of mental growth. Even in patterns of intellectual ability and in rates and timing of intellectual growth, monozygotic twins are more similar than are dizygotic twins (Wilson, 1974, 1975).

This pattern of greater similarity in the scores of identical than fraternal twins is more marked for tests of intellectual performance that attempt to be relatively culture free, such as intelligence tests, than it is for tests that are heavily culturally and educationally weighted such as achievement tests (Newman et al., 1937). Environmental factors play a greater role in performance on achievement tests than on intelligence tests (Burt, 1966) although they influence both. Other studies have suggested that the genetic contribution is higher in nonverbal tests, such as those involving visual-motor skills, than it is in verbal or linguistic measures.

Another type of study which is frequently used to investigate the contribution of genetic factors to intelligence involves comparisons of the intellectual performances of foster and adopted children with those of their biological or adoptive parents (Burks, 1928; Leahy, 1935, Scarr & Weinberg, 1977). Even if placement has been in the first year of life, the intellectual performance of school-age children correlates with those of their natural parents more closely than those of their adoptive parents.

The results of these studies of foster and adopted children cannot be assumed to indicate that the adoptive parents do not influence their children's IQs (Scarr-Salapatek, 1971). In the only study which included natural mothers' IQ scores rather than intellectual estimates made on the basis of education, it was found that adopted children often averaged 20 or more IQ points higher than their natural mothers. Since the adoptive parents tend to be more highly educated and more socially and economically advantaged than the natural parents, this may be due to the more stimulating environment provided by the brighter adoptive parents. The children's average IQs and the distribution of their IQs more closely resemble their adoptive (average IQ above 100) than natural parents (average IQ 85). However, the rank ordering of the children's IQs more closely resembles the rank ordering of their natural parents' IQs, which is what a correlation coefficient measures. Adopted children scored higher on intelligence tests than their natural mothers, but the children who had the slowest natural mothers were likely to have lower IQs than those who had brighter natural mothers even after years of living in an adoptive home. Although the *absolute* level of the adopted children's IQs were higher than might have been expected on the basis of their natural mothers' education or IQs, their performance *relative* to that of other adopted children was related to their natural mothers' intellectual level. It is this difference between absolute and relative levels that is critical to note.

Thus although twin studies and adoptive studies are in agreement in showing that genetic factors make an important contribution to individual differences in performance on intelligence tests, it cannot be concluded that environmental factors are not also salient in such variations. As we will see in Chapter 11, very poor environments can dramatically lower IQ scores, and cognitively stimulating environments or intervention programs can raise IQ scores radically.

Personality   The contribution of genetic factors to personality characteristics appears to be less than it is to intellectual characteristics. However, this may be attributable partially to the problems that exist in defining and measuring personality traits. Most investigators do not agree on precisely what attributes define assertiveness, sociability, dependency, nurturance, anxiety, and so on. The scales used to measure these characteristics vary more than do intelligence measures, and therefore personality measures tend to be less reliable than measures of intelligence.

In spite of these problems, one dimension of personality which seems to have a hereditary component is a trait which has been variously called *sociability* or *introversion-extraversion*. Sociability ranges from inhibited, apprehensive, and withdrawn behavior to outgoing, self-confident, and gregarious behavior. Monozygotic twins reared either together or apart are more similar than dizygotic twins in sociability (Buss, Plomin, & Willerman, 1973; Gottesman, 1963; Scarr, 1969; Shields, 1962). In a study in which the behavior of sets of identical and fraternal twins were rated once a month for the first year of life, sociability, smiling, and fear of strangers were very similar for identical twins but not for fraternal twins (Freedman & Keller, 1963).

In the photographs on the facing page it can be seen that Michael and

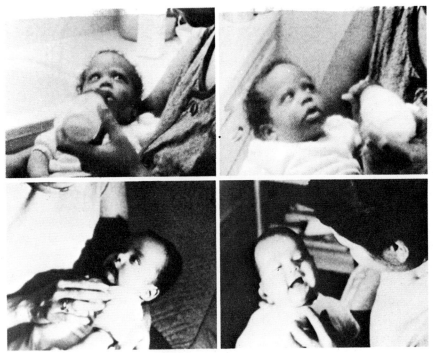

Pictures showing the similarity in social responses of identical twins, Michael and Peter, and the dissimilarity in social responses of fraternal twins, David and Jason. (Courtesy of Dr. Daniel G. Freedman)

Peter (fictitious names), who are monozygotic twins, exhibit the same sober visual fixation and orientation toward their mother's face during feeding at the age of 2 months. In contrast, David and Jason (fictitious names), who are dizygotic twins, display quite disparate behaviors when being touched by an adult. David smiles sleepily with his eyes closed; Jason looks intently and solemnly at the adult's face.

It is interesting that sociability is also a remarkably stable characteristic over time, according to findings from longitudinal studies of children (Kagan & Moss, 1962; Schaeffer & Bayley, 1963). This stability is more marked for boys than girls. Sociability and interpersonal apprehension in adolescence can be predicted for girls from the early school years, but in boys these behaviors are consistent from the first year of life.

A second personality characteristic which may be influenced by genetic factors and in which wide individual differences occur is a preference for different types and amounts of *stimulation.* Some individuals seem to enjoy an environment full of excitement and changing sights and sounds; others seem to prefer a quieter and less changing or turbulent milieu. It has been found that monozygotic twins are more similar than dizygotic twins in seeking thrills and adventures and in susceptibility to boredom (Buschsbaum, 1973).

It has been proposed that some people are *stimulus-reducers* and others are *stimulus-augmenters* (Petrie, 1967). On receiving the same actual amounts of stimulus input, stimulus-reducers subjectively experience the stimulus as less stimulating while stimulus-augmenters experience it as more stimulating. Thus, if an electric shock were administered, the reducers would phenomenally experience it as being less painful than the augmenters. A turbulent environment would seem no more stimulating to a stimulus-reducer than a relatively unchanging setting would to a stimulus-augmenter.

These two groups of individuals show divergent preferences for optimal levels of stimulation. A reducer prefers greater amounts of and more complex stimulation than an augmenter. Reducers have been demonstrated to drink alcohol and coffee, to smoke, to have more friends and be more active and attentive to others in social situations than are augmenters. They actually are more likely to seek out novel and complex social situations (Sales, 1972; Sales et al., 1974). Reducers are clearly more extraverted or sociable than augmenters. It has been argued that individual differences in the responsiveness of the nervous system to stimulation may underlie variations in both introversion-extraversion (sociability) and augmenting and reducing (Sales, 1972; Sales et al., 1974).

It has been suggested that so-called psychopaths (individuals who repeatedly get into difficulty, are thrill seekers, do not seem to learn from experience, and show few signs of guilt or remorse) are reducers, and neurotics (inhibited individuals who often show excessive anxiety and guilt) are augmenters. This leads to stimulus-seeking in psychopaths and avoidance of large amounts of stimulation in neurotics. What would happen to psychopaths and neurotics if we bombarded them with massive amounts of stimulation or isolated and restrained them and greatly reduced stimulation? Sykrzypek (1969) studied the effects of stimulus deprivation and exposure to large amounts of stimulation on responses to novelty and complexity and on anxiety scores of neutotic and psychopathic delinquents. Neurotic delinquents became more anxious and decreased their preference for complex stimuli following exposure to large amounts of stimulation. In contrast, psychopathic delinquents showed no effects following exposure to large amounts of stimulation but showed a marked increase in their preference for complex stimuli after being subjected to a period of stimulus deprivation. Apparently large amounts of stimulation were disruptive for neurotics but readily adapted to by psychopathic delinquents. Also, the effects of stimulus deprivation led to active stimulus-seeking in psychopathic delinquents. On the basis of such findings, it might be speculated that solitary confinement would be more distressing for psychopathic delinquents than for neurotic delinquents.

Even with much younger preadolescent children, ages 10 to 13, in a residential school for disturbed children, children who exhibited aggressive acting-out, antisocial behaviors were more likely than neurotic children to seek stimulation. In an experimental setting, children with conduct disorders were more likely than the neurotic children to prefer slides with diverse and constantly changing subject matter rather than monotonous, repetitious views of concrete buildings, and they pressed a button to change slides more rapidly (DeMyer-

Gapin & Scott, in press). These differences in stimulus-seeking have been attributed to differences in the rates of transmission of neural impulses that are at least in part genetically determined (Quay, in press; Wheeler, 1974).

Although most of the research on stimulus-seeking has been done on older children, adolescents, and adults, variations in response to stimulation by infants have also been studied. Some infants have the apparent ability to shut out unwanted stimulation by erecting a *stimulus barrier* composed of a group of responses similar to those found in deep sleep, such as changed patterns of electrical brain waves, decreased motor activity, and slow breathing. When the stimulation is too much, the infant turns it off (Brazelton, 1962).

Activity is a personality characteristic that might be conceived of as another form of stimulus-seeking. Reducers are more physically active and enjoy the stimulation of contact sports more than augmenters. Under boring or stimulus-depriving conditions they are more likely to stimulate themselves by moving about the room, shifting position, wiggling their feet and tapping their fingers, and talking to themselves. There is evidence that activity is influenced by hereditary factors. There is greater similarity in activity measures of monozygotic than dizygotic twins (Scarr, 1966; Willerman & Plomin, 1973). In addition, activity levels of children correlate with the activity levels of both their mothers and fathers when the parents were themselves children (Willerman & Plomin, 1973).

As was true in sociability, activity tends to be a relatively stable characteristic (Halverson & Waldrop, 1976). Fetuses that are most active in the last month before birth become the most active neonates and develop certain motor skills earlier. However, these active neonates are often more irritable and show more difficulties in early adjustment than less active neonates. These neonatal differences in activity tend to be stable into adolescence (Kagan & Moss, 1962; Neilon, 1948) and persist in a twenty-year period from adolescence into maturity (Tuddenham, 1959).

In addition to individual variations in preferences for different amounts of stimulation, variations occur in the types of stimulation preferred. In infants, differences in irritability, in responsiveness to different types of stimulation, and in the relative effectiveness of different types of stimulation in soothing also have been noted. Some infants are *cuddlers* and are soothed by physical contact, holding, and restraint; others, the *noncuddlers*, intensify their protests when such techniques are used and are more readily soothed by auditory and visual stimulation or by being walked (Schaffer & Emerson, 1964). Noncuddlers are generally more restless, physically active, and advanced in motor development than cuddlers.

Although genetically based temperamental predispositions in personality exist, the results of longitudinal studies indicate that the role of environmental factors in their expression cannot be ignored. The responsiveness of parents to the temperamental variations in their infants and to their stimulus preferences plays an important role in modifying the phenotypical expression of these traits. Depending on the responses of parents, the same temperamental genotype may be manifested in very different personality characteristics in children.

BOX 2-3
STABILITY OF TEMPERAMENTAL CHARACTERISTICS IN DIFFICULT CHILDREN

 In this study the relationship between early, presumably inherited, temperamental characteristics and later personality development was investigated. A total of 136 children from birth to ages 6 to 12 in 85 families were studied. A variety of methods were used to obtain information on the children over the course of the study, including frequent parent interviews, home and school observations, teacher interviews, and psychological tests. Measures of child behavior and temperament were obtained by parent interviews at three-month intervals during the first 18 months of age, at six-month intervals until 5 years, and at yearly intervals thereafter. Considerable consistency over the first two years of life was found in intensity of responses, rhythmicity (the regularity of cycles of such things as sleeping, eating, elimination, and irritability), adaptability, and threshold of responsiveness.

Before the age of 2 a group of fourteen *difficult children* with a set of specific temperamental characteristics were identified. These characteristics included biological irregularities in sleep, feeding, and elimination; avoidance, withdrawal, or distress in response to new stimuli or experiences; slow adaptability to new situations; and a prevalence of a negative mood including extremes of fussiness and crying. Of these children, 70 percent developed later behavior disorders, a much higher percentage than in the rest of the sample.

When these difficult children were infants, their parents did not seem to treat them markedly differently from other children, and therefore it is not possible to say their temperamental differences were caused by systematic differences in the way they were reared. However, as these children grew older, their parents started to cope with their behavior in a variety of ways—sometimes with guilt and self-blame, sometimes with anger, resentment, and punishment, and sometimes with flexibility and sensitivity to the needs of the child. The particular form of later behavior disorders to a large extent seemed to be determined by these parental responses, together with later social learning experiences. Some parents were able to moderate the behavior of these temperamentally difficult children; the responses of other parents led to intensification of their children's difficult behavior.

Thus although temperamental differences may have hereditary bases, their specific manifestations are shaped through social interactions, particularly early interactions within the family. ■

Source: Adapted from Thomas, A., Chess, S., Birch, H., Hertzig, M., & Korn, S. *Behavioral individuality in early childhood.* New York: New York University Press, 1963, and Chess, S., Thomas, A., & Birch, H. G. Behavioral problems revisited, in S. Chess & H. Birch (Eds.), *Annual progress in child psychiatry and child development.* New York: Brunner/Mazel, 1968, pp. 335–344.

Some infants can be identified in the earliest months of life as *difficult children* (Chess, Thomas, & Birch, 1968; Graham, Rutter, & George, 1973; Thomas, Chess, Birch, Hertzig, & Korn, 1963). These children are characterized by biological irregularities in sleep, feeding, and elimination; inflexibility; avoidance or distress in response to new experiences; slow adaptability to new situations; nonfastidiousness; and negative moods including extremes of fussiness and crying. A much higher rate of behavior disorders is found in later life in these children (70 percent) than is found in children who were not difficult infants. This may be attributable to two factors. First, that the less malleable child is likely to find adapting to environmental demands more difficult and be more prone to psychological damage. Second, that not only will the child with a difficult temperament be more vulnerable to stress, but he or she is also more likely to elicit different or adverse experiences. These children were found to serve as a target for parental irritability, and parents were more likely to take out their own stresses on these difficult children. Thus the child's temperament was not leading directly to psychiatric disorder, but it put the child at a higher risk of encountering adverse experiences in interacting with his or her environment.

Deviant Behavior   Twin studies have suggested that genetic factors may play a role in the development of a wide range of deviant behaviors such as neuroticism, depression, hysteria, suicide, alcoholism, manic-depressive psychosis, psychopathic personality, childhood behavior disorders, and crime. However, the form of psychopathology which has received the greatest attention is schizophrenia. Schizophrenia is a severe mental disorder in which emotional and cognitive disorders occur often, resulting in bizarre behavior and beliefs. In studies of specific disorders such as schizophrenia, rather than using a correlation as is done in studies of IQ, the *concordance rates* of monozygotic and dizygotic twins are compared. A concordance rate is a measure of the percent of time in which the disorder is present in both members of the twin pair. For example, a 100 percent concordance rate would indicate that when one twin had schizophrenia, the other twin also always had schizophrenia. One of the problems in using concordance rates in the study of mental disorders such as schizophrenia is that if one twin has the disorder at the time of the study and the other does not, the nondeviant twin may still develop it at a later time. This difficulty in controlling for age of occurrence has not yet been coped with adequately. Differences in specific populations studied, the ages of the subjects, and the criteria for labeling a person schizophrenic all contribute to variations in concordance rates. Table 2-5 presents a summary of concordance rates for a wide range of studies in a variety of countries. It can be seen that in all these studies monozygotic twins show significantly higher concordance rates than dizygotic twins.

Currently many studies of so-called high-risk children are being conducted. These children are regarded as being more vulnerable to the development of psychopathology because they have a parent who is emotionally disturbed or mentally retarded, or because they are being raised in a particularly stressful environment. Studies of children with a schizophrenic mother show that such children have a greater than average probability of developing problems even if they are separated from their mothers at an early age (Mednick, Schulsinger, & Schulsinger, 1975).

In a study by Heston (1966), a group of children of schizophrenic mothers, separated from their mothers at birth, were compared to offspring of nonschizo-

TABLE 2-5 CONCORDANCE RATES IN TWIN STUDIES OF SCHIZOPHRENIA

Investigator	Date	Monozygotic pairs			Dizygotic pairs		
		Number of twin pairs	Concordant twin pairs	Percent	Number of twin pairs	Concordant twin pairs	Percent
Luxenberger	1928	19	11	58	13	0	0
Rosanoff et al.	1934	41	25	61	53	7	13
Essen Moller	1941	11	7	64	27	4	15
Kallmann	1946	174	120	69	296	34	11
Slater	1953	37	24	65	58	8	14
Inouye	1961	55	33	60	11	2	18
Kringlen	1967	69	31	45	96	14	15
Fischer et al.	1969	25	14	56	45	12	26
Tienari	1971	20	7	35	23	3	13
Allen et al.	1972	121	52	43	131	12	9
Gottesman & Shields	1972	26	15	58	34	4	12

Source: Adapted from Gottesman, I. I., & Shields, J., Genetic theorizing and schizophrenia. *British Journal of Psychiatry*, 1973, **122**, 17–18.

phrenic mothers. About half of each group were placed in adoptive homes, and half remained in institutions. Both groups were compared on a variety of disorders at about age 35. The higher rates of deviant behavior in the offspring of schizophrenics, presented in Table 2-6, suggest that the genetic mechanisms involved may be manifested in a range of psychological anomalies, including schizophrenia, depending on the effects of life experiences. Investigators doing studies of high-risk children are trying to determine what these experiences may be (Garmezy, 1975). Some are even attempting to modify the experiences of high-risk children through intervention programs such as placing them in therapeutic nursery schools (Bell, B., Mednick, S., Raman, A. C., Schulsinger, F., Sutton-Smith, B., & Venables, P. A., 1975). As we will see in Chapter 11, some of these intervention programs for children at risk for mental retardation have been extremely successful.

Summary

One of the basic interests of geneticists and developmental psychologists is the study of how and when genetic and environmental factors transact throughout the course of development in shaping the phenotypical characteristics of the child.

Genetic factors play an important role in the emergence of many physical, intellectual, and behavioral characteristics. A simple one gene to one characteristic approach to the appearance of individual differences has been modified in accord with current understanding of the chemical processes and multiple gene interactions involved in genetic transmission and the modification of phenotypes

TABLE 2-6 COMPARISON OF SEPARATED OFFSPRING OF SCHIZOPHRENIC AND
NORMAL MOTHERS

	Offspring of normal mothers ($N = 50$)	Offspring of schizophrenic mothers ($N = 47$)
Age, mean	36.3	35.8
Adopted	19	22
Mental health ratings	80.1	65.2
Schizophrenia	0	5
Mental deficiency	0	4
Sociopathic	2	9
Neurotic disorder	7	13
More than one year in penal or psychiatric institution	2	11
Total years institution	15	112
Felons	2	7
Number serving in armed forces	17	21
Discharged from armed forces	1	8
Mean IQ	103.7	94.0
Years in school	12.4	11.6
Divorces	7	6

Source: From Heston, L., & Denny, D., Interactions between early life experiences and biological factors in schizophrenia. *Journal of Psychiatric Research*, 1968, **6**, 363–376.

through environmental factors. One genotype may lead to many different phenotypes, and a variety of genotypes may underlie the same phenotype.

The phenotypical appearance, transmission, and survival of genetically based characteristics depend on a variety of factors. Some of these are related to whether the characteristic is transmitted by a dominant or recessive gene or whether it is a sex-linked trait which is transmitted by the X chromosome and occurs more frequently in males. The phenotypical expression of genes may also be modified by interactions with other genes. In addition, biological factors— such as the age of the mother, intrauterine environment, physiological condition, and postnatal experiences—influence the phenotypical expression of the genotype.

The survival of mutations of individuals having certain attributes depends on how adaptive that characteristic is to the environment in which the individual lives. Sickle-cell anemia is an example of a disorder carried on a recessive gene which in its heterozygotic form of sicklemia is adaptive in high malarial regions but destructive in such areas as those having high altitudes.

Biologists have not been very successful in explaining the genetic processes involved in the development of social behavior and of intelligence. Some advances have been made in this area by behavior geneticists using twin studies and adoption studies. The results of these studies suggest that genetic factors play a role in the development of many physical and physiological characteristics, in intelligence, sociability, and emotional responsiveness, in the preference for certain types and levels of stimulation, and in some forms of psychopathology and deviant behavior. However, the occurrence of these disorders and the phenotypical manifestations of these genetic predispositions are also influenced by environmental and experiential factors. It is important to recognize that even if a characteristic is strongly influenced by heredity, it does not mean that it is not or cannot be modified by environment. Whether we are examining social, intellectual, or personality development, the transactions between genetic and environmental factors must be examined rather than genetic or experiential factors alone in understanding the emergence of individual differences.

References

Allen, G. Twin research: problems and prospects. In A. G. Steinberg & A. G. Bearn (Eds.), *Progress in medical genetics.* New York: Grune & Stratton, 1965, pp. 242–269.

Allison, A. C. Protection afforded by sickle-cell trait against subtertian malarial infections. *British Medical Journal*, 1954, **1**, 290–294.

Bartlett, H. W., Hurley, W., Brand, C., & Poole, E. Chromosomes of male patients in a security prison. *Nature*, 1968, **219**, 351–354.

Baumeister, A. A. The effects of dietary control on intelligence in phenylketonuria. *American Journal of Mental Deficiency*, 1967, **71**, 840–847.

Bell, B., Mednick, S., Raman, A. C., Schulsinger, F., Sutton-Smith, B., & Venables, P. A longitudinal psychophysiological study of three-year-old muuritian children: Preliminary report. *Developmental Medicine and Child Neurology*, 1975, **17**, 320–324.

Brazelton, T. B. Observations of the neonate. *Journal of American Academy of Child Psychiatry*, 1962, **1**, 38–58.

Burks, B. S. The relative influence of nature and nurture upon mental development: A comparative study of foster parent-foster child resemblance and true parent-true child resemblance. *27th Yearbook of the National Society for the Study of Education.* Chicago: University of Chicago Press, 1928. Part 1, pp. 219–316.

Burt, C. The genetic determination of differences in intelligence: A study of monozygotic twins reared together and apart. *British Journal of Psychology*, 1966, **57**, 137–153.

Buchsbaum, M. Visual and auditory AER in MZ and DZ twins. Paper presented at the 81st meeting of the American Psychological Association, Montreal, August, 1973.

Buss, A. H., Plomin, R., & Willerman, L. The inheritance of temperaments. *Journal of Personality*, 1973, **41**, 513–524.

Carter, C. O., & MacCarthy, D. Incidence of monogolism and its diagnosis in the newborn. *Britsh Journal of Social Medicine*, 1951, **5**, 83–90.

Chess, S., Thomas, A., & Birch, H. G. Behavioral problems revisited. In S. Chess & H. Birch (Eds.), *Annual progress in child psychiatry and development.* New York: Brunner/Mazel, 1968, pp. 335–344.

China Medical Journal, March 1975, **1**, 117.

Corney, G., & Aherne, W. The placental transfusion syndrome in twins. *Archives of Disease in Childhood*, 1965, **40**, 264–270.

Crow, J. F. A comparison of fetal and infant death rates in the progeny of radiologists and pathologists. *American Journal of Roentgenology, Radium Therapy and Nuclear Medicine*, 1955, **73**, 467–476.

DeMyer-Gapin, S., and Scott, T. J. Effects of stimulus novelty on stimulation seeking in anti-social and neurotic children. *Journal of Abnormal Psychology*, in press.

Erlenmeyer-Kimling, L., & Jarvik, L. F. Genetics and intelligence. *Science,* 1963, **142,** 1477–1479.

Forssman, H., & Hambert, C. Incidence of Klinefelter's syndrome among mental patients. *The Lancet,* 1966, **1** (7284), 1327–1328.

Freedman, D. An ethological approach to the genetical study of human behavior. In S. G. Vandenberg (Ed.), *Methods and goals in human behavior genetics.* New York: Academic, 1965, pp. 141–161.

Freedman, D. G., & Keller, B. Inheritance of behavior in infants. *Science,* 1963, **140,** 196–198.

Garmezy, N. The experimental study of children vulnerable to psychopathology. In A. Davies (Ed.), *Child personality and psychopathology* (Vol. 2). New York: Wiley, 1975, 171–220.

Gentry, J. T., Parkhurst, E., & Bulin, G. V., Jr. An epidemiological study of congenital malformations in New York State. *American Journal of Public Health,* 1959, **49,** 1–22.

Goodnight, C. J., Goodnight, M. C., & Gray, P. *General zoology.* New York: Reinhold, 1964.

Gottesman, I. I. Genetic aspects of intelligent behavior. In N. Ellis (Ed.), *Handbook of mental deficiency: Psychological theory and research.* New York: McGraw-Hill, 1963. (a)

Gottesman, I. I. Heritability of personality: A demonstration. *Psychological Monographs,* 1963, **77** (Whole No. 572) (b)

Graham, P., Rutter, M., & George, S. Temperamental characteristics as predictors of behavior disorders in children. *American Journal of Orthopsychiatry,* 1973, **43,** 328–399.

Halverson, C. F., & Victor, J. B. Minor physical anomalies and problem behavior in elementary school children. *Child Development,* 1976, **47,** 281–285.

Halverson, C. F., & Waldrop, M. F. Relations between preschool activity and aspects of intellectual and social behavior at age 7$^1/_2$. *Developmental Psychology,* 1976, **12,** 107–112.

Heston, L. Psychiatric disorders in foster-home reared children of schizophrenic mothers. *British Journal of Psychiatry,* 1966. **112,** 819–825.

Heston, L., & Denny, D. Interactions between early life experiences and biological factors in schizophrenia. *Journal of Psychiatric Research,* 1968, **6,** 363–376.

Hook, E. B. Behavioral implications of the human XYY genotype. *Science,* 1973, **179,** 131–150.

Howell, R. R., & Stevenson, R. E. The offspring of phenylketonuric women. *Social Biology Supplement,* 1971, **18,** 519–529.

Hsia, D. Y., Driscoll, K. W., Troll, W., & Knox, W. E. Detection by phenylalanine tolerance tests of heterozygous carriers of phenylketonuria. *Nature,* 1956, **178,** 1239–1240.

Huntley, R. M. C. A study of 320 twin pairs and their families showing resemblances in respect of a number of physical and psychological measurements. Unpublished Ph.D. thesis, University of London, 1966.

Jost, H., & Sontag, L. The genetic factor in autonomic nervous system function. *Psychosomatic Medicine,* 1944, **6,** 308–310.

Kagan, J., & Moss, H. A. *Birth to maturity.* New York: Wiley, 1962.

Kallman, F. J., & Sander, G. Twin studies in senescence. *American Journal of Psychiatry,* 1949, **106,** 2–26.

Lader, M., & Wing, L. Physiological measures, sedative drugs and morbid anxiety. *Maudsley Monographs* (No. 14). London: Oxford University Press, 1966.

Leahy, A. M. Nature-nurture and intelligence. *Genetic Psychology Monographs,* 1935, **17,** 235–308.

Lenneberg, E. H. *Biological foundations of language*. New York: Wiley, 1967.

Lerner, I. M. *Heredity, evolution and society*. San Francisco: Freeman, 1968.

Lerner, I. M., & Libby, W. L. *Heredity, evolution and society*. San Francisco: Freeman, 1976.

Lytton, H. Do parents create, or respond to, differences in twins? *Developmental Psychology*, 1976, **13**, 5, 456–459.

Matteny, A. P. Concordance for Piagetian-equivalent items derived from the Bayley mental test. *Developmental Psychology*, 1975, **11**, 2, 224–227.

Mednick, S. A., Schulsinger, H., & Schulsinger, F. Schizophrenia in children of schizophrenic mothers. In A. Davies (Ed.), *Child personality and psychopathology* (Vol. 2). New York: Wiley, 1975, pp. 221–252.

Mittler, P. Psycholinguistic skills in four-year-old twins and singletons. Ph.D. thesis, University of London, 1969.

Mittler, P. *The study of twins*. Baltimore: Penguin, 1971.

Money, J., & Mittenthal, S. Lack of personality pathology in Turner's syndrome: Relation to cytogenetics, hormones and physique. *Behavior Genetics*, 1970, **1**, 43–56.

Montague, A. *Human Heredity*. New York: Harcourt, Brace & World, 1959.

Neel, J. V. The inheritance of sickle cell anemia. *Science*, 1949, **110**, 64–66.

Neel, J. V., & Schull, W. J. Studies on the potential genetic effects of the atomic bombs. *Acta Genetics*, 1956, **6**, 183–189.

Neilon, P. Shirleys' babies after fifteen years: A personality study. *Journal of Genetic Psychology*, 1948, **73**, 175–186.

Newman, H. I., Freeman, F. N., & Holzinger, K. J. *Twins: A study of heredity and environment*. Chicago: University of Chicago Press, 1937.

Nichols, P. H., & Broman, S. H. Familial resemblance in infant mental development. *Developmental Psychology*, 1974, **10**, 442–446.

Petrie, A. *Individuality in pain and suffering*. Chicago: University of Chicago Press, 1967.

Pfeiffer, John (Ed.) *The Cell*. New York: Time, Inc., Life Science Library, 1964.

Price, B. Primary biases in twin studies: A review of prenatal and natal differences producing factors in monozygotic pairs *American Journal of Human Genetics*, 1950, **2**, 293–352.

Quay, H. C. Psychopathic behavior: Reflections on its nature, origins and treatment. In F. Weizmann & I. Uzgiris (Eds.), *The structuring of experience*. New York: Plenum. In press.

Quinn, R. & Rapaport, J. L. Minor physical anomalies and neurologic states in hyperactive boys. *Pediatrics*, 1974, **53**, 742–747.

Robinson, H. B., & Robinson, N. M. The mentally retarded child: A psychological approach. New York: McGraw-Hill, 1965.

Rugh, R., & Shettles, L. F. *From conception to birth: The drama of life's beginning*. New York: Harper & Row, 1971.

Scarr, S. Genetic factors in activity motivation. *Child Development*, 1966, **37**, 663–673.

Scarr, S. Environmental bias in twin studies. *Eugenics Quarterly*, 1968, **15**, 34–40.

Scarr, S. Social introversion-extraversion as a heritable response. *Child Development*, 1969, **40**, 823–832.

Scarr, S. V., & Weinberg, R. A. Intellectual similarities within families of both adopted and biological children. *Intelligence*. In press, 1977.

Scarr-Salapatek, S. Unknowns in the IQ equation. *Science*, 1971, **174**, 1223–1228.

Scarr-Salapatek, S. Genetics and the development of intelligence. In F. Horowitz (Ed.), *Review of child development research* (Vol. 4). Chicago: University of Chicago Press, 1975.

Schaeffer, W. W., & Bayley, N. Maternal behavior, child behavior and their intercorrelations from infancy through adolescence. *Monographs of the Society for Research in Child Development,* 1963, **28** (Serial No. 87), 1–127.

Schaffer, H., & Emerson, P. Patterns of response to physical contact in early human development. *Journal of Child Psychology and Psychiatry*, 1964, **5,** 1–13.

Scheinfeld, A. *Your heredity and environment.* Philadelphia: Lippincott, 1965.

Schull, W. J., & Neel, J. V. Radiation and the sex ratio in man. *Science*, 1958, **128,** 343–348.

Shields, J. *Monozygotic twins brought up together and apart.* London: Oxford University Press, 1962.

Shields, J., Gottesman, I., & Slater, E. Kallman's 1946 schizophrenia twin study in the light of new information. *Acta Psychiatrica Scandinavica*, 1967, **43,** 485–496.

Smith, R. T. A comparison of socioenvironmental factors in monozygotic and dizygotic twins; testing an assumption. In S. Vandenberg (Ed.), *Methods and goals in human behavior genetics.* New York: Academic, 1965, pp. 45–61.

Strong, S. J., & Corney, G. *The placenta in twin pregnancy.* New York: Pergamon, 1967.

Sykrzypek, G. J. Effects of perceptual isolation and arousal on anxiety, complexity preference and novelty preference in psychopathic delinquents. *Journal of Abnormal Psychology*, 1969, **74,** 321–329.

Telfer, M., Baker, D., Clark, G., & Richardson, C. Incidence of gross chromosomal errors among tall criminal American males. *Science*, 1968, **157,** 1249–1250.

Thomas, A., Chess, S., Birch, H., Hertzig, M., & Korn, S. *Behavioral individuality in early childhood.* New York: New York University Press, 1963.

Tuddenham, R. D. The constancy of personality ratings over two decades. *Genetic Psychology Monographs*, 1959, **60,** 3–29.

Waddington, C. H. *New Patterns in Genetics and Development.* New York: Columbia, 1962.

Waddington, C. H. *Principles of development and differentiation.* New York: Macmillan, 1966.

Waldrop, M. F., Bell, R. Q., & Goering, J. D. Minor physical anomalies and inhibited behavior in elementary school girls. *Journal of Child Psychology and Psychiatry*, **17,** 1976, 113–122.

Waldrop, M. F., & Halverson, C. F. Minor physical anomalies and hyperactive behavior in young children. In J. Hellmuth (Ed.), *Exceptional infant: Studies in abnormalities* (Vol. 2). New York: Brunner/Mazel, 1971.

Watson, J. B. What the nursery has to say about instincts. In C. Murcheson (Ed.), *Psychologies of 1925.* Worcester, Mass.: Clark University Press, 1926, pp. 1–35.

Watson, J. D., & Crick, F. H. C. Molecular structure of nucleic acid: A structure for deoxyribose nucleic acid, *Nature*, 1953, **171,** 737–738.

Wheeler, C. A. The relationship between psychopathy and the weak automatization cognitive style. *FCI Research Reports,* 1974, **6,** (No. 2).

Whitehill, M., DeMyer-Gapin, S., & Scott, T. J. Stimulation-seeking in antisocial preadolescent children. *Journal of Abnormal Psychology*, 1976, **85,** 101–104.

Willerman, L., & Plomin, R. Activity level in children and their parents. *Child Development*, 1973, **44,** 854–858.

Wilson, E. O. *Sociobiology.* Cambridge, Mass.: Belknap Press, Harvard University Press, 1975.

Wilson, R. S. Mental development in the preschool years. *Developmental Psychology*, 1974, **10,** 580–588.

Wilson, R. S. Twins: Patterns of cognitive development as measured on the Wechsler preschool and primary scale of intelligence. *Developmental Psychology*, 1975, **11,** 126–134.

Witkin, H. A., Mednick, S. A., Schulsinger, F., Bakkestrom, E., Christiansen, K. O., Goodenough, D. R., Hirchhorn, K., Lunsteen, C., Owen, D. R., Philip, J., Ruben, D. B., & Stocking, M. Criminality in XYY and XXY men. *Science*, 1976, **193,** 547–555.

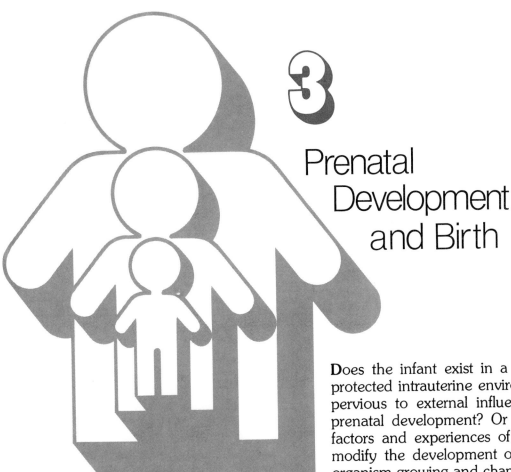

3

Prenatal Development and Birth

Does the infant exist in a benign and protected intrauterine environment, impervious to external influences during prenatal development? Or do external factors and experiences of the mother modify the development of the young organism growing and changing so rapidly in utero? Few of us would accept old beliefs that if a pregnant woman listens to classical music throughout the course of her pregnancy she will have a child who appreciates fine music; or if she reads the Bible assiduously her child will exhibit high ethical standards; or that the presence on her newborn infant of a birthmark shaped like the head of a dog might be attributable to the mother being frightened by a dog in early pregnancy. However, it is now recognized that the prenatal organism is vulnerable to a variety of factors that can influence the course of its development. Some of these factors are genetic mechanisms, and some are variations in prenatal environment due to the physical and possibly the emotional condition of the mother. A variety of adverse agents such as maternal disease, x-rays, drugs, and dietary deficiencies can contribute to deviations in development. Surprisingly, some of these agents previously regarded as harmless, such as commonly prescribed drugs which may have no deleterious effects on the pregnant mother, can lead to abnormalities in her unborn child.

In this chapter the effects of these genetic and environmental factors on prenatal development will be discussed. First, what are the most important factors? Second, how does the timing of variations in the prenatal environment modify their impact on the developing fetus? Third, what are the effects of conditions of birth and the status of the child at birth on later development? Finally, what postnatal environmental factors sustain or modify the effects of prenatal and perinatal factors?

Stages of Prenatal Development

Over the period of the 10 lunar months (usually about 280 days) of prenatal development, the new organism shows many varieties of change. Changes in the kinds, number, position, and size and shapes of cells, tissues, and somatic systems occur. Systems and structures usually increase in size and complexity. However, some prenatal structures actually decrease in size or disappear. For example, at the end of the third week gill arches appear, but by the middle of the second month they have been transformed into parts of the inner ear and neck and the cartilages of the larnyx. Another example would be the emergence and gradual disappearance of an external tail between the second and fourth months.

Prenatal development includes three periods: the period of the *ovum*, the period of the *embryo*, and the period of the *fetus*. These periods should be thought of as continuous phases of development, for from the moment the sperm penetrates the ovum, the development of the organism involves a systematic series of sequential changes by which the organism becomes increasingly complex and differentiated.

The Period of the Ovum

The period of the ovum includes approximately the first two weeks of life, extending from fertilization until the fertilized ovum, or zygote, proceeds down the fallopian tube and becomes implanted on the wall of the uterus. It is estimated that it would take 100 to 200 zygotes placed side by side to equal an inch, or more than 5 million such cells to weigh an ounce (Meredith, 1975). Tendrils from the zygote penetrate the blood vessels in the wall of the uterus, and the zygote forms the physiologically dependent relationship with the mother which will continue throughout the course of prenatal development. The establishment of this relationship marks the beginning of the second period, the period of the embryo, a state of rapid growth which lasts until the end of the eighth week.

The Period of the Embryo

Differentiation of the most important organs and physiological systems occurs at this time, and by the end of this period, the embryo is recognizable as a partially functioning tiny human being. From the time of fertilization until the end of this period the infant increases 2 million percent in size. Because rapidly developing and differentiating organisms are most vulnerable to adverse environmental effects, the period of the embryo is the phase in which environmental intrusions caused by such things as maternal disease, faulty nutrition, and drugs may result in devastating, irreversible deviations in development.

In the period of the embryo the inner mass of the zygote differentiates into three layers: the *ectoderm*, the *mesoderm*, and the *endoderm*. From the ectoderm develop the hair, nails, and part of the teeth; the outer layer of the skin and skin glands; and the sensory cells and the nervous system. From the mesoderm evolve the muscles, skeleton, excretory and circulatory systems, and inner skin layer; and from the endoderm come the gastrointestinal tract, trachea, bronchia, eustachian tubes, glands, and vital organs such as the lungs, pancreas, and liver.

In addition, in this period, three other important auxiliary structures develop: the *amniotic sac*, the *placenta*, and the *umbilical cord*. The amniotic sac contains *amniotic fluid*, a watery liquid in which the developing embryo floats and which serves as a protective buffer against physical shocks and temperature

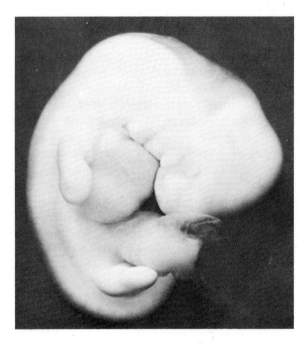

A human embryo at 38 days. (From Rugh, R., and Shettles, L., *Conception to Birth: The Drama of Life's Beginnings*, with permission)

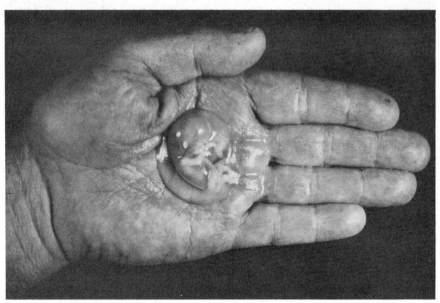

A human embryo at 2 months of age. (From Rugh, R., and Shettles, L., *Conception to Birth: The Drama of Life's Beginnings,* with permission)

changes. The tendrils which attach the embryo to the uterine wall increase in size and complexity to form a fleshy disc called the *placenta*. the embryo is joined at the abdomen to the placenta by the third accessory apparatus, the *umbilical cord*, which attains a final length slightly greater than that of the fetus and permits considerable fetal mobility. Although the umbilical cord is composed of blood vessels carrying blood to and from the infant and placenta, there is no direct connection between the bloodstream of the mother and child. The bloodstreams of the mother and child are separated in the placenta by semipermeable membranes, which permit transmission of chemicals with fine molecular structure, such as those found in nutrients and waste products. In this way the placenta carries nourishment to the child and removes its waste products. Early in gestation the nutrients in the mother's bloodstream exceed the needs of the embryo and are stored by the placenta for later use. Certain drugs, hormones, viruses, and antibodies from the mother, which may have desctructive effects on the embryo, are also transferred through the placental membranes. The rapid emergence and development of new organs and systems in this period make the embryo particularly vulnerable to environmental assault, and thus it is the period when most gross congenital anomalies occur.

The neural folds appear about day 19 and begin to close 2 days later; if they fail to close, spina bifida results. The future lens of the eye is recognizable at 28 days. The limb buds appear in the 5th week; the hand is defined at the 30th day, the fingers and toes about the 35th. The lateral elements of the future lips and palate are fusing in the 5th and 6th

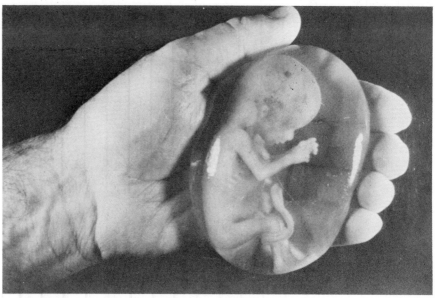

A human embryo at 12 weeks of age. (From Rugh, R., and Shettles, L., *Conception to Birth: The Drama of Life's Beginnings*, with permission)

weeks. In these same weeks, the heart and the great vessels are shifting toward their ultimate pattern. (Corner, 1961, p. 14)

By the end of the period of the embryo, the face and its features are delineated, and fingers, toes, and external genitalia are present. At 6 weeks the embryo can be recognized as a human being, although a rather strangely proportioned one in that the head is almost as large as the rest of the body. Primitive functioning of the heart and liver, as well as the peristaltic movement of ingestion, has been reported late in this period.

Most miscarriages or spontaneous abortions occur during this period; the embryo becomes detached from the wall of the uterus and is expelled. It has been estimated that the rate of spontaneous abortion is as high as 1 in 4 pregnancies but that many remain undetected because they occur in the first few weeks of pregnancy. This high rate of abortion may be advantageous to the species since the great majority of aborted embryos have gross chromosomal and genetic disorders. The most severely affected embryos are spontaneously eliminated.

The Period of the Fetus

The final stage of prenatal development, the period of the fetus, extends from the beginning of the third month until birth. During this time little further differentiation of the organs remains to be completed; however, muscular development is rapid, complete closure of the palate and reduction of the

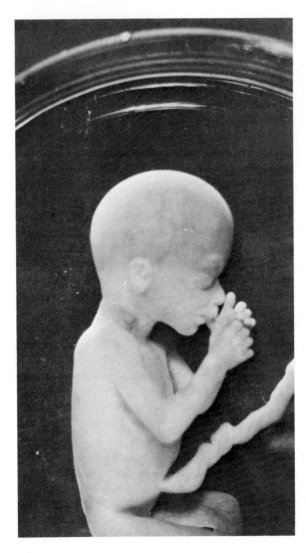

A human fetus at 17 weeks. (From Rugh, R., and Shettles, L., *Conception to Birth: The Drama of Life's Beginnings*, with permission)

umbilical hernia occur and differentiation of the external genitalia continues. The central nervous system develops rapidly in this period, although development of the central nervous system is not completed until several months after birth. By the end of the fourth month, mothers usually report movement of the fetus. By the age of 5 months reflexes such as sucking, swallowing, and hiccoughing usually appear. In addition, a Babinski reflex of a fanning of the toes in response to stroking of the foot occurs. After the fifth month, the fetus develops nails and sweat glands, a coarser, more adultlike skin, and a soft hair which covers the body. Most fetuses shed this hair in utero, but some continue to shed it after birth. By 6 months the eyes have developed, and opening and closing of the eyes occur. If an infant is born prematurely at 6 months, the regulatory processes

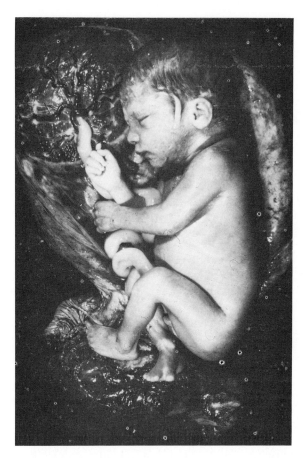

A human fetus at 8 months. (From Rugh, R., and Shettles, L., *Conception to Birth: The Drama of Life's Beginnings*, with permission)

and nervous and respiratory systems still are usually not mature enough for survival. The age of 28 weeks, sometimes referred to as the *age of viability*, is an important point in fetal development since at this time the physical systems of the fetus are sufficiently advanced so that if birth occurs, the child may survive.

Prenatal Influences on Development

During the course of prenatal development many agents may raise the incidence of deviations or produce malformations in the fetus. These agents are called *teratogens* and include maternal diseases and blood disorders, diet, irradiation, drugs, temperature, and oxygen level. In addition, maternal characteristics such as age, emotional state, and the number of children she has borne influence prenatal development.

In considering the effects of adverse prenatal and birth factors on development it is easy to concentrate on the resulting gross physical defects or mental impairments that sometimes result. However, an equally important issue to keep in mind may be how these factors change the life experiences of the child and the responses of those around the child. How does a parent who views the child as at risk because of such things as Rh factors or prematurity treat the baby? Is the parent more anxious, more protective, more rejecting? What happens to parent-child interaction if the infant is lethargic and unresponsive because of drugs administered during delivery? How is the emotional bond that usually forms between parent and child affected by early separation necessitated by the use of incubators for low-birthweight babies? It may be these experiential factors that are ultimately the most important in sustaining or in minimizing the long-term effect of early adversity.

Principles of the Effects of Teratogens

Certain general principles describe the effects of teratogens on prenatal development (for recent reviews on the topic, see Beck & Lloyd, 1965; Clegg, 1971; Tuchmann-Duplessis, 1975; and Wilson, 1961).

1 The effects of a teratogen vary with the developmental stage of the embryo. Teratogens acting on newly differentiated cells may damage developing but yet unformed organ systems. Since the various organ systems begin and end their prenatal development at different times, their sensitivity to agents varies over time. The vulnerable period for the brain is from 15 to 25 days, for the eye from 24 to 40 days, for the heart from 20 to 40 days, and for the legs from 24 to 36 days (Tuchmann-Duplessis, 1965). Before implantation and after the beginning of the fetal stage the organism is less vulnerable than during the embryonic period. During the fetal stage, teratogen-induced abnormalities tend to occur only in locations or systems which are still maturing such as the cerebellum, palate, and some cardiovascular and urogenital structures (Clegg, 1971). In addition some damage can be done to the continuously developing nervous system, or the differentiation of the external genitalia can be impaired resulting in pseudohermaphrodism (the appearance of both male and female sexual characteristics) (Clegg, 1971; Tuchmann-Duplessis, 1975).

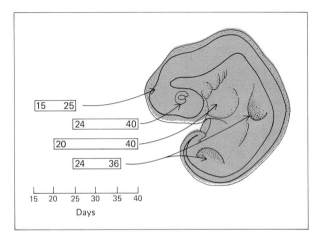

FIGURE 3-1 Critical periods for the vulnerability of the human embryo to teratogens. *(From Tuchmann-Duplessis, 1975, p. 42.)*

2 Since individual teratogens influence specific developmental processes, they produce specific patterns of developmental deviations. Rubella (German measles) affects mainly the heart, eyes, and brain; and the drug thalidomide results primarily in malformations of the limbs. This finding, in conjunction with the information on the critical vulnerable periods for these developing systems, reported in the first principle, suggests that although the form of the deviations resulting from rubella and thalidomide varies, the organism's period of greatest vulnerability to them is in approximatley the same time span during the embryonic period, that is, between the fourth and sixth weeks.

3 Both maternal and fetal genotypes can affect the developing organism's response to teratogenic agents and may play an important role in the appearance of abnormalities in offspring. Not all pregnant women who use the drug thalidomide or have German measles or poor diets produce defective infants. Those who do may themselves be genetically predisposed to being more vulnerable to those particular teratogens or may have fetuses who are so predisposed.

4 The physiological or pathological status of the mother will influence the action of a teratogen. Physiological factors, such as maternal nutritional and uterine condition and hormonal balance, will modify the impact of a teratogen. For example, not only will nutritional deficiencies themselves directly affect prenatal development, but they may intensify the adverse effects on the fetus of certain drugs ingested by the mother such as cortisone.

Pathological factors such as chronic and metabolic disease, obesity, toxemia, high blood pressure, and liver dysfunction may also increase the impact or frequency of damage by teratogens.

5 Levels of teratogenic agents which will produce malformations in the offspring may show no or mild detrimental effects on the mother. With a variety of drugs, diseases, x-irradiation, and dietary deficiencies the mother may show no abnormalities, but gross deviations may appear in the child.

6 One teratogen may result in a variety of deviations, and several different teratogens may produce the same deviation. Rubella may lead to deafness, cataracts, mental retardation, or heart disorders in the early months of pregnancy, depending on the time at which the disease was contracted. However, deafness in infants can be caused not only by maternal rubella but also by drugs such as quinine or streptomycin taken by the mother.

Maternal Diseases and Disorders

A wide range of maternal diseases and disorders can affect prenatal development, and, in accord with the principles noted previously, the effects are correlated with the stage of fetal development. Even mild attacks of rubella may produce cardiac disorders, cataracts, deafness, and mental retardation in the infant. It has been argued that the primary effects of rubella are the physical and sensory deficits such as blindness and deafness which limit the information available to the child and interfere with development. The suggestion is that the appearance of retardation in these children is one not directly produced by the rubella virus but is a result of these other physical and sensory liabilities which interfere with intellectual growth (Dodrill et al., 1974). The occurrence of deviations decreases from 50 percent if the mother contracts rubella in the first month to 17 percent if she contracts it in the third month; and there is almost no probability of abnormalities occurring if the mother contracts rubella after that time (Rhodes, 1961). Another maternal disease, mumps, also results in a higher incidence of malformations if contracted in the first trimester rather than later in pregnancy.

Chronic infections like venereal diseases (gonorrhea and syphilis), which invade the developing embryo and remain active, have their worst effects at later stages of development. The deleterious effects of the syphilis spirochete on the fetus do not occur before 18 weeks of age, and therefore early treatment of a syphilitic mother may avert abnormalities in the child. If the mother is untreated, invasion of the fetus by the syphilis spirochetes from the mother may result in abortion or miscarriage, mental retardation, blindness, or other physical abnormalities. In some cases the deleterious effects of syphilis are not apparent at birth but gradually emerge during the early years of development in the form of juvenile paresis, involving deterioration in thought processes, judgment, and speech, and in a decline in motor and mental abilities and eventual death.

Other maternal conditions such as high blood pressure, diabetes, and blood incompatibilities between mother and fetus may affect fetal development. The increases in miscarriage and infant and maternal mortality rates are directly correlated with the degree of high blood pressure in pregnant women suffering from hypertension. Infants of diabetic mothers have a relatively high proportion of infant mortality and abnormalities, particularly of the circulatory and respiratory systems (Gellis & Hsai, 1959). It is difficult to determine whether this relatively high incidence of malformations is attributable to the influence on the fetus of the mother's high blood sugar or to the effects of insulin, which the mother takes as medication for diabetes (Corner, 1961).

In addition, an incompatibility can occur between the blood types of mother and child. Although many forms of blood incompatibilities occur, Rh blood incompatibility is the most frequent and destructive. The incompatibility between an Rh-positive baby and an Rh-negative mother can cause miscarriage or infant death through *erythroblastosis*, a destruction of the red blood corpuscles resulting in an inadequate supply of oxygen to the fetus. Antigens are produced in the blood of the Rh-positive fetus and transmitted through the placenta to the blood of the Rh-negative mother; toxic antibodies are produced in the mother's blood and are returned to the infant, resulting in erythroblastosis. Maternal sensitivity to the Rh-positive antigens increases with successive pregnancies, and although the first pregnancy may be normal, later ones are less likely to be so.

Several advances have been made in treating this condition. One is to give the infant in utero blood transfusions to purge it of the destructive antibodies. A second and more promising method is to inoculate and immunize Rh-negative mothers prior to their first pregnancy before they have the opportunity of becoming sensitized to Rh-positive antigens. Finally, some very recent and promising work is being done in which maternal antibody level is controlled through drugs.

Drugs   Although most physicians and parents would probably agree that it is not good for pregnant women to take too many drugs during pregnancy, pregnant women consume an amazing number and variety of drugs. A recent study reported that 82 percent of pregnant women are given prescribed medication and in addition that 65 percent take self-medicated drugs (Marx, 1973). Another study found that pregnant women were prescribed an average of 3.6 drugs, and 4 percent were prescribed 10 or more drugs during pregnancy (Peckham & King, 1963). Some drugs are prescribed for therapeutic reasons; others are taken for stimulation, tension release, or pleasure by the mother.

Thalidomide   The *thalidomide* disaster in the late 1950s and early 1960s brought into public awareness the often unknown and potentially horrendous effects of the use of drugs by pregnant women. At this time an increase began to occur in the birth of children with an unusual group of abnormalities. The cluster of abnormalities included such things as eye defects, cleft palate, depressed bridge of the nose, small external ears, facial palsy, fusing of fingers and toes, dislocated hips, and malformations of the digestive and genitourinary tract and heart. However, the most unusual and characteristic deformity was *phocomelia*, an anomaly where limbs are missing and the feet and hands are attached directly to the torso like flippers (Karnofsky, 1965). It was partly the rarity of this anomaly that called attention to the fact that the mothers of these malformed infants had been prescribed thalidomide as a sedative or antinausea drug in the early months of pregnancy.

The problems in establishing the consequences of maternal intake of a drug during pregnancy on offspring are illustrated clearly in the case of thalidomide. The pregnant women showed no adverse effects of the thalidomide. (Even in instances where adults have ingested massive quantities of thalidomide in suicide attempts, it has resulted in nothing more serious than deep sleep, headaches, and nausea). Only a small percentage of pregnant women who used thalidomide produced deviant children, and in some of the animal species studied no effects of thalidomide on offspring were obtained.

Although there is some controversy about the intelligence of thalidomide babies, the evidence suggests that among noninstitutionalized infants who are reared in a normal home situation and who do not suffer from gross sensory deficits (such as blindness, deafness, or paralysis, which might be expected to seriously handicap the development of a child), the intelligence quotients of thalidomide babies differ little from those of normal children. However, in the study by Decarie (1969) of twenty-two thalidomide children under 4 years of age, who are suffering from malformations involving either or both the hands and arms or legs and feet, a typical profile of developmental abilities in thalidomide infants was found, which was rather unexpected. This study used both institutionalized and family-raised limb-deficient thalidomide children, and although the latter had a higher average intelligence quotient on the Griffith Developmental Scale, the configuration of the developmental profile was similar for both groups. The profile for the total sample is presented in Figure 3-2.

Surprisingly, the area of ability most adversely affected was language, as measured by the hearing and speech subscale; the area least affected was eye-hand coordination. In order to make the test appropriate for these limb-deficient children, the administration of the Eye-Hand Scale was made more flexible than in the standard test administration; thus, items such as "Can hold pencil as if to mark paper" were given credit when the pencil was held successfully with the toes, mouth, or hands. The pattern of findings on the subscales was attributed to two factors:

(1) interruption in the normal developmental sequence due to the limb deficiences which especially interfere with locomotor development thereby resulting in the impetus in fine motor development, and (2) lack of sufficient stimulation from the human milieu so that the child is forced to search for his satisfactions from the only other source available, the inanimate world of objects, with the only other instrument available, his deficient arms and hands. (O'Neill, 1965, p. 136)

Inadequate amounts of stimulation in institutional settings have been demonstrated frequently, and even in the home, handicapped children are not given sufficient stimulation from caretakers to compensate for their lack of initiative. There is less interaction between handicapped children and adult caretakers than between normal children and adults (Spock & Lerrigo, 1965). It may be that this lack of stimulation and interaction is partly responsible for the retardation in language development in thalidomide children. An active, talking, responsive adult is essential for the development of speech in the infant.

Although the deleterious effects of thalidomide are the most widely known, other drugs ingested by the mother also may affect the fetus. For example, the use of quinine for the treatment of malaria in pregnant women can result in congenital deafness in the child. In addition, it has recently been found that drugs which are commonly administered to pregnant women for therapeutic reasons may have deleterious effects. Maternal ingestion of reserpine, a tranquilizer, may lead to infant respiratory problems. Some of the drugs (such as

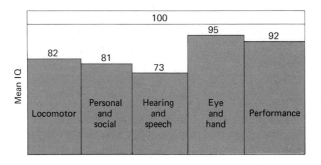

FIGURE 3-2 The Griffith Developmental Profile of a sample of thalidomide children. The overall mean IQ is 85. *(From Decarie, 1969.)*

the tetracyclins) used to combat maternal infections may depress infant skeletal growth. The intake of certain anticonvulsant drugs has been related to cleft lip and palate and problems in blood coagulation in the neonate. Even the common aspirin, if taken in high doses by pregnant women, may produce blood disorders in offspring (Eriksson, Catz, and Yaffe, 1973).

DES   The most recent example of a drug ingested by pregnant women having a tragic and delayed aftermath is that of a synthetic hormone called DES (diethylstilbestrol). This drug was frequently prescribed as an aid in preventing miscarriages between 1947 and 1964. It is estimated that as many as 2 million women may have taken DES. In the late 1960s it was found that many female offspring of women who had taken DES during pregnancy were developing vaginal abnormalities and cancer of the cervix. This case is notable for the delayed effects of the drug since they did not usually appear until the girls reached adolescence.

Labor and Delivery Medication   Recently concern has been focused on the administration of drugs to ease pain and sedate women during labor. Short-term effects of moderate to heavy obstetric medication on the newborn child have been demonstrated. Offspring of mothers who received certain drugs during labor show a decrease in cortical activity for several days after birth (Hughes, Ehemann, & Brown, 1948), disruptions in feeding responses (Brazelton, 1961; Kron, Stein, & Goddard, 1966), and general neonatal depression (Shnider & Moya, 1964). Attentional behavior, such as looking at pictures exposed at 1-minute intervals (Stechler, 1964b) and habituation to repeated bursts of noise as measured by a decrease in the startle response in the first five days of life, is also impaired by labor medication (Conway & Brackbill, 1970). In fact obstetrical medication results in impairment of attention and motor abilities that is still present at 1 month of age.

The timing of the administration of a drug during labor seems particularly important. Moya and Thorndike (1962) surveyed the results of a large group of studies on the use of a variety of narcotics during labor and found that if the infant is born less than one hour or more than six hours following a mother's intake of a drug, there is a decrease in its effects. Light levels of medication have few effects on infant behavior. There may be a critical cutoff drug level at which infants begin to be affected by obstetrical medication. Below that drug level no measurable deleterious effects on neonatal behavior can be observed (Tronick, Wise, Als, Adamson, Scanlon, & Brazelton, 1975). It has been suggested that this critical cutoff level may vary for different populations and for different individuals. Genetic factors, the physiological condition of the mother, and even maternal attitudes may modify the impact of obstetrical medications on the newborn (Horowitz, Ashton, Culp, & Gaddis, 1977).

How do mothers who receive a large amount of medication respond to the more lethargic, less adaptable and attentive behavior in their children? They attempt to stimulate and arouse their infants by touching and rocking and trying to get them to suck and attend (Brown, Bakeman, Snyder, Fredrickson, Morgan,

& Helper, 1975; Parke, O'Learey, & West, 1972; Richard & Bernal, 1971). It can be imagined that this could be a rather frustrating experience with a depressed, unresponsive infant. These effects may be compounded since although the neonate's deviant behavior may contribute to increased maternal anxiety, it may already have been the most anxious mothers who asked for or needed high levels of medication during labor and delivery. As we move on to discuss the effect of some self-administered drugs, it will be seen in Box 3-1 that disruptions in mother-infant interaction occur not only as a result of obstetrical medication but also because of drug addiction in mothers during pregnancy.

Heroin, Methadone, and LSD   In addition to drugs used for therapeutic reasons, in this "turned-on" age, the prenatal effects of drugs such as heroin, morphine, methadone, and LSD (lysergic acid diethylamide) are of increasing concern. Mothers who are heroin or morphine addicts have offspring who are also addicted and are observed to go through withdrawal symptoms such as hyperirritability, vomiting, trembling, shrill crying, rapid respiration, and hyper-activity which may result in death in the first few days of life (Brazelton, 1970). Female addicts seem to have reduced fertility; however, when they do conceive, their infants are often premature and of low birthweight, which makes them even less prepared to cope with the trauma of withdrawal symptoms (Eriksson et al., 1973). The severity of the neonate's symptoms are related to how sustained and intense the mother's addiction has been (Burnham, 1972). If the mother stops taking drugs in the months preceding birth, the infant usually is not affected in this way.

There has been a great controversy in the past ten years over the use of methadone as a less deleterious substitute for heroin. However, it has been found that the use of methadone by pregnant women leads to withdrawal symptoms in their infants that are believed by some experts to be even more severe than those resulting from heroin.

The evidence for the effects of LSD during pregnancy is less conclusive than that for heroin. Chromosomal breakages have been found in both humans and animals exposed to high and sustained doses of LSD. In animal studies some developmental anomalies have been associated with LSD, but in human studies no firm conclusions can be drawn about the relation between defects in children and maternal use of LSD (Eriksson, et al., 1973). In studies of maternal use of LSD, as in those of other illegally used drugs, it is difficult to isolate the specific effects of the drugs. Frequently these mothers have been multiple-drug users, are malnourished, and may have poor prenatal and delivery care, all of which could contribute to producing anomalies in their infants.

Nicotine and Alcohol   It is estimated that over 80 percent of pregnant women in the United States drink alcohol and 57 percent smoke. Although many pregnant women might avoid using hallucinogens, few would consider giving up their evening cocktails or cutting down on cigarettes for the sake of their unborn children. How wise is this?

The rate of abortions, prematurity, and low birthweight babies is higher for mothers who smoke or drink than for those who do not. Women who are

BOX 3-1
BEHAVIOR OF
NARCOTICS-ADDICTED NEWBORNS

How does the long-term in utero exposure to drugs that influence the nervous system influence the development of infants born to narcotic-addicted mothers?

The behavior of twenty-two infants born to methadone-treated heroin-addicted women and twenty-two infants of nonaddicted women was studied at 1 and 2 days of age. The groups were of comparable socioeconomic background, and the mothers had similar medical histories and comparable obstetric experiences in their most recent pregnancy. The Brazelton Neonatal Behavior Assessment Scale (Brazelton, 1973), a widely used scale which measures such things as response decrement and orientation to stimuli, alertness, motor maturity, activity, cuddliness, irritability, and other responses in infants, was used to assess the effects of the drugs. In addition, the frequency of startle responses and of tremors in response to both aversive stimuli and nonaversive stimuli such as in nondisturbed resting state and during handling was assessed. The investigators were particularly interested in the tremor measures because they thought these behaviors were likely to affect the mother's perception and care of her infant. Addicted infants were found to differ most from nonaddicted infants in responsiveness to stimulation, excitability, irritability, and frequency of tremors.

The investigators conclude that "although congenital addiction affects behavioral systems associated with arousal and with the development of maternal-infant affectional bonds, it is the deviations in the latter that are most significant. The addicted babies cry frequently and are likely to elicit increased attending from the caregiver. However, when these babies are held, they do not mold, nestle, or cuddle readily. In addition, motor stimulation and placing the infant on an adult shoulder, which reliably elicit alertness in normal babies (Korner & Thoman, 1970), have little effect on the addicted babies. This lack of responsiveness increases over the first two days of life (Ostrea, Chavez, & Strauss, in press). Cuddling, alerting, and visual regard are the primary means by which the neonate and infant initiate and maintain social interactions with the caregiver, that is, those not specifically limited to feeding and diapering (Brazelton, et al., 1974; Moss & Robson 1968). The behavior patterns of addicted neonates are likely to tax the caregiver's adaptability to the neonate . . . and may have long-term consequences for the development of infant-care-giver interaction patterns." (Strauss, Lessen-Firestone, Starr, & Ostrea, pp. 892–893) ■

Source: Strauss, M. E., Lessen-Firestone, J. K., Starr, R. H., & Ostrea, E. M. Behavior of narcotics-addicted newborns. *Child Development*, 1975, **46,** 887–893.

chronic smokers have premature infants almost twice as often as nonsmokers (Frazier, Davis, Goldstein, & Goldberg, 1961; Simpson, 1957); also, the rate of prematurity is directly related to the amount of maternal smoking. Even with full-term babies, infants of nonsmokers are heavier than those of smokers (Meredith, 1975). In observing such findings Bernard (1962) has commented that "the choice between a dessicated weed and a well cultivated seed often seems to be a quite difficult one" (p. 43).

Reports of abnormalities in the growth of children of alcoholic mothers can be found as early as 1800, when concern was expressed that the high con-

Smoking and consumption of alcohol by pregnant women may have adverse effects on the developing fetus. (Dixie M. Walker)

sumption of gin, euphemistically known as "mother's ruin," in English women was leading to increased rates of dwarfism in their offspring. More recently, a malformation syndrome called the *Fetal Alcohol Syndrome* in infants of alcoholic mothers has been discovered. These infants have a high incidence of facial, heart, and limb defects, are 20 percent shorter than average, and are often mentally retarded (Jones, Smith, Ulleland, & Streissguth, 1973). In addition, many children with Fetal Alcohol Syndrome exhibit abnormal behaviors such as excessive irritability, hyperactivity, distractibility, tremulousness, and stereotyped motor behaviors such as head banging or body rocking (Streissguth, 1977). It also has been suggested that heavy drinking in men may result in genetic damage that leads to birth defects in their offspring ("A man's drinking," 1975).

It would be easy to minimize the implications of these studies by saying disruptions in the behavior of infants occur only when the mother is an alcoholic rather than a moderate social drinker. However, abnormal behavioral patterns have also been found in the offspring of moderate drinkers (Landesman-Dwyar, Keller, & Streissguth, 1977). In addition, there seems to be an increased chance of developmental deviations if mothers both smoke and drink. Infants whose mothers used both alcohol and tobacco show greater prenatal growth deficiencies than do infants whose mothers used only alcohol or only tobacco (Little, 1975).

What can we conclude from the research on maternal drug intake and fetal development? The effects of drugs are difficult to predict. Many of the drugs which produce unfortunate effects had been tested on animals and nonpregnant adults and found to be harmless. We cannot make valid generalizations from tests performed on animals and human adults to the rapidly developing fetus since teratogens may affect different species at different stages of development in diverse ways. The problems in prediction are increased by the wide individual differences in infants and mothers in vulnerability to drug effects. It is apparent that great caution should be used in the ingestion of drugs by women during pregnancy and labor.

Maternal Diet   It is difficult to separate the effects of maternal malnourishment from those of a variety of other deleterious factors. The mother who is malnourished often exists in an environment of poverty and disadvantage characterized by poor education, inferior sanitation and shelter, and inadequate medical care (Birch & Gussow, 1970). In this country malnutrition and high maternal and infant mortality factors are associated not only with socioeconomic factors but also with ethnicity.

People who are both nonwhite and poor are exposed to more of these harmful environmental factors and experience more of their destructive effects. Figure 3-3 presents a table of infant mortality rates related to sex and race. It can be seen that males, particularly black and Indian males, are more likely to die in

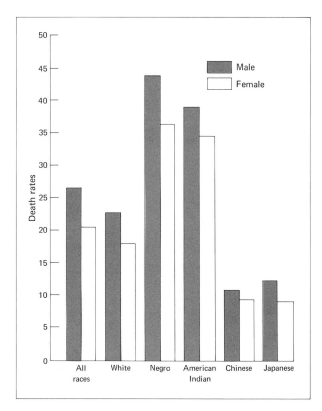

FIGURE 3-3 Infant mortality rates by sex, race, or national origin: United States, 1966. (Death rates under one year per 1,000 live births.) *(From the White House Conference on Children, 1970, p. 49.)*

infancy. In addition, infant and maternal mortality rates are higher in low-income families. The increase in infant mortality rates for Puerto Ricans and blacks with low income levels in New York City can be seen in Figure 3-4. In the United States, nonwhites tend to be less affluent, begin childbearing early and end it later, and have poorer diets, more illegitimate births, and poorer prenatal and delivery care. Adverse prenatal conditions are followed by the environment of poverty, which sustains and compounds their effects (Birch & Gussow, 1970), p. 44).

Middle-class mothers are more likely to have an adequate intake of protein, vitamins, and minerals than lower-class mothers, although there are no class differences in the consumption of fats, carbohydrates, and calories (McCance, Widdowson, & Verdon Roe, 1938). Studies on a variety of populations have shown that gross dietary deficiencies, especially in some vitamins and in protein, in the diets of pregnant women are related to increased rates of abortions, prematurity, stillbirths, infant mortality, and physical and neural defects in infants (Bayley, 1965; Burke, Beal, Kirkwood, & Stuart, 1943; Knoblock & Pasamanick, 1966; Pasamanick & Knoblock, 1966; Tompkins & Wiehl, 1951; Wortis, 1963). Even when gestation period and prematurity are controlled for, offspring of malnourished mothers are smaller in length and weight. Low birthweight is correlated with poor intellectual functioning. Even in identical twins, the twin with the lower birthweight is later found to perform less well on intelli-

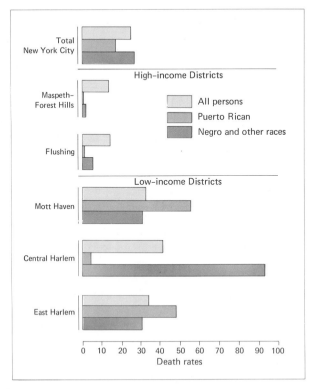

FIGURE 3-4 Infant mortality in selected health districts in New York City, by income, race, and ethnic group: 1966–1967. (Death rates per 1,000 live births.) *(From the White House Conference on Children, 1970, p. 48.)*

gence tests. This has been attributed to differences in intrauterine nutrition because of the arrangement of the blood supply to the twin fetuses.

Studies of severely malnourished animals and infants suggest that early malnutrition may interfere with the development of the nervous system, and, again, we find that the specific form the damage takes depends on the age at which malnutrition occurs. It has been proposed that there are periods of accelerated growth of the brain and that if malnutrition occurs during one of these growth spurts, the effects will be more deleterious than if it occurs at a time of slower growth. In humans this growth spurt is most marked from the last trimester of pregnancy through the first two years of life (Dobbing, 1970, 1973, 1974). At birth the infant's brain weighs 350 grams, about one-quarter of its adult weight, and in the first two years following birth it increases nearly 200 percent in weight. The rate of growth is markedly slower during the next ten years, when the additional weight increase is only 35 percent. By the age of 10, the child's brain has attained about 96 percent of adult size. Early gross malnutrition disrupts myelination, the development of an insulating fatty sheath around nerves, which facilitates the speed of transmission of neural impulses. If malnutrition occurs during the period of myelination of the brain, defective myelination may be associated with mental retardation (Davison & Dobbing, 1966).

In the prenatal period and in the first six months of life the brain grows mainly by cell division; after that time it grows through the intake of fats and proteins, not by the formation of additional cells (Winick, 1970). Autopsies on malnourished animals and children suggest that early malnutrition leads to a decreased number of cells in the brain and that later dietary deficiencies result in decreases in the size of the brain cells. Autopsy studies of malnourished children in Uganda (Brown, 1966) and India (Parekh, Pherwani, Udani, & Mukkerjie, 1970) show brain-weight deficits up to 36 percent. Similar findings were obtained in a study of 252 American urban children who were stillborn or died within forty-eight hours after birth, and who it is assumed were not as grossly malnourished as children in economically deprived countries. Autopsies on these American children showed that the brains of the lower-class infants weighed 15 percent less than those of children from more affluent families (Naeye, Diener, & Dellinger, 1969). In addition to changes in brain structure and weight resulting from maternal malnutrition, chemical changes in the brain and abnormal electrical brain-wave patterns have been found in the brains of malnourished infants. What really is not clearly understood is the relationship between these changes and mental development and how reversible these effects may be.

Impairment of intellectual development in children associated with prenatal malnutrition appears most marked when the mother has a history of dietary deprivation, when the malnutrition has been severe and long-lasting, and when the effects are sustained by adverse nutritional, social, and economic factors following birth. It seems to be this network of deleterious factors associated with prenatal malnutrition that leads to continued ill effects on the child.

In a study of Korean children adopted by American parents, it was found that early malnourished Korean children, after being raised in American homes where they received good nutrition, performed as well or better on intelligence and achievement tests as their American-born peers. However, the Korean children who suffered extreme early malnutrition performed less well than those who had been better nourished (Winick, Knarig, & Harris, 1975). In addition, dietary supplements provided to malnourished women during pregnancy have been successful in reducing delivery problems and mortality (Ebbs, Brown, Tisdall, Moyle, & Bell, 1942) and in increasing the birthweight of infants (Habicht, Yarborough, Lechtiz, & Klein, 1974). The study in Box 3-2 also suggests that there are no long-lasting intellectual deficits found in children if previously well-nourished mothers go through a temporary period of malnourishment during pregnancy and the child has a reasonably good diet following birth.

Maternal Emotional State

The causal factors in the frequently cited finding that emotionally disturbed women produce disturbed children are difficult to isolate. It might be attributable to genetic transmission of emotional characteristics or the fact that emotionality in a pregnant woman induces metabolic or biochemical changes, such as alterations in adrenalin level, which affect the fetus. It also seems probable that the woman who is emotionally disturbed during pregnancy is also more likely to be an emotionally unstable and inadequate caretaker following pregnancy when she will be the main social influence on the infant. Emotional stress in women may therefore be a contributing factor to both problems in pregnancy and delivery and later intellectual and emotional deviations in offspring. Genetic or prenatal factors or early infant learning and experiences could all play a role in the findings of the following studies.

Maternal emotional disturbance has been related to complications during both pregnancy and delivery. High maternal anxiety has been associated with nausea during pregnancy, prematurity, abortion, prolonged labor, and delivery complications (Ferreira, 1969; Joffe, 1969; McDonald, 1968). It might be expected that greater emotional stress would be found in women having psychiatrically diagnosed emotional disorders. Sameroff and Zax (1973) compared the difficulties during pregnancy and delivery of normal women and women diagnosed as schizophrenic, neurotic depressive, and personality disordered. Normal women had fewer difficulties during pregnancy and delivery than the women with severe emotional problems. However, there were no differences in the frequency of perinatal complications among the disturbed groups. The occurrence of obstetrical problems was related to the severity of disturbance rather than the psychiatric classification. Those who had had the most prolonged history of emotional disturbance with the most frequent contacts with psychiatrists and hospitalization, regardless of diagnostic classification, had the most perinatal difficulties.

Women who are anxious and emotionally disturbed during pregnancy have infants who are physically more active in utero. These infants also are hyperactive, are irritable, cry more, and have feeding and sleep problems after

BOX 3-2
FAMINE AND MENTAL COMPETENCE

During World War II a famine which lasted six months, from October 1944 to March 1945, occurred in the large cities of Western Holland. This famine was the result of an embargo imposed by the Nazis in reprisal for a strike of Dutch rail workers who were attempting to support Allied forces trying to cross the Rhine. This event provided an opportunity to do an important naturalistic study of the effects of prenatal malnutrition since the food intake was determined by rationing. Before the famine the ration was 2100 calories per day, whereas during the embargo it was estimated that intake dropped by one-half and was as low as 731 calories per day in February. This caloric decrease was accompanied by a reduction of 50 percent in available protein. It was found that the time at which pregnant women had experienced the malnutrition was an important factor in determining the effects on their offspring. Malnutrition in the last trimester of pregnancy was associated with the most marked decrements in weight, height, and head circumference. In addition, it was related to a high rate of infant mortality from seven to ninety days following birth. In contrast, a high rate of prematurity, stillbirth, and infant deaths in the first week following birth was associated with malnutrition in the first trimester.

Over 100,000 males conceived or born during the famine were studied at the time of their military induction when they were 19 years old. At that time their scores on intelligence tests indicated no cognitive impairment as a result of their adverse prenatal nutrition. The Dutch mothers in this study had reasonably good diets before and after the famine, and the children were well-nourished after birth. The investigators argue that since the first two years of life constitute 80 to 90 percent of the period of a marked brain growth spurt, good nutrition in that period can counter the possible effects of prenatal malnutrition on mental competence (Stein & Susser, 1976). However, a precautionary note may be in order. Severely handicapped or institutionalized men are unlikely to be inducted into the army. If the prenatally malnourished offspring are overrepresented in this population, the results of the study may present an unduly optimistic picture. ■

Source: Stein, Z. A., & Susser, M. W. Prenatal nutrition and mental competence. In J. D. Lloyd-Still (Ed.), *Malnutrition and intellectual development*. Littleton, Mass.: Publishing Sciences Group, 1976, 39–80.

birth (David, De Vault, & Talmadge, 1961; Montagu, 1950; Ottinger & Simmons, 1966; Sontag, 1941, 1944). It has even been argued that stress in the first trimester of pregnancy may lead to biochemical changes that inhibit the normal spontaneous abortion of malformed fetuses (Stott, 1971). More frequent reports of intense emotional stress during pregnancy are made by women who subsequently bear children with Down's syndrome or nonfamilial (thus unanticipated) cleft lip and palate (Drillien & Wilkinson, 1964; Drillien, Ingram, & Wilkinson, 1966).

The disturbance and apprehension of women during pregnancy may just be selected symptoms in a broader continuing pattern of maladjustment, and this pattern of disturbance may be continued later in the handling of their infants.

Pregnant mother with son. (Hanna Schreiber, Rapho/Photo Researchers, Inc.)

Women who have positive attitudes toward pregnancy have had happy childhoods and close family relationships and regard themselves as currently having satisfying marital, sexual, and social relationships; the reverse is true of women who have negative attitudes toward pregnancy.

Maternal Age and Parity

The development of offspring is related both to the age of the mother and to maternal parity, or the number of children she has borne, and these two factors interact. Women who have their first child when they are over 35 are likely to experience more problems during pregnancy and difficulties and complications during delivery than younger women. Mothers under age 35 tend to have lower rates of maternal and infant mortality and infant anomalies than older mothers do. The incidence of two-egg twinning, mental retardation, hydrocephaly (mental retardation resulting from the accumulation of fluid in the brain), microcephaly (mental retardation associated with a small skull and brain), Down's syndrome, low birthweight, and a variety of other congenital deviations increases in mothers over 35, particularly when the mother is bearing her first child.

The Effects of Birth Factors on Development

Although labor and birth are normal processes in human development and in the majority of cases occur with no lasting adverse influences, they sometimes do deleteriously affect the infant. More males than females are born with anomalies.

This has been attributed in part to the role of the sex chromosomes (discussed in the previous chapter) and in part to the larger size of, and hence greater pressure on, a male's head during birth. The majority of infants do not suffer serious impairment at birth, however. Less than 10 percent have any type of abnormality, and many of these disappear during the subsequent course of development. Such conditions as toxemia or bleeding and certain diseases during pregnancy, premature separation of the placenta, the development of the placenta in the lower portion of the uterus so that it blocks the uterine opening, or prolapse of the umbilical cord so that it precedes the baby through the cervix are all associated with greater intellectual and physical deficits in infants (Bishop, Israel, & Briscoe, 1965; Pasamanick & Lilienfeld, 1955). In prolonged labor or in difficult births (such as a breech birth where the buttocks appear first and the head last) the chance of neurological damage through pressure or hemorrhage in the brain or through anoxia (lack of oxygen in the brain) is greatly increased.

Other important birth factors that are related to developmental deviations and infant mortality are prematurity and low birthweight. In early studies an infant weighing less than $5\frac{1}{2}$ pounds was classed as premature; however, the sole use of weight as an indicator of prematurity has been criticized, and some investigators are now considering criteria such as weight relative to stature of the parent, gestational age, nutritional condition of the mother, and a variety of skeletal, neurological, and biochemical indexes of maturity (Drillien, 1964; Mitchell & Farr, 1965). One of the methods frequently used to assess the condition of the newborn infant is the Apgar scoring system (Table 3-1). At one minute and five minutes after birth, the obstetrician or nurse rates the heart rate, respiratory effort, reflex irritability, muscle tone, and body color of the infant. Each of the five signs is given a score of 0, 1, or 2. A high score indicates a more

TABLE 3-1   APGAR EVALUATION OF THE NEWBORN INFANT

	Score		
Sign	0		2
Heart rate	Absent	Less than 100 beats per minute	100 to 140 beats per minute
Respiratory effort	No breathing for more than one minute	Slow and irregular	Good respiration with normal crying
Muscle tone	Limp and flaccid	Some flexion of the extremities	Good flexion, active motion
Body Color	Blue or pale body and extremities	Body pink with blue extremities	Pink all over

Source: Adapted from Apgar, V. A. A proposal for a new method of evaluation of the newborn infant. *Current Research in Anesthesia and Analgesia*, 1953, **32**, 260–267, and Apgar, V. A., & James, L. S. Further observations on the newborn scoring system. *American Journal of Diseases of Children*, 1962, **104**, 419–428.

favorable condition. A total score of 7 to 10 indicates that the neonate is in good condition, a score below 5 indicates that there may be possible developmental difficulties, and a score of 3 or lower indicates that immediate emergency steps are necessary and that there may be a problem in survival.

Anoxia All infants undergo some oxygen deprivation and retention of carbon dioxide during the birth process; however, abnormalities in the mother and conditions during labor and delivery can lead to severe anoxia, which results in brain damage, functional defects, or even death of the infant.

Infants born with no complications during birth and with an average duration of labor of six to ten hours show fewest detrimental effects. It may seem surprising that extremely short as well as excessively long periods of labor are associated with severe anoxia. Infants delivered after a period of labor of less than two hours or those delivered by cesarean section suffer less brain injury from pressure or the use of instruments during birth but are often exposed to oxygen too suddenly, have difficulty beginning to breathe, and hence may be damaged by anoxia (Schwartz, 1956).

Longitudinal studies suggest that the effects of anoxia change or disappear with age. General intellectual and neurological impairments decrease. Distractibility and deficits in attentional abilities tend to be more sustained, and personality problems and lack of social adaptability may actually increase. It is interesting to speculate about what may lead to the later problems in social

Supportive father and elated mother at the time of delivery of their baby. (Black Star, Inc.)

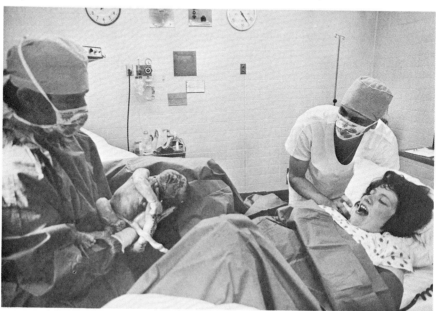

adjustment. It may be that parents respond to the early distractibility and motor and cognitive deficits with overprotection or rejection that results in later adjustment problems (Anthony, Painter, Stern, & Thurston, 1965; Graham, Ernhart, Thurston, & Craft, 1962).

**Prematurity and
Low Birthweight**

Both extremely low and extremely high birthweights are associated with intellectual impairment. Examination of the findings on low-birthweight children shows that significant impairment in IQ occurs only among children with extremely low birthweights, that is, under 4 pounds (Caputo & Mandel, 1970; Weiner, 1962). More low-birthweight children than normal-weight children are found among both institutionalized and noninstitutionalized mental retardates and high school dropouts. In contrast with anoxia, deficits associated with very low birthweights tend to be more enduring. Retardation in other cognitive skills such as reading, language, arithmetic, and spelling is also associated with prematurity and low birthweight. Deviant behavior of a disorganized, hyperactive type and disorders such as autism and accident-proneness are more frequently found in premature than in maturely born infants.

Since deviations in neurological functioning and motor and physical development are also characteristic of prematures and infants with extremely low birthweights, particularly in the early months of life, many of these children have often been considered to be suffering from *minimal brain dysfunction* (Knoblock & Pasamanick, 1966). Investigators who use this label are saying that the behavior exhibited by these children is similar to those of children with known organic brain damage and therefore they may be suffering from organic abnormalities which our neurological tests cannot detect. It is believed that in the syndrome of minimal brain damage many of the early neurological abnormalities often show gradual improvement over time. However, although neurological indicators of abnormality may disappear, a suggestion of an undetectable dysfunction remains in the lack of integrative and attentional abilities seen in the behavior and learning disorders of these children. Many psychologists have objected to the "I can't see it and I can't measure it, but it must be there" implications in the use of the concept of minimal brain dysfunction.

It has been pointed out that behavior associated with prematurity may also be the outcome of a number of related factors, such as delivery complications, low birthweight, the early period of isolation in an incubator, neonatal anomalies other than prematurity, the treatment by parents in response to the infants' apparent frailty and small size, and early separation of mother and infant (Braine, Heimer, Wortis, & Freedman, 1966; Klaus & Kennell, 1976; Parmalee & Haber, 1973).

In attempting to identify the factors that may be contributing to differences in development between premature and full-term children, let us look at the early experiences of these children and their parents. Most parents look forward to holding, cuddling, and feeding their infants soon after birth and to leaving the hospital within three or four days to assume full care of a healthy, vigorous baby. Instead, in most hospitals the premature baby is immediately taken from the parents and placed in an isolette where the parent usually can neither touch nor feed the infant. The infant is fed, cleansed, and changed by hospital staff through an opening in the isolette. Parents viewing their premature infants through the glass observation window in the nursery see a tiny, fragile-looking creature. Since the infant is not fully developed and has not formed the layer of subcutaneous fat found on full-term babies, the child appears thin, with wrinkled, transparent skin and a disproportionately large head. When the mother leaves to go home, she goes without her baby. The infant remains in the care of the hospital staff, often for several weeks until he or she is physically mature enough to leave the isolette.

Two aspects of these early experiences have concerned psychologists. The first is that the preterm infant in the early weeks of life in the isolette may be getting less and is certainly getting different sensory and social stimulation than the full-term baby does. The second is that the early parent-child separation may disrupt the formation of an affectionate bond between parent and infant.

In order to study these factors, experiments and programs have been introduced where the development of preterm babies who receive additional stimulation is compared to that of those who do not. Some experimenters have suggested that the stimulation used should approximate the conditions experienced by the infant in utero. Premature infants have been exposed to tape-recorded heartbeats with the sound intensity of that in the uterus of a pregnant woman (Barnard, 1973), or to rocking hammocks (Neal, 1968) or waterbeds within the isolettes (Korner, Kraemer, Hoffner, & Cosper, 1975) that permit rotation, movement, and rhythmical activity similar to the stimulation mediated through fetal flotation and movements in the amniotic fluid. Other investigators have used stimulation characteristic of the experiences of full-term infants such as mobiles, tape recordings of the mother's voice, manual rocking, talking and singing, and handling and cuddling (Powell, 1974; Rice, 1977; Scarr-Salapatek & Williams, 1973; Siqueland, 1970; Solkoff, Yaffe, Weintraub, & Blase, 1969). Both types of studies have found that additional stimulation can counteract some of the effects of the monotonous stimulation experienced by infants in isolettes. Stimulated premature infants have been found to be more advanced in mental development, in neurological development, as measured by infant reflexes (Rice, 1977), in sensorimotor and motor skills, in muscle tonus (Cornell & Gottfried, 1976), and in exploratory behavior than are unstimulated premature infants. In addition fewer incidents of apnea (temporary cessation of breathing which has been associated with later crib deaths) are found in stimulated infants (Korner et al., 1975). It is clear that stimulation has a salutary effect on the development of premature infants.

It has been suggested that even with full-term babies contact between the mother and neonate in the first few hours of life may facilitate the formation of emotional attachment between mother and child (Klaus & Kennell, 1976). However, in most hospitals even full-term babies and mothers are permitted only intermittent contact. With premature babies and their mothers this early contact is usually completely lacking. Mothers of premature babies report feelings of loss of self-esteem, guilt, failure, and alienation from their infants. In

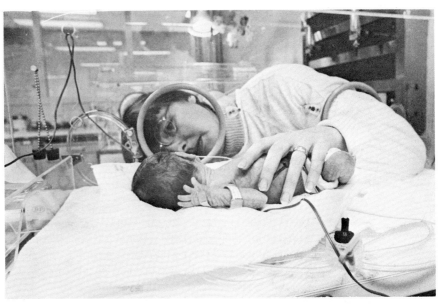

Mother handling premature baby in incubator. Although mother-child contact is established, it can be seen how awkward and atypical this mode of contact is. (Courtesy of M. H. Klaus, M.D.)

addition, mothers of premature babies who have been separated from their infants are apprehensive about handling and caring for their fragile-appearing infants. When mothers eventually are able to take their babies home from the hospital, these mothers still show less emotional involvement with them than do mothers of full-term babies. These effects are found as long as nine moths following hospital discharge (Brown & Bakeman, 1977).

When mothers have been directly observed interacting with their premature babies, it has been found that they exhibit less mutual gazing than mothers of full-term babies. They are more likely to hold their children on their laps away from their bodies at arm's length than they are apt to cradle the child in their arms or hold them close (Quinn & Goldberg, 1977; Leifer, Leiderman, Barnett, & Williams, 1972). In addition, the kind of mutual sensitivity and responsiveness where both mother and infant adapt to signals from the other found with full-term babies and their mothers is often lacking with mothers and their preterm babies.

Suggested evidence of disruption in the affectional bond between mothers and premature infants comes from several sources. First, in attempting to set up programs where mothers return to the hospital to handle or care for their premature babies in the isolettes, one of the greatest difficulties is in getting mothers to participate. Many mothers who have not previously had contact with their infants do not want to take the time required for such programs. In addition, when these mothers do visit their children, in spite of encouragement to touch their infants many will often just look at the child (Powell, 1974). Second, there is an extremely high incidence of premature babies among battered children and failure-to-thrive children who do not show normal weight and height gains in spite of no known organic impairments. In addition in the case of twins, the twin who has been retained in the hospital, and separated the longest from his or her mother, is more likely to be abused or be returned to the hospital as a failure-to-thrive child. These results could be attributed either to early separation and lack of emotional bonding or to characteristics of the low birthweight child that make the infant more likely to elicit adverse parental responses. The unattractive physical appearance, small size, high-pitched cry, feeding difficulties, low responsivity, and late development of smiling in premature babies may not make them as appealing to their parents, and also may increase parental anxiety and frustration leading to abuse (Lamb, in press).

How does increasing the amount of contact that mothers have with their premature infants affect mother-child relations? Mothers who are permitted early physical contact with their premature babies are initially more likely to feel self-confident and close to their babies and to cuddle and stimulate their infants than are mothers who were only able to look at their infants in the isolette (Barnett, Leiderman, Grobstein, & Klaus, 1970; Seashore, Leifer, Barnett, & Leiderman, 1973). However, many of these differences in the way mothers with or without contact handle their premature infants gradually disappear in the first few months after the infant goes home. Mothers of premature babies, whether or not they have been allowed to touch their babies, smile at their babies and hold them less than do mothers of full-term babies following hospital discharge (Leifer et al., 1972). It seems likely that the babies' small size, appearance, and behavior and the physical barrier presented by the isolette which necessitates a rather strained and unnatural encounter even for mothers who are attempting to touch and care for their infants may limit the effectiveness of early contact programs.

What are the long-term effects of prematurity and early separation from the infant on the family? This is a controversial issue. Some investigators have argued that the mother-child bond is irreversibly damaged; that the early days or even hours of contact are critical. Others have taken the more moderate position, and one that seems to be better supported by research findings, that attachment may be delayed, but eventually will occur. When disruptions in mother-child relations or in the cognitive development of the child are sustained, they seem to be attributable to a variety of factors associated with individual differences in the responsiveness of the child, the general competence of the mother, and environmental stresses (Sameroff, 1977). Disruptions seem to be more marked and enduring for economically deprived families than for middle-class families (Leiderman, 1978). In addition, the long-term effects associated with prematurity have been found more consistently in the relations between the parents than between parent and child. A high incidence of marital discord has been reported in the first two years following the birth of a premature infant (Leiderman, 1978). The stressful problems associated with prematurity such as delays in sleeping through the night, feeding problems, and a noxious cry may be reflected in tensions between the mother and father. These findings suggest that only by focusing on the entire family system will the effects of prematurity and early separation be understood.

Two Continuums: Reproductive Casualty and Caretaking Casualty

It has been proposed that there is a *continuum of reproductive casualty* (Pasamanick & Knoblock, 1966); that is, there are variations in the degree of reproductive complications which result in abnormalities in the child, ranging from relatively minor perceptual, attentional, intellectual, motor, and behavioral disabilities to extremely gross anomalies. However, more recently it has been suggested that in order to make predictions about the developmental course of such disorders, the transactions between the continuum of reproductive casualty and the *continuum of caretaking casualty* must be considered (Sameroff & Chandler, 1975). The continuum of caretaking casualty ranges from an environmental and family situation in which there are few adverse factors to one in which there are multiple, severe deleterious factors.

Although 10 percent of all children are born with some kind of handicap or anomaly (Niswander & Gordon, 1972), many of these defects decrease or disappear with age. How do these children overcome their deficits? What factors contribute to the retention and increase of these handicaps or the gradual overcoming of these liabilities?

Self-righting influences are powerful forces toward normal human development, so that protracted developmental disorders are typically found only in the presence of equally protracted, distorting influences. . . . Even if one continues to believe that a continuum of reproductive casualty exists, its importance pales in comparison to the massive influences of socio-economic factors on both prenatal and postnatal development. (Sameroff & Chandler, 1975)

In order to predict later development from neonatal condition the transactions between multiple measures of infant state and the environmental conditions in which the child will develop are necessary. This is vividly demonstrated in an outstanding longitudinal study of the effects of birth complications on the development of the entire population of 670 children born on the island of Kauai in the Hawaiian Islands in 1955 (Werner, Bierman, & French, 1971). At the time of birth 3 percent of the neonates showed severe complications, 13 percent showed moderate complications, 31 percent showed mild complications, and 53 percent showed no complications. Since all the mothers participated in a prepaid health plan and had good prenatal care, correlation between birth difficulties and socioeconomic status was not obtained.

When the children were reexamined at 20 months of age, 12 percent were rated as deficient in social development, 16 percent were deficient in intellectual functioning, and 14 percent were deficient in health. The more severe the complications of birth and the poorer the neonatal performance of the infants had been, the less adequate was the developmental level of children in these areas. Of more interest was the relationship between perinatal difficulties and environmental factors, notably those associated with socioeconomic status. Infants living in unstable, lower-socioeconomic family situations with mothers of low intelligence showed a 19- to 37-point difference in average IQ scores between the group with severe perinatal complications and the groups with mild or no complications. In contrast, infants in stable, high-socioeconomic family environments with mothers of high intelligence showed only a 5- to 7-point difference between the group with severe and the group with no perinatal complications.

By age 10 the effects of environmental variables had almost obliterated those of perinatal damage. No relationship was found between perinatal measures and a child's IQ at this age; instead the correlation between a child's intellectual performance and his parents' IQs and socioeconomic status increased with age, with lower-class children showing marked deficits on cognitive measures. The main effects of deviations caused by reproductive casualty occurred early in a child's development, and after that development was increasingly influenced by environment, or the continuum of caretaking casualty. The investigators note that at the conclusion of their study "ten times more children had problems related to the effects of poor early environment than to the effects of perinatal stress" (Werner et al., 1971).

Summary

The infant in utero goes through a sequence of three developmental stages: the periods of the ovum, the embryo, and the fetus. The infant is most vulnerable to the effects of teratogens (deviation- or malformation-producing agents) in the period of the embryo. A variety of factors such as maternal diseases and disorders, drugs, diet, radiation, blood incompatibilities, emotional state, age, and parity can all result in developmental deviations in the child.

The effects of teratogens are influenced by such things as the stage of development of the fetus, the physiological or pathological status of the mother, the organ systems that are developing at the time of exposure, and the genotypes of mother and child. An agent which may damage the infant may have no effects on the mother. This is dramatically exemplified in the results of the intake of thalidomide during pregnancy.

Anoxia and extremely low birthweight have also been found to be associated with a variety of physical, neurological, cognitive, and emotional deficits. The effects of low birthweight are more long-lasting than those of anoxia, which tend to disappear with age.

Prematurity is associated with cognitive, neurological, and motor impairment as well as disruptions in mother-child interactions. Programs of increased stimulation have been successful in improving the developmental status of premature infants. However, early increased contacts between mothers and their preterm babies have increased self-confidence and positive attitudes in mothers but have been less effective in obtaining enduring improvement in mother-infant relations.

It has been proposed that there are two interacting continuums which affect the appearance and maintenance of abnormalities in the child: the continuum of reproductive casualty and the continuum of caretaking casualty. Although in extreme instances of reproductive casualty (such as massive brain damage) the effects of environment cannot overcome the effects of perinatal complications, environmental conditions, in general, play a major role in sustaining or eliminating early deficits. The attitudes and behaviors of parents toward children who have experienced prenatal or perinatal damage and the socioeconomic milieu in which the child grows up are particularly important.

References

A man's drinking may harm his offspring. *Science News*, 1975, **107** (8), 116.

Apgar, V. A. A proposal for a new method of evaluation of the newborn infant. *Current Research in Anesthesia and Analgesia*, 1953, **32,** 260–267.

Apgar, V. A., Girdany, B. R., McIntosh, R., & Taylor, H. C. Neonatal anoxia—a study of the relation of oxygenation at birth to intellectual development. *Pediatrics*, 1955, **15,** 653–662.

Apgar, V. A., & James, L. S. Further observations on the newborn scoring system. *American Journal of Diseases of Children*, 1962, **104,** 419–428.

Barnard, K. A program of stimulation for infants born prematurely. Paper presented at the meeting of the Society for Research in Child Development, Philadelphia, 1973.

Barnett, C. R., Leiderman, P. H., Grobstein, K., & Klaus, M. Neonatal separation: The maternal side of interactional deprivation. *Pediatrics*, 1970, **45,** 197–205.

Bayley, N. Comparisons of mental and motor test scores for ages 1–15 months by sex, birth order, race, geographic location and education of parents. *Child Development*, 1965, **36,** 379–411.

Beck, F., & Lloyd, J. B. Embryological principles of teratogenesis. In J. M. Robson, F. M. Sullivan, & R. L. Smith (Eds.), *Symposium of embryopathic activity of drugs.* Boston: Little, Brown, 1965, pp. 1–17.

Bernard, H. W. *Human development in Western culture.* Boston: Allyn and Bacon, 1962.

Birch, H. G., & Gussow, J. D. *Disadvantaged children. Health, nutrition and school failure.* New York: Grune & Stratton, 1970.

Bishop, E. H., Israel, S. L., & Briscoe, C. C. Obstetric influences on premature infant's first year of development: A report from the collaborative study of cerebral palsy. *Obstetrics and Gynecology*, 1965, **26,** 628–635.

Braine, M. D. S., Heimer, C. B., Wortis, H., & Freedman, A. M. Factors associated with impairment of the early development of prematures. *Monographs of the Society for Research in Child Development*, 1966, **31** (106), 1–92.

Brazelton, T. B. Effects of maternal medication on the neonate and his behavior. *Journal of Pediatrics*, 1961, **58,** 513–518.

Brazelton, T. B. Effects of prenatal drugs on the behavior of the neonate. *American Journal of Psychiatry*, 1970, **126,** 1261–1266.

Brazelton, T. B. Neonatal behavioral assessment scale. *Clinics in Developmental Medicine*, No. 50. Philadelphia: Lippincott, 1973.

Brown, J. V., & Bakeman, R. Antecedents of emotional involvement in mothers of premature and fullterm infants. Paper presented at the biennial meeting of the Society for Research in Child Development, New Orleans, March 1977.

Brown, J. V., Bakeman, R., Snyder, P. A., Fredrickson, W. T., Morgan, S. T., & Helper, R. Interactions of Black inner-city mothers with their newborn infants. *Child Development*, 1975, **46,** 677–686.

Brown, R. E. Organ weight in malnutrition with special reference to brain weight. *Developmental Medicine and Child Neurology*, 1966, **8,** 512–522.

Burke, B. S., Beal, V. A., Kirkwood, S. B., & Stuart, H. C. The influence of nutrition during pregnancy upon the conditions of the infant at birth. *Journal of Nutrition*, 1943, **26,** 569–583.

Burnham, S. The heroin babies are going cold turkey. *New York Times Magazine*, Jan. 9, 1972.

Caputo, D. V., & Mandel, W. Consequences of low birth weight. *Developmental Psychology*, 1970, **3**, 363–383.

Clegg, D. J. Teratology. *Annual Review of Pharmacology*, 1971, **11**, 409–423.

Conway, E., & Brackbill, Y. Delivery medication and infant outcome: An empirical study. *Monographs of the Society for Research in Child Development*, 1970, **35** (137), 24–34.

Corah, N. L., Anthony, E. J., Painter, P., Stern, J. A., & Thurston, D. Effects of perinatal anoxia after seven years. *Psychological Monographs*, 1965, **79**, 3.

Cornell, E. H., & Gottfried, A. W. Intervention with premature human infants. *Child Development*, 1976, **47**, 32–39.

Corner, G. W. Congenital malformations: The problem and the task. In *Congenital malformations: Papers and discussions presented at the First International Conference on Congenital Malformations.* Philadelphia: Lippincott, 1961, pp. 7–17.

David, A., DeVault, S., & Talmadge, M. Anxiety, pregnancy and childbirth abnormalities. *Journal of Consulting Psychology*, 1961, **25**, 74–77.

Davison, A. N., & Dobbing, J. Myelination as a vulnerable period in brain development. *British Medical Bulletin*, 1966, **22**, 40–44.

Decarie, T. C. A study of the mental and emotional development of the thalidomide child. In B. M. Foss (Ed.), *Determinants of infant behaviour* (Vol. 4). London: Methuen, New York: Wiley, 1969.

Despres, M. A. Favorable and unfavorable attitudes toward pregnancy in primiparas. *Journal of Genetic Psychology*, 1937, **51**, 241–254.

Dobbing, J. Undernutrition and the developing brain. In W. Himwick (Ed.), *Developmental neurobiology*. Springfield, Ill.: Charles C Thomas, 1970.

Dobbing, J. Nutrition and the developing brain. *Lancet*, 1973, **1**, 48.

Dobbing, J. The later development of the brain and its vulnerability. In T. A. Davis & J. Dobbin (Eds.), *Scientific foundations of paediatrics*. Philadelphia: Saunders, 1974, pp. 565–577.

Drillien, C. M. *The growth and development of the prematurely born infant*. Baltimore: Williams & Wilkins, 1964.

Drillien, C. M., Ingram, T. T. S., & Wilkinson, F. M. *The cause and natural history of cleft lip and palate*. Edinburgh: Churchill Livingstone, 1966.

Drillien, C. M., & Wilkinson, E. M. Emotional stress and mongoloid birth. *Developmental Medicine and Child Neurology*, 1964, **6**, 140–143.

Ebbs, H. H., Brown, A., Tisdall, F. F., Moyle, W. J., & Bell, M. The influence of improven prenatal nutrition upon the infant. *Canadian Medical Association Journal*, 1942, **46**, 6–8.

Eriksson, M., Catz, C. S., & Yaffe, S. J. Drugs and pregnancy in H. Osofsky (Ed.), *Clinical obstetrics and gynecology: High risk pregnancy with emphases upon maternal and fetal well being* (Vol. 16). New York: Harper & Row, 1973, pp. 192–224.

Ferreira, A. *Prenatal environment*. Springfield, Ill.: Charles C Thomas, 1969.

Field, T. Effects of early separation, interactive deficits and experimental manipulations on mother-infant interaction. Paper presented at the biennial meeting of the Society for Research in Child Development, New Orleans, March 1977.

Frazier, T. M., Davis, G. H., Goldstein, H., & Goldberg, I. D. Cigarette smoking and prematurity: A prospective study. *American Journal of Obstetrics and Gynecology*, 1961, **81**, 988–996.

Gellis, S. S., & Hsai, D. Y. The infant of the diabetic mother. *American Journal of Diseases of Children*, 1959, **97**, 1.

Gottesmann, I. I., & Shields, J. Genetic theorizing and schizophrenia. *British Journal of Psychiatry*, 1973, **122**, 17–18.

Graham, F. K. Behavior differences between normal and traumatized newborns. I. The test procedures. *Psychological Monographs,* 1956, **70** (No. 20).

Graham, F. K., Ernhart, C. B., Thurston, D., & Craft, M. Development three years after perinatal anoxia and other potentially damaging experiences. *Psychological Monographs,* 1962, **76** (3 Whole No. 522).

Habicht, J. P., Yarborough, C., Lechtig, A., & Klein, R. E. Relation of maternal supplementary feeding during pregnancy to birth weight and other sociobiological factors. In M. Winick (Ed.), *Nutrition and fetal development, Vol. 2, Current concepts in nutrition.* New York: Wiley, 1974, p. 147.

Horowitz, F. D., Ashton, J., Culp, R., Gaddis, E., Leven, S., & Reichmann, B. The effects of obstetrical medication on the behavior of Israeli newborn infants and some comparisons with Uruguayan and American Infants. *Child Development*, 1977, **H8,** 1607–1623.

Hughes, J. G., Ehemann, B., & Brown, U. A. Electroencephalography of the newborn. *American Journal of Diseases of Children,* 1948, **76,** 626–633.

Joffe, J. M. *Prenatal determinants of behavior.* Oxford: Pergamon, 1969.

Jones, K. L., Smith, D. W., Ulleland, C. V., & Streissguth, A. P. Pattern of malformation in offspring of chronic alcoholic mothers. *Lancet*, 1973, **1,** 1267–1271.

Karnofsky, D. A. Drugs as teratogens in animals and man. *Annual Review of Pharmacology*, 1965, **5,** 477–482.

Klaus, M. H., & Kennell, J. H. *Maternal-infant bonding.* St. Louis: Mosby, 1976.

Knoblock, H., & Pasamanick, B. Prospective studies on the epidemiology of reproductive casualty: Methods, findings and some implications. *Merrill-Palmer Quarterly of Behavior and Development,* 1966, **12,** 27–43.

Korner, A. F., Kraemer, H. C., Hoffner, E., & Cosper, L. M. Effects of waterbed flotation on premature infants: A pilot study. *Pediatrics*, 1975, **56,** 3, 361–367.

Korner, A. F., & Thoman, E. B. Visual alertness in neonates as evoked by maternal care. *Journal of Experimental Child Psychology*, 1970, **10,** 67–79.

Kron, R. E., Stein, M., & Goddard, K. E. Newborn sucking behavior affected by obstetric sedation. *Pediatrics*, 1966, **37,** 1012–1016.

Lakin, M. Personality factors in mothers of excessively crying (colicky) infants. *Monographs of the Society for Research in Child Development*, 1957, **22,** 64.

Lamb, M. E. Influence of the child on marital quality and family interaction during the prenatal, perinatal and infancy periods. In Lerner, R. M., & Spanier, G. D. (Eds.), *Contribution of the child to marital quality and family interaction through the life-span.* New York: Academic, in press.

Landesman-Dwyer, S., Keller, S. L., & Streissguth, A. P. Naturalistic observations of newborns: Effects of maternal alcohol intake. Paper presented at the American Psychological Association Annual Meeting, San Francisco, 1977.

Leiderman, P. H. The Critical Period Hypothesis Revisited. Mother to Infant Social Bonding in the Neonatal Period, in press, 1978.

Liefer, A. D., Leiderman, P. H., Barnett, C. R., & Williams, J. A. Effects of mother-infant separation on maternal attachment behavior. *Child Development*, 1972, **43,** 1203–1218.

Little, R. Maternal alcohol use and resultant birth weight. Unpublished doctoral dissertation, Johns Hopkins University, 1975.

McCance, R. A., Widdowson, E. M., & Verdon Roe, C. M. A study of English diets by the individual method. III. Pregnant women at different economic levels. *Journal of Hygiene*, 1938, **38,** 596.

McDonald, R. L. The role of emotional factors in obstetric complications: A review. *Psychosomatic Medicine*, 1968, **30,** 222–237.

Meredith, H. V. Somatic changes during prenatal life *Child Development*, 1975, **46,** 603–610.

Mitchell, R. G., and Farr, V. The meaning of maturity and the assessment of maturity at birth. In M. Dawkins and W. G. MacGregor (Eds.). *Gestational age, size and maturity.* London: Spastics Society Medical Education and Information Unit, 1965, pp. 83–99.

Montagu, M. F. A. Constitutional and prenatal factors in infant and child health. In M. J. E. Senn (Ed.), *Symposium on the healthy personality.* New York: Josiah Macy, Jr., Foundation, 1950, pp. 148–175.

Moya, F., & Thorndike, V. Passage of drugs across the placenta. *American Journal of Obstetrics and Gynecology*, 1962, **84,** 1778–1798.

Naeye, R. L., Diener, M. M., & Dellinger, W. S. Urban poverty: Effects of prenatal nutrition. *Science*, 1969, **166,** 1206.

Neal, M. V. Vestibular stimulation and developmental behavior of the small premature infant. *Nursing Research Report*, 1968, **3,** 2–5.

Niswander, K. R., & Gordon, M. (Eds.). *The collaborative perinatal study of the National Institute of Neurological Diseases and Stroke: The women and their pregnancies.* Philadelphia: Saunders, 1972.

O'Neill, M. Preliminary evaluation of the intellectual development of children with congenital limb malformations associated with thalidomide. These de licence inedite, Universite de Montreal, 1965.

Ostrea, E. M., Chavez, C. J., & Strauss, M. E. A study of factors that influence the severity of neonatal narcotic withdrawal. *Journal of Addictive Diseases,* in press.

Ottinger, D. R., & Simmons, J. E. Behavior or human neonatal and prenatal maternal emotions. *Psychological Reports*, 1966, **14,** 391–394.

Parekh, V. C., Pherwani, A., Udani, P. M., & Murkerjie, S. Brain weight and head circumference in fetus, infant and children of different nutritional and socio-economic groups, *Indian Pediatrics*, 1970, **7,** 347–358.

Parke, R., O'Leary, S. E., & West, S. Mother-father-newborn interaction: Effect of maternal medication, labor and sex of infant. *Proceedings of the American Psychological Association*, 1972, **7,** 85–86.

Parmalee, A. H., & Haber, A. Who is the "risk infant"? In H. J. Osofsky (Ed.), *Clinical obstetrics and gynecology: High risk pregnancy with emphases upon maternal and fetal well being* (Vol. 16). New York: Harper & Row, 1973, pp. 376–387.

Pasamanick, B., & Knoblock, H. Retrospective studies on the epidemiology of reproductive casualty: Old and new. *Merrill-Palmer Quarterly of Behavior and Development,* 1966, **12,** 7–26.

Pasamanick, B., & Lilienfeld, A. Association of maternal and fetal factors with the development of mental deficiency. I. Abnormalities in the prenatal and perinatal periods. *Journal of the American Medical Association*, 1955, **159,** 155–160.

Powell, L. F. The effect of extra stimulation and maternal involvement on the development of low-birth-weight infants and on maternal behavior. *Child Development*, 1974, **45,** 106–113.

Quinn, B., & Goldberg, S. Feeding and fussing: Parent-infant interaction as a function of neonatal medical status. Paper presented at the biennial meeting of the Society for Research in Child Development, New Orleans, March 1977.

Rhodes, A. J. Virus infections and congenital malformations. *Papers and discussions presented at the First International Conference on Congenital Malformations.* Philadelphia: Lippincott, 1961, pp. 106–116.

Rice, R. D. Neurophysiological development in premature infants following stimulation. *Developmental Psychology*, 1977, **13,** 1, 69–76.

Richards, M. P., & Bernal, J. F. Social interactions in the first days of life. In H. R. Schaffer (Ed.), *The origins of human relations.* New York: Academic, 1971, pp. 3–13.

Sameroff, A. J. Caretaking or reproductive casualty determinants in developmental deviations. Paper presented at the meeting of the American Association for the Advancement of Science, Denver, February 1977.

Sameroff, A. J., & Chandler, M. J. Reproductive risk and the continuum of caretaking casualty. In F. Horowitz (Ed.), *Review of child development research* (Vol. 4). Chicago: University of Chicago Press, 1975.

Sameroff, A. J., & Zax, M. Perinatal characteristics of the offspring of schizophrenic women. *Journal of Nervous and Mental Diseases.* 1973, **46**, 178–185.

Scarr-Salapatek, S., & Williams, M. The effects of early stimulation on low-birthweight infants. *Child Development*, 1972, **43**, 509–519.

Schwartz, P. Birth injuries of the newborn. *Pediatric Archives*, 1956, **73**, 429–450.

Seashore, M. J., Leifer, A. D., Barnett, C. R., & Leiderman, P. H. The effects of denial of early mother-infant interaction on maternal self-confidence. *Journal of Personality and Social Psychology*, 1973, **26**, 369–378.

Shnider, S. M., & Moya, F. Effects of meperidine on the newborn infant. *American Journal of Obstetrics and Gynecology.* 1964, **89**, 1009–1015.

Simpson, W. J. A preliminary report on ciagarette smoking and the incidence of prematurity. *American Journal of Obstetrics and Gynecology*, 1957, **73**, 808–815.

Siqueland, R. R. Biological and experimental determinants of exploration in infancy. Paper presented at the First National Biological Conference, 1970.

Solkoff, N., Yaffe, S., Weintraub, D., & Blase, B. Effects of handling on the subsequent developments of premature infants. *Developmental Psychology*, 1969, **1**, 765–768.

Sontag, L. W. The significance of fetal environmental differences. *American Journal of Obstetrics and Gynecology*, 1941, **42**, 996–1003.

Sontag, L. W. War and fetal maternal relationship. *Marriage and Family Living*, 1944, **6**, 1–5.

Spock, B., & Lerrigo, M. *Caring for your disabled child*, New York: Macmillan, 1965.

Stechler, G. A longitudinal follow-up of neonatalapned. *Child Development*, 1964, **35**, 333–348. (a)

Stechler, G. New born attention as affected by medication during labor. *Science*, 1964, **144**, 315–317. (b)

Stein, Z. A., & Susser, M. W. Prenatal nutrition and mental competence. In J. D. Lloyd-Still (Ed.), *Malnutrition and intellectual development.* Littleton, Mass.: Publishing Sciences Group, 1976, 39–80.

Stewart, A. H., Weiland, I. H., Leider, A. R., Mangham, C. A., Holmes, T. H., & Ripley, H. S. Excessive infant crying (colic) in relation to parent behavior. *American Journal of Psichiatry*, 1954. **110**, 687–694.

Stott, D. H. The child's hazards in utero. In J. G. Howells (Ed.), *Modern perspectives in international child psychiatry.* New York: Brunner/Mazel, 1971.

Strauss, M. E., Lessen-Firestone, J. K., Starr, R., & Ostrea, E. M. Behavior of narcotics-addicted newborns. *Child Development*, 1975, **46**, 887–893.

Streissguth, A. P. Maternal Alcoholism and the Outcome of Pregnancy. In M. Greenwealth (Ed.), *Alcohol problems in women and children.* New York: Grune & Stratton, 1977.

Tompkins, W. T., & Wiehl, D. G. Nutritional deficiencies as a causal factor in toxemia and premature labor. *American Journal of Obstetrics and Gynecology,* 1951, **62**, 898–919.

Tronick, E., Wise, S., Als, H., Adamson, L., Scanlon, J., & Brazelton, T. B. Regional obstetric anesthesia and newborn behavior: Effect over the first ten days of life. Unpublished manuscript, Harvard Medical School, 1975.

Tuchmann-Duplessis, H. Design and interpretation of teratogenic tests. In J. N. Robson, J. M. Sullivan, & R. L. Smith (Eds.), *Symposium of embryopathic activity of drugs.* Boston: Little, Brown, 1965, 56–87.

Tuchmann-Duplessis, H. Drug effects on the fetus. *Monographs on Drugs* (Vol. 2). Sydney: ADIS Press, 1975.

Werner, E., Bierman, J. M., & French, F. F. *The children of Kauai*. Honolulu: University of Hawaii, 1971.

White House Conference on Children: *Profiles of children*. Washington: Government Printing Office, 1970.

Whitridge, J., & Davens, E. Are public health maternity programs effective and necessary? *American Journal of Public Health,* 1952, **42,** 508–515.

Wiener, G. Psychologic correlates of premature birth: A review. *Journal of Nervous and Mental Diseases*, 1962, **134,** 129–144.

Wilson, J. G. General principles in experimental teratology in congenital malformations. *Papers and discussions presented at the First International Conference on Congenital Malformations*. Philadelphia: Lippincott, 1961, pp. 187–194.

Winick, M. Nutrition and cell growth. *Nutrition Reviews*, 1969, **26,** 195–197.

Winick, M. Nutrition and nerve cell growth. *Federation Proceedings*, 1970, **29,** 1510–1515.

Winick, M., Knarig, K. M., & Harris, R. C. Malnutrition and environmental enrichment by early adoption. *Science*, **190,** 1975, 1173–1175.

Wortis, H. Social class and premature birth. *Social Casework*, 1963, **45,** 541–543.

4

Infancy and Growth

In the previous chapters genetic and pre-natal determinants of behavior were presented. In this chapter, we shall take a closer look at the outcome, the new-born child. How alert is the newborn and how do the states of alertness change? What is in the newborn's rep-ertoire of reflexes? What are the sen-sory and perceptual capacities of the neonate and how do these capacities improve as the infant develops? It has been stated that the newborn's world is a "blooming, buzzing confusion." However, research findings indicate that very young infants have a wide range of available reflexes and capacities, and even their primitive abilities permit them to respond selectively and organize the stimulation they are receiving. Recent methodological advances, particularly those in psychophysiology, have permitted developmental psychologists to gain a clearer understanding of the capabilities and response systems of the infant.

What are the motor achievements of the developing infant? When does the infant reach, crawl, and walk? Finally, what is the pattern of growth? Have growth patterns changed over past generations? Are we growing taller and, if so, why? These are the questions we shall explore in this chapter.

The Newborn Child

Unlike the beautiful creatures in the advertisements for diapers, cribs, and safety pins, the newborn, or neonate, is generally a homely organism. As one writer put it, "even a fond mother may experience a sense of shock at the first sight of the tiny, wizened, red creature that is her offspring" (Watson, 1962, p. 140). At birth the average child weighs approximately 7½ pounds and is about 20 inches long; from birth on, boys are slightly larger and heavier than girls. Part of the neonate's unusual appearance is derived from odd bodily proportions, odd at least in comparison with adults (see Figure 4-1). For example, the neonate seems to be "all head," and, in fact, the head represents ¼ of the body length (the head is only ⅛ of the full-grown adult).

What is this odd-looking creature capable of doing? An understanding of how well equipped, behaviorally speaking, the new arrival is on entering the world is crucial for understanding the relative importance of genetic and experiential variables. Is the neonate the passive, nonreacting organism that scientists for many years had thought? Hardly! In fact, as we shall see, the newborn is a highly competent organism with a surprisingly well-developed set of reflexes and sensory responses, even at birth. Nor are the responses random and disorganized; rather the newborn shows a capacity to respond in an organized, meaningful way from a much earlier time than was originally assumed. William James's claim that "the newborn baby's world is nothing more than a blooming, buzzing confusion" is clearly wrong!

Infant States and Soothability

Watch a young infant for a few hours and one of your most obvious insights will be that infants go through cycles of alertness, activity, quietness, and sleep. Just as adults have organized shifts in their sleep-wake patterns, so do infants. In fact one of the most fascinating aspects of the newborn infant's behavior is the periodic changes in his *state*. By state we mean the continuum of alertness or consciousness ranging from vigorous activity to regular sleep. Our exploration of the newborn begins with describing the baby's state for two reasons. First, it illustrates some important principles of early infant behavior, namely its spontaneity and its periodicity (Schaffer, 1977). As Schaffer notes:

The infant is by no means inert and passive, stirred into action only by outside stimulation. On the contrary, it appears that there are internal forces that regulate much of his behavior and account for changes in his activity. . . . periodicity is vividly illustrated by the cyclic alteration of states. There are it appears, certain fixed rhythms that underlie the spontaneously occurring state changes. (Schaffer, 1977, pp. 30 & 31)

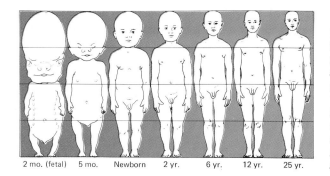

FIGURE 4-1 Changes in body form and proportion during prenatal and postnatal growth. *(From C. M. Jackson, 1933. Copyright 1933 by Blakiston Division, McGraw-Hill Book Company, and published with permission.)*

2 mo. (fetal)   5 mo.   Newborn   2 yr.   6 yr.   12 yr.   25 yr.

In addition, the state changes are not random, but are predictable and organized—another characteristic of newborn behavior.

A second reason for using the concept of state as a way to help understand the infant is that the impact of environmental stimulation will vary considerably with the baby's state. The presence, direction, and amount of the response to stimulation are dependent on the baby's state at the onset of stimulation. Even reflexes may not appear to be present in some states. Many investigators have been frustrated when after attaching a wide array of electrodes, wires, and recording equipment to an infant subject, the infant has burped and happily drifted off to sleep before the experimental procedures could be executed. In addition, at times some infants seem to sleep with their eyes open; although visually they appear to be awake, recordings of their physiological functioning suggest that they are really in a sleeplike state. In such cases failure to attend or respond on the part of the infant may be due to his state rather than his capacities.

In light of the central role of state in determining infant responsiveness, many researchers view state not only as an obstacle to be controlled for, but also as a phenomenon to be understood in its own right. It is clear that before the infant's reflex repertoire is examined and her sensory and perceptual capacities are probed, a look at the many states of the infant is necessary.

Classification of Infant States

How can infant states be classified? Wolff (1966) has offered the following criteria for infant states:

Regular sleep: His eyes are closed and he is completely still; respirations are slow and regular; his face is relaxed—no grimace—and his eyelids are still.

Irregular sleep: His eyes are closed; engages in variable gentle limb movements, writhing and stirring; grimaces and other facial expressions are frequent; respirations are irregular and faster than in regular sleep; interspersed and recurrent rapid eye movements.

Drowsiness: He is relatively inactive; his eyes open and close intermittently; respirations are regular, though faster than in regular sleep; when eyes are open, they have a dull or glazed quality.

Alert inactivity: His eyes are open and have a bright and shining quality; he can pursue moving objects and make conjugate eye movements in the horizontal and vertical plane. He is relatively inactive; his face is relaxed and he does not grimace.

Waking activity: He frequently engages in diffuse motor activity involving his whole body. His eyes are open, but not alert, and his respirations are grossly irregular.

Crying: He has crying vocalizations associated with vigorous diffuse motor activity.

Developmental Changes in States

To illustrate the state changes that occur as the infant develops, two extreme states are examined—sleep and crying.

Sleep   The proportion of time that an infant spends in these various states not only differs for individual infants, but also varies for each infant as he or she develops. As the infant becomes older, a larger proportion of time is spent in awake states, which provide increased opportunities to interact with the environment; in turn, the proportion of time spent sleeping is reduced. The newborn sleeps about 70 percent of the time, and, of course, not continuously; rather, sleep time is distributed across the day in a series of short and long naps. By 4 weeks of age, fewer but longer periods of sleep than those of the newborn are typical, and by the end of the first year, the infant sleeps through the night.

"Establishing a rhythm of diurnal waking and nocturnal sleep is in fact one of the more important developments in early infancy—it makes the baby so much easier to live with!" (Schaffer, 1977, p. 28). This shift to a culturally accepted pattern of sleep-wake cycles illustrates the way in which the infant's internal biorhythms become adapted to the demands of the external world.

However, not only the amount and temporal pattern of sleep change with age, but the kind of sleep changes as well. By recording brain activity of infants and adults at different ages, investigators have distinguished different phases of sleep. The most important distinction is between REM (rapid-eye-movement) and non-REM sleep. Often termed *dream sleep,* REM sleep is a period characterized by rapid eye movements as well as fluctuations in heart rate and blood pressure. In adults, dreaming occurs in this period, and one might expect increased motor activity; but the body is wisely organized so that there is no physical acting-out of dreams during REM sleep. Apparently dreaming is not simply a pleasant nighttime entertainment. We need a certain amount of REM sleep, and if we are deprived, we spend more of our later sleep in REM activity (Dement, 1960). There is some evidence that if people are wakened as soon as REM sleep begins, obtaining very little REM sleep, their subsequent waking behavior is irritable and disorganized.

Of particular interest is the change that takes place in the percentage of REM and non-REM sleep as the infant develops. In the newborn, 50 percent of sleep is REM sleep, and as the infant develops, the percentage drops dramatically (see Figure 4-2). As yet there is no way of determining if infants dream, and if this high amount of REM sleep is associated with dream activity. The organization and sequence of different phases of sleep also change from infancy to adulthood. For example, normal adults usually have an hour of non-REM sleep before drifting into REM sleep. In contrast, newborns enter REM sleep from almost any waking or sleeping state; only 25 percent of newborn REM sleep is preceded by non-REM sleep, and usually the babies go into REM sleep from a drowsy, crying, or waking state (Korner, 1968, 1972).

An *autostimulation* theory has been proposed to account for the high level of REM sleep in newborns: The REM mechanism provides stimulation to higher brain centers, and the high degree of REM activity in infancy may therefore stimulate the development of the central nervous system of the young infant (Roffwarg, Muzio, & Dement, 1966). As the infant develops and becomes increasingly alert and capable of processing external stimulation, this type of built-in stimulation becomes less necessary. Possibly the speed with which infants reduce their percentage of REM sleep will depend on how much external stimulation the infant receives. In fact, it has been found that newborns who were circumcised and hence received intense stimulation spent less time in REM sleep than noncircumcised infants—a finding that is consistent with the auto-stimulation theory (Emde, Harmon, Metcalf, Koenig, & Wagonfeld, 1971). It

FIGURE 4-2 Age changes in the total amounts of daily sleep and daily REM sleep and in percentage of REM sleep. The percentage of REM sleep is indicated by the non-shaded area of the graph. The percentage of REM sleep drops from 50 percent in the newborn period to only 25 percent in the 2- to 3-year-old child. *(From Roffwarg, Muzio, & Dement, 1966; revised since publication in Science by Dr. Roffwarg. By permission of the senior author.)*

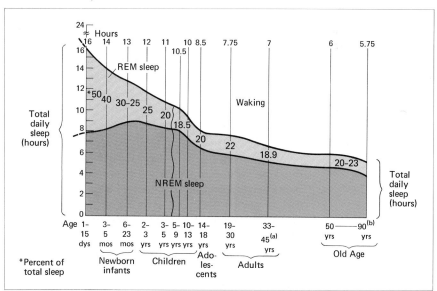

would be interesting to determine whether shifts in REM/non-REM sleep fluctuate with the social and physical environment of the home. Although it is speculative, the autostimulation theory makes good sense. Before leaving this discussion of sleep, turn to Box 4-1 for a brief look at "crib death," a syndrome that may be related to sleep dysfunctions.

Crying   At the other extreme of the continuum of infant states is crying, which, like sleep, is not a simple homogeneous state. Crying is considered important as one of the infant's earliest means of communicating his needs to his caretakers. In light of this communicative role, it is not surprising that different types of crying patterns can be distinguished. Three distinct patterns of crying have been identified:

1   A basic pattern, linked amongst other factors to hunger which starts arhythmically and at low intensity, but gradually becomes louder and more rhythmical.

2   The "mad" or angry cry, characterized by the same temporal sequence as the basic pattern (namely cry-rest-inspiration-rest) but distinguished from it by differences in the length of the various phase components.

3   The pain cry, which is sudden in onset, is loud from the start and is made up of a long cry, followed by a long silence (during which there is breath holding) and then by a series of short gasping inhalation. (Schaffer, 1971, p. 61)

Most mothers maintain that they are able to easily distinguish among these different types of crying, and research has demonstrated that this is true. For example, when mothers who were alone in a room heard a tape recording of a baby's pain cry from an adjacent room, they reacted with distress; but when they heard a tape in which the time sequences of the crying were changed by shortening the long silent pause, the mothers showed less concern (Wolff, 1969). The unique temporal characteristics of each cry pattern therefore have an important social signaling function.

Experience with infants helps in recognition of different types of crying patterns. In an extensive Swedish study, midwives, children's nurses, and mothers were superior to women who had less experience with children in identifying different crying patterns (Wasz-Hockert, Lind, Vuorenkoski, Partanen, & Valanne, 1968). However, even the least experienced women were able to identify the various crying patterns well above a level of accuracy that can be attributed to chance. Since comparative data on men are not available, we do not know whether women are superior to men in their sensitivity to crying because of their usual greater caretaking responsibility.

As every parent knows, crying is a very effective technique for eliciting adult attention. Moss and Robson (1968), in fact, found that 77 percent of the 2,461 crying episodes they studied were followed by maternal intervention but only 6 percent were preceded by contact with the mother. At first, crying is initiated by internal organic stimuli, but as a result of the consistent experience of having mother appear, crying becomes a deliberate means for the infant to gain contact with her caretakers. However, as the infant develops other means of signaling

BOX 4-1
SUDDEN INFANT DEATH SYNDROME (SIDS)

 Each year 10,000 infants in the United States die in their sleep from unknown causes. Often termed "crib death," or Sudden Infant Death Syndrome (SIDS), some progress has been made in identifying "who" are likely to be victims and "when" it is likely to occur. Low-birthweight male infants who have a prior history of neonatal respiratory difficulties and whose mothers have received little prenatal care are more likely to be victims—although it should be stressed that most infants with this history are not affected (Lipsitt, 1977; Steinschneider, 1975). Most often SIDS occurs during sleep during the winter months and often follows a minor respiratory ailment such as a cold. It occurs most commonly between 2 and 4 months of life and rarely after 6 months. It is not caused by suffocation, aspiration, or regurgitation, nor has there been any success in isolating a virus, although this is still a possibility. Another possibility is that apnea or the spontaneous interruption of respiration which occurs more often during REM sleep may be a factor in causing SIDS (Steinschneider, 1975). Currently researchers are investigating whether infants who have unusually long apnea periods during sleep may be more prone to crib death. Another possibility is that these infants have not developed adequate responses to nasal blockage and other threats to respiration (Lipsitt, 1977). It is clear that the possibilities far exceed firm knowledge, but research on early development of infant states, reflexes, and sensory and learning capacities will, it is hoped, contribute to solving this tragedy. ∎

Sources: Lipsitt, L.P. Perinatal indicators and psychophysiological precursors of crib death. In F.D. Horowitz (Ed.), *Early development hazards: Predictors and precautions.* American Association for the Advancement of Science, 1977.

Steinschneider, A. Implications of the sudden infant death syndrome for the study of sleep in infancy. In A.D. Pick (Ed.), *Minnesota symposia on child psychology* (Vol. 9). Minneapolis: The University of Minnesota Press, 1975.

her caretakers, the reliance on crying subsides. In fact, the changes in state that occur as the child develops can be viewed as part of a changing set of means of successfully interacting with the environment. Just as REM sleep decreases as the child's external input increases, so does the child's reliance on crying as a social signaling system decrease as her motor and language capacities increase.

Crying patterns can also be a sensitive diagnostic device that alerts nurses and pediatricians to possible abnormalities in early development. Brain-damaged infants and Down's syndrome infants take longer to cry in response to a painful stimulus, require a more intense stimulus to elicit a cry, and produce a less sustained and more arrhythmical cry than normal infants (Fisichelli & Karelitz, 1963). Using a sound spectrograph—a device for analyzing the frequency and amplitude characteristics of sounds—Ostwald and Peltzman (1974) compared the cries of normal, suspected abnormal, and definitely abnormal infants. The pitch levels were higher in the abnormal infants. Recently, the cry of the malnourished infant and the cry of the brain-damaged infant have been shown to be very similar—which suggests that malnutrition may be affecting the regulatory function of the central nervous system (Lester, 1976). In summary, the infant cry not only is an important communicative signal for parents, but is an early warning system for abnormality as well.

Soothing Techniques

Although general developmental changes from sleep to wakefulness and from agitation and crying to quieter states appear to follow a regular and preprogrammed course, there has been considerable interest in identifying specific techniques that are effective in shifting the infant's state. Of particular interest are soothing techniques, which can reduce agitation and distress in the baby.

Soothing techniques are obviously of practical importance for salvaging the nerves of the harried new mother. In addition, the state of the infant determines how much he will respond to his external environment, and therefore soothing techniques are important because they tend to shift the baby into a state that is more optimal for responding to the external world. The interesting sights and sounds in the outside environment are lost on the agitated crying baby; more optimal for the baby's development is a state of *alert inactivity.* As Korner (1972) recently noted, "the visual exploratory behavior which often attends this state may be one of the main avenues at the neonate's disposal for getting acquainted with his environment and for early learning" (Korner, 1972, p. 88). Infants who spontaneously spend a great deal of time in alert inactivity also tend to be most capable of fixating and following a visual stimulus (Korner, 1970). In short, the state of alert inactivity is optimal for early learning, and so there has been interest in determining whether certain types of stimulation that a mother or caretaker might provide an infant are effective in shifting the baby into this state.

The Caretaker as Soother   Korner and Thoman (1970) assessed the effectiveness of six different soothing techniques (see Figure 4-3), or kinds of stimulation, in shifting newborn infants from either a crying or sleeping state into

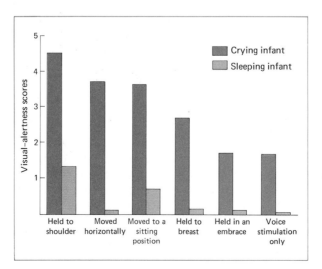

FIGURE 4-3   Effects of stimulation on visual alertness. *(From Korner and Thoman, 1970, by permission of the senior author and the publisher.)*

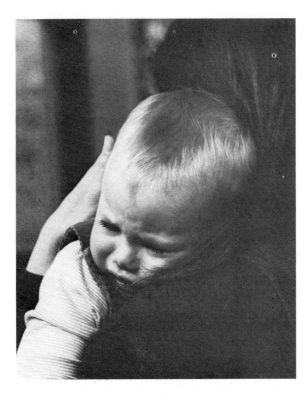

Picking up and placing the infant to the shoulder is an effective soothing technique. (Erika Stone)

a state of alert inactivity. Figure 4-3 indicates the results; by far the most effective technique for eliciting visual alertness was putting the infant to the shoulder; this position evoked bright-eyed scanning in 77.5 percent of the infants. Korner (1972) noted several implications of her findings.

Mothers, in soothing their crying infants by picking them up will inadvertently provide them with a great many visual experiences. . . . If the earliest forms of learning occur mostly through visual exploration, vestibular stimulation which evokes a great deal of visual alertness in the neonate may be the more important form of stimulation during this stage of development than . . . body contact. . . . It makes good sense for the vestibular system to be an excellent mediator for early stimulation. It appears that this system is one of the earliest to develop and is fully mature at birth. (Korner, 1972, p. 91)

Figure 4-3 also clearly illustrates that the same type of stimulation will have either a strong or minimal effect, depending on the infant's state at the time of intervention. For example, the same stimulation had a much greater impact on the infant who was crying than on the sleeping infant.

Of course, a variety of other techniques are effective in soothing infants, including rocking (Pederson & Ter Vrugt, 1973) and swaddling (Lipton, Steinscheider, & Richmond, 1965). Neither of these appears to be dependent on learning or experience, but they are effective shortly after birth. Centuries of mothers can testify on behalf of the effectiveness of them.

The Infant as a Self-Soother   To some extent, an infant is a self-sufficient pacifier and can shift from one state to another independently of outside stimulation. One way that an infant can often reduce distress is by *sucking*, a highly organized response pattern that is ready to operate at birth. Sucking, like state changes, is characterized by a high degree of periodicity and spontaneity. For example, infants in the early days of life often spontaneously show sucking movements, especially during light sleep. Most remarkable is the high degree of temporal organization of infant sucking. A number of investigators have described a burst-pause pattern, whereby the infant makes 5 to 20 sucks and then pauses for 4 to 15 seconds; generally the rate is about 2 sucks per second (Wolff, 1967; Sameroff, 1971). Just as state is not dependent solely on external stimulation, sucking is regulated by the infant's internal biological clock, as well as external events.

Sucking as the principal means of feeding is important for infant survival, and for many years it was assumed that the pacifying effects of sucking were due to the association of sucking and feeding. However, sucking on a pacifier—without any accompanying food—is an effective means of reducing distress. In fact, sucking on a pacifier functions as a stress reducer immediately after birth—even before the first postnatal feeding (Kessen, Leutzendoff, & Stoutsenberger, 1967). In short, sucking tends to reduce activity and movement in the newborn and may be viewed as a congenital stress reducer.

Soothability and Individual Differences   There are wide and reliable individual differences in babies, not only in their rhythms, states, and activity levels, but also in their ability to be soothed (Birns, Blank, & Bridger, 1966). There are sex differences: Moss (1967) found that boys are more difficult to pacify than girls. And there are race differences: Freedman and Freedman (1969), in assessing Chinese-American and European-American newborns, found marked differences in temperament and soothability. The European-American babies shifted between states of contentment and disturbance more frequently than the Chinese-American babies, and the Chinese-American babies tended to calm themselves more readily when upset (a self-quieting ability) and were more easily consoled by adult caretakers.

The Organized and Organizing Newborn

The Newborn's Repertoire of Reflexes

It is against this temperamental backdrop that the neurological assessment of newborn reflexes and the examination of the sensory and perceptual capacities must be executed. Next we take a brief look at the infant's initial equipment—the reflexes; then we discuss the sensory and perceptive capacities of the infant. In attempting to unravel the mysteries of infancy, it is becoming increasingly obvious how adaptively organized the young human organism really is. The confusion that psychologists traditionally have attributed to the newborn might better be attributed to the psychologists themselves. However, now that we are letting the organism speak for himself, even psychologists are becoming less confused.

First consider the newborn's repertoire of *reflexes*, which are involuntary responses to external stimuli. These may be elicited at birth as a test for the soundness of the infant's central nervous system. Moreover, a neurological examination of the newborn has predictive value; signs of abnormality which may be evident in the first days or weeks may disappear during a "silent period" and not reappear as abnormal functions until months or even years later (Prechtl & Beintema, 1964). In Table 4-1, some of the reflexes of the newborn are described. Note that some reflexes are permanent while others may disappear after a few months.

Sensory and Perceptual Capacities of the Infant

Problems of Investigation: Unlocking the Infant's Sensory Secrets

Neonates and young infants are not easy organisms to understand; in fact, they guard the secrets about their abilities extremely well. Part of the difficulty is that many of the methods used to investigate the sensory and perceptual capacities of older children and adults cannot be used with infants. Infants' motor repertoires are limited: they cannot reach or point with any degree of accuracy, nor can they crawl. In addition, they cannot be asked whether one tone is louder than another or whether they prefer red to green. Thus, many well-refined adult techniques of investigation which depend on motor and verbal responses are useless in studying infants. There are other problems as well. How can you be sure that the standards defined by the adults (for example, as to what constitutes a sweet, pleasant taste) apply to infants? Perhaps subjective judgments change with age.

Techniques of investigation have been developed to capitalize on the responses that the infant can make. The autonomic nervous system, which controls such things as heart rate, muscle reactions, and respiration, has been receiving much attention in recent years partly because the child psychologist can use psychophysiological functions to probe the infant's sensory capacities. A change in respiration contingent upon a change in the pitch of a sound suggests that the infant is sensitive to changes in this auditory dimension. The neonate's motor responses, although limited, can give a clue to her sensory systems as well. In fact, one of the earliest means of detecting sensory capacities was the stabilimeter, an apparatus that monitors changes in an infant's movement. Recently, researchers have capitalized on the infant's well-developed sucking pattern as an index of the effect of sensory input.

Listening: Development of Hearing

Although the neonate's hearing has not been as extensively investigated as vision, there have been some exciting discoveries about the newborn's auditory capacities in the last decade. Just how soon after birth the neonate begins to hear is still a controversial issue since fluid in the inner ear may prevent proper assessment of the infant's hearing capacities until a few hours after birth. It is clear, however, that as soon as a fair (for

TABLE 4-1 NEWBORN REFLEXES

Name	Testing method	Response	Developmental course	Significance
Blink	Light flash	Closing of both eyelids	Permanent	Protection of eyes to strong stimuli
Biceps reflex	Tap on the tendon of the biceps muscle	Short contraction of the biceps muscle	In the first few days it is brisker than in later days	Absent in depressed infants or in cases of congenital muscular disease
Knee jerk or patellar tendon reflex	Tap on the tendon below the patella or kneecap	Quick extension or kick of the knee	More pronounced in the first two days than later	Absent or difficult to obtain in depressed infants or infants with muscular disease; exaggerated in hyperexcitable infants
Babinski	Gentle stroking of the side of the infant's foot from heel to toes	Dorsal flexion of the big toe; extension of the other toes	Usually disappears near the end of the first year; replaced by plantar flexion of great toe as in the normal adult	Absent in defects of the lower spine
Withdrawal reflex	Pin prick is applied to the sole of the infant's foot	Leg flexion	Constantly present during the first ten days; present but less intense later	Absent with sciatic nerve damage
Plantar or toe grasp	Pressure is applied with finger against the balls of the infant's feet	Plantar flexion of all toes	Disappears between 8 and 12 months	Absent in defects of the lower spinal cord

116

Reflex	Stimulus	Response	Disappearance	Significance
Palmar or automatic hand grasp	A rod or finger is pressed against the infant's palm	Infant grasps the object	Disappears at 3 to 4 months; increases during the first month and then gradually declines; replaced by voluntary grasp between 4 and 5 months	Response is weak or absent in depressed babies; sucking movements facilitate grasping
Moro reflex	(1) Sudden loud sound or jarring (for example, bang on the examination table); or (2) head drop—head is dropped a few inches; or (3) baby drop—baby is suspended horizontally and the examiner lowers his hands rapidly about 6 inches and stops abruptly	Arms are thrown out in extension, and then brought toward each other in a convulsive manner; hands are fanned out at first and then clinched tightly; spine and lower extremities extend	Disappears in 6 to 7 months	Absent or constantly weak moro indicates serious disturbance of the central nervous system
Stepping	Baby is supported in upright position; examiner moves the infant forward and tilts him slightly to one side	Rhythmic stepping movements	Disappears in 3 to 4 months	Absent in depressed infants
Rooting response	Cheek of infant is stimulated by light pressure of the finger	Baby turns head toward finger, opens mouth, and tries to suck finger.	Disappears at approximately 3 to 4 months	Absent in depressed infants; appears in adults only in severe cerebral palsy diseases
Sucking response	Index finger is inserted about 3 to 4 centimeters into the mouth	Rhythmical sucking	Sucking is often less intensive and less regular during the first 3 to 4 days	Poor sucking (weak, slow, and short periods) is found in apathetic babies; maternal medication during childbirth may depress sucking
Babkin or Palmar-mental reflex	Pressure is applied on both of baby's palms when lying on his back	Mouth opens, eyes close, and head returns to midline	Disappears in 3 to 4 months	General depression of central nervous system inhibits this response

(a)

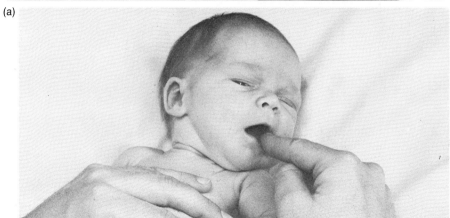

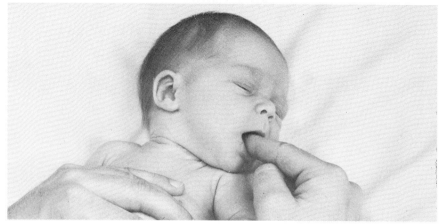

(b)

118

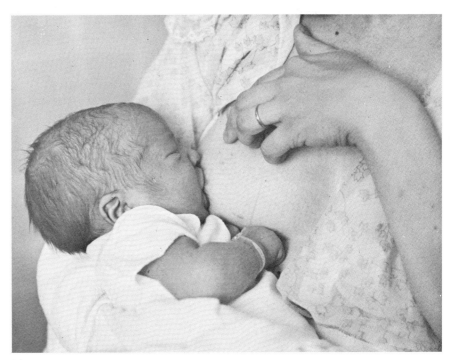

(c)

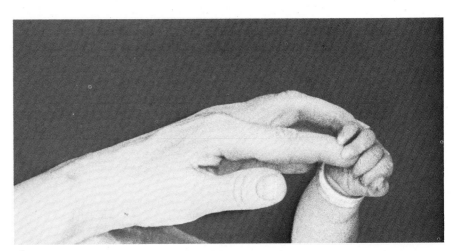

(d)

Some examples of newborn reflexes. The moro reflex (a) is the infant's response to the sudden loss of support at the back of the head. The rooting reflex (b) occurs when a finger stimulates the infant's cheeck causing the child to turn its head toward the stimulation, open its mouth, and try to suck the finger. The sucking reflex (c) occurs when stimulation is inserted 3 to 4 centimeters into the mouth causing rhythmical sucking. The grasp reflex (d) occurs when stimulation against the infant's palm causes the infant to grasp object.

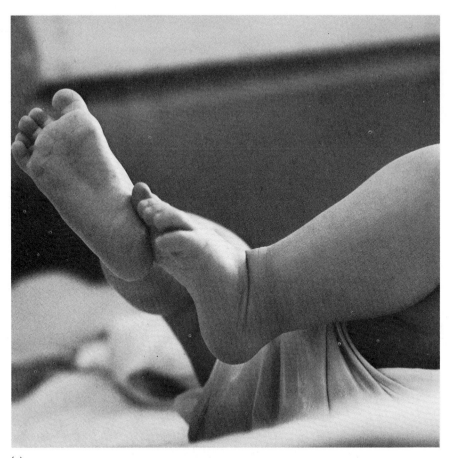

(e)

The withdrawal reflex (e) occurs when stimulation of the soles of the feet cause the infant to flex legs. (Photo (a) H. Prechtl and D. Beintoma, The neurological examination of the full-term newborn infant, *Little Club Clinics in Developmental Medicine*, 1964, number 12, 41. London: Spastics Society Medical Information Unit and William Heinemann Medical Books, Ltd. By permission. Photos (b) and (c) Eve Arnold, Magnum Photos, Inc. Photo (d) Roy Pinney, Monkmeyer. Photo (e) Nolan Patterson, Black Star.)

example, unobstructed) test can be made, the infant's hearing is remarkably well developed. In fact, the infant can localize sound and discriminate among sounds of different loudness and duration (Bartoshuk, 1964; Brackbill, 1970; Hammond, 1970). Continuous sound has a soothing impact on the infant (Brackbill, 1970). However, the effect of stimulus duration varies with the loudness of the sound; the softer the sound, the longer the sound needs to be presented in order to elicit an equivalent response from the infant (Clifton, Graham, & Hatton, 1968).

Not only can newborns discriminate among sounds of different duration and loudness, but they can discriminate among sounds of different *pitches* as well. It has been found that infants with a mean age of 58 hours can discriminate among tones of 200 and 1,000 cycles per second, as measured by bodily and leg movements and breathing patterns (Leventhal & Lipsitt, 1964). Sounds of a low pitch (ranging from 500 to 900 cycles per second) elicit more reliable and consistent responses than do high-pitched sounds (4,000 to 4,500 cycles per second) such as that of a whistle (Eisenberg, Coursin, Griffin, & Hunter, 1964). Moreover, the response patterns to different pitches are markedly varied: high-pitched sounds produce more marked startle responses than low-pitched sounds.

Together these studies suggest that infants respond to sounds in at least three different ways; soothing, alerting, or distressing reactions may occur depending on the duration, intensity, and pitch of the sound. Since experience can play only a minor role in accounting for these different response patterns, these findings suggest that human neonates are prepared at birth to respond differently to specific auditory characteristics, including duration, loudness, and pitch the first time they encounter them. Even more provocative evidence of the existence of a genetically based auditory mechanism comes from recent investigations of newborn responses to the human voice. Freedman (1971) found that newborns responded to the sound of a female voice more often and more vigorously than to the sound of a bell. Another group of investigators who have noted this selective responsivity to potentially important social stimuli have commented: "The structure of the human auditory apparatus at birth ensures . . . that the voice at normal intensities is nonaversive and pre-potent. The survival value of the differential responsivity may be in the part it plays in the development of the affectional bond between parent and child" (Hutt, Hutt, Lenard, Bernuth, & Muntjewerff, 1968).

Nor is this kind of selective responsivity to adult vocalizations limited to humans. Similar results have been found using young rhesus monkeys (Sackett & Tripp, 1968). After monkeys were reared for the first thirty days of life without hearing the vocalizations of adult monkeys, their responsivity to six levels of pitch was assessed. The monkeys were watched on closed-circuit TV, and a behavior change within 2 seconds of the onset of a tone was the criterion of responsivity. Sackett and Tripp found that response to pitch was selective: maximal response occurred at the low and high pitches, with significantly less response occurring at the three middle-frequency pitches. Of significance is the fact that the vocalizations of adult female monkeys have pitches with frequency ranges that are similar to the frequencies that the newborn monkeys responded to. Moreover, the vocalizations of younger monkeys do not have these frequency ranges, which suggests that the adult female vocalizations are unique. The implication is that "at birth or soon after rhesus monkeys possess a tuned auditory mechanism that produces maximal responsiveness to the vocalization of adult females. Thus, the neonate does not have to learn to respond to the mother's vocalization—the auditory system is prewired for these sounds" (Sackett, 1970, p. 12).

In humans, there is accumulating evidence that infants not only are born with a general sensitivity to sounds in the normal range of human speech, but also have a capacity to be "tuned in" to fine-grained aspects of adult speech.

Consider this recent observation: While infants listen to adult speech, they synchronize their body movements precisely to the sound patterns of the speech. Amazingly, this synchronization occurs as early as the first day of life. Condon and Sander (1974) used very sophisticated techniques to film and minutely analyze these infant movement patterns. Infants ranging in age from 12 hours to 2 weeks (most were 2 days old or younger) were filmed while listening to a variety of sounds, including natural speech (English or Chinese), disconnected vowel sounds, and tapping sounds. Analysis revealed that if the infants were already moving when the speech stimulus began, they quickly synchronized the movements of their heads, hands, elbows, hips, legs, and even toes to the exact acoustic structure of the speech. Coordinated segments of the infants' movements were found to start, stop, or change form in precise correspondence to the speech segments (for example, phonemes, syllables, or words). For instance, a movement pattern involving several of an infant's body parts might start exactly when a word (or syllable) began and stop exactly when the word (or syllable) ended. The time segments involved were only fractions of a second, and the precise synchrony was sustained by 2-day-old infants over sequences as long as 125 words.

Synchrony of movement to sound was equally precise for both English and Chinese speech. But this high degree of synchrony patterns to sound patterns was not observed in infants' responses to either the disconnected vowel sounds or the tapping sounds; nor was synchrony observed in a control condition in which the movement patterns of an infant filmed during silence were compared with those in response to speech samples used with the other infants. These results suggest that the phenomenon of movement synchronization may be specific to natural human speech. This research provides the earliest and perhaps the most dramatic evidence to date that from the beginning of life the human organism is genetically prepared to selectively attend and respond to human speech in very special ways.

In addition to these remarkable observations, there is other evidence of the early responsivity of the human infant to language sounds (Moffitt, 1971). It is becoming increasingly clear that at a very early age the infant is capable of auditory discriminations that have functional significance for later social and language development.

Looking: Visual Development   Some animals, such as kittens, cannot see at all for many days after birth, but at birth the eye of the human newborn "is physiologically and anatomically prepared to respond differentially to most aspects of its visual field" (Reese & Lipsitt, 1970, p. 36). In spite of this ability to respond to the visual environment, until recently little was known about how much the infant could actually see.

Visual sensitivity in infants   Let us begin with some of the simplest dimensions. First, is the newborn sensitive to changes in *brightness?* Using the pupillary reflex (closing of the eyelid in response to bright light) as their index of responsivity, a number of researchers have found that the infant is sensitive to brightness changes immediately after birth (for example, Sherman, Sherman, & Flory, 1936). More recently it has been demonstrated that brightness sensitivity undergoes rapid development in the first two months of life. The intensity of brightness required to elicit a response decreases as the infant matures. Similarly, other studies indicate that in response to brightness changes both the speed and amount of pupillary constriction increase with age.

Can the infant detect *movement* in her visual field? Haith (1966) exposed infants ranging in age from 24 to 96 hours to intermittent moving lights. To assess the infants' reactions to the light movement, they simultaneously monitored the newborns' sucking on a pacifier. It was found that infants engaged in measurably less sucking activity during the experimental trials with moving lights than during control trials employing nonmoving lights.

Moreover, it has been found that newborns have the capacity to follow a visual stimulus. Greenman (1963) presented a 4-inch red ring above infants' heads and moved it in a horizontal arc from one side to the other and then vertically. Immediately after birth 26 percent of the infants were able to follow the ring with their eyes, and in twelve to forty-eight hours 76 percent of the infants were able to do so. Also, it was found that following a horizontal stimulus is easier for the newborn than following a vertical stimulus. In relation to our earlier discussion of infant states, it is interesting to note that when cradled in the examiner's arms in the feeding position, many infants followed the stimulus who had not done so previously.

In spite of the unexpected visual capacities found in newborns, visual acuity is not fully developed at birth. Visual acuity is the ability to detect separation in parts of a visual target. Recall your last visit to an eye specialist, where you read the letters of a Snellen chart. If you can read the big E at a distance no greater than 20 feet away but you should be able to read it at 200 feet, you have 20/200 vision. The optimal level, of course, is 20/20 vision. Infants under 1 month of age range from 20/150 to 20/290, although a recent study suggests that this is a conservative estimate (Lewis & Maurer, 1977). This ability improves rapidly during the first year and appears to be within the range of normal adult vision by 6 months to 1 year (Cohen, De Loache, & Strauss, 1978).

In addition, the newborn infant cannot focus well at all distances. The newborn's ability to accomodate or bring a distant object into sharp focus is fixed at about 19 centimeters, and it is not until 4 months that the infant can focus as well as the average adult (Haynes, White, and Held, 1965). It is worth noting that this fixed distance allows the infant cradled in an adult's arms to see the adult's face fairly clearly. Closer objects and objects farther away remain blurry. This predisposition to be able to clearly focus on the caretaker's face from a common holding position is another small indication that the infant's sensory organization and capacities prepare him for social interaction from the earliest days of life.

Are infants color-blind, or can they distinguish colors? Not only can infants distinguish colors, but they can divide them into hue categories, such as red and blue, just as adults do (Bornstein, Kessen, & Weiskopf, 1976). Possibly, the perception of hue has a biological basis.

In summary, infants have a wide range of visual capacities that permit them to interact with their social and physical environment from a very early age.

Parts or patterns: Development of pattern perception in infancy Is the visual world of the infant organized into patterns, images, and forms, or does the infant see merely lines, angles, and edges? Two radical positions regarding these issues can be distinguished: one view, the nativist position, suggests that the infant comes into the world capable of perceiving forms and patterns; the empiricists, on the other hand, argue that only through experience can the infant develop the ability to construct "forms" out of the pieces of visual information coming from the environment. After a few years, hopes of resolving the controversy were dashed, and in place of this simply stated controversy has emerged a complex and fascinating developmental story of how the infant's perceptual world is organized.

In the hope of resolving long-standing questions concerning how perceptual development proceeds, a series of studies by Robert Fantz began to appear in the early 1960s. The early work of Robert Fantz on pattern discrimination is presented in Box 4-2. These early results indicated that infants can discriminate among patterns at a very early age. Generally, these studies have found that as infants develop, they prefer increasingly complex stimuli. This shift in preference may be based on changes in the neurological maturation of the visual system (see Cohen & Salapatek, 1975).

To what parts of the visual target does the infant attend? In order to find out, Salapatek and Kessen (1966) at Yale University substituted an infrared camera for the human observer. By this technique it was possible to determine not only that an infant was looking at an object, but precisely on what parts of the object his eyes were focused. When Salapatek and Kessen photographed the exact position of infants' eye movements on a triangle target, they found that the infants' attention was concentrated on the angles and was *not* distributed over the whole form. This suggests that certain elements of complex patterns may elicit infant attention, but it is not fair to conclude that young infants perceive a pattern. Instead, they appear to be attracted to specific elements of a pattern, particularly a vertex or boundary. Later research (Salapatek, 1969) found that the 4- to 6-week-old infants continue to show the fixation of the newborn on angles and edges but by 2 months of age, there is visual tracing of both the edge of the pattern and the center or internal areas. As Brennan and coworkers noted, "It seems possible that part of the age-related changes in response to complexity may be attributable to changes in patterns of scanning" (Brennan, Ames, & Moore, 1966, p. 356).

Scanning of forms clearly improves with age, but a question remains: Are the parts perceived as independent components or as a unified whole? If you show an infant a green square, will the infant respond to the green color and a square or to a green square as a compound figure? Investigators have employed a habituation technique in studying this problem. The infant habituates, that is, looks for shorter periods, over repeated presentations of the same stimulus; however, when a new or novel event appears, the infant responds at a higher level (that is, looks for a longer period). In vision studies, this technique is used to

BOX 4-2
PATTERN PERCEPTION IN INFANCY

Can the infant discriminate among patterns? To find out, Fantz (1961) developed a procedure in which he measured the amount of time that an infant would look at a visual target. An observer located above the baby recorded the amount of time that the infant directed his gaze at each target. If the infant looked longer at one form than another form, it was assumed that the infant preferred that form. In Figure 4-4 the results of one study are presented. These data support the *nativist* position: young infants can discriminate among visual patterns. The subjects looked longer at a face, newsprint, and bull's-eye pattern than at nonpatterned stimuli. However, the youngest infants in this study were 2 months of age at the commencement of testing; since opportunities for learning had been available, perhaps experi-ential factors did, in fact, contribute to the infants' ability to discriminate among patterns.

Fortunately, data on even younger infants are available. Fantz (1963), in a related study, found that babies under 48 hours of age looked longer at patterned targets, such as faces and concentric circles, than at targets of color, such as circles of red, white, or yellow. These results suggest that pattern perception in human organisms may be innate or at least acquired after very little environmental experience. ∎

Source: Adapted from Fantz, R.L. The origin of form perception. *Scientific American*, 1961, **204**, 66–72, and Fantz, R.L. Pattern vision in newborn infants. *Science*, 1963, **140**, 296–297.

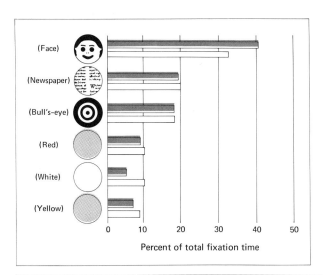

FIGURE 4-4 Importance of pattern rather than color or brightness was illustrated by the response of infants to a face, a piece of print-ed matter, a bull's-eye, and plain red, white, and yellow disks. Even the youngest infants preferred patterns. Brown bars show the results for infants from 2 to 3 months old; White bars show results for infants more than 3 months old. *(From Frantz, 1961: copyright by Scientific American, Inc. All rights reserved. By permission.)*

determine whether infants can tell different visual stimuli apart. Applying this technique to the parts and patterns problem, a green square is presented repeatedly until the infant visually habituates to this object as indicated by brief looking time. In order to determine whether the infant is responding to the shape (squareness) or the color (green), the infant is then shown either a green circle or a blue square. If the infant still does not look long at the green circle, it suggests that she is treating the green square and the green circle as similar. She is responding to color—not shape. Similarly, if she has learned to respond to the shape of the object, she will not look long at the blue square, since it is shape, not color, that is important. However, if the infant has remembered the green square as a compound figure, she would treat an object that differed in either color or shape as a novel stimulus and therefore look longer at it than at the familiar object. Recent studies suggest that before 5 months of age infants perceive color forms in terms of their components such as color or shape and those over 5 months perceive the compound as well (Fagan, 1977; L.B. Cohen, et al., 1978).

Face perception: The beginnings of social responsiveness   Faces have attracted the attention of babies and researchers alike. How early can infants recognize faces? Does the recognition of social stimuli such as faces follow the same developmental course as recognition of checkerboards and colored squares? These are important questions since they provide some early clues concerning infants' social responsiveness and their ability to recognize familiar and unfamiliar people. Just as 1-month-old infants scan only a small section of the outermost contours of a triangle, they do the same when they look at a line drawing of a face. However, when 2-month-old infants are shown a drawing of a face, they do not stay fixated at the outer edge, but quickly move their eyes to the internal aspects of the figure (Maurer & Salapatek, 1976). Figure 4-5 illustrates these developmental changes in scanning patterns.

More recently, researchers have documented the developmental shifts in scanning of real faces (Haith, Bergman, & Moore, 1977). Using a technique that permitted them to determine which parts of the face were being scanned, these investigators found that 3- to 5-week-old infants fixated on the face only 22

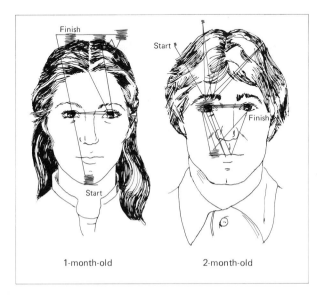

FIGURE 4-5   How 1- and 2-month-old infants scan the human face. *(From Maurer & Salapatek, 1975, with permission of the authors and the Society for Research in Child Development.)*

1-month-old   2-month-old

percent of the time, while 7- and 9- to 11-week-old infants fixated 88 and 90 percent of the time. Figure 4-6 shows the parts of the face that the infants at different ages focused on. Not only did the older infants spend less time on the contours, but they looked at the eyes more than the younger infants did. "It is possible that between 5 and 7 weeks, the eyes have become meaningful to the infants as signals of social interaction. Whatever the case it is highly likely that increased face looking and, especially eye contact, carries special social meaning for the infant's caretakers and play an important role in the development of the social bond" (Haith et al., 1977, p. 8).

By 5 months, the infant has mastered another important developmental task; instead of a face being a mere collection of interesting elements, such as eyes and nose, infants now perceive faces as distinct patterns and can even distinguish between dissimilar faces (L.B. Cohen et al., 1978). This shift from the perception of parts to the perception of patterns appears to be similar for both objects and faces.

Some later visual landmarks: Depth perception and size constancy   Our survey of the infant's visual capacities would not be complete without a discussion of two other aspects of visual behavior: *depth perception* and *size constancy*.

Depth perception   As adults we possess the ability to distinguish depth; the adaptive value of this capacity is obvious—it prevents us from routinely walking off cliffs and the edges of tall buildings. But how soon does the infant show depth perception? To investigate this issue, Gibson and Walk (1960) developed an apparatus that they termed the *visual cliff* (see Figure 4-7). As you can see, it

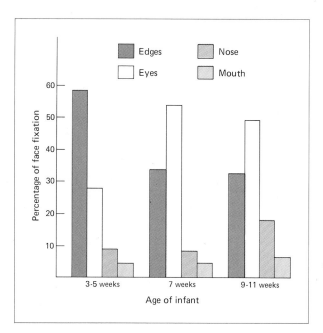

FIGURE 4-6   Shifts in face fixation of 3- to 11-week-old infants. *(Drawn from data of Haith, Bergman, & Moore, 1977.)*

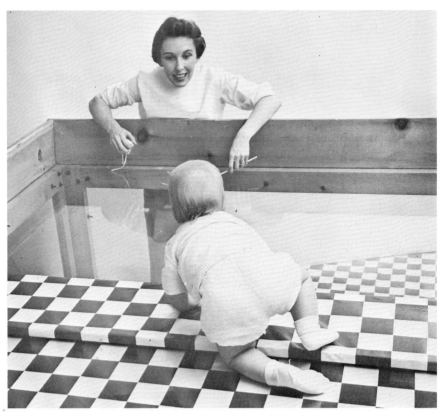

FIGURE 4-7   The visual cliff. (From Gibson and Walk, 1960. Photo by William Vandivert. Used with permission.)

consists of an elevated glass platform divided into two sections. One section has a surface that is textured with a checkerboard pattern, while the other has a clear glass surface with a checkerboard pattern several feet below it. The investigators hypothesized that if an infant can, in fact, perceive depth, he should remain on the "shallow" side of the platform and avoid the "cliff" side since it has the appearance of a chasm. In the natural world, of course, it is possible to misjudge the perception of depth; for example, the reflections from the surfaces of water may mislead a person to think that the water is not deep. However, in this visual-cliff apparatus, the glass surfaces are lighted in such a way as to eliminate any reflections. Thirty-six infants ranging in age from 6 to 14 months were tested. All infants eagerly approached their mothers when the mothers were on the "shallow" side of the platform but refused to cross the "deep" side in spite of the mothers' encouragements.

This study is important for it suggests not only that human infants can discriminate depth as soon as they can crawl, but that the ability to avoid a visual brink may not be as dependent on experience as was once assumed. However, six months may be sufficiently long to acquire this ability through experience, and therefore tests with younger human infants are necessary before it can be concluded that depth perception is an innate ability.

More recently, Campos, Langer, and Krowitz (1970) overcame the problem of testing the premotor infant for depth perception and provided a test using very young infants. Instead of indexing whether or not infants would crawl over the deep side of the visual cliff they placed 44- to 115-day-old infants on both the deep and shallow sides of the visual cliff and measured changes in their heart rates. It was hypothesized that if the infant is capable of depth perception, his heart rate should increase when he is placed on the deep side. The infants' heart rates did increase, which clearly supports the hypothesis that infants as young as $1\frac{1}{2}$ months perceive depth. This finding is consistent with experiments involving animals with independent locomotion shortly after birth, which show that chicks, kids, and lambs avoid the deep side of the visual cliff when they are 1 day old. Together these studies support an interpretation that the ability to perceive depth is innate.

Even if the ability to perceive depth is innate, early environmental experience may be important in *maintaining* early visual skills. Recent evidence (Aslin & Banks, 1978; Banks, Aslin, & Letson, 1975) suggests that children with a history of convergent strabismus (crossed-eyes) may not develop normal binocular vision—an ability that helps us detect distance and depth. Studies of children who have experienced corrective surgery at different ages indicate that the period during which the "cross-eyed" condition is most detrimental appears to begin several months after birth, to reach a maximum during the second year of life, and to decline by 6 to 8 years of age (Salapatek & Banks, 1977). For children born with this condition, early corrective surgery before age 2 usually prevents long-term visual deficits. This research underlines the importance of the early environment for sustaining the proper development of the infant's perceptual systems. We will return to this general issue of the importance of early experience in the next chapter.

Size constancy. Next, we turn to the origins and development of size constancy. As adults we are able to judge the size of an object, regardless of its distance from us; for example, even though a truck looks toylike at a great distance, we still recognize it as a "truck" with real-life proportions. This ability is called *size constancy* and is defined as the tendency of an object to retain its size in our perception regardless of changes in viewing distance, even though the size of the retinal image changes (Bower, 1966). (See Figure 4-8.) Again, the question arises: How early does the infant show size constancy? This question is, of course, important. If the ability does not depend on experience, very young infants should possess it; on the other hand, failure to demonstrate this ability in early infancy would support the empiricist view, namely, that size constancy is a capacity acquired through direct experience with real objects at varying distances. Progress in resolving this controversy has been hampered by inadequate research techniques for assessing this ability in young infants. As the study in Box 4-3 indicates, Bower (1966) has removed the methodological roadblock and demonstrated that infants do possess this capacity very early in life.

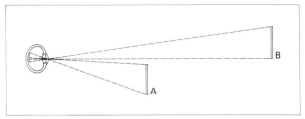

FIGURE 4-8 Size constancy. Two objects of the same physical size may produce very different retinal image sizes and yet be seen as the same size. *(From Bower, 1966. Reprinted with permission. Copyright 1966, by Scientific American, Inc. All rights reserved.)*

Smell and Taste   To conclude our excursion through the sensory world of the infant, we turn to two other senses—smell and taste. Just as we have seen in the case of vision and hearing, we will see that smell and taste are also well developed from a very early age. The infant's competence is not restricted to a few senses, but characterizes all sensory systems.

Smell   Neonates can discriminate among a variety of odors (Lipsitt, Engen, & Kaye, 1963). Moreover, newborn infants are sensitive to the spatial location of odors, and they turn away from an unpleasant odor more frequently than they turn toward it (Rieser, Yonas, & Wikner, 1976). From an evolutionary viewpoint, a mechanism for the avoidance of an aversive odor is highly adaptive and serves to protect the infant from potentially harmful stimulation. Smell sensitivity does, of course, improve with age; the intensity of an odor necessary for detection by an infant decreases as the infant develops (Lipsitt et al., 1963). After a few days, smell may even play a role in early social interaction and provide one of the early means by which the infant comes to recognize his mother. In a recent study in England, Macfarlane (1975) showed that 1-week-old infants can distinguish their mother's odor from those of other people. In this clever demonstration, two used breast pads from nursing mothers were positioned above the infant's head. Infants turned to look at their mother's breast pad more often than a stranger's pad. The preference was not evident in the first few days of life and seems to depend on the infant learning to recognize his mother's special smell. For young infants, smell provides another early guide to things and people in their world. In view of the value of smell for infants, maybe it is fortunate that our efforts to create an odorless environment have not yet reached early infancy! Once developed, our sense of smell is remarkably stable. There is a high degree of consistency between 6 and 94 years of age, with little evidence of a decline even in the oldest subjects. This, of course, is in marked contrast to the decline in visual and auditory sensitivity that occurs in old age. In view of the fact that the olfactory sense is one of the earliest to be acquired prenatally, it has been suggested that "these sensitivities which develop the earliest will be those which are sustained longest in the lifetime of the individual, relative to those more recently acquired" (Rovee, Cohen, and Shlapack, 1975, p. 318).

BOX 4-3
SIZE CONSTANCY IN INFANCY

 How early do infants show size constancy? To find out, Bower (1966) rewarded a group of 6- to 8-week-old babies for a simple head-turning response with a "peek-a-boo!" Once the head turning was well established, he reinforced an infant for head turning only when a 12-inch cube was present 3 feet in front of the infant. Now to determine whether the infant possessed *size constancy*, the experimenter systematically varied the size and distance of the cube. An empiricist would predict that an infant should maintain a high rate of head-turning response even if the original stimulus object, the cube, were changed as long as the new stimulus object continued to project onto the retina an image identical to that of the original stimulus.

To produce this condition, Bower displayed a 36-inch cube at a distance of 9 feet from the infant; the retinal image produced by this arrangement is the same as the retinal image produced by the original 12-inch cube presented at 1 foot (see Figure 4-9). If the infant does not yet have size constancy, and is responding on the basis of retinal image, she should respond equally in these two conditions. However, as a nativist would argue, if the infant does have size constancy and can respond to the actual size of the original stimulus (12-inch cube) and not simply to the retinal image produced by the cube, she should maintain a high rate of head turning to the 12-inch cube—regardless of its distance from her.

To evaluate the adequacy of these viewpoints, infants were tested with either 12- or 36-inch cubes placed 9 feet away from them. The infants turned to the 12-inch cube regardless of distance, while they did not turn their heads when only the retinal image was the same as the original. In summary, the infants demonstrated size constancy: they did not use the retinal image as their guide for responding, but the true size of the object. The change in distance did not affect the infant's recognition of the original stimulus—even though a retinal image from a distance of 9 feet would be, of course, much smaller than its image at a distance of 3 feet. The results support the nativist viewpoint: size constancy may be an innately determined ability. ∎

Source: Adapted from Bower, T.G.R. The visual world of infants. *Scientific American*, 1966, **215**, 80–92.

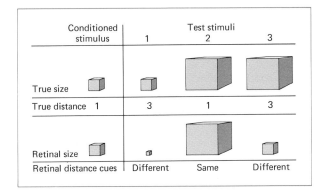

FIGURE 4-9 Size constancy was investigated with cubes of different sizes placed at different distances from the infants. The conditioned stimulus was 30 centimeters on a side and 1 meter away. Test stimuli 30 or 90 centimeters on a side and/or 3 meters away were related to the conditioned stimulus in various respects. *(From Bower, 1966. Reprinted with permission. Copyright 1966, by Scientific American, Inc. All rights reserved.)*

Taste Although controversy still exists concerning the exact taste preferences of the human newborn, there is little doubt that the neonate is selectively responsive to different gustatory stimuli. Over forty years ago, Jensen (1932) utilized changes in sucking as an index of taste and found that infants' sucking responses to water and glucose and various concentrations of salt solutions differed from their responses to milk; moreover, their sucking responses varied for different concentrations of salt solutions. Recently, a number of investigators have confirmed that newborn infants can discriminate between concentrations of sweet solutions (Desor, Maller, & Turner, 1973) and that they may even slow their rate of sucking after tasting a sweet solution in order to "savor" the sweet taste! (Crook & Lipsitt, 1976). However, even in the earliest days of life, there are sex differences in taste: females prefer sweet formula more than males (Nisbett & Gurwitz, 1970).

In summary, the sensory and perceptual apparatus of infants is well developed very early in life, which suggests that infants are well prepared to profit from interactions with both their social and physical environments. Next, we turn to a brief examination of infants' motor development and then finally to a discussion of growth.

Motor Development

What course does the infant's motor development follow? How soon can an infant crawl and walk? The remarkable achievement of the development of posture and locomotion in infants was plotted by Shirley (1933), and her results are shown in Figure 4-10. One of the important implications of these motor achievements is the increasing degree of independence that children gain. They can explore their environment more fully and initiate social contact with peers and caretakers.

There are variations in the age at which walking begins. Some of these differences seem to be attributable to experiential or cultural factors, and some are based on biologically determined individual differences. It has been found

FIGURE 4-10 Sequence of motor development in locomotion. *(From Shirley, 1933. Reproduced by permission from Mary M. Shirley. Copyright renewed, 1961.)*

that children raised in different European cities, such as London, Paris, and Stockholm, show variations in the average age of onset of walking (Hindley et al, 1966). French children, for example, walk earlier than their peers in London or Stockholm. Not only are the differences in the cities noteworthy, but even more striking are the wide range of differences in individual children. Although neither sex nor social class can account for these differences, it is possible that nutritional and environmental factors may contribute to these patterns.

Recent cross-cultural evidence indicates that variations in opportunities for practice can have an effect on emerging motor skills. Consider two different cultures. In one culture, Zambian infants are carried everywhere in a sling on the mother's back until the infant is able to sit. The infant receives a great deal of visual, auditory, and tactual-kinesthetic stimulation. After learning to sit, the infant is often left sitting alone for considerable periods of time; thus the infant has plenty of opportunity to practice emerging motor skills. In another culture— the Zinacantecos of Mexico—the infants are carried, but always tightly swaddled and even have their faces covered for the first three months of life. The mother's aim is a quiet infant, and so she tries to anticipate the infant's needs. The infants in these two cultures develop very differently. The Zambian infants, like many African infants, show early development of motor behavior (Goldberg, 1972), while the Mexican infants show a lag in their development of motor skills (Brazelton, 1972).

The timing of different environmental opportunities is important as well. For example, Yucatecan infants show advanced motor development up to 10

Running steps of a 15-month-old baby photographed with pulsating strobe. (Vivienne, Photo Researchers, Inc.)

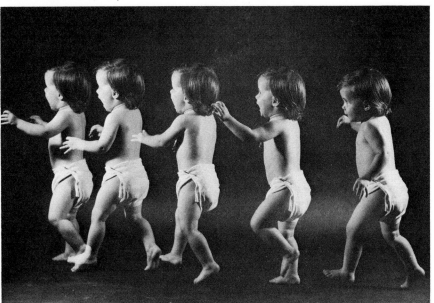

months, but are below normal at 12 months (Solomons & Solomons, 1975). Examination of their rearing conditions indicates that they are carried everywhere in early infancy, but once they can sit, they are *not*—like the Zambian infants—given the chance to practice their motor skills such as standing and reaching. The result—loss of their advanced level of motor performance. Together these cross-cultural glimpses illustrate how early infant rearing environments can alter motor development.

Finally, studies of the effects of restriction and practice provide further support for the modifiability of motor skills. For example, studies by Dennis and Najarian (1957) have indicated that very severe restriction of opportunities for practice of motor skills (such as found in some orphanages) may, in fact, retard motor development. Under extreme conditions, therefore, the onset of walking may be delayed. As Box 4-4 illustrates, walking can be facilitated by extra practice.

As these data indicate, walking is not immune from environmental influences; rather, the general limits may be set by a maturational pattern, but the timing of the emergence of this behavior may be either enhanced or slowed by particular environmental factors.

Motor Development in Blind Infants   Another way to find out what factors influence motor development is to examine the effects of various disabilities, such as blindness. As Figure 4-12 shows, the lack of sight clearly slows motor development, especially reaching and independent walking (Adelson & Fraiberg, 1974). Limited mobility of the blind infant may have serious consequences: "It lessens his ability to explore independently, to discover by himself the objective rules that govern things and events in the external world" (Fraiberg, 1977, p. 270).

Can these blind infants be helped? On the assumption that the blind infants needed to learn to associate sound with touch activities, Fraiberg (1977) has developed a program which maximizes the opportunities to use sound as a guide for touch. For example, parents were encouraged to talk to their blind infants when approaching and during routine activities such as feeding and dressing. Or they provided toys within easy reach to encourage coordinated two-hand activity and to increase exploration of objects that made sounds. Through these experiences the infants learned to use a combination of sound and touch as a way of identifying people and things. And it did make a difference. In comparison to other blind children who did not receive the intervention, delays in standing and walking were lessened—although the blind children were still behind sighted infants.

And other help may be on the way. Recently some experiments in Scotland suggest that an electronic device that produces echoes from objects may aid blind babies to "see." You can learn to use the echoes from objects to judge distance and even size. By outfitting a blind infant with this echo-producing device, Bower (1977) has successfully increased the reaching ability of a 6-month-old infant who had worn the echo device for 4 months. Although it is not clear whether this skill will persist, "this baby can do things with the aid of the

BOX 4-4
"WALKING" IN THE NEWBORN

Recent evidence indicates that walking can be elicited earlier by providing extra practice. As we noted earlier, stepping or walking is a reflexive pattern exhibited by newborn infants. Zelazo, Zelazo, and Kolb (1972) sought to determine whether this reflex could be altered by exercise and whether this would affect voluntary and unaided walking. From 2 to 8 weeks, mothers provided walking practice for a few minutes a day for one group of infants, while another group received only passive exercise, which consisted of flexing the limbs, but no walking experience. Other groups received no training but only periodic testing, and a final group received only the final test to evaluate the effect of the repeated testing. Figure 4-11 shows the results. The intervention increased the number of walking responses over the training period; moreover, mothers reported that the infants in the active exercise group walked sooner than infants who had not received this type of intervention. Experience does contribute to the age of onset of walking, but it is unlikely that walking at an early age confers a permanent advantage! ■

Source: Adapted from Zelazo, P.R., Zelazo, N.A., & Kolb, S. "Walking" in the newborn. *Science*, 1972, **176**, 314–315.

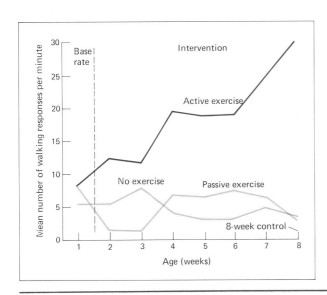

FIGURE 4-11 Newborn children given active exercise of the walking reflex showed an increase in this response and also walked earlier than newborn children in the controlled condition. *(From Zelazo, Zelazo, & Kolb. Copyright 1972 by the American Association for the Advancement of Science, reproduced by permission.)*

echo-sounding device that are more typical of a sighted than a blind baby" (Bower, 1977, p. 105).

These studies of the slow motor development of blind infants underline an important principle, namely, the interdependence among various sensory and motor systems.

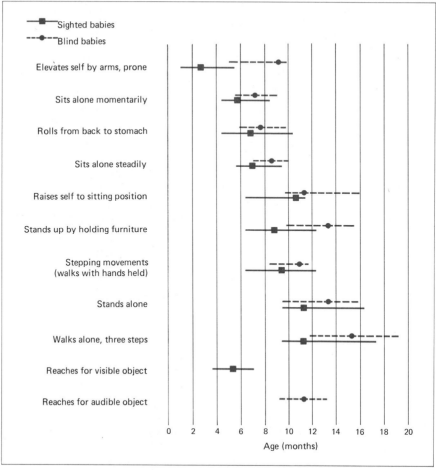

FIGURE 4-12 Comparative development of blind and sighted babies. *(Data from Adelson & Fraiberg, 1974; graph from Bower, 1977, with permission of author and publisher.)*

Growth   One of the most heavily investigated areas of child development is physical growth. For many years psychologists have tracked and plotted the manner in which the young infant grows. A brief description of the general growth trends is in order before we discuss some of the determinants of growth.

As a culture, we are very concerned about how tall and heavy we are. Parents hope that their boys won't be too short or their girls too tall. Consider these interesting observations of our concern about height that appeared in a Sunday newspaper supplement:

The Metropolitan Life Insurance Company reports that average life insurance coverage is twice as much for six-footers; bishops average 5′10-1/2″, rural preachers 5′8-3/4″, presidents of major universities are 1′ taller than those of smaller colleges and of high school principals; sales managers hit 5'10", their salesmen average 1" shorter, railroad presidents are 5'11", station agents 5'9-1/2"; in the depression of the 1930s shorter men were first to be laid off; in fifteen presidential elections victory went to the taller candidate (Lincoln was the tallest at 6'4", L.B.J. next at 6'3"). (Summarized by Krogman, 1972, pp. 28–29)

Although taller isn't necessarily better, it seems to help. It is not just height that we are concerned about. The monthly appearance of another new diet book or the announcement of a recently formed Weight Watchers club also testifies to our concern about weight.

Age and Sex Differences in Height and Weight   How do a child's height and weight change with age? Are the patterns of growth similar for boys and girls? Are there national, ethnic, and socioeconomic differences in height and weight? Figure 4-13 summarizes curves for height and weight for boys and girls in the United States. Of interest are the sex differences: in height the girls' curve crosses the boys' curve at about 9½ years of age, and until 13½ the girls are taller than boys on the average. Similarly, notice the weight curves: girls are lighter than boys until nearly 9 years of age and then are heavier than boys until about age 14. However, these curves do not tell the complete story; it is of interest not only

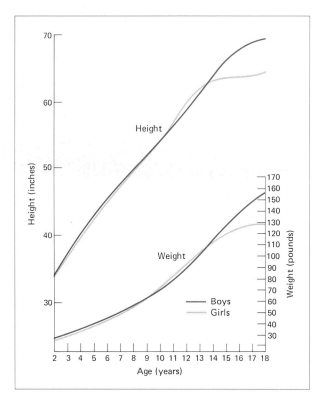

FIGURE 4-13 Growth in height & weight from 2 to 18 years. *(From National Center for Health Statistics: NCHS Growth Charts, 1976.)*

to determine the average height and weight at various age points, but to isolate periods of accelerated growth. The periods of peak growth occur at different ages for boys and girls. Between 7 and $10^{1}/_{2}$ for both boys and girls the differences between successive age groups are relatively consistent. For boys the greatest mean change occurs at $13^{1}/_{4}$ years, while for girls the peak is earlier at $11^{3}/_{4}$ years. Not only does their growth spurt occur earlier, but girls reach their mature height earlier than boys. A similar pattern is evident for weight: Boys start their spurt in weight gain at $12^{1}/_{4}$ years, while girls start their weight spurt about $1^{1}/_{2}$ years earlier when they are $10^{3}/_{4}$ years old. Table 4-2 summarizes these growth spurt data for boys and girls.

These differences have important implications for the social and emotional adjustment of boys and girls, and these issues will be discussed in later chapters.

National Differences in Height and Weight   There are ethnic and national differences in growth as well as age and sex differences. For example, there are variations within Europe. Northwestern and western Europeans, especially Scandinavians, are taller than southern Europeans, such as Italians. And, of course, there are even more extreme examples in Africa, where the Niloties grow 7 feet tall, while Pygmies are approximately 4 feet tall.

Are We Growing Taller?   Height is on the rise. Estimates of the average Englishman between the eleventh and fourteenth centuries have been made by careful measurements of bones exhumed from British cemeteries, and he was approximately 5 feet 6 inches tall. In contrast, in 1976 the average male was 3 inches taller at 5 feet 9 inches. Serious measurement of these group trends in size has indicated that we need to be constantly updating our norms of height and weight. Figure 4-14 documents these shifts between 1880 and 1960, and in

TABLE 4-2 PERIODS OF SPURT GROWTH FOR BOYS AND GIRLS

	Height			
	Start	Peak	End	Duration
Boys	$11^{3}/_{4}$	$13^{1}/_{4}$	$14^{1}/_{2}$	$2^{3}/_{4}$
Girls	$10^{1}/_{4}$	$11^{3}/_{4}$	$12^{1}/_{2}$	$2^{1}/_{4}$
	Weight			
Boys	$12^{1}/_{4}$	$13^{3}/_{4}$	15	$2^{3}/_{4}$
Girls	$10^{3}/_{4}$	$12^{1}/_{4}$	$13^{1}/_{4}$	$2^{1}/_{2}$

Source: From Hamil, P., Johnston, F., & Lemeshow, S. *Vital Statistics*, Series 11, No. 124; 1973. The National Center for Health Statistics, Health Resources Administration, Department of Health, Education, and Welfare. By permission.

most parts of the culture we are still growing bigger. There are also social-class differences in height and weight; as the 1976 government survey revealed, children in families of over $10,000 annual income were both taller and heavier than children of families with less than $3,000 in yearly income. Moreover, the changes were more marked for the upper-income groups. However, recent indications are that in the upper 75 percent of the United States population, the increases have stopped; the majority of individuals—at least in our current social, nutritional, and medical environment—have apparently reached their maximum growth potential (Hamill et al., 1976). Increases in the remaining segments of society continue. However, should major changes occur in the environment, such as a famine or spectacular medical discoveries, the average height of the population could again undergo progressive change.

There are several possible reasons for the trends that Americans are growing taller and heavier (Krogman, 1972):

1 Health and nutrition have both improved; specifically there has been a decline in growth-retarding illness, particularly in the first five years. There has been an improvement in the amount and balance of nutritional intake. Medical care and personal health practices have improved.

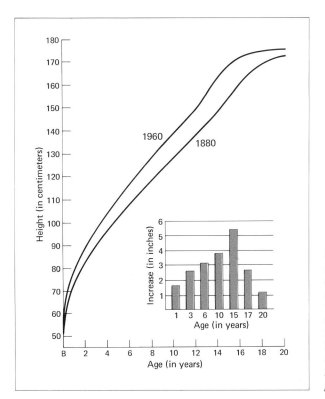

FIGURE 4-14 Schematic curves of mean stature of North American white boys for 1880 and 1960. Inset shows differences between the curves at selected ages. *(From Meredith, 1963. By permission of author and publisher.)*

2 Socioeconomic conditions have improved; child labor is less frequent, and living conditions have improved.

In the 19th century child labor in coal mines and the big mills extracted a repressive toll upon the health and stamina of the growing child. . . . Additionally, the crowding within and around industrial centers made for wretched living conditions. Child labor in England and Scotland, as in the USA, has been greatly reduced so that children are freed to grow up under far less represssive circumstances. (Krogman, 1972, p. 40)

3 Genetic factors, including interbreeding which produces increases in height and weight in the offspring. An additional factor may be selective mating of tall individuals.

Finally, we are not only growing taller, but our feet are growing longer due to the fact that we are growing taller. Your grandfather probably wore a size 7 A or B, while now the average American male wears a size 9 to 10 B. This represents about a $1/3$-inch gain in length each generation. Krogman (1972) has spelled out the economic implications of this change: "About 650 million pairs of shoes are sold annually; add $1/3$ inch of leather needed per generation and you get about 6,800 miles of additional shoe leather—diagonally from Maine to California" (Krogman, 1972, p. 42). If this demand continues, we may have a leather crisis in addition to an energy crisis.

Are We Reaching Sexual Maturity Earlier?   Not only are we growing taller and heavier, but we are achieving sexual maturity earlier as well. Puberty is occurring earlier in prosperous countries. A recent comparison of the age at which mothers and daughters reached puberty tells the tale: American mothers reached menarche at 14.38 years, while their daughters reached this developmental landmark nearly two years earlier—at 12.88 years (Damon, Damon, Reed, & Valadian, 1969). In fact, it is estimated that puberty is achieved $2^1/2$ to $3^1/2$ years earlier than it was a century ago (Tanner, 1968). However, this trend to earlier menarche is slowing down among middle-class girls in the United States. Just as in the shifts in height and weight, there are limits on the extent of change that is likely to occur.

Obesity in Childhood, or Are We Growing Fatter?   As the proliferation of clubs, magazines, and fad diets indicate, we are a weight-conscious society. The problem of obesity begins in infancy and childhood. Obese infants are more likely to become obese children and adolescents, who, in turn, are more likely to become overweight adults than their skinny or average-weight peers (Winick, 1975). For example, one study found that 86 percent of overweight boys and 80 percent of overweight girls became overweight adults, in contrast to 42 percent of average-weight boys and 18 percent of average-weight girls (Abraham, Collins, & Nordsieck, 1971). The odds against an overweight adolescent becoming an average-weight adult are 28 to 1 (Stunkard & Burt, 1967). Having fat parents doesn't help. If you have one fat parent, your chances of being a fat adult are 40 percent, and 80 percent if you have two fat parents (Winick, 1974). Nor is it much fun being overweight: obese children and adolescents suffer from a variety of physical and psychological problems including hypertension and diabetes. Psychologically, they suffer as well, as indicated by less acceptance from peers, discrimination by adults, greater body image disturbances, and poorer self-concepts (Coates & Thoresen, 1976).

Recently, a wide variety of treatments have been developed for helping fat children "take it off and keep it off." Treatments range from straightforward dietary approaches, which usually involve less food and more exercise, to more exotic approaches, such as anorexigenic drugs, therapeutic starvation, and even bypass surgery. Unfortunately, the success rate to date has not been very striking.

"Most obese persons will not stay in treatment for obesity. Of those who stay in treatment, most will not lose weight, and of those who do lose weight, most will regain it" (Stunkard, 1958). Recent behavioral approaches, which recognize the important role that cues in the everyday environment play in regulating eating, appear to be promising.

In early adolescence, girls mature more rapidly than boys, as these two 13-year-olds illustrate.

Fat children usually become fat adults. (United Press International)

Individuals are instructed in methods for changing their personal, social and physical environments to change their eating and exercise behaviors. . . . typically these techniques include monitoring and recording the quality and circumstances of eating, restricting the range of cues associated with eating (e.g.-eating only at certain times and places) altering the act of eating (e.g.-eating more slowly) and changing physical and social cues associated with eating (e.g.-food storage, stressful interaction with family members at mealtime). (Coates & Thoresen, 1976, p. 14)

Until recently, this was only a promise. But recent reports seem to be fulfilling this promise; children and adolescents who maintain weight losses are those who show more self-control rather than relying on parental restrictions, and who get more exercise (Cohen, Gelfand, Dodd, Jensen, & Turner, 1978). In spite of this recent success, it is still easier to put it on than take it off!

Nutrition and Growth   Growth is determined not only by genetic factors which set limits to normal adult stature, but also by the environmental context. In a favorable environment, there is a great deal of similarity in the growth curves; when nutrition is inadequate, however, growth rates are seriously depressed. Evidence of the controlling role of nutrition in physical growth comes from studies comparing growth before and during wartime periods in which nutritional intake was reduced. During World Wars I and II, there was a general growth retardation, while there was a general secular increase during 1920 to 1940, the between-war period. However, weight was affected more than height and boys more than girls. Age of puberty is affected by nutritional factors as well. During World War II, girls in occupied France did not achieve menarche until an average age of 16 years, approximately three years later than the prewar norm (Howe & Schiller, 1952).

A variety of other environmental factors affect growth as well, including illness, disease, climate, and psychological disturbance (Tanner, 1970). In addition, there is a season of the year effect: growth in height is fastest in the spring and growth in weight fastest in the fall.

Overcoming environmental deficiencies: catch-up growth   As we have seen earlier in our discussions of the effects of prenatal deficiences on later development, there is a strong corrective tendency to regain the normal course of development after an early setback. A similar corrective principle operates in the case of physical growth following environmental injury or deprivation. As Tanner notes:

Children, no less than rockets, have their trajectories governed by control systems of their genetical constitution and powered by energy absorbed from the natural environment. Deflect the child from its growth trajectory by acute malnutrition or illness, and a restoring force develops so that as soon as the missing food is supplied or the illness terminated the child catches up toward its original curve. When it gets there, it slows down again to adjust its path onto the old trajectory once more. (Tanner, 1970, p. 125)

A child who had reduced food intake during two periods of psychological disturbance showed a compensatory increase in growth rate after each period of reduced growth. However, the degree of "catch-up" will depend on a variety of factors: duration, severity of timing of the deprivation, and the nature of the subsequent treatment or therapy. The effects of intervention following severe malnutrition will illustrate (Graham, 1966). When infants with varying degrees of malnutrition were treated, those with a 5 percent deficit in body length caught up; those with a 15 percent deficit benefited only somewhat, but remained significantly shorter. In general, the earlier and more prolonged the stress, the more difficult it is for regulation to be fully effective in achieving the normal level of growth.

Summary

The newborn infant is not a "blooming, buzzing confusion." Rather, the newborn has a well-organized set of reflexes and sensory capacities. Since assessment of the newborn's capacities is affected by the state of alertness, developmental changes in sleep and crying patterns were examined. A state of alert inactivity is optimal for responding to external stimulation. Soothing techniques such as holding the baby on the shoulder, rocking, swaddling, and sucking were discussed. There are wide differences among individuals, sexes, and races in soothability.

The newborn's repertoire of reflexes—involuntary responses to an external stimulus—was examined; these assessments are employed as a test of the soundness of the infant's central nervous system. Next the sensory capacities of the newborn were examined. At birth the infant can discriminate sounds of different intensity, duration, and pitch. Some evidence suggests that the newborn may be particularly responsive to human voices and is capable of discriminating certain aspects of language.

Visual capacities are also well developed in the infant. The newborn is sensitive to changes in brightness and movement and can track a moving object. Pattern preferences are evident early, with indication that infants prefer facelike stimuli. Other evidence suggests that very young infants respond to only small segments of a visual stimulus such as angles and lines and only later does true pattern perception develop. By 5 months, infants appear to be able to recognize patterns rather than only parts of a figure. Infants possess depth perception and size constancy in the first months of life.

Changes in the infant's locomotion skills from creeping to walking were discussed next. Although these kinds of motor skills are to a large degree maturationally determined, extreme variations in the early environment can retard the developmental sequence of motor skills. Motor development in blind infants tends to progress at a slower rate.

Finally, growth patterns in height and weight from infancy on were discussed. Sex differences were noted, with girls showing faster rates of maturation than boys. Cross-generation comparisons indicate that we are growing taller and heavier; however, the upper classes appear to have reached their growth potential, but the remaining segments of the population continue to show this increasing trend. The problem of childhood obesity was discussed as well as recent weight-reduction programs. Growth is a self-regulating process which compensates for temporary interference by illness or dietary deficiency by a period of accelerated growth.

References

Abraham, S., Collins, G., & Nordsieck, M. Relationship of childhood weight status to morbidity in adults. *Public Health Reports*, 1971, **86**, 273–284.

Adelson, E., & Fraiberg, S. Gross motor development in infants blind from birth. *Child Development*, 1974, **45**, 114–126.

Aslin, R. N., & Banks, M. S. Early visual experience in humans: Evidence for a critical period in the development of binocular vision. In H. L. Pick, Jr., H. W. Leibowitz, J. E. Singer, A. Steinschneider, & H. W. Stevenson (Eds.), *Psychology: From research to practice*. New York: Plenum, 1978.

Banks, M. S., Aslin, R. N., & Letson, R. D. Sensitive period for the development of human binocular vision. *Science*, 1975, **190**, 675–677.

Bartoshuk, A. K. Human neonatal cardiac responses to sound: A power function. *Psychonomic Science*, 1964, **1**, 151–152.

Birns, B., Blank, M., & Bridger, W. H. The effectiveness of various soothing techniques on human neonates. *Psychosomatic Medicine*, 1966, **28**, 316–322.

Bornstein, M. H., Kessen, W., & Weiskopf, S. The categories of hue in infancy. *Science*, 1976, **191**, 201–202.

Bower, T. G. R. The visual world of infants. *Scientific American*, 1966, **215**, 80–92.

Bower, T. G. R. *A primer of infant development.* San Francisco: Freeman, 1977.

Bower, T. G. R., Watson, J. S., Umansky, R., & Magoun, M. Auditory surrogates for vision in sensory motor development. Unpublished manuscript, University of Edinburgh, 1976.

Brackbill, Y. Continuous stimulation and arousal level in infants: Additive effects. *Proceedings, 78th Annual Convention, American Psychological Association*, 1970, **5**, 271–272.

Brazelton, T. B. Implications of infant development among the Mayan Indians of Mexico. *Human Development*, 1972, **15**, 90–111.

Brennan, W. M., Ames, E. W., & Moore, R. W. Age differences in infants' attention to patterns of different complexities. *Science*, 1966, **151**, 354–356.

Campos, J. J., Langer, A., & Krowitz, A. Cardiac responses on the visual cliff in prelocomotor human infants. *Science*, 1970, **170**, 196–197.

Clifton, R. K., Graham, F. K., & Hatton, H. M. Newborn heart rate response and response inhibition as a function of stimulus duration. *Journal of Experimental Child Psychology*, 1968, **6**, 265–278.

Coates, T. J., & Thoresen, C. E. Treating obesity in children and adolescents: A review. Unpublished manuscript, Stanford University, 1976.

Cohen, E., Gelfand, D., Dodd, D., Jensen, J., & Turner, C. The role of self-regulation in maintenance of weight-loss in obese children. Presented at the Western Psychological Association, San Francisco, 1978.

Cohen, L. B., DeLoache, J. S., & Strauss, M. S. Infant visual perception. In J. Osofsky (Ed.), *Handbook of infancy.* New York: Wiley, 1978.

Cohen, L. B., & Salapatek, P. (Eds.), *Infant perception from sensation to cognition: Basic visual processes* (Vol 1). New York: Academic, 1975.

Condon, W. D., & Sander, L. W. Neonate movement is synchronized with adult speech: Interactional participation and language acquisition. *Science*, 1974, **183**, 99–101.

Crook, C. K., & Lipsitt, L. P. Neonatal nutritive sucking: Effects of taste stimulation upon sucking rhythm and heart rate. *Child Development*, 1976, **47**, 518–522.

Damon, A., Damon, S. T., Reed, R. B., & Valadian, I. Age at menarche of mothers and daughters, with a note on accuracy of recall. *Human Biology*, 1969, **41**, 161–175.

Dement, W. C. The effect of dream deprivation. *Science*, 1960, **131**, 1705–1707.

Dennis, W., & Najarian, P. Infant development under environmental handicap. *Psychological Monographs*, 1957, **71** (Whole No. 436).

Desor, J., Maller, O., & Turner, R. Taste in acceptance of sugars by human infants. *Journal of Comparative and Physiological Psychology*, 1973, **84**, 496–501.

Eisenberg, R. B., Coursin, D. B., Griffin, E. J., & Hunter, M. A. Auditory behavior in the human neonate: A preliminary report. *Journal of Speech and Hearing Research*, 1964, **7**, 245–269.

Emde, R. N., Harmon, R. J., Metcalf, D., Koenig, K. L., & Wagonfeld, S. Stress and neonatal sleep. *Psychosomatic Medicine*, 1971, **33**, 491–497.

Fagan, J. F. An attention model of infant recognition. *Child Development*, 1977, **48**, 345–359.

Fantz, R. L. The origin of form perception. *Scientific American*, 1961, **204**, 66–72.

Fantz, R. L. Pattern vision in newborn infants. *Science*, 1963, **140**, 296–297.

Fisichelli, V., & Karelitz, S. The cry latencies of normal infants and those with brain damage. *Journal of Pediatrics*, 1963, **62**, 724–734.

Fraiberg, S. *Insights from the blind.* New York: Basic Books, 1977.

Freedman, D. G. Behavioral assessment in infancy. In G. B. A. Stoelinga & J. J. Van Der Werff Ten Bosch (Eds.), *Normal and abnormal development of brain and behavior.* Leiden: Leiden University Press, 1971, pp. 92–103.

Freedman, D. G., & Freedman, N. C. Behavioral differences between Chinese-American and European-American newborns. *Nature,* 1969, **224,** 1227.

Gesell, A., & Amatruda, C. S. *The embryology of behavior.* New York: Harper, 1945.

Gibson, E. J., & Walk, R. R. The "visual cliff." *Scientific American,* 1960, **202,** 2–9.

Goldberg, S. Infant care and growth in urban Zambia. *Human Development,* 1972, **15,** 77–89.

Graham, G. G. Growth during recovery from infantile malnutrition. *Journal of American Medical Women's Association,* 1966, **21,** 737–742.

Greenman, G. W. Visual behavior of newborn infants. In A. J. Solnit & S. A. Provence (Eds.), *Modern perspectives in child development.* New York: Hallmark, 1963.

Haith, M. M. The response of the human newborn to visual movement. *Journal of Experimental Child Psychology,* 1966, **3,** 235–243.

Haith, M. M., Bergman, T., & Moore, M. J. Eye contact and face scanning in early infancy. Unpublished manuscript, University of Denver, 1977.

Hamill, P., Drizd, T. A., Johnson, C. L., Reed, R. B., & Roche, A. F. NCHS Growth Charts, 1976. *Monthly Vital Statistics Report,* 1976, **25,** Supp (HRA) 76–1120.

Hamill, P., Johnston, F., & Lemeshow, S. Height and weight of youths 12–17 years. *Vital and Health Statistics,* 1973 (ser. 11, No. 124).

Hammond, J. Hearing and response in the newborn. *Developmental Medicine and Child Neurology,* 1970, **12,** 3–5.

Haynes, H., White, B. L., & Held, R. Visual accomodation in human infants. *Science,* 1965, **148,** 528–530.

Hindley, C. B., Filliozat, A. M., Klackenberg, G., Nicolet-Neister, D., & Sand, E. A. Differences in age of walking for five European longitudinal samples. *Human Biology,* 1966, **38,** 364–379.

Howe, P. E., & Schiller, M. Growth responses of the school child to changes in diet and environmental factors. *Journal of Applied Physiology,* 1952, **5,** 51–61.

Hutt, S. J., Hutt, C., Lenard, H. G., Bernuth, H. V., & Muntjewerff, W.J. Auditory responsivity in the human neon. te. *Nature,* 1968, **318,** 888–890.

Jackson, C. M. (Ed.). *Human anatomy* (9th ed.). New York: McGraw-Hill, 1933.

Jensen, K. Differential reactions to taste and temperature stimuli in newborn infants. *Genetic Pschology Monographs,* 1932, **12,** 363–479.

Kessen, W., Leutzendoff, A. M., & Stoutsenberger, K. Age, food deprivation, non-nutritive sucking and movement in the human newborn. *Journal of Comparative and Physiological Psychology,* 1967, **63,** 82–86.

Korner, A. F. REM organization in neonates: Theoretical implications for development and the biological function of REM. *Archives of General Psychiatry,* 1968, **19,** 330–340.

Korner, A. F. Visual alertness in neonates: individual differences and their correlates. *Perceptual and Motor Skills,* 1970, **31,** 499–509.

Korner, A. F. State as variable, as obstacle and as mediator of stimulation in infant research. *Merrill-Palmer Quarterly,* 1972, **18,** 77–94.

Korner, A. F., & Thoman, E. Visual alertness in neonates as evoked by maternal care. *Journal of Experimental Child Psychology,* 1970, **10,** 67–78.

Krogman, W. M. *Child Growth.* Ann Arbor: University of Michigan Press, 1972.

Lester, B. M. Spectrum analysis of the cry sounds of well nourished and malnourished infants. *Child Development,* 1976, **47,** 237–241.

Leventhal, A. S., & Lipsitt, L. P. Adaptation, pitch discrimination, and sound localization in the neonate. *Child Development,* 1964, **35,** 759–767.

Lewis, T. L., & Maurer, D. Newborns' central vision: Whole or hole? Paper presented at the meeting of the Society for Research in Child Development, New Orleans, March 1977.

Lipsitt, L. P. Perinatal indicators and psychophysiological precursors of crib death. In F. D. Horowitz (Ed.), *Early developmental hazards: Predictors and precautions.* American Association for the Advancement of Science, 1977.

Lipsitt, L. P., Engen, T., & Kaye, H. Developmental changes in the olfactory threshold of the neonate. *Child Development*, 1963, **34**, 371–376.

Lipton, E. L., Steinschneider, A., & Richmond, J. B. Swaddling, a child care practice: Historical, cultural and experimental. *Pediatrics*, 1965, **35**, 521–567.

Macfarlane, J. A. Olfaction in the development of social preferences in the human neonate. In M. A. Hofer (Ed.), *Parent-Infant interaction.* Amsterdam: Elsevier, 1975.

Maurer, D., & Salapatek, P. Developmental changes in the scanning of faces by young infants. *Child Development*, 1976, **47**, 523–527.

Meredith, H. V. Changes in the stature and body weight of North American boys during the last 80 years. In L. P. Lipsitt & C. C. Spiker (Eds.), *Advances in child development and behavior* (Vol. 1). New York: Academic, 1963, pp. 69–114.

Moffitt, A. R. Consonant cue perception by twenty- to twenty-four-week old infants. *Child Development*, 1971, **42**, 717–732.

Moss, H. A. Sex, age and state as determinants of mother-infant interaction. *Merrill-Palmer Quarterly*, 1967, **13**, 19–36.

Moss, H. A., & Robson, K. S. The role of protest behavior in the development of mother-infant attachment. Paper presented at the American Psychological Association, San Francisco, 1968.

Nisbett, R., & Gurwitz, S. Weight, sex and the eating behavior of human newborns. *Journal of Comparative and Physiological Psychology*, 1970, **73**, 245–253.

Ostwald, P. F., & Peltzman, P. The cry of the human infant. *Scientific American*, 1974, March.

Parmalee, A. H., Wenner, W. H., & Schulz, H. R. Infant sleep patterns from birth to 16 weeks of age. *Journal of Pediatrics*, 1964, **65**, 576–582.

Pederson, D. R., & Ter Vrugt, D. The influence of amplitude and frequency of vestibular stimulation on the activity of two-month-old infants. *Child Development*, 1973, **44**, 122–128.

Prechtl, H. F. R., & Beintema, D. J. *The neurological examination of the full term newborn infant.* Little Club Clinics in Developmental Medicine (No. 12). London: Spastics Society Medical Information Unit and William Heinemann Medical Books, 1964.

Reese, H. W., & Lipsitt, L. P. (Eds.), *Experimental child psychology.* New York: Academic, 1970.

Rieser, J., Yonas, A., & Wikner, K. Radial localization of odors by human newborns. *Child Development*, 1976, **47**, 856–859.

Roffwarg, H. P., Muzio, J. N., & Dement, W. C. Ontogenetic development of the human sleep-dream cycle. *Science*, 1966, **152**, 604–619.

Rovee, C. K., Cohen, R. Y., & Shlapack, W. Life span stability in olfactory sensitivity. *Developmental Psychology*, 1975, **11**, 311–318.

Sackett, G. P. Innate mechanisms, rearing conditions and a theory of early experience effects. In M. R. Jones (Ed.), *Miami symposium on the prediction of behavior: Early experience.* Coral Gables: University of Miami Press, 1970.

Sackett, G. P., & Tripp, R. Innate mechanisms in primate behavior: Identification and causal significance. Paper presented at the US–Japan Seminar on Regulatory Mechanisms, Emory University, Atlanta, July 1968.

Salapatek, P. The visual investigation of geometric pattern by the one- and two-month-old infant. Paper presented at the meeting of the American Association for the Advancement of Science, Boston, December 1969.

Salapatek, P., & Banks, M. S. Infant sensory assessment: Vision. In F.D. Minifie & L. L. Lloyd (Eds.), *Communicative and cognitive abilities—early behavioral assessment*. Baltimore: University Park Press, 1977.

Salapatek, P., & Kessen, W. Visual scanning of triangles by the human newborn. *Journal of Experimental Child Psychology*, 1966, **3**, 155–167.

Sameroff, A. J. Can conditioned responses be established in the newborn infant? *Developmental Psychology*, 1971, **5**, 1–12.

Schaffer, H. R. *The growth of sociability*. London: Penguin, 1971.

Schaffer, H. R. *Mothering*. Cambridge, Mass: Harvard University Press, 1977.

Sherman, M., Sherman, I.C., & Flory, C.D. Infant behavior. *Comparative Psychology Monographs*, 1936, **12** (No. 4).

Shirley, M. M. *The first two years*. Minneapolis: University of Minnesota Press, 1933.

Solomons, G., & Solomons, H. S. Motor development in Yucatecan infants. *Developmental Medicine and Child Neurology*, 1975, **17**, 41–46.

Steinschneider, A. Implications of the sudden infant death syndrome for the study of sleep in infancy. In A. D. Pick (Ed.), *Minnesota symposia on child psychology* (Vol. 9). Minneapolis: University of Minnesota Press, 1975.

Stunkard, A. J. The management of obesity. *New York Journal of Medicine*, 1958, **58**, 79–87.

Stunkard, A. J., & Burt, V. Obesity and the body image: II. Age at onset of disturbances in the body. *American Journal of Psychiatry*, 1967, **123**, 1443–1447.

Tanner, J. M. Earlier maturation in man. *Scientific American*, 1968, **218**, 21–27.

Tanner, J. M. Physical growth. In P. H. Mussen (Ed.), *Carmichael's manual of child psychology* (Vol. 1). New York: Wiley, 1970, pp. 77–155.

Watson, R. I. *Psychology of the child*. New York: Wiley, 1962.

Wasz-Hockert, O., Lind, J., Vuorenkoski, V., Partanen, T., & Valanne, E. *The infant cry: A spectrographic and auditory analysis*. Suffolk: Lavenham Press, 1968.

Winick, M. Childhood obesity. *Nutrition Today*, 1974, **9**, 6–12.

Winick, M. *Childhood obesity*. New York: Wiley, 1975.

Wolff, P. H. The causes, controls and organization of behavior in the neonate, *Psychological Issues*, 1966, **5** (1, Whole No. 17).

Wolff, P. H. The role of biological rhythms in early psychological development. *Bulletin of the Menninger Clinic*, 1967, **31**, 197–218.

Wolff, P. H. The natural history of crying and other vocalizations in early infancy. In B. Foss (Ed.), *Determinants of infant behavior* (Vol. 4). London: Methuen, 1969.

Zelazo, P. R., Zelazo, N. A., & Kolb, S. "Walking" in the newborn. *Science*, 1972, **176**, 314–315.

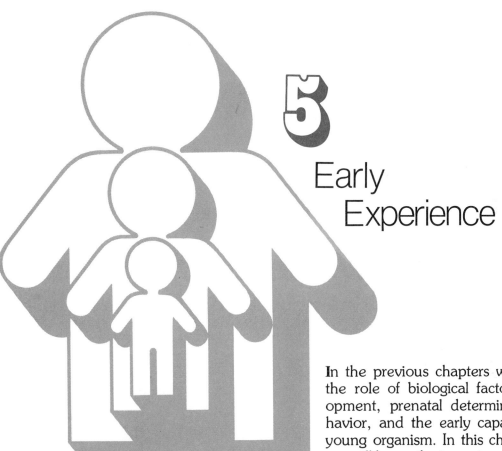

5

Early
Experience

In the previous chapters we examined the role of biological factors in development, prenatal determinants of behavior, and the early capacities of the young organism. In this chapter the focus will be on the importance of the early environment for the child's normal development. Since the late 1940s under the influence of Donald Hebb's classic work, *The Organization of Behavior*, in which he elegantly argued that a certain minimal amount of environmental stimulation of the sense organs was necessary for the proper development of the central nervous system, there has been a flurry of activity aimed at determining the effects of variations in the early environment on later development. A number of questions can be asked. Do normal patterns of behavior—motoric, intellectual, and social—emerge in a predetermined fashion regardless of the nature of the early experiences of the child? Or are there some minimal conditions that are necessary for proper development? Another issue concerns the timing of experience. Are early experiences more important than later ones? Are some periods of development more critical for proper development than others? Finally, can patterns of behavior that are established early be modified by later experience? How much plasticity is there in human development?

In order to answer these questions, psychologists have employed two closely related approaches, both of which involve a systematic tampering with the environmental rearing conditions of the organism. On the one hand, the effects of reductions in the normal level of sensory, perceptual, and social stimulation have been examined in order to isolate the necessary conditions for normal development. In contrast to this deprivation approach, another technique has been to provide the organism with "extra experience" in which the environment is enriched beyond the typical amount of sensory and perceptual stimulation typically found in the normal rearing environment.

To illustrate these two approaches to understanding the effects of early experience, a series of experimental and naturalistic studies employing a wide range of species will be presented. First, a series of experimental studies of the impact of environmental deprivation and enrichment on the development of the underlying physiological structures of the central nervous system will be examined. Second, the effects of social and sensory deprivation on the development of social and intellectual competence in monkeys will be discussed. Third, naturalistic studies of human deprivation found in orphanages and institutions will be presented. In all sets of studies the prime interest will be the modifiability of the effects of early environmental deprivation on later behavior. Finally, the importance of early opportunities for social interaction with other members of the species for normal social and intellectual development will be emphasized.

Early Experience and the Modification of the Central Nervous System's Early Development

The importance of the early environment for the proper development of the central nervous system was demonstrated many years ago. In fact, at the turn of the century A.J. Carlson (1902) demonstrated that the physiological structures of the visual system of birds could be altered by variations in stimulation. However, Carlson was much ahead of his time, and his demonstration had little impact on psychological views of development. Rather, the maturationalists were to have their heydey before a similar kind of demonstration over forty years later would point the way to serious consideration of the effects of early experience. In 1947, Austin Reisen reported his classic experiments on the effects of reduced sensory stimulation on the development of the visual system of the chimpanzee. He found that the retinal structures of a chimp that had spent the first sixteen months of life in the dark failed to develop properly. Specifically, there was a loss of ganglion cells in the retina, those neurons whose axons form the optic nerve, which connects the retina with the rest of the nervous system. Moreover, even when the animals were returned to lighted conditions, their retinas failed to develop properly and they became permanently blind. Other studies (Reisen, 1950) have confirmed these original results. It is clear that even the anatomical structures of the central nervous system, the foundation blocks of maturation, require a certain amount of early environmental stimulation for proper development.

More recent research has indicated that the physiological effects of variations in early experience are not restricted to the peripheral aspects of the visual system but may actually modify the size of the brain itself (Krech, Rosenzweig, & Bennett, 1962; Rosenzweig & Bennett, 1970). In order to test the modifiability of the brain, these investigators, in Rosenzweig's words:

. . . decided to set up two markedly different experimental situations, to put the rats in one or the other at an early age when their brains might be most plastic and to maintain the animals in these situations for a prolonged period. Animals were therefore assigned at weaning (about 25 days of age) and kept for 80 days in either an enriched environment—environmental complexity and training (ECT)—or in an impoverished condition (IC). . . . In the enriched situation the animals are housed in groups of 10 to 12 in a large cage that is provided with "toys" such as ladders, wheels, boxes, platforms, etc. . . . The toys are selected each day from a larger group. To enrich the rats further, we gave them a daily half-hour exploratory session in groups of 5 or 6 . . . in a 3 × 3 foot field with a pattern of barriers that is changed daily. . . . After about 30 days some formal training is given in a series of mazes. In contrast the animals in the impoverished condition live in individual cages with solid side walls, so that an animal cannot see or touch another. These cages are placed in a separate, quiet, dimly lighted room, while the ECT (enriched) cages are in a large, brightly lighted room with considerable incidental activity. (Rosenzweig, 1966, pp. 321–322)

What impact do these different rearing conditions have on brain weight and on brain chemistry? In the early stages of their research program, these investigators disregarded brain anatomy, since they, like most psychologists and physiologists, had accepted the dogma of absolute stability of brain weight. Records of brain weights were routinely recorded, however, and after two years it became apparent that their environmental manipulations *were* affecting the *actual weight of the animal's brain*—in spite of historical beliefs to the contrary. As Figure 5-1 indicates, separate analyses were performed for the cerebral cortex and the rest of the brain; this was fortunate, since not all areas, it turned out, were equally affected. The variations in early environment had their greatest impact on the cortex region, with the enriched animal's cortex weighing about 4 percent more than the cortex of the restricted littermates. Not only does the cerebral cortex differ from the rest of the brain in its response to the differential rearing experiences, but all regions of the cortex are not equally altered. The occipital region, which controls vision, shows the largest changes in weight, 6 percent, whereas the somesthetic area, the touch region, showed only 2 percent increase in weight. Other experiments indicate that there may be systematic relationships between the nature of the enrichment program and the particular

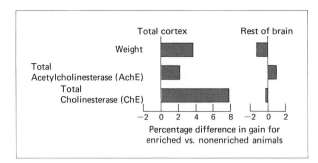

FIGURE 5-1   The effects of enriched rearing environment on brain chemistry and brain weight in rats. (Note that the enriched animals made the larger gains.) *(From Rosenzweig. 1966, with permission of the author and the American Psychological Association.)*

region of the cortex that is affected. Rearing rats in darkness results in a shrinkage of the visual cortex. There is some suggestion of parallel effects at the human level. Donaldson in 1892 (cited by Rosenzweig, 1966) carried out a postmortem examination of the brain of a human blind deaf-mute and found deficient development of the cortical areas controlling speech and visual and auditory functions. The skin senses region of the cortex, on the other hand, was apparently normally developed. Careful investigation may show that there is an anatomical as well as a behavioral basis for the overcompensation phenomenon wherein loss of one sense results in heightened sensitivity in the other sense organs.

Brain size may not be the only important factor; as recent experiments have indicated, the biochemistry of the brain as well as the structure of neurons, or nerve cells, is affected by early experience. First, the neurons increase in complexity, as measured by the number of branches and subbranches that develop from the neuron (Greenough, 1976). These branches, or dendrites, may, in part, account for the difference in brain size. In addition, these changes in neuron structure mean that there will be a considerably greater number of synapses per neuron in animals reared in complex environments. Since synapses are junctions or switching stations between neurons, the amount of information that can be transmitted may be greater in these enriched animals. Second, brain chemistry is affected. To assess these effects, Rosenzweig and his colleagues (1970) measured the activity of two enzymes, acetylcholinesterase (AchE) and cholinesterase (ChE). These enzymes play an important role in synaptic transmission of nerve impulses between neurons. Specifically, they act on acetylcholine, the chemical transmitter that conveys messages from one neuron to the next. Examination of Figure 5-1 reveals that the total activity of both enzymes increases significantly as a result of the enriched rearing experience. As in the case of the weight changes, the cortex is again the area most responsive to the rearing conditions.

The rats used in the original studies were young, and for good reason: it was assumed that their brains would show their greatest plasticity prior to maturity. However, later studies showed that the weight and biochemical effects are *not* restricted to the immature brain. Rats exposed to the deprived or enriched experience after spending their early days under normal laboratory rearing conditions showed similar weight and biochemical effects. "The cortex of the adult brain is as capable of adaptive growth as is the cortex of the young animal" (Rosenzweig, 1966, p. 327)

Do these changes in brain size, complexity, and biochemistry result in brighter rats? Although there is still debate, mounting evidence (Greenough, Wood, & Madden, 1972; Greenough, 1975) indicates that animals from a complex environment may be able to process and remember environmental information more rapidly or efficiently than animals reared under more impoverished conditions (Greenough, 1975).

Although it is clear that these results are not restricted to rats (La Torre, 1968), the implications for human development are still only suggestive. In any case, these studies dramatically illustrate the impact of the environment on the development of the central nervous system.

Effects of Early Experience on Social and Emotional Development

Variations in the early environment may exert profound effects on the individual's emotional and social development and possibly on intellectual development. The child's capacity for responding flexibly and adaptively to changing stimulus conditions, a necessity for proper development, may be impaired if his early experience is impoverished. A wide range of species have participated in studies of early experience, including dogs, monkeys, fish, birds, and even humans. Although the details of the particular kinds of effects have varied considerably across species, the broad picture that emerges is clear: an animal reared in an environment that is low in sensory and perceptual stimulation and does not allow opportunities for interaction with other members of its species during some period of its early life will be socially, emotionally, and perhaps intellectually inadequate. To document this proposition two sets of studies will be examined in detail: Harlow's studies of the effects of sensory and social deprivation on the development of the rhesus monkey, and studies of children reared in impoverished institutional environments.

There are a number of reasons for examining the monkey data. First, the deprivation studies simply could not be carried out on children for ethical and humanitarian reasons. Second, although cross-species generalization is always risky, the recent monkey research may have implications for human development, since monkeys undergo "a relatively long period of development analogous to that of the human child" (Harlow & Harlow, 1962, p. 138). Third, because these are carefully controlled experimental studies, they permit quite refined statements about cause-and-effect relationships. By comparing these experimental findings with the nonexperimental data yielded by the studies of institutionalized children, firmer conclusions about the impact of variations in early experience on human development may be possible.

Effects of Social and Sensory Isolation on Monkeys

One of the most thorough and systematic attempts to investigate the effects of early environmental deprivation on later development has been the work of Harry Harlow and his colleagues at the University of Wisconsin. To study the impact of depriving young rhesus monkeys of sensory and social stimulation, Harlow has devised a number of experimental rearing procedures.

In some cases the animals were reared in total social isolation which the Harlows have described as follows:

At birth the monkey is enclosed in a stainless steel chamber where light is diffused, temperature controlled, air flow regulated and environmental sounds filtered. Food and water are provided and the cage is cleaned by remote control. During its isolation the animal sees no living creature, not even a human hand. (Harlow & Harlow, 1972, p. 276)

In another condition, partial isolation, animals are reared alone in wire cages; but in contrast to the totally isolated monkeys, they can see and hear other young monkeys. Although they do have some sensory and perceptual input and some social stimulation, no physical interaction with other monkeys is allowed.

These drastic modifications in the natural early environment of young monkeys are appreciated more fully in contrast to the rearing conditions of control or normal monkeys. The animals with the most "normal" backgrounds are, of course, feral monkeys who are born in the jungles of Southeast Asia and are brought to the laboratory for study at various ages. Close approximations of "normality" in the laboratory are achieved in two ways: the mother-peer rearing condition, in which animals are raised by a real mother in a large cage where the infants have daily access to age-mates in an adjacent play area; and the nuclear family environment (Harlow, 1971), in which the infants have continual access to their mothers, fathers, and siblings. Characterizing all three of these conditions is a healthy dose of sensory and perceptual stimulation and plenty of opportunity to interact with other monkeys.

In some cases, observations of animal behavior were made when the animals were in their cages. More extensive tests of the social and emotional competence of the monkeys took place in a playroom, where two isolation-reared animals were paired with two other cage-reared monkeys. Trained observers recorded the "monkey business" from behind a one-way-vision screen; the frequency of behaviors such as exploration, play, and fear were systematically noted. Since duration of the deprivation experience may be important, animals were isolated for varying periods of time. Some were deprived for the first three months of life, and others were sentenced to a six-months stay, while a third group spent a full year in isolation prior to being tested.

What are the effects of isolation on the development of young rhesus monkeys? First, let us examine the *partial isolates*, who were totally deprived of mothering, fathering, and the opportunities for physical interaction with their peers (Cross & Harlow, 1965). Compared to monkeys raised by real monkey mothers and permitted extensive peer play, these isolates showed a number of abnormal behavior patterns, such as self-biting and self-clasping, fear grimacing, rocking, huddling, and a variety of stereotyped movements. When presented with a fear stimulus (a black-gloved hand), the mother-peer-raised monkeys responded appropriately—they directed their threats toward either the fear

The total withdrawal of an isolated monkey. (Wisconsin Primate Laboratory)

object or the experimenter. In contrast, the isolates engaged in episodes of self-biting and ignored the external fear elicitor. In summary, depriving the animal of opportunities for physical contact with other monkeys resulted in abnormal motor patterns, agitation and disturbance, and an inability to direct hostility toward appropriate targets.

To examine the effects of even further environmental deprivation, we turn to the *total isolation* studies. Confining the animal for only the first three months in this highly impoverished situation does not appear to produce serious or long-lasting effects. In fact, when tested in the playroom, they did not differ from wire cage-reared age-mates, the partial isolates. They experienced a post-isolation depression for a few weeks, but after recovery they showed no behavioral deficits (Griffin & Harlow, 1966). Total isolation, then, if it lasts for three months, is no more damaging than the partial isolation treatment. But if the confinement period is six months, the effects are more dramatic. As Figure 5-2 shows, these animals exhibited a much higher level of general emotional disturbance, a composite of fear, withdrawal, rocking, and huddling behaviors. Their social inadequacy was not permanent, and although they were never as socially competent as their control group partners, they did improve with age. To produce a full-fledged social incompetent, a full year of isolation was necessary. Unlike normal monkeys, these social misfits played and explored very little; were generally inactive, fearful, and withdrawn; and were frequently the victims of aggressive attacks by their test partners (see Figure 5-3). "Whereas 6-month isolates are social misfits, monkeys isolated for the first year of life seem to be little more than semi-animated vegetables" (Suomi & Harlow, 1971, pp. 506–507).

However, the length of deprivation is not the only important temporal

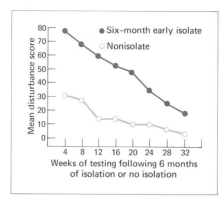

FIGURE 5-2 Amount of disturbed behavior (fear, withdrawal, rocking, and huddling) after isolation for the first six months for rhesus monkeys. *(From Rowland, 1964.)*

variable; the timing of the *onset* of the deprivation experience is critical as well. To investigate this issue, another group of animals were reared in wire cages in an enclosed cage with a cloth surrogate mother for the first six months of life. The second half of the first year was spent in total isolation. Does the partial isolation experience of the first six months serve to reduce the impact of the total isolation experience? Not completely. These animals were both hyperactive and hyperaggressive in contrast to the withdrawn animals isolated for the *first* six months of life. However, these late isolates displayed higher levels of play and exploration than the monkeys in their comparison group, which suggests that these monkeys were still capable of engaging in some positive social behaviors. In spite of their abnormal behavior patterns, they were clearly superior to their peers who experienced a similar duration of deprivation but who experienced the isolation from birth. Both *duration* and *timing* are important determinants of the impact of early deprivation. As Sackett pointed out in a summary of these studies:

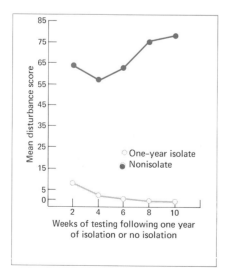

FIGURE 5-3 Amount of disturbed behavior (fear withdrawal, rocking, and huddling) after one year of isolation for rhesus monkeys. *(From Rowland, 1964.)*

there was a critical age for exposure to social stimulation at which later qualitative changes in the characteristics of social behavior can be produced. . . . This critical age seems to be between 3 to 6 months for quantitative deficits and 6 to 8 months for producing complete destruction of social ability. (1968, p. 7)

Later Effects of Isolation   Do the social deficiencies of these isolated monkeys persist, or are they merely transitory? To find out, Sackett (1967) tracked the social development of the early isolates and found clear evidence that as adolescents and adults these monkeys were still *social misfits.* At 3$^1/_2$ and 4$^1/_2$ years of age, the social behavior of totally or partially isolated animals was compared with animals reared with both mother and peer experience. Reactions displayed in the presence of a strange monkey constituted the test for social adequacy. Social initiative and motor activity were both depressed in the total isolates, whereas fearfulness was high, especially in the case of the animals isolated for a full year.

Other research confirms this general picture of social inadequacy (Mitchell, Raymond, Ruppenthal, & Harlow, 1966). When tested in a playroom with a range of partners—age-mates, younger juveniles, and older adults—the total isolates were more fearful and less playful than mother-peer-raised monkeys. Their main social behavior was a high level of misdirected hostility; unlike normal animals, they aggressed against infant monkeys. "Or the isolates make a

Self-biting by an adult male monkey raised in isolation for the first 6 months of life. (Wisconsin Primate Laboratory)

single, sacrificial, suicidal sortee against a large adult: an act never attempted by socially experienced adolescents" (Harlow & Novak, 1973, p. 468). The total isolates are sexual incompetents, even though they are endocrinologically adequate sexually by 2 or 3 years of age.

Their gymnastic qualifications are only quaint and cursory as compared with sexual achievement customary at these ages. Isolates may grasp other monkeys of either sex by the head and throat aimlessly, a semierotic exercise without amorous achievements. . . . This exercise leaves the totally isolated monkey working at cross purposes with reality. (Harlow & Novak, 1973, p. 468)

The above describes the six-month total isolate; twelve-month isolates did not even bother to engage in these misguided sexual overtures. These sexual failings may be a virtue in disguise since those isolate females that have become pregnant (artificially or accidentally) are generally inadequate mothers that often reject or brutally mismanage their young offspring.

Females: The Buffered Sex   One interesting and provocative sidelight: Males are more devastated by isolation than females. Male monkeys reared in total or partial isolation for the first year show more fear and disturbance than their deprived female peers. Females engage in more exploratory behavior than males and more nonsocial play in the lab (Sackett, Holm, & Landesman-Dwyer, 1975) (see Figure 5-4). Nor are these sex differences restricted to the laboratory. To determine whether prior isolation experiences would affect the animals' later survival in a natural environment, 7- to 8-year-old animals who had experienced early isolation were released onto an island off Puerto Rico (Sackett, Wescott, &

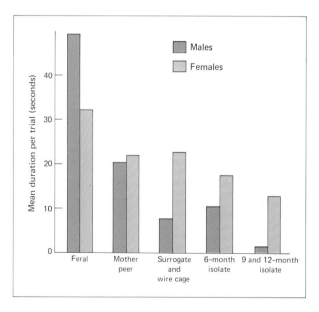

FIGURE 5-4 Amount of exploration of novel environments in differently reared monkeys. *(From Sackett, 1972, with permission of the author and the American Psychological Association.)*

Wescott, 1977). While some of the female isolates survived, none of the isolate males survived in the wild environment. Apparently, deviantly reared females can survive under conditions that lead to death in males. As Sackett and his colleagues note:

Under various social sensory deprivation conditions, females are "buffered" against permanent rearing-induced deficits and are more able to modify their behavior in species-typical ways. Such adaptive changes are rarely seen in males reared in isolation conditions. (1975, p. 74)

Are All Species Equally Affected by Isolation?   As repeatedly stressed, experience interacts with genetic factors in determining behavior. This principle is well illustrated by recent isolation studies which compared a different species of monkey—pigtails—with the rhesus monkeys used in the original Harlow studies. These investigators (Sackett, Holm, & Ruppenthal, 1976) found that rhesus monkeys reared for the first seven months in total isolation exhibited many more profound disturbances than pigtail monkeys reared under similar isolation conditions. In contrast to the rhesus monkeys, the pigtail monkeys had less abnormal behavior and showed more positive social interaction. Since the rearing conditions for the two groups were similar, the data suggest that genetic differences between the two species are responsible for this buffering effect observed in the pigtail monkeys. Experiential factors are important, but clearly are filtered through the genetically determined behavior dispositions of the animals.

Reversibility of Early Deprivation   The monkey data clearly suggest that early rearing environments influence social and emotional development. However, are the effects of early rearing permanent and irreversible? Many theorists (for example, Scott, 1962) have championed a critical-period view of development, which postulates that certain periods in development are of particular importance and if the individual does not receive the appropriate experience during this phase, permanent deficits will result.

Recent findings have strongly challenged this viewpoint, by showing that monkeys reared in total social isolation for the first six months of life can be rehabilitated. In Box 5-1, Suomi, Harlow, and McKinney (1972) demonstrate the important role of peer therapists in reversing the effects of early isolation.

In a later study, Novak and Harlow (1975) tackled an even more difficult task—the rehabilitation of monkeys isolated for the first twelve months of life. Using a six-month dose of a similar peer therapy procedure, they were able to demonstrate a remarkable degree of recovery for these former "total misfits." The self-clasping, rocking, and biting were reduced, while the levels of play, social contact, exploration, and locomotion were similar to their therapist partners. "By adolescence these subjects were actively interacting with other monkeys, formed stable and well-established dominance hierarchies with a minimum of inappropriate aggression and displayed age-appropriate sexual behavior" (Suomi, 1976, p. 19).

BOX 5-1
THE REVERSIBILITY OF EARLY DEPRIVATION: THE MONKEY THERAPISTS

Can the effects of total isolation be reversed? Suomi, Harlow, and McKinney (1972) have demonstrated that the devastating impact of six months of isolation can be overcome. Since most efforts to rehabilitate isolates by exposing them to normal age-mates have failed, these investigators tried a new approach. Normal animals overwhelm the socially inexperienced and incompetent isolate; therefore instead of normal age-mates, they paired the isolates with 3-month-old animals. Unlike older animals, monkeys of this age would initiate social contact without displaying social aggression and would exhibit simple social responses which gradually became more sophisticated. Four male monkeys that had served six months in total isolation were the "patients"; after their isolation ordeal they showed little exploration or locomotive behavior but high levels of rocking, huddling, and self-clasping. Four 3-month-old females that had been reared with peers and were socially normal served as "therapists." Individual therapy sessions involving one isolate and one therapist were held two hours a day, three days a week, while group therapy periods (two isolates and two therapists) were held on two other days each week. After six months of therapy, the isolates were virtually indistinguishable from the therapists in terms of their social behaviors (see Figure 5-5). After this six-month period, the isolates and therapists were placed in a large group living pen. At 2 years of age, the isolates showed complete recovery—even sexual behavior was normal. More recently, Harlow and Novak (1973) have reported considerable success in treating 12-month isolates by the use of 4-month-old therapists.

These findings bring into question critical-period notions that suggest the importance of particular time periods for adequate social development, and they clearly stress the modifiability of early established patterns by later experience.

■

Source: Suomi, S.J., Harlow, H.F., & McKinney, W.T. Monkey psychiatrists. *American Journal of Psychiatry*, 1972, **128**, 41–46.

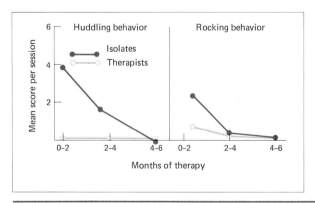

FIGURE 5-5 The effects of peer therapy on rhesus monkeys after isolation rearing. The figure shows the amount of huddling and rocking behavior during the therapy period. *(From Suomi, Harlow, & McKinney. 1972, with permission of the authors and the American Psychiatric Association.)*

What are the implications of these reversals? "They directly contradict the critical period notion that social deficiencies developed in impoverished early rearing environments are necessarily permanent and irreversible. It is true that spontaneous recovery rarely, if ever, occurs in an isolate. However, social rehabilitation is possible—if the proper social agents can be discovered" (Suomi, 1976, p. 19).

Institutionalization: Studies of Early Deprivation in Humans

At the human level, the environment that most closely resembles the isolation rearing conditions of Harlow's rehsus monkeys is the old-fashioned orphanage or institution. In fact, institutional rearing environments are an unfortunate but naturally occurring deprivation which permits us to determine the impact of depriving the young child of a single caretaker and the effect of considerable reduction in sensory and perceptual stimulation as well. Here is the description of one institution studied in the 1940s by Goldfarb, one of the pioneering investigators of the effects of this kind of environment:

The children had been reared in institutions outstanding for their standards of physical hygiene. To prevent epidemic infection babies below nine months of age were kept singly in separate cubicles. They had brief, hurried contacts with adults when they were cleaned and fed by the nurse. During the first year of life, therefore, each child lived in almost *complete isolation.* (Goldfarb, 1955, p. 108)

Nor is this institution very different from other institutions studied in the 1930s and 1940s, as the following description by Spitz indicates:

The infants lay in cots with bed sheets hung over the railings so that the child was effectively screened from the world. . . . Probably owing to the lack of stimulation, the babies lay supine in their cots for many months and a hollow is worn into their mattresses . . . this hollow confines their activity to such a degree that they are effectively prevented from turning in any direction. (Spitz, 1945, p. 63)

Add to these descriptions the following characteristics: a typical caretaker-child ratio of 1:8, little individualized attention, propped bottles, few if any toys, and minimal opportunities for peer-peer interaction. The result is a fairly accurate picture of these childrearing environments.

Compared to the infant reared in a normal home environment, the institutionalized child is markedly deprived both in terms of the amount and variation of sensory stimulation and in terms of the degree of social attention. It is, of course, always hazardous to describe a "typical" institution, and fortunately most modern orphanages and other child-care centers do not conform to this dismal picture. However, institutions of the kind described did exist in the 1930s and 1940s and even in the 1950s, and it is the impact of these deprived rearing environments that is our concern. As a result of increased awareness of the debilitating effects of these situations that we are about to describe, these types of institutions are part of history for much of the world.

The Effects of Institutionalization

What are the effects of this kind of impoverished early environment on the child's social, emotional, and intellectual development? (For detailed reviews, see Yarrow, 1961, 1964; Casler, 1961, 1967.) As in the case of the Harlow monkeys, social development is markedly affected, with the major disturbances centering around interpersonal relationships. Children tended to show two predominant patterns. On the one hand, some were socially indifferent, with little motivation or capacity to form meaningful social attachments with their caretakers or later with their peers. Social discrimination was also retarded; institutionalized infants often show similar reactions to both familiar caretakers and total strangers. In contrast to this picture of social apathy, some children show a second pattern characterized by an *affect hunger*, to borrow Spitz's term, which is characterized by a seemingly insatiable desire for individual social attention and affection. Nor are these personality and social abnormalities limited to the young child. Goldfarb (1943, 1949), for example, has reported that even as adolescents, many institutionalized children continue to show social deficiencies in the form of heightened aggression, impulsivity, and antisocial behavior. Intellectual behavior is affected by institutionalization. Many studies have reported severe retardation with the severity of the IQ deficit typically increasing with the length of the institutional stay. Language development, in particular, is often markedly affected, and a number of researchers have reported evidence of deficiencies in abstract thinking and conceptual abilities as well. The one area that is least affected is motor development, although some studies do find evidence of retarded emergence of motor skills, such as walking (Dennis, 1960). More often investigators have noted extremes in activity level. These variations, either hyperactivity or marked passivity and withdrawal, present an interesting parallel in the motor sphere to the social apathy and heightened attention-seeking characterizing the social behavior of institutionalized children. In addition, bizarre motor patterns similar to Harlow's "rocking and huddling" monkeys have been reported. This summary of the effects of institutionalization suggests the importance of the child's early environment for later social and intellectual development.

Alternative Explanations of Institutionalization Effects

Although these studies of institutionalization have been severely criticized on methodological grounds, there is general agreement that this kind of early environment does have devastating emotional, social, and intellectual effects on the developing child. The issue is no longer *what* happens, but *why* it happens. In this section we shall examine alternative explanations for the effects of institutionalization.

The Perceptual-Deprivation Position   Some investigators have argued that it is the lack or deficit of perceptual and sensory stimulation that is responsible for the low level of intellectual and social functioning of the institutionalized child. This approach is, of course, consistent with the theme that has been developed in this chapter: sensory stimulation is necessary for proper development. The chief spokesman for this viewpoint is Lawrence Casler (1961, 1967), who specifically suggests that "the physical, intellectual and emotional defects often observed in individuals deprived of 'mothering' during early infancy can best be explained in terms of perceptual deprivation" (1961, p. 42). Evidence from studies of the effects of perceptual stimulation on institutionalized infants (Casler, 1965; Schaffer, 1966) provides some support for this position. White's study, in Box 5-2, suggests that the development of visually directed reaching can be enhanced by extra sensory and perceptual stimulation. This evidence suggests that the lack of perceptual stimulation is probably *one* of the contributors to the poor social and cognitive development of the institutionalized child. But it is probably not the only reason. Even monkeys do not develop adequately by sensory stimulation alone.

We have already seen that monkeys reared in cages that permitted a good deal of auditory, visual, and olfactory stimulation, but no opportunities for physical interaction with other animals, were still impaired in their later social development. Pratt (1967) attempted to overcome the effects of isolation by providing extra visual stimulation to isolated monkeys in the form of color slides. In spite of extra perceptual variation, they were still socially inept. Stimulation, at least of the kind and dosage provided, was not sufficient to ensure the proper development of these animals raised without mothers; however, those provided with an opportunity to interact with age-mates did develop adequate social behavior repertoires.

The Importance of a Responsive Social Environment   These data suggest that we need to reformulate the issue and ask not whether stimulation per se is important, but in what forms, in what amounts, and in what ways and by whom should stimulation be provided to ensure adequate development. More specifically, the monkey research points to the necessity of sustained interaction with other members of the species as a necessary condition for adequate social development. Are there any human data to support this viewpoint?

A recent study of the impact of opportunities for sustained social interaction on the development of institutionalized children helps answer this question. As the report of this study in Box 5-3 clearly demonstrates, it is probably the quality of stimulation, not merely the quantity, that is important for proper intellectual development. Moreover, as Rheingold (1956) has shown, personalized contact clearly increases social responsiveness in institutionalized infants as well.

Consideration of the consequences of growing up without a responsive caregiver provides us with important insights concerning early development. Under the typical orphanage regime the child had less frequent contact with caretakers; responsibility for the child's care was distributed among a large group

BOX 5-2
EXPERIMENTAL MODIFICATION OF VISUALLY DIRECTED REACHING

 Evidence of the plasticity of the human organism comes from a series of experimental studies of the modification of visual-motor behavior. During the first half year of life, normal infants in average environments proceed through a rather remarkable set of landmarks that culminate in visually directed reaching for objects at about 5½ months of age. Before this time, the hand and eye are simply not well coordinated. At first, the infant may attend to an object placed in her visual field, but only in the second month can any swiping action be seen. Gradually the young infant learns to use her eye and hand together, so that she not only swings at the target but eventually can accurately and consistently contact the object with her hand. Burton White and his colleagues (White, Castle, & Held, 1964; White & Held, 1966; White, 1967) have shown, however, that the speed of development of visual-motor coordination can be rather drastically altered by enriching the visual world of infants whose environments were deficient in opportunities and rewards for visually directed reaching. The subjects were institutionalized infants, whose visual-motor development generally lags behind the pace of normal home-reared infants due to the rather monotonous visual environment of the institution. In order to enrich the infants' surroundings, these investigators suspended a colorful stabile over the cribs, substituted printed multicolored sheets for the standard white ones, and adorned the side of the baby beds with brightly colored bumpers (see photos). In addition, the infants were given extra handling by their caretakers and placed in a prone position for a short time each day to further enrich their visual input. These "treated" infants exhibited visually guided reaching by ninety-eight days, an advance of forty-five days over the control babies, who were given only routine institutional care. In another related experiment, visually enriched subjects reached this developmental milestone even earlier, at day 89. Stating these findings somewhat differently, the experimental infants developed visually directed reaching in approximately 60 percent of the time required by the control-group children. The White study leaves little question that severely deprived environments can have delaying effects which, in turn, can be overcome by extra perceptual and sensory stimulation.

These data illustrate another point in addition to clearly demonstrating the plasticity of visual-motor development. Timing of the enrichment is important, as the early studies of the effects of practice on the emergence of maturational skills clearly indicated (for example, Gesell & Thompson, 1929; Hilgard, 1932). White's infants who were given too large a dose of visual stimulation too early tended to show less rather than more looking behavior during the first five weeks of the procedure. Once the infants began to engage in prehensory contacts with the stabile over their beds and the figured bumpers along the sides of their cribs, visual attention increased sharply. However, in the initial period they not only ignored the novel objects but showed much more crying than did the control subjects. Enrichment that comes too early and in too large a dose may slow down development. Stimulation can be helpful, but the dosage and timing must be carefully considered if maximal effectiveness is to be achieved. Probably the most effective enrichment provides a proper match of input to internally developing structures. Maturation, then, clearly limits the effect of externally imposed stimulation; the problem of producing maximal acceleration involves providing the child with new experiences that are paced just ahead of emerging capacities, but not so far ahead that with effort the child

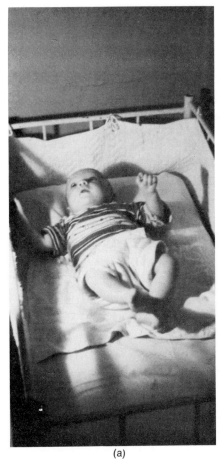

(a)

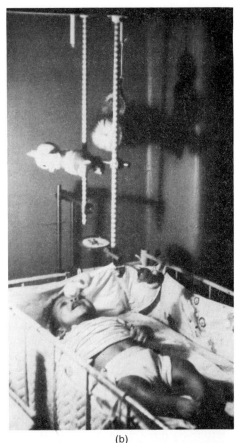

(b)

The typical nursery ward facility (a) for control infants 1 to 4 months of age. Massive enrichment condition (b) featuring many brightly colored objects around the infant at distances of 5 to 36 inches. Modified enrichment condition (c) with two high-lighted pacifiers placed according to postural and visual characteristics of the 4- to 8-week-old infant. (From White and Held, 1966, with permission of the authors and Allyn and Bacon)

cannot incorporate these inputs into an emerging response repertoire. We will discuss this issue again in our consideration of Piaget's theory of cognitive development. ■

Source: White, B.L., & Held, R. Plasticity of sensorimotor development in the human infant. In J. Rosenblith & W. Allinsmith (Eds.), *The causes of behavior: Readings in child development and educational psychology.* Boston: Allyn and Bacon, 1966, pp. 60–70.

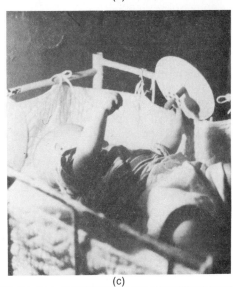

(c)

BOX 5-3
THE EFFECTS OF PART-TIME MOTHERING ON INSTITUTIONALIZED CHILDREN

 The aim of this study was to determine the impact of extra individualized attention on the development of institutionalized children. Two institutions which were similar in staff, organization, and degree of physical and intellectual stimulation were studied. The children ranged in age from 16 months to 6 years. In contrast to the 1940s institutions, these were "model" institutions. The two institutions differed in one respect: a foster-grandparent program was introduced in one of the institutions. Foster-grandparents were impoverished elderly persons who were employed part-time to provide personal relationships for the children. The typical routine was as follows:

Foster-grandparents worked 5 days a week, 4 hours per day. Each was assigned two children as his "own." Their specific activities naturally varied according to the age of the children. For example, in the nursery, the foster-grandparents rocked, fed, walked, talked to, and played with "their" babies. For an older child, in any one day a foster-grandparent might read stories or play a special game, take the child for a walk on the grounds (including visits to other cottage units where the child might have a sibling), encourage him to practice skills, talk with him and listen to his complaints or tales of accomplishments, or simply sit on the side-lines and watch him play, being available as required to tie his shoelace or offer comfort after a bump. Generally, regardless of the specific activity, there was a pronounced affective quality to the interactions between each foster-grandparent and his or her "own" children. (Saltz 1973, p. 167)

Does this personalized care make any difference to the child's intellectual development? Yes; the children in the foster-grandparent program scored significantly higher on a standard IQ test than did children in a similar institution without the extra personal interaction. Moreover, the effects were most marked after a long period of institutionalization (thirty-five months), which suggests that the foster-grandparent program aided in maintaining an average rate of intellectual development. What aspects of the program were responsible for the effects? It is unlikely that the effects were simply due to an increase in the quantity of stimulation, since both institutions offered the children extensive physical and sensory stimulation. Rather, "the primary contribution of the foster-grandparents was to improve the quality of stimulation" (Saltz, 1973, p. 169). This type of program benefited not only the infants and children; the opportunity to perform a useful function enhanced the self-esteem and self-worth of the foster-grandparents as well. ∎

Source: Saltz, R. Aging persons as child-care workers in a foster-grandparent program: Psychosocial effects and work performance. *Aging and Human Development*, 1971, **3**, 314-340, and Saltz, R. Effects of part time "mothering" on IQ and SQ of young institutionalized children. *Child Development*, 1973, **9**, 166-170.

of individuals; and most importantly, the child was treated in a highly mechanical and routinized fashion. It is simply easier and less time-consuming to care for the child according to a fixed schedule. Demands on the caretaking staff allowed little opportunity to adjust routines to accommodate the idiosyncracies and special demands of individual children. They were picked up when it was feeding time, and were changed when it was diaper-changing time; but their bids for attention at other times generally passed unnoticed. The child was assigned a passive role in the infant-caretaker interaction schedule. This analysis of the caretaking routines of an orphanage suggests that the amount of stimulation per se is not the only dimension along which an institutional environment may differ from the home situation. Rather the schedule and tempo of the caretaker-infant interaction differ as well. Specifically, in this impoverished situation, input is less likely to be contingent on (that is, closely follow) the infant's behavior; rather it is more likely to be on a schedule that is to a large degree independent of the behavior of the child.

What are the implications of growing up in an environment that allows infants so little opportunity to shape and alter their environmental inputs and provides them with little direct encouragement in the form of consistent and contingent feedback for their emerging social and language skills such as smiling, crying, and vocalizing? There are at least two important implications. First, some degree of contingent feedback from the environment attendant upon the performance of certain social responses may be necessary for the adequate development of these responses. An environment that is responsive to emerging behaviors and skills is necessary for adequate development.

Learning to Control the Environment   There is a second and possibly more important implication of the kinds of caretaking regimes found in these orphanages and institutions. There are few opportunities for the kind of social interaction in which children gain experience in successfully modifying the behavior of other individuals. In fact, this type of experience may be necessary for the development of a generalized expectancy or belief in their own ability to control their social environment (Lewis & Goldberg, 1969). Moreover, this lesson is probably learned independently of the acquisition of specific social behaviors of the kind discussed above. The institutionalized environment, however, promotes the development of a precisely opposite expectation, namely, that little if anything that one does will make any difference in what happens to one. The world proceeds on schedule, regardless of individual needs and demands. In light of this, it is not at all surprising that such descriptive adjectives as apathetic, passive, and withdrawn are frequently applied to institutionalized infants. In an environment one is helpless to alter, one simply gives up and stops trying to have any effect on others. It is interesting to note that this pattern of passive withdrawal is not seen initially in infants who have had six months or more home-rearing experience prior to being institutionalized. (As we will see in a later chapter, the first half year of life is a particularly important period for the infant to learn the lesson that he can control his caretaker's behavior.) Rather than being passive, these infants often vigorously attempt to elicit responses from their institution handlers, as they were able to do in the more personalized home environment. Of course, these early attempts to elicit the attention of their new caretakers typically fail, and a new and familiar phase in the life of the institutionalized child ensues—passivity and withdrawal. The child learns that it is useless to try, so he simply does not try any longer. In the language of the learning theorist (and the next chapter), the child's efforts are extinguished.

Helplessness in Children   Some recent experimental work by Watson and Ramey (1969, 1972) illustrated how "helplessness" can develop. To compare the effects of exposure to visual stimulation that was either contingent on the infant's behavior or independent of his activities, these investigators designed a special remotely controlled "mobile." In one case, by means of a pressure-sensitive pillow, the mobile made a one-second turn each time the infant moved his head. In this condition, the infant had control; the movement of the mobile was contingent on the infant's behavior. During the fourteen days of exposure, the infants in the other two groups were powerless to control the activity of their mobiles. In one case, during the ten-minute daily exposure period, the mobile remained stationary. In the other condition, the mobile periodically turned by itself. The movement was independent of the infant's behavior in the same way that environmental changes are often on a noncontingent basis in an institutional environment. Of central interest is the impact of experiencing this dose of noncontingent input on later behavior. Specifically, what will happen when the infants have the opportunity to control external events at some later time? Will they remain passive as a result of their earlier failure to exercise control over their environment? To find out, Watson and Ramey exposed the infants to the mobiles again, but on this occasion all the infants could control the movement of their mobiles. All of the infants who had viewed the noncontingently turning mobile were unsuccessful in controlling the mobiles. Even after six weeks without further exposure to the mobiles, the results were the same: the infants who had experienced the uncontrollable mobile failed to exercise control even when they had the opportunity to do so. Like the institutionalized child, these infants apparently learned that they were unable to control their environment and so gave up trying to exercise any control.

Nor is this effect restricted to only the situation in which it was originally encountered. It has been recently shown that infants who learned to behave in a passive, helpless fashion on one task were likely to behave this same way on a different learning task (Finkelstein & Ramey, 1977). This finding suggests that infants may acquire a general belief about their ability to control people and events in their environment. It is possible that the institutionalized infant's general apathy is a result of the failure to develop this expectation. This belief not only is important in infancy, but remains an important determinant of both social and cognitive progress throughout childhood. As we will discover in later chapters, children who believe their academic success is due to their own effort often achieve more and persist longer in the face of failure. Perhaps these later differences have their early antecedents in infancy.

Finally, before closing this section, it is worthwhile examining Russian institutions, which indicate quite clearly that "competent" infants can develop in an institutional setting if attention is paid to social and cognitive as well as physical development (see Box 5-4).

BOX 5-4
A MODEL INSTITUTION

Not all institutions are as unstimulating and devastating to the child's development as the institutions that we have described. In fact, some of the Russian institutions for infants and preschoolers are highly effective environments for childrearing. Bronfenbrenner, in an exerpt from his *Two Worlds of Childhood: U.S. and U.S.S.R.,* describes these settings.

From the very beginning, considerable emphasis is given to the development of self-reliance, so that by 18 months of age the children are expected to have completed bowel and bladder training and are already learning more complex skills such as dressing themselves. Physical activity outdoors is encouraged and it is usually followed by rest,

with the windows wide open and the smallest children swaddled in thick quilts.

During the first year of life, especial attention is focused on language training. The following passage from the official manual on the preschool programme provides an accurate summary of our own observations:

The upbringer exploits every moment spent with the child for the development of speech. In order that the infant learns to discriminate and understand specific words, the upbringer speaks to him in short phrases, emphasizes by her intonation the main words in a given sentence, pauses after speaking to the child, and waits for him to do what was asked. It is important that the words coincide with the moment when the child engages in the action, looks at the object which the adult has named, or is watching a movement or

Children in the Soviet Union are placed in these group cribs in order to build up an early sense of collective belonging and to minimize individuality. (Sovfoto, Inc.)

activity being performed by the adult. The speech of the upbringer should be emotional and expressive, and should reflect her loving, tender relation to the child.

The development of speech becomes the vehicle for developing social behaviour. Thus, in speaking of the nine to twelve months age level, the manual states:

It is important to cultivate in the baby a positive attitude toward adults and children. At this age the child's need to relate to the adults around him increases. Interest develops in what others are doing. Sometimes children of this age play together: they throw balls into the same basket, roll downhill one after the other, smile at each other, call to one another. If the upbringer is not sufficiently attentive to the children, negative relations may arise among them; for example, the result of the attempt by one child to take a toy held by another. From the very beginning, stress is placed on teaching children to share and to engage in joint activity. Frequent reference is made to common ownership: "Moe eto nashe; nashe moe" (mine is ours, ours is mine). Collective play is emphasized. Gradually, the adult be-

gins to withdraw from the role of leader or coordinator in order to forge a "self-reliant collective," in which the children cooperate and discipline themselves—at meal times and in play activities, too.

Play itself often takes the form of role playing in real-life social situations, which gradually increase in complexity (taking care of baby, shopping, in the doctor's office, at school). Beginning in the second year of nursery and continuing through kindergarten children are expected to take on ever-increasing communal responsibilities, such as helping others, serving at table, cleaning up, gardening, caring for animals, and shoveling snow. The effects of these socializing experiences are reflected in the youngsters behaviour, with many children giving an impression of self-confidence, competence and camaraderie.

■

Source: Bronfenbrenner, U. Two worlds of childhood: U.S. and U.S.S.R. New York: Russell Sage Foundation, 1970.

The Importance of Early Experience in Normal Home Environments

Nor are the beneficial effects of a stimulating perceptual and social environment restricted only to institutionalized infants or even to the period of early infancy. Recent studies of the effects of variations in normal home environments on children's development have underlined the importance of the early physical setting and social stimulation for promoting adequate cognitive, motor, and social development.

In a careful investigation of 5-month-old infants it was found that mothers who attended to and stimulated their infants in response to an infant signal, such as vocalization or a distress call, had more developmentally advanced infants. The social input of these mothers was contingent upon the behavior of the infant and was not merely a random occurrence. Social stimulation that is responsive to the infant's signals is an extremely important contributor to early development. In addition, both the complexity of toys and the variety of play materials and household objects available to the infant were significantly related to a variety of measures of infant development, such as reaching and grasping, exploratory behavior, and preference for novel stimuli (Yarrow, Rubinstein, & Pedersen, 1975). Other studies with older infants (12 to 24 months) have yielded similar results. Wachs (1976) found not only that the variety and number of toys, mobiles, and magazines were important, but that the freedom to visually and physically explore his or her environment was an important determinant of the child's cognitive development. These early opportunities to explore varied objects, spaces, and places probably strengthen the child's emerging curiosity and encourage later inquisitiveness and questioning.

The Reversibility of Early Experience in Humans

An important question remains. Can the effects of early experience be reversed? Can children who grow up in a deprived environment overcome the impact of their early rearing if they are placed in more adequate environments?

In Box 5-5, we examine a study by Harold Skeels that attempted to answer this question. Mentally retarded women served as substitute mothers for a group of institutionalized infants, and the infants' social and intellectual development markedly improved.

Nor is the Skeels study an isolated case. More recently a number of studies have found reversibility of early deprivation (Clarke & Clarke, 1976)—not only in North America, but in a number of different cultures. Dennis (1973), in his book *Children of the Creche*, reports the outcome of a natural experiment in which a Lebanese social agency shifted its policy and began to substitute adoption for institutionalization of unwanted infants and children. By comparing the progress of the infants who were adopted with the infants who had spent their childhood in the institution, Dennis provided further insight into the modifiability issue. In contrast to the low intelligence of children who had stayed in the institution throughout childhood, the children adopted prior to age 2 reached normal intelligence levels. Those who were adopted later gained as a result of being in a more stimulating environment, but were still below normal levels by age 16. As Dennis notes, "The greater the age of adoption, the lower the eventual mean IQ attained" (1973, p. 106). However, again we see the problem of determining causality in field research. This conclusion is open to challenge. Possibly, brighter children were adopted at an earlier age or the younger children were placed in better homes—both possibilities could account for the Dennis findings.

A similar story comes from Guatemala, where Kagan and Klein (1973) found severe retardation among infants living in an isolated farming area. Compared to their American peers, they were behind on a variety of cognitive and social skills. Examination of the environment may help understand this slow development:

During most of the first year, the infant is tightly clothed and restricted to the inside of a windowless hut. . . . the infant has no conventional toys with which to play and adults are minimally interactive with him. . . . Play and vocalization directed at the baby by others occurred less than 10% of the time, in contrast to 25 to 40 percent of the time in American homes. (Kagan, 1976, pp. 106–107)

But that is only in infancy:

By 13 to 16 months when the baby becomes mobile and is allowed to leave the hut he encounters the greater variety inherent in the outside world. He engages in an environment that includes domestic animals, other children, trees, rain, clouds and makes

BOX 5-5
THE REVERSIBILITY OF EARLY EXPERIENCE DEFICITS: THE SKEELS STUDY

 In the late 1930s, Skeels set out to determine whether the debilitating impact of early institutionalization could be overcome by exposure to a more enriched environment. Two groups of children were involved. Due to crowding, one group was transferred from the orphanage to a mental retardation institution; children in the comparison group remained in the orphanage. The two environments were in marked contrast. The orphanage offered little social or perceptual stimulation. The institution for the mentally retarded could easily be described as "enriched" in comparison to the orphanage. It was a more varied and stimulating environment, and provided abundant opportunities for social and emotional development as well, with frequent one-to-one adult-child relationships.

The thirteen children who were sent to this setting at an average age of 19 months were considered mentally retarded, with an average IQ of 64.3. The average IQ of the twelve children who stayed in the orphanage was 86.7. To assess the impact of living under these contrasting conditions, the children's IQs were reassessed about $1\frac{1}{2}$ years after the transfer. The experimental subjects showed a marked increase in mental growth, with the average gain being a dramatic 28.5 IQ points. These "mental retardates" now had an average IQ of 91.8. The average loss was 26.2 IQ points for the other children who stayed in the institution ($\overline{X}$ IQ=60.5).

The two groups had reversed positions over the two-year period. Skeels was interested in determining whether the gains achieved by the experimental subjects would last. His first follow-up study was conducted $2\frac{1}{2}$ years after the termination of the initial study. Of the original group of thirteen children, eleven were adopted while two remained institutionalized until adulthood. The adopted children maintained their intellectual status: the mean IQ for these children was 101.4, but the reinstitutionalized children dropped in IQ. The unfortunates in the control group, of course,

remained wards of the state and in spite of slight gains were still classified as mentally retarded; the mean IQ for this group was 66.1.

To illustrate more convincingly the reversibility of the effects of early environmental deprivation, Skeels (1966) assessed the adult status of the two groups and found no evidence of any late-emerging defects in the experimental subjects. Twenty-one years elapsed between the first follow-up study and this final assessment; by this time the "children" were between 25 and 35 years of age. All the subjects in the experimental group were self-supporting, including the nonadopted children. Of the twelve children in the control group, one died in adolescence after continued institutionalization, while another four children were still under state care. The educational and occupational achievements of the two groups were markedly different as well; for example, half of the experimental group completed the twelfth grade; in contrast, half of the control subjects had not completed the third grade. In fact, in terms of education, occupation, and income, the eleven adopted children were indiscriminable from the rest of the "normal" population, as assessed by the 1960 United States census figures. According to Skeels, "Their adult status was equivalent to what might have been expected of children living with natural parents in homes of comparable sociocultural levels" (Skeels, 1966, p. 55). Although no IQ data were available, it seems safe to conclude that the eleven adopted children were functioning as normal adults. Also, children of the experimental subjects were in no way retarded. Of their twenty-eight offspring, the mean IQ was 104, and school progress was normal.

The implication of this study is clear: the deleterious effects of early environmental restriction can be effectively reversed. ∎

Source: Skeels, H. Adult status of children with contrasting early life experiences. *Monographs of the Society for Research in Child Development*, 1966, *31* (No. 3).

the accomodations those experiences require. The 8–10 year-old is assigned tasks and responsibilities, such as helping the father in the field, caring for infants, cooking, cleaning, and carrying water. (Kagan, 1976, p. 107)

Does this shift in the environment permit these infants to overcome their slow start? To find out, Kagan and Klein administered a variety of cognitive tests which tap universal and culture-free skills such as memory and perceptual analysis to groups of children from this area ranging from 5 to 12 years of age. By 10 years of age, the children in this village were as capable as American children on the memory and perceptual tests. The experiences during infancy did not affect the abilities of the preadolescents. Again, the evidence supports the view that behavior is modifiable at a variety of developmental points and later behavior is not necessarily predetermined in a fixed way by early experiences.

A word of caution is in order. While early experiences can be reversed, it is still probably easier to acquire some behaviors at certain ages than at others. And it is still easier to acquire new skills than reverse the effects of earlier acquired behaviors.

In summary, early experience is important, but the detrimental impact of drastic modifications in the early rearing environment can be altered. Of particular importance for the proper development of behavior—motoric, social, and intellectual—is not only sensory and perceptual stimulation, but a responsive environment that permits the acquisition of a critical belief, the belief that children can modify their social and nonsocial world.

Summary

The impact of early experience on later development was the focus of this chapter. Two approaches to understanding this problem were employed; a deprivation approach involving modification of the normal environment by a reduction in sensory, perceptual, and social stimulation, and an enrichment approach involving an increase in the level of normal stimulation.

First, a series of experimental studies of the modifiability of the central nervous system by rearing rats in an enriched environment were discussed. Significant increases in the size, weight, and complexity of the cortex were obtained as a result of being reared in an enriched situation; these increases are associated with more efficient learning.

Next, investigations of the effects of severe sensory, perceptual, and social deprivation on the social and intellectual development of monkeys were presented. A number of factors, such as the length, the completeness, and the timing of the deprivation experience, were important determinants of both the short-range and long-range effects of deprivation. Total isolation involving reduced sensory and perceptual stimulation as well as no contact with other animals was more debilitating than partial isolation wherein the monkey could see and hear but not physically interact with other monkeys. The impairment in social behavior increased as the length of the deprivation increased, with one year of total isolation producing a total social misfit. Deprivation immediately after birth was more damaging than deprivation after a period of social experience. Some species are more affected by deprivation than others, and males are more severely affected than females by early deprivation. Finally, the impact of early deprivation is reversible. A technique involving the use of younger age-mates as therapists was found to be particularly effective.

Institutionalization in which there was a reduction in sensory and perceptual stimulation as well as limited opportunities for social interaction had a debilitating effect on the child's social, intellectual, and motor development. However, as in the case of the monkeys' these effects of early deprivation are reversible. Evidence was presented which indicated that perceptual and sensory stimulation was important, but the critical factor for adequate development was a responsive social environment. Institutional effects often occur because of the development of a state of helplessness in infants and young children.

References

Bronfenbrenner, U. *Two worlds of childhood: U.S. and U.S.S.R.* New York: Russell Sage Foundation, 1970.

Carlson, A. J. Changes in Nissl's substance of the ganglion and the bipolar cells of the retina of the brandt cormorant phalacrocorax pencillatus during prolonged normal stimulation. *American Journal of Anatomy*, 1902/3, **2**, 341–347.

Casler, L. Maternal deprivation: A critical review of the literature. *Monographs of the Society for Research in Child Development*, 1961, **26** (No. 2).

Casler, L. The effects of extra tactile stimulation on a group of institutionalized infants. *Genetic Psychology Monographs*, 1965, **71**, 137–175.

Casler, L. Perceptual deprivation in institutional settings. In G. Newton & S. Levine (Eds.), *Early experience and behavior*. New York: Springer, 1967.

Clarke, A. M., & Clarke, A. D. B. (Eds.). *Early experience: Myth and evidence*. New York: Free Press, 1976.

Cross, H. A., & Harlow, H. F. Prolonged and progressive effects of partial isolation on the behavior of macaque monkeys. *Journal of Experimental Research in Personality*, 1965, **1**, 39–49.

Dennis, W. Causes of retardation among institutional children: Iran. *Journal of Genetic Psychology*, 1960, **96**, 47–59.

Dennis, W. *Children of the creche*. New York: Appleton-Century-Crofts, 1973.

Finkelstein, N. W., & Ramey, C. T. Learning to control the environment in infancy. *Child Development*, 1977, **48**, 806–819.

Gessell, A., & Thompson, H. Learning and growth in identical twin infants. *Genetic Psychology Monographs*, 1929, **6**, 1–124.

Goldfarb, W. Effects of early institutional care on adolescent personality. *Child Development*, 1943, **14**, 213–223.

Goldfarb, W. Rorschach test differences between family reared, institution-reared, and schizophrenic children. *American Journal of Orthopsychiatry*, 1949, **19**, 625–633.

Goldfarb, W. Emotional and intellectual consequences of psychological deprivation in infancy: A revaluation. In P. H. Hock and J. Zubin (Eds.), *Psychopathology of childhood*. New York: Grune & Stratton, 1955.

Greenough, W. T. Experiential modification of the developing brain. *American Scientist*, 1975, **63**, 37–46.

Greenough, W. T. Enduring brain effects and differential experience and training. In M. R. Rosenzweig and E. L. Bennett (Eds.), *Neural mechanisms of learning and memory*. Cambridge, Mass.: M.I.T. Press, 1976.

Greenough, W. T., Wood, W. E., & Madden, T. C. Possible memory storage differences among mice reared in environments varying in complexity. *Behavioral Biology*, 1972, **7**, 717–722.

Griffin, G. A., & Harlow, H. F. Effects of three months of total social deprivation on social adjustment and learning in the rhesus monkey. *Child Development*, 1966, **37**, 533–547.

Harlow, M. K. Nuclear family apparatus. *Behavioral Research Method and Instrumentation,* 1971, 301–304.

Harlow, H. F., & Harlow, M. K. Social deprivation in monkeys. *Scientific American*, 1962, **207,** 137–146.

Harlow, H. F., & Harlow, M. K. The young monkeys. *Readings in psychology today.* Delmar Publishers, CRM Books, 1972.

Harlow, H. F., & Novak, M. A. Psychopathological perspectives. *Perspectives in Biology and Medicine*, 1973, **16**, 461–478.

Hebb, D. O. *The organization of behavior.* New York: Wiley, 1949.

Hilgard, J. R. Learning and maturation in preschool children: *Journal of Genetic Psychology*, 1932, **41**, 36–56.

Kagan, J. Resistance and continuity in psychological development. In A. M. Clarke and A. D. B. Clarke (Eds.), *Early experience: Myth and evidence.* New York: Free Press, 1976, pp. 97–121.

Kagan, J., & Klein, R. E. Cross-cultural perspectives on early development. *American Psychologist*, 1973, **28,** 947–961.

Krech, D., Rosenzweig, M., & Bennett, E. L. Relations between brain chemistry and problem-solving among rats raised in enriched and impoverished environments. *Journal of Comparative and Physiological Psychology*, 1962, **55,** 801–807.

La Torre, J. C. Effect of differential environment enrichment on brain weight and on acetylcholinesterase and cholinesterase activities in mice. *Experimental Neurology*, 1968, **22,** 493–503.

Lewis, M., & Goldberg, S. Perceptual-cognitive development in infancy: A generalized expectancy model as a function of mother-infant interaction. *Merrill-Palmer Quarterly*, 1969, **15,** 81–100.

Mitchell, G. D., Raymond, E. J., Ruppenthal, G. C., & Harlow, H. F. Long-term effects of total social isolation upon behavior of rhesus monkeys. *Psychological Reports*, 1966. **18,** 567–580.

Novak, M. A., & Harlow, H. F. Social recovery of monkeys isolated for the first year of life: I. *Developmental Psychology*, 1975, **11,** 453–465.

Pratt, C. L. Social behavior of rhesus monkeys reared with varying degrees of early peer experience. Unpublished M. A. thesis, University of Wisconsin, 1967.

Reisen, A. H. Arrested vision. *Scientific American*, 1950, **183,** 16–19.

Rheingold, H. L. The modification of social responsiveness in institutional babies. *Monographs of the Society for Research in Child Development*, 1956, **21** (No. 63).

Rosenzweig, M. R. Environmental complexity, cerebral change and behavior. *American Psychologist,* 1966, **21,** 321–332.

Rosenzweig, M. R., & Bennett, E. L. Effects of differential environments on brain weights and enzyme activities in gerbils, rats and mice. *Developmental Psychobiology*, 1970, **2,** 87–95.

Rowland, G. L. The effects of total social isolation upon learning and social behavior in rhesus monkeys. Unpublished doctoral dissertation, University of Wisconsin, 1964.

Sackett, G. P. Exploratory behavior of rhesus monkeys as a function of rearing experiences and sex. *Developmental Psychology*, 1972, **6,** 260–270.

Sackett, G. P. Some persistent effects of differential rearing conditions on pre-adult social behavior of monkeys. *Journal of Comparative and Physiological Psychology*, 1967, **64,** 363–365.

Sackett, G. P. The persistence of abnormal behavior in monkeys following isolation rearing. In R. Porter (Ed.), *The role of learning in psychotherapy.* London: J & A Churchill, Ltd., 1968.

Sackett, G. P., Holm, R. A., & Landesman-Dwyer, S. Vulnerability for abnormal development: Pregnancy outcomes and sex differences in macaque monkeys. In N. R. Ellis (Ed.), *Aberrant development in infancy.* New York: Erlbaum Associates, 1975, 59–76.

Sackett, G. P., Holm, R. A., & Ruppenthal, G. C. Social isolation rearing: Species differences in behavior of macaque monkeys. *Developmental Psychology*, 1976, **12,** 283–288.

Sackett, G. P., Wescott, J. T. & Wescott, R. Effect of rearing on survival in a free-ranging environment. Unpublished Manuscript. University of Washington, 1977.

Saltz, R. Aging persons as child-care workers in a foster-grandparent program: Psychosocial effects and work performance. *Aging and Human Development*, 1971, **3,** 314–340.

Saltz, R. Effects of part time "mothering" on IQ and SQ of young institutionalized children. *Child Development*, 1973, **9,** 166–170.

Schaffer, H. R. Activity level as a constitutional determinant of infantile reaction to deprivation. *Child Development*, 1966, **37,** 595–602.

Scott, J. P. Critical periods in behavioral development. *Science*, 1962, **138,** 949–958.

Skeels, H. Adult status of children with contrasting early life experiences. *Monographs of the Society for Research in Child Development,* 1966, **31** (No. 3).

Spitz, R. A. Hospitalism: An inquiry into the genesis of psychiatric conditions in early childhood. *Psychoanalytic Study of the Child*, 1945, **1,** 53–74.

Suomi, S. J. Early experience and social development in rhesus monkeys. Unpublished manuscript, University of Wisconsin, 1976.

Suomi, S. J., & Harlow H. F. Abnormal social behavior in young monkeys. In J. Helmuth (Ed.), *Exceptional infant: Studies in abnormalities.* Vol. 2. New York: Brunner/Mazel, 1971, pp. 483–529.

Suomi, S. J., Harlow, H. F., & McKinney, W. T. Monkey psychiatrists. *American Journal of Psychiatry,* 1972, **128,** 41–46.

Wachs, T. D. Utilization of a Piagetian approach in the investigation of early experience. *Merrill-Palmer Quarterly*, 1976, **22,** 11–30.

Watson, J. S., & Ramey, C. T. Reactions to responsive contingent stimulation in early infancy. Paper presented at the biennial meeting of the Society for Research in Child Development, Santa Monica, Calif., March 1969.

Watson, J. S., & Ramey, C. T. Reactions to responsive contingent stimulation in early infancy. *Merrill-Palmer Quarterly*, 1972, **18,** 219–227.

White, B. L. An experimental approach to the effects of environment on early human behavior. In J. P. Hill (Ed.), *Minnesota symposium on child psychology* (Vol. 1). Minneapolis: University of Minnesota Press, 1967.

White, B. L., Castle, P., & Held, R. M. Observations on the development of visually directed reaching. *Child Development*, 1964, **35,** 349–364.

White, B. L., & Held, R. Plasticity of sensorimotor development in human infant. In J. Rosenblith & W. Allinsmith (Eds.), *The causes of behavior: Readings in child development and educational psychology.* Boston: Allyn and Bacon, 1966.

Yarrow, L. Maternal deprivation: Toward an empirical and conceptual re-evaluation. *Psychological Bulletin*, 1961, **58,** 459–490.

Yarrow, L. J. Separation from parents during early childhood. In M. L. Hoffman & L. W. Hoffman (Eds.). *Review of child development research.* (Vol. 1). New York: Russell Sage Foundation, 1964, pp. 89–136.

Yarrow, L. J., Rubinstein, J. L., & Pedersen, F. A. *Infant and Environment.* New York: Halsted, 1975.

6

Learning

In this chapter we begin a long and interesting exploration of how children learn. Few topics have so successfully captured the imagination and attention of professional researchers, educators, and parents. Genetics sets the course for development, but learning principles and processes are important channels for shaping, molding, and directing the course of *genetically based* capacities. The principles of learning presented in this chapter act together with the genetic, hereditary, and maturational factors discussed in earlier chapters.

Learning covers a wide variety of processes, and this chapter is a sampling of some of the traditional approaches to learning. First, two well-established approaches to learning will be examined: classical and operant conditioning. What factors determine the effectiveness of these two forms of learning in children? How early can infants be classically or operantly conditioned, and what is the developmental course of these types of conditioning? Next, observational learning will be examined. What are the processes involved in this type of learning, and how long do the effects last? How important is observational learning from real-life and televised models for cognitive and social development? How do children learn to discriminate between relevant and irrelevant information in their environment? Alternatively, how do children learn to generalize and transfer their behaviors to new situations? Next, techniques for decreasing undesirable behavior, including extinction and punishment, are explored. Again, the factors that modify the effectiveness of these methods of controlling behavior are examined. What are the negative side effects associated with the use of punishment? Is punishment an ethical technique? In subsequent chapters, other more complex cognitive functions such as memory and problem solving will be featured. So remember this is just our first glance at the issue of "how children learn."

Classical and Operant Conditioning

Classical Conditioning

The first and most famous demonstration of the kind of learning termed *classical conditioning* was carried out by Ivan Pavlov over sixty years ago. A harnessed dog heard a bell ring just as food was placed in his mouth. The dog, of course, salivated. What was significant was the fact that after a series of occasions in which the bell and food were presented together, the dog began to salivate whenever he heard the bell. The presentation of the food was unnecessary; the bell had become an effective elicitor of the salivary reaction.

With this example in mind, let us examine the characteristic features of this type of learning. The food in our example is termed the *unconditioned stimulus,* or *US:* It is a reliable elicitor of a particular response. The presentation of food always evokes salivation, which is termed the *unconditioned response,* or *UCR.* The stimulus that is paired with the US (that is, the bell) is labeled the *conditioned stimulus,* or *CS.* The main characteristic property of this stimulus, the bell, is its inability to evoke salivation reactions prior to being systematically paired with the unconditioned stimulus. In classical conditioning, the UCS and US generally occur together, or the UCS is sometimes presented before the US. To complete this procedure we have a *conditioned response,* or *CR,* the response (salivary response) that closely resembles but is not identical with the unconditioned response originally produced by the unconditioned stimulus, but which is now evoked by the conditioned stimulus alone. The CR may differ from UR, for example, in terms of strength of response.

This type of conditioning can be found frequently in everyday life. Consider the child who cries when he sees a physician who gave him a painful injection on a previous visit. On the first visit, he did not cry when he saw the physician. It was only as a result of the pairing of the painful needle (unconditioned stimulus) with the physician (conditioned stimulus) that the sight of the doctor alone elicited crying. Figure 6-1 illustrates this conditioning process.

Operant Conditioning

Unlike classical conditioning, operant conditioning requires that the organism first make a response and then experience some consequence for his behavior. The strength of the response that is followed by a reinforcing or rewarding outcome is increased (that is, conditioned).

Consider two examples—one is famous; the other is relevant. First, the famous demonstration of instrumental conditioning will be discussed. A lowly white rat is wandering about its cage and accidentally presses a bar extending out of one wall of its cage. Immediately after the press, a click is heard and a food pellet drops into a cup near the bar. The rat presses the bar again, and again food is delivered. Soon the rat has given up its tour of the cage and is seen avidly pressing the bar and eating food pellets. It has been conditioned to press the bar. Or as one rather precocious white rat once commented, "I've sure got him (that is, the experimenter) conditioned; every time I press the bar he gives me another food pellet."

Now, let us consider an example of operant conditioning with children, for this type of learning is extremely important in understanding the development of infant and child behavior. Rheingold, Gewirtz, and Ross (1959) demonstrated that vocalizing in 3-month-old infants could be modified by the use of operant conditioning. First, an adult leaned over the baby's crib and recorded the frequency of the infant's vocalizations. However, during this early session, the adult gave no reaction to the vocalization. To determine whether positive feedback would increase vocalizing, the adult began to smile, say "tsk," and touch the infant immediately after a vocalization. In short, through operant conditioning the infant's vocalizations had been modified.

Unlike classical conditioning where the response to be conditioned is readily and reliably elicited by the unconditioned stimulus, the operant conditioning method can be used to increase the frequency of behaviors that are often not emitted by the child. The process is termed *shaping*, and the following example of a child who seldom attended to his teacher's actions will illustrate this process.

FIGURE 6-1 Three stages of classical conditioning.

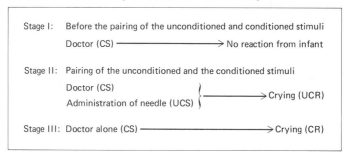

This pupil spent most of his day either looking at classmates, gazing out the window, or staring blankly at his desk. The school year might have been over before the child ever looked at the teacher, so it would have been highly inefficient to wait for the desired response to spontaneously occur. The solution is to reinforce or reward (by approval, candy, etc.) the child for approximations of the final response that is desired. For example, whenever the child looked to the front of the class, the "experimenter" dispensed a candy, even though the child didn't look directly at the teacher. By gradually reinforcing the child for closer and closer approximations of the final response, the child eventually begins to look at his teacher.

The complexity and variety of behavior patterns that can be learned through operant shaping procedures are virtually unlimited; the only restrictions are the ingenuity and patience of the parent, teacher, or experimenter. Skinner (1953) received considerable recognition for demonstrating that pigeons could even be taught to play Ping-Pong through shaping tactics. In fact, numerous animal trainers have used these techniques for teaching seals, lions, and other assorted circus performers to do complex and amusing stunts.

For an illustration of the ways in which operant conditioning can be used in real-life settings, turn to Box 6-1, which describes the successful application of operant conditioning to the control of hyperactive children.

Factors Affecting Operant Conditioning A variety of variables affect the success of operant conditioning, particularly the timing and the schedule of reinforcement. In general, reinforcement that is delivered immediately upon the execution of the response is more effective than a delayed reinforcement.

The age of the child makes a difference; for young infants, even brief delays may severely disrupt learning. In a recent study of operant conditioning of the vocalization rate in 3-month-old infants, Ramey and Ourth (1971) found that delaying the presentation of the reward by a mere three seconds prevented the occurrence of operant conditioning. This is not simply due to an inability to learn. As we saw in the study of infant vocalization, 3-month-old infants can be operantly conditioned if the positive reinforcement is delivered immediately after the response. Probably the increase in memory capacity that occurs with age contributes to the greater ability of the older child to learn under conditions of longer reinforcement delays. The child is able to remember the response that she has made until the time that the reinforcement is delivered.

Another important factor is the schedule of reinforcement, or the pattern with which reinforcement is delivered. There are a variety of schedules of reinforcement. Under ratio schedules, the reinforcement is delivered only after the child has made a certain number of responses. For example, the reinforcement is delivered every third or every fifth response, not every response. Under interval schedules, reinforcement is delivered only after a certain time interval since the last reinforcement has elapsed. Ratio and interval schedules can be either fixed or variable. A fixed schedule is one where every fifth or tenth response is reinforced or reinforcement comes a set interval (for example, thirty

BOX 6-1
OPERANT PRINCIPLES IN ACTION: HYPERACTIVE CHILDREN

In nearly every classroom in the country there is a hyperactive child—a child who has difficulty sitting still, attending to the teacher, finishing school tasks. Drug therapy has been a popular solution to this problem. However, not only may drugs produce undesirable side effects, such as growth suppression and increased blood pressure, but in 30 to 50 percent of the cases, drug treatments are ineffective. An alternative is the use of operant learning principles to control this type of child. Daniel O'Leary and his colleagues (1976) assigned nine children to a therapy program for ten weeks and compared them with a group of eight nontreated but equally hyperactive children in the third to fifth grades. In the authors' words,

The primary treatment consisted of a home-based reward program. This program had five components: 1) specification of each child's daily classroom goals; 2) praising the child for efforts to achieve those goals; 3) end-of-day evaluation of the child's behavior relevant to the specified goals; 4) sending the parents a daily report card on their child's daily progress; and 5) rewarding of the child by the parent for progress toward his goals. (p. 511)

During the program period, the teacher advised the parents on their child's progress by means of a daily report card. At the end of each day, the teacher completed the daily report, to be taken home by the child to his parents. They, in turn, rewarded him every time he had met his goals for the day, as indicated by the teacher's report. (p. 512)

To assess the effectiveness of using parents as therapists, two measures were made before and after treatment. First, a teacher's rating scale was employed which measured the degree of inattentiveness, anxiety, conduct problems, and hyperactivity displayed by the child. Second, a specifically designed problem behavior rating scale was established for each child; this consisted of an 8-point rating of the severity of four or five problem behaviors for each child.

The results were clear: In comparison to the nontreated children, the children in the operant therapy group showed significant improvement on both of the rating scales. They were rated as less hyperactive by their teachers and exhibited fewer problem behaviors. In a related study, Susan O'Leary and William Pelham (1977) have made an even more dramatic demonstration. Hyperactive children who were being treated by medication were taken off their drug and received behavior therapy. The children who received behavior modification therapy improved just as much as those children who were treated with medication. Together these studies not only demonstrate the value of operant principles in real-life settings, but illustrate that operant principles can be an effective alternative way of treating hyperactivity. ■

O'Leary, K. D., Pelham, W. E., Rosenbaum, A., & Price, G. H. Behavioral treatment of hyperkinetic children. *Clinical Pediatrics*, 1976, **15**, 510–515. O'Leary, S. G., & Pelham, W. E. Behavior therapy and withdrawal of stimulant medication with hyperactive children. *Pediatrics*, 1977, **60**, 101–115.

seconds) after the last reinforcement. In everyday life, mealtimes, the presence of father, or opportunities for interaction among school-age siblings usually occur on a fixed-interval schedule. That is, they occur with predictable regularity at the same times of the day. Fixed-ratio schedules are less common in naturalistic settings. Perhaps the most usual reinforcement patterns are variable-ratio and interval schedules. In the case of variable-ratio schedules, the reinforcement comes after differing numbers of responses (3, 5, 2, 6), but the average is one reinforcement for every so many responses (for example, 4). Similarly, according to a variable-interval schedule, reinforcement comes on an average of every thirty seconds, but the actual intervals between reinforcement may vary (for example, sixty, twenty, or ten seconds). In most everyday situations, most reinforcement is intermittent; that is, a combination of schedules is employed whereby both the ratio of responses to reinforcement and the interval between reinforcements vary. Mothers don't praise their children on a regular schedule; on some days praise may be frequent, but on other occasions when mother is tired and irritable, even the most loving mother may reward infrequently.

How Early Can Children Be Conditioned?

For the past forty years there has been considerable controversy over the issue of how early children can be conditioned, and the controversy is not yet over (Fitzgerald & Brackbill, 1976; Sameroff & Cavanaugh, 1978).

Some investigators (for example, Spelt, 1948) have attempted to demonstrate classical conditioning in the unborn fetus; however, the results were inconclusive due to methodological inadequacies. But can the newborn infant be classically conditioned? In spite of some skeptics (Sameroff, 1971, 1972), there appears to be evidence that a limited set of responses can be classically conditioned even in newborns (Fitzgerald & Brackbill, 1976). Generally, the responses which have been successfully conditioned do not involve motor behavior such as sucking or movement, but involve behavior such as heart rate (Clifton, 1974; Stamps & Porges, 1975); it appears that the infant's autonomic nervous system which controls heart rate and respiration may be more conditionable in the early days of life than complex motor behavior.

Moreover, a variety of factors are important determinants of early infant learning, including the infant's state. Awake and alert infants clearly learn more effectively than awake and drowsy ones, a not surprising phenomenon to students who try to stay awake in a boring lecture (Clifton, Siqueland, & Lipsitt, 1972). Another factor is the interstimulus interval—the time between the unconditioned stimulus (for example, doctor) and the conditioned stimulus (for example, needle), to use our earlier example. The optimal interstimulus interval is longer for younger than older subjects, which suggests that "the more immature the organism, the more time needed to process stimulus information" (Fitzgerald & Brackbill, 1976, p. 365).

Less controversy surrounds the modifiability of the infant's behavior by operant conditioning. Sameroff (1968) has demonstrated that the sucking response of the newborn can be modified by the presentation or withholding of milk. Specifically, sucking can be divided into two distinct components: an expression response involving the squeezing of the nipple between the tongue and palate, and a suction component in which the floor of the mouth is lowered and creates a partial vacuum in the oral cavity during the suction. Sameroff provided milk for the babies either as a direct consequence of suction applied to the nipple or in response to direct sucking or squeezing the nipple. The infants were able to adjust their style of sucking depending on the component that was followed by milk. If the milk was contingent upon the suction component, suction sucking increased; pressure sucking increased if milk delivery was contingent on this type of sucking action. This study clearly indicates that operant conditioning involving very subtle and complex discriminations is possible in the first few days of life.

However, this study and other successful demonstrations of operant conditioning in the newborn have involved *existing* organized patterns of behavior such as sucking or head turning, a component of rooting-feeding behavior, which are of considerable biological importance to the infant's survival. Some responses are apparently more easily modified than others. Newborn infants, like members of any species, have certain response systems that are biologically prepared to operate efficiently very early in life. For the human newborn infant, these *prepared responses*, to use Seligman's (1970) terms, are associated with feeding and through evolution have been selected as a result of their importance for survival. The infant is best organized in early life to perform behaviors that are functionally adaptive (Sameroff, 1972).

As studies in this section show, basic learning processes appear to be present very early in life; what changes over development seems to be the nature of the information that the child is capable of learning and possibly the speed and efficiency with which learning proceeds.

The issue of developmental changes in conditioning over the first three months of life is addressed by Papousek in Box 6-2. Not only does this study demonstrate changes in conditioning in the early months of life, but the investigation illustrates the way in which the two types of conditioning—operant and classical—can often be used in combination to facilitate the child's learning. Nor is it just in experiments that the two types of learning occur together; in real-life situations operant and classical conditioning often work together in altering behavior.

In the next section, we turn to another type of learning—observational learning.

Learning through Observation

Although a great deal of learning takes place through direct contact with the environment, as we have seen in the cases of operant and classical conditioning, learning can occur vicariously as well. Merely observing the behavior of peers, parents, and teachers can significantly expand the behavioral repertoire of the observer. Research has clearly demonstrated that new responses can be acquired and old responses elicited and modified through imitation. Indeed, it would be extremely unfortunate if a child were forced to acquire all of her repsonses through either operant or classical conditioning. For example, consid-

BOX 6-2
DEVELOPMENTAL TRENDS IN INFANT CONDITIONING

 In addition to knowing how early learning can occur, child psychologists have been interested in determining whether the child's capacity to learn in this way improves with age. Papousek (1967), a Czechoslovakian investigator, has provided the most systematic data on this issue. Using a combination of operant and classical conditioning techniques, he studied the development of conditioning in infants at three age levels: newborn, three months, and five months. Head turning, the unconditioned response employed in these studies, was elicited by a tactile stimulus to the side of the mouth. A bell, paired with the tactile unconditioned stimulus, served as the conditioned stimulus. Up to now, this paradigm is an example of classical conditioning. However, when the infant turned his head to the US, he received a milk reinforcer. The addition of the milk brings this procedure close to an operant conditioning paradigm. It is a mixed classical-operant conditioning paradigm. To review, on a typical trial, a bell sounded followed by presentation of milk whenever the infant turned his head to one side. The bell continued to sound until the baby began sucking the milk. Gradually the sound of the bell alone was sufficient to elicit the head-turning response. However, the number of trials necessary to reach a criterion of five consecutive head-turning responses in the ten trials of a daily session clearly depended on the age of the child. For newborns, an average of 177 trials was required to reach this criterion, while 42 trials were sufficient for the 3-month old infants; by five months, still more rapid conditioning occurred; only 28 trials were necessary. In short, conditionability does improve with age. These findings are consistent with the notion that the opportunity for experience with auditory stimuli in the natural environment is a prerequisite for conditioning. Although additional opportunities to interact with the environment are probably important, maturation of the central nervous system may be important as well. There is evidence that the dramatic improvement over the first three months found by Papousek may, in fact, be due to changes that take place in the organization of the central nervous system around the third month of life. First, it is at this age that Ellingson (1967) has reported that the infant electroencephalographic, or EEG, activity patterns first approximate adult patterns. A second indication of the increasing maturity of the central nervous system is the disappearance of a number of primitive reflexes at this age. Finally, autopsy analyses of a group of South American children who died in the first six months of life of respiratory ailments found that the deoxyribonucleic acid (DNA) content in the brain showed a rapid increase during the first few months and reached a peak at the three- to four-month age period (Winick, unpublished; cited by Lewis, Goldberg, & Campbell, 1969, p. 25). ■

Source: Papousek, H. Conditioning during early postnatal development. In Y. Brackbill & G. G. Thompson (Eds.), *Behavior in Infancy and early childhood.* New York: Free Press, 1967, pp. 259–274.

er how uneconomical it would be to learn to drive a car through operant conditioning alone. Bandura offers the following rather humorous analysis of such a predicament:

As a first step our trainer, who has been carefully programmed to produce head nods, resonant hm-hms, and other verbal reinforcers, loads up with an ample supply of candy, chewing gum and filter-tip cigarettes. A semi-willing subject who has never observed a person drive an automobile, and a parked car complete the picture. Our trainer might have to wait a long time before the subject emits an orienting response toward the vehicle. At the moment the subject does look even in the general direction of the car, this response is immediately reinforced and gradually he begins to gaze longingly at the stationary automobile. Similarly, approach responses in the desired direction are promptly reinforced in order to bring the subject in proximity to the car. Eventually, through the skillful use of differential reinforcement, the trainer will teach the subject to open and to close the car door. With perseverance he will move the subject from the back seat or any other inappropriate location chosen in this trial-and-error ramble until at length the subject is shaped up behind the steering wheel. It is unnecessary to depict the remainder of the training procedure beyond noting that it will likely prove an exceedingly tedious, not to mention an expensive and hazardous enterprise. (1962, pp. 212–213)

Origins of Imitation   Imitation begins early in life and provides another route for the acquisition and modification of developing behavior patterns. Imitation of at least some behaviors can occur in the first weeks of life. Twelve- to twenty-one-day-old infants imitated tongue protrusions and mouth openings (Meltzoff & Moore, 1977). These findings suggest that infants may be ready for social interaction and learning by imitation at a much earlier age than previous theories thought possible. However, imitation undergoes changes in terms of the accuracy of imitation and the kinds of behaviors that are imitated as the child develops. Recently, McCall, Parke, and Kavanaugh (1977) investigated developmental shifts in imitative behavior in infants from 12 to 24 months of age. Infants watched a live adult display a series of different behaviors such as vocalizing, making a wooden puzzle, and manipulating toy rings. After each behavior that the adult modeled, the infant's imitation of the adult's behavior was recorded. Figure 6-2 indicates clearly that the amount of perfect imitation increases dramatically between twelve and twenty-four months of age. However, the figure indicates that not all behaviors are imitated to the same degree. Three types of behaviors were investigated: (1) motor, (2) social, and (3) coordinated sequences. The series of motor behaviors refer to three types of motor actions: (1) motor behaviors with an object, such as placing rings over one's neck, (2) motor behavior with a product, such as making a stroke or series of dots with a crayon or putting a puzzle together, and (3) motor behavior which results in a sound, such as striking a can. Social behaviors include vocalizations and playing peek-a-boo with the infant. Finally, coordinated sequences represent complex patterns; for example, the adult places a cube inside a small cup, which, in turn, is placed in a larger one, and *then* the combination of cups is rattled. A coordinated series of actions is required of the child to imitate this sequence.

First, both motor and social behaviors show a clear-cut developmental

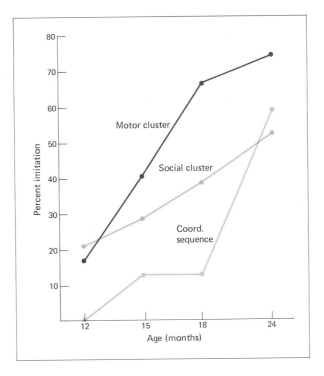

FIGURE 6-2 Developmental changes in imitation from 12 to 24 months. *(From McCall, Parke, & Kavanaugh, 1977, by permission of the authors and the Society for Research in Child Development.)*

increase during the second year of life. Second, infants imitate motor and gestural behaviors more often than social and vocal behaviors. However, the infants did not imitate coordinated sequences until 24 months.

Nor did the infants show deferred imitation—that is, imitation that is delayed for some period of time after the modeled display—before 2 years of age. Although the delay period was only thirty minutes in this study, these same investigators showed in a later investigation that two-year-olds were able to imitate even after a twenty-four-hour delay. In fact, there was no difference in the amount of imitation exhibited by children who were tested immediately and those tested after a delay of one day. By 2 years of age, then, children show a substantial capacity to defer imitation, which makes observational learning an increasingly powerful avenue for learning as the child develops. Probably this shift in imitative ability that occurs at two years is, in part, due to shifts in memory development—a topic that we will discuss in Chapter 10.

Can Infants Learn from Television?

Even for infants and young children, TV is an important medium for observational learning. In a typical home, a TV set is on for over six hours a day, and parents often use TV as a baby-sitter for infants. Some of the important ways in which TV can enhance cognitive development and alter aggressive and prosocial behavior have already been described in Chapter 1. How early does the TV

Even infants and toddlers can learn by watching television. (Ken Heyman)

influence begin? Even in the first year of life, TV is a successful competitor for the infant's attention. In one study, 6-month-old infants looked at a TV screen 49 percent of the available time while it portrayed children's TV programs (Slaby and Hollenbeck, 1977). However, the extent to which infants attend to and imitate TV presentations changes as the infant develops. In a recent study, infants between 18 months and 3 years were exposed to either a televised or live model playing with toys (McCall et al., 1977). Children at all ages attended to the live model nearly all of the time, but there were developmental changes in the amount of time that the children watched the televised model. The 18-month-olds only looked at the TV presentation 68 percent of the time, while this figure jumped to 78 percent by 24 months and 95 percent by 3 years. To find out if the children's imitation of the model's unique toy play showed the same increase as their viewing patterns, these researchers observed the children's toy play after either live or TV presentations. At the younger ages (18 and 24 months), the infants imitated the live model more than the TV model; by 36 months, the amount of imitation of live and TV models was similar. Over the first three years, television becomes an increasingly important contributor to the development of social and cognitive skills in young children.

We know children can learn through observing others, but how does observational learning occur? Is it merely another form of conditioning, or are different processes involved in this type of learning? We turn to these issues in the next section.

Another Form of Conditioning?

Are we justified in treating imitation as another form of learning, a form governed by a set of principles that are separate and discrete from either operant or classical conditioning? Many theorists have tried to reduce imitation to a special case of either operant or classical conditioning. Skinner (1953) has argued that it is the frequent rewarding of a child for imitating that increases the frequency of modeling. Imitation, according to this viewpoint, is simply a set of response tendencies that are developed and maintained according to well-established operant conditioning principles. The most serious challenge to this position comes from Bandura and his colleagues at Stanford University. They argue that imitation is, in fact, a separate and distinct form of learning, and a separate set of principles is required for its understanding.

An Illustrative Experiment   To illustrate, let us consider an early but classic experiment. In this study, Bandura, Ross, and Ross (1963) brought nursery-school-age children into a room to sit and watch an adult pummel, hit, and kick a large inflated Bobo doll. Some of the model's verbal and motor responses are both bizarre and novel, unlike anything the typical nursery schooler has likely ever seen before, much less ever performed previously. The adult model is neither praised nor punished for his antics; similarly no consequences in the form of either rewards or punishment accrue to the children as they watch the model. So neither observers nor model is reinforced. To determine whether any learning has taken place under these seemingly impoverished conditions, the children are left alone with the same Bobo doll that had previously been the object of the model's aggression. And for comparison purposes, other children who had not observed the model were left alone with the Bobo toy. Hidden assistants recorded the frequency with which a child's behavior matched the behavior of the model. The children who had been exposed to the model were much more likely to exhibit matching responses than the children in the no-model condition. Moreover, many of the bizarre and novel responses exhibited by the adult were accurately reproduced by the child observers. Learning, in the absence of any reinforcers delivered to either the model or the viewer, clearly had taken place; imitation, then, is another means by which novel responses can be acquired. In addition, the experimenters noted the frequency of forms of aggressive behavior that were different from the model's aggressive responses. Again, the children who observed the model scored higher. Watching a model apparently serves another function, namely, eliciting previously acquired responses that belong to the same class of behaviors as those of the model. In the case of the present example, other forms of aggressive expression that already existed in the observer's behavior repertoire, such as poking and name calling, were more likely to be displayed after watching the model act aggressively.

In summary, new responses can be acquired and previously acquired responses can be elicited by observing the behavior of another individual. Moreover, reinforcement is not necessary for these acquisition and eliciting processes to operate.

The Acquisition-Performance Distinction Although responses can be acquired in the absence of reinforcement, this does not imply that the reinforcement contingencies associated with the model's behavior are unimportant. Consider a related study by Bandura (1965). In one condition, the young children saw the adult lavishly rewarded with candy and juice for performing the aggressive acts, while in a second condition, other children saw the model punished. The kind of consequences that the model experienced was important; in the subsequent test for imitation, children who saw the model rewarded displayed more aggressive responses, both imitative and nonimitative, than the children who viewed the punished model. Is our earlier conclusion that reinforcement is unnecessary for acquisition by observation incorrect? To answer this question, it is necessary to examine the second part of Bandura's experiment. In this phase, which followed immediately after the test for imitation, the children in all of the experimental conditions were offered candy incentives to reproduce as many of the model's responses as possible. In spite of the earlier differences between the model-rewarded and model-punished groups, both sets of child observers reproduced almost exactly the same number of model responses. The question is answered: The children who viewed different outcomes to the model differed in their performance of the observed acts, but as the follow-up phase indicates, both groups had "learned," or acquired, the same amount of information during the viewing period. Response consequences, in other words, affect the child's likelihood of performing the model's behavior; these consequences have little effect on the acquisition of responses through imitation.

Long-Term Effects The effects of exposure to models may have long-lasting effects. Hicks (1965) exposed preschool boys and girls to filmed aggressive models. In addition to assessing the immediate effects of exposure, Hicks brought his subjects back to the experimental setting after a six-month period and assessed the amount of imitative aggressive behavior they displayed in a free-play session. Although the amount of imitative aggressive behavior markedly decreased over time, in comparison to control subjects who had never viewed a model, there was still evidence that exposure to an aggressive model had an effect even up to six months after the initial viewing. More recently Eron and his colleagues (1972, 1974) reported that TV viewing may affect aggressive behavior even after a ten-year period. High exposure to televised violence at 8 years of age was positively related with interpersonal aggressiveness in boys at age 19. Clearly, early exposure to aggressive models can have a long-lasting impact.

Representational Processes in Observational Learning

In order to account for the occurrence of imitative learning in the absence of reinforcement, Bandura has offered an information processing theory of observational learning. He has summarized the theory as follows: "While the observer views the model's behavior, the observer codes the modeled actions in the form

Children learn the strangest things from viewing TV. (Alice Kandell, Photo Researchers, Inc.)

of verbal or symbolic images that can later be retrieved when the observer performs the model's actions'' (Bandura, 1971, p. 17). According to this theory, the observer's symbolic or representational responses in the form of images and verbal associates of the model's behavior are clearly central in accounting for imitative learning. The role that symbolic representation plays in observational learning is illustrated in an experiment by Bandura, Grusec, and Menlove (1966). On the assumption that the observer's verbalizations would affect the representational process, a group of 6- to 8-year-old boys and girls were instructed to verbalize the actions of a film model who was exhibiting some novel play behaviors. This verbalization procedure was intended to facilitate the development of symbolic representations of the models' responses. While other children passively observed, a third group was instructed to count, an activity that was assumed to interfere with and retard the acquisition of imaginal correlates of the model's behavior. In support of the theory, subjects in the facilitating symbolization condition were clearly superior in reproducing the model's responses (see Figure 6-3). Later research by Coates and Hartup (1969), however, suggests that the importance of verbalization for acquisition and retention of imitative responses is dependent on the age of the child. In a study of 4- and 7-year-old children, they compared passive observation with two

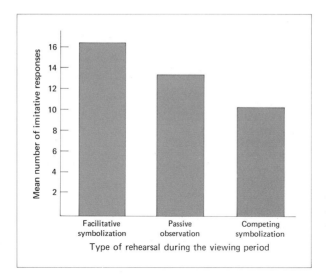

FIGURE 6-3 The effects of different types of viewer rehearsal on observational learning. *(Plotted from Bandura, Grusec, & Menlove, 1966.)*

types of verbalization: *induced verbalization*, in which the subjects were told how to describe the model's actions during exposure, and *free verbalization*, in which the subjects were asked to describe the model's actions in their own words during exposure. A number of interesting findings emerged from this experiment. Since children tend to verbalize spontaneously to a greater extent as they grow older, it was not surprising to find that the verbalization procedures benefited the younger children more than their older peers. While both induced and free verbalization increased the younger children's reproduction of the model's responses, the induced verbalization procedure was superior. Probably this is due to young children's limited practice in verbalization production which, in turn, resulted in the children in the free verbalization condition emitting fewer accurate verbalizations during the exposure period than subjects in the induced verbalization group.

In order to understand the development of imitative learning, both age and the type of coding activity clearly need to be considered. However, these experiments indicate that the nature of the observer's activity during the viewing period can markedly influence observational learning. More specifically, this research suggests that symbolization clearly enhances the acquisition of and retention of imitative responses. For an applied example of the role of symbolic mediators in observational learning from TV, see Box 6-3. Finally, these experiments question the adequacy of theories which stress the necessity of reinforcement for the occurrence of imitative learning.

It should be noted that learning by imitation is not restricted to mere mimicry, whereby the observer is limited to the exact reproduction of the model's responses. Children are able to abstract conceptual rules from instances of modeled behavior that permit a wide degree of transfer to new tasks and new situations (Bandura, 1977). Observational learning, for example, has been

BOX 6-3
LEARNING PROSOCIAL BEHAVIOR FROM TV VIEWING

In spite of the indictments of TV as a "prep school for delinquents," it should be remembered that TV can be a constructive learning source. Prosocial as well as aggressive lessons can be learned from TV viewing. To assess the impact of watching segments from "Mister Rogers Neighborhood," a program focusing on understanding the feelings of others, expressing sympathy, and helping, was the aim of a recent study. Five- and six year-olds either watched a prosocial TV program once a day for four days or watched a neutral program. The children not only *learned* from watching "Mister Rogers Neighborhood" the specific presocial content of the TV program, but also were able to apply that learning to other situations involving children. In comparison to those who saw the neutral TV shows, then, the children who saw the prosocial programs learned some generalized rules about prosocial behavior. Two procedures designed to increase learning and retention were examined. First, a verbal labeling training was used in which the themes from the program were labeled in storybooks. At the end of each program the children read the story and repeated the labels from the story and gave

Research indicates that the amount of television violence seen by preschool children can affect them in different ways. *Mister Rogers' Neighborhood* is a prosocial television show in comparison to other shows which stress aggression. (Sandy Speiser, courtesy of *Mr. Rogers' Neighborhood*, Family Communications, Inc.)

examples of the behaviors or feelings labeled. This is similar to a verbal rehearsal strategy. Other children received role-play training, in which the program themes were rehearsed using hand puppets. Finally, some children experienced both types of training. The verbal-labeling training, which involved listening to a story and rehearsing the labels had the greatest impact on verbal measures of learning, particularly for girls. To measure the impact of the exposure and training on behavior, a helping situation was devised in which children were given the opportunity to aid another child in completing a picture collage that had been accidentally knocked over. Role playing, in combination with exposure to the prosocial program, increased helping behavior for both boys and girls, but boys were most dramatically affected by the role-play experience.

In summary, exposure to prosocial TV not only increases knowledge about prosocial behavior, but when combined with other training aids such as verbal labeling and role playing, can increase helping behavior in a situation that is very different and far removed from the television program. TV is clearly an important learning medium, not only for aggressive behavior, but for prosocial behavior as well. ■

Source: Freidrich, L. K., & Stein, A. H. Prosocial television and young children: The effects of verbal labeling and role playing on learning and behavior. *Child Development*, 1975, **46**, 27–36.

---

found to be effective in teaching children generalized language rules, concepts, and problem-solving and question-asking strategies (Zimmerman, 1977). Children have learned rules for using prepositions, passive tenses, and other particulars of English grammar through imitation. In summary, observational learning is an important avenue for the acquisition of new behaviors and the modification of old response patterns, and most importantly, it is a technique for the acquisition of not only specific, but highly generalizable and flexible, response patterns. Throughout the remaining chapters, numerous instances of observational learning will be presented.

Generalization and Discrimination

Classical conditioning, operant conditioning, and observational learning are highly useful techniques for changing children's behavior, but our discussion has focused on the learning of specific behavior patterns exhibited in particular situations. To understand how children learn to behave appropriately in many different situations and to account for the obvious fact that the children do not have to learn the appropriate behaviors for each new situation that they encounter, we turn to two important learning principles—discrimination and generalization.

Generalization

Stimulus Generalization   One of the important features of learning is the child's ability to recognize similarities between new stimuli and previously experienced objects and events. In other words, a child need not learn to respond to every situation as a unique and novel experience; she can draw upon her past history to help her decide how to react by noticing the similarities between the present context and past situations. This process of transferring previously acquired responses or habits from one stimulus situation to a new context is known as *stimulus generalization*. Its importance stems from the time and energy that it saves the child; generalization makes daily living a much more economical and effortless business, and therefore this capacity has clear adaptive significance. But generalization can have unfortunate and detrimental consequences as well. The following example will serve two functions: to illustrate the principle of stimulus generalization and to indicate some of the negative, maladaptive consequences of overgeneralization.

The following letter was taken from an advice column of a metropolitan newspaper:

Dear Abby:
My girlfriend fixed me up with a blind date and I should have known the minute he showed up in a bow tie that he couldn't be trusted. I fell for him like a rock. He got me to love him on purpose and then lied to me and cheated on me. Every time I go with a man who wears a bow tie, the same thing happens. I think girls should be warned about men who wear them.

AGAINST BOW TIES

Dear Against:
Don't condemn all men who wear bow ties because of your experience. I know many a man behind a bow tie who can be trusted.

(Cited by Bandura & Walters, 1963)

As the amusing exchange indicates, overzealous generalization can lead to unfortunate consequences; discrimination is necessary as well. Bandura and Walters point out the lesson of these letters as follows:

A generalized response is inappropriate when it occurs to a stimulus element that is not regularly correlated with the other elements of the stimulus complex in which the response was originally learned. The letter-writer had generalized a whole pattern of behavior to the bow tie, an object which one would not expect to be regularly associated with the response characteristics of the wearer. (Bandura & Walters, 1963, p. 9)

A number of variables affect the degree of stimulus generalization. The physical similarity of the two stimulus situations is one important determinant. A 5-year-old boy who is chased by a large Afghan hound is more likely to react with fear and flight at the sight of a German shepherd than a miniature poodle; the physical similarity between the Afghan and the German shepherd is likely to suggest that their reactions to small boys might be similar as well.

This observation can be summarized by the following principle: The greater the similarity that exists between the original and the generalization situations, the greater the probability that the same behavior will be exhibited in the two situations. This principle is termed a *gradient of generalization*.

Other types of stimulus generalization occur as well; these depend not so much on the physical similarity that exists between two situations, but rather on the perceived similarity as a result of the two situations sharing the same meaning or the same conceptual label or belonging to the same class or linguistic grouping. We will encounter examples of this in Chapter 8.

Response Generalization   Children generalize not only along stimulus dimensions, but along response dimensions as well; they learn to substitute different but related responses to the same stimulus. Let us turn again to our dog-fearing child to illustrate this type of generalization. One reaction to the sight of a dog might be to cry. However, the emotion of fear can be expressed in a variety of ways, and crying is only one manifestation of fear. The child could have hidden his face in his hands, screamed for help, or run away from the frightening animal. The same fear stimulus can evoke a slightly different response, illustrating the principle of response generalization.

Or consider some examples of response generalization of aggression. Children who are encouraged to punch tend to kick and scratch often as well, even though these behaviors were never involved in the original training. These other responses generalized from the original training in punching behavior. Response generalization can often occur between verbal and physical behaviors as well; for example, a child who attacks with angry, hostile words may on a later occasion generalize the aggressiveness and punch his or her target rather than simply call him a nasty name. Recent research has shown that young children or adolescents who were rewarded for speaking aggressive words were more likely to act in a physically aggressive fashion toward one of their peers (Slaby, 1974). These findings illustrate the process of response generalization.

Discrimination   Not only must children develop the ability to detect similarities among stimuli that they encounter; they must learn to notice differences as well. One of the important lessons is learning to discriminate among objects, events, people, and situations. Children must learn to discriminate their mother from strangers, licorice from chocolate, A's from Z's, and antelopes from zebras.

Moreover, children not only learn to discriminate among different objects, but also among different situations and the responses that are appropriate to these situations. For example, children quickly learn they can run outside on the playground, but this behavior is taboo in the classroom. Similarly, children learn that they may be able to use their brother for practicing their boxing skills, but punching their father is not a good idea. This is an important form of learning, and much effort has been spent on discovering ways of improving children's discrimination skills.

In a typical discrimination learning task, the child is presented with two or more different stimuli either both at once (simultaneous discrimination) or one after the other (successive discrimination). Typically by rewarding one and not rewarding the other(s), the child's speed of learning to choose the correct one increases. Generally, simultaneous discriminations are easier to learn than successive ones.

Finally, various techniques have been developed to help children make discriminations among objects in both the laboratory and the world about them. For example, labeling an object with a special name can aid children in discriminating one object from another. To demonstrate this beneficial effect of verbal labels on discrimination, Norcross and Spiker (1957) taught one group of children to give specific names to two different faces, such as Megan and Amy. Other children did not label the two pictures. When the children were required to discriminate between one of the faces and a different face, children who had been trained to label the faces were better able to discriminate these faces from other faces. Labeling helped them discriminate among different faces. Moreover, the distinctiveness of the label is important too. It is probably easier for children to learn to recognize the different girls in their classroom at the start of the new school year if all the girls have different names than if there are three Susans and two Jills. Distinctive verbal labels or names play an important role in helping us discriminate among people and events. We will discuss this role of verbal processes in discrimination learning again in Chapter 10.

Inhibition of Behavior

Not only are procedures that increase the occurrence of a behavior important, but tactics to weaken or eliminate undesirable behaviors are also of both practical and theoretical interest. Indeed, during childhood socialization the child must learn acceptable, prosocial behavior, but in addition, he or she must learn to inhibit or suppress undesirable and unacceptable behaviors. Moreover, maladaptive responses, such as excessive fears, often require weakening in order to permit adequate development. Procedures that inhibit behavior, therefore, play an important role in naturalistic socialization and in therapeutic situations as well.

In this section, two methods of weakening or inhibiting children's responses will be discussed—extinction and punishment.

Extinction   In the case of operant conditioning, the presentation of the reinforcement maintains behavior; similarly, withholding the reinforcement following the response will weaken and eventually eliminate the behavior. In the case of classical conditioning, if the conditioned stimulus continues to be presented without pairing it with the unconditioned stimulus, eventually the conditioned stimulus will lose its power to elicit the conditioned response. These procedures are termed experimental *extinction*.

The effectiveness of an extinction procedure is nicely illustrated by a case study of excessive crying reported by Williams (1959). The subject was a 21-month-old child who regularly protested being separated from his parents at bedtime by insistently screaming and crying until someone attended to him. The attention that his tantrum behavior produced, however, served only to increase the strength of this undesirable behavior. The parents tried a new approach; they ignored his crying behavior after bedtime routines had been completed. As Figure 6-4 illustrates, the results were dramatic. There was a marked decrease in the duration of the tantrum episode, and within a week the troublesome behavior had virtually disappeared. It was necessary to repeat the extinction procedure a short time later due to the intervention of a "helpful" grandmother who insisted on responding to the infant's crying. However, extinction was again successful, and no adverse side effects were apparent after a two-year follow-up.

One factor that affects the rate of extinction is the previous reinforcement history of the individual. Extinction is slower following intermittent reward than after continuous reinforcement. A study by Brackbill (1958) on infant smiling provides an illustration of this principle. Using eight infants between $3^{1}/_{2}$ and $4^{1}/_{2}$ months of age as subjects, she first measured the amount of smiling to a motionless and expressionless face. Following this period, Brackbill placed four infants on a continuous reinforcement schedule and the remaining four infants first on a continuous, then on an intermittent, schedule. Reinforcement consisted of the experimenter smiling, speaking softly to, picking up, patting, and talking to the infant. When reinforcements were discontinued, the experimenter stood motionless and expressionless when the infants smiled. During the extinction period there was a decline in the mean number of responses given by both groups of infants. However, the intermittently reinforced infants smiled at a higher rate during extinction than did the continuously reinforced subjects. These data illustrate another feature of the early stages of extinction, namely a

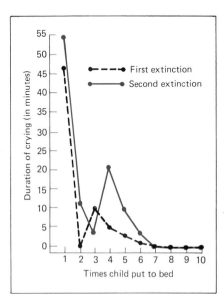

FIGURE 6-4 Length of crying in two extinction series as a function of successive occasions of being put to bed. *(From Williams, 1959, with permission of the author and the American Psychological Association.)*

heightened rate and intensity of responding. That is, the infant appears to be protesting the fact that reinforcement has stopped and therefore exerts a greater effort in order to reinstate the vanished rewards. Often emotional responses different from the behavior previously reinforced can be detected as well. In the Brackbill experiment this can be seen quite clearly; the incidence of crying and fussing increased in the early stages of extinction.

Intermittently reinforced children have greater difficulty determining when reinforcement has occurred for the last time, whereas continuously rewarded subjects should experience an abrupt and easily recognized shift when extinction begins. Research with children (Kass & Wilson, 1966), in fact, has supported this explanation of the persistence of intermittently reinforced behaviors.

Punishment
In punishment, a noxious stimulus is associated with a particular response and thereby makes this response less likely to occur. The anxiety or fear that is generated by the unpleasant event (for example, a swat on the bottom, a verbal rebuke, or an electric shock) comes to be associated via classical conditioning with the originally pleasant and rewarding response. The result is suppression of the punished behavior. Punishment has been used for many years by parents, although the "experts" in psychology assumed that punishment was an extremely ineffective means of controlling human behavior. Possibly the harried and harrassed parents who have used punishment as a way of disciplining their

There is still some controversy regarding how beneficial punishment really is. (*Science World*, vol. 22, no.4, March 1, 1971)

Punishment–Does It Help or Hurt?

charges have been wiser than the experts, for recent research has shown that punishment can, under certain circumstances, be an effective control technique (Parke, 1972, 1977).

Factors Affecting the Operation of Punishment   Recent laboratory studies of the effects of punishment on children's behavior have revealed that its effectiveness is dependent on a variety of factors, just as we saw in the case of positive reinforcement. The factors that seem to be most important in punishment are the timing, the severity, the consistency, the relationship between agent and recipient of punishment, and the type of rationale that accompanies the punishment. As in the case of positive reinforcement, temporal factors are critical, as the following study of the effects of timing of punishment on children's behavior illustrates (Walters, Parke, & Cane, 1965). These investigators presented 6- to 8-year-old boys with pairs of toys, one attractive and one unattractive, over a series of trials. Punishment consisting of a verbal rebuke, "No that's for the other boy," was delivered when they chose the attractive toy. One group of children was punished as they approached the attractive toy, but before they actually touched it. For the remaining boys, punishment was delivered only after they had picked up the critical toy. Following the punishment training session, the boys were left alone with the attractive toys for a fifteen-minute period. The extent to which the child touched the toys in the absence of the adult was recorded by an observer hidden behind a one-way screen. The timing of the punishment clearly affected the children's behavior: the early punished children touched the taboo toys less than did the boys punished late in the response sequence. Extensions of this experimental model indicate that this finding is merely one aspect of a general relation: The longer the delay between the initiation of the act and the onset of punishment, the less effective the punishment for producing response inhibition (Aronfreed, 1968).

The delay periods in all these studies were relatively short. In everyday life, detection of a deviant act is often delayed many hours, or the punishment may be postponed, for example, until the father returns home. In light of the evidence already described, it is not surprising that this type of delayed discipline is often ineffective. One way of increasing the effectiveness of delayed discipline involves describing the reason for punishment just before punishing the child (Verna, 1977).

Another determinant of punishment effectiveness is intensity, and laboratory studies (Parke, 1969) using noises of different levels of loudness as punishment have indicated that as the "intensity" of punishment increases, the amount of inhibition increases. However, it is highly questionable whether high-intensity punishment, such as severe physical punishment, is justified as a disciplinary technique under real-life circumstances. Particularly, if adults are careful in the timing and consistency of their discipline, high-intensity punishment is probably unnecessary in order to achieve control. Moreover, ethical and practical considerations must serve as important guides concerning the choice of intensity levels; the routine use of *severe* punishment, in fact, may often be a first step in the development of child abuse (Parke & Collmer, 1975). Obviously, parental control is a prerequisite to the effective utilization of punishment as a method of child control.

The nature of the relationship between the agent and recipient of punishment is a third determinant. Punishment delivered by a parent who has previously established a warm and nurturant relationship with a child is much more likely to be effective than the same kind of punishment delivered by a cool and aloof parent (Parke, 1969; Sears, Maccoby, and Levin, 1957).

One of the most difficult problems faced by parents, teachers, and other disciplinary agents is being consistent in their disciplinary actions. On a busy day, a parent may ignore a disruptive child, while on another day, the parent may punish the child for the same misbehavior. Or sometimes parents disagree. A father may laugh at his son's headstands in the living room, while a mother may punish her son for these same gymnastic antics. Regardless of the type of inconsistency, erratically administered punishment is less effective in achieving control than consistently delivered discipline (Parke & Deur, 1972; Sawin & Parke, 1977). There are other consequences of being inconsistent as well. Once you have been inconsistent, it is more difficult to gain control even with consistent techniques. Consider this experiment by Deur and Parke (1970) in which some children were punished and rewarded by an adult while others were rewarded either consistently or half of the times that they punched a Bobo doll—the measure of aggression used in this study. Subsequently they were either punished consistently or received no reward or punishment. In learning-theory terms, these latter subjects were on an extinction schedule. Figure 6-5 shows the results. The punished boys made fewer hitting responses than did subjects in the extinction condition, which suggests that punishment was

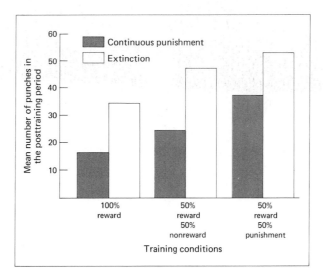

FIGURE 6-5 The effects of different types of reward and punishment training on persistence during extinction and continuous punishment for 6- to 9-year-old boys. *(After Deur & Parke, 1970, with permission of the American Psychological Association.)*

effective in inhibiting the aggressive behavior. However, the boys who had previously been inconsistently punished showed the greatest resistance to extinction. Moreover, these previously punished children tended to persist longer in the face of consistent punishment than did the boys in the other training groups. The implication is clear: The socializing agent using inconsistent punishment builds up resistance to future attempts to either extinguish it or suppress it by consistently administered punishment. It is possible that parents who inconsistently punish their children may build up strongly established patterns of aggressive and deviant behavior which are highly resistant to the use of punitive control.

Is punishment more effective when the parent or teacher provides a reason for the punishment they administer? According to both field studies of childrearing (Sears et al., 1957) and laboratory studies (Parke, 1969), punishment is more effective when accompanied by a rationale. Moreover, the importance of such factors as the timing, intensity, and the parent-child relationship is lessened when a rationale accompanies the punishment. For example, the relative superiority of early versus late-timed punishment or high- versus low-intensity discipline disappears when the child is given a reason for being punished. However, the effectiveness of different types of reasoning procedures for producing inhibition varies with the developmental level of the child. The

Discipline is most effective when accompanied by a verbal explanation. (Christy Park, Monkmeyer)

successful disciplinarian chooses a rationale that fits the cognitive level of the child, so that the child will readily understand the adult's reasons. Young children (3-year-olds), for example, are more effectively controlled by a very concrete explanation ("Don't touch the toy; it's fragile and may break"), while an abstract property rationale ("Don't touch the toy; it belongs to someone else") is more effective with 5-year-olds (Parke, 1974). The length of the explanation as well as content of the rationale determines the effectiveness of different rationales at different ages. Since young children have shorter attention spans and are able to process less information than older children, lengthy explanations may not be very effective with young children. Hetherington (1975), for example, found that parents who used brief explanations with young children gained better control over their offspring's behavior than parents who used long and involved explanations. Long-windedness—particularly with young children—simply isn't very effective! Together the findings emphasize the importance of considering developmental factors in studies of different types of control tactics.

Finally, before closing this discussion, turn to Box 6-4, which serves as a reminder that children play an active role in shaping adult disciplinary choices.

Applications of Punishment   In recent years, punishment has been increasingly employed by child clinical psychologists as a therapeutic procedure. A recent highly dramatic study of this type will illustrate not only the effectiveness of punishment, but its application as a treatment technique as well.

To illustrate that severe punishment in the form of electric shock can have therapeutic value, consider the work of Ivor Lovaas, who has applied punishment techniques to the treatment of retarded and mentally disturbed children. Here is one case:

John was a seven-year-old boy, diagnosed as retarded (IQ 25), with psychotic-like behaviors. He had been self-injurious since he was two years of age, a behavior which necessitated his hospitalization one year prior to his being studied at UCLA. During that year he had to be kept in complete restraints (legs, waist, and with a camisole to restrain his arms) on a 24-hour a day basis. When removed from restraint he would immediately hit his head against the crib, beat his head with his fists, and scream. He looked extremely frightened when removed from restraints. He was so unmanageable that he had to be fed in full restraints; he would not take food otherwise. His head was covered with scar tissue, and his ears were swollen and bleeding. (Bucher & Lovaas, 1968, p. 86)

Only after other techniques had failed did Lovaas resort to electric shock. Consider the results for a simple extinction procedure, for example. On the assumption that attention in the form of sympathetic comments by ward personnel often increased rather than decreased self-destructive behavior, the child was left alone without restraints with no attention given to his self-destructive actions. Although after eight days the child's self-destructive behavior was nearly extinguished, he still hit himself nearly 10,000 times in the process.

Box 6-4
THE CHILD'S ROLE IN SPARING
THE ROD

 Children are not passive recipients of adult behavior; children shape adults just as adults shape children. Even in disciplinary contexts, this principle operates, and the following studies illustrate how children can modify adult disiciplinary choices.

In one study, adult females were given the opportunity to administer rewards and punishments to a 7-year-old boy. They were first shown a videotape of two boys sitting at desks in a school-like context. They were asked to assist in assessing "how adults and children can interact by means of a remote closed-circuit television monitoring and control system that might be used in understaffed day-care facilities to supplement regular person-to-person contacts." The adult was asked to evaluate the boys' behavior by delivering or removing points that could be later traded in for varying amounts of free-play time. In fact, the children's behavior on the videotapes

was prerecorded and the adult's feedback to the child was surreptitiously recorded by the experimenter. To evaluate the impact of children's behavior on adult disciplinary actions, adults saw one of four videotaped sequences, which were similar except for one section of the tape. All tapes showed one boy pushing a second child's workbook off his desk. Prior to the adult's opportunity to discipline or reward the child, the deviant child gave one of four reactions: (1) reparation—offered to pick up the book, (2) pleading—pleaded for leniency, (3) ignoring—turned his back to the adult, (4) defiance—acted in a defiant fashion by saying "It was a dumb book anyway." Although all the children were punished, the amount of punishment varied. The adults who saw the reparative child, who offered to correct his misbehavior, delivered the least amount of punishment, while the adults who saw the child ignore the adult or behave in a defiant fashion delivered the harshest punishment. The way that a child reacts after

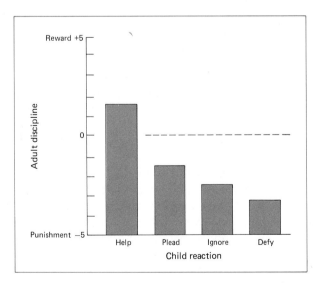

FIGURE 6-6 Adult discipline in response to children's reactions to prior punishment. *(From Parke & Sawin, 1977, with permission of the senior author.)*

misbehaving but before the adult administers punishment can significantly modify the severity of the adult's disciplinary behavior.

In a related study, the impact of the child's reaction *after* being disciplined on the adults' later disciplinary actions was examined. As in the earlier study, an adult monitored children on a videotape. Again, one of the children misbehaved, but this time the adult was allowed to finish punishing the child before viewing the child's reaction to being punished. One of four reactions followed: (1) reparation, (2) pleading, (3) ignoring, or (4) defiance. Immediately following the target child's reaction to being punished, the adult was signaled to respond again; this was the crucial test trial since it followed immediately on the child's reaction to the prior discipline. As Figure 6-6 illustrates, the subsequent discipline was significantly affected by the child's reaction to the earlier adult discipline. In fact, the adults who witnessed the child make reparation were *not* even punitive, but were mildly rewarding. As in the earlier study, the defiance and ignoring reactions elicited the most severe punitive reactions from the adults. The study clearly demonstrates that children's reactions to discipline serve as determinants of how severely they will be dealt with on future occasions. Children can play a role in sparing the rod! ■

Source: Parke, R. D., & Sawin, D. B. The child's role in sparing the rod. Unpublished manuscript, University of Illinois, 1977.

Punishment, an electric shock, produced dramatic results. The self-destructive behavior was virtually eliminated by the administration of a total of twelve shocks over fifteen sessions. In addition, the child cried less and avoided attending adults less following the treatment. In this case, at least, the punishment not only was an effective therapeutic procedure, but even resulted in some positive side effects. However, this is probably not always true, and only in the most unusual circumstances would the use of such severe punishment be ethically and morally justified. In the present case, there is little question; punishment was a humane treatment.

Side Effects of Punishment Punishment can have undesirable side effects, which may limit its usefulness. Parents who use physical punishment may be inadvertently providing an aggressive model. Bandura has summarized this viewpoint:

When a parent punishes his child physically for having aggressed toward peers for example, the intended outcome of this training is that the child should refrain from hitting others. The child, however, is also learning from parental demonstration how to aggress physically. And, the imitative learning may provide the direction for the child's behavior when he is similarly frustrated in subsequent social interactions. (Bandura, 1967, p. 43)

Support for this possibility comes from childrearing field studies (Becker, 1964; Eron, Walder, Huesmann, & Lefkowitz, 1974), as well as from laboratory studies (Parke, 1972; Gelfand, Hartmann, Lamb, Smith, Mahan, & Paul, 1974). Another negative side effect is the avoidance of the punishing agent. This is illustrated in a recent study by Redd, Morris, and Martin (1975) in which 5-year-old children interacted with three different adults who employed various control strategies. One adult behaved in a positive manner and smiled and made positive comments ("Good," "Nice boy," "Tremendous") while the child performed a color-sorting task. A second adult dispensed mild verbal reprimands whenever the child deviated from the sorting task (for example, "Stop throwing the tokens around," "Don't play with the chair"). A third adult was present but didn't comment on the child's behavior. While the results indicated that the punitive adult was most effective in keeping the children working on the task, the children tended to prefer the positive and neutral agents more than the punitive adult. When asked to indicate which adult they wished to work with a little longer, the children always chose the positive adult. Similarly, the children always avoided the punitive adult as their partner on other tasks or as a playmate. The implication is clear: Punishment may be an effective modification technique, but the use of punishment by adults may lead the child to avoid that socializing agent and therefore undermine the adult's effectiveness as a future influence on the child's behavior.

This review leaves little doubt that punishment can be an effective means of controlling children's behavior. The operation of punishment, however, is a complex process, and its effects are quite varied and highly dependent on such parameters as timing, intensity, consistency, and the affectional relationship between the agent and recipient of punishment.

It is unlikely that a socialization program based solely on punishment would be very effective; the child needs to be taught new appropriate responses in addition to learning to suppress unacceptable forms of behavior.

In fact, in real-life situations the suppressive effect of punishment is usually only of value if alternative pro-social responses are elicited and strengthened while the undesirable behavior is held in check. The primary practical value of studies of parameters that influence the efficacy of punishment is . . . to determine the conditions under which suppression will most likely occur. (Walters & Parke, 1967, p. 217).

From this viewpoint, punishment is only one technique which can be used in concert with other training techniques, such as positive reinforcement, to shape, direct, and control the behavior of the developing child. As Box 6-5 illustrates, reinforcement of incompatible responses is an effective alternative to punishment. The advantage of this technique is that the unwanted side effects associated with punishment can be avoided.

TABLE 6-1 AVERAGE NUMBER OF RESPONSES IN THE VARIOUS CATE-GORIES OF AGGRESSION

Time of observation	Categories of aggression		
	Physical	Verbal	Total
Pretreatment	41.2	22.8	64.0
First treatment	26.0	17.4	43.4
Follow-up	37.8	13.8	51.6
Second treatment	21.0	4.6	25.6

BOX 6-5
REINFORCEMENT OF
INCOMPATIBLE BEHAVIOR

The encouragement of alternative responses that are inconsistent with the expression of disruptive classroom behavior, such as cooperative behaviors, is a particularly important technique for controlling undesirable behavior.

Brown and Elliott (1965) applied this technique to a practical problem: controlling aggression in a nursery school class of twenty-seven boys. Instead of disrupting the routine by introducing experimenters who would interact with the children, these investigators trained the teachers to carry out their research program. The following instructions to the teachers nicely illustrate the aim:

We will try to ignore aggression and reward cooperative and peaceful behavior. Of course, if someone is using a hammer on another's head, we would step in, but just to separate the two and leave. It will be difficult at first, because we tend to watch and be quiet when nothing is happening, and now our attention will, as much as possible, be directed toward cooperative, or nonaggressive behavior. It would be good to let the most aggressive boys see that the others are getting the attention if it is possible. A pat on the head, "That's good Mike," "Hello Chris and Mark, how are you today?," "Look what Eric made," etc., may have more rewarding power than we think. On the other hand, it is just as important during this week to have no reprimands, no "Say you're sorry," "Aren't you sorry?" Not that these aren't useful ways of teaching proper behavior, but they will only cloud the effects of our other manner of treatment. It would be best not even to look at a shove or small fight if we are sure no harm is being done; as I mentioned before, if it is necessary we should just separate the children and leave.

Prior to the treatment phase, observations of the boys' aggressive responses were gathered for a week. Two weeks later the first treatment period was initiated, and it lasted for two weeks. Ratings were taken during the second week of this period. Teachers were then told that the experiment was over and that they were no longer constrained in their behavior toward aggressive acts. In order to assess the durability of the treatment, a set of ratings was taken three weeks later. Finally, the treatment was reinstituted for two weeks. The results summarized in Table 6-1 show dramatic reduction in the frequency of aggressive responses following treatment.

This study not only illustrates the importance of reinforcement of prosocial behavior for controlling aggression, but also demonstrates the often paradoxical role played by teacher "attention." Note that when the teachers were allowed to attend to the aggressive behaviors that they were previously ignoring as part of the treatment, the frequency of physical aggression increased. Naturally, the teacher in "paying attention" to the aggressive child hopes to decrease the frequency of this kind of behavior. However, as this study and a variety of other systematic observational studies (for example, Harris, Wolf, & Baer, 1964) have clearly shown, attending to deviant responses with a mild rebuke or reprimand may often serve to maintain or even increase aggressive and troublesome behaviors. Possibly, behaving aggressively is used by children as an attention-seeking tactic. However, as the Brown and Elliott study suggests, this is less likely to occur in situations where the child is provided alternative means of gaining adult attention. There is another important feature of this technique. It avoids some of the undesirable consequences usually associated with the use of punishment for suppressing aggression. For instance, it is unlikely that this approach would lead to an increase in aggressive behavior in situations different from the disciplinary context. ∎

Source: Brown, P., & Elliott, R. Control of aggression in a nursery school class. *Journal of Experimental Child Psychology,* 1965, **2**, 103–107.

Summary

A variety of different aspects of learning were presented in this chapter. First, classical and operant conditioning were distinguished. Classical conditioning involves the pairing of two events, such as a noise and food, with the result that *both* the noise and the food elicit reactions (salivating) that were previously only linked with the food. Even in infancy this type of learning occurs, although there is still some controversy concerning how early infants can be classically conditioned. Operant conditioning, unlike classical conditioning, requires that the child first make a response and then experience some consequence for her behavior. According to this type of learning, conditioning occurs when a response is followed by a reinforcing event. Even newborn infants can learn in this way, but only if the delay interval between response and reward is brief. The schedule of reinforcement is an important determinant of the effectiveness of operant learning. Under extinction, a condition when no reinforcing consequences follow a response, children who experience intermittent schedules persist for a longer period than children exposed to continuous reinforcement.

Imitation or learning by observation of others is another effective learning technique. Children acquire new responses and modify existing behaviors as a result of exposure to peer and adult models. A variety of factors affect this type of learning, particularly the consequences (reward or punishment) experienced by the model. Age changes in observational learning occur, as do shifts in the effectiveness of different types of strategies for coding and remembering the model's behavior. Television is one of the most widespread ways that children learn by observation; both new cognitive skills and social behaviors can be learned by TV viewing, and old behaviors can be modified and maintained.

Next we explored two related processes: discrimination and generalization. Effective learning requires that children learn to notice distinctive features or parts of objects and people in order to distinguish among parts of their environment. Labeling often helps this discrimination process.

Not only do children develop the ability to detect differences among stimuli, but they learn to notice similarities. The process of transferring previously acquired responses to a new situation is known as stimulus generalization. Response generalization involves the substitution of a different but related response to a similar stimulus. Children cry on one occasion but may run at the sight of the same fear stimulus on another occasion.

Procedures that weaken or eliminate behaviors were considered. Extinction, a procedure involving the removal of the conditions that maintain a behavior, was discussed. The decrease in the occurrence of a response after removal of reinforcement illustrates extinction. Punishment, another technique for producing inhibition, was discussed. It was suggested that punishment can be effective, but a variety of controlling factors, such as timing, intensity, the nature of the adult-child relationship, and consistency, need to be considered.

Some of the side effects of punishment, such as increasing aggressiveness in children and avoiding the punishing adult, were noted. Reinforcement of incompatible behaviors was recommended as an alternative to punishment.

References

Aronfreed, J. *Conduct and conscience.* New York: Academic, 1968.

Bandura, A. Social learning through imitation. In M. R. Jones (Ed.), *Nebraska symposium on motivation: 1962.* Lincoln: University of Nebraska Press, 1962, pp. 211–269.

Bandura, A. Influence of model's reinforcement contingencies on the acquisition of imitative responses. *Journal of Personality and Social Psychology*, 1965, **1,** 589–595.

Bandura, A. The role of modeling processes in personality development. In W. W. Hartup & N. L. Smothergill (Eds.), *The young child* (Vol. I). Washington: National Association for the Education of Young Children, 1967, pp. 42–58.

Bandura, A. (Ed.). *Psychological modeling.* Chicago: Atherton, 1971.

Bandura, A. *Social learning theory.* Englewood Cliffs, N.J.: Prentice-Hall, 1977.

Bandura, A., Grusec, J., & Menlove, F. L. Observational learning as a function of symbolization and incentive set. *Child Development*, 1966, **37,** 499–506.

Bandura, A., Ross, D., & Ross, S. A. Imitation of film-mediated aggressive models. *Journal of Abnormal and Social Psychology*, 1963, **66,** 3–11.

Bandura, A., & Walters, R. H. *Social learning and personality development.* New York: Holt, 1963.

Becker, W. C. Consequences of different kinds of parental discipline. In M. L. Hoffman & L. W. Hoffman (Eds.), *Review of child development research* (Vol. 1). New York: Russell Sage Foundation, 1964.

Brackbill, Y. Extinction of the smiling response in infants as a function of reinforcement schedules. *Child Development*, 1958, **29,** 115–124.

Brown, P., & Elliott, R. Control of aggression in a nursery school class. *Journal of Experimental Child Psychology*, 1965, **2,** 103–107.

Bucher, B., & Lovaas, I. Use of aversive stimulation in behavior modification. In M. R. Jones (Ed.), *Miami symposium on the prediction of behavior 1967: Aversive stimulation.* Miami: University of Miami Press, 1968.

Clifton, R., Siqueland, E. R., & Lipsitt, L. P. Conditioned head turning in human newborns as a function of conditioned response requirements and states of wakefulness. *Journal of Experimental Child Psychology*, 1972, **13,** 43–57.

Clifton, R. K. Heartrate conditioning in the newborn infant. *Journal of Experimental Child Psychology*, 1974, **18,** 9–21.

Coates, B., & Hartup, W. W. Age and verbalization in observational learning. *Developmental Psychology*, 1969, **1,** 556–562.

Deur, J. L., & Parke, R. D. The effects of inconsistent punishment on aggression in children. *Developmental Psychology*, 1970, **2,** 403–411.

Ellingson, R. J. The study of brain electrical activity in infants. In L. P. Lipsitt & C. C. Spiker (Eds.), *Advances in child development and behavior* (Vol. 3). New York: Academic, 1967.

Eron, L. D., Lefkowitz, M. M., Huesmann, L. R., & Walder, L. O. Does television violence cause aggression? *American Psychologist*, 1972, **27,** 253–263.

Eron, L. D., Walder, L. O., Huesmann, L. R., & Lefkowitz, M. M. The convergence of laboratory and field studies of the development of aggression. In J. de Wit and W. W. Hartup (Eds.), *Determinants and origins of aggressive behavior.* The Hague: Mouton, 1974.

Fitzgerald, H. E., & Brackbill, Y. Classical conditioning in infancy: Development and constraints. *Psychological Bulletin*, 1976, **83,** 353–376.

Freidrich, L. K., & Stein, A. H. Prosocial television and young children: The effects of verbal labeling and role playing on learning and behavior. *Child Development*, 1975, **46,** 27–38.

Gelfand, D. M., Hartmann, D. P., Lamb, A. K., Smith, C. L., Mahan, M. A., & Paul, S. C. The effects of adult models and described alternatives on children's choice of behavior management techniques. *Child Development*, 1974, **45,** 585–593.

Harris, F. R., Wolf, M. M., & Baer, D. M. Effects of social reinforcement on child behavior. *Young Children*, 1964, **20,** 8–17.

Hetherington, E. M. Children of divorce. Paper presented at the biennial meeting of the Socty for Research in Child Development, Denver, 1975.

Hicks, J. Imitation and retention of film-mediated aggressive peer and adult models. *Journal of Personality and Social Psychology*, 1965, **2,** 97–100.

Kass, N., & Wilson, H. Resistance to extinction as a function of percentage of reinforcement, number of trials, and conditioned reinforcement. *Journal of Experimental Psychology*, 1966, **71,** 355–357.

Lewis, M., Goldberg, S., & Campbell, H. A developmental study of information processing within the first three years of life: Response decrement to a redundant signal. *Monographs of the Society for Research in Child Development*, 1969, **34** (Serial No. 133).

McCall, R. B., Parke, R. D., & Kavanaugh, R. Imitation of live and televised models in children 1–3 years of age. *Monographs of the Society for Research in Child Development*, 1977, **42** (Serial No. 173).

Meltzoff, A. N., & Moore, M. K. Imitation of facial and manual gestures by human neonates. *Science*, 1977, **198,** 75–78.

Moely, B. E., Olsen, F. A., Hawles, T. G., & Flavell, J. H. Production deficiency in young children's clustered recall. *Developmental Psychology*, 1969, **1,** 26–34.

Norcross, K. J., & Spiker, C. C. The effects of type of stimulus pretraining on discrimination performance in preschool children. *Child Development*, 1957, **28,** 79–84.

O'Leary, K. D., Pelham, W. E., Rosenbaum, A., & Price, G. H. Behavioral treatment of hyperkinetic children. *Clinical Pediatrics*, 1976, **15,** 510–515.

O'Leary, S. G., & Pelham, W. E. Behavior therapy and withdrawal of stimulant medication with hyperactive children. *Pediatrics*, 1977, **60,** 101–115.

Papousek, H. Conditioning during early postnatal development. In Y. Brackbill & G. G. Thompson (Eds.), *Behavior in infancy and early childhood*. New York: Free Press, 1967, pp. 259–274.

Parke, R. D. Effectiveness of punishment as an interaction of intensity, timing, agent nurturance and cognitive-structuring. *Child Development,* 1969, **40,** 213–235.

Parke, R. D. Some effects of punishment on children's behavior. In W. W. Hartup (Ed.), *The young child* (Vol. 2). Washington: National Association for the Education of Young Children, 1972, pp. 264–283.

Parke, R. D. Rules, roles, and resistance to deviation: Explorations in punishment, discipline, and self-control. In A. Pick (Ed.), *Minnesota Symposia on Child Psychology*. Minneapolis: University of Minnesota Press, 1974.

Parke, R. D. Punishment in children: Effects, side effects and alternative control strategies. In H. Hom & P. Robinson (Eds.), *Early childhood education: A psychological perspective*. New York: Academic, 1977, pp. 71–97.

Parke, R. D., & Collmer, C. Child abuse: An interdisciplinary analysis. In E. M. Hetherington (Ed.), *Review of child development research* (Vol. 5). Chicago: University of Chicago Press, 1975.

Parke, R. D., & Deur, J. L. Punishment and inhibition of aggression in children. *Developmental Psychology*, 1972, **7,** 266–269.

Parke, R. D., & Sawin, D. B. The child's role in sparing the rod. Unpublished manuscript, University of Illinois, 1977.

Ramey, C. T., and Ourth, L. L. Delayed reinforcement and vocalization rates of infants. *Child Development,* 1971, **42,** 291–297.

Redd, W. H., Morris, E. K., & Martin, J. A. Effects of positive and negative adult-child interactions on children's social preferences. *Journal of Experimental Child Psychology*, 1975, **19**, 153–164.

Rheingold, H., Gewirtz, J. L., & Ross, H. W. Social conditioning of vocalizations in the infant. *Journal of Comparative and Physiological Psychology*, 1959, **52**, 68–73.

Sameroff, A. J. The components of sucking in the human newborn. *Journal of Experimental Child Psychology*, 1968, **6**, 607–623.

Sameroff, A. J. Can conditioned responses be established in the newborn infant: 1971? *Developmental Psychology*, 1971, **5**, 1–12.

Sameroff, A. J. Learning and adaptation in infancy: A comparison of models. In H. W. Reese (Ed.), *Advances in child development and behavior* (Vol. 7). New York: Academic, 1972, pp. 169–214.

Sameroff, A. J., & Cavanaugh, P. J. Learning in infancy: A developmental perspective. In J. Osofsky (Ed.), *Handbook of infant development*. New York: Wiley, 1978.

Sawin, D. B., & Parke, R. D. The effects of inter-agent inconsistency on aggression in children. Unpublished manuscript, University of Texas, 1977.

Sears, R. R., Maccoby, E., & Levin, H. *Patterns of child rearing*. Evanston, Ill.: Row, Peterson, 1957.

Seligman, M. E. P. On the generality of the laws of learning. *Psychological Review*, 1970, **77**, 406–418.

Skinner, B. F. *Science and human behavior*. New York: Macmillan, 1953.

Slaby, R. G. The effects of aggressive and altruistic verbalizations on aggressive and altruistic behaviors. In J. de Wit & W. W. Hartup (Eds.), *Origins and determinants of aggression*. The Hague: Mouton 1974.

Slaby, R. G., & Hollenbeck, A. R. Television influences on visual and vocal behavior of infants. Paper presented at the biennial meeting of the Society for Research in Child Development, New Orleans, March 1977.

Spelt, D. K. The conditioning of the human fetus in utero. *Journal of Experimental Psychology*, 1948, **38**, 375–376.

Stamps, L. E., & Porges, S. W. Heartrate conditioning in newborn infants: Relationships among conditionability, heartrate variability and sex. *Developmental Psychology*, 1975, **11**, 424–431.

Verna, G. B. The effects of four-hour delay of punishment under two conditions of verbal instruction. *Child Development*, 1977, **48**, 621–624.

Walters, R. H., & Parke, R. D. The influence of punishment and related disciplinary techniques on the social behavior or children: Theory and empirical findings. In B. A. Maher (Ed.), *Progress in experimental personality research* (Vol. 4). New York: Academic, 1967, pp. 179–228.

Walters, R. H., Parke, R. D., & Cane, V. A. Timing of punishment and the observation of consequences to others as determinants of response inhibition. *Journal of Experimental Child Psychology*, 1965, **2**, 10–30.

Williams, C. D. The elimination of tantrum behavior by extinction procedures. *Journal of Abnormal and Social Psychology*, 1959, **59**, 269.

Zimmerman, B. J. Modeling. In H. Hom & P. Robinson (Eds.), *Psychological processes in early education*. New York: Academic, 1977.

7

Emotional Development

Children show a wide range of emotional reactions. Sometimes they are elated and happy; at other times, depressed and sullen; and on other occasions, angry. What are the determinants of emotions? How do emotional responses originally develop, and how do they shift with age? In this chapter we will explore the origins and development of emotions and show how early emotional development and social development are related. Smiling, an early index of positive affect, will be examined. Next we will explore the development of attachment, the process by which the infant develops a special affection for particular people. To illustrate the emergence of negative emotions, fear will be examined, with special attention to the development of social fears, particularly fear of strangers. Finally, questions concerning the ways in which children learn to recognize and label their own emotions and emotions in other people will be discussed.

The Functions of Emotions

Children laugh and cry and show fear, anger, love, and affection. What functions do these emotional expressions serve? Emotions can be viewed as forms of communication by which the infant and child can communicate to others information about their current feelings, needs, and desires. By smiling, for example, an infant tells others that an event or object is pleasurable, while by frowning an infant can communicate displeasure. Second, emotions serve to regulate social distance. By smiling, the infant is more likely to maintain contact with his or her caregiver. Similarly, anger may help to keep a stranger at a distance, while sadness and crying cause adults to attend. Emotional signals such as smiles, frowns, and angry outbursts serve other social functions as well. Smiling can be viewed as a form of greeting behavior—a welcome sign to a person who enters a situation. Or children often use emotional expressions to regulate conflict; expressions of anger and threat may deter a potential aggressor, while smiling may serve as a signal of appeasement in a losing-conflict situation. Through emotional displays, then, the infant and young child can communicate their needs and desires and provide one of the earliest means for gaining control over their social world.

We begin our exploration of emotional development with one of the infant's earliest social and emotional expressions—smiling.

Children show a wide range of different emotions. (Photos (a, b, and c) by Erika Stone; photo (d) by Suzanne Szasz)

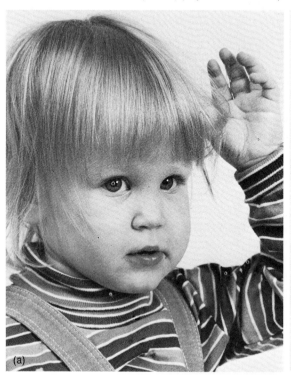

(a)

(b)

(c)

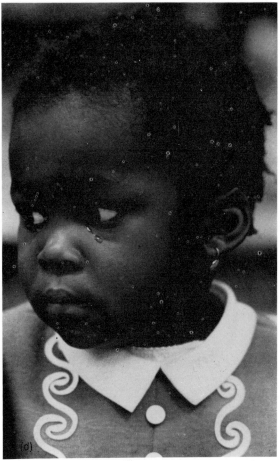

(d)

Early Emotional Development: The Smile as a Social Signal

Infants are organized to emit a wide number of social responses—even from birth. One of the most interesting early social signals for both parents and researchers is the smile. When do infants begin to smile, and how does smiling change over development? Why do they smile? Let us try to answer these questions.

The Developmental Course of Smiling

Smiling begins early, and if you watch closely, you can see smiles even in newborn infants. The earliest phase of smiling in the human infant has been termed *spontaneous* or *reflex* smiling (Gewirtz, 1965). An infant smile that is elicited by stroking the lips or cheek is an example of a reflex smile. Most early smiling is spontaneous and appears to depend on the infant's internal state.

Early smiles have been attributed to "gas," but support for this theory has evaporated. The exact nature of the internal stimulus remains a mystery. In the first three or four weeks infants are likely to smile when they are comfortable or in REM (rapid eye movement) periods of sleep (Emde, Gaensbauer, & Harman, 1976). Even in the newborn period there are sex differences in smiling. Girls show more spontaneous smiles than boys (Korner, 1974). Some have suggested that girls may be genetically better prepared for social interaction than boys (Freedman, 1971).

Between 3 and 8 weeks of age, infants move to the next period of smiling, in which they are no longer responsive to only internal events but to a wide range of external elicitors—including social stimuli such as faces and voices. Although the earliest elicitor of the smile appears to be a high-pitched human voice, a combination of voice and face, particularly a moving face, is the most reliable elicitor of smiling in the first six months of life.

However, the critical aspects of the human face that are effective elicitors of smiling in normal infants change as the infant matures (Ahrens, 1954). Figure 7-1 illustrates this developmental sequence; at first the configuration of the eyes is important, followed by the mouth, and finally the details of the face and expressions become important. All social agents are not equally effective elicitors of smiles. Three-month-old infants show greater increases in smiling when their smiles are reinforced by smiles and vocalizations of their mothers than when they are reinforced by equally responsive female strangers (Wahler, 1967). Nor are all environments equally effective in promoting the development of smiling. As

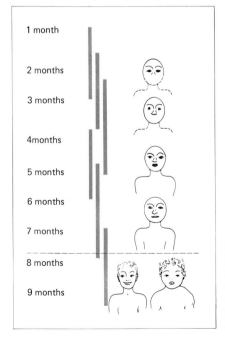

FIGURE 7-1 The stimulus features that elicit smiling in infants of different ages. *(Adapted from Ahrens, 1954, with permission of the publisher.)*

BOX 7-1
THE DEVELOPMENT OF SMILING IN DIFFERENT CHILDREARING SETTINGS

The development of smiling was examined in three different childrearing settings in Israel: the kibbutz, the normal family, and a residential institution. Infants in both the kibbutz (a collective settlement) and the normal family had plenty of opportunities to interact with adults. In the kibbutz, although the responsibility for childrearing was shared by the mother and metapelet, a professional caretaker, the infant was in no sense deprived of human social contact. On the other hand, in the residential institution, interaction between the infants and their caretakers is much less frequent. Smiling should develop at a slower rate in the institutional environment. Examination of Figure 7-2 indicates that this is the case. The family and kibbutz curves peak at four months, while the institution curve reaches its peak about one month later, at five months. The development of smiling varies with the type of childrearing environment, with the highest rate of smiling occurring in the family environment. ∎

Source: Gewirtz, J. L. The course of infant smiling in four child-rearing environments in Israel. In B. M. Foss (Ed.), *Determinants of infant behavior* (Vol. 3). London: Methuen, 1965, pp. 205–248.

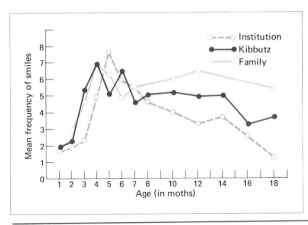

FIGURE 7-2 Frequency of smiling among infants raised in three different environments. *(From Gewirtz, 1965, with permission of the author, the publisher, and the Tavistock Institute of Human Relations.)*

Gewirtz (1965) shows in Box 7-1, children reared in a family environment exhibited more smiling than infants reared in either a kibbutz or an institution.

From Smiling to Laughter

By 4 months infants not only are skilled smilers, but begin to laugh (Sroufe, 1978). Laughter, like smiling, may play an important role in caretaker-infant interaction; specifically, the infant's laughter may serve to maintain the proximity of the mother or other caretaker and hence is a very adaptive response pattern. Until recently, little was known about the early development of laughter.

Sroufe and Wunsch (1972) have helped fill this gap in our knowledge by their investigation of laughter in the first years of life. Using mothers as their experimental assistants, these investigators examined the amount of laughter elicited by a wide array of visual (human mask, disappearing object), tactile (bouncing on knee, blowing in hair), auditory (lip popping, whispering, a whinnying horse sound), and social (peek-a-boo, covering baby's face, and sticking out tongue) stimuli. Infants from 4 to 12 months participated, and Figure 7-3 shows their results.

After the onset of laughter at the age of 4 months, there is a clear increase with age in the number of situations eliciting laughter; the increase is most apparent between the second and third trimesters of life. Moreover, the nature of the stimuli that elicit laughter changes as the child develops. While stimulation, such as tactile stimulation, may be effective for a 5-month-old, older infants lose interest in mere stimulation; in the third quarter of the first year infants respond more to social games (peek-a-boo), visual spectacles, and other activities in which they can participate, such as covering and uncovering the mother's face with a cloth or playing tug-of-war with a blanket. By the end of the first year and throughout the second year of life, infants increasingly smile and laugh in response to activities that they create themselves. For example, an infant may repeatedly bat a mobile to make it turn and then laugh uproariously.

The Explanation of Smiling and Laughter

Few phenomena have a single explanation, and smiling and laughter are no exceptions. Some theorists regard smiling as innately determined (Spitz, 1946), while others have emphasized the role of learning (Gewirtz, 1965). Finally, some theorists have championed a perceptual-recognition hypothesis to explain smiling and laughter.

Is smiling innate? Some support for the view that smiling and laughter have a strong maturational basis comes from twin studies and from investigations of premature infants. It has been found that identical twins exhibit greater concordance than fraternal twins in the time of onset and in the amount of social smiling.

Studies of smiling in premature infants also point to the role of maturational factors in the onset of smiling. The normal conceptual age for an infant at birth is

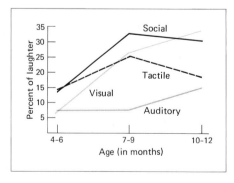

FIGURE 7-3 Laughter of infants in the first year of life in response to four different classes of stimuli. *(From Sroufe & Wunsch, 1972, with permission of the authors and the Society for Research in Child Development.)*

40 weeks. Most normal full-term infants begin to smile at 6 weeks, or at a conceptual age of 46 weeks. Premature infants, who are born at 34 weeks, often do not smile until 12 weeks after birth, or when they are 46 weeks old in terms of their conceptual age (Dittrichova, 1969). The fact that chronological age is not the best predictor of the onset of smiling underlines the role that maturational factors play.

Although the timing of the beginning of smiling may be biologically determined, it is highly unlikely that genetic factors alone would be able to account for differences in the rate of development of smiling and laughter. As we have already seen, frequency of smiling seems to vary with the type of rearing environment. To account for these variations in smiling, learning-theory explanations have been suggested. Stimulation from adults, particularly familiar caregivers, that follows infant smiling can increase the rate of smiling (Brackbill, 1958; Etzel & Gewirtz, 1967; Wahler, 1967). Although some recent skeptics have questioned the adequacy of these early demonstrations (Bloom & Esposito, 1975), it is likely that smiling can be modified by social stimulation.

An adequate explanation of smiling and laughter not only should account for the frequency of smiling, but also should explain why different events cause smiling and laughter at different ages. Why will young infants smile at simple toys, while older children will be more likely to smile or laugh when playing interactive games? The perceptual-recognition viewpoint provides the best explanation of these aspects of smiling and laughter. According to this theory, development of smiling can best be understood by viewing the infant as an information-processing organism who is attempting to impose structure or meaning on incoming stimulation. One way in which the infant makes sense of the external world is by forming mental representations of external events; these internal pictures are called *schemas*. This process of schema development will be discussed in detail in Chapter 9. Achieving a match between the schema and an incoming stimulus is the infant's means of understanding. This achievement, the creation of a schema for an event, is a source of pleasure which is signaled by a smile (Kagan, 1967).

A study of 4-month-old infants illustrates interesting relationships between the nature of the facial configuration, age of the infant, and smiling behavior (Kagan, Henker, Hen-Tov, Levine, and Lewis, 1966). When infants were shown either a photograph of a regular face or a three-dimensional sculptured face, they smiled much more often than they smiled at either a schematic version of a face or a distorted, disordered version of a face. Why does this occur? One interpretation is that the smile can be elicited when the infant matches stimulus to schema—when she has an "aha" reaction, that is, when she makes a cognitive discovery. The 4-month-old infant is cognitively close to establishing a relatively firm schema of a human face. When a regular representation of a face is presented to her, there is a short period during which the stimulus is assimilated to the schema and then after several seconds a smile may occur. The smile is released following the perceptual recognition of the face and reflects the assimilation of the stimulus of the infant's schema, a small but significant act of creation. This hypothesis is supported by the fact that the typical latency between the onset of looking at the regular face (in the 4-month-old) and the onset of smiling is about three to five seconds. The smile usually does not occur immediately, but only after the infant has studied the stimulus. If one sees this phenomenon in real life, it is difficult to avoid the conclusion that the smile is released following an act of perceptual recognition.

This perceptual-recognition view can nicely explain Ahren's observations of the developmental changes in the facial stimuli necessary for smiling behavior. As the Gewirtz study (Box 7-1) indicates, the extent to which the infant has opportunities to learn the characteristics of social stimuli, such as faces, will determine the speed with which he or she reaches each of these developmental points.

In summary, the onset of smiling and laughter may be biologically predetermined, but the developmental course of these behaviors is shaped by both shifts in cognitive abilities and the child's social experiences.

From Smiling to Attachment

A 3-month-old smiles more at his mother than at a stranger; three months later the infant may cry when his mother leaves; and a few months later he may crawl to his mother's side in an unfamiliar situation. These developments are part of a most remarkable achievement—the development of a specific social attachment, whereby the infant seeks to be near certain people—not just anyone. Few topics have generated as much interest as the process of attachment formation. It is of interest not only because it is a widespread and often extremely intense and dramatic phenomenon, but also because attachment is thought to enhance the parents' effectiveness in later socialization of the child. The child who has developed an attachment to his parent is more likely to be concerned about maintaining parental affection and approval through adopting socialized behaviors than is a child who has failed to develop this special social relationship with some adults in his environment.

The issues in attachment which have been the focus of greatest theorizing and research have been the parental characteristics and childrearing practices associated with attachment, the sequence and timing of attachment behaviors, and the consequences of attachment for later social and emotional development.

Theories of Attachment

A variety of theories have been offered to explain the development of attachment, including psychoanalytic theory, learning theory, and ethological theory. Each position makes different assumptions about the role of the infant in the development of attachment, the variables that are important for the development of attachment, and the processes underlying the development of attachment.

Psychoanalytic Theory   Much of the work on the development of attachment has been directly or indirectly influenced by psychoanalytic theory. According to this viewpoint, parental caretaking activities, such as feeding, which are essential for the survival of the child are critical in attachment formation. Specifically, Freudians postulate that the infant has an innate need to suck, which interacts with and is modified by actual feeding experiences. The need for oral gratification through sucking and other forms of stimulation of the mouth results in the infant becoming attached to the satisfying mother's breast and ultimately to the mother herself.

Learning Theory   Learning theorists as well as psychoanalytic theorists have stressed the importance of the feeding situation for the development of attachment (Sears, Maccoby, & Levin, 1957). According to a learning view, the caretaker acquires positive value through association with the satisfaction and reduction of hunger, a primary drive. The mother, as a result of being paired with drive-reducing feeding activity, acquires secondary reinforcement properties and consequently is valued in her own right. In other words, eventually just the presence of the mother becomes satisfying and the child develops an acquired need for contact with the mother, which is referred to as attachment.

Few people accept the view that the feeding situation is the critical context for the development of social attachment. The most famous challenge to this traditional view came from the Harlow and Zimmerman (1959) study of cloth-and-wire surrogate mother monkeys, which showed that infants preferred cloth "mothers" even though they were fed on the wire "mother." Hunger reduction is clearly not necessary for the development of attachment.

Human studies tell a similar story: variations in routine caretaking practices are poor predictors of infant attachment. For example, in one study of attachment in Scotland, it was found that infants formed attachments to some individuals, such as fathers and other relatives, who played little or no role in routine child care, such as feeding or diapering (Schaffer & Emerson, 1964).

Adults, however, do more than feed; they provide a wide variety of other types of stimulation for the infant. Some learning theorists suggest that the visual, auditory, and tactual stimulation that adults provide in the course of their daily interactions with the infant provides the basis for the development of attachment (Gewirtz, 1969). The infant is initially attracted to people because they are the most important and reliable sources of stimulation. As a result of *specific* individuals regularly providing this satisfying stimulation, these individuals are valued by the infant and become the objects of attachment. The important feature of the learning-theory explanation, however, is that attachment is not an innate or instinctual process, but rather develops over time as a result of satisfying interaction with key people in the child's environment. Learning theorists, as well as others, view attachment as a two-way process with both the infant and the parent developing attachment to each other. As we have seen in earlier chapters, the process of parent-to-infant attachment probably begins very soon after birth, while infant-to-parent attachment develops more gradually over the first six to seven months of life.

Ethological Theory   Another theoretical view that has emphasized the reciprocal nature of the attachment process is John Bowlby's ethological theory (1958, 1969, 1973). Under the influence of both evolutionary theory and observational studies of animals, Bowlby has suggested that attachment is a result of a set of instinctual responses which are important for the protection and survival of the species. These infant behaviors—crying, smiling, sucking, clinging, and following—elicit necessary parental care and protection for the infant and promote contact between mother and infant. The mother is biologically prepared to respond to these infant elicitors, just as the infant is predisposed to respond to the sights, sounds, and nurturance provided by her human caretakers. It is as a result of these biologically programmed systems that both mother and infant develop mutual attachment to each other. Bowlby, like other current theorists, minimizes the importance of the feeding situation. The value of this position lies in its explicit emphasis on the active role of the infant's early social signaling systems, such as smiling and crying, in the formation of attachment. Another attractive feature of the theory is its stress on the development of mutual attachment, whereby both partners, not just one, form attachments. Of some question, however, is the value of Bowlby's suggestion that these early behaviors are biologically preprogrammed. Learning theory probably can more adequately account for the shifting role that different signaling systems play at different developmental points. Less controversial than the theoretical viewpoints are the empirical findings concerning the developmental determinants and consequences of attachment. Next we turn to these issues.

The Developmental Course of Attachment

Attachment does not develop suddenly and unheralded, but emerges in a consistent series of steps in the first six months of life. Three general steps have been distinguished: First, the infant is attracted to all social objects and comes to prefer humans to inanimate objects. Second, the infant gradually learns to discriminate familiar and unfamiliar people. Finally, the infant develops the capacity to form a special relationship with certain specific individuals with whom he or she actively seeks to maintain contact. This final phase is the onset of attachment.

As we saw in our earlier discussions of infant perceptual preferences, infants are attracted to faces from a very early age. In fact, one recent study suggests infants can recognize their mothers as early as 2 weeks of age (Carpenter, 1975). When babies were presented with either the mother's face or a stranger's face through a porthole in their cribs, the infants looked longer at their mothers. This learning continues, and by 2 months infants can discriminate not only their parents from strangers but mothers from fathers as well (Yogman, Dixon, Tronick, Als, & Brazelton, 1977).

The process of familiarization continues over the next few months with parents becoming increasingly acquainted with the unique characteristics of their infants. They learn what makes them smile and laugh, and they learn how to calm and soothe their infants. In turn, the infants learn the unique features of their caretakers—their faces, their voices, their movements. But during this period the infant does not protest the departure of familiar people.

At about 6 to 7 months, a new phase begins—the attachment phase. Now the infant actively seeks contact with specific individuals and may protest when they depart. This general sequence of the emergence of attachment is well illustrated in a famous study of sixty Scottish infants by Schaffer and Emerson (1964). The infants were studied at four-week intervals during the first year of life, with an additional follow-up session at 18 months. The amount of protest behavior manifested by the children in a variety of specific separation situations (for example, being left in a pram outside shops, being left in a crib, etc.) was reported by the mothers in monthly interviews, and monthly observations were made of the infants' fear responses to the increasing approach of the strange interviewer.

In the first six months of life the infants developed indiscriminate attachments to people: they cried for attention and contact from strangers or close acquaintances alike. However, at about 7 months of age very intense attachments to specific people appeared. The children protested only when separation from certain people occurred. The mother was usually, but not always, the main person to whom the child became attached, and many children were attached to more than one person. Other studies have found the same pattern in the development of separation protest and have found that protest is highest between 12 and 18 months (Kotelchuck, 1972). The developmental course of these attachments is presented in Figure 7-4. In looking at Figure 7-4, it is important to remember that these ages represent averages and that there is considerable variation among babies in the timing of attachments.

Although other studies show cultural influences and individual differences in the time these behaviors emerge, this general developmental pattern is frequently found. A study of infants in Uganda, Africa, showed that specific attachments emerged slightly earlier and fear of strangers later than in the Scottish sample (Ainsworth, 1963; Ainsworth, Salter, & Wittig, 1967).

The child's level of cognitive development plays an important role in the emergence of specific attachments. Before such responses can occur, the infant not only must be able to differentiate between mother and stranger, but must be aware that people still exist when they are not visible. The child must have developed *object permanence*, or the knowledge that objects, including humans, have a continuous existence. The child is unlikely to protest or call for a person who is out of sight if she is not aware that the person still exists when she

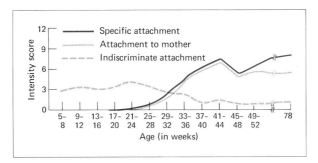

FIGURE 7-4 Developmental course of attachments. *(From Schaffer & Emerson, 1964.)*

cannot see him. Other findings suggest that cognitive factors play a role in the amount of protest children show at separation from a parent. Increased protest is likely to occur when children are able to recognize that they are in an unfamiliar situation, that they are with strange people, or that something unexpected is occurring. Children protest less when the mother leaves them at home than in the laboratory, and they protest more in the home when the mother leaves them through a door she seldom uses than when she departs through a door she uses often (Littenberg, Tulkin, & Kagan, 1971).

Advances in the infant's cognitive development can also account, in part, for the gradual shift in the ways that attachment is expressed. Physical proximity becomes less important as the child develops, and hence departures tend to result in less upset in the older child. Children also are better able to understand the reasons for separation and can appreciate that separations are temporary. With increasing understanding, parents are able to reduce the impact of separation by providing explanations for their departures. The role of explanation in altering children's reactions to separation was illustrated in a recent investigation (Weinraub, 1977; Weinraub & Lewis, 1977). Mothers left their 2-year-olds alone in a room, but varied in their style of departure in order to determine the impact of verbal explanations on children's reactions to separation. In one condition, mothers were instructed to slip out unobtrusively and without any explanation. Other mothers informed the child of their departure and/or eventual return ("I'm going out now for just a minute, but I'll be right back"), while mothers in a third group not only informed the child but suggested an activity that the child could do in the mother's absence. The results were clear: The boys of mothers who verbally structured their departure played more in their absence than boys of mothers who just slipped out without any explanation. Further evidence of the role of cognitive factors in regulating reactions to separation comes from the relationship between the child's cognitive ability and his or her activity during separation. Children with higher levels of cognitive development coped better and played more during mother's absence than less cognitively advanced children (Weinraub & Lewis, 1977). Reactions to separation vary with a variety of factors, including the context in which the separation occurs, the other people present, and the age of the child. In general, as the child develops, reactions to separation lessen as the child learns that the mother will return.

Parental Behavior and the Development of Attachment	What determines the quality of the infant's attachment to his parents? What parent-child interactions in early infancy are important? In their Scottish study, Schaffer and Emerson (1964) tried to answer these questions. Infants were attached to adults who responded quickly to their demands and cries and who spontaneously sought and initiated interactions with them. Hence, when a relatively unstimulating mother, that is, one who tends to avoid contact with her infant except for routine physical care, is combined with an attentive, stimulating father, the child is more likely to form a paternal attachment despite the greater

amount of routine contact with the mother. As was true in the studies of the effects of early institutionalization, stimulation and a sense of control over the environment seem to be critical factors in the development of early infant attachment. Longitudinal studies which have used direct observational measures of mother-child interactions rather than maternal reports have also found that parental stimulation, particularly in response to the infant's signals, is important in attachment formation (Ainsworth, 1973; Ainsworth & Bell, 1969; Caldwell, Wright, Honig, & Tannenbaum, 1970).

In another study Ainsworth and her colleagues observed a group of white middle-class mothers interacting with their infants for four-hour sessions every three weeks from birth until 54 weeks of age. At about 1 year of age, observations of the infants' attachment and exploratory behavior were made in a series of standard situations involving various combinations of the infant with the presence or absence of the mother and a stranger. This sequence is known as the "strange situation." There are striking differences in the infants' responses to the strange situation, and through this test the *quality* of the infant-mother relationship can be assessed. One group of infants were clearly or "securely" attached to their mothers, as shown by occasional seeking to be close to and touching the mother when she was present, and intensified contact-maintaining behavior following being left alone in a strange situation. This group felt secure enough to explore and manipulate a strange environment when their mothers were present. They did not cling and whine, but were curious and manipulative in dealing with toys and other objects in the unfamiliar situation when their mothers were with them. In familiar situations such as the home, with ordinary minor separations these children were minimally disturbed although they greeted the mother's return with enthusiasm. All children in this group had mothers who had permitted them to play an active role in determining the pacing, onset, and termination of feeding early in life. It should be noted again that it is not the particular child-care practice but the responsiveness and sensitivity to the infant's needs that are important in attachment.

Some of the infants showed frequent intense distress and crying when the mother was either present or absent, and either lacked interest in contact with the mother or showed ambivalence about contact by such things as intermittent proximity seeking accompanied with angry pushing away and rejection of the mother. These infants were termed "anxiously attached" and had mothers who had been rated as being insensitive in their interactions with their infants during earlier feeding situations.

Other studies indicate that the antecedents of "securely" and "anxiously" attached infants can be found in a variety of interaction contexts, including face-to-face play. During the first few months of life, the beginnings of later attachment can be seen in the playful frolic that often characterizes early parent-infant interaction. As described in Box 7-2, even 3-month-old infants and their mothers engage in highly involved, intricate, and delicately orchestrated play bouts. Not all infants and parents are able to adapt successfully to each other and achieve the interactive "waltz" described in Box 7-2.

BOX 7-2
THE ROOTS OF ATTACHMENT:
THE DEVELOPMENT OF
CARETAKER-INFANT SYNCHRONY

Well before the infant shows evidence of a specific attachment, the early beginnings of mutual adaptation and regulation are evident. Just as sucking, sleeping, and other early behaviors are highly organized, so are interpersonal relationships. Only recently have we fully appreciated how early and how finely tuned the interaction patterns between infants and their caretakers actually are.

Let us take a close look at a mother and a 3-month-old infant playing together. To permit a detailed analysis, Stern (1974) filmed the face-to-face interaction between 3-month-old infants and their mothers. Rather than a disorganized pattern, the play behavior is a highly orchestrated interchange with both mother and infant adjusting their behavior throughout the play period. Both mothers and infants show a pattern of mutual approach and withdrawal which permits the mutual regulation of stimulation at some optimal and presumably pleasurable level for the infant. Each partner makes a unique contribution to this early dialogue. Mothers constantly shift their behavior in order to elicit and maintain the baby's attention. One technique that mothers use to hold their infant's attention is to exaggerate their speech. For example, they talk louder and slower and use longer vowels. A mother might say, "Hi swee-eeet-ee, Hiii, Hi-i-iya, watcha lookin at? Hu-u-uh?

O-o-o-o-o-o, yeah, it's mommy ye-e-a-ah" (Stern, 1974, p. 192). Similarly facial expressions are often exaggerated, slower to form, and longer in duration. The infant contributes to the regulation largely through the control of gaze, which allows him to regulate the amount of stimulation that he is receiving. When the amount of stimulation is too much, the infant turns away. In turn, the mother reduces her input. Stern has characterized the mutual regulatory actions of both partners who are constantly making readjustments in their behavior during play as a "waltz." The infant during this period is learning in a more precise way the features of his caretaker's face, the regulation of his attention, and an early lesson in social control. The caretaker is learning a variety of important lessons as well. Through this interaction, adults are learning to more sensitively and accurately "read" their baby's early social signals and learn to adjust their behavior to maintain the baby's attention and interest. It is out of these early dialogues that adults become increasingly more attached to their infants as well as the infants developing an attachment to their caregivers. Play, in short, is serious business! ■

Source: Stern, D. N. Mother and infant at play: The dyadic interaction involving facial, vocal and gaze behaviors. In M. Lewis & L. A. Rosenblum (eds.), *The effect of the infant on its caretaker*. New York: Wiley, 1974.

Unfortunately, some of those parent-infant dyads that fail to achieve early interactive synchrony also fail later to develop secure infant-parent attachment. Blehar, Leiberman, and Ainsworth (1977) examined adult-infant face-to-face play patterns between 6 and 15 weeks and then assessed the quality of attachment at 12 months. Infants identified as securely attached at 1 year were more responsive in earlier playful encounters with their mothers than infants judged to be anxiously attached; their mothers encouraged social interaction and were more likely to respond in a sensitive and contingent manner to their infant's behaviors. The anxiously attached infants were more unresponsive and negative in early face-to-face play than securely attached infants; their mothers were more likely to be impassive or abrupt. Even at these early ages, the securely attached infants were more positively responsive to their mothers than to an unfamiliar figure in face-to-face episodes, while anxiously attached infants responded equally to familiar and unfamiliar people.

Stability of Attachment

Are the differences in the patterning of attachment that we have discussed stable over time? Infants tested in the strange situation at 12 months and again at 18 months were generally classified in the same way at the two time points. Infants who showed secure attachment at 12 months were rated as secure at 18 months, just as the infants with avoidant and ambivalent attachment patterns showed stability over the 6-month interval. Of interest is the fact that discrete behavior (for example, crying, touching, approaching, vocalizing) was relatively unstable across this time period. This suggests that the general pattern of infant-parent attachments may be stable, but the particular behaviors that are used to express this relationship may shift as the child develops. The younger child may cling to maintain maternal contact, while the older child maintains contact through subtler verbal communications (Waters, 1978).

Multiple Caretakers and Attachment: Day Care and the Kibbutz

Is the development of attachment impaired if care is distributed among a number of caretakers as well as the parents? This question is frequently asked by researchers, parents, and policymakers since nearly 5.5 million children in the United States each year are involved in day care (Bronfenbrenner, Belsky, & Steinberg, 1977). Day care involves leaving the child with other caretakers, usually in a group setting, for a period during the day while the parent works or attends school. If the quantity of time that parent and infant spend together is critical for the development of attachment, infants in day care who spend less total time with their parents than home-reared infants may show disruptions in the formation of attachment. As Box 7-3 illustrates, day care does not appear to have adverse effects on attachment. Quality of the interaction is the important determinant of adequate social and emotional development.

Similar findings come from studies of the Israeli kibbutz, where childrearing is shared between the parents and professional caretakers. There is no indication that rearing by multiple caretakers interferes with the development of infant-mother attachment (Fox, 1977: Maccoby & Feldman, 1972).

Multiple Attachments: Fathers and Peers as Attachment Figures

Fathers as Attachment Figures   Infants develop attachments not only to their mothers, but to a variety of other persons—including their fathers. With changing cultural views, fathers often take a much more active role in early infancy, which makes it even more likely that they will develop an attachment to their infant as well as serve as an attachment figure for their offspring. Margaret Mead's famous claim that "fathers are a biological necessity, but a social accident" is no longer valid.

BOX 7-3
DAY CARE AND ATTACHMENT:
A CONTINUING CONTROVERSY

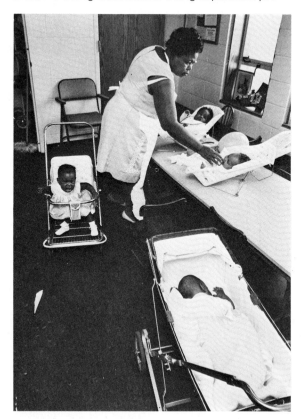

Under the influence of John Bowlby and early studies of institutionalization which stressed the adverse effects of being deprived of a single mother figure during infancy, there has been a national debate over the impact of day care on infant-mother attachment. The issue is being hotly debated and equally hotly researched. The most comprehensive study to date involved longitudinal comparisons of infants who either were enrolled in a day-care program or stayed at home (Kagan, Kearsley, & Zelazo, 1977). The infants were assessed between 3½ and 29 months on a variety of cognitive, language, and social measures, including attachment. Using separation pro-

test to measure attachment, these investigators found no differences between home-reared and day-care infants. Day care, then, does not necessarily weaken the infant's attachment to the mother. Nor does the infant necessarily develop a preference for their teachers over their mother—another unfounded fear. Infants continue to prefer their mothers over their teachers when bored or apprehensive, although teachers are preferred to strangers (Farran & Ramey, 1977).

Moreover, day care may even yield some beneficial effects: infants with prior day-care experience adapt more quickly and explore more in an unfamiliar environment and play more with their peers. In summary, day care does not appear

The effects of day-care centers continue to be a controversial issue. (Ken Heyman)

to disrupt the mother-infant relationship and may even promote the child's exploration of her social and physical environment. Day care, like institutionalization, means many things, and just as variations in the quality of home environments can either facilitate or slow the child's development, the quality of day care is an important determinant of the impact of this experience on the child. The debate continues, and the definitive answer concerning the "best" kind of day care is not yet available. ■

Sources: Kagan, J., Kearsley, R. B., & Zelazo, P. R. The effects of infant day care on psychological development. *Educational Quarterly*, 1977, **1**, 109–142; and Ricciuti, H. Effects of day care experience on behavior and development: Research and implications for social policy. Unpublished manuscript, Cornell University, 1976.

Even in the newborn period, fathers take an active interest in their infants. Although this is often through the looking glass of the newborn nursery, fathers who are given the opportunity to have contact with their infants hold, touch, vocalize, and kiss them just as much as mothers (Parke & O'Leary, 1976).

This early father involvement is reciprocated by infants, who show just as much attachment to their fathers as their mothers later in the first year. This is well illustrated in a recent observational study by Lamb (1977), who studied 7-to-8- and 12-to-13-month-old infants when both parents and a friendly but unfamiliar, visitor were present in the home. Although the infants were more "attached" to their parents than to the visitor, they showed no preference for either parent in terms of their attachment behaviors. They were just as likely to touch, fuss, approach, and be near their fathers as their mothers. "There was certainly no evidence to support the popular assumption that infants of this age should prefer—indeed be uniquely attached to—their mothers" (Lamb, 1977, p. 180). Infants form attachments not to a single individual, but to *both* mother and father in the first year of life.

Fathers and mothers, however, may play unique roles. Fathers are not merely substitute caretakers in their infant's social world, and in spite of current trends they are still less likely than mothers to be the primary caretaker. The father's special role is as a playmate, with fathers spending four to five times as much time playing with their infants as taking care of them. In his home observational study, Lamb (1977) found that fathers are more likely to hold babies to play with them while mothers are far more likely to hold them for caretaking purposes.

Moreover, the quality of play is different. Generally, mothers stimulate their infants verbally, while fathers treat them more physically. These differences in parental play patterns are evident during the first months of life and continue throughout infancy (Yogman et al., 1977). Studies with 8-month-old infants indicate that fathers engage in more unusual and physically arousing games, such as rough-and-tumble play, while mothers verbally stimulate their babies and play more conventional games such as peek-a-boo (Lamb, 1977; Clarke-Stewart, 1978). Finally, infant reactions to father play seem to be more positive than to mother play. If given a choice of play partners, 18-month-old infants in one study (Clarke-Stewart, 1978) chose their fathers more than their mothers, probably because a father is a more exciting and unpredictable play partner.

Fathers and mothers have different styles of playing with infants. (Photo (a) by Hanna Schreiber, Rapho/Photo Researchers, Inc.; photo (b) by Virginia Hamilton)

Fathers are not the preferred partner on all occasions. In times of stress, mothers are generally preferred. Infants were introduced to a stranger in a laboratory situation when both parents were present. The infant, in this unfamiliar and presumably stressful situation, showed a clear preference for the mother over the father (Lamb, 1976). In view of the different roles played by mothers and fathers, with mother assuming primary caretaking responsibility, the infant's choice of mother in time of stress is sensible. Mother is presumably the parent that has most often served in this capacity in other situations in the past.

In summary, fathers as well as mothers are important attachment figures and play an important role in the early social and emotional development of the infant. Although fathers and mothers are usually the most significant attachment objects, it should be stressed that a variety of other individuals are important in the infant's social world including peers, siblings, and relatives such as grandparents. Box 7-4 dramatically illustrates that peers can become important attachment figures—even for young children. Emotional development in early life can best be understood by appreciating the complexity and diversity of the infant's social network.

Consequences of Attachment

Does the quality of early infant-parent attachment have implications for the child's later cognitive and social adaptation? Early social interactions with attachment figures *do* shape the child's later behavior. In cognitive development this is most notable in exploratory behavior and problem-solving style. An early "secure" attachment promotes more complex exploratory behavior at 2 years of age (Main, 1973). In addition, as the child develops, this intellectual curiosity is reflected in a heightened involvement, persistence, and enjoyment in problem-solving situations seldom found in toddlers who have been insecurely attached infants (Matas & Sroufe, cited by Sroufe, 1978).

Early social relationships with the mother affect not only other adult-child interactions, but also the child's developing peer relationships. To illustrate these links between attachment and peer relations, Leiberman (1977) assessed the quality of attachment in a group of 3-year-olds through the laboratory strange situation, a home visit, and an interview with the mother. Four months later, an independent measure of peer competence was secured in order to determine how effectively children are able to relate to their age-mates. Children were observed interacting with an unfamiliar same-age playmate in a laboratory setting. Children who showed a "secure" attachment with their mothers exhibited more extensive reciprocal interaction (for example, sharing, giving, social initiations) and less negative peer behavior (crying, physical aggression, verbal threat). The quality of the mother-child relationship is clearly related to peer-peer interactions. While no clear cause-effect link can be established from this study, the pattern that emerges suggests that a secure relationship with an adult may promote better peer relations.

In summary, a healthy attachment to parents facilitates rather than stifles exploration, curiosity, and mastery of the social and physical environment. At

BOX 7-4
PEERS AS ATTACHMENT FIGURES

 A famous study (Freud & Dann, 1951) of six German-Jewish orphans, separated from their parents at an early age because of World War II and placed in an institution, tells how the children formed intense, protective attachments to each other while ignoring or being actively hostile to their adult caretakers. The children had lost their parents before the age of 1, most commonly in gas chambers. When they were in their fourth year of life, they arrived at Bulldog Banks, a small English country home which had been transformed into a nursery for war children. They had lived together in various concentration camps and institutions since their first year of life. Their stay at Bulldog Banks was their first experience in living in a small, intimate setting.

In their early days at Bulldog Banks they were wild and uncontrollable. They destroyed or damaged much of the furniture and all of their toys within a few days. Usually they ignored adults, but when they were angry they would bite, spit, or swear at them, often called them bloder ochs (stupid fools), which seemed to be their favorite epithet for their caretakers.

The contrast between their hostile behavior toward their caretakers and their solicitous, considerate behavior toward other children in their group was surprising. In one case, when a caretaker accidentally knocked over one of the children, two of the other children threw bricks at her and called her names. The children resisted being separated from each other even for special treats such as pony rides. When one child was ill, the others wanted to remain with her. They showed little envy, jealousy, rivalry, or competition with each other. The sharing and helping behavior the children showed was remarkable in children of this age.

The following are typical incidents in their first seven months at Bulldog Banks:

The children were eating cake, and John began to cry when he saw there was no cake left for a second helping. Ruth and Miriam, who had not yet finished their portions, gave him the remainder of their cake and seemed happy just to pet him and comment on his eating the cake.

On another occasion when one child lost his gloves, although it was very cold another child loaned his gloves without complaining about his own discomfort.

The investigators cited the following incidents when even in fearful situations children were able to overcome their trepidation to help the others in the group:

A dog approaches the children, who are terrified. Ruth, though badly frightened herself, walks bravely to Peter who is screaming and gives him her toy rabbit to comfort him. She comforts John by lending him her necklace.

On the beach in Brighton, Ruth throws pebbles into the water. Peter is afraid of waves and does not dare to approach them. In spite of his fear, he suddenly rushes to Ruth, calling out: "Water coming, water coming," and drags her back to safety. (Freud & Dann, 1951, pp. 150-168).

When finally positive relations with adults began to be formed, they were made on the basis of group feelings and had none of the demanding, possessive attitudes often shown by young children toward their own mothers. They began to include adults in their group and to treat them in some ways as they treated each other. This seemed to be a phase of general attachments which for some of the children was eventually followed by specific attachment toward an individual caretaker, with clinging and possessiveness appearing. During their year's stay at Bulldog Banks the intensity of the children's attachment to their surrogate mothers was never as intense as in normal mother-child relations and never as binding as those to their peers. ■

Source: Freud, A., & Dann, S. An experiment in group upbringing. In *The psychoanalytic study of the child* (Vol. 6). New York: International Universities Press, 1951.

the same time, early attachment increases the child's trust in other social relationships and permits the later development of mature affectional relationships with peers. Longitudinal studies aimed at specifying the links between early parent-infant interaction and later relationships in adolescence and adulthood would help us determine the long-term stability of these positive cognitive and social effects of an early secure attachment.

The Other Side of Early Emotions: The Development of Fear

At the same time as the infant is developing a positive emotional relationship with a few special individuals, he is learning to be wary of strangers. In our continuing search for regularities in early development, few phenomena have captured as much time, effort, and interest as the following type of exchange between an infant and a stranger.

Timothy, age 8 months, is exploring some toys in his playpen, looks up and sees a strange woman standing beside his playpen. He turns back to his toys briefly, then again solemnly looks up at the stranger, whimpers, turns away and begins to cry.

Fear of strangers, as this reaction to unfamiliar people is usually called, was at one time thought to be inevitable and universal and has become enshrined in the psychological literature as a developmental milestone. However, as we will see below, this reaction is neither inevitable nor universal. Instead, the appearance of fear is determined by a host of variables, including the identity and the behavior of the stranger, the setting, and the developmental status of the child. In fact, Rheingold and Eckerman (1973) have recently criticized the continued treatment of stranger fear as a typical reaction, and suggest that greeting and smiling may be a frequent reaction to strangers for some infants.

The Development of Fear of Strangers

In spite of this controversy, there is little doubt that some infants do show fear or at least wariness in reaction to unfamiliar people, but the timing of onset, the frequency of occurrence, and the intensity of the reaction are modified by a variety of factors. The emergence of fear, like the emergence of smiling, is gradual. In the early weeks of life, fear reactions depend on internal-biological factors, and only gradually does the infant become responsive to external events. In general, full-blown fear reactions develop more slowly than the emergence of positive, emotional reactions such as smiling. In a recent longitudinal study, Emde and his colleagues (Emde, Gaensbauer, & Harmon, 1976) traced the development of fearful reactions in infants over the first year. By 4 months, infants smile less at unfamiliar adults than at their mothers. They are showing early signs of recognition not by distress, but by less smiling to a stranger. However, infants show a great interest in novel people as well as novel objects, and a 4- or 5-month-old will often look longer at a stranger than at her familiar caretaker. In addition, these investigators found a comparison period in

Fear of strangers is not universal, but some infants occasionally show fear when a stranger is too intrusive. (Photos by Suzanne Szasz)

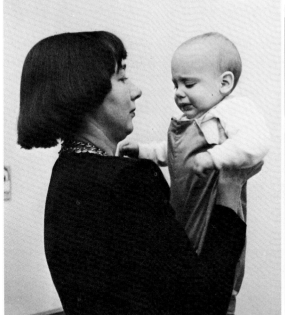

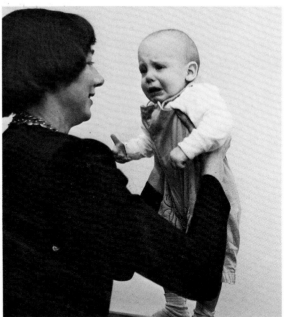

which the infant at 4 months looked back and forth between the mother's face and the stranger's face. A little later—at 5 to 7 months—the infant exhibited a sober expression, and finally in the 7- to 9-month period, the infant showed distress in the presence of the stranger. This sequence is summarized in Figure 7-5 and indicates that the development of fearful reactions to strangers is

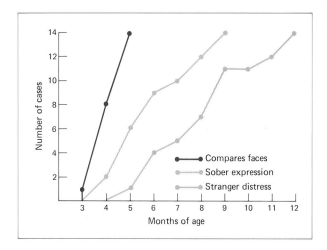

FIGURE 7-5   Onset of social fear. *(From Emde, Gaensbauer, and Harmon, 1977, with permission of the authors and the publisher.)*

preceded by a series of less intense emotional responses and does not make an abrupt appearance.

Fear reactions—not just to strangers—but to a number of different events—begin to occur between 5 and 9 months of age. For example, infants show more fear of the visual cliff—a test of depth perception—at 9 months than at 5 months (Schwartz, Campos, & Baisel, 1973). Of particular interest is the finding that infants' heart-rate patterns show similar shifts from 5 to 9 months for both the visual cliff and reactions to strangers. At 5 months infants show a decelerating heart-rate pattern—an indication that they are attending closely to the object. In contrast, at 9 months, an acceleration pattern occurs, which indicates that the infant is shutting out or avoiding stimulation. This suggests that changes in the organization of the central nervous system and related shifts in cognitive and perceptual processes may underlie the onset of fear reactions in this period. As we will show, this does not mean that fear is an inevitable reaction to all strangers, by all infants at this or other ages, in all situations. Many factors will determine how an infant reacts to a stranger, and next we examine some of these determinants.

The Influence of Context   Another determinant of children's reactions to strangers is the context or setting in which the assessment is conducted. Infants who sit on their mothers' laps while a stranger approaches rarely show any fear reaction; but when placed in infant seats a few feet away from their mothers, they will gaze apprehensively, whimper, or cry as a stranger comes near (Morgan & Ricciuti, 1969).

Just as the presence of a familiar caretaker may affect the child's reaction to strangers, the familiarity of the context is important as well. Sroufe, Waters, and Matas (1974) reported few signs of fear when 10-month-old infants were tested at home for their reaction to a stranger, but nearly 50 percent of the infants showed fear when tested in an unfamiliar laboratory. Even the amount of time that the infant is allowed to become familiar with the new setting can make a marked difference. While only 50 percent of the infants were "fearful" if they were given a ten-minute familiarization period, 65 percent of the infants showed negative reactions after only a three-minute adaptation, and nearly all (93 percent) of the infants were upset if the tests began immediately (thirty seconds). Familiarity of the context, then, is an important determinant of the infant's emotional reaction.

Are All Kinds of Strangers Equal? Do infants show fear reactions to all unfamiliar people—children as well as adults? To find out, Lewis and Brooks (1974) examined the reactions of infants between 7 and 19 months of age to strange male and female adults, a strange child (4-year-old girl), their mothers, and the self (as reflected in a mirror). The infants' responses were measured at four distances: 15 feet away, 8 feet away, 3 feet away, and touching the infants. Reactions were measured on a 5-point scale: a score of 3 indicates a neutral response, with 1 being the most negative and 5 being the most positive responses. The facial expression scale varied from a broad smile to a puckering crylike expression, while the motor scale varied from reaching toward the person to twisting away and reaching to mother. Figure 7-6 shows the results. First, it is not the mere *presence* of a stranger that elicits negative emotional reactions; the child's affective reaction depends on the distance of the stimulus person from the infant. As the individuals came closer, both positive and negative reactions were greater; the negative reaction to the strange adults became clear, while the positive reactions to the mother and mirror image of the self were more marked. Of principal interest is the child's reaction to the unfamiliar child; in contrast to their reaction to the adult, the infants showed a mild positive reaction. The

FIGURE 7-6   The amount of positive and negative facial and motor responses of human infants in reaction to self and to familiar and unfamiliar individuals. (*From Lewis & Brooks, 1974, with the permission of the senior author and the publisher.*)

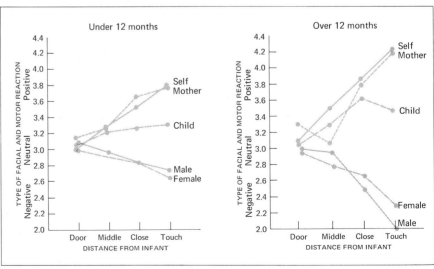

stimulus characteristics of the stranger are an important determinant of whether or not a stranger will elicit fear. It is clear that infants do not show fear to all kinds of strangers. In an ingenious follow-up study, Brooks and Lewis (1976) evaluated adults, children, and a midget as strangers in order to determine whether it is height or facial configuration that elicits fear. The 7- to 24-month-old infants showed more negative reactions to the adults—frowning and moving away from both the adult and midget—than to the child, which suggests that size alone is not a cue that infants use in evaluating strangers; facial configuration also is important. It is unfortunate that a "baby-faced" adult was not available for comparison purposes!

Physical characteristics, however, are not the only important factors; the *behavior* of the stranger makes a difference as well. As adults, we are more likely to respond positively if another person is friendly, outgoing, and active than if a person is quiet and passive. So, in infancy, the behaviors of the stranger determine how the infant will react (Ross & Goldman, 1977). When confronted by an active, friendly stranger who "talked, gestured, smiled, imitated and offered toys," 12-month-olds showed little fear. In fact, the infants were highly sociable with the stranger and imitated him, devised and played games with him, and exchanged and played with toys together. In contrast, if the stranger was passive and quiet, the infant spent less time with, touched less, and played less with this passive stranger than with the active stranger. A stranger is not just a stranger—it's the way the stranger behaves that makes the difference!

Explanation of Fear Development

Fear of strangers as well as fear of situations and objects may develop in a variety of different ways. Let us consider some alternative routes to the development of fear.

Fear as a Genetically Determined Phenomenon   According to this viewpoint, fear has a constitutional basis and is not dependent on specific learning experiences. Freedman (1965) has offered some evidence that the age of onset of fear of strangers is influenced by genetic factors. Specifically, he found greater concordance of onset age between identical than between fraternal twins. Although it is possible that the experiences, such as frequency of exposure to strangers, may be more similar for identical than for fraternal twins, this is a rather weak and unlikely possibility.

Another kind of evidence in favor of a constitutional argument comes from cross-cultural studies of the development of fear of strangers. In spite of childrearing practices that differ greatly from Western customs, both infants raised in Uganda (Ainsworth, 1963) and babies reared on a Hopi Indian reservation (Dennis, 1940) show the stranger-anxiety reaction at approximately 8 months, the same time as Western infants. Probably the most convincing evidence of the genetic basis of fear comes from a study of fear emergence in rhesus monkeys by Sackett (1966). In this experiment a group of eight monkeys were raised from birth to 9 months in isolation. Their only input was a series of colored slides depicting monkeys of various ages engaged in a range of typical monkey activities, such as threatening, exploring, and playing. In addition, a set of control slides of nonmonkey scenes were included. Two methods of slide presentation were employed: In one case, the slides were projected for a two-minute period in a daily exposure session, but the monkey had no direct control over the onset or duration of the picture. Under the second procedure the animal could expose itself to the pictures by touching a lever which turned on the picture for a fifteen-second period. Behavioral reactions to the slides, such as vocalization, disturbance, playing, and exploration, were recorded by an observer hidden behind a one-way-vision screen. Of particular interest was the disturbance reaction, which includes rocking, huddling, self-clasping, fear, and withdrawal. Figure 7-7 shows that the isolated monkeys were highly selective in their fear reaction in terms of both the object and the timing. Only one slide evoked much disturbance, the threatening monkey picture. Throughout the 9-month period the other slides provoked little fear response. Even more striking is the fact that the fear reaction began abruptly at 2 to $2^1/2$ months and peaked at about 3 months. By $3^1/2$ months, there was a decline in fear of the picture. When the monkey had control over the things that it looked at, a similar pattern emerged.

Since the isolation rearing conditions precluded opportunities for learning the significance of the visual threat of another monkey, the data suggest that this threat pattern may be an *innate releasing stimulus* for fearful behavior in rhesus monkeys. Although the initial onset may be maturationally governed, it is unlikely that the decline observed in this experiment would be found under normal rearing conditions where the threat is often backed up with actual physical attacks. These data suggest that while certain aspects of communication may lie in acquisition through social learning processes during interactions with other animals, the initial evocation of such complex responses may have an inherited species-specific structure. (Sackett, 1966, p. 1472)

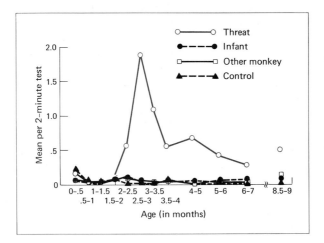

FIGURE 7-7 The amount of disturbance behavior of infant rhesus monkeys in response to different types of pictures viewed during nine months of isolation. *(From Sackett, 1966, with permission of the author and the American Association for the Advancement of Science.)*

Fear as a Learned Phenomenon   According to other theorists, fear is not innate or constitutionally determined; rather, children *learn* to fear certain aspects of their environment. Sometimes this can be accomplished in a very direct manner through either instrumental conditioning or classical conditioning, learning paradigms that were discussed in Chapter 6. A familiar example of instrumental fear conditioning is the young child who touches a hot stove; the *consequence* of touching the stove is pain, and as a result of this unpleasant outcome the child learns to fear the hot stove and avoids it on later occasions.

Another approach is the classical conditioning position, which stresses not the outcomes but rather the events that are temporarily associated with a particular response. According to this viewpoint, the young child learns to fear objects and even people in his environment by their association with an unlearned fearful stimulus. For example, as we noted in an earlier chapter, children who are punished by an adult may avoid this parent or socializing agent. In classical conditioning terms, the loud noise would be the unconditioned stimulus, or UCS; any object that was temporarily linked with this UCS would be termed the conditioned stimulus, or CS. The theory assumes that as a result of the frequent pairing of the previously neutral or nonfearful stimulus with the anxiety-arousing event, this neutral event would serve as a fear elicitor as well.

The case of "little Albert" illustrates this approach to fear development. Watson and Raynor (1920) found that the loud noise produced by striking a steel bar evoked fear reactions in this 11-month-old boy; few other things caused him any anxiety or fear. A white rat, to which the child showed no fear, was chosen as the object to be conditioned. Over a series of trials, Watson and Raynor presented the white rat but, at the same time, clanged the steel bar. Although the child had not previously feared the white rat, presentation of the animal—without the noise—was sufficient to produce marked fear reactions. Little Albert had been classically conditioned to fear the rat. Moreover, the child showed evidence of generalized fear of similar objects: furry and wooly objects in his environment, such as a white rabbit, a dog, a fur coat, cotton, and wool. In fact, he even showed a fear reaction to a Santa Claus mask! To determine whether the generalization effect was merely transitory, Watson and Raynor retested Albert after one month. Although the emotional reactions were reduced, there was still evidence of generalized conditioned fear. Later studies with both children (Jones, 1931) and animals (Miller, 1948) have confirmed this classical conditioning theory of fear acquisition.

However, direct experience with the critical object is not the only way in which fears are learned. Observation of the emotional reactions of other people to environmental events will often shape the onlookers' reactions to these events. In a recent experiment Venn and Short (1973) exposed nursery-school-age children to a film showing a 5-year-old male model scream and withdraw when the mother presented a plastic figure of Mickey Mouse; in response to another previously neutral stimulus, a plastic figure of Donald Duck, the film model gave only a neutral reaction. A later test revealed that the children avoided Mickey Mouse, the fearful stimulus, more than Donald Duck, the neutral stimulus. In this study, classical conditioning had been achieved, but merely through observation. In other naturalistic situations, a similar phenomenon may occur. Parents, for example, may be inadvertently teaching their children to fear certain objects by showing marked fear themselves in the presence of the object. Children who witness a parent jumping back and screaming at the sight of a snake may show a similar fear reaction when they themselves directly encounter a snake on some future occasion. In this case the child's fear of snakes develops through observing the parent's emotional reactions.

The Perceptual-Recognition Viewpoint   Just as smiling and laughter could be understood as a perceptual-recognition achievement, some reactions also can be viewed this way. A classic experiment by Hebb in 1946 on the development of fear in the chimpanzee will illustrate this viewpoint. There were two critical conditions in this study. In the first condition, the chimps were given normal visual experience, including the experience of seeing other chimpanzees. In the second condition, the animals were reared with a blindfold which prevented them from seeing the other chimps. Both groups were then exposed to the critical stimulus, a plaster replica of the head of a chimpanzee. The results were striking: for the animals who had been reared under normal conditions and allowed to interact with age-mates, the sight of the "chimpanzee head" caused extreme fear and flight; for the animals lacking this opportunity for visual learning, the sculpture caused either little reaction or a mild curiosity. The main thing is that these animals showed no fear reaction. Why the difference? Hebb (1946, 1949) proposed that the normally reared chimps had learned a particular perceptual pattern which defined the concept of "chimpanzee." This familiar pattern included not only a head, but, of course, a body, legs, and arms as well. It was the sight of the head alone, partially familiar but incomplete, that caused the animals' upset. Their expectation, based on past experience with the familiar object, the chimpanzee, was violated by this incomplete duplication of the familiar pattern. It was, according to Hebb, this violation of the expectation that evoked fear. It is now easy to see why the blindfolded animals failed to show any fear. They were deprived of the opportunity to build a standard of familiarity. Until the pattern has been learned or centrally coded, incongruous or violating stimulation is precluded.

At the human level, the phenomenon that most closely resembles the reactions of Hebb's chimpanzees is a fear of strangers anxiety reaction, such as crying, whimpering, and withdrawal, whenever a strange adult is present. Part of the reason for this reaction may be due to the apparent discrepancy the infant notices between his familiar caretaker and the stranger. They share some similarities, just as the plaster head shared some similarities with the chimp's familiar experiences, but there were some discrepancies as well. It may be that the discrepancy between the familiar and the partially familiar causes the anxiety. If this position has any merit, certain predictions would follow. Since the central proposition involves the learning of a unique pattern—the characteristics of the mother, for example—then the extent of the anxiety reaction should vary with the exclusiveness of the mother-infant relationship. The infant who sees only his mother is more likely to notice or detect the difference between the well-established pattern of mother and a strange female. On the other hand, a child who sees baby-sitters, grandmothers, day-care center aids, and the next-door neighbors, as well as the mother, will have a more diffuse concept of "mother" and will, therefore, be less likely to show a fear of strange adults. Evidence in support of this prediction comes from a study by Schaffer (1966). Using human infants, he found that fear of strangers was evidenced earlier in families with a small number of children and when the number of strangers typically seen by the child was small. These findings, then, are clearly consistent with the perceptual recognition approach to fear development.

Which Explanation Is Correct?   It should be obvious to the reader by now that no single viewpoint is "correct"; all views have some evidence in their favor. It is not unreasonable to assume that different types of fear may, in fact, develop according to different sets of principles. Moreover, it is possible, as Bronson (1968) has proposed, that the contribution and importance of these viewpoints may vary with the developmental stage of the infant. For example, in the first few months of life, the constitutional and classical conditioning positions are probably much more useful in explaining "fear" than is the perceptual-recognition hypothesis. This latter viewpoint will be relevant only "when the child is cognitively mature enough to distinguish between familiar and unfamiliar and to recognize discrepancies in the appearance of a familiar stimulus" (Bronson, 1968, p. 424). These cognitive attainments are related to Piaget's concepts of schema and object permanence, which will be discussed in Chapter 9. The task, then, is not to decide which explanation is correct, but to determine how each set of principles contributes to our understanding of the development of this complex emotional response pattern. Just as we saw in the case of smiling and attachment, different theoretical perspectives may be required at different developmental periods.

In summary, fear, like smiling, is a complex response which depends on a variety of factors including the type of stimulus, the infant's familiarity with the situation, the social agent, and the infant's developmental level. Only by considering these factors can the emergence of fear be understood. Without consideration of these factors, it is very unlikely that you would know when to expect a smile or a frown.

Developmental Changes in Specific Fears

It is likely that the specific objects and situations that evoke fear change as children develop. In fact, tracking the development of specific fears has been a favorite task of psychologists since the 1930s.

For an up-to-date look at the nature of children's fears, we turn to a recent study by Barnett (1969). A group of 228 seven- to twelve-year-old girls participated in this project. She found that overall fear did not differ at various age levels, but several specific categories of fear changed with age. Figure 7-8 illustrates age changes in particular fears. Notice that as the child grows older,

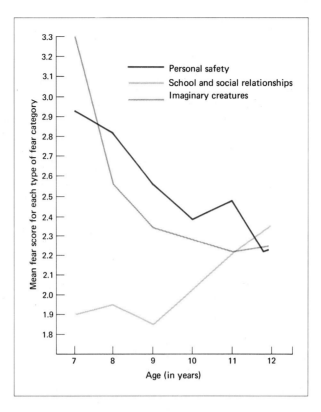

FIGURE 7-8 Variation in children's fears with age for imaginary creatures, school and social relationships, and personal safety. *(From Barnett, 1969.)*

fears concerning imaginary creatures and personal safety show a decline; probably this trend is due to the child's more sophisticated understanding of the laws governing physical reality. As adolescence approaches, there is another marked change: school and social concerns show a rapid rise. These developmental changes move the child closer to the adult fear profile, which is characterized by a high degree of social fear and little concern of imaginary fears.

Fear Measurement: The Integration of Various Indexes of Fearfulness

Although many studies of children's fear have relied on verbal reports of what children (or their parents) *say* they fear, until recently little attention has been directed to the interrelationships between verbal reports and actual fear behavior. In other words, do children who say they are afraid *act* afraid? Similarly, do emotional measures of fear relate to verbal and behavioral indexes? The importance of these questions is underlined by recent studies of fear in adults. Lang (1968), for example, found little relationship among verbal responses and overt responses, both in the form of avoidance of the feared object and in physiological measures of fear among college students. Saying one is not afraid is a poor predictor of how one will act or how one's heart will react when confronted by the actual fear object. Whether or not the three systems of fear are integrated to a greater extent during childhood is one of the questions that Barnett (1969) tried to answer. Two groups of girls participated: ten 9- to 11-year-olds drawn from local Brownie and Girl Scout organizations and twenty 9- to 11-year-olds from a local Catholic school. Children came individually to the university laboratory, where a variety of measures of fear were collected. First, the girls watched a series of slides depicting neutral pictures of nonfrightening animals, such as deer, raccoons, and rabbits, and then a series of three critical slides of three different snakes. To measure the children's physiological reaction, heart rate was continuously monitored during the slide show. To index the children's verbal expressions of fear, the subjects rated their fear of the snake pictures. As a further measure of the children's reactions to snakes generally, the snake questionnaire for children was administered. This instrument is composed of eleven items describing scenes with harmless snakes; the children merely indicate how fearful they would be if they were in each scene. Confrontation with a live snake followed. In this behavioral assessment phase of the study, each girl was asked to execute a series of increasingly intimate acts, first with a small kitten and then with the test animal, a 4-foot boa constrictor. Here is a list of the eleven acts that the children were asked to perform:

1   Walk up to a white line 2 feet from the cage.
2   Walk directly up to the cage.
3   Look directly at the animal in the cage.
4   Put hand on the glass of the cage.
5   Remove the cover from the cage.
6   Place hand in the cage.
7   Touch the animal for the count of one.
8   Stroke the animal for the count of three.
9   Stroke the animal for the count of five.
10 Lift the animal an inch off the ground.
11 Lift the animal out of the cage.

The child's behavior fear score was the number of tasks actually completed, with the higher scores representing less fear. Finally, the child was asked to rate her own fear during the snake test. Now let us examine the results. Barnett confirmed the fact that most children, or girls at least, are not afraid of kittens. Twenty-five out of twenty-seven girls completed all tasks with the live kitten. In contrast, only seven children completed the eleven tasks with the live boa constrictor. Of particular interest is the relationship of the girls' behavior with other fear measures, the self-report and heart rate. The children's self-ratings during the slide presentation and their evaluations of their own fearfulness in the presence of the snake both predicted accurately the actual behavioral performance. Children who said earlier that they feared snakes hovered around the back of the room and would not touch the snake. Those who said they were not afraid touched, picked up, and even held the snake close to their bodies. Similarly, the high correlation between the snake questionnaire results and children's performance suggests that this is a valid instrument for fear assessment in children. Apparently children do as they say. However, the self-reported overall fear level, measured by the children's Fear Survey Schedule which measured fear of a wide range of objects, did *not* relate to the children's behavior in the snake test. The close link between word and deed is present only in the case of specific fears. Knowing that a child regards herself as highly fearful in *general* may be a poor predictor of how she will actually behave in *particular* fear situations.

The relationships between emotional reactions indexed by heart rate and the self-report and behavioral measures of fear were also impressive. With the snake questionnaire scores as a basis, the children were divided into high- and low-fear groups and then the heart-rate responses in reaction to the snake slides of these two samples were examined. Heart-rate acceleration was higher for the high-fear girls than for their peers who reported being less afraid of snakes. Similarly, heart-rate acceleration was greater for the girls who rated their fear of the snake as greater. Finally, the verbal rating of fear during performance with the live snake followed the same pattern of relationship of heart-rate measure. In summary, somatic and self-report indexes among these girls showed a consistent and positive relationship. Again evidence of a high degree of interrelation between these two fear indexes was found: the high-fear subjects as indexed by the completion of few tasks with the snake showed greater heart-rate acceleration than the low-fear girls.

Unlike adults, in children the three fear systems—self-report, behavioral, and psychophysiological—show a well-integrated pattern. Girls who say they are afraid tend to react that way both behaviorally and physiologically. As Barnett suggested, "It may be the case that while in adults separate variables control the various systems of fear response, the extent of this differential learning has not taken place with children 7 to 12 years of age" (Barnett, 1969, p. 33). Clearly, data on older children would be of interest in tracking the emergence of the highly differentiated control of fear responsivity that is observed in adults. Moreover, in light of Bronson's (1970) data concerning the sex differences in stability of fear reactions over time, one wonders whether the same degree of integration would be present for boys. Cultural norms dictating less fearfulness for boys may contribute to weaker links between self-report measures and other indexes of fear.

Overcoming Children's Fears

Fears of dangerous animals and hot stoves are adaptive and useful, but fears of harmless household pets, heights, and dentists are only debilitating. One advantage of a learning-theory approach to fear development is that it points directly to therapeutic techniques for reducing children's fears. Just as conditioning and modeling could be used to account for fear acquisition, these same principles can aid in fear reduction.

Counterconditioning For counterconditioning, the fearful stimuli that typically evoke emotional reactions are presented in conjunction with pleasant activities. In a classic application of this technique, Mary Cover Jones (1924) used food as the pleasant stimulus. The subject, Peter, a boy of 34 months, showed many of the same reactions as "little Albert," the infant in the Watson and Raynor study.

Both children showed strong fear reactions to furry objects, such as fur coats, feathers, cotton, wool, and animals, especially rabbits. To reduce his fear of the rabbit, Jones placed the caged animal in the room with the child at the same time that he was eating. She was careful not to put the cage too close so that Peter's eating was disrupted. Each day the cage was moved a little closer, and finally the animal was released from his cage. At the end of the treatment period, the child showed no fear, even when the rabbit was placed on the eating table. In fact, the child spontaneously expressed his fondness for the animal; by pairing the animal with the highly pleasant activity of eating, the positive affect associated with eating generalized to the rabbit and counterconditioned Peter's fear of the rabbit. Generalization tests, moreover, indicated that his previous fears of furry objects had been successfully eliminated as well.

Desensitization   A more recent approach to overcoming children's fear is *desensitization.* The basic premise in this technique is that the physical states such as muscle relaxation which are associated with nonstressful states are incompatible with and can counteract responses associated with fear. According to this approach, the therapist trains the child in physical relaxation techniques, constructs a graduated list of fearful stimuli, and then asks the child to imagine events in increasing order of fearfulness. Each time that a fearful stimulus is visualized, the child is required to relax. By inducing a state of calm in the presence of the fearful stimulus, the associated anxiety is extinguished, or counterconditioned. Relaxation, then, instead of food is used in this procedure. As the child overcomes his or her fear of weaker events, the therapist gradually moves up the fear scale so that eventually the most fearful event becomes completely neutralized and elicits no anxiety. Instead of visualizing fear items, more concrete techniques of stimulus presentation, such as slides and pictures of the fear stimuli, have been employed with children.

To illustrate the procedure, here is an example for a snake-fearing child. The child and therapist first construct a list of snake-related objects that the child fears. There may be as many as twenty steps between the least and most feared items. The least feared item might be seeing a snakeskin belt on a department store counter, while a middle-level item might be seeing a snake 20 feet ahead on a path in the forest. The highest item might be picking up and handling a nonpoisonous snake. After a few sessions of relaxation training, the child in the first desensitization session is asked to imagine seeing the belt and to relax. He has repeated visualization of this first item with relaxation instructions until he no longer reports fear and anxiety upon visualizing the belt on the store counter. Then he moves on to the next item in his hierarchy and goes through repeated exposure to this item while he engages in the incompatible muscle relaxation procedure. Gradually, the child works up to the point where he can even pick up and handle the previously feared snake without anxiety.

This technique has been applied to a wide range of fears in both children and adults, including fear of spiders, snakes, airplanes, hospitals, and schools. Children with severe examination anxiety have had their performance on tests improved through desensitization (Mann & Rosenthal, 1969). Reading achieve-

Children can overcome fear of snakes. (Jeanne Tifft, Photo Researchers, Inc.)

ment scores of desensitized children improved and their anxiety test scores dropped significantly in contrast to a group of nontreated control children. Moreover, observers of the treatment procedure benefited to the same extent as the direct participants; this suggests a further manner in which fears can be reduced: modeling. In the next section we will examine the effectiveness of modeling techniques for promoting fear reduction.

Exposure to a Fearless Model   Just as many fears can be acquired merely by observing the actions of other individuals, many fearful responses can be eliminated in this same manner. A study by Bandura, Grusec, and Menlove (1967) illustrates that a fear of dogs can be overcome by exposure to a fearless peer model. Qualifications for participation in this project were few: one merely had to be a nursery schooler who exhibited a strong fear of dogs. Then each child was assigned to one of four treatment conditions designed to help overcome the dog phobia. Children in one group watched a 4-year-old model perform increasingly "brave" and intimate interactions with a dog over a series of eight brief sessions. For example, in the first session the child merely stayed close to the dog, who was enclosed in a wooden pen. In later sessions the child climbed into the pen and fearlessly played with the animal. All the sessions took place in the context of a "jovial party" to determine whether a positive viewing atmosphere would further reduce and counteract the young children's anxieties. A child assigned to the second condition would see the same graduated series of model-dog interactions, but in a neutral rather than a party context. Since repeated exposure to the feared animal alone might be therapeutic, some of the children merely watched the dog, and although the party atmosphere was retained, no peer model ever appeared. Finally, for the last group, the only experience offered would be the jovial party; neither dog nor model was ever present. Following treatment, the children's fear behavior in reaction to two different dogs was assessed twice: once immediately after the final session and again a month later.

According to Bandura:

The avoidance test consisted of a graded sequence of interactions with the dog. The children were asked, for example, to approach and pet the dog, to release it from the playpen, remove it from its leash, feed it with dog biscuits and spend a fixed period of time alone in the room with the animal. The final and most difficult set of tasks required the children to climb into the playpen with the dog and after having locked the gate, to pet it and remain alone with it under these confining fear-arousing conditions. (Bandura, 1968, p. 203)

As Figure 7-9 indicates, the modeling treatment was successful in producing stable *and* generalized reduction in the children's avoidance of dogs. In comparison to the other two groups, children exposed to the fearless peer model displayed significantly greater approach behavior, not only toward the experimental dog, but to an unfamiliar dog as well. A generalized reduction in fear had been produced by these modeling procedures. Modeling alone apparently accounted for these changes since the party atmosphere contributed little to the fear reduction. Stating the results differently, an impressive 67 percent of the children in the modeling treatment conditions were eventually able to remain alone in the room and confined with the dog in the playpen; only a few children in the control conditions could manage this terminal task.

More recently, these fear-reduction techniques have been applied to children's fear of the dentist (Melamed, Hawes, Heiby, & Glick, 1975). These investigators exposed 5- to 11-year-old children to a film of a child experiencing

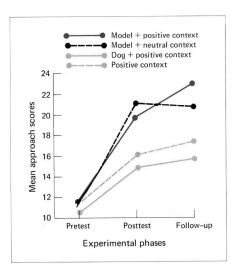

FIGURE 7-9   Mean approach scores achieved by children in each of the treatment conditions on the three different periods of assessment. *(From Bandura, Grusec & Menlove, 1967, with permission of the authors and the American Psychological Association.)*

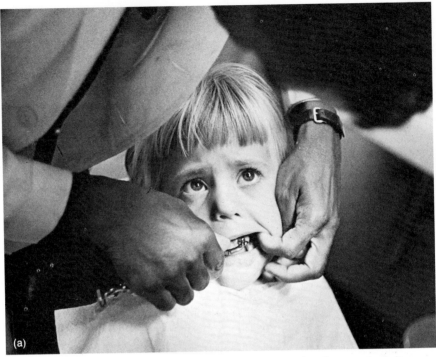

Many children are fearful of dentists and doctors, but modeling therapy can help children reduce these fears. (Photo (a) by Richard Frear, Photo Researchers, Inc.; photo (b) by Ed Lettau, Photo Researchers, Inc.)

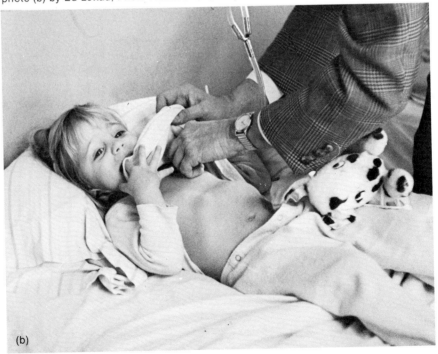

a typical dental procedure with a sensitive and friendly dentist. The child was shown coping with her anxiety and clearly discovering that there was nothing to fear. The film child was praised for cooperating and received a prize at the end of the procedure. Compared to children who saw a film unrelated to dentistry, these children showed fewer disruptive behaviors during a tooth-filling session and were rated as less fearful (see Figure 7-10). Together, these demonstrations illustrate the effectiveness of film models for reducing children's fears.

Recognition and Labeling of Emotions

It is interesting not only to understand the development of emotions in children, but to determine when infants learn to recognize the emotional states of others. Well before the infant is capable of understanding verbal language, her caretakers communicate their feelings and wishes by a whole array of emotional expressions. As Darwin (1872) observed over a century ago, "Movements of expression in the face and body . . . serve as the first means of communication between the mother and her infant; she smiles approval and thus encourages her child on the right path or frowns disapproval" (1872, p. 364).

Recent studies indicate that infants as young as 4 months of age can discriminate among different emotions. Four- and six-month-old infants saw slides of an adult face expressing joy or anger or a neutral emotion (La Barbera, Izard, Vietze, & Parisi, 1976). Infants looked longer at the joy expression than at either the anger or neutral expressions. This ability to distinguish joy before

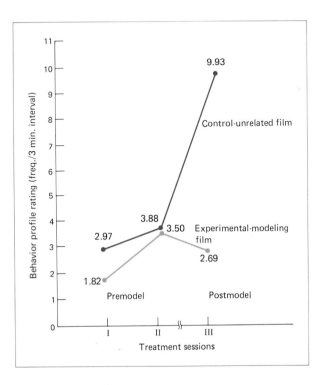

FIGURE 7-10 The effects of modeling on reducing children's fear of dentists. Sessions I and II involved teeth cleaning and a dental examination. In session III, children saw a film and then had a cavity filled. *(From Melamed, Hawes, Heiby, & Glick, 1975, with permission of the senior author and the publisher.)*

being able to recognize anger is consistent with the developmental course of the infant's own emotional expression. Smiling and laughter—positive emotions—develop before fear—a negative emotional state. The findings are consistent with the view that

Biological mechanisms underlying a particular discrete emotion become functional as that emotion becomes adaptive in the life of the infant. . . . Recognition of joy can provide rewarding and self-enhancing experiences for the infant. Such recognition can also strengthen the mother-infant bond and facilitate mutually rewarding experiences, particularly if the joy recognition leads to joy expression . . . anger recognition is not adaptive in the first half year of life. It seems reasonable that the threat of an anger expression would call for coping responses that are beyond the capacity of the 6 month-old. (La Barbera et al., 1976, p. 537)

Although the process of distinguishing among emotional expressions of other people begins early in infancy, the developmental progression to the full sophistication of adulthood continues throughout childhood. Moreover, recognition of emotions involves more than merely discriminating between different facial expressions. Children must learn which emotions are appropriate in different situations. How early do children know that sharing candy will make someone happy, while getting lost in the woods makes someone sad or afraid? To find out, Borke (1971) presented 3- to 8-year-old children with stories which described situations that might make another child feel happy, fearful, sad, or angry. The child was shown happy, fearful, sad, and angry faces and was asked to point to the one which indicated how the other child felt in the situation. The age at which children understood other people's feelings varied according to the type of emotion being assessed. By age 3½ to 4 almost all the children identified happy stories correctly. In stories in which the story character might be expected to be fearful, 3- to 3½-year-olds were unsuccessful, and only by 4½ years of age were most of the children aware that another child would be fearful in these situations. Children were least successful in correctly recognizing sadness and anger. The recognition process develops at different rates for different emotional states.

The child must learn not only to distinguish among expressions, but to be able to produce them as well. "The expressions of others serve to communicate significant information to the child about the people and things around him while his own productions of expression function to communicate attitudes and needs to others" (Odom & Lemond, 1972, p. 359).

Just as we saw in the case of children's ability to recognize different emotions, children can *produce* positive emotions earlier than negative emotions (Buck, 1975). But children do improve over age in their ability to both discriminate and reproduce facial expressions (Odom & Lemond, 1972). This developmental increase probably contributes to the more frequent and successful peer-group participation and increasingly more sustained and sophisticated social interactions (Buck, 1975). Moreover, facial expressions such as joy, sadness, disgust, and anger are universal; facial expressions of emotion are similar across a wide range of both literate (for example, Brazil, Japan, United States) and primitive cultures (for example, Fore & Dori tribes of New Guinea) (Ekman, 1971).

Sometimes emotional messages may be contradictory. For example, criticism may be delivered in a pleasant voice or may be accompanied by a smile. The father who smiles benignly at his son as he says blandly, "Don't swear at your mother," is communicating a very different message than the father who makes the same communication in a stern voice accompanied by a scowl. It has been found that in interacting with their children, mothers are more likely to make this type of inconsistent communication than fathers. When a father smiles while talking to his child, he is likely to be making a more positive approving statement than when he is not smiling. In contrast it has been found that mothers are likely to smile when criticizing their children as well as when praising them. (Bugental, Love, & Gianetto, 1971).

It is interesting that children are aware that the female smile is an unreliable indicator of true emotion. In a paper aptly entitled "Perfidious Feminine Faces" it was reported that when children view mothers making joking messages such as criticism with a smile, they are more likely to regard this as hostile than when the same inconsistent message is delivered by a father. If mother smiles and says, "You're a complete idiot," the child accepts her words. Father's smile means the communication is a teasing, more positive, even affectionate message.

Children differ from adults in their ratings of how positively or negatively they view such communications. Children in the presence of conflicting information, particularly from women, are more likely than adults to resolve the incongruity by assuming the worst. Adults tend to place less credence in a critical statement if the speaker smiles (Bugental et al., 1971).

To Laugh or Cry: Learning to Recognize Our Own Emotions

These studies tell us when capacities for labeling and recognition of emotions may occur. But what is the nature of the process by which we decide when we are happy rather than sad, angry, or disgusted? Attempts to define emotions by identifying stimuli that elicit different emotions have not been successful. In fact, the *same* stimulus can produce laughter at one time and fear on another occasion. Let us take an example: Scarr and Salapatek (1970), in their study of fear, found that a mask worn by a stranger produced withdrawal and fear in their infants, while Sroufe and Wunsch (1972) reported that a similar mask worn by the infant's mother elicited laughter. Rothbart (1973) offers a parallel illustration of the paradox:

If a man suddenly appears to a child and says, "I'm going to get you," and the man is a stranger, the child is likely to run away. If, however, the man saying "I'm going to get you" is the child's father, the child may laugh and beg the father to repeat the threat. In the former case, the child is aroused in a situation subsequently labeled dangerous; in the latter case he is aroused in a "safe" situation. (Rothbart, 1973, p. 251)

It is clear that the *same* stimulus, whether it is a loud sound, a mock attack, or a masked face, is capable of eliciting either fear *or* laughter.

Perhaps there are different physiological correlates of emotions such as fear, anger, and embarrassment. But emotions appear to be more than physiological states, and those early attempts to discover different physiological bases of emotions were largely unsuccessful. Rather, it appears that the physiological reactions determine only the *intensity* of our emotional reactions; they do not provide information concerning the *identity* of the emotion that is being experienced. In fact, the physiological states appear to be surprisingly similar for all emotions. We learn to label or catalog these similar states of arousal by reference either to clues in the present environment or to our past experience in related situations. For example, the infant knows that her father is playing when he says, "I'm going to get you," and so the baby laughs; when hearing these words from a stranger, the baby interprets them as threatening and so exhibits fear. In short, we have to learn to interpret the events that produce our physiological states; only then do we have *emotions.*

Summary

Emotions serve a variety of functions including the communication of needs, moods, and feelings; through emotional expressions children can regulate their social environment such as greet another person, gain and maintain social contact, or appease an attacker.

Smiling, an early positive emotional expression, follows a general developmental progression from an early dependence on internal stimulation to a later responsiveness to external input by 3 months of age. At about 5 months, laughter emerges. Alternative explanations have been offered to account for the origins and development of smiling. The onset of smiling may be biologically predetermined, but prior learning probably determines the rate of smiling. A perceptual-cognitive interpretation which stresses the pleasure and subsequent expression of smiling that results from the infant's understanding of a moderately discrepant event has also been advanced to explain some of the developmental changes in smiling and laughter.

The development of attachment is an important experience in the infant's emotional development. Early in the first year, infants begin to discriminate familiar and unfamiliar caretakers. At 6 to 7 months, the development of attachment to specific individuals emerges. Alternative theories of how attachment develops include psychoanalytic, learning, and ethological viewpoints. A sensitive and responsive caretaker is critical for the development of attachment. Infants form multiple attachments, and fathers and peers as well as mothers are frequently attachment objects. Fathers have a special role as an early play partner. Finally, the quality of early attachments may affect later patterns of play and exploration as well as peer relationships.

Fear, like positive emotions, is under internal regulation in early infancy, while later fear is evoked by external events and objects. The expression of fears, including fear of strangers, a reaction that is neither inevitable nor universal, is influenced by a variety of factors. These include the nature of the setting, the type of fear object, and the behavior of the social agent. Alternative explanations for fear development have been offered, including genetic, learning, and perceptual recognition. The perceptual-recognition hypothesis suggests that incongruous or unfamiliar events that cannot be readily understood by the child may evoke fear.

Evidence indicates that the nature of children's fear changes with age; as the child grows, fears concerning imaginary creatures and personal safety decline, while school and social anxieties begin to predominate.

Three frequently used approaches to overcoming children's fears are counterconditioning, desensitization, and modeling. In counterconditioning, the fear stimulus is associated with a pleasant activity (for example, eating) and the child's fear is gradually reduced. Desensitization involves teaching the child to relax in the presence of increasingly fearful stimuli and gradually eliminating the fear. Another technique to lessen children's fears involves exposing a fearful child to a nonfearful model. Children who feared dogs were eventually able to interact without fear or flight after watching a peer play with the originally feared animal.

Finally, children learn to recognize emotions in others and to label their own emotions. Children can recognize and produce positive emotional expressions sooner than negative emotions.

References

Ahrens, R. Beitrag zur entwicklun des physionomie und mimikerkennens. *Z. F. Exp. U. Angew. Psychol.,* 1954, **2,** 599–633.

Ainsworth, M. D. The development of infant-mother interaction among the Ganda. In D. M. Foss (Ed.), *Determinants of infant behavior* (Vol. 2). New York: Wiley, 1963, pp. 67–104.

Ainsworth, M. D. The development of infant-mother attachment. In B. Caldwell & H. Ricciuti (Eds.), *Review of child development research* (Vol. 3). Chicago: University of Chicago Press, 1973.

Ainsworth, M., Salter, D., & Wittig, B. A. Attachment and exploratory behavior of one-year-olds in a strange situation. In B. M. Foss (Ed.), *Determinants of infant behavior* (Vol. 4). New York: Wiley, 1967.

Ainsworth, M. D., & Bell, S. M. Some contemporary patterns of mother-infant interaction in the feeding situation. In J. A. Ambrose (Ed.), *Stimulation in early infancy.* London: Academic, 1969.

Buck, R. Nonverbal communication of affect in children. *Journal of Personality and Social Psychology,* 1975, **31,** 644–653.

Bandura, A. Modeling approaches to the modification of phobic disorders. In R. Porter (Ed.), *The role of learning in psychotherapy.* London: Churchill, 1968, pp. 201–217.

Bandura, A., Grusec, J. E., & Menlove, F. L. Vicarious extinction of avoidance behavior. *Journal of Personality and Social Psychology,* 1967, **5,** 16–23.

Barnett, J. T. Development of children's fears: The relationship between three systems of fear measurement. Unpublished M.A. thesis, University of Wisconsin, 1969.

Blehar, M. C., Lieberman, A. F., & Ainsworth, M. D. Early face-to-face interaction and its relation to later infant-mother attachment. *Child Development,* 1977, **48,** 182–194.

Bloom, K., & Esposito, A. Social conditioning and its proper control procedures. *Journal of Experimental Child Psychology,* 1975, **19,** 209–222.

Borke, H. Interpersonal perception of young children: Egocentrism or empathy? *Developmental Psychology,* 1971, **5,** 263–296.

Bowlby, J. The nature of the child's tie to his mother. *International Journal of Psychoanalysis,* 1958, **39,** 35.

Bowlby, J. *Attachment and loss,* Vol. 1, *Attachment.* New York: Basic Books, 1969.

Bowlby, J. *Separation and loss.* New York: Basic Books, 1973.

Brackbill, Y. Extinction of the smiling response in infants as a function of reinforcement schedule. *Child Development,* 1958, **29,** 115–124.

Bronfenbrenner, U., Belsky, J., & Steinberg, L. Day care in context: An ecological perspective on research and public policy. In *Policy issues in day care.* U.S. Department of Health, Education, and Welfare report, Washington, 1977.

Bronson, G. W. The development of fear in man and other animals. *Child Development,* 1968, **39,** 409–431.

Bronson, G. W. Fear of visual novelty. *Developmental Psychology,* 1970, **2,** 33–40.

Brooks, J., & Lewis, M. Infants' responses to strangers: Midget, adult and child. *Child Development,* 1976, **47,** 323–332.

Bugental, D. E., Love, L. R., & Gianetto, R. M. Perfidious feminine faces. *Journal of Personality and Social Psychology,* 1971, **17,** 314–318.

Caldwell, B. M., Wright, C., Honig, R., & Tannenbaum, J. Infant day care and attachment. *American Journal of Orthopsychiatry,* 1970, **40,** 397–412.

Carpenter, G. Mother's face and the newborn. In R. Lewin (Ed.), *Child alive.* London: Temple Smith, 1975.

Clarke-Stewart, K. A. And daddy makes three. *Child Development,* 1978, **49,** 466–478.

Darwin, C. *The expression of emotions in man and animals,* London: John Murray, 1872.

Dennis, W. Does culture appreciably affect patterns of infant behavior? *Journal of Social Psychology,* 1940, **12,** 305–317.

Dittrichova, J. The development of premature infants. In R. J. Robinson (Ed.), *Brain and early development.* London: Academic, 1969.

Ekman, P. Universals and cultural differences in facial expression of emotion. In J. K. Cole (Ed.), *Nebraska symposium on motivation.* Lincoln: University of Nebraska Press, 1971, pp. 207–283.

Emde, R., Gaensbauer, T., & Harmon, R. Emotional expression in infancy: A biobehavioral study. *Psychological Issues Monograph,* 1976, **10** (No. 37).

Etzel, B. C., & Gewirtz, J. L. Experimental modification of caretaker-maintained high rate operant crying in a 6- and a 20-week-old infant: Extinction of crying with reinforcement of eye contact and smiling. *Journal of Experimental Child Psychology,* 1967, **5,** 303–317.

Farran, D. C., & Ramey, C. T. Infant day care and attachment behaviors toward mothers and teachers. *Child Development,* 1977, **48,** 1112–1116.

Fox, N. Attachment of kibbutz infants to mother and metapelet. *Child Development,* 1977, **48,** 1228–1239.

Freedman, D. G. Hereditary control of early social behavior. In B. M. Foss (Ed.), *Determinants of infant behavior* (Vol. 3). London: Methuen, 1965, pp. 149–156.

Freedman, D. G. An evolutionary approach to research on the life cycle. *Human Development,* 1971, **14,** 87–99.

Freud, A., & Dann, S. An experiment in group upbringing. In *The psychoanalytic study of the child* (Vol. 6). New York: International Universities Press, 1951.

Gewirtz, J. L. The course of infant smiling in four child-rearing environments in Israel. In B. M. Foss (Ed.), *Determinants of infant behavior* (Vol. 3). London: Methuen, 1965, pp. 205–248.

Gewirtz, J. L. Mechanisms of social learning: Some roles of stimulation and behavior in early human development. In D. A. Goslin (Ed.), *Handbook of socialization theory and research.* Chicago: Rand-McNally, 1969.

Harlow, H. F., & Zimmermann, R. R. Affectional responses in the infant monkey. *Science,* 1959, **130,** 421–432.

Hebb, D. O. On the nature of fear. *Psychological Review,* 1946, **53,** 250–275.

Hebb, D. O. *The organization of behavior.* New York: Wiley, 1949.

Izard, C. *The face of emotion.* New York: Appleton-Century-Crofts, 1971.

Jones, H. E. The conditioning of overt emotional responses. *Journal of Educational Psychology,* 1931, **22,** 127–130.

Jones, M. C. The elimination of children's fears. *Journal of Experimental Psychology,* 1924, **7,** 383–390.

Kagan, J. On the need for relativism. *American Psychologist,* 1967, **22,** 131–147.

Kagan, J., Henker, B., Hen-Tov, A., Levine, J., & Lewis, M. Infants' differential reactions to familiar and distorted faces. *Child Development,* 1966, **37,** 519–532.

Kagan, J., Kearsley, R. B., & Zelazo, P. R. The effects of infant day care on psychological development. *Educational Quarterly,* 1977, **1,** 109–142.

Korner, A. The effect of the infant's state, level of arousal, sex and ontogenic stage on the caregiver. In M. Lewis & L. Rosenblum (Eds.), *The effect of the infant on its caregiver.* New York: Wiley, 1974.

Kotelchuck, M. The nature of a child's tie to his father. Unpublished doctoral dissertation, Harvard University, 1972.

La Barbera, J. D., Izard, C. E., Vietze, P., & Parisi, S. A. Four and six-month-old infant's visual responses to joy, anger and neutral expressions. *Child Development,* 1976, **47,** 535–538.

Lamb, M. E. Twelve-month-olds and their parents: Interaction in a laboratory playroom. *Developmental Psychology,* 1976, **12,** 237–244.

Lamb, M. E. Father-infant and mother-infant interaction in the first year of life. *Child Development,* 1977, **48,** 167–181.

Lang, P. J. The mechanics of desensitization and the laboratory study of human fear. In C. M. Franks (Ed.), *Assessment and status of the behavior therapies.* New York: McGraw-Hill, 1968.

Leiberman, A. F. Preschooler's competence with a peer: Relations with attachment and peer experience. *Child Development,* 1977, **48,** 1277–1287.

Lewis, M., & Brooks, J. Self, other and fear: Infants' reactions to people. In M. Lewis & L. Rosenblum (Eds.), *The origins of fear.* New York: Wiley, 1974.

Littenberg, R., Tulkin, S., & Kagan, J. Cognitive components of separation anxiety. *Developmental Psychology,* 1971, **4,** 387–388.

Maccoby, E. E., & Feldman, S. S. Mother-attachment and stranger-reactions in the third year of life. *Monographs of the Society for Research in Child Development,* 1972, **37** (Serial No. 146).

Main, M. Exploration, play and level of cognitive functioning as related to child-mother attachment. Unpublished dissertation, Johns Hopkins University, 1973.

Mann, J., & Rosenthal, T. L. Vicarious and direct counterconditioning of test anxiety through individual and group desensitization. Unpublished manuscript, University of Arizona, 1969.

Melamed, B. G., Hawes, R. R., Heiby, E., & Glick, J. The use of filmed modeling to reduce uncooperative behavior of children during dental treatment. *Journal of Dental Research,* 1975, **54,** 797–801.

Miller, N. E. Studies of fear as an acquirable drive. I. Fear as motivation and fear reduction reinforcement in the learning of new responses. *Journal of Experimental Psychology,* 1948, **38,** 89–101.

Morgan, G. A., & Ricciuti, H. Infants' responses to strangers during the first year. In B. M. Foss (Ed.), *Determinants of infant behavior* (Vol. 4). London: Methuen, 1969, pp. 253–272.

Odom, R. D., & Lemond, C. M. Developmental differences in the perception and production of facial expressions. *Child Development,* 1972, **43,** 359–370.

Parke, R. D., & O'Leary, S. E. Father-mother-infant interaction in the newborn period: Some findings, some observations and some unresolved issues. In K. Riegel and J. Meacham (Eds.), *The developing individual in a changing world: Social and environmental issues* (Vol 2). The Hague: Mouton, 1976.

Rheingold, H. L., & Eckerman, C. O. The fear of strangers hypothesis: A critical review. In H. Reese (Ed.), *Advances in child development and behavior* (Vol. 8). New York: Academic, 1973, pp. 185–222.

Ricciuti, H. Effects of day care experience on behavior and development: Research and implications for social policy. Unpublished manuscript, Cornell University, 1976.

Ross, H. S., & Goldman, B. D. Infant's sociability toward strangers. *Child Development,* 1977, **48,** 638–642.

Rothbart, M. K. Laughter in young children. *Psychological Bulletin,* 1973, **80,** 247–256.

Sackett, G. P. Monkeys reared in isolation with pictures as visual input: Evidence for an innate releasing mechanism. *Science,* 1966, **154,** 1468–1473.

Scarr S., & Salapatek, P. Patterns of fear development during infancy. *Merrill-Palmer Quarterly,* 1970, **16,** 53–90.

Schaffer, H. R. The onset of fear of strangers and the incongruity hypothesis. *Journal of Child Psychology and Psychiatry,* 1966, **7,** 95–106.

Schaffer, H. R., & Emerson, P. E. The development of social attachments in infancy. *Monographs of the Society for Research in Child Development,* 1964, **29** (3, Serial No. 94).

Schwartz, A., Campos, J., & Baisel, E. The visual cliff: Cardiac and behavioral correlates on the deep and shallow sides at five and nine months of age. *Journal of Experimental Child Psychology,* 1973, **15,** 85–99.

Sears, R. R., Maccoby, E. E., & Levin, H. *Patterns of child rearing.* New York: Harper & Row, 1957.

Shultz, T. R., & Zigler, E. Emotional concomitants of visual mastery in infants: The effects of stimulus movement on smiling and vocalizing. *Journal of Experimental Child Psychology,* 1970, **10,** 390–402.

Spitz, R. A. The smiling response: A contribution to the ontogenesis of social relations. *Genetic Psychology Monographs,* 1946, **34,** 67–125.

Sroufe, L. A. Emotional development in infancy. In J. Osofsky (Ed.), *Handbook of infancy.* New York: Wiley, 1978.

Sroufe, L. A., Waters, E., & Matas, L. Contextual determinants of infant affectional response. In M. Lewis and L. Rosenblum (Eds.), *Origins of fear.* New York: Wiley, 1974.

Sroufe, L. A., & Wunsch, J. P. The development of laughter in the first year of life. *Child Development,* 1972, **43,** 1326–1344.

Stern, D. N. Mother and infant at play: The dyadic interaction involving facial, vocal and gaze behaviors. In M. Lewis & L. A. Rosenblum (Eds.), *The effect of the infant on its caregiver.* New York: Wiley, 1974.

Venn, J. R., & Short, J. G. Vicarious classical conditioning of emotional responses in nursery school children. *Journal of Personality and Social Psychology,* 1973, **28,** 249–255.

Wahler, R. G. Infant social attachments: A reinforcement theory interpretation and investigation. *Child Development,* 1967, **38,** 1079–1088.

Waters, E. The reliability and stability of individual differences in infant-mother attachment. *Child Development,* 1978, **49,** 483–494.

Watson, J. B., & Raynor, R. Conditioned emotional responses. *Journal of Experimental Psychology,* 1920, **3,** 1–14.

Weinraub, M. Children's responses to maternal absence: An experimental study.

Paper presented at biennial meeting of the Society for Research in Child Development, New Orleans, March 1977.

Weinraub, M., & Lewis, M. The determinants of children's responses to separation. *Monographs of the Society for Research in Child Development* (Serial No. 172), 1977.

Yogman, M. J., Dixon, S., Tronick, E., Als, H., & Brazelton, T. B. The goals and structure of face-to-face interaction between infants and fathers. Paper presented at the biennial meeting of the Society for Research in Child Development, New Orleans, March 1977.

This chapter draws substantially from the language chapter of the first edition which was written by Diana Arezzo Slaby.

8

Language and Communication

One of the most outstanding of the child's developmental achievements is the mastery of language. Language is one of the most complex systems of rules a person *ever* learns, but all children in a wide range of different environments and cultures learn to understand and use language in a remarkably short period. In this chapter, we will try to unravel some of the complexities of language development and communication. How well prepared are infants for learning language? Is there any relationship between early infant vocal behavior and later language development? By tracing the child's development from one-word utterances to the mastery of complex sentences, we will explore how the child learns grammar. How similar is grammar in different cultures and in deaf children? Can animals learn grammatical rules? Next, how does the child's understanding of the meaning of words and sentences develop? Children not only gain new language skills as they develop but gain insight into their own language behavior. How and when does this understanding develop? Another set of questions concerns the ways in which children learn to communicate. What skills are necessary to be an effective speaker or listener? Tracing the developmental course of these communication skills in children will be the final aim of this chapter. By exploring this series of questions we will determine how children acquire the rules of grammar, how they come to understand the meaning of language, and how they learn to use language for effective communication.

Functions of Language, or Why Language?

Few developments that are discussed in this book have such wide-ranging consequences as language. In all aspects of our daily life, language plays an important function. Recently, Halliday (1975) has suggested the following seven functions of language:

1 *Instrumental function.* Language permits the child to satisfy his needs and to express his wishes. This is the "I want" function.

2 *Regulatory function.* Through languge the child is able to control the behavior of others; this is the "do that" function.

3 *Interpersonal function.* Language can be used for interacting with others in the child's social world; this is the "me and you" function.

4 *Personal function.* A child expresses his unique views, feelings, and attitudes through language; through language the child establishes his personal identity.

5 *Heuristic function.* After the child begins to distinguish himself from his environment, he uses language to explore and understand his environment. This is the questioning, or "tell me why," function.

6 *Imaginative function.* Language permits the child to escape from reality into a universe of his own making. This is the "let's pretend," or poetic, function of language.

7 *Informative function.* Children can communicate new information through language; this is the "I've got something to tell you," function.

As this list suggests, language serves a wide range of purposes for the developing child. In this and other chapters we will see numerous examples of how language aids in organizing our perceptions, directing our thinking, controlling our actions, aiding our memory, and modifying our emotions. Without it you wouldn't be reading this page. Language development is a complex process and is most easily understood by dividing up language into a series of subtopics. Next we examine the four faces of language.

The Four Faces of Language: Phonology, Semantics, Syntax, and Pragmatics

The study of language has usually been divided into three areas: phonology, semantics, and syntax. *Phonology* describes the system of sounds for a language, that is, how the basic sound units (phonemes) are put together to form words and how the intonation patterns of phrases and sentences are determined. A *phoneme* can be defined as the shortest speech unit in which a change produces a change in meaning, for example, the difference in meaning between "*bat*" and "*cat*" is accounted for by the different initial phoneme; "*bat*" and "*bit*" differ in their middle phoneme.

Although we will not emphasize phonology in this chapter, it is important to realize that phonological rules, like rules at other linguistic levels, are generative. That is, speakers and listeners know the proper stress and intonation patterns for novel sentences they have never heard before, as well as the sound relationships allowable in novel words. For example, a native speaker knows that the nonsense word "kib" is a possible sound pattern in the English phonological system, but that the nonsense word "bnik" is not possible. Thus, even the rules of phonology form a system, and they are general rules in the sense that they are applicable beyond the cases from which they are derived.

Semantics is the study of the meaning of words and of sentences. The study of semantics is a relatively new area and involves a number of issues. First, when and how does the child understand the meaning of different words and sentences? Second, how does the child learn to use words correctly to communicate her meaning?

Knowledge of the many aspects of meaning requires not only experience with words themselves, but also an understanding of features and relationships in the world. Thus, semantic knowledge continues to increase substantially throughout the school years as the child matures intellectually. A preschool child may use the words "animal" and "dog" appropriately in many contexts. However, his incomplete understanding of the meanings of these words might be demonstrated when he calls a pony a dog, or when he makes statements such as "Lassie is not an animal, she's a dog."

Syntax describes the structure of a language, the underlying rules which specify the order, and the function of words in a sentence. Application of syntactic rules provides the greatest opportunity for linguistic creativity. Each language has specific syntactic rules for expressing grammatical relations, such as negation, interrogation, possession, and juxtaposition of subject and object. Because we share the same syntactic knowledge of sentence structure, when someone says either "Bill hit John" or "Bill was hit by John," we know who did the hitting and who got hit. We can agree that the sentence "You didn't go, did you?" is an acceptable (grammatical) sentence, whereas "You didn't go, didn't you?" is unacceptable and ambiguous.

One category of syntactic rules consists of those which specify how to vary or form words to express grammatical relations. Syntactic word variations are called *inflections*. The following are examples of inflections: go-going, mouse-mice, Mary-Mary's, be-is, was-am, and he-him. The syntax of some languages, such as Latin and Russian, depends much more heavily on inflections than does English. In English the order of words is relatively important for expressing syntactic relations. Linguists have demonstrated the vast complexity of the underlying syntactic system. Yet, in contrast to semantic development, acquisition of the basics of syntactic competence is nearly complete by 4 or 5 years of age.

Developmental psycholinguists initially focused almost exclusively on the syntax of children's earliest sentences. Little emphasis was placed on semantics per se. However, syntax and semantics are not fully separable. The structure of a sentence and its meaning are intrinsically related. There has recently been an increased effort to combine the study of syntax and semantics and to specify the relationship between structure and meaning.

A fourth face of language has recently appeared: *pragmatics*. Pragmatics can be defined as rules governing the use of language in context, by real speakers and listeners in real stiuations (Bates, 1974). For example, when do children learn to use polite forms, how do children adjust their speech for younger children, and why do children talk differently in classrooms and playgrounds? This subfield of language has emerged out of the recognition that much of child language (as well as adult) cannot be understood without knowledge of the context and setting in which it occurs. Context refers to such things as information about the identity of the speaker and listener and the speaker's goal and the immediate physical setting. Finally, pragmatics concerns how children learn conversational rules and so provides a clear link between language development and one of the purposes of language—communication.

In this chapter, we will examine each of the four faces of language so that you will know how sounds develop, what they mean, how children learn grammar, and how they learn to communicate.

Let us begin by briefly reviewing the major theoretical orientations that have helped shape the current research in language development.

Some Contrasting Views on Language Development

Linguistics: Old and New

The field of language development has been influenced heavily by certain theoretical views. Some argue that language is innate, while others contend that learning can account for the development of language. Most current theorists maintain a more middle ground and recognize the role that both genetic and environmental factors play in language development.

A Nativist View   According to this view, language is probably innate, but the theory may take many forms. A representative example is Chomsky's proposal that the human nervous system contains a mental structure which includes an innate concept of human language (Chomsky, 1968). Some nativists maintain that specific aspects of language are innate. For example, they may claim that certain "universal features," common to all human languages, are innate; or that a set of innate "language hypotheses" are used by the child in deriving rules from the language "data" he hears.

These more extreme or literal statements of the nativist position are highly controversial. It has been argued, for instance, that the theories are not testable and that the "innateness" label is simply being used to explain away behavior we do not yet understand. Nativist speculation involving deep structure (for example, McNeill, 1966) is especially questionable because the linguistic concept of deep structure itself is controversial and very much in flux.

Most nativists have not spelled out exactly what they consider to be innate. They do agree, however, that at the very least, every normal human child is in some way biologically "ready" or "predisposed" to learn any human language with ease. They uniformly view language as an abstract system of rules which is not learned by way of traditional learning principles. These more general aspects of the nativist position have become fairly widely accepted and have been influential even among empirical psychologists.

By far the most thorough and precise case for biological determinants of language has been presented, with considerable supporting data, by Eric Lenneberg (1967). Lenneberg's position is that the uniquely human ability to generate and understand language is an inherited species-specific characteristic of humans. He argues that language is based on highly specialized biological mechanisms which not only predispose but actually shape the development of language in the child. These biological determinants include, among other things, the articulatory apparatus, specific brain centers for language, and a specialized auditory system which processes speech sounds in a qualitatively different way than other sounds. Lenneberg points out that the unfolding "milestones" of language acquisition occur in a regular and fixed order in all normal children around the world, and that they occur at very much the same rate despite cultural or environmental variation. For example, children all over the world begin babbling at about 6 months, say their first word near the end of the first year, begin using two-word combinations near the end of the second year, and master the basic syntax of their language by the time they are 4 or 5 years old. Lenneberg considers this regular unfolding process to be tied to biological maturation, in much the same manner as the stages involved in learning how to walk are maturationally determined. In fact, he has demonstrated the correspondence in time between milestones in motor development and milestones in language. Lenneberg suggests that the only requirement for this preprogrammed "unfolding" of language milestones is exposure to a minimal number and variety of normal language examples. In cases in which maturation is abnormally slow, such as in Downs' syndrome, the language milestones develop in the same order as in normal children, but correspond to the slower overall maturation of the child.

Another source of support for specific biological involvement is evidence that humans learn language far more easily and quickly during a certain period of biological development, that is, from infancy to puberty. Before puberty, a child can achieve the fluency of a native speaker in any language (or even in two or more languages simultaneously) without special training. After puberty, language learning is more difficult and usually requires study, and the speaker rarely approaches the fluency of a native speaker. When a family moves to a foreign country, the parents sometimes must depend on their young children, who pick up the language quickly, to serve as translators. Furthermore, in cases of speech disruption due to brain damage, young children often recover their language capacity rapidly and completely; if the brain damage occurs after puberty, the prognosis for the recovery of language is poor (Lenneberg, 1967).

If language ability is an inherited species-specific characteristic, all languages of the species must share common basic characteristics, or universal features. In examining features such as the sounds used in speaking, the way words are organized, and how meaning is determined in various languages, investigators have concluded that a set of common principles underlies all human languages (Greenberg, 1966). For instance, speakers of all languages create a vast number of spoken words by combining a small set of meaningless sounds of a particular type. All languages use only a limited sample of vocal sounds, of all the possible sounds humans can make; for example, no language makes use of snorting or clapping sounds. Words are always combined into structured sequences we call sentences. All languages have grammars, and linguists claim that these grammars share certain formal properties as well.

Although the organism is probably biologically prepared for learning language, it is unlikely that biological principles alone will account for all aspects of language development.

Learning-Theory Approaches to Language   Some theorists have adopted the extreme position that language can be accounted for by traditional learning principles. Some theorists stress reinforcement principles (Skinner, 1957), while others give more weight to imitation (Bijou 1976). According to the operant or reinforcement view, the parent first selectively reinforces those parts of the child's babbling sounds which are most like adult speech, thereby increasing the frequency of vocalization of these sounds by the baby. Parental reinforcement serves to gradually shape the child's verbal behavior through "successive approximations" until it becomes more and more like adult speech. Others propose that the child learns through imitation. According to this view, the child picks up words, phrases, and sentences directly by imitation, and then through reinforcement and generalization the child learns when it is appropriate to use and combine these responses.

What's Wrong with Learning-Theory Accounts?   Learning-theory accounts of language acquisition have not fared well. Critics have pointed out that the number of specific stimulus-response connections that would be necessary to even begin to explain language is so enormous that there would not be enough time to acquire these connections in a whole lifetime, not to mention a few short years. Moreover, naturalistic studies of parent-child interaction fail to support this account. Mothers are just as likely to reward their children for truthful but grammatically incorrect statements as they are to reinforce their children for grammatically correct utterances. In short, parents often respond to the child's meaning and not to the grammar. Therefore it is difficult to see how adult reinforcement can easily explain the child's learning of correct grammar (Brown,

1973). Furthermore, the vast majority of language utterances can in no way be directly predicted from specific "environmental eliciting cues." Utterances which are closely tied to environmental cues, such as "Hello," "Watch out!" or "You're welcome," are rare. For most sets of circumstances, language affords an enormous degree of creative latitude, which linguists argue is not accounted for by learning theories. Nor have learning-theory accounts explained the regular sequence in which language develops. Children in our culture and other cultures seem to learn the same types of grammatical rules and in the same order. For example, active constructions are learned before passive constructions. Finally, behavioral theories basically portray the child as playing a passive role in the language acquisition process; in contrast, linguists argue that the child plays an active and creative role in discovering and applying general rules of language.

Learning theorists respond by arguing that linguists have interpreted learning-theory principles too narrowly, and that traditional concepts (such as reinforcement, imitation, and generalization) may in fact be important in explaining language development. This conclusion is based in part on experimental demonstrations that certain aspects of verbal behavior can be modified. For instance, the types of questions produced by an adult model have been shown to affect the types of questions subsequently produced by sixth-grade children; this finding indicates the influence of imitation (Rosenthal, Zimmerman, & Durning, 1970). Learning principles obviously play some part in language learning and in shaping subsequent language behavior as well.

Here is an example (Liebert, Odom, Hill, & Huff, 1969). An adult modeled (or gave examples of) ungrammatical sentences which ended with a preposition; for example, "The boy went *the house to*," or "The goat was *the door at*." These sentences were considered to embody a "new rule." Children in three different age groups were required to make up sentences and were told to pay close attention to those sentences the experimenter would indicate were especially good. When the adult model said a "new rule sentence," the experimenter praised him (for example, "I like that sentence"); then the experimenter asked the child to repeat the sentence. When the child said a new rule sentence of his own, he was also praised and, in addition, was given a token reward.

Children in the oldest group (averaging 14 years of age) showed a dramatic increase in their use of the new ungrammatical rule. Children in the middle group (averaging 8 years of age) showed some increase in their use of the new rule, though a much less substantial increase than the 14-year-olds. However, children in the youngest group (averaging about $5^1/_2$ years of age) showed no tendency to learn the new rule. The authors concluded that "the results of this experiment lend additional support to the general hypothesis that children's adoption of language rules may be influenced by a combination of modeling and reward procedures . . ." (Liebert et al., 1969, p. 185).

However, a qualification is necessary since psycholinguists have shown that the vast majority of actual language rules are "adopted" by children even *younger* than the youngest group used in the study. This experiment, therefore, though perhaps relevant to the rule-learning behavior of older children, provides no evidence that modeling and rewards influence *initial* language acquisition.

A demonstration that modeling or reinforcement can shape language in an older child is not evidence that the child actually learns language initially through these strategies. In fact, psychologists have thus far not been able to demonstrate that traditional learning principles play a *critical* role in the normal acquisition of language rules by the young child. However, learning principles may play a very important and useful role in modifying language usage and in overcoming language deficits in some individuals. Lovaas (1967), for example, has made remarkable demonstrations of the usefulness of imitation and reinforcement principles in overcoming speech deficits in autistic children.

A Synthesis   Most modern theorists recognize that language is learned in the context of spoken language and that humans are biologically prepared for learning to speak. The human organism is specifically prepared for language learning, but extensive experience with expressed language is also a condition of language acquisition. Students of language disagree about the extent to which the child has to be directly taught to speak. In contrast to the learning-theory account, where the child is viewed as playing a passive role, most current theorists emphasize the active role that the child plays in acquiring language.

Children compile specific information from what they hear and formulate hypotheses concerning the nature of this language. Children are instrumental in the language development process. . . . Not only do they formulate, test and evaluate hypotheses concerning the rules of their languages, but they also actively compile linguistic information to use in the formulation of hypotheses. (Tagatz, 1976, p. 90)

Not only has the child's role received increased emphasis, but the role of socializing agents as active facilitators of the child's language acquisition has been recognized. Parents and other adults use a variety of devices that aid the child's learning of language. Although the techniques do not fit easily into a learning-theory framework, these techniques may, nevertheless, facilitate the child's acquisition of language.

First, parents and other adults modify their speech when they talk to children. Mothers' speech to children is special and much simplified. In fact, mothers' speech has been described as "language lessons in miniature" (Clark & Clark, 1977, p. 327). Sentences are typically short, well-formed, and simple in structure. Mothers talk slower, with a higher pitch, and use more intonation and more repetition and fewer tenses when talking to children (Newport, 1976; Bates, 1976). Children, in turn, are more attentive to simplified speech. Spring (1974) gave 12-month-old infants a choice between two tape-recorded speech segments—a mother talking to her own 12-month-old infant and talking to another adult. The infants could select either tape by pushing one of two plastic panels. Over a 20-minute period, the year-old infants pushed the panel more that activated the simplified rather than the adult speech. Moreover, some parts of maternal speech, such as repetition, not only increase the child's attention, but may increase the chances that the child will understand the message. In a recent study of 9- to 16-month-olds, Benedict (1975) found that repetition of a request increased attention as well as the likelihood that the infant would follow the mother's instruction. In short, some of these peculiar characteristics of adult speech to infants and children have clear functional value.

Moreover, parents have to adjust their speech as the child develops; it is assumed that there is some optimum level of language complexity.

Talking in baby talk to a child for the first 5 years of his life would surely hinder his learning, but so would speaking in the language of an encyclopedia or a diplomatic treaty. (Dale, 1976, p. 144)

In fact, in one study, the investigators found that children responded appropriately more frequently—if they were past the one-word stage—to an adult form of a command (Throw me the ball) than to a simplified form (Throw ball). Just as we have seen in other areas, a level of complexity that is slightly ahead of the child may be the most effective elicitor of attention and provide the maximal opportunity for learning (Shipley, Smith, & Gleitman, 1969).

Children and adults use a simplified form of speech when talking to infants. (Richard Frieman, Photo Researchers, Inc.)

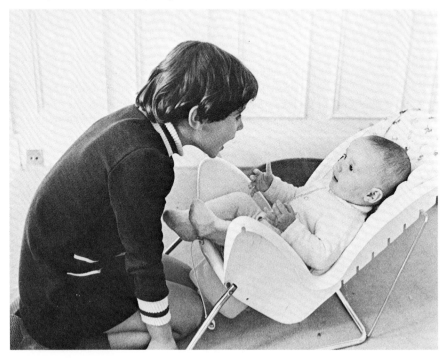

Not only do adults adjust their speech when talking to children, but the form of these adjustments may vary according to the age of the child (Nelson, 1973; Moerk, 1974). Adults use a wider range of words and parts of speech as children develop (Phillips, 1973). What are the consequences of these early language lessons?

First, by listening to adults who speak slowly and exaggerate their pauses and who repeat phrases and words, the child potentially learns some early segmentation rules, which indicate how utterances should be divided up into words and phrases. Second, the child learns the relationship between words and objects; in other words, the child's first lessons in the meaning of words may come from these early interchanges. Finally, children may learn *conversational* rules from these early interactions. These rules include turn-taking, knowing when they are being addressed, and clues concerning the right words for the right situation (Clark & Clark, 1977).

The final question, does the use of a simplified code facilitate children's language learning? has no answer at this point. The fine tubing that adults engage in *should* help children learn, and recently there is some evidence that certain language patterns (verb auxilaries) are, in fact, learned by their use in maternal speech (Newport, Gleitman, & Gleitman, 1977). However, the *fact* of "motherese" is much better established than the long-term impact of these speech patterns on children's language acquisition.

Other Influence Techniques A variety of other tactics that parents use to facilitate early language should be mentioned. Consider the following exchanges between a mother and her child:

Child: baby highchair
Adult: baby is in the highchair
Child: throw daddy
Adult: throw it to daddy (Brown & Bellugi, 1964)

These exchanges illustrate the technique of *expansion*. As you can see, the adult imitates and expands, or adds to, the child's statement. Roger Brown (1973) has estimated that middle-class parents used this expansion technique about 30 percent of the time; lower-class parents used this tactic much less often.

Not only do parents expand on their children's utterances, but the children, in turn, may imitate the parent's expansions. Of particular interest is the fact that children's imitations of their parent's expansions are often grammatically more advanced than their free speech. Table 8-1 illustrates these types of exchanges between parent and child. Although the results have been mixed, some laboratory studies have yielded support for the role of expansions in the acquisition of language, particularly aspects of syntax, such as verbal auxilaries and questions (Nelson, Carskadden, & Bonvillian, 1973; Nelson, 1976). More recently, expansions have been shown to be an effective technique for increasing 2-year-old children's use of adjective-noun combinations (Hovell, Schumaker, & Sherman, 1978).

TABLE 8-1 IMITATIONS OF EXPANSIONS

Type of Imitation	Example		Relative Frequency[a] Adam	Eve
Unexpanded	Child:	Just like cowboy.	45	17
	Adult:	Oh, just like the cowboy's.		
	Child:	Just like cowboy.		
Reduced	Child:	Play piano.	7	29
	Adult:	Playing the piano.		
	Child:	Piano.		
Expanded	Child:	Pick-mato.	48	54
	Adult:	Picking tomatoes up?		
	Child:	Pick 'mato up.		

[a]These figures cover Adam from age 2;3 to age 2;10 and Eve from 1;6 to 2;2.
Source: From Dan I. Slobin, Imitation and grammatical development in children. In Norman S. Endler, Lawrence R. Boulter and Harry Osser (Eds.), *Contemporary Issues in Development in Psychology*, New York: Holt, Rinehart and Winston. 1968. Reprinted by permission.

Parents and adults use other techniques as well, including prompting and echoing. *Prompting* is illustrated by the following interchange:

Adult: What do you want?
Child: no response
Adult: You want what? (Dale, 1976, p. 146)

By rephrasing the parent may make it easier for the child to understand. Or the parent may use *echoing*.

Child: I going owa nah
Mother: You're going where?
Child: I going (Dale, 1976, p. 146).

In this case, the mother tries to imitate part of the child's utterance but "replaces the unintelligible part with one of the 'wh' words of English producing questions like 'you're going where' and 'you're gonna do what?'" (Dale, 1976, p. 146).

These are just a few of the tactics that parents use in trying to facilitate their children's language.

What are the implications of these influence techniques? Although the child is probably biologically prepared for learning language, it is increasingly necessary to formulate a more interactional theory—one that recognizes the role of both environmental input and biological predispositions as important determinants of language development.

Environmental influences are prevalent in all areas of language development—phonology, syntax, semantics, and pragmatics. Now let us turn to a closer look at how language development proceeds.

Infancy: The Antecedents of Language Development

Language involves both the production of sounds and the ability to understand speech. These two aspects of language are often referred to as productive and receptive language. Well before the infant is able to speak, she is capable of selectively attending to certain features of speech sounds. As we saw in Chapter 4, even newborns synchronize their body movement in coordination with the sound patterns of adult speech (Condon & Sander, 1974). From the end of the first month, infants can distinguish human voices from other sounds, and by 2 months they respond differentially to the voice of their mother and an unfamiliar female (Horowitz, 1974). Nor does this exhaust the young infant's receptive abilities. One of the most remarkable discoveries of recent years is the finding that infants can discriminate among consonants such as "pah" and "bah" just as well as adults. Box 8-1 describes one of these demonstrations. This ability is present in infants as young as 1 month of age (Eimas, 1975).

Thus, even young infants demonstrate specialized language abilities, including selective attention, voice discrimination, imitation of aspects of speech, movement synchronized to speech patterns, and specialized phoneme perception. This evidence supports either that there is an innate capacity and readiness in the human infant to learn language or that there is a period of very rapid language learning in the early days and weeks of life.

Productive Abilities of Infants: Babbling and Other Early Sounds

It is not just receptive language abilities that are rapidly developing in infancy. The infant is actively producing sounds—even though not language—from birth onward. Anyone who has been awakened in the middle of the night by a crying 3-week-old baby knows that infants are neither quiet nor passive! But are the early sounds that an infant makes just random noise, or do they occur in some specific, meaningful sequence? And are early speech sounds related to later language development? These are some of the questions that have intrigued researchers. The production of sounds in the first year of life follows an orderly sequence. Four stages have been identified: (1) crying, which begins at birth; (2) other vocalizations and cooing, which start at the end of the first month; (3) babbling, which begins at the middle of the first year; and (4) finally patterned speech at the close of year 1 (Kaplan & Kaplan, 1971). Not only does early sound production follow an orderly sequence; these early sound scenarios, such as babbling, are universal and similar across different linguistic communities (Atkinson, McWhinney, & Stoel, 1970).

Even before their first words, infants are capable of modifying their vocalizations to suit the physical and social setting. Their babbling is different in different situations—in the crib, looking at a mobile, or sitting on mother's lap (Delack, 1976). Infants under 1 year of age modify their own babbling according to the pitch levels and intonation patterns of their adult caretakers. For example, compared to the babbling of American babies, the babbling of 6-month-old Chinese babies shows much more pitch variation, reflecting the Chinese language they hear (Weir, 1966). Infants also adjust their pitch levels to match the pitch of the person that is present. Two infants—10 and 13 months

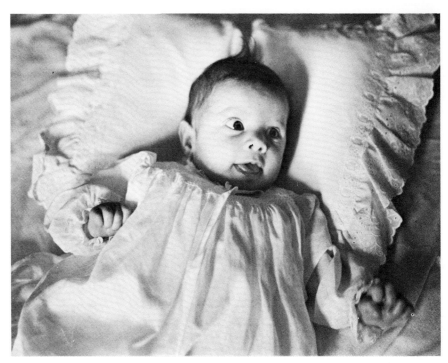

Babbling is more complex and meaningful than earlier theorists suggested. (Alice Kandell, Photo Researchers, Inc.)

old—babbled at a higher pitch on their mother's lap than when they were with their fathers (Lieberman, 1967). Even in the first year of life infants are sensitive to variations in context and tell us by shifts in their vocalizations.

The toughest question still remains. Is there any relationship between early babbling and later meaningful speech? Although linguists have favored a discontinuity view (Jakobson, 1968), which suggests that there is no relationship between early vocalizations and later speech, recent evidence has challenged this view. Specifically, studies of the early babblings of five infants over the first year have found that babbled syllables resemble the child's first meaningful words in a variety of ways (Oller, Wieman, Doyle, & Ross, 1976). As the investigators note:

The research disputes the traditional position on babbling by showing the phonetic content of babbled utterances exhibits many of the same preferences for certain kinds of phonetic elements and sequences that have been found in the production of meaningful speech by children in later stages of language development (Oller et al., 1976, p. 1).

In summary, the child's early productions not only are orderly, but relate to later speech. In both production and receptivity, the infant is surprisingly well prepared for learning to talk.

BOX 8-1
LANGUAGE DETECTORS
IN EARLY INFANCY

 Can the 5-month-old infant discriminate between consonants, such as "bah" and "gah"? Until very recently it was virtually impossible to find out if infants could make such a discrimination, but advances in techniques for measuring infants' heart rates have given investigators access to the infants' perceptual and linguistic capacities. Babies' heart rates show a habituation, or response decrement, with repeated testing. In short, an infant quits reacting to the same old sight or sound; however, upon presentation of a novel, or new stimulus, the infant's heart rate may show renewed responsivity. The change associated with the new input tells the investigator that the baby knows the difference between the old and new stimuli. This was precisely the paradigm that Moffitt (1971) adopted to determine whether his 5-month-old infants could distinguish consonants, just as adults can. One group of babies heard sixty "bah" syllables and then ten "gah" trials; babies in a second group heard "gah" sixty times, followed by ten presentations of "bah"; a final group heard only "bah" throughout the series. Heart rate was monitored throughout to determine if the infants' reactions changed with the presentation of the new consonant. The answer was positive: babies listening to repeated "bah" showed only limited cardiac reaction, but showed a marked recovery when the other consonant ("gah") was presented. A similar effect emerged for the "gah-bah" sequence; the control babies exhibited the same level of reaction throughout the series; after all, nothing changed. Very young infants, then, are able to perceive and discriminate speech sounds, in spite of no experience in producing these sounds, relatively limited exposure to speech, and certainly with little if any differential reinforcement for this form of behavior. "It would appear that infants enter the world with some knowledge of the phonological structure of language already available to them" (Moffitt, 1971, p. 729). At least some of language is probably innate; how much is yet to be determined. ■

Source: Moffitt, A. R. Consonant cue perception by 20 to 24 week old infants. *Child Development*, 1971, **42,** 717–732.

One Word at a Time

The title of this section, which is also a title of a book (Bloom, 1973), reflects our continuing fascination with the young child's first halting steps on the road to language mastery, namely, her early one-word utterances. Between 10 and 13 months, the child speaks her first word (McCarthy, 1954), and for the next few months language occurs "one word at a time." In a recent study of the first fifty words, Nelson (1973) classified words into six categories. Figure 8-1 illustrates the different kinds of words used by young children. Children show considerable uniformity in their early vocabulary, but early words are still highly selective. Children learn words that represent objects that they can act on and that produce a change or movement. For example, the words "shoes," "socks," and "toys" are more common than words denoting objects that are just "there,"

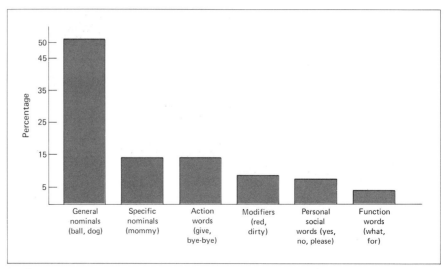

FIGURE 8-1 Types of first words used by young infants and children. *(Based on data from Nelson, 1973.)*

such as "tables," "stove," and "trees." Language—from the first words onward—is always closely linked to function. The child learns those words which are perceptually salient and meaningful in terms of her own world, for these words are most important for identifying objects that she may wish to interact with.

However, children use words differently than adults. Children may use a word in a highly restricted and individualistic way. A child may only use the word "car" when she sees her father's yellow Porsche and call all other automobiles trucks. Or later children overgeneralize; everyone has heard a young child term horses, cows, and other four-legged animals, "doggie." The child is not just making an error; he or she is trying to find the relationship between a linguistic form and an element of experience. As Bloom notes:

It seems entirely reasonable for the child to use an available word to represent different but related objects—it is almost as if the child were reasoning, "I know about dogs, that thing is not a dog, I don't know what to call it, but it is like a dog." (1977, p. 23)

For the child, applying words in different contexts is a type of hypothesis testing, a process that will continue throughout childhood. This process manifests itself particularly in the first three years when the process of relating the word form with the object begins (Bloom, 1973, 1976). Gradually as the child's discriminations improve and their conceptual categories become more stable, the child's accuracy in the use of words increases. But are they just single words?

When a young child points to a toy airplane on a high shelf and says "down" or when he takes a spoon from his mother and says "me," is there more than meets the ear? In the first case, the child may be requesting that the toy be taken down off the shelf, or in our second example, the child may be saying "I want to do it myself." As Dale notes:

First words seem to be more than single words. They appear to be attempts to express complex ideas, ideas that would be expressed in sentences by an adult. The term "holophrastic speech" is often used to capture this idea of "words that are sentences." (1976, p. 13)

Whether or not children are really expressing sentences in a word remains more an intriguing idea than a proven fact at this point.

These early observations do underline one of the important insights about language development: children do not acquire different skills—grammar, meaning, and communication skills—separately. Rather there is a constant interplay among these three faces of language. Well before children can formulate the correct grammatical form, they are actively trying to communicate to others around them and to indicate what they mean. It is out of these early attempts to make themselves and their wishes understood and meaningful for others that their grasp of grammar gradually emerges. The next step is from one word to two words.

Beyond Single Words

The next important step in language development is the use of not just a single word but two words together. Children generally take this step around 18 to 20 months of age. At this point, language is still simpler than adult language and more selective since although nouns, verbs, and adjectives are generally present, others, such as articles, prepositions, etc., are often absent. However, the child's speech is still novel and creative and not merely a copy of adult language. Table 8-2 shows some of the kinds of two-word sentences used by young children not only in English, but in other cultures as well. Notice the high degree of similarity of the semantic relations of the two-word sentences used by children in cultures as different as Finnish, English, and Samoan. As Slobin observed:

If you ignore word order and read through transcriptions of two word utterances in the various languages we have studied, the utterances read like direct translations of one another. (1970, p. 177)

Nor are these patterns limited to oral language. As Box 8-2 shows, children acquire sign language in the same way as oral language.

Why are the early utterances of children similar? Language can be viewed as a way of expressing what one understands about the world at a particular age. The content of what children say is closely related to their general level of intellectual functioning at any given stage in development. Children who are beginning to speak are also beginning to understand various environmental relationships, such as self-other distinctions, primitive concepts of causality, and notions about the permanence of objects. Therefore, beginning speakers all over

TABLE 8-2 SOME SEMANTIC RELATIONS IN STAGE I SPEECH FROM SEVERAL LANGUAGES

Relation	English	German	Russian	Finnish	Luo	Samoan
Recurrence	more milk	mehr Milch (more milk)	yesche moloka (more milk)	lisaa kakkua (more cake)	piypiy kech (pepper hot)	fa'ali'i pepe (headstrong baby)
Attributive	big boat	Milch heiss (milk hot)	papa bol-shoy (papa big)	rikki auto (broken car)	kom baba (chair father)	paluni mama (balloon mama)
Possessive	mama dress	Mamas Hut (mama's hat)	mami chashka (mama's cup)	tati auto (aunt car)	odhi skul (he-went school)	tu'u lala (put down)
Action-locative	walk street	Sofa sitzen (sofa sit)		viedaan kauppa (take store)		
Agent-action	Bambi go	Puppe kommt (doll comes)	mama prua (mama walk)	Seppo putoo (Seppo fall)	chungu biro (European comes)	pa'u pepe (fall doll)
Action-object	hit ball		nasbla yaechko (found egg)	ajaa bmbm (drives car)	omoyo oduma (she dries maize)	
Question	where ball	wo Ball (where ball)	gdu papa (where papa)	missa pallo (where ball)		fea Pupafu (where Punafu)

Source: Adapted from Table 1 of D. I. Slobin, Universals of grammatical development in children. In G. B. Flores d'Arcais and W. J. M. Levelt (Eds.), *Advances in psycholinguistics*, Amsterdam: North-Holland, 1970, pp. 178–179.

BOX 8-2
LANGUAGE LEARNING IN THE DEAF: SIGN LANGUAGE

Sign language, the system used by deaf individuals, has been of interest to students of language. A central question concerns the similarity in the child's acquisition of oral language and sign language. Just as there are cross-cultural similarities in two-word phrases, the same semantic relations which occur in oral language appear in the first two sign strings in sign language. Compare the following examples observed in a child using sign language:

1 daddy work: daddy is at work

2 Barry train: her brother's train

3 bed shoes: referring to slippers

4 daddy shoe: trying to persuade her father to take off his shoes and play in the sand

with the examples in Figure 8-2. We see instances of (1) locative, (2) possessive, (3) attributive, and (4) agent-object strings that are remarkably similar to those observed in the language of speaking children. Similarly, the length of strings increases in a steady fashion, and just as in spoken language, children who use sign language tend to overgeneralize. Nor are young signing children always accurate; like the early language of their speaking peers, early signs are not always perfect. Instead of pointing to their mouth they may miss

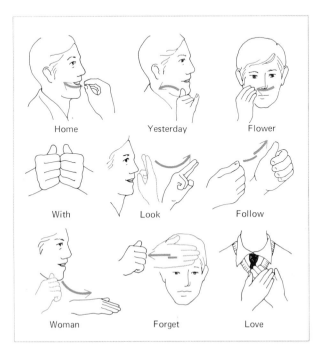

FIGURE 8-2 Some signs of American sign language. *(From Riekehof, 1963. Reprinted by permission.)*

and point to their chin! Other evidence indicates that vocabulary rates show the same growth pattern. One young 3-year-old girl knew 384 signs and four months later increased her repertoire of signs to 604—an expansion often seen in speaking children.

What do these observations mean?
The really important aspects of language and the really important abilities the child brings to the problem of language learning are independent of the modality in which the linguistic system operates. Language is a central process, not a peripheral one. The abilities that children have are so general and so powerful that they proceed through the same milestones of development as do hearing children. (Dale, 1976, p. 59) ■

Source: Dale, P. S. *Language development: Structure and function* (2d ed.). New York: Holt, 1976, pp. 54–59.

These deaf children are learning to use sign language: "signing" follows the same developmental course as spoken language. (Hanna Schreiber, Rapho/Photo Researchers, Inc.)

the world use similar types of relations in their early speech, such as agent-action relations, possessives, disappearance, and reappearance. This is presumably because these particular relations are significant in the children's cognitive processes at that time. That is, semantic development and cognitive or intellectual development are probably closely related (Bloom, 1970; Nelson, 1973).

These early utterances of children cannot easily be understood by an examination of the syntax or grammatical relations alone. A knowledge of the context in which early speech occurs is critical for capturing the child's meaning. For instance, 21-month-old Kathryn, who was studied by Bloom (1970), was observed to say "Mommy sock" in two separate contexts: when Kathryn picked up her mother's sock, and when mother was putting Kathryn's sock on Kathryn. In the first context Kathryn was probably describing the sock as belonging to Mommy, whereas in the second context she probably meant that Mommy was doing something involving a sock. Theoretically, "Mommy sock" might express many things, including "Mommy is that a sock?" "Mommy, give me the sock," or perhaps even "Mommy, go sock Daddy!" As another example, Bloom (1970) has pointed out that the observed negative sentence "No dirty soap" could be interpreted in at least four ways: There is no dirty soap; the soap isn't dirty; that isn't dirty *soap;* and I don't want the dirty soap.

Since the meaning is ambiguous from word order alone, Bloom has made the important suggestion that the child's immediate behavior and the context in which the language occurs be carefully recorded and evaluated as a clue to the meaning. She sees this as necessary in studying the child's progress in expressing meaning syntactically. Even as children move from words to sentences, in order to understand language the context in which it occurs must be considered. In the next section, we watch the children's grammatical skills unfold as they begin to move from words to sentences.

The Acquisition of Grammar: From Words to Sentences

Read over the passages in Box 8-3 of the speech of the same child at 28 months and again at 38 months. It will be clear that a great deal has happened in this short time. Both the length and the complexity of the utterances have increased. Trying to understand these shifts has been one of the concerns of the last two decades. These speech samples come from a longitudinal study of children's spontaneous speech; the strategy of studying a few children over an extended period of time has provided a wealth of information about children's early speech development. Its main advantage over the manipulative experimental approach is that only by studying the same child extensively over a period of time is it possible to analyze in detail how the individual child's language system changes and develops. So far, very few children have been involved, perhaps a few dozen in total, including children in non-English-speaking countries. However, the enormous quantity of language acquisition data that have been collected from these children has permitted analysis and reanalysis by the original investigators as their thinking changed. Also, other researchers have analyzed these data with different goals in mind. The best-known children were initially studied by Roger Brown and associates (Brown, 1973). In the literature they are called Adam and Sarah (each studied for over two years) and Eve (studied for nine months).

Telegraphic Speech One striking fact that has emerged from the longitudinal studies is that young children often omit words or word endings that would be found in adult speech, and that these omissions are not random. Children omit the small words (such as "of," "on," "the," etc.) and word endings, both of which carry relatively little

BOX 8-3
SPEECH SAMPLES,
TEN MONTHS APART

 These samples of speech are from the records of Brown and Bellugi (1964). The first is from a boy at 28 months of age, and the second is from the same boy at 38 months of age.

Child—28 months	Adult
What dat . . .	Whose pencils are they?
somebody pencil	
Floor	Floor?
Where birdie go? Birdie Birdie up dere Birdie Read dat? Read dat?	Will you read it to me?
What innere?	Is that a hammer, Adam?
Hammer Hit Hammer, Mommy, No Cromer_____, mommy? Hurt	Poor Adam. Did you hurt yourself? What happened, Adam?
Screw (did) happen	Screw happened? You didn't even have a screw.
have screw _____no down there . . . table . . . get broom	Does that one fit?
Yep, it fit Yep, it fit	Does it fit?
No . . . fit Put suitcase . . . for?	What did you put it in the suitcase for?
What dat?	That's tape. We'll use that one tomorrow.

Source: Cited in McNeil, D. *The acquisition of language: The study of developmental psycholinguistics.* New York: Harper & Row, 1970, pp. 16–19.

All right' morrow	Shall we use it tomorrow?
Yep	
Use morrow, yep	
Sure, use 'morrow	

Child—38 months	**Adult**
I like a racing car	
D'you like some?	
I broke my racing car	Oh, did you used to have one?
Yes	
Look at dat one	
Like dis part broke	What part broke?
Dis part broke, like that	
It's got a flat tire	
What is dat?	
It's a what?	
He . . . his mouth is open	
What shall we shall have?	
Why he going to have some seeds?	
Why it's not working?	
You got some beads?	Yes
Just like me?	
I got bead 'round myself	
Hit my knee	Hit my knee
Hit your knee	
What dat teacher will do?	
Why you pull out?	
Who put dust on my hair?	Dust in your hair
	Can you tell Ursula what the lesson is . . . on the blackboard?
On the black which board?	
We going see another one	
We can read 'bout dis	
You wanto read?	
What is dat?	
What is dat got?	
It's got a flat tire	
When it's got flat tire, it's needs to go to the . . . to the station.	
The station will fix it.	
Tank come out through what?	
Really . . . tank come out through . . . here	

Mommy don't let my buy some

What is dis? | That's a marble bag

A marble bag for what? | For marbles. It would be good to carry tiny cars.

What is dat?
Can I keep dem?
Why I can keep dem?
We don't do some games
It's broked? ∎

---

meaning. The words they do speak are the most important meaningful words, called *content words.* The resulting speech has been called *telegraphic,* and this speech includes sentences such as "There no more these." In addition to the selection of certain types of words to speak, the child usually orders these words in a systematic way. For instance, one of the first syntactic rules used by children seems to be that the subject comes before the verb; this has been found in several different countries for children learning their native language (Slobin, 1973). The words that are spoken in a telegraphic sentence are usually in the same order as in the corresponding adult sentence. Even when a young child is imitating an adult sentence (spontaneously or on request), she will usually produce a telegraphic version. No matter how long the model sentence is, the child's imitation will be only about as long as the sentences she makes up on her own at that point in her development. Here are some examples:

Adult	*Child*
"I showed you the book."	"I show book."
"He's going out."	"He go out."
"No, you can't write on Mr. Cromer's shoe."	"Write Cromer shoe."

The Emergence of Meaning Modifiers

One of the interesting achievements during the early phases of grammar acquisition is the way in which children learn to qualify the meaning of their simple sentences. Roger Brown (1973) has provided the most complete description of the course of this type of grammatical development in children. Based on his longitudinal study, he noted that children acquire certain morphemes in a remarkably regular order. By morphemes he means modifiers that help give more precise meaning to words that children use. For example, during this period, children acquire qualifiers to indicate plurality or to indicate a possessive. Table 8-3 lists the fourteen morphemes that Brown studied and the order in which they occur in English. Although the rate that Adam, Eve, and Sarah acquired these morphemes varied, the order for each child was the same. Can we generalize from these three children? Fortunately we don't have to rely

TABLE 8-3 SUFFIXES AND FUNCTION WORDS
Fourteen suffixes and function words in English

Form	Meaning	Example
1. Present progressive: -ing	Ongoing process	He is sitt*ing* down.
2. Preposition: in	Containment	The mouse is *in* the box.
3. Preposition: on	Support	The book is *on* the table.
4. Plural: -s	Number	The dog*s* ran away.
5. Past irregular: e.g., went	Earlier in time relative to time of speaking	The boy *went* home.
6. Possessive: -'s	Possession	The girl*'s* dog is big.
7. Uncontractible copula be: e.g., are, was	Number; earlier in time	*Are* they boys or girls? *Was* that a dog?
8. Articles: the, a	Definite/indefinite	He has *a* book.
9. Past regular: -ed	Earlier in time	He jump*ed* the stream.
10. Third person regular: -s	Number; earlier in time	She run*s* fast.
11. Third person irregular: e.g., has, does	Number; earlier in time	*Does* the dog bark?
12. Uncontractible auxiliary be: e.g., is were	Number; earlier in time; ongoing process	*Is* he running? *Were* they at home?
13. Contractible copula be: e.g., -'s, -'re	Number; earlier in time	That*'s* a spaniel.
14. Contractible auxiliary be: e.g., -'s, -'re	Number; earlier in time; ongoing process	They*'re* running very slowly.

Based on R. Brown (1973). Cited in Clark, H. H., & Clark, E. V. Psychology and language: An introduction to psycholinguistics. New York: Harcourt Brace Jovanovich, 1977.

on this evidence alone. In a cross-sectional study, the deVilliers (1973) studied not just three but twenty-one children and provided confirmation of Brown's order of acquisition of morphemes. Notice that the order is a sensible one. In terms of complexity, simpler morphemes are acquired earlier than more complex ones. For example, plurals, such as "s," are learned before the copula "be." We will see that this same general principle of development from simple to complex characterizes children's cognitive development as well. This parallel in the development of language and cognition has led some theorists to suggest that language development is dependent on the child's prior level of cognitive development.

As we noted earlier, language learning would not be a very efficient process if children had to learn specific rules for each new set of words that they encountered. Imagine how time-consuming it would be if a child had to learn that two dogs was dogs, but had to have a separate lesson to learn how to pluralize other words, such as cat or house. Fortunately, children learn general grammatical rules, which can be used with new as well as familiar words. Box 8-4 illustrates this general rule-learning principle for children's use of plural endings.

Unfortunately, adult language does not always follow the rules and is full of exceptions and irregularities. When first learning a language, children ignore these irregularities and apply the rules in a rigid way. In other words, children show *overregularization* of rules they acquire. They apply a rule to form regularities in cases where the adult form is irregular and does not follow the rule. For instance, a young child may use the words "went" and "came" correctly. But after learning that "-ed" forms the past tense for many verbs, the child will use this ending on *all* verbs and will switch to saying "goed" and "comed" (Ervin, 1964). Similarly a child often uses the word "feet" until the regular plural ending "-s" is learned; at that time he or she switches to "foots" (or sometimes "feets"). In some cases it has been reported that after learning that some plurals are formed by adding "-es" (such as "boxes"), the child may then say "footses" for a time.

Children also sometimes "create" regularized singular words from an irregular plural. For example, a child the authors knew used the word "clothes" and insisted on calling one piece of clothing a "clo." A different type of overregularization was demonstrated by a child who said, "I'm magic, amn't I?" It has been observed that young children in the Soviet Union and other countries also broadly apply the rules they learn to form novel "regularized" words and phrases that do not occur in adult speech (Slobin, 1966).

Overregularization is only one example of the fact that children's speech is unique and qualitatively different from adult speech in many ways.

Some Other Achievements: Questions and Negations

There are a variety of other grammatical landmarks that warrant attention, since they follow their own course of development. How do children formulate questions?

In the early stages of question formulation, children simply place a question word, such as "where," "what," or "why" (or "why not"), at the beginning of an otherwise declarative sentence without further modifying its form (Klima & Bellugi, 1966). Examples of spontaneous early questions from Adam, Eve, and Sarah are:

Where my mitten?
What the dollie have? (Klima & Bellugi, 1966)

BOX 8-4
ONE WUG OR TWO? CHILDREN'S USE OF THE PLURAL

Berko (1958) studied children's productive use of word inflections. Examples of common English inflections are the plural ending "s," the past tense ending "ed," and variations of each. Berko presented a series of nonsense words, such as "wug" or "bix," in conjunction with drawings. For instance, she showed children drawings of strange birdlike creatures and said, "This is a wug. Now there is another one. There are two of them. There are two———" (see Figure 8-3). It should be noted that the sound of the required plural endings varies with the word,

for example, wug(z), bix(es), and zat(s). Even 4-year-olds could produce the proper plural forms of the nonsense words in a large proportion of test sentences. Similar demonstrations have used other inflections, such as the past tense endings. They clearly demonstrate that children learn *general rules* for plural inflection and not just individual plural words. Since general rules can be applied to novel material, they form the core of any generative language system. ■

Source: Berko, J. The child's learning of English morphology. *Word*, 1958, **14**, 50–177.

This is a wug.

Now there is another one. There are two of them.

There are two _____

FIGURE 8-3 One of the drawings used to test children's productive use of word inflections.

Or they may simply use an assertion such as *sit chair* or *see hole* but raise their voice at the end to indicate that it is a question and not merely a statement. Only later do children learn to invert subject and verb when asking questions. Some question forms are easier to learn than others. Positive questions are easier for children than negative ones. This is illustrated in the following exchange between a child and a puppet who was dressed up as an old lady:

Adult: Adam, ask the Old Lady (puppet) what she'll do next.
Adam: Old Lady what will you do now? (Bellugi 1971)

Compare that exchange with this one:

Adult: Adam, ask the Old Lady why she can't sit down.
Adam: Old Lady why you can't sit down? (Bellugi, 1971)

These contrasting dialogues illustrate that subject-verb inversions are acquired sooner in positive than negative questions.

Many of the same stages found for children's question development hold for the development of negatives. For example, the earliest negative sentences are formed by adding a negative word, usually "no" in English, to an affirmative sentence. For example, a child might say, "No sit there" or "no the sun shining." Only later do children learn to say, "I not said" or "I not hurt him," which involves placing the negative in the correct order in a sentence.

Children in the Soviet Union, Japan, and France apparently form early negative sentences in the same way as American children. They choose *one* negative word and consistently add that one word to sentences. This is especially interesting because the rules of negation in the adult grammars of these languages are different: single negation is the rule in English, double negation is common in the Soviet Union, and two words are required in French (for example, "no . . . pas") (McNeill, 1968; Slobin, 1970).

The development of these two systems—negatives and questions—is only a sample of a wide range of grammatical accomplishments during the preschool years. By 3 years of age, children begin to use complex sentences through the use of relative clauses. Again, progress is gradual but orderly. At first children tack on clauses, for example, "See the ball that I got," and only later do they interrupt a main clause with a subordinate clause, "The owl who eats candy runs fast" (Slobin & Welsh, 1973).

Another accomplishment is the gradual ability to use and understand passive as well as active sentences. In one study of sentence comprehension, 3-year-olds were presented with pairs of sentences and corresponding pictures. Then, after hearing one of the sentences repeated, they were asked to point to the appropriate picture. For example, they were asked to point to the picture of either "The boy pushes the girl" or "The girl pushes the boy." The children had little trouble understanding this type of sentence, which is called an *active* sentence. However, most of them misinterpreted the corresponding *passive* sentence. That is, when asked to show "The boy is pushed by the girl," they pointed instead to the boy pushing the girl. This systematic error suggests that 3-year-olds process passive sentences as if they were active sentences, incorrectly assuming the first noun is the actor (Fraser, Bellugi, & Brown, 1963). This finding is consistent with the observation that in their own early speech, children almost always place the subject before the verb.

Of course, the process of grammar acquisition is not over in the preschool years. As the study of children's understanding of complex syntax in Box 8-5 illustrates, specific complex aspects of syntax continue to develop into the elementary school years. And individuals continue to develop even more complex syntax as any comparison of an eighth-grade English lesson and a college lecture on Shakespeare will indicate.

Finally, are these accomplishments unique to humans? As the remarkable studies of two chimpanzees discussed in Box 8-6 show, some animals—with a lot of human help—can achieve many of the same language landmarks.

BOX 8-5
COMPREHENSION OF
COMPLEX SYNTAX

In order to make sense of a number of English sentences, children must learn to violate some of the rules they have previously acquired. These semantically complex sentences may resemble simpler forms at the surface level. For example, in the two sentences "John is eager to please" and "John is easy to please" the subject, John, takes on two very different functions. In "John is eager to please" John is doing the pleasing. But in "John is easy to please," John is the logical object, the one being pleased; this sentence is unusual in that the subject of a sentence is more often the actor than the recipient of action. Most children younger than 8 or 9 years old are not able to understand this type of sentence in which the subject is also the logical object.

This phenomenon was investigated by Carol Chomsky (1969). In one of her experiments she used a sentence with the same form as "John is easy to please." Her subjects were individually presented with a blindfolded doll and asked, "Is the doll easy to see or hard to see?" After re-

sponding, the child was asked, "Why is the doll easy/hard to see?" Finally, the child was asked to make the doll easy or hard to see (opposite to his or her previous response).

Most of the youngest children (the 5-year-olds) misinterpreted the sentence. They initially said the blindfolded doll was "hard to see," and then took off the doll's blindfold in an effort to make her "easy to see." In contrast, all the 9-year-olds said the doll was "easy to see," and then hid the doll or covered their own eyes in an effort to make her "hard to see," thus demonstrating the correct interpretation of the sentence. The 6-, 7-, and 8-year-olds showed intermediate levels of correct interpretations. This is one of several recent experiments which demonstrate that children's use of specific aspects of syntax continues to develop well into the school years, although the basic syntactic system is acquired in the preschool years. ■

Source: Chomsky, C. *The acquisition of syntax in children from 5 to 10.* Cambridge, Mass.: M.I.T. Press, 1969.

The Meaning of Sentences	Not only do children need to know how to speak grammatically correct sentences; they need to learn to *understand* the meaning of sentences. Knowledge of single words alone is insufficient. Children use a variety of types of information to make sense of sentences. Consider this situation:

Imagine listening to a conversation on a noisy telephone line. Parts of words are obliterated by the noise. Often a word cannot be completely identified on the basis of the acoustic signal alone, but identification is generally easy because we have heard other words in the sentence and can narrow down the range of possibilties. For example, after *the boy* a verb is extremely likely; after *the red* a noun is very probable. If the conversation is a sensible one and if we know something about the topic, stronger predictions can be made on semantic grounds. After *the boy* the verb *lectured* is unlikely, though grammatically correct. (Dale, 1976, p. 189)

BOX 8-6
LANGUAGE IN CHIMPANZEES: WASHOE AND SARAH

In two different parts of the country, Reno, Nevada, and Santa Barbara, California, two chimps have been taught language. This accomplishment is amazing in light of earlier failures. In spite of valiant attempts by the Kelloggs in the 1930s and by the Hayes family in the 1950s, the world's record for the number of words spoken by a chimp was held by Vicki, who learned 4 words! (Fleming, 1974). It wasn't the chimp's fault; animals are not equipped with the proper vocal equipment for speaking. But they can learn to talk in other ways.

The Gardners in Nevada have successfully used the sign language of the deaf to teach their chimpanzee, Washoe, to talk. Beginning in 1966,

Washoe lived in a fully-equipped house trailer. The Gardners designed her living arrangements to exploit the possibility that she would engage in conversations—ask questions as well as answer them, describe objects as well as request them. They gave her a stimulus-rich environment, minimal restraint, constant human companionship while she was awake, and lots of games that promoted interaction between Washoe and human beings. Her teachers used no language except sign language in her presence. (Fleming, 1974, p. 32)

Just as we have seen with children, Washoe learned one word at a time at first. Within a year, she began to produce combinations of signs—even though she was never given sentence lessons. Some were the same as her teachers, while others were invented by Washoe herself. Table 8-4 presents some of the utterances made by Washoe. Notice how similar they are to children's early speech. By age 4, Washoe had had a vocabulary of 160 signs and could understand even more.

Sarah, the California chimp, learned language in a very different way from her teacher, David Premack (1971).

Sarah did not live, like Washoe, in a language-rich, stimulating environment with daily invitations from human friends to play language games. She lived under standard laboratory conditons: wire cage, cement-block walls, a few toys. Her exposure to both human beings and her special language was largely limited to the one hour of language training she received five days a week. (Fleming, 1974, p. 33)

Instead of signs, Premack developed a set of plastic shapes which were used as words (see Figure 8-4). Each shape had a metal back and could be placed on a magnetic board. Sarah learned through a combination of imitation, shap-

TABLE 8-4 SOME OF WASHOE'S UTTERANCES
Each English word represents a separate sign in Ameslan (sign language)

Washoe sorry	Out open please hurry	Clothes yours
Baby down	You me in	You hat
Go in	Gimme flower	Roger tickle
Hug hurry	More fruit	You more drink
Open blanket	Baby mine	Comb black

Gardner, B. T., & Gardner, R. A. Two-way communication with an infant chimpanzee. In A. M. Schrier & F. Stollnitz (Eds.), *Behavior of nonhuman primates* (Vol. 4). New York: Academic, 1971.

ing, prompting, and conditioning. Her teacher would present an object and she would receive a reward if she picked the right symbol. For example, she would receive a food reward if she picked up the triangle when an apple was presented. Premack has been remarkably successful:

At the end of two and a half years of training, Sarah possessed a staggering list of language functions. She used words, sentences, the interrogative, class concepts, negation, pluralization, conjunction, quantifiers, the conditional, and the copula. Washoe's abilities cover only the first five on this list. (Fleming, 1974, p. 35)

Together, these experiments in language acquisition offer impressive evidence that chimpanzees can acquire some aspects of language; in short, language may not be uniquely human. However, it is well to remember that very spe-

cial training was necessary in order to teach these chimps language. And many questions remain:

How much language can chimpanzees be taught? Will chimpanzees brought up on sign language spontaneously transmit it to their young? Will they use sign language to communicate with other chimpanzees brought up in the same way? Will their young "pick up" language in the rather casual way human children do or will they require intensive coaching? Definite answers to these questions may not come for many years. (Clark & Clark, 1977, p. 522) ■

Source: Gardner, B.T., & Gardner, R.A. Two way communication with a chimpanzee In A.M. Schrier & F. Stollnitz (Eds.) *Behavior of nonhuman primates* (Vol. 4) New York: Academic, 1971. Premack, D., Language in the chimpanzee? *Science* 1971, **172**, 808–822.

The bottom row forms the sentence "Red is not the color of chocolate."

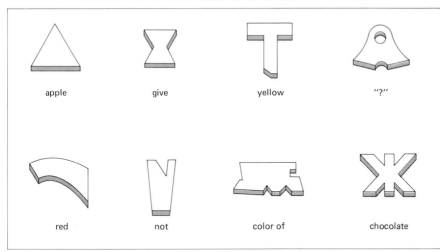

apple   give   yellow   "?"

red   not   color of   chocolate

FIGURE 8-4 Some plastic shapes used as forms. The bottom row forms the sentence "Red is not the color of chocolate." (*From Premack & Premack, 1972.*)

Can children use syntactic and semantic cues to help them understand sentences, and does the ability to use these kinds of information improve with age? A recent study utilized the "noisy telephone" technique with 6- to 9-year-old children. The children heard the following sentences with superimposed noise and were required to repeat the sentences. Since the noise blocked out part of the sentence, the children had to rely on their prior knowledge of how sentences are generally formed to fill in the missing words.

Meaningful: Bears steal honey from the hive.

Anomalous: Trains steal elephants around the house.

Scrambled: From shoot highways the passengers mothers.

The meaningful sentence was correct in terms of both syntax and semantics and therefore should be the easiest for the listener. Both grammar and meaning could serve as guidelines. The anomalous sentence doesn't make much sense, but it is syntactically correct. Grammar, not meaning, is the only guide. In the last type of sentence, neither syntax nor semantics is in order, and therefore this should be the most difficult for children to reproduce. Figure 8-5 confirms these predictions and indicates that as children develop, they are better able to use the syntactic and semantic information that is available.

Just as children fill in the word gaps in sentences, children learn to make sense out of groups of sentences. Without this integrative ability, few of us could understand the first page of a novel, a short story, or even this textbook. In fact, as adults we are generally better able to understand the meaning than to recognize the particular syntax (active versus passive form) used in a paragraph (Sachs, 1967). Consider these three sentences:

The bird is inside the cage.

The cage is under the table.

The bird is yellow.

We all know that the bird is not on top of the table, but under the table—even though no specific sentence gave us this information. Even 7- and 10-year-olds

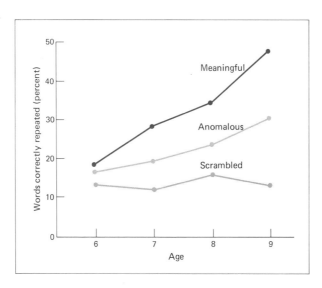

FIGURE 8-5 Percent of words repeated at four age levels as a function of syntactic and semantic structure. *(From Entwisle & Frasure, 1974. Reprinted by permission of the senior author and the American Psychological Association.)*

can tell you the location of the bird, as Paris and Carter (1973) found in their study of constructive memory. They asked their child listeners which sentences had occurred. Some had actually occurred, and others were new. The cage is over the table is similar to a sentence that occurred, but incorrect, while the bird is under the table was also not said, but is semantically consistent with the other sentences. Over 55 percent of the listeners recognized this type of sentence as familiar—even though it had not, in fact, occurred. The children had constructed a semantically consistent story based on the sentences and used their story as their guide.

Later studies (Paris & Lindauer, 1976) have found that constructive memory increases with age. Moreover, "children could scarcely carry on everyday conversations if they could not make spontaneous inference, integrations, elaborations and reorganizations. . . . A great deal has to be assumed, presupposed or otherwise added by a listener in understanding and remembering what a speaker says; a surprising amount of what gets said in an ordinary conversation is inexplicit and elliptical" (Flavell, 1977, p. 194).

Metalinguistic Awareness, or Knowing about Language

One of the crowning achievements in language development and one of the latest to develop is the ability to know language not merely in the sense of being able to speak and understand it, but to know *about* language. By this we mean that children know that they know language and can think and talk about language. This ability, or metalinguistic awareness, does not emerge until about age 5 and is generally evaluated by asking children to judge between grammatical and ungrammatical sentences and acceptable and unacceptable word order. Here is one example. In this investigation, deVilliers and deVilliers (1974) tested children's ability to judge and correct word order in active sentences. Using the clever technique of asking children to teach a puppet to talk correctly, they were required to correct the puppet's language. Sometimes the puppet spoke in correct word order (for example, "Eat the cake"), while at other times the puppet "spoke" in reversed ("Dog the pat") or in a semantically anomalous fashion ("Drink the chair"). The children both indicated whether the puppet was right or wrong and were required to help the puppet say it the "right way." There was a clear relationship between the children's level of language development and their metalinguistic awareness: as their ability to produce and comprehend sentences increased, their awareness increased. But insight lags behind production and comprehension:

A child may "know" a particular linguistic rule, in the sense of following the rule in producing sentences and understanding sentences when the only clue is the structure described by the rule long before he can consciously state the rule or use it to make judgments of grammatical or ungrammatical sentences. . . . the process of becoming aware of language is one that continues throughout development. In its highest form, it becomes the basis of aesthetic pleasure in poetry and prose. (Dale, 1976, p. 128)

Communication in Children: Speaking and Listening

Even with syntax solvable and meaning meaningful, you still wouldn't be fully equipped to be an effective speaker. You must learn another set of rules, namely, when to use what language in which situations. The subfield concerned with language use is called *pragmatics*. To illustrate the importance of these pragmatic rules, let us consider one of the most important functions of language—communication. To be an effective communicator requires a complicated set of skills. A number of things are required. First, you have to engage the attention of your listeners so they know that you want to address them and that they should listen. Second, you have to be sensitive to the characteristics of the listeners. You don't address visitors from Russia in English and expect them to understand. Nor do you use unique landmarks (the Trevi fountain) to help lost visitors on their first trip to Rome. It won't help to talk to a 2-year-old in a day-care center using the same vocabulary as you would to students in a college lecture hall. Being a good communicator requires that you adapt your message to take into account "who the listener is, what the listener already knows and what the listener needs to know" (Glucksberg, Krauss, & Higgins, 1975, p. 329). In addition, effective communicators have to be sensitive to listeners' feedback. If a child doesn't know that he is not being understood, and doesn't know how to change his message to make it clear, he is not going to be a very successful communicator. Finally, you must learn to adjust your speech to suit the situation. Children learn to talk differently on a street or playground than in a church or classroom. Box 8-7 provides a clear demonstration of how children learn to shift their style of speech in different settings.

Communication is a two-way process—an effective speaker is not enough. To have a conversation, for example, requires not only a competent speaker but a skilled listener as well. For effective communication, learning to listen is just as important as learning to speak.

Listeners can do at least three things within a communicative interaction. First, they can judge or estimate their confidence or certainty of understanding. That is they can recognize ambiguous or noninformative messages as such. Second, if they recognize that a message or communication is inadequate, they can make this known to the speaker. Finally, they can specify the additional information that is needed in order to clarify the message. (Glucksberg et al., 1975, p. 331)

Finally, children's understanding of the effectiveness of their own communicator or listener skills is another important determinant of their effectiveness in communication situations. In other words, when do children know that their own messages are clear and helpful and when do they know when someone else's message to them is unclear and inadequate? Just as children gain insight into their own memory abilities—metamemory—or language abilities—metalanguage—there is another meta—namely, metacommunication skills, which refers to children's understanding of their own communicative skills.

How early do children acquire these various communication skills? How do they develop? How do they shift across different types of communicative situations? We will explore these questions next.

BOX 8-7
BLACK ENGLISH: A CASE
OF DIALECT DIFFERENCES

 Black children often learn two dialects—standard English and black English—which are used in different situations. Houston (1970) showed that poor black children used different modes of communication in school and play. The "school register" is used with persons in authority and is characterized by nonfluency, shortened utterances, simplified syntax, and lack of expressiveness. However, the "nonschool register," used with friends and in natural settings is very expressive and shows all the syntactic characteristics expected of 11-year-olds. Houston noted that the children engaged in constant language games, verbal contests, and narrative improvisations. She wrote, "To the observer able to elicit the nonschool register . . . the natural linguistic creativity and frequent giftedness of the so-called linguistically deprived child become apparent" (Houston, 1970, p. 953).

Similarly, it has been pointed out that the poor black adolescent gang members studied by Labov (1970) display an extremely sophisticated verbal system and place a very high value on verbal skill. Individual gangs often have a "verbal leader" who leads other members in the ritualized tradition of "toasts," or gang-originated epic poems partly recited from memory and partly invented, which frequently have high literary value. The linguistic skills demonstrated by the boys among themselves stand in marked contrast to the consistent failure of these same boys in the school system.

These studies also demonstrate that black English has its own complex structure with a complete and consistent set of rules. Labov wrote, "When linquists say that black English is a system we mean that it differs from other dialects in regular and rule-governed ways, so that it has equivalent ways of expressing the same logical content" (Labov, 1970, p. 185). Thus, black English is functionally equivalent to standard English. It definitely is not a collection of sloppy or random mistakes, or a simplified version of standard English, as has been assumed by many researchers and educators. The incorrect assumption that black English is inferior has undoubtedly put black children at a disadvantage on standardized tests and in school.

Communication ability varies with the situation, and by sampling only a limited set of contexts, we may sometimes underestimate a child's language skills. ■

Source: Labov, W. The logic of nonstandard English. In F. Williams (Ed.), *Language and poverty*. Chicago: Markham, 1970; and Houston, S. H. A re-examination of some assumptions about the language of the disadvantaged child. *Child Development*, 1970. **41,** 947–963.

Not by Word Alone: Gestures as an Aspect
of Early Communication

Communication is not only achieved by words; and by restricting ourselves to verbal communication, one can easily misjudge how early communication begins. Even before language, infants and adults communicate by means of gestures. From 3 or 4 months on, adults offer and show things to infants, and by 6 or 7 months, infants reciprocate. Similarly, by 7 or 8 months, adults begin to point to draw attention of the infant to an object or event. Within a few months,

(a) (b)

Even before learning to talk, infants use pointing as a means of communication. (Photo (a) Ken Heyman; photo (b) John Rees, Black Star)

infants begin to actively use pointing gestures, an early form of communication. At the end of the first year, children show a surprisingly high degree of communicative knowledge. They can use gestures to communicate; for example, children not only point but check to make sure that their gesture has been successful in getting their partner to look in the right direction. All of us have seen a child tug at the pant leg of a distracted father and then point again. And they can respond to pointing as a communicative gesture. By a year, infants look in the direction that an adult is pointing and not at the adults' face or the pointing hand (Lempers, Flavell, & Flavell, 1977). Of course, there are other common gestures such as reaching, grasping, or staring, and some children develop their own unique gesturing tactics.

As language develops, words and gestures are often used together for more effective communication. A child may point to an object and then verbally comment or gesture to emphasize the meaning of her words.

Early Communication Skills: Preschoolers As Communicators

Communication skills develop rapidly, and by 2 years of age, children show a surprisingly sophisticated set of communication abilities. To find out just how capable 2-year-olds are, Wellman and Lempers (1977) recently videotaped the interactions of ten 2-year-olds in their day-to-day interaction in a nursery school. They scored 300 referential communicative interactions where the communicator's intent was to point out, show, or display a particular object or referent to another child. The results were striking in their demonstration of the competence of 2-year-olds as communicators. First, these toddlers were sensitive to situational determinants of effective communication. The communicator addressed her listener when the two were either interacting or playing together (82 percent) or when the listener was at least not involved with someone else (88 percent), when they could see each other (97 percent), when they were physically close to each other (91 percent), and to a lesser extent when the listener was looking at her (41 percent). Similarly, the children made sure that they—as communicators—were close to the referent (92 percent) and so was the receiver (84 percent), to make it more likely that the receiver would understand the message.

In light of these precautions on the part of our young communicators, it is not surprising that they were effectively able to engage their receivers. In fact, 79 percent of the messages met with an adequate response from the listener. Moreover, the children showed an awareness of the difficulty of the situation and adjusted their communications accordingly: they communicated more in difficult situations (for example, where there might be a visual obstacle or where the object is hard to locate, such as a single toy in a toy box) and used shorter messages in easy situations. Finally, these children were responsive to feedback from their partners. For example, in 54 percent of the cases where the communicators received no response, they repeated their message in some form; in only 3 percent of the cases where they received an adequate response did they repeat. Or if the listener either just looked or gave a negative verbal reaction—an indication that the listener didn't understand—the children always recommunicated. In sum, these 2-year-olds show a surprisingly sophisticated display of communicative competence.

A closer look at the verbal language that young children use in communicating with partners of different ages confirms this picture. As the studies in Box 8-8 clearly show, 4-year-olds are sensitive to their partner's verbal abilities and talk differently to 2-year-olds, other 4-year-olds, and adults. Young children, then, are able to shift their language style to suit their listener's level of competence.

These findings present a serious challenge to some traditional viewpoints. One popular hypothesis was advanced by Piaget (1926), who argued that children younger than about 7 years of age were trapped within their own egocentric perspective and unable to accommodate to the perspective of their listener. According to Piaget the child is egocentric when:

He does not bother to know to whom he is speaking nor whether he is being listened to . . . the talk is egocentric because he does not attempt to place himself at the point of view of his hearer. . . . He feels no desire to influence his hearer nor to tell him anything; not unlike a certain type of drawing-room conversation where everyone talks about himself and no one listens." (Piaget, 1926, p. 9)

BOX 8-8
SPEECH ADJUSTMENTS
IN 4-YEAR-OLDS

Skilled communicators adjust the level of their speech and the content of their message to fit the competence of their listeners. Adults talk differently to 2-year-olds than to adolescents or other adults. Do children adjust their messages to suit their listeners as well? Shatz and Gelman (1973) recorded the conversations of 4-year-olds who were introducing a new toy to partners of different ages—2-year-olds and adults. Even 4-year-olds switch their speech patterns to accommodate their audience. When speaking to a 2-year-old, they used shorter utterances than when speaking to adults (see Figure 8-6). Consider these contrasting utterances to an adult listener and a 2-year-old listener.

A. M. to ADULT: . . . You're supposed to put one of these persons in, see? Then one goes with the other little girl. And then the little boy. He's the little boy and he drives. And then they back up. And then the little girl has marbles . . . [Questions from adult and responses from S.] And then the little girl falls out and then it goes backwards.

A.M. to YOUNGER CHILD: . . . Watch, Perry, Watch this. He's backing in here. Now he drives up. Look, Perry. Look here, Perry. Those are marbles, Perry. Put the men in here. Now I'll do it.

As these speech samples show, not only are the utterances shorter, but 4-year-olds use more attention-getting and attention-holding words with 2-year-olds than with adults. These 4-year-old communicators apparently recognized that adults have better attentional capacities than 2-year-olds, and they vary their language accordingly by using more attentional devices with their young listeners. Finally, they adjusted the complexity of their grammatical constructions to suit their listener as well: they used less complex utterances such as fewer coordinate construc-

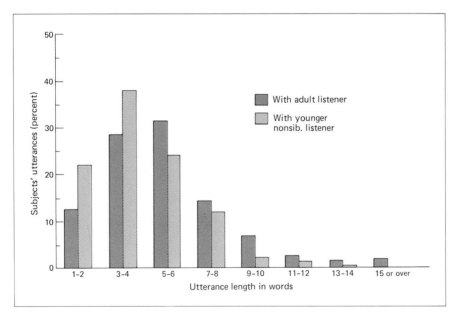

FIGURE 8-6 Distribution of utterances of various lengths in 16 adult-non-sibling sessions. (*From Shatz & Gelman, 1973.*)

tions (and, but, so, etc.), fewer subordinate conjunctions (when, where, while, etc.), and fewer predicate complements (for example, "I think *that* this goes here; I'll show you *how* to do it") with 2-year-olds. Even when 4-year-olds do occasionally use complex constructions with young listeners, they use them differently than with adults. For 2-year-olds, even the complex utterances such as: "I'll show you how to do it," are used to direct the interaction or for "show and tell" purposes. There are no references to the listener's thoughts or mental state, no requests for information, or no modulation of their statements to indicate any uncertainty. In contrast, 4-year olds are less bold and blunt and are more polite and cautious—in recognition of the status and knowledge level of the adult. In short, children not only shifted their speech in a variety of ways, but shifted both the kinds of topics that they talked about and the degree of politeness that they showed in addressing listeners of different ages. Four-year-olds have already learned one of the basic rules of effective communication, namely, the need to adjust one's language to suit the competence level of their listeners. ∎

Source: Shatz, M., & Gelman, R. The development of communication skills: Modifications in the speech of young children as a function of listener. *Monographs of the Society for Research in Child Development*, 1973, **38** (5), 1–37; and Gelman, R., & Shatz, M. Appropriate speech adjustments: The operational restraints on talk to two year olds. In M. Lewis & L. Rosenblum (Eds.), *Interaction, conversation and the development of language*. New York: Wiley, 1977.

In contrast, adult speech is nonegocentric since the adult takes the audience into account.

As the studies above show, when you look more closely at children's communications, it is clear that the children are sensitive to their listener's perspective much earlier than Piaget's egocentricism hypothesis suggests.

Developmental Changes in Communication Effectiveness

These demonstrations of early communicative skill do not mean that 5-year-olds are as effective as adults. Sensitivity to the listener's feedback, for example, improves with age, as children become responsive to more subtle forms of feedback. Young children (4-year-olds) do not benefit as much from subtle feedback such as a puzzled look or "I don't understand" as older children (7-year-olds). In response to this feedback, the 4-year-olds rarely reformulated their message, while the 7-year-olds produced a different message after finding out that their listener wasn't understanding their original message. However, the verbal feedback was much better than the facial expression—even for the older children. If you give clear and explicit feedback, even 4-year-olds shift their strategies. By telling them to "Look at it again, what else does it look like? Can you tell me anything else about it?" the 4-year-olds produced different messages. Even young children can benefit from feedback, but it apparently has to be more direct than for older communicators (Peterson, Danner, & Flavell, 1972). Similarly, all communication situations are not alike, and some may require more sophisticated skills. Communicative competence is present early for some kinds of situations, but continues to develop throughout childhood. In the Wellman-Lempers study, for example, children communicated about single familiar objects that were present in their immediate environment. But children

may have more difficulty communicating about absent objects (in time or space), internal referents (one's own feelings, motivations, thoughts, etc.), and relationships of one or more referents (relationships over space and time, the functions of referents, etc.) (Wellman & Lempers, 1977).

Let us examine a series of studies by Krauss and Glucksberg, which put children's communication skills to a much more stringent test. At the same time they showed that different communication situations require different skills, which may develop at different rates in children. Specifically, they asked how well children could communicate with a partner when they could talk to but not look at each other and when they were required to communicate about unfamiliar objects. In some ways, it is like trying to describe a new toy to a friend over the telephone. To find out, Krauss and Glucksberg gave children at four age levels, kindergarten and grades 1, 3, and 5, the task of communicating a description of a set of novel graphic designs to a partner of the same age. Table 8-5 illustrates the novel figures which are printed on wooden blocks. In the experimental situation there are two subjects, designated the speaker and listener, each of whom has a duplicate set of the design blocks. The speaker is required to stack his blocks on a peg and at the same time to instruct his partner, the listener, which block to stack on her peg. No restrictions are placed on verbal

TABLE 8-5 TYPICAL INITIAL DESCRIPTIONS OFFERED BY FIVE NURSERY SCHOOL SPEAKERS FOR EACH OF THE FORMS ARE SHOWN HERE. UNLIKE ADULT DESCRIPTIONS, THEY WERE BRIEF AND HIGHLY IDIOSYNCRATIC

Form		Child				
		1	2	3	4	5
1		Man's legs	Airplane	Drapeholder	Zebra	Flying saucer
2		Mother's hat	Ring	Keyhold	Lion	Snake
3		Somebody running	Eagle	Throwing sticks	Strip-stripe	Wire
4		Daddy's shirt	Milk jug	Shoe hold	Coffeepot	Dog
5		Another Daddy's shirt	Bird	Dress hold	Dress	Knife
6		Mother's dress	Ideal	Digger hold	Caterpillar	Ghost

Source: Krauss, R. M., & Glucksberg, F. Social and nonsocial speech. *Scientific American*, 1977, 236, 100–105.

communication, and the object of the game is to tell the partner the correct block so that listener and speaker have identical stacks of blocks at the end of the trial. Success is rewarded by a small plastic trinket. Before using the novel forms, the children were given practice trials with animal-shaped blocks in full view of one another. After they learned the game, they were separated by an opaque screen and provided eight trials with the novel figures.

Table 8-5 shows some of the children's descriptions; not only are the descriptions often not very helpful in discriminating among the objects, but notice that the first child uses the same description—Daddy's shirt—to describe two different objects. To illustrate how the youngest children often forget the limitations of the situation—they couldn't see each other or the other child's objects—consider this exchange between two 4-year-olds:

Speaker (referring to one of the geometric figures): It's a bird.

Listener: Is this it?

Speaker: No.

In light of this sample exchange the results—shown in Figure 8-7—are not surprising. There were clear developmental trends. While the kindergarten-age

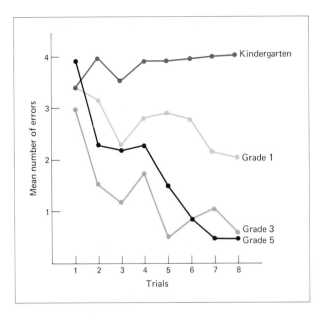

FIGURE 8-7 Development of communication skill across age. *(From Krauss & Glucksberg, 1969, by permission of the authors and the Society for Research in Child Development.)*

subjects failed to show any improvement, the older subjects in grades 3 and 5 steadily reduced their error rate so that by the last few trials they were performing the game without a mistake. Clearly, communication effectiveness does improve as the child develops. However, in combination with the other evidence that we have reviewed, it is clear that communication skills develop at different rates for different kinds of communication tasks.

Learning to Listen

Nor is it just speaker skills that improve as the child develops. Listening skills improve over development as well. Being a good listener requires that you know when a message is clear. Young children are often unaware that they do not understand a message. In a recent experiment, Markman (1977) gave first and third graders instructions for a game that left out critical information which made it impossible to play the game. The younger children were unaware of the inadequacy of the communicator's message and often had to be urged to try to play the game before becoming aware of the problems. In contrast, the third graders noticed the inadequacy of the message more readily. Recently, it has been shown that 6- to 10-year-old children can be taught to be better listeners; children who were encouraged to ask the speaker clarifying questions performed more effectively than children who were not given this lesson in listening (Cosgrove & Patterson, 1977). Four-year-olds, however, did not benefit from the instruction, which suggests that this type of listener strategy may be a moderately advanced communication skill.

Other evidence not only confirms that listener skills improve with age, but indicates that metacommunication skills, namely, awareness of the adequacy of one's own communications, improve as the child develops as well. To demonstrate these shifts, children at three grade levels—2, 4, and 6—were asked to evaluate the adequacy of two types of messages—their own and someone else's (Asher, 1976). In both cases, some of the messages were poor and unhelpful, while in other cases the messages were clear and helpful. As the children developed, they were more accurate in their discrimination of good and poor messages—whether they were their own or another child's communication. In summary, insight into one's own communication skills is a late-developing, but important, aspect of communicative competence.

Summary

Language serves a variety of functions and facilitates interpersonal communication, thinking, and learning. The study of language can be divided into four areas: phonology, semantics, syntax, and pragmatics. Phonology describes the system of sounds for a language and how the basic sound units, or phonemes, are combined to form words and how the intonation patterns of phrases and sentences are determined. Semantics is the study of the meaning of words and of sentences, while syntax describes the structure of a language, the rules which specify the order, and the function of words in a sentence. Finally, pragmatics describes the rules that govern how children use language in different social contexts.

Various theoretical positions have guided research in language development. To account for the development of language, some theorists have taken a nativist position, which suggests that some aspects of language are innate. Evidence that young infants can respond to different phonemes has given support to this position. The regularity and similarity of children's mastery of language in a wide variety of cultures are additional support for this position.

In contrast, behavioral or learning-theory accounts of language development have minimized innate factors. According to this view, language can be acquired through principles of classical and operant conditioning and imitation. Although learning principles are important in modifying language usage and in overcoming language deficits in children, there is considerable doubt that these principles can account for language acquisition.

An interactionist position, which recognizes that children are biologically prepared for language, but require extensive experience with expressed language for adequate language development, provides the most reasonable theoretical acocunt.

Children's early language development was traced from babbling through one- and two-word utterances. Children's language follows a similar course in most cultures and in both oral and sign languages. Early speech is often restricted; children tend to use words either in an overly specific way or overgeneralize later. Context is very important in attempting to understand the meaning of children's early utterances; word order alone is often insufficient.

Children's early sentences are characterized as telegraphic, since children often omit words or word endings. Even these early sentences follow a set of rules—characteristic of all language development. Next the child's progress in mastering morphemes such as possessives and plurals and major constructions such as questions and negations was reviewed.

Children not only learn sentence structure, but use this knowledge of syntax to help in understanding the meaning of sentences. An advanced accomplishment is metalinguistic awareness, by which the child not only can understand and produce language, but can articulate the rules of the language.

Communication, one aspect of pragmatics, involves a variety of skills for both speaker and listener. Communication begins early, and 1-year-olds often use gestures in their first communicative attempts. During the preschool years, children exhibit a remarkable range of communicative abilities including an ability to adjust their communications for the age of their listeners. Communication skills show developmental changes, and the skills required for different kinds of communication tasks develop at different rates. Finally, listener skills, such as recognizing when a message is unclear, show parallel improvement as the child develops.

References

Asher, S. R. Children's ability to appraise their own and another person's communication performance. *Developmental Psychology*, 1976, **12**, 24–32.

Atkinson, K., McWhinney, B., & Stoel, C. An experiment on the recognition of babbling. Papers and reports on child language development, Committee on Linguistics, Stanford University, 1970 (No. 1).

Bates, E. Acquisition of pragmatic competence. *Journal of Child Language*, 1974, **1**, 277–281.

Bates, E. Pragmatics and sociolinguistics in child language. In D. Morehead & A. Morehead (Eds.), *Directions in normal and deficient child language*. Baltimore: University Park Press, 1976.

Bellugi, U. Simplification in children's language. In R. Husley and E. Ingram (Eds.), *Methods and models in language acquisition*. New York: Academic, 1971.

Benedict, H. The role of repetition in early language comprehension. Paper presented at the biennial meeting of the Society for Research in Child Development, Denver, 1975.

Berko, J. The child's learning of English morphology. *Word*, 1958, **14**, 50–177.

Bijou, S., *Child development: The basic stage of early childhood*. Englewood Cliffs: Prentice Hall, 1976.

Bloom, L. *Language development: Form and function in emerging grammars*. Cambridge, Mass.: M.I.T. Press, 1970.

Bloom, L. *One word at a time*. The Hague: Mouton, 1973.

Bloom, L. An interactive perspective on language development. Keynote address, Child Language Research Forum, Stanford University, 1976.

Bloom, L. The integration of form, content and use in language development. Unpublished manuscript, Columbia University, 1977.

Brown, R. *A first language*. Cambridge, Mass.: Harvard University Press, 1973.

Brown, R., & Bellugi. U. Three processes in the child's acquisition of syntax. In E. H. Lenneberg (Ed.), *New directions in the study of language*. Cambridge, Mass.: M.I.T. Press, 1964.

Chomsky, C., *The acquisition of syntax in children from 5 to 10*. Cambridge, Mass.: M.I.T. Press, 1969.

Chomsky, N. *Language and mind.* New York: Harcourt, Brace & World, 1968.

Clark, H. H., & Clark, E. V. *Psychology and language: An introduction to psycholoinguistics.* New York: Harcourt Brace Jovanovich, 1977.

Condon, W. S., & Sander, L. W. Neonate movement is synchronized with adult speech: Interactional participation and language acquisition. *Science,* 1974, **183,** 99–101.

Cosgrove, J. M., & Patterson, C. J. Plans and the development of listener skills. *Developmental Psychology,* 1977, **13,** 557–564.

Dale, P. S. *Language development: Structure and function* (2d Ed.). New York: Holt, 1976.

Delack, J. B. Aspects of infant speech development in the first year of life. *Canadian Journal of Linguistics,* 1976, **21,** 17–37.

deVilliers, J. G., & deVilliers, P. A. A cross-sectional study of the acquisition of grammatical morphemes in child speech. *Journal of Psycholinguistic Research,* 1973, **2,** 267–278.

Eimas, P. D. Speech perception in early infancy. In L. B. Cohen & P. Salapatek (Eds.), *Infant perception.* New York: Academic, 1975, pp. 193–231.

Entwisle, D. R., & Frasure, N. E., A contradiction resolved: Children's processing of syntactic cues. *Developmental Psychology,* 1974, **10,** 852–857.

Ervin, S. Imitation and structural change in children's language. In E. H. Lenneberg (Ed.), *New directions in the study of language.* Cambridge, Mass.: M.I.T. Press, 1964.

Flavell, J. H. *Cognitive development.* Englewood Cliffs, N.J.: Prentice-Hall, 1977.

Fleming, J. D. The state of the apes. *Psychology Today,* 1974, **8.**

Fraser, C., Bellugi, U., & Brown, R. Control of grammar in imitation, comprehension and production. *Journal of Verbal Learning and Verbal Behavior,* 1963, **2,** 121–135.

Gardner, B. T., & Gardner, R. A. Two-way communication with an infant chimpanzee. In A. M. Schrier & F. Stollnitz (Eds.), *Behavior of nonhuman primates* (Vol. 4). New York: Academic, 1971.

Gelman, R., & Shatz, M. Appropriate speech adjustments: The operation of conversational restraints on talk to two year olds. In M. Lewis & L. Rosenblum (Eds.), *Interaction, conversation and the development of language.* New York: Wiley, 1977.

Glucksberg, S., Krauss, R., & Higgins, E. T. The development of referential communication skills. In F. D. Horowitz (Ed.), *Review of child development research* (Vol. 4). Chicago: University of Chicago Press, 1975.

Greenberg, J. H. *Language universals.* The Hague: Mouton, 1966.

Halliday, M. A. K. *Learning how to mean: Exploration in the development of language.* London: Arnold, 1975.

Horowitz, F. D. (Ed.). Visual attention, auditory stimulation and language discrimination in young infants. *Monographs of the Society for Research in Child Development,* 1974, **39** (No. 5, Series No. 158).

Houston, S. H. A re-examination of some assumptions about the language of the disadvantaged child. *Child Development,* 1970, **41,** 947–963.

Hovell, M. F., Schumaker, J. B., & Sherman, J. A. A comparison of parents' models and expansions in promoting children's acquisition of adjectives. *Journal of Experimental Child Psychology,* 1978, **25,** 41–57.

Jakobson, R. *Child language, aphasia, and phonological universals.* The Hague: Mouton, 1968.

Kaplan, E., & Kaplan, G. The prelinguistic child. In J. Elliot (Ed.), *Human development and cognitive processes.* New York: Holt, 1971, pp. 359–381.

Kilma, E. S., & Bellugi, U. Syntactic regularities in the speech of children. In J. Lyons and R. Wales (Eds.), *Pyscholinguistic papers.* Edinburgh: Edinburgh University Press, 1966, pp. 183–207.

Krauss, R. M., & Glucksberg, S. Social and nonsocial speech. *Scientific American*, 1977, **236,** 100–105.

Labov, W. The logic of nonstandard English. In F. Williams (Ed.), *Language and poverty*. Chicago: Markham, 1970.

Lempers, J. D., Flavell, E. R., & Flavell, J. H. The development in very young children of tacit knowledge concerning visual perception. *Genetic Psychology Monographs*, 1977.

Lenneberg, E. *Biological foundations of language*. New York: Wiley, 1967.

Lieberman, P. *Intonation, perception, and language*. Cambridge, Mass.: M.I.T. Press, 1967.

Liebert, R. M., Odom, R. D., Hill, J. H., & Huff, R. L. Effects of age and rule familiarity on the production of modeled language constructions. *Developmental Psychology*, 1969, **1,** 108–112.

Lovaas, I. A behavior therapy approach to the treatment of childhood schizophrenia. In J. P. Hill (Ed.), *Minnesota symposia on child development* (Vol. 1). Minneapolis: University of Minnesota Press, 1967, pp. 108–159.

Markman, E. M. Realizing that you don't understand: A preliminary investigation. *Child Development*, 1977, **48,** 986–992.

McCarthy, D. Language development in children: In L. Carmichael (Ed.), *Manual of child psychology*. New York: Wiley, 1954, pp. 452–630.

McNeill, D. Developmental psycholnguistics. In F. Smith & G. Miller (Eds.), *The genesis of language*. Cambridge, Mass.: M.I.T. Press, 1966.

McNeill, D. On theories of language acquisition. In D. Horton & T. Dixon (Eds.), *Verbal behavior and general behavior*. Englewood Cliffs, N.J.: Prentice-Hall, 1968.

McNeill, D. *The acquisition of language: The study of developmental psycholinguistics*. New York: Harper & Row, 1970.

Moerk, E. Change in verbal child-mother interactions with increasing language skills of the child. *Journal of Psycholinguistic Research*, 1974, **3,** 101–116.

Moffitt, A. R. Consonant cue perception by twenty to twenty-four week old infants. *Child Development*, 1971, **42,** 717–732.

Nelson, K. Structure and strategy in learning to talk. *Monographs of the Society for Research in Child Development*, 1973, **38** (Nos. 1 and 2).

Nelson, K. Early speech in its communicative context. Unpublished manuscript, Yale University, 1976.

Nelson, K., Carskaddon, G., & Bonvillian, J. D. Syntax acquisition: Impact of experimental variation in adult verbal interaction with the child. *Child Development*, 1973, **44,** 497–504.

Newport, E. L. Motherese: The speech of mothers to young children. In N. J. Castellan, D. B. Pisoni, & G. R. Potts (Eds.), *Cognitive theory* (Vol II). Hillsdale, N.J.: Lawrence Erlbaum, 1976.

Newport, E. L., Gleitman, H., & Gleitman, L. R. Mother, I'd rather do it myself: Some effects and non-effects of maternal speech style. In C. A. Ferguson & C. E. Snow (Eds.), *Talking to children: Language input and acquisition*. Cambridge: Cambridge University Press, 1977.

Oller, J. W., Wieman, L. A., Doyle, W. J., & Ross, C. Infant babbling and speech. *Journal of Child Language*, 1976, **3,** 1–11.

Paris, S. G., & Carter, A. Y. Semantic and constructive aspects of sentence memory in children. *Developmental Psychology*, 1973, **9,** 109–113.

Paris, S. G., & Lindauer, B. K. Constructive processes in children's comprehension and memory. In R. V. Kail & J. W. Hagen (Eds.), *Memory in cognitive development*. Hillsdale, N. J.: Lawrence Erlbaum, 1976.

Peterson, C. L., Danner, F. W., & Flavell, J. H. Developmental changes in children's responses to three indications of communication failure. *Child Development*, 1972, **43,** 1463–1468.

Phillips, J. R. Syntax and vocabulary of mother's speech to young children: Age and sex comparisons. *Child Development*, 1973, **44,** 182–185.

Piaget, J. *The language and thought of the child.* New York: Harcourt Brace, 1926.

Premack, A. J., & Premack, D. Teaching language to an ape. *Scientific American,* 1972, **227,** 92–99.

Premack, D. Language in chimpanzee? *Science,* 1971, **172,** 808–822.

Riekehof, L. Talk to the deaf. Springfield, Mo.: Gospel Publishing House, 1963.

Rosenthal, T. L., Zimmerman, B. J., & Durning, K. Observationally induced changes in children's interrogative classes. *Journal of Personality and Social Psychology*, 1970, **16,** 681–688.

Sachs, J. S. Recognition memory for syntactic and semantic aspects of connected discourse. *Perception and Psychophysics*, 1967, **2,** 437–442.

Shatz, M., & Gelman, R. The development of communication skills: Modifications in the speech of young children as a function of listener. *Monographs of the Society for Research in Child Development*, 1973, **38** (5, Serial No. 152), 1–37.

Shipley, E. S., Smith, C. S., & Gleitman, L. R. A study in the acquisition of language: Free responses to commands. *Language*, 1969, **45,** 322–342.

Skinner, F. F. *Verbal behavior.* New York: Appleton-Century-Crofts, 1957.

Slobin, D. I. The acquisition of Russian as a native language. In F. Smith & G. Miller (Eds.), *The genesis of language.* Cambridge, Mass.: M.I.T. Press, 1966, pp. 129–148.

Slobin, D. I. Imitation and grammatical development in children. In N. S. Endler, L. R. Boulter, & Harry Osser (Eds.), *Contemporary issues in development in psychology.* New York: Holt, 1968.

Slobin, D. I. Universals of grammatical development in children. In G. B. Flores d'Arcais & J. M. Levelt (Eds.), *Advances in Psycholinguistics.* New York: American Elsevier, 1970, pp. 174–184.

Slobin, D. I., & Welsh, C. A. Elicited imitation as a research tool in developmental psycholinguistics. In C. A. Ferguson & D. I. Slobin (Eds.), *Studies in child language development.* New York: Holt, 1973, pp. 485–497.

Spring, D. R. Effects of maternal speech on infant's selection of vocal reinforcement. Unpublished paper, University of Washington, 1974.

Tagatz, G. E. *Child development and individually guided education.* Reading, Mass.: Addison-Wesley, 1976.

Weir, R. H. Some questions on the child's learning of phonology. In F. Smith & G. Miller (Eds.), *The genesis of language,* Cambridge, Mass.: M.I.T. Press, 1966, pp. 153–168.

Wellman, H. M., & Lempers, J. D. The naturalistic communicative abilities of two-year-olds. *Child Development*, 1977, **48,** 1052–1057.

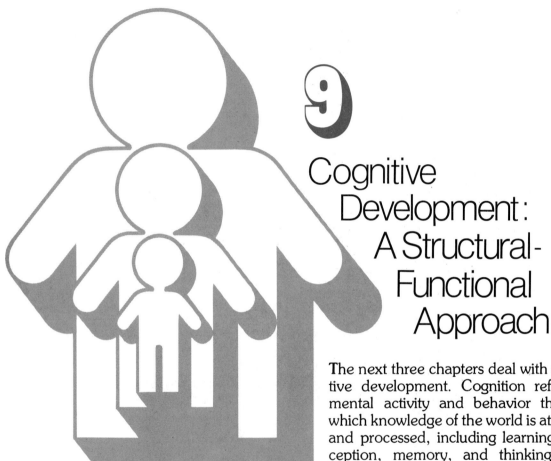

9

Cognitive Development: A Structural-Functional Approach

The next three chapters deal with cognitive development. Cognition refers to mental activity and behavior through which knowledge of the world is attained and processed, including learning, perception, memory, and thinking. The concept of cognition is such a broadly integrative one that most of the topics covered in the previous chapters of this book have relevance for cognitive development. Biological factors, environmental and experiential factors, social factors, emotions, and motivation all play a role in cognitive development.

In this chapter and the next we will examine psychological processes and events which underlie cognitive functioning. In Chapter 11 we will focus on individual differences in mental abilities and the factors that contribute to these differences.

Two models of the psychological processes and events which underlie cognitive development will be presented in this chapter and Chapter 10. The first model is one which emphasizes developmental changes in the organization or structure of intelligence, and how differences in these structures are reflected in the learning of children at different ages. In this chapter Piaget's monumental theory of cognitive development, which evolved from his own interest in natural science and initially from observations largely of his own children, will be presented as an example of this approach. In addition, the development of social cognition will be discussed. How do children perceive, understand, and think about the social world—about themselves, other people, social interactions, and social institutions? How are changes in the organization of intelligence reflected in age differences in social cognition?

In the next chapter the second model of cognitive development, the cognitive processing model, which emerged from the experimental laboratory and from a more behavioristic approach to psychology, will be examined. This model, rather than focusing on structural changes in intelligence or problems of learning presented in Chapter 6, explores the role of cognitive operations in processing information. The cognitive processing theorists study the operations involved in receiving, attending to, discriminating, transforming, storing, and recalling information. The developing child is viewed as having an array of cognitive processes and strategies that help her learn about herself and about objects and events in the world and which facilitate adaptive intelligent problem solving.

Piaget's Cognitive Developmental Theory of Intelligence

The single most important, detailed, and controversial theory of intellectual development is that of the Swiss scientist Jean Piaget. He has been the major figure responsible for a great surge of interest in cognitive development in the past decade. If two criteria for the significance of a theory are its comprehensiveness and the amount of research it stimulates, Piaget's theory is unique in the area. Whether or not they agree with his theories, hundreds of psychologists currently are investigating Piaget's provocative formulations.

A Historical Overview

Piaget has been writing since 1907, when at the age of 10 he published his first article on a rare albino sparrow in a natural history journal. Four years later some of his writings on mollusks led to an inquiry being made as to his possible interest in the position of curator of the mollusk collection in the Geneva Museum of Natural History. The chagrined director of the museum reneged on his offer when he discovered that the creative young biologist was a schoolboy. Piaget continued to be interested in biology and by 1920 was concerned with the relationship between biology and psychology. In the following two decades he published a remarkable series of books on the intellectual development of children. He has produced over 30 books and more than 200 articles, and his writing still continues. Since he had such a long history of prolific study and writing on cognitive development, why was it not until the early 1960s that his influence began to really shape the course of American developmental psychology? What was it about the climate of American psychology that made it inhospitable to the ideas of a theorist like Piaget?

Child psychology in the 1930s and 1940s was largely a descriptive, atheoretical field. Interest in intelligence focused on mental measurement. Psychologists were more interested in the number of questions a child could answer correctly on an intelligence test than in qualitative differences in how children of different ages arrived at these answers. When theory did impinge on child psychology in the late 1940s, it was predominantly in the form of stimulus-response theories—derived from the behaviorism of John B. Watson—which had dominated the mainstream of psychology for twenty years. Stimulus-response theorists emphasized the role of learning rather than any innate predispositions, processes, or structures in intellectual development. They were not truly concerned with differences in learning over age, but tried to apply the same principles of learning across all ages. Standard laws of conditioning, reinforcement, generalization, and extinction were invoked to explain the behavior of children of all ages as well as the behavior of rats from which these principles were derived. The preferred method of behaviorists was to investigate groups of subjects by using controlled manipulative experimental procedures, rather than to observe a few subjects intensively and repeatedly under naturalistic conditions. As the student reads further into the work of Piaget, it will become clear why this behavioristic approach was incompatible with Piagetian theory and methods.

Jean Piaget. (Yves DeBraine, Black Star)

By the end of the 1950s child psychology was in a period of great growth and flux. No completely satisfying developmental theory existed. The psychoanalytic developmental theory had never been accepted by experimentally oriented academic American psychologists. The attempts to translate psychoanalytic theory into the more familiar terms of learning theory had not proved fruitful and were abating. Moreover, disenchantment with learning theory itself had set in. Some psychologists claimed it was not a real developmental theory since it did not allow for the different capacities of children at different ages. In learning theory, development was explained as a function of learning, whereas Piaget argued that learning was a function of development. Some behavioral scientists also said the child played a more active role in learning than contemporary learning theory allowed. Others, including Piaget, argued that American learning theory had little relevance or influence on educational or other practical human problems since it had evolved from work in animal laboratories. In addition to this theoretical need, the launching of Sputnik and our government's concern with competing in achievement with the Russians led to a heightened interest in understanding how intellectual abilities develop. Piaget presented an attractive alternative to the available theories of the time. His theory was a genuinely developmental theory derived from direct observations of children.

One of the major obstacles to Piaget's acceptance in this country was that he is difficult to read. His terminology was unfamiliar to American psychologists. His theory was complex and at times obscure. He did not define his constructs operationally, and he seemed to use terms with inconsistent meanings. American psychologists who had gone to Geneva to study with Piaget at the Centre of Genetic Epistemology began to return and present his work in a more readily understandable fashion. In 1963 John Flavell published *The Developmental Psychology of Jean Piaget*, a lucid, comprehensive summary and analysis of Piaget's work, and the Piaget boom was well underway.

Early in his career Piaget had worked in the Binet Laboratory in Paris with Theophile Simon, one of the developers of the first intelligence test. In contrast to the other psychologists in the laboratory, who were interested in standardizing and measuring children's ability to answer questions correctly, Piaget became interested in the similarity of the incorrect responses made by children of the same age and how they differed from errors of older or younger children. The qualitative differences in the responses made by children of different ages seemed to reveal varying developmental strategies or processes in thinking. The understanding of these developmental differences in thinking became the central goal of Piaget's investigations. For Piaget the study of *what* children know was only an avenue to understanding age changes in *how* children think.

In order to attain this goal Piaget used an unstructured method of questioning children. The child's responses and not a standardized procedure directed the questioning. Many of his conclusions are derived from detailed observation and question sessions with his own three children, Laurent, Lucienne, and Jacqueline. Later Piaget attempted to test some of his hypotheses with more controlled experiments; nevertheless the looseness of his early methodology is frequently criticized by more rigorously oriented psychologists.

**Structure and
Function**

Piaget's theory of cognitive development (Piaget, 1952) is one which tries to explain how the child adapts to and interprets objects and events in the world about him. How does the child learn about the characteristics and functions of objects such as toys, furniture, clouds, and food and about social objects such as self, parents, and peers. How does the child learn to group objects to identify similarities and differences in objects, to understand what causes changes in objects or events, and to form expectations about objects and events. Piaget views the child as playing an active role in constructing his knowledge of reality. The child does not passively take in information. Although the child's thought processes and conceptions of reality are modified by his encounters with the world about him, the child also plays an active role in interpreting the information he is gaining from experiences, and in adapting it to the knowledge and conceptions of the world he already has.

Piaget uses the term *schemata* to refer to the cognitive structures underlying organized patterns of behavior. These schemata, or cognitive structures, are the processes or ways of organizing and responding to experiences. Even in infants, it is apparent that the child's behavior reflects some organized patterns of relating to or "knowing" the environment. It is not the same kind of process involved in "knowing" the world by older children and adults, where internal mental representations and the use of symbols, such as those in language, are involved in adapting to the world.

In the newborn most of the schemata are inherited reaction patterns and reflexes. The newborn will suck anything that touches her lips. In adapting to her environment, she carries out organized sucking behaviors in response to a wide range of suckable objects. She may be said to possess a sucking *schema* (the singular of schemata). She possesses many other schemata such as grasping, kicking, looking, and hitting which are manifested in organized sensorimotor activities. These early schemata are rapidly modified as the infant interacts with the world about her. Although in younger children these schemata are largely based on the interaction of sensory input and physical activity, the infant shows intelligent behavior in manipulating, responding, and adapting to objects in an organized way.

There is a gradual shift with age and experience from mental activities based on overt behavior to symbolically represented schemata. In older children schemata are more internalized and more mental. Piaget calls these mental equivalents of behavioral schemata *operations*. They can be viewed as involving plans or strategies and rules of problem solving and classification. The older child utilizes internal cognitive structures increasingly similar to those used in adult thought, whereas the mental operations of younger children are based on sensorimotor activities.

Certain unlearned principles of processing and responding to experience result in the continuous modification of schemata. The most important of these inherited principles of functioning are *organization* and *adaptation*.

Organization is the predisposition to integrate and coordinate physical or psychological structures into more complex systems. In the previously cited example of the sucking schema, the infant may initially have a sucking response, a looking response, and a grasping response which function independently.

However, these separate simple behaviors are gradually organized into a high-order system involving the coordination of all these activities.

The second functional principle, that of adaptation, involves two processes: *assimilation* and *accommodation*. When a child has a new experience, the child relates and modifies it, that is, assimilates it in accordance with his or her existing schemata. Through assimilation, the child's current cognitive structures and level of understanding alter his or her response to the environmental event. Piaget regards fantasy play where the childs' imaginative processes are relatively independent of reality as pure assimilation. A child may swoop about his room saying "I'm the wicked witch of the west flying over the castle" with little response to the realities of the situation. However, most instances of assimilation involve more responding to events and objects in their surroundings. For example, children reared in primitive cultures who have never seen an airplane may assimilate their first view of an airplane into a familiar conceptual framework by calling it a great white bird. A more familiar example of assimilation may be the sometimes embarrassing one of the child calling "Daddy" to a male stranger.

Accommodation is a complementary process to that of assimilation. It involves the adjustment of the organism to environmental demands. This coping with the environment results in the continuous modification of schemata. Thus, the child eventually modifies the schema of "daddy" so that it includes only one person; then a new schema, "man," evolves for other male adults. Piaget views imitation, where the child matches her behavior to that of someone else, as the purest form of accommodation.

Most environmental encounters involve both assimilation and accommodation. The infant may try his sucking schema on many objects. He may suck his bottle, his thumb, his pacifier, the ear of his teddy bear, or the plastic birds on his mobile. Some of these objects, such as bottles, thumbs, and pacifiers, are more appropriately "suckable" than others and may involve more assimilation than accommodation. In response to objects such as the plastic birds, sucking may not be a satisfactory response. The wings may be sharp and the plastic distasteful. In addition, a winged creature is awkard to get into the mouth. The child will have to modify or accommodate schema to fit the characteristics of the object. In adapting to his bird mobile, the child may accommodate by just sucking on the soft body and avoiding the wings, or he may give up his sucking schema and use a hitting or kicking response which makes the birds move.

Cognitive development therefore is based on alterations in intellectual structures resulting from innate predispositions to organize and to adapt experience in certain ways. These processes are found in all normal children and continue to operate throughout the life span. Children are constantly changing schemata, or cognitive structures.

Piaget's Developmental Stages

Piaget viewed the course of intellectual growth in terms of progressive changes in cognitive structures. All children do not go through the stages at the same age; however, all children pass through the stages in the same order. The attainments in earlier stages are essential for those in later stages, and some of the earlier intellectual processes may extend into later periods of development. The stages are in no way discrete but involve gradual and continuous changes.

Piaget identifies the four main periods of intellectual development (presented in Table 9-1): the sensorimotor period, the preoperational period, the concrete operational period, and the period of formal operations.

As children pass through these periods, they change from organisms incapable of thought, and dependent on their senses and motor activities in knowing the world about them, to individuals capable of great flexibility of thought and abstract reasoning.

Sensorimotor Period During the first period, the sensorimotor period, which encompasses approximately the first two years of life, the child makes a dramatic

TABLE 9-1 CHARACTERISTICS AND ACHIEVEMENTS IN STAGES OF INTELLECTUAL DEVELOPMENT ACCORDING TO PIAGET

Stage	Approximate age range, years	Major characteristics and achievements
Sensorimotor period	0–2	Infant differentiates himself from other objects; seeks stimulation and prolongs interesting spectacles; attainment of object permanence; primitive understanding of causality, time, and space; means-end relationships; beginnings of imitation of absent, complex nonhuman stimuli; imaginative play and symbolic thought
Preoperational period	2–6	Development of the symbolic function; symbolic use of language; intuitive problem solving; thinking characterized by irreversibility, centration, and egocentricity; beginnings of attainment of conservation of number and ability to think in classes and see relationships
Period of concrete operations	6 or 7 through 11 or 12	Conservation of mass, length, weight, and volume; reversibility, decentration, ability to take role of others; logical thinking involving concrete operations of the immediate world, classification (organizing objects into hierarchies of classes), and seriation (organizing objects into ordered series, such as increasing height)
Period of formal operations	11 or 12 on	Flexibility, abstraction, mental hypotheses testing, and consideration of possible alternatives in complex reasoning and problem solving

transition from a reflexive organism to one possessing rudimentary symbolic thought, that is, from a *reflexive* to a *reflective* organism.

In this period the infant shifts from an organism focused only on immediate sensory and motor experiences to one who becomes oriented toward understanding objects in the world about him. The child becomes aware of spatial relationships through such motor activities as reaching and grasping. He develops concepts of a time dimension having a before and after rather than only immediate experience, and an awareness of causality, of how one event leads to another. Basic to these concepts is knowledge that objects continue to exist when the child is not perceiving them. This is called object permanence. Because understanding the permanence of objects is such an important cognitive attainment, we will discuss it in a separate section at the end of the presentation of the sensorimotor period.

In addition, in the sensorimotor period, the child gradually comes to see the relation between goals and the means to attain those goals. The child begins to imitate the behavior of people who are not present, and he shows intentionality in his behavior. Through the actions of sensing and manipulating the body and objects around him, he acquires knowledge about the properties of his environment. The infant's physical actions are essential in his evolving discovery, organization, and knowledge of reality.

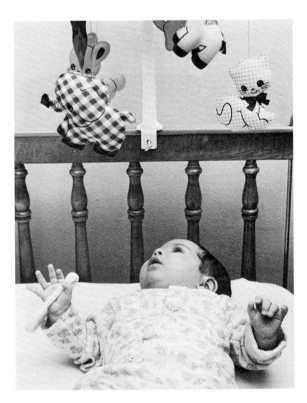

Child in sensorimotor period. (Erika Stone, Peter Arnold Photo Agency)

Piaget speaks of the *plane of action* in the sensorimotor phase preceding and being essential for the later development of the *plane of thought*.

Piaget divides the sensorimotor period into six substages. Again it should be emphasized that these stages involve gradual rather than abrupt transitions in behavior.

Stage of reflex activity　In the first month of life, the stage of reflex activity, infants refine their innate responses. They become more proficient in the use of reflexes, such as the sucking reflex, and in finding stimulation which will permit the functioning of these responses.

Stage of primary circular reactions　In the stage of primary circular reactions (1 to 4 months) the infant repeats and modifies actions which initially may have occurred by chance and which seem to be satisfying. These behaviors are primary in that they are basic reflexive or motoric functions of his or her own body; they are circular in that they are repeated. The primary circular reactions are focused on the infant's activities and body rather than on objects. The functioning of assimilation and accommodation is clearly seen in this period as schemata are altered and integrated.

Primitive anticipations begin to occur. In the neonate, sucking had occurred mainly when the infant's mouth was in contact with the nipple. Now anticipatory sucking may occur when the child is first placed in a reclining position in the mother's arms. The sucking schema has come to include postural cues, in addition to sucking and the satisfaction of hunger.

Stage of secondary circular reactions　It is not until the stage of *secondary circular reactions* (4 to 8 months) that the infant's attention becomes centered on the manipulation of objects rather than focused on her body, as it was in primary circular reactions. It appears that the child now repeats behavior which will reproduce stimulating events which may first have occurred by chance. The child will grasp and shake a rattle in order to hear the interesting sound it makes. The reaching, grasping, and shaking motions necessary for the movement and noise of the rattle are learned. The infant has begun to intentionally manipulate and change her environment.

Stage of coordination of secondary schemata　In the stage of *coordination of secondary schemata* (8 to 12 months) the child begins to use or combine previously acquired schemata as a means of attaining goals. He or she intentionally utilizes schemata previously used in one situation to solve problems in a new situation. For example, a previously acquired hitting schema developed as a means of moving a mobile will be used in order to strike away a barrier in front of a toy. Two things are noticeable about this achievement. First, schemata are generalized from one situation to another; second, a schema may be used as an intermediate step, as a means of attaining a goal.

The child in this stage starts to imitate responses initiated by other people. In the earlier stages, imitation consisted of repeating responses initiated by the infant which might be copied by someone else. If the child was babbling and his or her mother repeated the sounds, the child would listen to her and then repeat the sounds again. This type of imitation really involved only the infant's repetition of his or her own behavior. Now if the mother initiates a new response which is similar to one the child can already perform, the child will attempt to modify the familiar response to match hers. The mother may make a new response of waving "bye-bye." This response is not too different from the child's hand-closing response in an existing grasping schema. The child will attempt to change the action of the hand closing to match the mother's finger movements. The shift here is from subject-initiated to model-initiated behavior in imitation, but the behavior involved must resemble one in an already existing schema.

Stage of tertiary circular reactions   In the stage of tertiary circular reactions (12 to 18 months) children actively use trial and error methods to learn more about the properties of objects. Interest is no longer focused on their own behavior and their own bodies. Their curiosity leads them to experiment with objects. Children become interested in the properties of falling objects; they experiment by dropping different toys and by varying the way the toy is dropped, the position and distance of the drop, the place from which the object is dropped, and the characteristics of the surface on which it lands. This

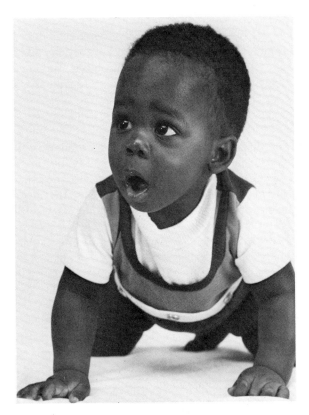

Surprise is often used as an indicator of expectancies in infants. (Erika Stone)

exploration is a kind of early problem solving which leads children to accommodate to new aspects of their environment and assimilate them into their constantly changing schemata. Through experimenting they learn about characteristics of objects around them and new means of attaining goals.

Stage of the invention of new means through mental combination   It is not until the sixth and last stage of the sensorimotor period, *the stage of the invention of new means through mental combination*, that the beginnings of thought using symbolic representations occur.

This internal representation facilitates problem solving through the invention of new means through mental combinations rather than through the overt explorations, manipulations, and behavioral experimentation which occurred in the previous stage. This primitive ability to think through problems leads to the emergence of sudden solutions to problems with little or no overt trial and error behavior. Piaget believes this type of insightful solution to problems occurs when the child discovers new relationships among familiar elements. Piaget describes Laurent's behavior on being presented with a stick at various ages. Over the course of the first year of life, although he manipulated the stick and gradually came to hit objects with the stick, he did not use it to bring attractive objects closer to him. Even at 14 months, when he was holding the stick, he would futilely attempt to reach for distant objects by hand rather than extend the stick and pull them toward them. He was over 16 months of age when he finally grasped the stick in the middle and attempted unsuccessfully to pull some bread toward him. He soon grasped the stick by the end and obtained the bread. After that he stopped reaching for distant objects, such as toys, with his hand and immediately used the stick. Laurent seemed suddenly to discover the usefulness of the stick with little overt trial and error. The exploration and experimentation had been interiorized. It is not until this stage that the child begins to think without acting.

The emergence of the ability to represent an object, which is not present through mental imagery, is manifested in the occurrence of deferred imitation. Without the presence of a model, the child now is able to imitate complex behavior exhibited by a model at a previous time. Piaget cites an occasion when Jacqueline, who did not have temper tantrums, viewed with amazement a wild tantrum in the playpen by a visiting child. The next day when Jacqueline was placed in her playpen, she exhibited the same pattern of behavior, complete with the screaming, foot stamping, and pen rattling, that she had observed in her little visitor. She must have maintained some image of the boy's tantrum in order to match his behavior so closely.

The Construction of a World of Permanent Objects   It is difficult for adults to conceive of a world in which objects do not have a continuing existence, that is, a world in which objects cease to be when we are not perceiving them. As adults, when we can no longer see or hear or touch an object we do not assume that it no longer exists. That would seem to be more like a science fiction "instant destruct" fantasy than an accurate reflection of reality. Adults are able to accept the existence of objects or people as being independent of their own interaction with these objects. But Piaget proposes that young infants do not have this ability to conceive of the permanence of objects. For the very young child, when mother goes out of the room or when a favorite toy drops over the edge of the crib, it is not only "out of sight, out of mind" but "out of sight, out of existence" (Flavell, 1977).

Piaget believes that the process of learning that objects exist when the child is not in direct contact with them is one that occurs gradually and in a predicted sequence over the course of the sensorimotor period. Table 9-2 summarizes the progression of the concept of object permanence. In the first two stages of the sensorimotor period the child shows no comprehension of objects having an existence of their own. When a toy vanishes or when mother's face disappears from over the crib, the infant does not actively seek to find the lost object. When an object is not being perceived, the child behaves as though it does not exist.

It is not until about 4 months of age, in the stage of secondary circular reactions, that some increased awareness of the permanence of objects is found. For the first time the child recognizes a partly concealed object. If a favorite toy is only partly covered by a blanket, the child will reach for it. However, if the child sees someone else placing the toy under a blanket which completely conceals it, he or she does not search for the toy under the blanket. A child who drops a toy may look around briefly for it but makes no new movements to attempt to regain the toy. The child then exhibits visual search, but no manual search, for the missing toy. If the loss of the object is associated with interruption of the child's own movements, visual searching is more likely to ensue than if it has been hidden by another person. What is even more surprising is that the child does not attempt to retrieve an object even when he or she is holding it! If both the child's toy and the hand in which the child is holding it are quickly concealed by an opaque cloth, the child may release the toy without looking for it, or may continue to hold the toy but not attend to it, as if he or she is unaware that it is still in the hand (Gratch, 1972; Gratch & Landers, 1971). If a transparent, rather

TABLE 9-2   STAGES IN THE ATTAINMENT OF OB-JECT PERMANENCE

Approximate ages	Search behavior
0–4 months	No visual or manual searching
4–8 months	Searches for partially concealed objects
8–12 months	Searches for completely concealed objects
12–18 months	Searches after visible displacements of objects
18 months and older	Searches after hidden displacements of objects

than an opaque, cloth is used to cover the hand and toy, the child will retrieve it in a normal fashion (Bower, 1974).

In the subsequent stages, although marked improvement in the development of object permanence occurs, these transitions are gradual.

In the stage of coordination of secondary schemata, the child's concept of object permanence continues to evolve. Early in this stage if a child's favorite toy, say a teddy bear, is hidden under a blanket and is surreptitiously replaced by a truck, the child will look surprised, but will proceed to play with the truck. By the end of this period when the teddy bear disappears and a truck takes its place, the child looks baffled and searches for the bear.

In the period of tertiary circular reactions (about 12 to 18 months), the infant finally is able to recognize the permanence of a visible object. A child, seeing an object being moved and hidden, will track it visually and search for it in the position where it disappeared. Piaget describes hiding his watch alternately between two cushions. His son, Laurent, consistently searched for the watch under the cushion where it had just disappeared. However, if the child saw the watch placed in a box, saw the box taken behind a cushion where it was emptied, and was then handed the empty box, he would not search for it behind the cushion. Laurent manifested object permanence only when he could observe the sequential displacement of the watch. He could not make the inferences necessary to understand invisible displacements of the watch when it had vanished into the box and then the box disappeared.

It is not until the last stage of the sensorimotor period that true object permanence is attained. The child is finally able to make inferences about the position of unseen objects, for example those of the watch in the box described above. The child, upon not finding the watch in the box, will search for it behind the cushion where the box containing the watch last disappeared. One thing that the student should note is that in all situations and procedures described and used by Piaget to track the development of object permanence, the child's behavior used to evaluate the attainment of this concept is search behavior. Is it possible that the child may have attained object permanence but not be able to reveal it in search activities because of other developmental limitations? For example, could it be that the child is aware that the object which has disappeared

As children begin to develop a primitive sense of object permanence, they delight in playing peek-a-boo. (Alice Kandell, Rapho/Photo Researchers, Inc.)

BOX 9-1
THE ROLE OF MEMORY IN PERFORMANCE ON OBJECT PERMANENCE TASKS

Do Infants acquire object permanence earlier than can be indicated through studies involving search procedures? What role do differing memory abilities in infants of different ages play in the manifestation of object permanence? These questions were examined in an experiment which studied object permanence in 20-, 40-, 80-, and 100-day-old infants. If the student reviews Table 9-2, it can be seen that little evidence of object permanence will be exhibited in search behavior by infants this young. In this study each baby was propped in a sitting position in order to look at an object such as a ball. As the infant was viewing the ball, a screen moved over the ball and concealed it from the infant's sight. The screen remained in front of the ball for 1½, 3, 7½, or 15 seconds and then was removed. In one-half of the trials the ball was still there when the screen was removed. In the other half of the trials the ball had disappeared when the screen was removed. What might the different reactions to these two circumstances be of a child who had or had not developed some primitive notion of object permanence? The experimenter reasoned that if infants have some conception of the permanent existence of objects, they would show surprise when the ball had disappeared and none when it remained. In contrast, if infants have no notion of object permanence, they will have no expectation

that the ball is still behind the screen and will reappear when it is removed. These infants should be surprised to see the object appear and not surprised when it has disappeared. Facial expressions of surprise were used to measure the expectations of infants.

Both the age of the infant and the length of time the ball had been concealed influenced the infant's response. If the ball had been hidden for only 1½ seconds, babies in all age groups were surprised when the ball was gone and were not when the ball remained. It seems that with a short concealment period even 20-day-old infants show some object permanence. However, if the ball had been hidden for 15 seconds, the oldest babies, but not the 20-day-old infants, were more startled to see the ball disappear than reappear. The difference in the behavior of the older and younger infants under short and long periods of concealment suggests that limitations in memory may interfere with the younger infant exhibiting object permanence. The younger child may understand that objects continue to exist, but may be unable to remember for an extended period of time that the ball previously was there and had been hidden. ■

Source: Bower, T. G. R. The object in the world of the infant. *Scientific American*, 1971, **225**, 30–38.

still exists, but hand-eye coordination (that is, coordination of reaching movements with visual regard) is not yet developed enough to permit effective searching; or alternatively, could it be that young infants have such a short memory span that they rapidly forget about the object? The findings of the study presented in Box 9-1 suggest that both of these factors may play a role in the outcome of object permanence studies.

Progress in the Sensorimotor Period   The child's intellectual development in the first two years of life is a monumental attainment. Through rapid central nervous system development and active interaction with the environment, the child has changed from a being focused on reflex activity and sensory and motor experiences into an organism with a considerable understanding of realities in the environment and an ability to adapt to them. The child has now developed new behaviors and strategies to attain goals and has begun to use symbolic thought processes to help solve problems. It is the increasingly efficient use of these symbolic processes that leads to the rapid changes in thought which occur in the preoperational period.

Preoperational Period   Piaget divides the preoperational phase into two sub-periods: the preconceptual period (2 to 4 years) and the intuitive period (4 to 7 years).

Preconceptual period   The major characteristic of the preoperational phase is the appearance of systems of representation, such as language, which Piaget calls the *symbolic function.*

The symbolic function   In the preconceptual period the emergence of the symbolic function is shown in the rapid development of language, in imaginative play, and in the increase in deferred imitation. In the intuitive phase it is manifested in changes in thought process involving such things as new understandings of relationships, numbers, and classifications. All these behaviors suggest that the infant is able to produce mental symbols which mediate his or her performance.

The acceleration of language development in the preconceptual period is regarded as an outcome of the development of symbolization rather than as its precursor. Once the use of language symbols begins, it greatly broadens the child's problem-solving abilities and also permits learning from the verbalization of others.

Piaget's notion that cognitive development precedes and is the foundation for the development of language is in direct opposition to the frequently advanced position that improvement in reasoning and problem solving is a result of advances in speech. Piaget's theory is supported by studies of deaf children; the results of these studies show that children with severely restricted language development are able to reason and solve most problems as well as normally hearing children (Furth, 1971). As we saw in our earlier discussion of language it has been proposed that deaf children evolve their own nonlinguistic symbols as they are required for thinking and problem solving.

The symbolic process is also apparent in imaginative play. The child who has seen a train going down the track may push a series of blocks and say "toot toot"; the child has assimilated the blocks into a schema formerly involving a real train. Although Piaget's main interest was in the intellectual rather than the emotional development of the child, he does discuss the emotional importance of play in this period. Symbolic play is an attempt to cope with the demands of reality. At a time when increasing demands are being placed upon the child, he or she is able to act out conflicts with reality in a gratifying, nonstressful manner.

Limitations in preconceptual thought: Animism and egocentrism Two marked limitations of thought in the preconceptual period are found in *animistic* and *egocentric* thinking. Children in this period attribute life to inanimate objects. Plants may hurt when they are picked. The wind may be talking to his friends the trees. One preschool child explained that he was diligently making an elaborate hat and waterbed for his pet rock George so that George would feel snazzy and have sweet dreams. Consider the animistic conception of the sun revealed in the following interchange between Piaget and a preconceptual child.

Piaget: Does the sun move?
Child: Yes, when one walks it follows. When one turns around it turns around too.
　　　Doesn't it ever follow you too?
Piaget: Why does it move?
Child: Because when one walks, it goes too.
Piaget: Why does it go?
Child: To hear what we say.
Piaget: Is it alive?
Child: Of course, otherwise it wouldn't follow us, it couldn't shine. (Piaget, 1960, p. 215)

The lifelike characteristics attributed to the sun are clear. In addition, this dialogue reveals another characteristic of preconceptual thought: *egocentrism*. The sun follows the child, imitates the child's turning, and listens to the child. The child believes the universe is organized and created for him and is centered on him. He has difficulty seeing any point of view but his own. Although egocentrism is most marked in the preconceptual period, Piaget feels that it continues throughout the entire preoperational stage and into the concrete operational stage.

The inability of the preoperational child to solve Piaget's famous three-mountain problem also demonstrates his or her difficulty in seeing things from the perspective of others. Three mountains of varying sizes are set on a square table with one chair at each side of the table. The child is seated on one chair, and a doll is placed sequentially on the other chairs. The child is asked to identify what the doll is seeing from each of three positions, either by selecting from a set of drawings or by using cardboard cutouts of the mountain to construct the doll's views (see Figure 9-1). On the three-mountain task it is not until about age 9 or 10 that children can consistently pick the picture showing what the doll would see from each of the other locations. However, again we find that the perspective-taking task and the type of response required to solve it affect the child's performance on the task. If children view through a peephole three familiar objects such as a doll in a high chair looking at a toy television, and then move and look at the same scene through a peephole on the other side, children as young as 4 years old show surprise if the scene has surreptitiously been rotated so that the toys remain in the same spatial orientation relative to the child (Shantz & Watson 1970, 1971). Although they show surprise indicating that the scene is not what they had expected, at this age they are unable to select a picture representing the correct perspective.

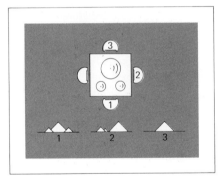

FIGURE 9-1 The three-mountain problem. *(From Phillips, 1969.)*

There are many different kinds of perspective taking in addition to the perceptual role taking measured in the three-mountain task. Many of these role-taking skills involve the ability to understand what another person is thinking, for example, to anticipate what strategies another person will take in a game-playing or problem-solving situation. Others involve an awareness of people's emotions and the situations which evoke them. These role-taking skills involve understanding the responses of others and will be discussed in greater detail later in the chapter in the section on social cognition. Although the ability to take the perspective or role of others on different kinds of tasks has been found to increase with age and experience and to be related to the general level of intellectual performance as measured on standarized tests, it has been found to be only modestly interrelated (Rubin, 1973) or on some sets of measures not to be related at all (Rubin, in press). This suggests that different types or levels of cognitive skills may be required for different types of perspective- or role-taking tasks.

Intuitive period   The term *intuitive* is applied to the child in the period from 4 to 7 years; this term is appropriate because although certain mental "operations" (such as ways of classifying, quantifying, or relating objects) occur, the child does not seem to be aware of the principles he or she has used in the performance of these operations. Although the child can solve problems involving these operations, he or she cannot explain the reasons for solving a problem in a certain way.

Although the child's symbols are becoming increasingly complex, reasoning and thinking processes have certain characteristic limitations which are manifested in a variety of tasks. Some of these limitations are reflected in the preoperational child's inability to order things on the basis of a particular dimension, for example, to order a group of sticks in a series from shortest to longest. Limitations are also found in problems of *part-whole relations*. This is vividly illustrated in the child's response on a bead task where she is given seven blue beads and three white beads. All of the beads are wooden. If she is asked if there are more blue or white beads she can answer correctly. However, if she is asked if there are more blue beads or wooden beads, she is unable to respond

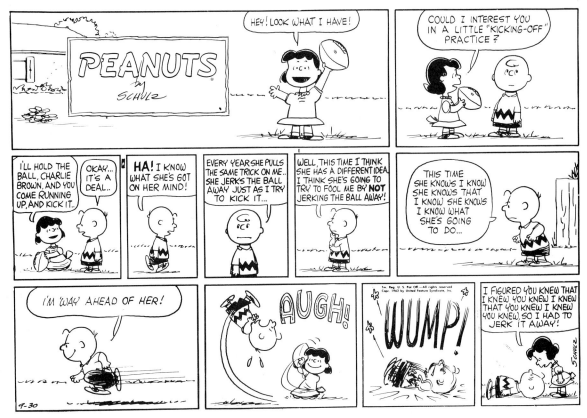

(King Features Syndicate)

correctly because she is unable to focus simultaneously on the parts (white and blue) and on the whole (wooden). Although the preoperational child can conceive of an object belonging to a class such as blue or wooden, and even that two classes can exist simultaneously, she cannot cope with the concept that classes formed on the basis of color (blue and white) can be included in a larger class based on material (wood). The child cannot simultaneously focus on multiple aspects of parts and wholes in order to solve this problem of class inclusion.

The type of problem in which the multiple limitations in preoperational thought are most clearly manifested and on which there has been the most extensive research is in *conservation* problems. When superficial changes in an object or situation occur, the child is unable to understand that certain attributes of the object remain the same, or have been *conserved*.

For example, a preoperational child presented with two equal-sized balls of clay and asked if they are the same size will report that they are equal in size. If the child then sees the experimenter roll one of the balls into a long sausagelike form and again is asked the same question, he or she will examine the clay objects and will report that one or the other is larger. Asked if anything was added or taken away from each clay form, the child will say no, but will still insist they now differ in size because of the variation in either height or length of the two objects. What processes are at work that lead to this remarkable error in judgment, this lack of conservation, when the child has viewed the entire procedure?

The most important characteristic of preoperational reasoning is *irreversibility*. The child does not see that every logical operation is reversible—in this case, that if one of two balls of clay of the same size can be rolled into a sausage-shaped form, by rerolling it can be transformed back into its previous round shape again. Irreversibility is found in many different types of problems in the preoperational child.

A four-year-old subject is asked:
"Do you have a brother?" He says, "Yes."
"What's his name?" "Jim."
"Does Jim have a brother?" "No." (Phillips, 1969, p. 61)

Irreversibility is associated with another type of error, the focusing on the successive states of a changing perception rather than on the process or *transformations* by which the change occurs. Piaget uses the analogy of the child viewing a motion picture as a series of successive but unrelated still pictures instead of the continuous movie which an older person would see. Likewise, in the transformation of the clay the child ignores how the experimenter changed the ball of clay by gradually reducing its height and extending its width through rolling. Flavell (1963) reports a vivid illustration of the preoperational child's difficulty in seeing transformations. The child has difficulty in arranging in order a series of drawings to reconstruct the movements of a ruler or stick which is held in a vertical position and then let fall into a horizontal position, as in Figure 9-2. He cannot identify the sequence of movements necessary for the shift of the ruler from its upright to its prone position, nor does he follow the transition stages in this process. In a similar way, in the problem with the ball of clay he does not pay attention to the gradual transition in the shape of the clay as it becomes longer and narrower as the experimenter rolls it.

Finally, our example of the lack of conservation of mass in the clay balls demonstrates *centration* in thinking. The child focuses on one dimension of the object, that is, on either height *or* length, in giving his reasons for why he thinks the clay is no longer equal. One child may say one ball is bigger because it is

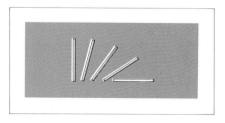

FIGURE 9-2 Falling stick. *(From Phillips, 1969.)*

taller; another child that the other ball is bigger because it is longer. This attention to only one attribute of the objects and not to reciprocal changes between dimensions (that is, as it gets shorter some of the clay is being displaced into making it longer) contributes to the child's inability to solve the problem.

The conservation of many attributes other than mass has been studied, and the age of attainment of conservation varies for different characteristics. Some of the problems used to test conservation are illustrated in Figure 9-3. Conservation of number has usually been achieved by about age 6, conservation of mass and

FIGURE 9-3 Some simple tests for conservation. *(From Lefrancois, 1973.)*

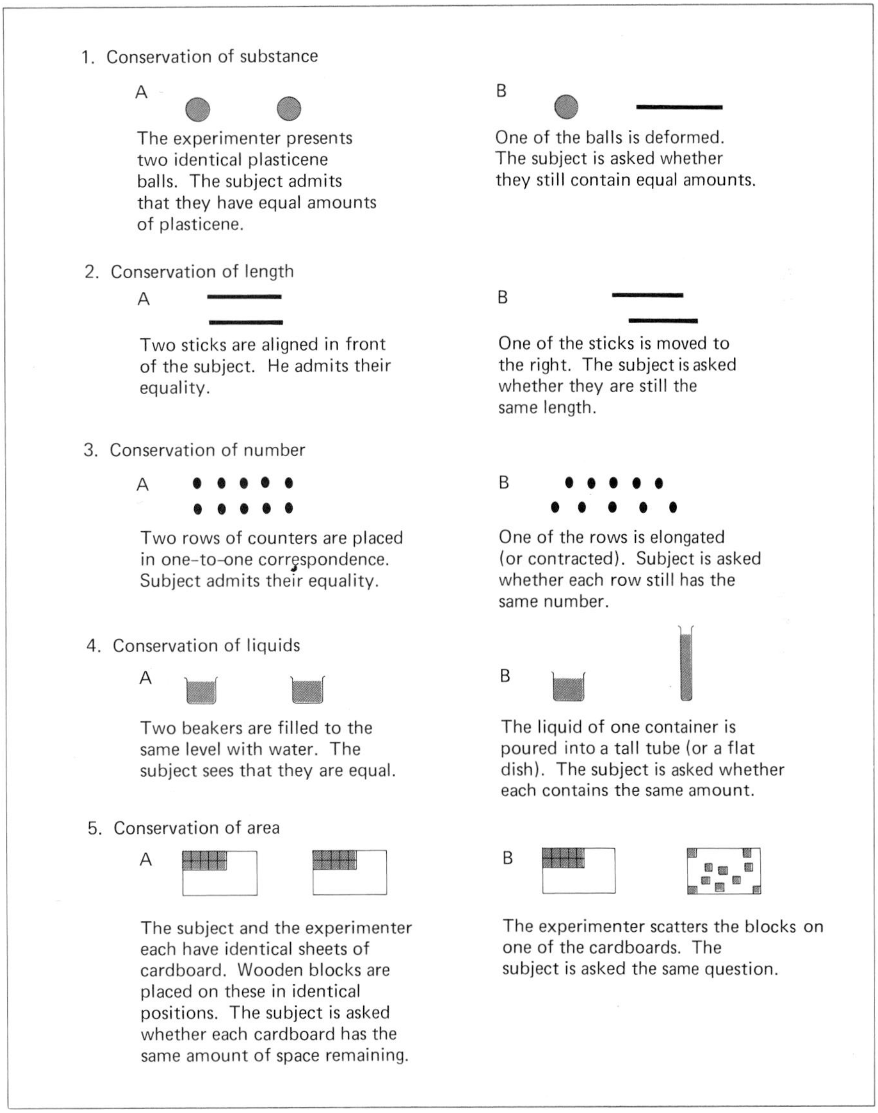

1. Conservation of substance

   A

   The experimenter presents two identical plasticene balls. The subject admits that they have equal amounts of plasticene.

   B

   One of the balls is deformed. The subject is asked whether they still contain equal amounts.

2. Conservation of length

   A

   Two sticks are aligned in front of the subject. He admits their equality.

   B

   One of the sticks is moved to the right. The subject is asked whether they are still the same length.

3. Conservation of number

   A

   Two rows of counters are placed in one-to-one correspondence. Subject admits their equality.

   B

   One of the rows is elongated (or contracted). Subject is asked whether each row still has the same number.

4. Conservation of liquids

   A

   Two beakers are filled to the same level with water. The subject sees that they are equal.

   B

   The liquid of one container is poured into a tall tube (or a flat dish). The subject is asked whether each contains the same amount.

5. Conservation of area

   A

   The subject and the experimenter each have identical sheets of cardboard. Wooden blocks are placed on these in identical positions. The subject is asked whether each cardboard has the same amount of space remaining.

   B

   The experimenter scatters the blocks on one of the cardboards. The subject is asked the same question.

length between 6 and 7, weight around 9, and finally volume sometime after 11. Cross-cultural studies have found considerable variation in the age at which conservation is attained in different societies, but only moderate differences in the order in which different types of conservation occur. In order to illustrate this, we return to the problem of the clay balls. A child of 7 who has attained the concept of conservation of mass will respond that the two different-shaped balls are the same size after seeing one rolled out. However, when the child sees the two identical round balls of clay weigh equally on a balance and then sees one ball rolled and is asked whether the sausage-shaped and round-shaped clay weigh the same, the response will be that they do not. The child will offer the same reasons that were given at a younger age for his belief that they differed in mass. Then at about age 9 the child will be able to say they weigh the same but will say they differ in volume when they are rolled, although he has previously seen that they displace the same amount of water when they are placed in beakers of water in their round shape.

Piaget says the separation and sequence in achieving these three kinds of conservation are due to *horizontal decalage*. Horizontal decalage refers to the fact that even in tasks requiring similar operations there is an age separation in the chief ability to deal with the problems. He believes that mass, weight, and volume differ in degree of abstraction, with mass requiring the least abstract operations and volume the most. He also believes that the attainment of the earlier concept is essential for the development of the one of greater abstraction, and that increasing age is essential for progress from one concept to the next.

Child solving a conservation task. (George Roos, Peter Arnold Photo Agency)

The acceleration of conservation   Because the attainment of the processes underlying conservation is regarded by Piaget as such an important intellectual achievement, many psychologists have attempted to accelerate the development of conservation through a variety of training procedures (Brainerd, 1972, 1974; Botvin & Murray, 1975; Denny, Zlytinogler, & Selzer, in press; Gelman, 1969; Goldschmid, 1968; Inhelder, 1968; Kingsley & Hall, 1967; Sigel, Roeper, & Hooper, 1966; Zimiles, 1966). These investigators question whether the operations Piaget assumes are basic in the development of conservation are the critical ones. Could children be trained to conserve without attempting to alter their notions of such things as reversibility? Although children's performance on a conservation task may appear inadequate, perhaps they have the capacity to conserve under the right circumstances. The inability of children to perform on certain of Piaget's tasks may not be a result of limitations in their cognitive ability. Instead, it may be a limitation in certain necessary prerequisites for the use of those cognitive functions. It has been proposed that failure to conserve may occur because the child attends to irrelevant aspects of the stimulus, such as shape, length, height, color, and so on. Training procedures which modify children's attentional processes have been effective in facilitating conservation in children who were previously nonconservers. In one study children were made aware that objects possess many attributes by having them look at pairs of objects, for example, an orange and a banana, and describe how they are the same and how they are different (Sigel et al., 1966). In another study they were trained through discrimination-learning procedures to attend to the relevant dimensions of the stimuli (Gelman, 1969). Not only have such attentional-training procedures improved the children's conservation on the conservation task on which they were trained, but the effects have also generalized to other forms of conservation. Thus, if a child was given attentional training involving conservation of number, where the same number of pennies are grouped closely or strung out in a long row, in addition to improvement in number conservation, the attentional training would also generalize to improved conservation of mass, on which the child had had no training (Gelman, 1969). Nonconserving children have also improved their performance on conservation tasks through observational learning by watching children or adults who were able to conserve solve problems or by discussing their solutions with them (Charbonneau, Robert, Bourassa, & Glady-Bissonnette, 1976; Murray, 1972; Rosenthal & Zimmerman, 1972; Zimmerman & Lanaro, 1974). Most psychologists agree with Piaget in recognizing that preoperational children have difficulty in solving conservation problems. However, the importance of these training studies lies in their casting doubt on whether the acquisition of conservation is based on underlying operations, such as reversibility, as is proposed by Piaget. Some investigators even argue that there is no reason to assume the existence of underlying cognitive structures. In addition, these results suggest that more information is needed on the role of experience in the development of conservation.

Concrete Operational Period   Dramatic changes in the characteristics of thought occur in the concrete operational period, which extends from about age

7 to about age 11. In this period increased mobility of thinking due to increased understanding of reversibility, and a decrease in centration and the ability to take the role of others, leads to a new understanding of reality. Logic and objectivity increase. Children begin to think deductively. If all dogs are animals, then this dog is an animal. If 1 foot is equal to 12 inches, then 12 inches put together will equal 1 foot. Children are able to conserve quantity and number, to form concepts of space and time, and to classify or group objects *if the objects are present.* However, they are still tied to the concrete operations of the immediate world. They seem to be able to solve problems only if the objects necessary for the solution of the problem are physically present. For example, if three children of varying heights are presented in pairs so that in pair 1 a child sees that Joan is taller than Sandra, and in pair 2 Sandra is taller than Mary, without seeing Joan and Mary together the child can reason that Joan is taller than both Sandra and Mary. However, if the visual stimuli are not present and the problem is presented verbally as "Joan is taller than Sandra and Sandra is taller than Mary; who is the tallest of the three?" the concrete operational but not the formal operational child will have difficulty with its solution.

Again it has been questioned whether the solution of such problems is based on the underlying changes in mental operations proposed by Piaget. Some investigators have suggested that in tests of inference, such as the one just cited dealing with height, the deficits of the concrete operational child do not lie in being tied to the physical presence of stimuli, but in memory capacity. It is a complex series of propositions to remember. If the child could be trained to remember the rather complicated components of the problem, perhaps he or she could solve it in the absence of the stimuli, the three girls. Bryant and Trabasso (1971), in a study involving a similar problem of inferences about the length of sticks, demonstrated that when procedures are used to assure that the information is retained, even very young children can make logical inferences. The difference in memory capacity of younger and older children therefore is one of the critical factors in differences in performance on tests of logical inference (Harris & Bassett, 1975).

Although memory capacity is an important factor in age differences in logical inference, it has been found that children between the ages of 8 and 18 solve problems of inference presented with concrete examples more easily than those with verbal presentations (Glick & Wapner, 1968).

Humor   We have emphasized how the marked changes in thinking, particularly in logical processes and symbolic thought, which occur across the preoperational and concrete operational periods, affect performance on such tasks as classification, ordination, perspective taking, and conservation. However, there is another area in which changing cognitive processes radically affect performance and that is in children's appreciation of humor. Most parents have been deluged by the jokes and riddles of a precocious pint-sized stand-up comic. Why do 6-year-olds find the following two versions of a joke equally funny and 8-year-olds regard the first version as funnier?

Order, order in the court.
Ham and cheese on rye, your honor.
and
Silence, silence in the court
Ham and cheese on rye, your honor. (Schultz, 1974, p. 102)

It has been proposed that incongruity, defined as a conflict between a person's expectancy and what actually occurs, frequently plays a role in humor responses. The person perceives a discrepancy and then engages in problem solving to explain or resolve the discrepancy. In the first version of the joke the 8-year-old, but not the 6-year-old, is able to go over the joke and see that the apparently ludicrous response was elicited by the call to "order."

It has been proposed that the attainment of logical thought processes in the concrete operational child facilitates her appreciation of the relationships between the incongruous elements in joking humor (McGhee, 1974; Schultz & Horibe, 1974; Schultz, 1976). As children grow older, they appear to appreciate humor which is more cognitively complex and challenging and which involves logical forms of incongruity rather than illogical incongruity (Sutton-Smith, 1976; Whitt & Prentice, 1977).

Formal Operations Period   In the period of concrete operations the child was beginning to utilize symbolic thought and was building the foundation for logical thinking which characterizes the adolescent child. The period of formal operations begins at about age 12. How do thought processes in this period differ from those in the concrete operational period?

The adolescent is able to think about fanciful problems not based in reality. She realizes that logical rules can be applied to ideas that violate reality. For example, take the problem "If all blue people live in red houses, are all people who live in red houses blue?" The concrete operational child would have difficulty getting beyond the fact that there is no such thing as blue people. In contrast, the child in the formal operations period would focus on applying logical solutions to the problem regardless of the unrealistic content.

During adolescence the child's thought also becomes increasingly flexible and abstract. To solve problems the child uses logical processes in which all the possibilities in a situation are considered. In contrast to the concrete operational child, who under most circumstances can solve problems of classification only in a real situation with the objects actually present, the adolescent considers a number of possible alternatives or hypotheses in a problem-solving situation and thinks of what could occur.

In addition to this system of deducing consequences from a variety of alternative hypotheses, the child can assimilate and combine information from a variety of sources. Rather than evaluating single factors in solving a problem, as the concrete operational child does, the child at this stage is able to consider combinations of factors and simultaneous interactions of factors which will effect the solution.

It is in this flexibility, mental hypotheses testing, and appreciation of the many possibilities in a situation, as well as in the awareness of the complexity of problems, that the adolescent differs from the concrete operational child.

Inhelder and Piaget (1958) describe a task in which children are allowed to experiment with an assortment of objects and water and are asked to arrive at a law to explain why some objects float and others do not. The children are being asked to derive Archimede's law of floating bodies, which states that an object will float if its weight per unit (its density) is less than that of water. Thus, if two objects are of equal weight, the larger object is more likely to float than the smaller. Concrete operational children may focus on weight (because it is heavy) or on size (because it is bigger) as a reason why things float or sink. They may even arrive at a double classification which involves the categories large and heavy, large and light, small and heavy, and small and light. However, they always base their solutions on the observable characteristics size and weight. They are perplexed when their rules do not fit contradictory observations. For example, a large piece of wood may be heavier than a small lead weight, but will float while the weight sinks. They are still unable to consider alternatives not directly observable in the physical world. In contrast, the child in the formal operations period is able to free herself from the obvious cues of weight and size and conceptualize a variety of possible alternatives and arrive at the concept of density. Piaget describes the comments of a formal operational child grappling with this problem: "It sinks because it is small, it isn't stretched enough. . . . You would have to have something larger to stay at the surface, something of the same weight and which would have a greater extension (Inhelder & Piaget, 1958, p. 38).

The stage of formal operations and the flexible problem solving associated with it are not attained by all adolescents, nor for that matter by all adults. This is attributable partly to cultural and educational factors and partly to general intellectual level. Subjects who score below average on standard tests of intelligence do not attain formal operational thought (Inhelder, 1966; Jackson, 1965; Stephens, McLaughlin, & Mahoney, 1971). In contrast, very bright children have been found to perform as well or better than some adults (Neimark, 1975; Neimark & Lewis, 1967). In addition, scientific training in such subjects as physics, chemistry, or logic has been found to be associated with greater ability to use formal operations.

Summary of Piaget's Theory of Cognitive Development

The theory of cognitive development of Jean Piaget is the most influential and elaborate attempt to describe and explain the development of rational thought processes in children. The basic cognitive structures of the infant are modified and new schemata emerge through the interaction of the processes of assimilation and accommodation. Assimilation involves the modification of sensory input in accord with existing schemata. Accommodation involves a reciprocal process of adapting the mental structures or transforming the existing schemata to the characteristics of the stimuli or experiences to which the child is exposed. Through the interaction of these two processes involving reorganization of and adaptation to experience, increasingly complex cognitive structures emerge.

The child goes through an invariant sequence of cognitive growth in which the attainments of one period depend on those of the preceding period. Piaget describes the course of this development of thought in four stages, which must be regarded as subdivisions of a continuous course of cognitive change.

During the first two years of life the sensorimotor period occurs. During this first period the child responds with simple motor responses to the sensory stimuli to which he or she is exposed. In these early years remarkable intellectual development occurs in such things as comprehending the permanence of objects; understanding means-ends relationships; using complex forms of imitation; and understanding primitive concepts of space, time, and causality. By the end of this period the child is clearly exhibiting behaviors which involve the beginnings of symbolic thought.

These symbolic thought processes become increasingly apparent in the child's use of language and elaborated symbolic play in the period of preoperational thought extending from 2 to 6 years. However, the thinking of the preoperational child in such things as solving problems dealing with numbers, concepts, relations, or classes is still limited because of certain restrictive characteristics of his or her cognitive processes. The movement away from the limitations of preoperational cognitive thought, such as egocentrism, irreversibility, and centering, is associated with the emergence of concrete operations.

During the period of concrete operations the child begins to appreciate the dynamic changing aspects of objects and to understand the relations between different attributes of objects. He or she can take the role of others and understand their perceptions, cognitions, and feelings, as well as elaborate his or her concepts of causality, time, space, and number and the operations of conservation.

Although the concrete operational child is clearly a reasoning organism capable of complex problem solving, thought processes of the child in this period differ markedly from those of the adolescent in the period of formal operations. The concrete operational child can solve problems if the stimuli are present but has difficulty in verbal and mental manipulations.

The formal operational child is able to consider the many possible solutions to a problem and understand the relationships between many attributes or classes simultaneously. In problem solving, in this period the child uses the kind of systematic deductive reasoning that is characteristic of scientific thought, in that it involves the consideration of all possible alternative solutions and the logical elimination of those which are untenable. Everyone does not attain the level of formal operations, which is influenced by IQ and educational and cultural variables. Moreover, unlike concrete operational thought, which seems to be attained to some degree in all societies, the attainment of formal operations is influenced by culture (Goodnow & Bethos, 1966). In groups which do not emphasize symbolic skills or in which educational experiences are limited, the stage of formal operations may occur late in development or may even be absent.

Even in the attainment of concrete operations there are marked cultural variations in the time they are achieved and the means through which they are attained (Dasen, 1972; Glick, 1975). For example, fewer children from non-pottery-making than pottery-making families in Mexico can conserve quantity. This may be attributable to less experience in manipulating the shape, appearance, and size of clay in the non-pottery-making families (Price-Williams, Gordon, & Ramirez, 1969).

These cultural variations are not incompatible with Piaget's theory as long as the order of the acquisition of operations is constant for children in different societies. After all, Piaget has emphasized the important role which children's active processing of experience has on cognitive development, and cultural differences in such experience might be expected to have impact upon intellectual development.

Commentary and Evaluation of Piaget's Theory

The student might ask why the theory of Jean Piaget has been discussed in such great detail. It is because of his profound impact on contemporary developmental psychology. The current concern with cognitive factors in development and the establishment of many centers for the study of cognitive psychology throughout the country are largely attributable to his influence.

Piaget presents the only well-elaborated and integrated theory of cognitive development. There are no comparable theories of intellectual growth. In spite of the frequently noted limitations and lack of objectivity of his methodology, he has asked and answered important questions in an innovative way, and his provocative theory has stimulated a vast amount of research and theorizing by other behavioral scientists. It is inconceivable that our understanding of the intellectual development of children could have advanced to its present stage without the monumental work of Jean Piaget.

However, Piaget's theory and observations have received considerable criticism on the basis of recent evidence. The current findings in infant conditionability and perceptual ability, presented in the chapters on infancy and on learning, suggest that the infant may know more than Piaget discerned (Flavell, 1977). Piaget based many of his inferences about infant cognitive development on observations of motor activity. It may be that the infant's motoric skills are incapable of reflecting his cognitive level (Charlesworth, 1968). In addition, investigators have proposed that the emergence of some of the behaviors Piaget thinks occur only as a result of considerable practice and experience, such as the coordination of visual and motor behavior in the development of grasping, may be strongly innately programmed (Bruner & Koslowski, 1972). In a recent thought-provoking paper Bower (1976) presents evidence that many of the behaviors regarded by Piaget as manifestations of progressive intellectual development do not emerge in a cumulative incremental fashion, but seem to appear and then disappear. Stepping behavior and reaching for visible objects or objects which infants have localized only by sound occur in the first few weeks of life and then disappear and emerge again later in development. Even more complex behaviors, such as imitation and conservation of weight, appear early and then fade away. Infants in the first week of life are able to exhibit a complex behavior such as imitating an adult sticking out her

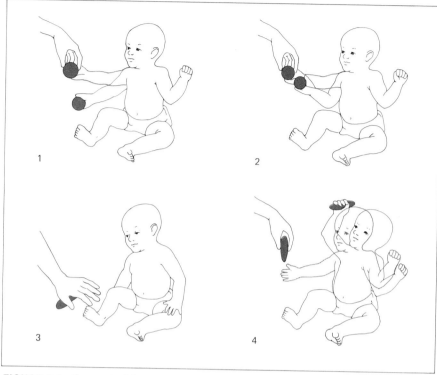

FIGURE 9-4 Concept of the conservation of weight may be acquired not just once but three times in the course of a child's development. If a 1-year-old child is handed a ball of modeling clay, he will typically misjudge its weight the first time it is presented to him (1). Soon, however, his behavior indicates that he has learned to estimate the weight of the object before he holds it (2). The ball of clay is then rolled into the shape of a sausage with the child watching (3). When the child holds the sausage, typically his arm flies up (4), indicating that he thinks the sausage is heavier than the ball because it is longer. This erroneous behavior disappears by the age of about 18 months, only to reappear and disappear twice more much later. A child finally acquires a stable concept of the conservation of weight early in his teens. *(From Bower, 1976.)*

tongue. This ability soon disappears and reemerges toward the end of the first year of life. A similar cyclical pattern which occurs for conservation of weight can be seen in Figure 9-4. The child's arm flying up when he holds the sausage-shaped, but not the round-shaped, ball of clay is used as an indicator of lack of conservation because the child apparently conceives of the elongated clay as lighter. Using this criteria, the child at 1 year has not mastered conservation of weight, but she has by 18 months. However, two years later she is behaving as she did at 1 year. She has lost the concept of conservation of weight. This reappears at 7 or 8, again vanishes at 11 or 12, and finally emerges in a stable form at age 13 or 14. It is difficult to explain these repetitive processes in development on the basis of Piagetian theory.

Finally, the results of cross-cultural studies indicate that the sequence of

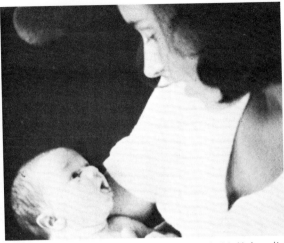

Six-day-old infant imitating mother sticking out her tongue. (Jane Dunkeld, University of Edinburgh, Edinburgh, Scotland)

intellectual growth that Piaget proposes may not be as unvarying as he suggests and that it may be modified by cultural and experiential factors, as well as by training in problem-solving strategies. In addition, there is some question that attainment of the underlying operations regarded by Piaget as necessary in solving certain problems is really essential in those tasks.

Whatever reevaluations of Piaget may occur as more investigators systematically test his theory, he will remain a giant in the history of developmental psychology. Jean Piaget must be considered one of the very few individuals whose theories, even if they are eventually rejected, have led to massive alterations in the course of developmental psychology.

Social Cognition

Thus far we have been discussing mainly how children understand nonsocial objects and events in their world. We will now turn to the development of *social cognition*, that is, how children come to understand the viewpoints, emotions, thoughts, and intentions of themselves and of others, and how they think about social relations and institutions.

In many ways the changes in social cognition and the processes underlying them are parallel to those in nonsocial cognition. Children come to recognize that social objects have a permanence and existence of their own and that certain attributes of people are invariant. The children become less egocentric and more able to understand the viewpoints, feelings, and thoughts of others. They move from viewing people in terms of immediately observable attributes to more abstract characteristics involving motives, intentions, and emotions of others. They are able to view the multiple aspects of people and hypothesize about the complexities of their relationships to their environments, past experiences, and future expectations. In addition, they become increasingly aware of

Children enjoy looking in a mirror long before they can identify the reflection as their own. (Suzanne Szasz, Photo Researchers, Inc.)

the psychological processes associated with their own and other people's feelings, motives, emotions, values, problems, and cognitions. They speculate about what others think of them and examine their own thinking about themselves and others. Let us examine some of the areas in which developmental changes in social cognition occur.

Who Am I? The Development of the Self System

When do children begin to recognize themselves as different from other people? How is this related to other aspects of cognitive development such as object permanence? How does the complex network of cognitions associated with the person's sense of personal identity evolve?

We have all experienced the power of our own reflection. Mirrors in a room are like television sets. People seem compelled to look at them. Children as young as 18 weeks of age will gaze at their reflection in a mirror, but they do not seem to recognize that they are attending to a reflection of themselves until sometime in the second year of life.

How would investigators go about studying the problem of self-identity in infants? A number of investigators have used the clever procedure of putting a bright spot of rouge on the child's nose and watching the child's response to the rouge when she looks in the mirror (Amersterdam, 1972; Brooks-Gunn & Lewis, 1975; Bertenthal & Fischer, 1978). It is assumed that if the child recognizes the reflection in the mirror as belonging to her, she is likely to touch her nose. Children under 1 year of age do not touch their nose (Brooks-Gunn & Lewis, 1975). One-year-olds seem to believe the reflection is another child and may touch it or try to look behind the mirror to attempt to find the other child.

Sometime during the second year of life children seem to recognize their own image. By 2 years of age almost all children give evidence of self-recognition. In the earlier stage of this self-recognition the child may show signs of embarrassment or silly or coy behavior upon seeing the rouge on her nose, and only at about 20 months of age does the child fairly consistently locate or touch the spot of rouge on her own nose rather than on the reflection (Amsterdam, 1972). It is not surprising that the development of object permanence has been found to be related to the development of self-recognition (Bertenthal & Fischer, 1978). The development of an understanding of the continued permanent existence and continuity of the self would seem to be a critical part of self-identity.

The interaction of the many factors which contribute to the elaboration of this early self-recognition into the complex network of cognitions, emotions, motives, values, and behaviors composing the individual's self-concept is not well understood.

The developmental changes in characterizations of the self seem to parallel those in descriptions of others, which will be discussed in considerable detail in the next section. The individual's view of himself becomes more differentiated and involves more descriptions of motives, values, intentions, and other internal psychological states as he grows older. Views of the self, however, tend to be less stereotyped and involve a greater variety of possible behaviors than those of others. For example, as we will see in Chapter 15, children perceive their own behavior as much less rigidly confined by culturally determined sex-role stereotypes than they do the behavior of others. A girl may think of herself as competitive and achieving and as having the option to enter occupations regarded as masculine occupations, but she is likely to view her female peers in a more sex-stereotyped manner.

It has been suggested that there are four basic dimensions in the person's sense of self-identity (Guardo & Bohan, 1971). The first is *humanity*—the sense of having capacities and experiences found only in humans. The second is *sexuality*—the awareness of femaleness or maleness. The third is *individuality*—the sense of being a unique person. The fourth is *continuity*—the sense of being the same person over time.

What Is the Other Like?

People of all ages often are asked about and frequently attempt to describe themselves or the people around them. What is your mother like? Tell me about your new teacher? What did you think of the new boy we met at the party? How would the responses of an older person to these questions differ from those of a younger child? Six- or seven-year-old children are more likely to describe people in concrete observable terms, in terms of appearance, possessions, or behavior or in egocentric terms involving what the other person does to the child. (She gives me candy. She hits me.) They tend not to use inferential statements or psychological statements involving intentions, motives, or feelings, such as shy, considerate, or friendly. When these young children do use a psychological description, it tends to be stereotyped, diffuse, or value laden, such as "nice" or "bad." The following description by a 7-year-old reveals some of these characteristics:

She is very nice because she gives my friends and me toffee. She lives by the main road. She has fair hair and glasses. . . . She sometimes gives us flowers. (Livesley & Bromley, 1973, p. 214)

As children grow older, they are more likely to increase in the number and proportion of psychological statements used in describing people, and to use abstract inferential categories more frequently (Livesley & Bromley, 1973; Peevers & Secord, 1973). The most marked increase in the use of psychological descriptions and the number of categories used occurs between 7½ and 8½ years of age. In fact, the differences between ages 7 and 8 are greater than those between 8 and 15. This has led some investigators to conclude that "the eighth year is a critical period in the development of person perception" (Livesley & Bromley, 1973, p. 147). Although great changes do occur in this period, the descriptions of people by children in the middle childhood years are often poorly organized, inconsistent, and lacking in explanations. They often present strings of unrelated or even contradictory attributes of people rather than an integrated picture of an individual in describing others. This is illustrated in the following description by a 10-year-old:

He smells very much and is very nasty. He has no sense of humor and is very dull. He is always fighting and is very cruel. He does silly things and is very stupid. He has brown hair and cruel eyes. He is sulky and 11 years old and has lots of sisters. I think he is the most horrible boy in the class. He has a croaky voice and always chews his pencil and picks his teeth and I think he is disgusting. (Livesley & Bromley, 1973, p. 217)

It is not until adolescence or early adulthood that people become aware of the full complexity of human thoughts, feelings, and intentions, or become aware that characteristics of behavior may vary with situations, internal states, or other transitory factors. In the following description of his brother by a 16-year-old boy some of these characteristics are revealed.

My kid brother is a funny kid. He loves to be with people especially his older brothers. Most of the time he's good natured and a lot of fun but sometimes he turns mean. Like when we play soccer. He's a good athlete but he can't keep up with teenagers. He gets mad when he loses the ball and will kick or swear at people. Later I've found him crying in his room. He knows he's made an ass of himself but he gets so frustrated he can't help it. It's tough being the youngest.

Egocentric Perspectives and Role Taking

As children grow older, they are better able to decenter from their own perspectives, motives, and feelings and understand the perceptions, intentions, thoughts, and emotions of others. It has been suggested this shift away from an early egocentric orientation underlies improved communication skills, the development of moral standards involving concern for the feelings and welfare of others, and the development of empathic understanding, which are basic in socialization. The development of these abilities are described in detail in other chapters in the book.

TABLE 9-3 PERSPECTIVE TAKING (RELATION BETWEEN PERSPECTIVES OF SELF AND OTHERS)

Stage 0—Egocentric or undifferentiated perspectives

The child does not distinguish her own perspective from that of others. The child does not recognize that another person may interpret experiences differently than she does.

Stage 1—Subjective or differentiated perspectives

The child realizes that the self and other may have the same or different perspectives. The child is concerned with the uniqueness of the cognitions of each person. However, although she recognizes that different people may have different perspectives she can't accurately judge what the other person's perspectives will be.

Stage 2—Self-reflective or reciprocal perspectives

The child is able to see herself from another's perspective and is aware that the other person can do the same thing. This permits her to anticipate and consider the thoughts and feelings of others.

Stage 3—Mutual perspectives

In this stage not only is the child able to understand her own perspectives and that of another person and be aware that the other person can do the same thing simultaneously, but she can view this mutual perspective from the position of a third person. She can think of how some member of another group (parents, teachers, the other kids on the team) might view both persons' perspectives.

Stage 4—Societal or in-depth perspectives

People are able to see networks or systems of perspectives, such as society's perspectives, or the Republican point of view, or the Black perspective. These systems of perspectives among people are seen not only to exist on the plane of common expectations or awareness, but also to involve deeper levels of communication such as unverbalized feelings or values.

Source: Selman, R. L., & Jacquette, D. Stability and oscillation in interpersonal awareness: A clinical-developmental analysis. In C. B. Keasy (Ed.), *The XXV Nebraska symposium on motivation,* 1977, in press. By permission of the University of Nebraska Press Copyright © 1978 by the University of Nebraska Press.

Selman and his colleagues have recently proposed that this decentering process involves a developmental sequence of role-taking ability in learning how to differentiate between perspectives of the self and others and the relationship between these perspectives (Selman, 1976; Selman & Byrne, 1974; Selman & Jacquette, 1977). These role-taking stages are presented in Table 9-3.

Selman and his colleagues have gone on to study the developmental progression of these stages. The study presented in Box 9-2 clearly shows that with increasing age children are more likely to attain higher levels of perspective taking.

BOX 9-2
HOW DO I SEE YOU? HOW DO YOU SEE ME?

 Is there a systematic developmental progression in role-taking skills? The results of this study by Selman and Byrne suggest that there is.

Groups of 4-, 6-, 8-, and 10-year-old children were presented with filmed stories and questioned about the perspectives and thoughts of the characters in the story. A sample story is as follows:

Holly is an 8-year-old girl who likes to climb trees. She is the best tree climber in the neighborhood. One day while climbing down from a tall tree she falls off the bottom branch but does not hurt herself. Her father sees her fall. He is upset and asks her to promise not to climb trees any more. Holly promises.

Later that day, Holly and her friends meet Sean. Sean's kitten is caught up in a tree and cannot get down. Something has to be done right away or the kitten may fall. Holly is the only one who climbs trees well enough to reach the kitten and get it down, but she remembers her promise to her father. (Selman & Byrne, 1974, p. 805)

The questions were structured to assess the levels of role taking attained by the child. These are levels 1, 2, and 3 in Table 9-3. The questions were as follows.

Level 1—Subjective Role taking
a) Does Holly know how Sean feels about the kitten? Why?

b) Does Sean know why Holly cannot decide whether or not to climb the tree? Why or why not?

c) Why might Sean think Holly will not climb the tree if Holly does not tell him about her promise?

Level 2—Self-reflective Role Taking
a) What does Holly think her father will think of her if he finds out?

b) Does Holly think her father will understand why she climbed the tree? Why is that?

Level 3—Mutual Role Taking
a) What does Holly think most people would do in this situation?

b) If Holly and her father discussed this situa-

TABLE 9-4   PERCENTAGE OF CHILDREN REACHING A GIVEN ROLE-TAKING LEVEL AT EACH LEVEL OF CHRONOLOGICAL AGE

Stage	Age 4	Age 6	Age 8	Age 10
0	80	10	0	0
1	20	90	40	20
2	0	0	50	60
3	0	0	10	20
Total	100	100	100	100

Source: Selman, R. L., & Byrne, D. F. A structural-developmental analysis of levels of role-taking in middle childhood. *Child Development,* 1974, **45,** p. 806.

tion, what might they decide together? Why is that?

c) Do you know what the Golden Rule is (explain if the child says no)? What would the Golden Rule say to do in this situation? Why? (Selman & Byrne, 1974, p. 805).

The percentage of children in each age group reaching a given role-taking level is presented in Table 9-4 on page 337.

A steady progression can be seen through these role-taking stages. No 4- or 6-year-old children have attained stage 2 or 3 role taking, whereas most age 8- and 10-year-old children have reached at least stage 2 and some have attained level 3. ■

Source: Selman, R. L., & Byrne, D. F. A structural-developmental analysis of levels of role taking in middle childhood. *Child Development*, 1974, **45**, 803–806.

Some individuals reach higher levels of social role-taking abilities than others, or may attain them earlier. What kinds of factors contribute or are related to individual differences in role-taking abilities?

Performance on standard intelligence tests shows a modest relation to social role-taking ability. In addition, some studies have found positive relations between prosocial behavior such as helping and sharing and role-taking skills (Iannotti, 1975; Rubin & Schneider, 1973). In one study (Krebs & Sturrup, 1974) children's offers of help, offers of support, and responsible suggestions to other children on the playground and in classrooms were observed and recorded. The frequency with which altruistic behaviors occurred correlated with laboratory measures of role taking.

In deviant or emotionally disturbed populations, such as in schizophrenic or mentally retarded subjects, and in institutionalized emotionally disturbed or delinquent children highly significant deficits in social role-taking skills have been reported (Anthony, 1959; Chandler, 1973). In fact in some cases training in role taking has been found to reduce antisocial behavior. In one study, delinquent adolescents received a ten-week training program in role taking involving making up skits, playing various roles, filming the skits, and viewing themselves in the films. During an eighteen-month period following the training they committed only half as many delinquent acts as did a group not receiving training (Chandler, 1973).

Family influences on social role-taking skills have also been found. Parental childrearing practices which emphasize social relations, the feelings and intentions of others, and the importance of making reparations to mistreated victims rather than the power of parents, status factors, or appeals to conformity are associated with role-taking skills (Bearison & Cassell, 1975). Parents who use appeals such as "Your brother will feel lonely" or "Your teacher will feel sad" rather than "All children should" have children who take the role of others more readily. In addition, when parents make maturity demands of their children by expecting them to maintain and act in accord with high standards and assume responsibilities appropriate to their level of maturity, their children are more likely to demonstrate role-taking skills and empathy in their relations with others.

Summary

In this chapter we examined Jean Piaget's theory of cognitive development and the development of social cognition. Piaget evolved the most detailed and influential theory of intellectual development. Much of this theory was based on the naturalistic observation of children. It emphasizes the modification and evolution of cognitive structures through the functions of organization and adaptation. A balance between the two complementary processes involved in adaptation, those of assimilation and accommodation, results in intelligent behavior.

Piaget proposes that intellectual growth goes through an invariant sequence of stages of development. Each of the four major stages, the sensorimotor stage, the preoperational stage, the concrete operational stage, and the stage of formal operations, is characterized by different kinds of thought. The cognitive attainments in any stage are built upon and require those of the earlier stages. Over the course of development the individual shifts from being an infant focused only on immediate sensory and motor experiences to being a mature organism capable of symbolic thought and complex abstract reasoning and able to consider all possible solutions to a problem.

In the sensorimotor period, through sensing, exploring, and manipulating objects in the world about them, children begin to construct a knowledge of reality. They develop an understanding of means-ends relations, the permanence of objects, and an ability to use symbolic thought processes and language.

The use of symbolic thought processes increases rapidly in the preoperational period and is reflected in children's involvement in imaginative play and improved problem-solving ability. However, certain limitations in cognitive functioning such as animism, egocentrism, centration, and irreversibility may limit children's performances on tasks such as classification, part-whole problems, or conservation tasks.

In the period of concrete operations many of the limitations of thought found in the preoperational period have gone. Logic and objectivity increase, and children are able to think deductively. Children are able to conserve quantity and number, to form concepts of space and time, and to classify objects; however, they are still tied to the concrete operations of their immediate world. Not until the period of formal operations is the thought of the individual characterized by flexibility, mental hypotheses testing, and the appreciation of the interaction of multiple factors and possibilities in a problem-solving situation.

Cultural and experiential factors have a marked impact on the attainment of thought processes characteristic of each stage of development, but these are most marked in the formal operations period.

There are progressive developmental steps in understanding social objects, events, and institutions just as in understanding nonsocial objects. Children become increasingly able to decenter and take the role of others and to understand the complex interaction between self, others, and situations in evaluating their own and other's thoughts, perceptions, feelings, and intentions.

REFERENCES

Amsterdam, B. Mirror self image reactions before age two. *Developmental Psychology*, 1972, **5**, 297–305.

Anthony, E. T. An experimental approach to the psychopathology of childhood autism. *British Journal of Medical Psychology*, 1959, **32**, 18–37.

Bearison, D. J., & Cassell, T. Z. Cognitive and decentration and social codes: Communicative effectiveness in young children from differing family contents. *Developmental Psychology*, 1975, **11**, 29–36.

Bertenthal, B. I., & Fisher, K. W. Development of self recognition in the infant. *Developmental Psychology*, 1978, **14**, 44–50.

Botvin, G. J., & Murray, F. B. The efficacy of peer modeling and social conflict in the acquisition of conservation. *Child Development*, 1975, **46**, 796–799.

Bower, T. G. R. The object in the world of the infant. *Scientific American*, 1971, **225**, 30–38.

Bower, T. G. R. *Development in infancy*. San Francisco: Freeman, 1974.

Bower, T. G. R. Repetitive processes in child development, *Scientific American*, 1976, **235**, 38–47.

Brainerd, C. J. Reinforcement and reversibility in quantity conservation acquisition. *Psychonomic Science*, 1972, **27**, 114–116.

Brainerd, C. J. Training and transfer of transitivity conservation and class inclusion. *Child Development*, 1974, **45**, 324–334.

Brooks-Gunn, J., & Lewis, M. Mirror-image stimulation and self recognition in infancy. Unpublished paper, Educational Testing Service, Princeton, N.J., 1975.

Bruner, J. S., & Koslowski, B. Visually preadapted constituents of manipulatory action. *Perception*, 1972, **1**, 3–14.

Bryant, P. E., & Trabasso, J. Transitive inferences and memory in young children. *Nature*, 1971, **232**, 456–458.

Chandler, M. J. Egocentrism and antisocial behavior: The assessment and training of social perspective-taking skills. *Developmental Psychology*, 1973, **9**, 326–332.

Charbonneau, C., Robert, M., Bourassa, G., & Gladu-Bissonette, S. Observational learning of quantity conservation and Piagetian generalization tasks. *Developmental Psychology*, 1976, **12**, 211–217.

Charlesworth, W. R. Cognition in infancy. Where do we stand in the mid-sixties? *Merrill-Palmer Quarterly*, 1968, **14**, 25–46.

Dasen, P. R. Cross-cultural Piagetian research: A summary. *Journal of Cross-Cultural Psychology*, 1972, **3**, 23–29.

Denny, N. W., Zlytinogler, S., & Selzer, S. C. Conservation training in four year olds. *Journal of Experimental Child Psychology*, in press.

Flavell, J. H. *The developmental psychology of Jean Piaget*. Princeton, N.J.: Van Nostrand, 1963.

Flavell, J. H. *Cognitive development*. Englewood Cliffs, N.J.: Prentice-Hall, 1977.

Furth, H. C. Linguistic deficiency and thinking: Research with deaf subjects, 1964–1969. *Psychological Bulletin*, 1971, **76**, 58–82.

Gelman, R. Conservation acquisition: A problem of learning to attend to relevant attributes. *Journal of Experimental Child Psychology*, 1969, **7**, 167–187.

Glick, J. Cognitive development in cross-cultural perspective. In F. D. Horowitz, E. M. Hetherington, S. Scarr-Salapatek, & G. M. Siegel (Eds), *Review of child development research* (Vol. 4). Chicago: University of Chicago Press, 1975.

Glick, J., & Wapner, S. Development of transitivity: Some findings and problems of analysis. *Child Development*, 1968, **39**, 162–638.

Goldschmid, M. L. The relation of conservation to emotional and environmental aspects of development. *Child Development*, 1968, **37**, 579–589.

Goodnow, J., & Bethon, G. Piaget's task: The effects of schooling and intelligence. *Child Development*, 1966, **37**, 573–582.

Gratch, G. A study of the relative dominance of vision and touch in six-month old infants. *Child Development*, 1972, **43**, 615–623.

Gratch, G., & Landers, W. F. Stage IV of Piaget's theory of infant's object concepts: A longitudinal study. *Child Development*, 1971, **42**, 359–372.

Guardo, C. J., & Bohan, J. B. Development of a sense of self identity in children. *Child Development*, 1971, **42**, 1909–1921.

Harris, P. L., & Bassett, E. Transitive inference by four year old children. *Developmental Psychology*, 1975, **11**, 875–876.

Iannotti, R. J. The many faces of empathy. Paper presented at the biennial meeting of the Society for Research in Child Development, Denver, April 1975.

Inhelder, B. Cognitive development and its contribution to the diagnosis of some phenomena of mental deficiency. *Merrill-Palmer Quarterly*, 1966, **12**, 299–319.

Inhelder, B. Recent trends in Genevan research. Paper presented at Temple University, 1968.

Inhelder, B., & Piaget, J. *The growth of logical thinking from childhood to adolescence.* New York: Basic Books, 1958.

Jackson, S. The growth of logical thinking in normal and subnormal children. *British Journal of Educational Psychology*, 1965, **35**, 255–258.

Kingsley, R. C., & Hall, V. C. Training conservation through the use of learning sets. *Child Development*, 1967, **38**, 1111–1126.

Krebs, P., & Sturrup, B. Altruism, egocentricity and behavioral consistency in children. Paper presented at the meeting of the American Psychological Association, New Orleans, September 1974.

Lefrancois, G. R. *Of children*, Belmont, Calif.: Wadsworth, 1973.

Livesley, W. J., & Bromley, D. B. *Person perception in childhood and adolescence.* London: Wiley, 1973.

McGhee, P. E. Cognitive mastery and children's humor. *Psychological Bulletin*, 1974, **81**, 721–730.

Murray, F. B. Acquisition of conservation through social interaction. *Developmental Psychology*, 1972, **6**, 1–6.

Neimark, E. D. Intellectual development during adolescence. In F. Horowitz (Ed.), *Review of research in child development* (Vol. 4). 1975.

Neimark, E. C., & Lewis, N. The development of logical problem-solving strategies. *Child Development*, 1967, **38**, 107–117.

Peevers, B. H., & Secord, P. F. Developmental changes in attribution of descriptive concepts to persons. *Journal of Personality and Social Psychology*, 1973, **27**, 120–128.

Phillips, J. *The origin of intellect: Piaget's theory.* San Francisco: Freeman, 1969.

Piaget, J. *The origins of intelligence in children.* New York: International Universities Press, 1952.

Piaget, J. *The child's conception of the world.* London: Routledge, 1960.

Price-Williams, D., Gordon, W., & Ramirez, M. III. Skill and conservation: A study of pottery-making children. *Developmental Psychology*, 1969, **1**, 769.

Rosenthal, T. L., & Zimmerman, B. J. Modeling by exemplification and instruction in training conservation. *Developmental Psychology*, 1972, **6**, 392–401.

Rubin, K. H. Egocentrism in childhood: A unitary construct? *Child Development*, 1973, **44**, 102–110.

Rubin, K. H. Role-taking in childhood: Some methodological considerations. *Child Development*, in press.

Rubin, K. H., & Schneider, F. W. The relationship between moral judgement, egocentrism and altruistic behavior. *Child Development*, 1973, **43**, 661–665.

Schultz, T. R. Development of the appreciation of riddles. *Child Development*, 1974, **45**, 100–105.

Schultz, T. R. A cognitive-developmental analysis of humor. In A. J. Chapman & H. C. Foot (Eds.), *Humor and laughter: Theory, research and applications*. London: Wiley, 1976.

Schultz, T. R., & Horibe, F. Development of the appreciation of verbal jokes. *Developmental Psychology*, 1974, **10**, 13–20.

Selman, R. L. Stages of role-taking and moral judgement as guides to social interaction. In T. Lickona (Ed.), *A handbook of moral development*. New York: Holt, 1976.

Selman, R. L., & Byrne, D. F. A structural-developmental analysis of levels of role taking in middle childhood. *Child Development*, 1974, **45**, 803–806.

Selman, R. L., & Jacquette, D. Stability and oscillation in interpersonal awareness: A clinical-developmental analysis. In C. B. Keasy (Ed.), *The XXV Nebraska symposium on motivation*, 1977, in press.

Shantz, C. B., & Watson, J. S. Assessment of spatial egocentrism through expectancy violation. *Psychonomic Science*, 1970, **18**, 93–94.

Shantz, C. V., & Watson, J. S. Spatial abilities and spatial egocentrism in the young child. *Child Development*, 1971, **42**, 171–181.

Sigel, I. E., Roeper, A., & Hooper, F. H. A training procedure for acquisition of Piaget's conservation of quantity: A pilot study and its replication. *British Journal of Educational Psychology*, 1966, **36**, 301–311.

Stephens, B., McLaughlin, J. A., & Mahoney, E. J. Age at which Piagetian concepts are achieved. *Proceedings, APA*, 1971, 203–204.

Sutton-Smith, B. A developmental structural account of riddles. In B. Kirschenblatt-Gimblett (Ed.), *Speech play: Research and resources for studying linguistic creativity*. Philadelphia: University of Pennsylvania Press, 1976.

Whitt, J. K., & Prentice, N. M. Cognitive processes in the development of childrens' enjoyment and comprehension of joking riddles. *Developmental Psychology*, 1977, **13**, 129–136.

Zimiles, H. The development of conservation and differentiation of number. *Monographs of the Society for Research in Child Development*, 1966, **31** (No. 6).

Zimmerman, B. J., & Lanaro, P. Acquiring and retaining conservation of length through modeling and reversibility cues. *Merrill-Palmer Quarterly*, 1974, **20**, 145–161.

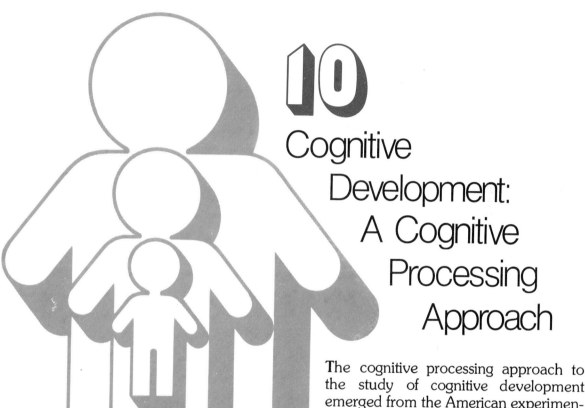

10
Cognitive Development: A Cognitive Processing Approach

The cognitive processing approach to the study of cognitive development emerged from the American experimental tradition in psychology. Psychologists taking this approach are interested in many of the same phenomena which concerned Piaget and his followers. Both groups of investigators are interested in the basic issue of how children of different ages process information when performing logical operations or solving cognitive tasks. However, the cognitive processing theorists have developed a different vocabulary and have tended to investigate more specific cognitive processes in contrast to Piaget's attempt to build an all-encompassing theory of cognitive development.

The cognitive processing approach focuses on the processes involved in perception, selective attention, memory, and cognitive strategies. It addresses questions such as, in solving cognitive tasks, how does the child perceive and selectively attend to events in her environment? How does she organize her perceptions and develop sets of concepts and problem-solving strategies that will facilitate the acquisition and retention of information? In addition, how does the child learn to discriminate among situations and problems in which a given cognitive strategy is appropriate or inappropriate?

The processes involved in all these types of information processing are intermeshed and cannot validly be viewed as separate components. It is obvious that in order to remember, the child must have perceived an event. It is also apparent that the child's perceptions and memory in large part will be determined by the aspects of an event to which she has attended. This selective attending will in turn be shaped by the problem-solving strategies or hypotheses being used by the child. She will attend to those aspects of the situation she thinks most relevant to reaching her goal.

Perception

When a group of children are in the same situation and are exposed to the same sensory stimulation, they do not necessarily perceive the situation in the same way. In the same classroom one child focusing in rapt attention on the teacher's words may hear and understand her lesson and view it as an exciting learning experience. Another child more interested in a whispered message from a neighboring peer may perceive the teacher's voice as no more than an annoying buzz. Perception is the person's interpretation of sensory information, of the sights, sounds, smells, touches, and movements in the world about her. Perception involves both the subjective awareness of events occurring in the individual's environment and selective responding to stimuli in the immediate surroundings (Gibson, 1969). What are the developmental processes underlying this subjective awareness of events and this selective responding to stimuli? Two main theories of the way in which experience affects perceptual learning and development have been advanced.

An *enrichment theory*, such as that of Piaget discussed in the previous chapter, proposes that each time a child perceives an object, she learns a little more about that object. The first time a child sees a cat, it may be viewed as little more than another fuzzy four-footed animal. The next time she sees the cat, it may be drinking milk and meowing. She elaborates her cat schema to include "likes milk and meows." Finally, the child may attempt to pick the cat up and be scratched. Cats then become fuzzy four-footed animals that drink milk, meow, and are dangerous. With experience, information is added to the existing schema of an object, and the schema becomes more detailed and elaborated. The sensations that are received from the stimulus are meaningless until they are modified and enriched by information from other schemata. Meager sensory information is reorganized and elaborated by the child. As this enrichment of schemata for many different objects occurs, the child is better able to discriminate among objects (Bruner, 1957; Vernon, 1955).

In contrast to the enrichment theory, the *differentiation theory* of Eleanor Gibson emphasizes that sensory input is a rich, not a meager, source of information. The sensory information does not have to be enriched through schemata or associations as is proposed in the enrichment theory. Instead, the task of the child is to gradually attend to, identify, and discriminate features of objects, such as size, shape, and color, or relationships in this very complex sensory stream. Through experience the child learns to make increasingly fine discriminations among objects and events and to attend to the relevant attributes of objects. The child learns that although cats and dogs are both furry four-footed animals, there are many characteristics which differentiate them.

In addition, the child becomes aware of *invariants*, that is, of characteristics of objects, or relationships among objects, that do not change under different conditions. Although when an object is near the child, it will produce a larger retinal image than when it is farther away, the child rapidly learns to make correct judgments of size. A small nearby cat and a large distant tiger are not confused, although they may produce similar retinal images. Similarly, although the retinal image changes in relation to an object's spatial orientation, even young infants are able to perceive the real shape of the object. A child knows the surface of his dish is round even if he views it from the side and the retinal image is elliptical.

Enrichment and differentiation theories are not necessarily incompatible but may be viewed as complementary (Stevenson, 1972). Children may both identify distinctive attributes of objects and build up mental representations or schemata. When a child must distinguish among several objects, she may pick out their distinctive features. When the child must identify one object, she may compare it with existing mental representations. The child may have developed a schema for her pet cat. Eventually through matching experiences with different kinds of animals with her schema and through identifying the distinctive features of various animals, she will begin to discriminate her friendly neighborhood cat from the king of the jungle.

Selective Attention

Because the growing child is exposed to such a complex mosaic of stimulation and can process only a limited amount of information, it is essential that she learn to focus her attention on selected aspects of her experience. The child must learn to focus on the objects that have the most *functional value* for her, that are relevant for her goals. Initially the child is attracted by objects that are bright, gaily colored, or large because these stimulus dimensions are particularly salient for her. As the child has more experience with the world about her, she starts to selectively attend to attributes that are relevant to the task or problem before her. Although Gibson has emphasized the importance of selective attention in perception, it is also critical in memory, thought, and problem solving (Pick, Frankel, & Hess, 1975).

It has been suggested that there are four developmental changes in attentional processing by children (Flavell, 1977). As the child develops, there are shifts in control of attention, adaptability, planfulness, and deployment of attention over time.

Control Two of the requirements for successful information processing are the ability to sustain attention and to attend to relevant and ignore irrelevant information in the environment. Obviously everything is not equally important, and directing and controlling attention is one of the most important abilities that children acquire as they develop.

Very young children can sustain their attention for only short periods of time. No teacher or parent expects a preschool child to show the persistence in play or in task-oriented activities that is found in older children. Even within the preschool period marked differences in distractibility are found. In a recent study (Anderson & Levin, 1976), children ranging in age from 2 to 4 were observed while watching a segment of "Sesame Street." The youngest children often looked away from the screen. They frequently wandered around the room touching or playing with toys and chatting with other people. In contrast, the

In order to solve this spatial task, children must attend to the correct dimensions of stimuli. (F. J. Dias, Photo Researchers, Inc.)

older children were less distracted and spent more time with their attention directed toward the television program.

In learning situations, it is not only the amount of time spent attending to the task that is important, but also focusing attention on relevant aspects of a task which facilitates learning. In learning situations very young children are easily distracted by irrelevant features and therefore learn the critical aspects of the task at a slower rate. As children mature, they pay less attention to irrelevant information and learn to concentrate on the central and critical aspects of a task.

There are a variety of ways to study the deployment of attention in children. One technique for studying attention is to photograph children's visual scanning patterns by means of an eye camera, which takes a picture of the object to which the child is attending as well as exactly where the child is focused. Vurpillot (1968) asked children between the ages of 6 and 9 to examine pairs of pictures and decide whether they were the same or different. Of course to correctly make this kind of judgment, children ought to scan both pictures in detail before deciding. But, in fact, the younger children were not very systematic in their scanning strategies; rather they looked only at parts of the pictures and as a result made more errors than the older children, who more systematically scanned the features of the pictures. This is, of course, reminiscent of the behavior of young infants who spend a large amount of time investigating the angles of a triangle, but rarely scan the full outline of the figure (Salapatek & Kessen, 1966). With increasing age, children improve in their capacity to attend selectively with their eyes to those portions of visual stimuli which contain the most information.

However, it is not just the lack of systematic scanning, but the young child's failure to distinguish irrelevant from relevant information, that often accounts for poor learning. A study by Hagen (1967) will illustrate this process. Children in grades 1, 3, 5, and 7 saw cards containing two pictures: an animal and a household object. Half the children were instructed to remember the locations of the animals, while the remaining children were asked to remember the household objects. After going through the cards, the children were unexpectedly asked to pair each animal with the household object with which it had appeared. In other words, children had to remember and relate both animals and household objects on the cards, although they had originally been asked to attend to only one of the objects. There were two measures: the *central memory score*, consisting of the number of correct responses for objects that adults asked the child to remember, and the *incidental memory score*, consisting of the number of correct responses for objects the child had not originally been asked to remember. Both central memory performance and incidental performance increased with age through the fifth-grade group, indicating little differentiation between relevant and irrelevant information by these children. However, at the oldest age level, that is, in the grade 7 students, the increase in the learning of relevant information continued but there was a dramatic decrease in incidental learning. Moreover, younger children who performed well on the central task also did well on the incidental task; but for the oldest children, those who did best on central memory recalled little of the incidental information. What differences in the way the older and younger children process information might be contributing to these findings? In a study using a similar task, it was reported that older children usually only scanned and covertly named relevant objects in the pictures, while younger children reported more scanning and naming of both central and incidental objects (Druker & Hagen, 1969). Older children were therefore better able to focus on aspects of the picture which were relevant to solutions of the task as it was originally presented by the experimenter.

Studies of retarded children show that they have some of the same problems as younger children in not selectively attending to the relevant aspects of the stimuli in a discrimination-learning task. However, once the retarded children begin to focus on those dimensions of the stimuli leading to rewarded solutions, they frequently learn as rapidly as nonretarded children (House & Zeaman, 1963). Let us take a task where the child is looking at squares that vary in size and color: large or small, black or white squares provide the stimuli, and the relevant rewarded dimension is size. The large square is always rewarded whether it is black or white. The child goes through a series of trials. On each trial the child is presented with two squares and asked to select the correct square. If he selects the large square, he gets a reward of candy. If he selects the small square, he gets nothing. Retardates are slower than nonretarded children in attending to the dimension of size and ignoring color. However, once they begin to focus on size, they make as many correct responses as the nonretarded children.

A question remains. Can young children be trained to attend selectively to relevant features of their environment? The answer is clearly yes. If children are given training in distinguishing critical features of an object (for example, color versus size) *before* a discrimination test so that they are aware of the multiple dimensions of the stimuli, the trained children's discrimination performance will be markedly superior to their nontrained peers (Tighe & Tighe, 1969). The reader will recall, from the previous chapter, that a very similar effect was obtained in improving children's performances on conservation tasks by training them to attend to the multiple attributes of stimuli. Such findings are certainly compatible with Gibson's perceptual-differentiation theory which argues that the principal process underlying successful learning is the discovery and attention to distinctive features that separate objects in the environment. According to Gibson's view, reinforcement is unnecessary for learning. Reinforcement may serve to increase motivation and maintain persistence and interest, but the basic learning process is essentially a perceptual-differentiation process.

Adaptability With increasing age children can more easily adapt their attentional strategies to the demands of specific tasks or situations. There is no one attentional strategy that is appropriate to all situations or problems. Older children are more flexible than younger children in modifying their attention in accord with the requirements of the task (Pick & Frankel, 1974). Eight-year-olds, more frequently than five-year-olds, focus on multiple aspects of a stimulus when that is adaptive in problem solving and on a single dimension of a stimulus when that has functional value (Hale & Taweel, 1974).

The adaptive role of selective attending may be established by cultural demands. A frequently reported finding is that in Western children there is a shift from preference of stimuli based on color to preferences based on form (shape) at about age 5 (Suchman & Trabasso, 1966). This increase in the salience of form occurs at about the time the child is beginning to read. Attention to form is more adaptive than attention to color in the detection of letters and words. Is this shift in salience due to the demands of the educational system or to some biologically determined developmental change? Studies of children in an Islamic school in Nigeria suggest that environmental factors may play an important role in such shifts. In Islamic schools emphasis is placed upon memorizing and reciting extensive sections from the Koran rather than on reading. Islamic children not only failed to show a preference for form in the early school years, but were still exhibiting no preference for form over color in adolescence (Suchman, 1966). Such cultural differences again provide evidence for the adaptive role of selective attending.

Planfulness Adaptive attending involves being ready to process certain selected types of useful information in accord with a plan or strategy. If the child knows beforehand what information must be gathered, she can plan how to focus her

Selective attending is necessary for reading. (Charles Gatewood)

attention in order to solve the problem efficiently, as can be seen in the study reported in Box 10-1. Such systematic directing of attention is facilitated if the child has foreknowledge of the task she is to solve. Older children are more apt to utilize foreknowledge and use more systematic strategies in attending to stimuli than are younger children (Pick, Christy, & Frankel, 1972). In addition, it has been suggested that even when younger children are using planful looking strategies, they often seem unaware and unable to report what they are doing. In contrast, older children are usually more conscious of their strategies than are younger children (Flavell, 1977).

Attention over Time As children grow older, they are able to process complex *sequences* of information, modifying their attentional focusing as the information they receive changes or as they get feedback on the success or failure of the strategies they are using. They become more flexible and better able to alter and adapt their attentional plans to changes in the situation *over time*. Flavell (1977) has described the entire process of the development of attentional selectivity as follows:

> My own mental image of a cognitively mature information processor is that of a conductor who directs his ensemble of musicians (attentional processes and resources)—now calling forth one instrument, now another, now a blended combination of several or all depending upon the effect desired. I think we do not so much "pay attention" as "play our attentional system." That is, we intentionally exploit and deploy it in a flexible, situation-contingent, adaptive fashion. (Flavell, 1977, pp. 169–170)

Memory and How Children Learn to Remember

Up to now we have focused on how children process and attend to sensory information and changing facets of their environment. But that is only one aspect of cognitive processing. Children not only must learn, but also must retain information and be able to recognize, recall, and use it when it is needed. Think of how difficult solving any kind of problem would be if we could not draw on our vast store of memories of past experiences and similar situations.

Researchers investigating memory generally make a distinction between two types of memory: short-term and long-term. *Short-term memory* refers to the process by which people remember over a brief period of time (for example, thirty seconds). An example of short-term memory would be trying to remember an unfamiliar telephone number long enough to dial it after looking it up in the phone book. Short-term memory can store only a very restricted amount of knowledge at any one time. In contrast, *long-term memory* involves our knowledge of the world, our memory of past events and experiences. Its capacity is large, and once information is stored in long-term memory, it is relatively difficult to lose. There are modest developmental differences in short-term memory. For example, the average 3-year-old child can only recall a series of three orally repeated numbers, whereas the average 7-year-old can

BOX 10-1
AUDITORY ATTENTION, OR
LEARNING TO LISTEN
SELECTIVELY

Children learn to attend selectively to information coming from their auditory environment as well as from their visual world. Often two people are talking, but we are able to tune out one conversation while we attend to the other. Similarly, we ignore street noise and barking dogs and "hear" a TV program or a call for dinner. An experimental analogue of this type of double auditory message is the dichotic listening situation in which two different messages are presented through earphones to the two ears simultaneously. In a series of dichotic listening studies by Maccoby (1967, 1969) a man's voice was presented in one ear and a woman's voice in the other. The child was instructed to attend to the messages (simple English words) and to repeat them after the voice stopped. It was found that the child's ability to listen selectively improved between ages 5 and 14. In addition, instructions

before the listening task, which permitted the child to plan which voice to attend to, greatly improved learning. Children were told either before or after the presentation of the message which voice they would have to remember.

As Figure 10-1 illustrates, hearing the instructions before the two messages were received markedly improved the child's ability to selectively report a particular message. The opportunity to plan how to attend is an important determinant of success in a dichotic listening task. ■

Source: Maccoby, E. E. Selective auditory attention in children. In L. P. Lipsett & C. C. Spiker (Eds.), *Advances in child development and behavior* (Vol. 3). New York: Academic, 1967, pp. 99–125; and Maccoby, E. E. The development of stimulus selection. In John P. Hill (Ed.), *Minnesota symposia on child psychology* (Vol. 3). Minneapolis: University of Minnesota Press, 1969, pp. 68–96.

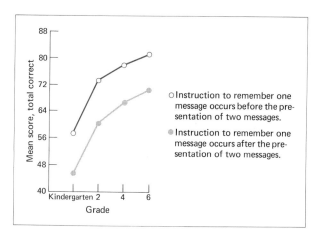

○ Instruction to remember one message occurs before the presentation of two messages.

◍ Instruction to remember one message occurs after the presentation of two messages.

FIGURE 10-1 The effects of the age of a child and the timing of an instruction to listen to a particular message on selective auditory attention. *(From Maccoby, 1967.)*

recall five numbers. Not a very substantial increase in four years. However, differences across ages are most marked in long-term memory, and seem to be associated with differences in the cognitive processes involved both in how children store or retain information and in how they go about retrieving or bringing the information into awareness when they need it.

In order to examine some of these developmental differences in memory processes, we will use Brown's (1975) distinction between memory as knowing, memory as knowing how to know, and memory as knowing about knowing.

Memory as Knowing   Children remember people, places, and events that are no longer present. This vast fund of knowledge that is built up with experience influences how the individual stores and retrieves new information. What the individual already knows will greatly influence how he learns and remembers.

The Construction of Memory

The information the child receives is not stored in a fragmentary random fashion, but is reorganized and reconstructed in a way to make it more meaningful and hence easier to remember. How does this process of actively altering and rebuilding information vary for children of different ages? One of the main ways is through the increasing use of categories and verbal labels. As children grow older, they are better able to group and to give names or labels to events and objects (Flavell & Wellman, 1977). A child on seeing a new taciturn neighbor for the first time may classify him as a "fearsome person" along with a hostile teacher, the unfriendly policeman on the corner, and the wicked witch of the west. This labeling and categorization helps make the new experience more personally meaningful and easier to remember.

In addition to using such processes as classifying and labeling which assist in

Bushman traditions are passed on to the younger generation orally. The bushman elder who transmits these traditions must have an exceptional memory. (From Jens Bjerre's *Kalahari*, Hill and Wang, New York)

remembering, children may remember things in a way which seems logically correct to them. They extend or reinterpret information on the basis of reasoning or meaning. This is called *semantic integration*. Studies have shown that both children and adults may have difficulty in distinguishing, for example, an actual sentence from their logical elaboration of that sentence (Bransford & Franks, 1971; Paris & Mahoney, 1974; Paris & Lindauer, 1977). If a child first hears the two sentences "The box is to the right of the tree" and "The chair is on top of the box," the child may later incorrectly identify "The chair is to the right of the tree" as one of the sentences previously presented to her. The child does not recall the specific word order or form of the sentences, but remembers their meaning. This process is so pervasive that the child may be even more insistent and certain that her logically reconstructed sentence had been presented previously than that she had ever seen the sentences which were actually presented.

Eidetic Imagery: A Help or a Hinderance to Memory?   Between 5 and 10 percent of children and very few adults possess *eidetic imagery*, that is, a remarkable ability to visualize for several seconds or even minutes things they have seen for only a short period of time. They speak of the image as being localized in space in front of their eyes and can describe it in great detail. An example of the unusual precision with which these images are reported is presented in Box 10-2.

At this point you may be thinking what a wonderful advantage to memory it would be to have eidetic imagery! How great to be able to visualize a page in an address book, a road map, mathematical formulas, a list of French vocabulary words!

Unfortunately, eidetic imagery may prove to be more of a hindrance than a help to long-term memory. The image itself seldom lasts more than a minute or two. When people with eidetic imagery are able to recall the images after longer periods of time, they are unable to break down the images and reconstruct them in a meaningful way (Luria, 1968). In fact, a conscious attempt to label or categorize features in the image may actually interfere with the formation of an image (Haber, 1969). Children with eidetic imagery can thus reproduce what they have seen, but may not be able to differentiate what is important from what is unimportant. This nonselectivity in memory results in "a kind of junk heap of impressions" (Bruner, 1968) that is not useful in abstract thinking or in generalizing to solving problems in new situations, and which may not be as useful in long-term memory as the processes of reconstruction we have described previously.

Memory as Knowing How to Know, or "You Gotta Have a Gimmick"

Thus far we have emphasized that memory involves actively reconstructing and reorganizing information in ways that make it more meaningful. We also have suggested that the more effective memory of adults over that of children is in part because adults know more. They already have more existing cognitive schemes which can organize and give meaning to new information. Are there any other

BOX 10-2
EIDETIC IMAGERY IN A
10-YEAR-OLD BOY

How accurately can children report the details in an eidetic image? A 10-year-old boy was allowed to study the picture of Alice in Wonderland in Figure 10-2 for half a minute. The picture was removed, and he continued to stare at the blank easel and discuss his image of the absent picture with the experimenter.

Experimenter: Tell me what else you see.
Subject: And I can see the flowers on the bottom. There's about three stems, but you can see two pairs of flowers. One on the right has green leaves, red flower on bottom with yellow on top. And I can see the girl with a green dress. She's got blonde hair and a red hair band and there are some leaves in the upper left-hand corner where the tree is.
Experimenter: Can you tell me about the roots of the tree?
Subject: Well, there's two of them going down here (points) and there's one that cuts off on the left-hand side of the picture.
Experimenter: What is the cat doing with its paws?
Subject: Well, one of them he's holding out and the other one is on the tree.
Experimenter: What color is the sky?
Subject: Can't tell.
Experimenter: Can't tell at all?
Subject: No. I can see the yellowish ground though.
Experimenter: Tell me if any of the parts go away

FIGURE 10-2   Picture from *Alice in Wonderland* used in a study of eidetic imagery. *(From Haber, 1969.)*

or change at all as I'm talking to you. What color is the girl's dress?
Subject: Green. It has some white on it.
Experimenter: How about her legs and feet? (The subject looks away from the easel and then back again.)
Experimenter: Is the image gone?

Subject: Yes, except for the tree.
Experimenter: Tell me when it goes away.
Subject: (pause) It went away. ∎

Source: Haber, R. N. Eidetic images. *Scientific American*, 1969, **220**, 36–44.

---

reasons why adults or older children remember some things more effectively than do younger children? Certain strategies can be used intentionally to improve memory. We have all used some of these strategies in attempting to study for exams. We may underline or outline important points in a book. We may repeatedly say English words and equivalent foreign word pairs aloud in studying for a language exam. We may list or group similar important principles, or we may try to visualize mathematical formulas or verb conjugations. Younger children are likely to use fewer and less effective memory strategies than older children or adults.

The most common strategies used to enhance memory are *rehearsal imagery and organization.* Suppose a child is shown a series of pictures of the following objects and is asked to remember them: red, pig, parsley, truck, banana, hat, bicycle, green, dog, jacket. How might the child use rehersal, imagery, and organization in improving her memory of these items? She might use *rehearsal* by repeatedly going through the pictures and naming the objects aloud. She also might try to improve her memory through the use of *imagery* by visualizing the objects. She might not just use the strategy of visualizing objects one at a time, but she may try to make her imagery more vivid and meaningful by combining the stimuli in unique ways. For example, she might visualize a pig wearing a red jacket who is munching a banana as he drives a truck. Or she might visualize a dog wearing a hat decorated with parsley and riding a green bicycle. Finally the child might try to improve her memory through *organization* by clustering the objects in a meaningful way such as by pairing the pig and the dog because they are animals, parsley and banana because they are food, truck and bicycle because they are vehicles, and red and green because they are colors.

Let us examine some of the differences in the way children of various ages use rehersal, imagery, and organization in facilitating memory.

Rehearsal   How do older and younger children differ in their use of rehearsal? John Flavell and his colleagues (Flavell, 1970) performed a series of studies using a task similar to the one just described to examine the effects of rehearsing by verbally naming objects or pictures to be remembered. If children ranging in age from kindergarten to fifth grade are shown a series of pictures and are asked to recall the sequence in which the experimenter points to a subset of the pictures, younger children exhibit very different behavior than do older children. Flavell found that when the children's lip movements were observed for a sign that they were *rehearsing* by naming the pictures as a memory aid, the children who used spontaneous verbal rehearsal demonstrated better memory for the pictures. In addition, the use of spontaneous verbal rehersal increased dramatically with age. Only about 10 percent of kindergarten children spontaneously named the common objects in the pictures, whereas over 60 percent of second graders and about 85 percent of fifth graders did so. Does this mean that the younger children were unable to use the verbal mediators when they were available (that is, have a *mediational deficiency*)? No! The evidence suggests that the problem with the kindergarten children was that of a *production deficiency*, that is, they did not spontaneously produce verbal mediators. When verbal labeling occurred, either by the experimenter naming the objects in the pictures or by instructing the child to name the pictures, the young child's memory was greatly improved. In fact, in a study of first graders, when children who had not spontaneously named the pictures were required to do so, memory performance differences between children who did and did not spontaneously rehearse were eliminated. Since older children already spontaneously rehearse, it has been found that training and induced rehearsal in the use of verbal mediators are of less benefit to them than to their younger peers.

Not only does the tendency to spontaneously rehearse increase with age, but there are developmental changes in the type of rehearsal used. In learning a

(King Features Syndicate)

BOX 10-3
IMAGES: AIDS FOR REMEMBERING

How does forming mental images improve the memory of older and younger children? In a recent study, children in kindergarten and third grade were presented with pairs of toys (for example, giraffe-truck, watch-airplane). Later, only one toy was presented and the child was asked to recall the other toy in the pair. Children received one of four different kinds of training. Children in the control condition were shown the pairs and told to remember which toys went together. In the imagery group, they were in structed to form a mental image of the toys in each pair "playing together." Children in another condition were instructed to manipulate the toys in a manner described by the experimenter (for example, the bear jumped into the truck). Subjects in the final condition were asked to devise their own ways of having the toys in each pair play together by actually manipulating the toys.

As Figure 10-3 illustrates, active manipulation of the toys resulted in improved memory regardless of whether the experimenter or the child initiated the manipulation sequence. However, the mental imagery instructions were effective only for the third graders; the kindergarten children did not benefit from these instructions. Motor manipulation appears to be a helpful aid for the 5-year-old, while more abstract techniques like imagery are effective only at older ages. ■

Source: Wolff, P., & Levin, J. R. The role of overt activity in children's imagery production. *Child Development*, 1972, **43**, 537–548.

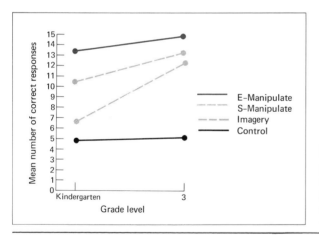

FIGURE 10-3 The effects of different ways of presenting information on children's ability to remember. Mean number of correct responses by kindergarten and third-grade children in each of four presentation conditions. *(From Wolff & Levin, 1972.)*

list of items, sixth graders are more likely than third graders to rehearse several items together. Thus, in learning the list given in an earlier example, the young child is more likely to repeat red over and over, then pig several times, then move on to parsley. The older child would be more likely to repeat "red, pig, parsley"; then "truck, banana, hat"; and so on (Ornstein, Naus, & Liberty, 1975). Again we find that training younger children, such as second graders, in effective rehearsal strategies by having them name several items together makes them perform as well as untrained sixth graders (Ornstein, Naus, & Stone, 1977).

Mental Imagery Older and younger children differ not only in their use of rehearsal, but also in the way they use mental images. This is demonstrated by a recent study by Wolff and Levin (1972), which is presented in Box 10-3.

It can be seen that rehearsal through labeling, motor manipulation of toys, and formulation of mental images can be used to improve memory in some children. However, the effectiveness of any of these strategies varies according to the cognitive level of the child and the particular task conditions (Ferguson & Bray, 1976; Bray, Justice, Ferguson, & Simon, 1977).

Organization Finally, one of the most interesting recent advances in our understanding of developmental differences in memory strategies is in the role of *organization* of material. When faced with the task of remembering a set of pictures or words, children tend to cluster the material into different conceptual categories. Moreover, again there is a relationship between increasing recall and clustering with age. Not only do young children show the same type of transitional production-deficiency pattern in clustering as they do in verbal rehearsal, but they seem to use a different cognitive basis for clustering objects than do older children. The organizational basis for memory appears to change with age (Moely, Olson, Hawles, & Flavell, 1969; Neimark, Slotnick, & Ulrich, 1971). Rossi and Wittrock (1971) found marked differences in the organizational bases for free recall among children with mental age ranges from 2 to 5 years. They used a list of words (for example, sun, hand, men, peach, hat, bark, apple, dogs, fat) that could be organized in a number of different ways during recall. At the youngest age (mental age 2) rhyming (for example, sun-fun, fat-hat) was the predominant mode of organizing the words. At the next age level (mental age 3) syntactical organization (for example, dog-bark, men-work) was the most evident strategy. Clustering (for example, peach-apple, leg-hand) was higher than the other techniques at age 4, while the children at the oldest mental age level (5) used serial ordering (for example, the order in which they heard the words) most often. These results are consistent with Piaget's theory of a development from concrete to abstract functioning and from perceptual to conceptual responding.

Just as spontaneous rehearsal and spontaneous labeling increase with age, it has been observed that the spontaneous clustering of items increases with age and that this clustering is related to the number of items subsequently recalled (Moely et al., 1969). In addition, just as memory can be enhanced in children who do not spontaneously label, by training them to use labels, memory can also be improved by training children to use conceptual categories (Moely & Jeffrey, 1974).

Memory Strategies Used in Retrieval Most of the strategies we have discussed thus far have focused on developmental differences in strategies used by a child when she knows that she will wish to recover that information later, that is, the strategies used when the child is learning or memorizing the material. However, investigators are now becoming interested in retrieval strategies, that is, in strategies used in attempting to retrieve previously learned information,

Children use many different strategies in trying to remember. (James H. Karales, Peter Arnold, Inc.)

whether that information was intentionally or incidentally (nonintentionally) learned. The study by Kobasigawa presented in Box 10-4 again shows developmental differences in the strategies used by children of different ages and in their ability to use different kinds of retrieval cues. In memory, as was found in perception and attention processing, the use of plans and strategies is more common in older children.

Knowing about Knowing

What does the child know about how people remember? The growing child becomes increasingly aware of the limits of his own memory ability, of what things are difficult or easy to remember, and of when a task or situation needs special strategies to aid memory. This knowledge about memory is sometimes called *metamemory*.

Older elementary school children are more likely than younger children to predict that when material is organized or meaningful it will be easier to remember. For example, items which can be grouped in categories, such as food items, furniture items, or items of clothing, will be easier to remember than unrelated items (Moynahan, 1973). They also realize that words that are meaningfully related, such as opposites (for example, big-small, light-heavy) or words making a story, are easier to remember than unrelated words (Kreutzer, Leonard, & Flavell, 1975). In addition, as children mature, they become more aware of the limitations of their memory. Younger children tend both to

BOX 10-4
THE USE OF RETRIEVAL CUES IN RECALL

When children are trying to remember something, what kinds of retrieval cues are useful in recall? Are children increasingly likely to make efficient use of available retrieval cues as they get older? Children in grades 1, 3, and 6 were presented with eight sets of pictures of three items belonging to a given category and told that they would later have to recall them. The sets included such items as three things associated with music, three types of fruit, three pieces of furniture, and three pieces of playground equipment. Each set of pictures was accompanied by a cue card; the seesaw, slide, and swing were accompanied by a picture of a park; the pear, grapes, and bananas were accompanied by a picture of a fruit stand; the monkey, camel, and bear sat by a picture of a zoo with three empty cages, and so on. All the children were asked to recall as many of the items as possible. However, one-third of the children were instructed to recall as many items as possible with no cue cards present (free-recall condition); one-third were given the cue cards face down in their laps and told that they could use them if they thought it would help their remembering (cue condition). The remaining third were presented with the cards one by one and told that there were three small pictures that went with the picture on the card and to attempt to remember the three small

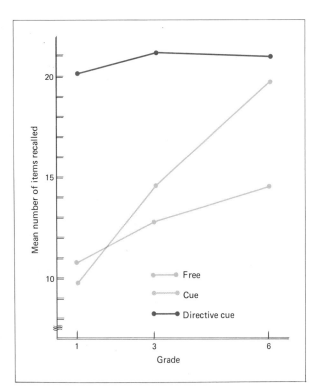

FIGURE 10-4 Mean number of items correctly recalled as a function of grade and recall condition. *(From Kobasigawa, 1974.)*

pictures (directive-cue condition).

It can be seen in Figure 10-4 that the presence of a cue improved the recall of the oldest children whether or not they were instructed to use it. When the cue was present, they were able spontaneously to initiate a retrieval strategy. In contrast, the first graders did no better under the cue condition, when the cue was available but they were not directed to use it, than under the free-recall condition. Only when a strategy for use of the cue was presented to them and they were directed to use it did their recall improve, and then they remembered as well as the sixth graders. ■

Source: Kobasigawa, A. Utilization of retrieval cues by children in recall. *Child Development*, 1974, **45**, 127–134.

overestimate their memory ability and to understimate the amount of time and effort they require to learn something. In planning for a test, fifth graders are much more likely than first graders to study harder for a difficult test than for an easy test, to use appropriate memory aids, and to be able to predict realistically when they have studied enough to retain the material (Flavell & Wellman, 1977; Markman, 1973). Thus, the developing child becomes increasingly aware of how attributes of the task, the person doing the learning, and strategies used interact and affect the outcome of memory.

Hypothesis Testing and the Use of Cognitive Strategies

The final aspect of cognitive processing that we will discuss is hypothesis testing. Piaget recognized that an important characteristic of an individual in the formal operations period was that he could generate and test hypotheses. Psychologists approaching cognition from the perspective of information processing also would agree that the generation and confirmation or disconfirmation of hypotheses play a critical role in effective problem solving.

Many of us have played the game twenty questions, where one player thinks of an object or a person and the other players must guess what or who it is within twenty questions. Most adolescents and adults will use a strategy of asking planned and increasingly constrained categorical questions. Is it alive? Yes. Is it an animal rather than a vegetable? Yes. Is it a person rather than another form of animal? Yes. Is it someone living now rather than in the past? And so on. In contrast, younger children ask very specific questions directed to very specific objects in no planned order. Is it R2D2? Is it straw with a daisy on it? (mother's hat). Is it Pooh Bear?

This hypothesis-testing process has been studied more systematically with discrimination-learning tasks in the laboratory (Levine, 1966; Phillips & Levine, 1975). Marvin Levine and his colleagues have developed a cue-selection procedure in which subjects are presented with stimulus pairs that vary on a variety of attributes. For example, the series of stimulus pairs presented in Figure 10-5 vary on dimensions of size (large or small), position (left or right), color (black or white), and letter (X or T). The person views the pair and selects the figure she thinks is correct.

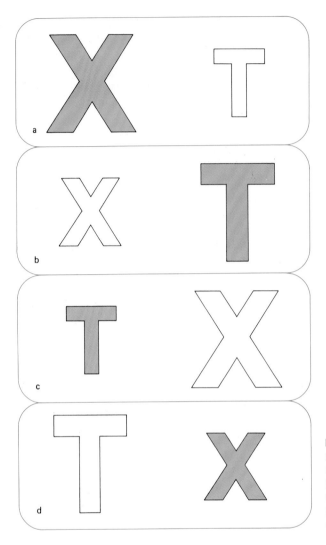

FIGURE 10-5 An example of four stimulus pairs presented in Levine's cue-selection procedure. *(From Levine, 1966.)*

Most adult subjects will begin with a hypothesis that one dimension is correct and test that hypothesis. Levine is able to assess the hypothesis the person is testing by observing the pattern of responses across pairs. The experimenter responds right or wrong to the choices on some, but not all, trials. Blank trials, that is, trials in which the child is not informed of the correctness of her choice, are randomly interspersed between the trials on which the child gets feedback. The child's performance on the blank trials allows the experimenter to see what strategy the child is using in attempting to solve the problem. When the experimenter says right or wrong on the initial pair, a number of attributes may be the correct one. If the X on the left is chosen in the first pair, it can be the letter

X, the left position, the large size, or the color that is correct. However, with continued feedback from the experimenter, if the person used a strategy called *focusing*, which consists of narrowing down the field by logically eliminating all disconfirmed attributes, it is possible to solve the problem in Figure 10-5 in only four trials. Try it. Other less efficient strategies may be used. *Dimension checking* involves systematically checking all four dimensions, one dimension at a time. Even less effective is *hypothesis checking*, where all eight attributes are singly checked. Finally, the individual may use an extremely maladaptive response of *stimulus preference*, which involves repeatedly selecting the same attribute even when she has been told it is wrong.

The frequencies with which these four different strategies were used by second, fourth, and sixth graders and adults are presented in Figure 10-6. It can be seen that only the adults used the most efficient strategy, focusing, a significant proportion of the time. However, note that dimension checking, the next most effective strategy, was used frequently by all age groups, and stimulus preference, a stereotyped maladaptive response, was infrequently used by persons of all ages (Gholson, Levine, & Phillips, 1972). Later studies have shown that kindergarten children use even less effective strategies than second graders, almost never utilizing focusing, dimension checking, or hypothesis checking. They most frequently used a response of *stereotyped position alternation*, first selecting the figure on the left, then on the right, then on the left, and so on. They also often demonstrated a *stimulus preference* or a *field-position preference*, always selecting on one side, fixing on either the left or right position. These three strategies are rarely adopted by second graders. This marked difference in the problem-solving strategies of children in kindergarten and second grade parallels the timing of differences we have reported in more effective attentional-focusing strategies and memory mediation techniques in this period.

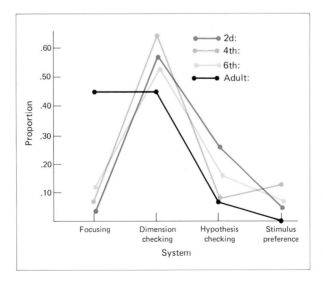

FIGURE 10-6 The proportion of choices made involving four different problem-solving strategies by four different age groups. Strategies are ordered from most (focusing) to least effective (stimulus preference). *(From Levine, 1974.)*

Individual Differences in Cognitive Processing: Cognitive Style

This section will in some ways serve as a bridge between the previous two chapters, which have emphasized cognitive structure and processes, and the next chapter, which focuses on individual differences in performance on standardized tests of intelligence. Some children manifest relatively consistent individual differences in the way they process, perceive, remember, or use information. They show a preferred *cognitive style* that may be related to differences in motivation, personality, attention, or cognitive organization. Cognitive style does not refer to the level of intellectual ability as much as to the manner in which congitive functions are executed. Cognitive styles show individual differences among children and systematic changes with age, and are associated with a variety of other social and cognitive measures. One of the types of cognitive style which has been most extensively investigated is that of impulsivity-reflectivity.

On a variety of cognitive tasks there are relatively stable differences in the degree to which a child will wait and evaluate his response before answering. When children are asked to respond in situations where there is response uncertainty, for example, in the Matching Familiar Figures Test, some children respond slowly and with accuracy and others respond rapidly and with many errors. The former type Kagan calls *reflective* children; the latter he calls *impulsives.* Although all children become more reflective with increasing age, some children tend to be more reflective and others more impulsive relative to other children in their age group. The Matching Familiar Figures Test is a test in which the child is asked to match a standard figure, say a picture of a teddy bear sitting on a chair, with the identical stimulus in an array of six pictures of teddy bears on chairs which vary only in tiny details from the standard. Figure 10-7 presents two items from the Matching Familiar Figures Test.

The Matching Familiar Figures Test taps two individual-difference components; anxiety over errors and tempo of information processing. Impulsives and reflectives show different styles of scanning stimuli which may be related to concern about making errors. Studies have been performed in which the eye movements of children were photographed while they scanned the pictures in the Matching Familiar Figures Test (Siegelman, 1966; Drake, 1970; Wright & Vliestra, 1977; McCluskey & Wright, 1975). Reflectives carefully inspect the standard and check between each picture in the array and the standard before making a response. Impulsives check back and forth between the array and the standard less, and frequently do not even look at all alternatives in the array before responding. In addition, impulsives make fewer informative comparisons between the standard and stimuli. That is, they show fewer successive fixations on corresponding areas of the standard and the stimulus array figures particularly in the area where the critical differences between the figures occur. The scanning strategies of reflectives are more systematic and planful than those of impulsives.

Since much learning in the classroom requires the careful, considered,

The joy of problem solving. (Alice Kandell, Rapho/Photo Researchers, Inc.)

systematic behavior of the reflective, it is not surprising that impulsives have greater difficulty in the school situation. Impulsive children are less attentive and more distractible on a variety of learning tasks and more frequently show reading disabilities than do reflectives. Boys who are not promoted in the first grade are often more impulsive than their classmates who go on to second grade, although the two groups of children do not differ in scores on standard intelligence tests (Messer, 1970). In general, the relationship between IQ and reflectivity-impulsivity is small, although it is higher for girls than for boys.

Reflectives also do better than impulsives on certain standard laboratory tests of discrimination learning, reasoning, memory, and Piagetian measures of conservation and formal operations (Neimark, 1974; Pascual-Leone, 1973). It has often been suggested that impulsivity is related to the use of less efficient and less advanced problem-solving strategies. However, it has recently been proposed that the superiority of the reflective children's strategies in processing information depends on the nature of the task. If the task requires detailed analysis, reflectives perform better. If the task requires a global response, no superiority in performance of reflectives is found. For example, on match-to-sample visual tasks such as those found in the Matching Familiar Figures Test, sometimes the change to be detected is inside the visual form and sometimes it is in the contour or edge of the object. It is assumed that a more detailed response is required to identify the internal embedded change and a more global response for the change in contour. Reflective children make fewer errors when

FIGURE 10-7 Sample items from the Matching Familiar Figures Test. The child is asked to find the object in the six-item stimulus array which is identical to the single stimulus above them. *(From Kagan, Rosman, Day, Albert, & Phillips, 1964).*

the change is located inside the figure than they do when it is on the contour. Impulsive children show the opposite profile (Zelniker & Jeffery, 1976). Thus if the significant variation in Figure 10-7 was in the length of one of the chair legs, an impulsive would be more likely to detect it, whereas a reflective might be more likely to detect a change in facial expression, such as a smile.

Differences in social behavior and personality are also found between reflectives and impulsives. Impulsive children run around a room picking up toys, play with them for only a few minutes, and then dart off to the next plaything. In their play they are curious, exploratory, and distractible. However, in social relations they are more socially responsive than reflectives are. In contrast, reflective children consider with which toys they would prefer to play, will play with the same toy for longer periods of time, and are less dependent on the teacher.

In addition to the relation between impulsivity and reflectivity and social responses, variations in cognitive style are related to different types of pathology (S. Wientraub, as reported in Kagan & Kagan, 1970). Children who show overinhibited, internalized symptoms, such as feelings of guilt and self-criticism, fears, and phobias, tend to score more reflective on the Matching Familiar Figures Test. Boys who have been diagnosed as hyperactive, learning-disabled, or epileptic are more impulsive than children in nonclinical populations (Campbell, 1974). Preadolescent boys who externalize their conflicts and show aggressive, antisocial, uncontrolled delinquent behavior also score high on impulsivity.

Modification of Reflectivity-Impulsivity

The early appearance of differences in cognitive tempo and the correlation of reflectivity-impulsivity with measures assumed to be partially genetically or constitutionally based (such as heart-rate lability, activity level, and IQ) have led some investigators to conceive of cognitive style as a relatively unmodifiable attribute. However, this is not the case. Shifts in cognitive style have been induced or observed in both laboratory and naturalistic settings. In general it has been found easier to modify response time than number of errors, although both can be altered. Experimenters have found a variety of techniques to be partially successful in these studies. These include giving the child verbal descriptions of other response styles and direct instructions on appropriate response tactics, and reinforcing or modeling a different response style where a model may demonstrate to the impulsive how to respond slowly (Briggs, 1966; Debus, 1970; Kagan, Pearson, & Welch, 1966; Nelson, 1968; Barstis & Ford, 1977; Zelniker & Oppenheimer, 1976). Another effective technique involves demonstrations of scanning strategies, in which the impulsive child is shown how to check back and forth between the standard and each alternative on the Matching Familiar Figure 5 Test (Ridberg, Parke, & Hetherington, 1971), which is the strategy used by reflective children.

In the classroom even the presence of reflective or impulsive teachers can affect the cognitive style of pupils (Yando & Kagan, 1968). Children's response styles become more similar to those of their teachers, with the clearest effects occurring when impulsive boys are in a class with an experienced reflective teacher. Perhaps our impulsive, fidgety children with reading disabilities should be taught by careful, methodical, reflective teachers.

These studies demonstrate that although there may be a predisposition to respond in a reflective or impulsive manner, cognitive styles can be altered through experience and training.

Although, in general, problem-solving strategies and behaviors of impulsive children seem to be associated with more difficulties and learning problems in the school situation, greater playfulness, curiousity, and social responsiveness may be an advantage in some situations over the more constrained behavior of reflectives. The goal of training projects should perhaps not be to transform all children into reflectives, but to develop a little more planfulness in impulsives and a little more playfulness in reflectives (Wright & Vliestra, 1977).

Summary

In this chapter the cognitive processing approach to cognitive development was examined. The cognitive processing theorists focus on the processes involved in perceiving, attending to, discriminating, transforming, and recalling information. With increasing age children learn to attend to and process information in the environment that has functional value to them. They attend to more task-relevant aspects of the environment. In addition, as children grow older, they deploy their attention in a more adaptive planful manner and are able to change attentional stretegies as the demands of situations change over time.

Similar developmental changes are reflected in memory where older children are more effective than younger children in reconstructing information in ways to make it more memorable through such things as labeling and categorizing the information to be remembered. In addition, older children are more likely to use semantic integration of information, that is, to logically elaborate and integrate information.

With increasing maturity, individuals are more likely to use strategies such as rehearsal, imagery, and organization to facilitate remembering. In many cases younger children do not seem to spontaneously produce the kinds of responses or strategies which assist in memory, but can use them if they are introduced or taught by others. Younger children apparently have a production deficiency rather than a mediational deficiency.

The growing child becomes increasingly able to think about how people remember. The child becomes aware of the limitations of his or her own memory ability and of how attributes of a cognitive task, the person doing the learning, and cognitive strategies affect memory.

One of the most marked developmental changes in cognitive processes is in the growing ability to use sophisticated, complex, task-appropriate hypotheses or strategies in solving problems.

There are individual differences in the cognitive styles or approaches taken to processing cognitive information. One of the most extensively studied dimensions of cognitive style is reflectivity-impulsivity. Reflectivity-impulsivity is associated with a variety of intellectual, social, and personality factors. Attempts to modify cognitive style have been successful. However, it seems to be easier to modify response time than number of errors.

References

Anderson, D. R., & Leven, S. R. Young children's attention to Sesame Street. *Child Development*, 1976, **47,** 806–811.

Barstis, S., & Ford, L. Reflection-impulsivity, conservation, and the development of ability to control cognitive tempo. *Child Development*, 1977, **48,** 953–959.

Bransford, J. D., & Franks, J. J. The abstraction of linguistic ideas. *Cognitive Psychology*, 1971, **2,** 331–350.

Bray, N. W., Justice, E. M., Ferguson, R. P., & Simon, D. L. Developmental changes in the effects of instructions on production-deficient children. *Child Development*, 1977, **48,** 1019–1026.

Briggs, C. H. An experimental study of reflection-impulsivity in children. Unpublished doctoral dissertation, University of Minnesota, 1966.

Brown, A. L. The development of memory: Knowing, knowing about knowing, and knowing how to know. In H. W. Reese (Ed.), *Advances in child development and behavior* (Vol. 10). New York: Academic, 1975.

Bruner, J. S. On perceptual readiness. *Psychological Review*, 1957, **64,** 123–152.

Bruner, J. S. Introduction. In A. R. Luria, *The mind of a mnemonist*. New York: Basic Books, 1968.

Campbell, S. Cognitive styles and behavior problems of clinic boys. *Journal of Abnormal Child Psychology*, 1974, **2,** 307–312.

Debus, R. L. Effects of brief observation of model behavior on conceptual tempo of impulsive children. *Developmental Psychology*, 1970, **2,** 22–32.

Drake, D. M. Perceptual correlates of impulsive and reflective behavior. *Developmental Psychology*, 1970, **2,** 204–212.

Druker, J. F., & Hagen, J. W. Developmental trends in the processing of task-relevant and task-irrelevant information. *Child Development*, 1969, **40,** 371–382.

Ferguson, R. P., & Bray, N. W. Component processes of an overt rehearsal strategy in young children. *Journal of Experimental Child Psychology*, 1976, **21,** 490–506.

Flavell, J. H. Developmental studies of mediated memory. In H. W. Reese & L. P. Lipsitt (Eds.), *Advances in child development and behavior* (Vol. 5). New York: Academic, 1970.

Flavell, J. H. *Cognitive development*. Englewood Cliffs, N. J.: Prentice-Hall, 1977.

Flavell, J. H., & Wellman, H. M. Metamemory. In R. V. Kail & J. W. Hagen (Eds.), *Memory in cognitive development*. Hillsdale, N. J.: Lawrence Erlbaum, 1977.

Gholson, B., Levine, M., & Phillips, S. Hypotheses, strategies, and stereotypes in discrimination learning. *Journal of Experimental Child Psychology*, 1972, **13,** 423–446.

Gibson, E. J. *Principles of perceptual learning and development.* New York: Appleton-Century-Crofts, 1969.

Haber, R. N. Eidetic images. *Scientific American*, 1969, **220,** 36–44.

Hagen, J. W. The effect of distraction on selective attention. *Child Development*, 1967, **38,** 685–694.

Hale, G. A., & Taweel, S. S. Age differences in children's performance on measures of component selection and incidental learning. *Journal of Experimental Child Psychology*, 1974, **18,** 107–116.

House, B. J., & Zeaman, D. Miniature experiments in the discrimination learning of retardates. In L. P. Lipsitt & C. C. Spiker (Eds.), *Advances in child development and behavior* (Vol. 1). New York: Academic, 1963.

Kagan, J., & Kagan, N. Individual variation in cognitive processes. In P. Mussen (Ed.), *Carmichael's manual of child psychology*. New York: Wiley, 1970, pp. 1273–1365.

Kagan, J., Pearson, L., & Welch, L. Modifiability of an impulsive tempo. *Journal of Educational Psychology*, 1966, **57,** 359–365.

Kagan, J., Rosman, B. L., Day, D., Albert, J., & Phillips, W., Information processing in the child: Significance of analytic and reflective attitudes. *Psychological Monographs*, 1964 (Whole No. 578).

Kobasigawa, H. Utilization of retrieval cues by children in recall. *Child Development*, 1974, **45,** 127–134.

Kreutzer, M. A., Leonard, C., & Flavell, J. H. An interview study of children's knowledge about memory. *Monographs of the Society for Research in Child Development*, 1975, **40** (1, Serial No. 159).

Levine, M. Hypothesis behavior by humans during discrimination learning. *Journal of Experimental Psychology*, 1966, **71,** 331–338.

Levine, M. The development of hypothesis testing. In R. M. Liebert, R. W. Poulos, & C. D. Strauss, *Developmental psychology*. Englewood Cliffs, N.J.: Prentice-Hall, 1974.

Luria, A. R. *The mind of a mnemonist*. New York: Basic Books, 1968.

Maccoby, E. E. Selective auditory attention in children. In L. P. Lipsett & C. C. Spiker (Eds.), *Advances in child development and behavior* (Vol. 3). New York: Academic, 1967, pp. 99–125.

Maccoby, E. E. The development of stimulus selection. In John P. Hill (Ed.), *Minnesota symposia on child psychology* (Vol. 3). Minneapolis: University of Minnesota Press, 1969, pp. 68–96.

Markman, E. Factors affecting the young child's ability to monitor his memory. Unpublished doctoral dissertation, University of Pennsylvania, 1973.

McClusky, K. A., & Wright, J. C. Reflection-impulsivity and age as determinants of visual scanning strategy and preschool activities. Paper presented at the meeting of the Society for Research in Child Development, Denver, April 1975.

Messer, S. Reflection-impulsivity: Stability and school failure. *Journal of Educational Psychology*, 1970, **61,** 487–490.

Moely, B. E., & Jeffrey, W. E. The effect of organizational training on children's free recall of category items. *Child Development*, 1974, **45,** 135–143.

Moely, B. E., Olson, F. A., Hawles, T. G., & Flavell, J. H. Production deficiency in young children's clustered recall. *Developmental Psychology*, 1969, **1,** 26–34.

Moynahan, E. D. The development of knowledge concerning the effect of categorization upon free recall. *Child Development*, 1973, **44,** 238–246.

Neimark, E. D. Intellectual development during adolescence. In F. Horowitz (Ed.), *Review of research in child development* (Vol. 5). 1974.

Neimark, E. A., Slotnick, N. S., & Ulrich, T. Development of memorization strategies. *Development Psychology*, 1971, **5,** 427–432.

Nelson, T. F. The effects of training in attention deployment on observing behavior in reflective and impulsive children. Unpublished doctoral dissertation, University of Minnesota, 1968.

Ornstein, P. A., Naus, N. J., & Liberty, C. Rehearsal and organizational processes in children's memory. *Child Development*, 1975, **46,** 818–830.

Ornstein, P. A., Naus, N. J., & Stone, B. P. Rehearsal training and development differences in memory. *Developmental Psychology*, 1977, **13,** 15–24.

Paris, S. G., & Lindauer, B. K. Constructive processes in children's comprehension and memory. In R. V. Kail & J. W. Hagen (Eds.), *Memory in cognitive development*. Hillsdale, N.J.: Lawrence Erlbaum, 1977.

Paris, S. G., & Mahoney, G. J. Cognitive integration in children's memory for sentences and pictures. *Child Development*, 1974, **45,** 633–642.

Pascual-Leone, J. *Cognitive development and cognitive style.* Lexington, Mass: Heath, 1973.

Phillips, S., & Levine, M. Probing for hypotheses with adults and children: Blank trials and introtacts. *Journal of Experimental Psychology: General*, 1975, **104,** 327–354.

Pick, A. D., Christy, M. D., & Frankel, G. W. A developmental study of visual selective attention. *Journal of Experimental Child Psychology*, 1972, **14,** 165–175.

Pick, A. D., & Frankel, G. W. A developmental study of strategies of visual selectivity. *Child Development*, 1974, **45,** 1162–1165.

Pick, A. D., Frankel, D. G., & Hess, V. L. Children's attention: The development of selectivity. In E. M. Hetherington (Ed.), *Review of child development research* (Vol. 5). Chicago: University of Chicago Press, 1975.

Ridberg, E., Parke, R., & Hetherington, E. M. Modification of impulsive and reflective cognitive styles through observation of film mediated models. *Developmental Psychology*, 1971, **5,** 369–377.

Rossi, S., and Wittrock, M. C. Developmental shifts in verbal recall between mental ages two and five. *Child Development*, 1971, **42,** 333–338.

Salapatek, P., & Kessen, W. Visual scanning of triangles of the human newborn. *Journal of Experimental Child Psychology*, 1966, **3,** 155–167.

Siegelman, E. Observing behavior in impulsive and reflective children. Unpublished doctoral dissertation, University of Minnesota, 1966.

Stevenson, H. W. *Children's learning.* New York: Appleton-Century-Crofts, 1972.

Suchman, R. G. Cultural differences in children's color and form preferences. *Journal of Social Psychology*, 1966, **70,** 3–10.

Suchman, R. G., & Trabasso, T. Stimulus preference and cue function in young children's concept attainment. *Journal of Experimental Child Psychology*, 1966, **3,** 188–198.

Tighe, L. S., & Tighe, T. J. Facilitation of transposition and reversal learning in children by prior perceptual training. *Journal of Experimental Child Psychology*, 1969, **8,** 366–374.

Vernon, M. D. The functions of schemata in perceiving. *Psychological Review*, 1955, **62,** 180–192.

Vurpillot, E. The development of scanning strategies and their relation to visual differentiation. *Journal of Experimental Child Psychology*, 1968, **6,** 632–650.

Wolff, P., & Levin, J. R. The role of overt activity in children's imagery production. *Child Development*, 1972, **43,** 537–548.

Wright, J. C., & Vliestra, A. G. Reflection-impulsivity and information-processing from 3 to 9 years of age. In M. J. Fine (Ed.), *Principles and techniques of intervention with hyperactive children.* Springfield, Ill.: Charles C Thomas, 1977.

Yando, R. M., & Kagan, J. The effect of teacher tempo on the child. *Child Development*, 1968, **39,** 27–34.

Zelniker, T., & Jeffrey, W. Reflective and impulsive children: Strategies of information processing underlying differences in problem solving. *Monograph of the Society for Research in Child Development*, 1976, **41,** 1–59.

Zelniker, T., & Oppenheimer, L. Effect of different training methods on perceptual learning in impulsive children. *Child Development*, 1976, **47,** 492–497.

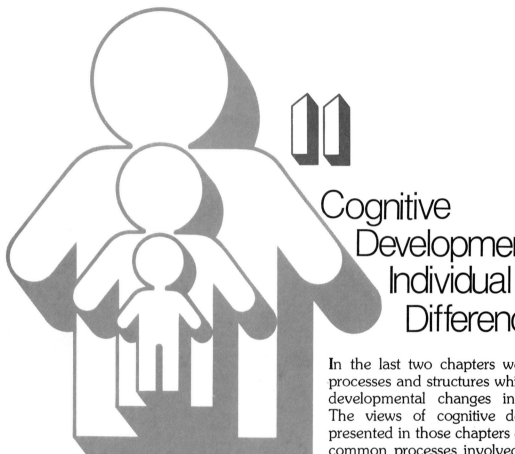

Cognitive Development: Individual Differences

In the last two chapters we discussed processes and structures which underlie developmental changes in cognition. The views of cognitive development presented in those chapters emphasized common processes involved in the development of cognition and how these processes change with age. In this chapter we will take a very different perspective. We will examine individual differences in intellectual performance, how these differences can be measured, what contributes to these differences, and what these individual differences predict about performance in other situations. The two approaches to cognition have sometimes been labeled the "process" versus the "product" approach. The most common approach to assessing cognitive products is by administering a standardized intelligence test which yields a score, whereby an individual's performance can be compared to the performance of others. This score often takes the form of an *intelligence quotient*, or IQ.

Many of the students reading this book probably had never heard of cognitive schemata or information-processing strategies until they read the last two chapters. However, all will have heard of the IQ, or intelligence quotient. Many will confess their own IQ at the slightest provocation, and many who do not know their IQ often wish they did. IQ is a term which is widely used and often misconstrued by a great many people. It is frequently regarded as some kind of innate, fixed endowment, like a baritone voice, big ears, or "your father's family's nose." It sometimes comes as a shock to find that IQs vary over age, can be modified by experience, and depend to some extent on which test is being administered and under what circumstances.

Since there are many definitions and theories of intelligence, it is not surprising that there are a wide variety of intelligence tests constructed in different ways and with different goals.

Definitions of Intelligence

Since few topics in psychology have generated a more voluminous literature than that of intelligence, it seems strange that there is no widely accepted definition of intelligence. It is apparent that conceptions of the nature of intelligence will influence views of the methods most appropriate for its assessment, its stability or modifiability, and its usefulness in predicting other behaviors.

Alternative views of intelligence have centered on three questions. First, is intelligence a unitary, generalized function, or is it composed of a group of relatively separate abilities? If it is a generalized function, an intelligent child should perform well across a variety of intellectual tasks; if it is composed of independent factors, an individual could excel on some cognitive tasks and perform poorly on others. Second, how modifiable is intelligence? Is its development determined primarily by genetic factors, or is it more dependent upon learning experiences in environments with varying degrees of stimulation or deprivation? Finally, is intelligence an underlying construct, trait, ability, or capacity which can never be directly assessed, or should it be defined only in terms of performance on specific cognitive tests? If the latter position is accepted, the most appropriate definition of a child's intelligence might be his or her score on a particular intelligence test under particular circumstances.

Differing positions on these issues are reflected in the frequently cited definitions of intelligence which follow: Intelligence is "innate, general cognitive ability" (Burt, 1955, p. 162). Intelligence is "the aggregate or global capacity of the individual to act purposefully, to think rationally and to deal effectively with his environment" (Wechsler, 1958, p. 7). "Manifest intelligence is nothing more than an accumulation of learned facts and skills . . . innate intellectual potential consists of tendencies to engage in activities conducive to learning, rather than inherited capacities as such" (Hayes, 1962, p. 337). Some psychologists have even gone to the empirical extreme and defined intelligence as being what intelligence tests test. Thus, it is obvious that the experts are by no means in agreement concerning the definition of intelligence; and as we are about to learn, the uses and interpretations of scores on intelligence tests have also been subject to controversy.

Let us now examine some alternative models of intelligence and their implications for the construction of intelligence tests.

Factor-Analytic Models of Intelligence

A technique called factor analysis has been used to answer questions about the organization of intelligence. One of the main questions factor analysis attempts to answer is whether intelligence is unitary or whether different kinds of intellectual abilities might vary within the same individual. Can people accurately be described in general terms as very intelligent or below average? Or is it more accurate to describe people in terms of specific intellectual skills, for example, "He's very articulate and verbally fluent, but is a bit of a dolt at arithmetic."

Factor analysis is a statistical procedure which groups test items which are highly related to each other and relatively independent from other clusters of items. These clusters of intercorrelated items are regarded as intellectual factors. It would be expected that an individual who does well on one item within a cluster would be likely to do well on other items within the same cluster, whereas his performance on this item would be less likely to predict his performance on items in other clusters. If there was a verbal reasoning cluster and someone had performed well on one of the items within the cluster, for example, explaining the meaning of a proverb (such as "A bird in the hand is worth two in the bush"), this would probably relate more closely to other verbal reasoning items, such as explaining the similarity between an eye and an ear, than it would to items involving arthmetical computations.

The earliest attempt at defining intellectual factors through factor analysis was performed by Charles Spearman (1927), who concluded that intelligence comprises a "g," or general, factor and a number of "s," or specific, factors. He regarded g as general mental energy or ability which would be involved in all cognitive tasks, and s factors as factors unique to a particular task. Thus someone with a high g would be expected to do well on all intellectual tasks. Variations in performance among tasks would be attributable to differential amounts of s.

Later Thurstone (1938, 1947) analyzed a large number of tests and identified seven factors of primary mental abilities: perceptual speed, numerical ability, word fluency, verbal comprehension, space visualization, associative memory, and reasoning. He went on to construct seven tests, each of which would measure one of his seven independent primary mental abilities. However after all his careful efforts in attempting to derive pure measures of his seven mental abilities, he found scores on these abilities tended to be correlated. Spearman's general mental ability factor appeared to be emerging again, in addition to the specific primary abilities.

One of the most complex contemporary factor-analytic models of intelligence is that developed by Guilford (1966), which proposes that intelligence is composed of 120 factors classified in terms of subdivisions of three major dimensions: operations, products, and contents. The subclassifications of these three basic dimensions are presented in Figure 11-1.

Intellectual activities can be classified in terms of the interaction of four types of contents or material involved in a task, with five types of processes or operations performed to respond to the problem, resulting in six possible different kinds of cognitive products. For example, a frequently used item on intelligence tests is recall of a series of digits said aloud by an examiner. In Guilford's terms the task would require the operation of "memory" and the production of numbers which are "units" having "symbolic" content. Since this is such a complicated model of intelligence, the student will not be burdened with all of the details of the subcategories within the three dimensions. Guilford has been attempting to systematically build tests to tap each of the 120 cells, but this monumental task is not yet completed. At this point he has items to assess about 75 of the 120 cells. Each individual's intelligence would be composed of a unique combination of these separate intellectual abilities.

Guilford, like other factor analysts, has focused mainly on the structure of intelligence rather than on its developmental aspects or modifiability. However, he does suggest that although even the intellect of infants must be conceived of in terms of complex factors rather than general intellectual ability, the child is able to deal with different kinds of information and experiences at different ages.

Much of the initial optimism about the usefulness of factor analysis as an instrument to further the understanding of intelligence has dissipated. Not only do different psychologists disagree on the number of factors; they even disagree on the names of the factors of intelligence. The type of factor analysis used, the

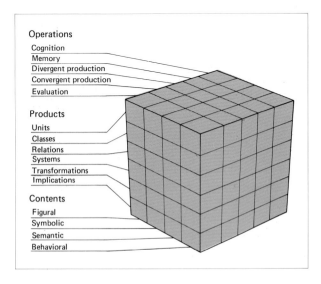

Operations
Cognition
Memory
Divergent production
Convergent production
Evaluation

Products
Units
Classes
Relations
Systems
Transformations
Implications

Contents
Figural
Symbolic
Semantic
Behavioral

FIGURE 11-1   Guilford's structure of intellect. *(From Guilford, 1966.)*

selection of items serving as the initial pool for analysis, the characteristics of the subjects answering the items, and the subjectivity in the interpretation and naming of the factors lead to wide variations in results. Most of the factors obtained, even in recent factor-analytic studies, such as those of Guilford, tend to be dependent and show some degree of correlation with each other. This has led many psychologists (Humphreys, 1962; McNemar, 1964; Vernon, 1965) to question both the conceptual and practical utility of such a fractionated approach to the study of intelligence. After a careful analysis of the most important of such studies, McNemar states, "The structure of intellect that requires 120 factors may very well lead the British, and some of the rest of us, to regard our fractionalization and fragmentation of ability, into more and more factors of less and less importance, as indicative of scatterbrainedness" (McNemar, 1964, p. 872). He concludes that the notion of general intelligence still has a rightful and practical place in psychology.

From an applied as well as theoretical point of view the notion of general intelligence has never been discarded. Intelligence tests based on the concept of global intelligence which yield a single IQ score continue to be widely used by practicing psychologists in clinical, academic, and industrial settings.

Some theory of mental organization acknowledging both general intelligence and some differentiated clusters of mental abilities would seem to most adequately fit current evidence about cognitive development. Mental abilities do tend to be correlated. Studies of exceptionally bright children (Terman, 1925) show that these children excel in a wide variety of cognitive tasks; but although their performance is above average on most tasks, they still score higher in some areas than in others.

Studies of changes in intellectual performance with age show that although general ability is marked in the preadolescent years, more specialized talents appear with increasing age (Garrett, 1946; Dye & Very, 1968). This evolving cognitive differentiation could of course be attributed to varied training and experience.

The Assessment of Intelligence

The strategies used in constructing intelligence tests will depend to some extent on the model of intelligence held by the test constructor. Psychologists who believe in a factor of general intellectual ability may select items which intercorrelate with each other. Others who believe in relatively independent factors of intellectual abilities may select items to measure these postulated abilities and would not expect these items to be interrelated. Guilford in refining his tests carefully selected items presumed to measure his dimensions of intellectual abilities. He selected items to fit the cells in his theoretical model of intellectual ability.

In spite of the fact that different views of intelligence influence the selection of test items, certain common goals or principles are utilized in the construction of all intelligence tests.

Norm-Referenced Assessment and Standardization

The performance of an individual on an intelligence test is always described in terms of the individual's position relative to the performance of other members in a group. The individual may be described as being above average, average, or below average in relation to his or her comparison group. Establishing norms is accomplished through administering the test items to groups having particular characteristics. One of the important issues in establishing norms is what the critical similarities between the subject and the members of the comparison group should be. Age is always one of the critical factors considered in setting up norms for children. The actual performance on the test items generally improves throughout childhood. When a child is 10, she is usually able to answer more items than when she was 6. However, it is the maintenance of her position relative to other children her age that is regarded as significant in evaluating her intellectual development. Although most psychometricians would agree that age should be considered in establishing norms, there is less consensus on whether comparison groups should be further broken down on the basis of factors such as education, socioeconomic class, ethnic group, and sex. It is always important to consider how similar the attributes and experiences of the individual being tested are to the normative group in evaluating test performance. It would be inappropriate to use the same set of norms in evaluating the performance of children raised in an isolated New Guinea tribe with no access to formal schooling as is used in evaluating the performance of middle-class American children. Less extreme cultural variations such as those found within American children may also make application of the same norms to different subcultural groups inappropriate.

It is also important to consider the similarity in the administration of the test from one test session to another. For this reason the stimuli, instructions, and scoring of test items are carefully standardized so that the test procedures will be identical when they are administered by different examiners. We will see later that some people will argue that even if we carefully control test administration, factors such as the child's familiarity with the test setting and test administrator and the child's ease in the situation may affect his or her performance.

Test Validity

The *validity* of a test refers to whether it measures what it claims to measure. In the case of an intelligence test, does it measure problem-solving skills, the ability to learn, or whatever other definition of intelligence the test constructor might ascribe to? In evaluating the validity of a test, performance on the test is usually correlated with a criterion measure or measures which are assumed to reflect the attribute being assessed. Achievement test scores, grades in school, teacher's ratings of cognitive ability, and performance on other intelligence tests are the most frequently used criteria in establishing the validity of intelligence tests. It is apparent that a very restricted range of problem-solving and adaptive skills is being sampled with such criteria and that a limited view of what constitutes intelligent behavior is held by psychometricians using such criteria. That is probably why intelligence tests are much more successful in predicting school performance than in predicting adaptive ability in social situations or performance in some skilled occupations. Even within school performance there is more relation between intelligence test scores and history, mathematical problem solving, and reading comprehension than with drama, art, or music.

Test Reliability

Reliability refers to the consistency or stability of a test. If an individual's test scores fluctuate capriciously, they are not very useful measures of intellectual functioning. The most frequently used method of assessing test reliability is to correlate the scores of the same individuals on repeated administrations of the test. However, sometimes the individual's performance on alternative forms of the same test is correlated, or internal consistency within a single administration may be assessed by correlating scores on the odd-numbered items with those on the even-numbered items. The most widely used intelligence tests are fairly reliable when internal consistency measures are used or when repeated test intervals are not too widely spaced.

Intellectual Performance versus Intellectual Capacity

It should be kept in mind that what is measured on an intelligence test is intellectual performance, not intellectual ability. Although intellectual capacity and performance may be correlated, intellectual capacity always remains only an inference on the basis of the child's responses to test items. It cannot be directly measured. Even the type of intellectual performance measured on any given test is limited by the criteria used to select items and validate the test. In addition, situational, emotional, and experiential factors will influence the child's performance in any given test situation. Let us move on now and look at how some of these factors were handled in the development of the most frequently used intelligence scales for children.

Intelligence Tests

In 1904 the administrators in the overcrowded Paris school system presented Alfred Binet and Theophile Simon with the challenging task of devising a means of identifying children who were mentally retarded and unable to learn in traditional classroom settings and who should be given the opportunity for special education. Binet and Simon were remarkably successful in developing a measure to serve their original goal of an academic screening device. It is a tribute to these testing pioneers that the modern version of the Binet-Simon intelligence test remains one of the best predictors of academic success. Their approach to their task was particularly notable in three ways: they took an empirical approach to item selection; they attempted to measure higher mental processes rather than simple functions; and they were sensitive to the chronology of intelligence, that is, to the fact that older children are able to solve a greater number of and more complex problems than are younger children.

Binet and Simon were critical of earlier psychologists who had attempted to assess intelligence through simple sensory or motor responses which had failed to correlate with school achievement or with each other. They argued that in order to differentiate between individuals, higher mental functions involving judgment, comprehension, and reasoning must be examined. They proceeded to develop an array of intellectual tasks varying in difficulty. They included such things as the ability to recognize logical absurdities, memory for digits, attentional tests, and also some skills which were taught in school such as counting coins, naming the days of the week, and recalling details of a story after reading it. To some extent, a sample of academic achievement was being used to predict future achievement in school settings. It should be noted that Binet and Simon did not emphasize a general factor of intellectual ability, although they did refer to the "faculty of reasoning" as being a pervasive factor which is the basis of what most people mean by intelligence. They were selecting items to sample cognitive abilities they thought might be unrelated. However, the fact that their tests yielded a single score led many people to view this as support for a unitary model of intelligence. In refining their tests they administered large numbers of items to children who had been labeled as having bright or dull characteristics by their teachers and retained items which discriminated between these children.

In later revisions of their test, they used the criterion that if items were to be included in their test, they must be effective in sorting children by their ages. Items were selected to reflect the competence of children at different age levels. Items which were passed by about 60 percent of 6-year-olds and were passed by fewer 5-year-olds and significantly more 7-year-olds were assumed to reflect the performance of the average 6-year-old.

Binet originated the concept of *mental age*. Mental age is based on the number of items the child gets correct relative to the number of items the average child of various chronological ages gets correct. Thus, if a 6-year-old child has a mental age of 7, he or she is performing as well as the average child whose actual chronological age is 7. Later, William Stern, a German psychologist, conceived of the intelligence quotient, which is a ratio of the child's mental age (MA) divided by his chronological age (CA) and multiplied by 100.

$$IQ = \frac{MA}{CA} \times 100$$

It can be seen that if a child had an IQ of 100, his performance would be average for a child of his age. As the IQ rises above 100, his performance is increasingly superior to other children his age; as it drops below 100, he is doing relatively less well than his peers.

Subsequent revisions of the Binet-Simon scale and many other contemporary intelligence tests are designed to include items which are less directly influenced by academic experience. It is clear that items such as vocabulary items involving definitions of words or mathematical problem solving are heavily weighted by different experiences. However, the extent to which learning and education affect form-board tasks, building designs out of blocks, or assembling objects which have been broken up like a jigsaw puzzle is less clear. These last items are often referred to as performance items. Since language and mathemat-

A child identifies parts of the body in one section of a standardized intelligence test. (Suzanne Szasz)

ics are heavily culturally and educationally influenced, much effort has been put into attempting to design tests which do not solely emphasize skills in these areas.

In contrast to the Binet tests, a series of intelligence tests was developed by David Wechsler (Wechsler, 1952, 1958) which puts less emphasis on verbal items. In fact, the Wechsler scales yield a separate verbal and performance IQ as well as a full-scale IQ based on the combination of these two scores. The student can look at the type of items included under the verbal and performance scales presented in Table 11-1 and see that the performance items are less likely to be influenced by formal education or cultural factors.

Wechsler does not use mental age to estimate intelligence; rather he uses a score called a deviation IQ, which is determined by the relation of a person's score to the distribution curve of scores for people her age. The deviation score indicates how far above or below the mean the individual's score lies relative to children of the same age in the standardization group. In the most recent revision of the Binet scale, a shift to the use of deviation scores has also occurred.

Many other types of intelligence tests have been designed since Binet and Simon's ingenious first scale and which differ from both the Binet and the Wechsler scales. Tests for newborns, such as the Brazelton Neonatal Assessment Scale, or for older infants, such as the Bayley Scales of Infant Development,

TABLE 11-1   THE WECHSLER INTELLIGENCE SCALE FOR CHILDREN*

Verbal scale	Performance scale
1. General information: A series of questions involving a sample of information which most children will have been exposed to (for example, Where does the sun rise? How many weeks are there in a year?)	1. Picture completion: The child is asked which part is missing in each picture in a series of twelve pictures of common objects (for example, a car with a wheel missing, a rabbit with an ear missing)
2. General comprehension: Items in which the child must explain why certain practices are desirable or what course of action is preferred under certain circumstances (for example, Why should people not waste fuel? What is the thing to do if you lose a friend's toy?)	2. Picture arrangement: A series of sets of pictures in which the pictures will tell a story if they are arranged in the correct order. These are rather like wordless comic-strip pictures.
3. Arithmetic: A series of arithmetic questions ranging from easy ones involving simple counting to more difficult ones involving mental computations and reasoning.	3. Block design: The child receives a set of small blocks having some white, some red, and some half-red and half-white sides. She is shown a series of red and white designs which she must reproduce with the blocks.
4. Similarities: The child is asked to tell in what way a series of paired words are alike. (for example, In what way are a shoe and a slipper alike? In what way are a boat and a car alike?)	4. Object assembly: The child must assemble jigsawlike parts of common objects into the whole puzzle (for example, a chair, a foot)
5. Vocabulary: A series of increasingly difficult words are presented and the child is asked what each word means.	5. Coding: A task in which symbols are to be matched with numbers on the basis of a code given to the child.
6. Digit span: A series of numbers of increasing length are presented orally and the child is asked to repeat them either in the same order or in a reverse order.	6. Mazes: The child must trace the correct route from a starting point to home on a series of mazes.

*The examples given are similar, but not identical, to items on the Wechsler Intelligence Scale for Children.

which rely largely on sensorimotor skills, have been developed (St. Clair, 1978). In addition, scales based on Piagetian constructs have been devised. Tests which can be administered in groups rather than individually also often are used. However, performance on all these tests is influenced to varying degrees by cultural factors. These cultural influences are less marked with children under 1 year of age (Golden & Birns, 1976). At the present time IQ is best conceived of as a measure representing the interaction of a multitude of factors including those of innate capacity and experience.

Stability of IQ

If it is assumed that intelligence tests largely measure a capacity to learn, it might be expected that the IQ would remain stable over time. Most of the information on the consistency of performance on intelligence tests over age has been obtained from longitudinal studies in which the same children were repeatedly tested over long periods of time. In some cases these multiple testings have extended from the first month of life until adulthood.

Investigators who have collected and analyzed the results of a large number of these longitudinal studies conclude that infant intelligence tests in the first year of life do not accurately predict IQ performance later in childhood although they may be useful in identifying neuromotor abnormalities or extreme intellectual deficits (Honzik, 1976; Lewis, 1976, McCall, Hogarty, & Hurlburt, 1972). The types of tasks used in the first year of life are largely sensorimotor tasks involving such things as reaching and grasping an object or visually following a moving object. These tasks differ considerably from the type of task used with older children which frequently tap problem-solving ability and verbal skills. After about 18 months when items of the latter type are included on intelligence tests, the prediction of later test performance from early IQ scores improves. In general it has been found that the shorter the period is between repeated test sessions and the older the child is at the time of the initial testing, the more stable are the IQ scores. This is clearly illustrated in Figure 11-2, in which the correlations between infant and preschool test scores and IQ at age 8 derived from three different studies are presented. It can be seen that although different infant tests

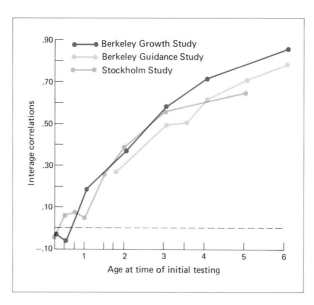

FIGURE 11-2 Prediction of IQs on the Stanford-Binet at 8 years from earlier scores on the Berkeley Growth Study and the Berkeley Guidance Study and from earlier scores on the Brunet-Lezine Scale in the Stockholm Study. *(From Honzik, 1976.)*

were used in the Stockholm studies and in the two Berkeley studies, none of the studies were able to effectively predict IQ at age 8 from tests in the first few years of life. However, as the child gets older and the interval between the earlier test and the 8-year-old test is shorter, prediction becomes very efficient.

Although IQ tests from the middle childhood years onward are reasonably good predictors of adult intelligence, there is still considerable variability in the IQs of individual children. An investigation of the stability of test IQs of 140 children in the longitudinal Fels Institute study was summarized as follows:

Normal home-reared middle-class children change in IQ performance during childhood, some a substantial amount. In the present sample, the average individual's range of IQ between 2½ and 17 years of age was 28.5 IQ points, one of every three children displayed a progressive change of more than 30 points, and one in seven shifted more than 40 points. Rare individuals may alter their performance as much as 74 points. High-IQ children are likely to show greater amounts of change than low-IQ children. (McCall, Appelbaum, & Hogarty, 1973, p. 70).

The rate of mental growth varies among different children. Just as different children may experience a spurt or a plateau in physical growth at different ages, the ages at which sudden accelerations or leveling in cognitive development occur vary among children. These variations in rate of growth will obviously affect the reliability of IQ scores. When changes in IQ over age are examined, it is found that the changes are most likely to occur at ages 6 and 10. It has been proposed that the 6-year change may be associated with a shift to higher levels of abstract reasoning and conceptual process that Piaget and other investigators have discussed. The reason for the variability at age 10 is less clear.

Some evidence suggests that the intelligence of girls is more stable and predictable from infancy than that of boys, and that the developmental course of cognition varies for the two sexes. Vocalization and speech competence in the first two years of life are predictive of later intellectual performance for girls but not for boys (Cameron, Livson, & Bayley, 1967; McCall, Hogarty, & Hurlburt, 1972; Moore, 1967). In contrast, a factor of social orientation and active play in the first year of life seems to relate inversely to later childhood intellectual and verbal skills for boys but not for girls. Thus, early verbal behavior is associated with later cognitive development in girls, and low sociability and low activity in infant boys are related to subsequent intellectual development in boys. However, by age 2½ intensely active behavior, which may be a precursor of distractibility, is predictive of poor intellectual performance in the school years not only for boys, but for girls as well (Halverson & Waldrop, 1976).

Boys have shown larger gains in IQ with age, whereas girls more often show decreases in IQ (Sontag, Baker, & Nelsen, 1958). This is even present in young adulthood when male scores on the verbal scale of the adult Wechsler increase, in contrast to females, who drop on performance scores and only remain stable on verbal scores between the ages of 26 and 36 years (Bayley, 1970).

The correlates of IQ growth for the two sexes show some similarities and a few marked differences. Children of both sexes who show marked IQ gains between ages 3 and 12 are described as independent, problem-solving, self-initiating, and academically competitive (Sontag, Baker, & Nelsen, 1958). IQ gains after 18 years seem to be related to introversion and a detachment and distancing in interpersonal relations (Honzik & MacFarlane, 1970). Boys who show IQ growth tend to be better adjusted and happier than those whose IQs decrease; however, IQ gains in girls are associated with poorer social adjustment and unhappiness (Haan, 1963). It is interesting that a more masculine orientation and interests are associated with IQ growth for both boys and girls (Rees & Palmer, 1970). Perhaps independence, competitiveness, persistence, and self-confidence which are associated with IQ gains are regarded as more appropriate for males in our culture. It may be only the girl who resists social pressure to accept the stereotyped passive feminine role who develops a strong motivation toward coping with intellectual problems. Perhaps as intellectual and professional achievement becomes more acceptable for females, these relationships will change.

Correlates of Intellectual Performance

Genetic and Constitutional Factors

The role of genetic factors in intellectual development is clearly supported by the studies reported in Chapter 2 on the greater similarity of IQs of monozygotic than dizygotic twins, and in studies involving comparisons between children raised by natural parents or by foster-parents. Even the most rabid environmentalist would not deny that heredity has some influence on cognitive development. The question is how these genetic factors are manifested in intellectual performance and what factors interact with and modify the effects of genetic and constitutional predispositions.

There is evidence that some intellectual abilities are more influenced by experience than are others, and that there may be individual differences in vulnerability to environmental influences. Bayley speculates that genetically determined nonintellective behaviors associated with temperamental or personality factors may shape the expression of inherited intellectual capacities. Thus, characteristics such as social orientation, thresholds of physiological arousal, activity, fearfulness, and attention span may retard or enhance cognitive development or performance. Support for the relationship between such temperamental characteristics, which are probably genetically based, and mental development was obtained in a recent longitudinal study in which neonatal physiological activity was compared with differences in intellectual and personality measures at age $2^{1}/_{2}$ (Bell, Weller, & Waldrop, 1971). Infants who were categorized as "low-intensity" neonates because they showed low respiration rates, low tactile sensitivity, and little response to interrupted sucking were described at $2^{1}/_{2}$ years as being advanced in speech development, manipulative skills, geographic orientation, and modeling of adults. These associations were more marked for boys than for girls.

In addition to the influence of these genetically based influences on intellectual performance, physiological effects of such things as conditions of pregnancy and birth, nutrition, drugs, disease, and physical injury shape the cognitive skills of the child.

Environmental Improverishment and Stimulation

It has been stated that

Trying to predict what a person's IQ will be at 20 on the bases of his IQ at age one or two is like trying to predict how heavy a two-week-old calf will be when he is a two-year-old without knowing whether he will be reared in a dry pasture, in an irrigated pasture or in a feed lot. (Hunt, 1972, p. 41)

It is apparent that the quality, amount, and patterning of stimulation received by children in different environments vary greatly. One of the problems in studying such environmental variations is that of trying to specify which attributes of the environment are the salient ones affecting cognitive perform- ance. It is easier to identify groups of children who do not perform well on standardized tests of intelligence or achievement than it is to report what it is about their culture, homes, education, or communities which result in these deficits.

Some of the most extensively investigated groups of children who have been found to show deviations in cognitive performance are children living in isolated communities, those of low socioeconomic class, and minority-group children.

Social Isolation and Cognitive Development Many studies have dealt with the intelligence test performance of children living in isolated conditions, which are frequently associated with both educational and economic deprivation. An increasing intellectual deficit is also found among rural children and children living under isolated conditions. Several studies have been done on isolated mountain children in the United States. The IQs of children living in lonely hollows of the Blue Ridge Mountains of Virginia were significantly lower than those of children in nearby villages, and the IQ scores of the isolated children decreased with age (Sherman & Key, 1932). This might be attributable to selective migration; the brighter individuals may leave to seek out a more exciting environment. However, a recent longitudinal study with repeated measures of the same child permits us to see if IQ in the same children is actually declining with age (Kennedy, VanDeRiet, & White, 1963; Kennedy, 1969). Eighteen hundred black children in five Southeastern states were tested. A subgroup of the children was retested five years later. Again the result was that the older the rural child was, the lower was his or her IQ. And again it was found that community size was correlated with IQ. The mean IQ for the children in metropolitan areas was 83.96, in urban areas 79.37, and in rural areas 78.70. Although these residential trends were present, the most marked effect on IQ was one associated with socioeconomic level. The lower the socioeconomic level, the lower the IQ.

It may be that different environments stimulate and facilitate the develop-

(a)

(b)

Children living in iso-
lated rural environments
often do not perform as
well on intelligence tests
as do urban children.
(Photo (a) Jean Pierre,
Laffont/Sygma; photo (b)
Robert Perren, Photo
Researchers, Inc.)

ment of different cognitive abilities and that standard intelligence tests do not measure a wide enough array of these abilities. One study showed that children living in remote Newfoundland outpost communities had highly developed motor and perceptual abilities which might be considered adaptive in that setting, whereas their verbal and reasoning skills which might be less necessary for survival were below average (Burnett, Beach, & Sullivan, 1963).

The Pulawat islanders, who live a primitive, isolated, seafaring existence in a society with little technology or formal education, have developed an amazing navigational system. This system, which reveals an understanding of navigational rules and the relationship between winds, tides, currents, and direction, permits the islanders to navigate over long distances out of the sight of land. It seems probable that these remarkable navigators would not perform well on a standard test of intelligence or even on one of the frequently used Piagetian tasks of formal operations, although on problems which are culturally relevant they are clearly demonstrating very advanced deductive reasoning. On navigational tasks they have certainly attained the stage of formal operations. It has been argued that such observations show the importance of analyzing intellectual performance within the naturalistic, cultural context in which they occur (Gladwin, 1970). This has been advanced as an important issue not only in cross-cultural studies and studies of isolated communities but also in studies of social class, race, and ethnicity in the United States.

Social Class, Race, and Cognitive Development Differences in performance on standardized intelligence tests among children from various ethnic and racial groups and social classes have been frequently noted (Dreger & Miller, 1960, 1968; Jensen, 1969; Kennedy, VanDeReit, & White, 1963; Kennedy, 1969; Shuey, 1966). Low socioeconomic class children score 10 to 15 IQ points below middle-class children, and black children score on the average 15 to 20 IQ points below white children. These differences are present by first grade, and are sustained throughout the school years (Kennedy, 1969). A similar 20 percent deficit on achievement tests such as the California Reading and Arithmetic Test appears in the early school years and increases with age in blacks (Osborne, 1960). It has been found that in poor environmental circumstances, such as those in the rural south, deficits on both verbal and performance IQ in blacks increase with age from 5 to 18 years (Jensen, 1977). However, in better environmental circumstances, such as in California, a deficit is found for verbal but not performance IQ, and this verbal difference between blacks and whites increases with age.

In many studies the effects of race and social class have not been clearly separated, since in our country a disproportionate number of blacks are found in the lower classes. However, when these factors are controlled, a consistent finding emerges that social-class differences are found on cognitive measures that involve language as early as the first year of life, and that starting around 2 years of age these measures are highly correlated with performance on standardized intelligence tests (Golden & Birns, 1976).

Some investigators have argued that a more fruitful approach to racial and

Children with different ethnic backgrounds show different profiles of mental abilities. (Ed Lettau, Photo Researchers, Inc.)

socio-economic differences is to look at differences in the patterns of cognitive skills rather than at overall level of IQs. On what kinds of intellectual dimensions do members of different groups show the greatest relative strengths or weaknesses? Such an approach leads to construction of a profile of patterns of abilities. The carefully designed study presented in Box 11-1 investigated the relative standing on tests of verbal, reasoning, number, and spatial abilities of middle- and lower-class Chinese, Jews, Puerto Ricans, and blacks. The findings of this study are even more impressive when one realizes that it has been replicated and similar ethnic patterns of ability were found with a different sample of children.

Interpretations of Racial and Social-Class Differences in Cognitive Performance Three main types of explanations have been advanced to explain the ethnic and social-class differences in intellectual performance: a position which emphasizes the inappropriateness of the tests for lower-class children, a genetic position, and an environmental position.

Test bias and IQ Advocates of the first position argue that the most widely used intelligence tests have not been standardized on minority groups, and that

BOX 11-1
ETHNIC GROUP, SOCIAL CLASS, AND MENTAL ABILITIES

 This study investigated the relationship of social class and ethnic group in performance on tests of verbal ability, reasoning, number facility, and space conceptualization.

Eighty New York City children between the ages of 6 years 2 months and 7 years 5 months were selected from each of four ethnic groups: Jewish, Chinese, Puerto Rican, and black. The children in each group were equally divided between lower- and middle-class children.

The investigators tried to use test materials and items that were equally familiar to all the social classes and cultural groups used in the study. The test administrators were from the same cultural background as the subjects and spoke the language of the child being tested. The test was administered in the language most familiar to the child. The items involved no writing or reading, and no time limits on responding were used. Thus, a careful, systematic attempt was made to develop measures that were culture-fair. To establish rapport and reduce test anxiety, long periods of adapting to the test situation and extensive practice materials were used.

The relative standing of the four ethnic groups is presented in Figure 11-3. It can be seen that distinctive profiles of mental ability scores emerge for the four ethnic groups: Puerto Ricans and Chinese show higher spatial abilities relative to their verbal abilities, whereas the pattern is reversed for blacks and Jews.

It was found that social class influenced the elevation but not the pattern of scores, whereas ethnicity influenced both pattern and level. When the groups were separated on the basis of socioeconomic class, the profiles of abilities for lower-class ethnic groups parallel the middle-class profiles but they are lower on all abilities. The difference between the levels for the lower- and middle-class is greatest for blacks, which suggests relatively greater socioeconomic disadvantage for lower-class blacks. ■

Source: Lesser, G. S., Fifer, G., & Clark, D. H. Mental abilities of children from different social class and cultural groups. *Monographs of the Society for Research in Child Development*, 1965, **30** (4, Serial No. 102), 1–115.

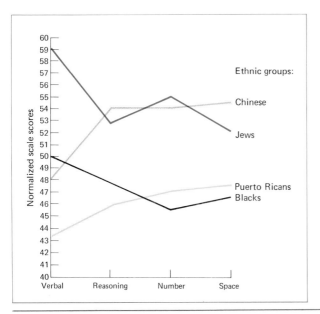

FIGURE 11-3 Pattern of verbal, reasoning, number, and spatial mental ability scores for 6- and 7-year-old children of ethnic groups (*Reproduced from Lesser, Fifer, & Clark, 1965.*)

the items contained on these tests are not a true measure of adaptive ability or problem solving for the circumstances within which lower-class children and some ethnic groups live. The content of the usual intelligence tests draws heavily on white middle-class language, vocabulary, experience, and values. Attempts to cope with the possible bias in both tests and the testing conditions have not been very successful, and some of the proposed solutions seem naive.

If the test items are experientially inappropriate, attempts to deal with such cultural bias by developing lower norms for blacks based on the performance of a large sample of blacks on a standard test such as the Stanford-Binet test or by translating these biased items into black dialect are not very sensible solutions to the problem. An example of cultural bias on the current revision of the Binet scale is cited by Williams (1970). Correct responses to the Binet item "What's the thing for you to do if another boy hits you without meaning to do it?" are such things as "That's alright. I know it was an accident,' and walk away." Williams says that in some black communities a child must fight back as a means of survival and to walk away would mean suicide.

A little different kind of cultural bias is demonstrated in the test presented in Box 11-2. The "Dove Counterbalance General Intelligence Test," or the "Chitling Test," was facetiously developed by Adrian Dove, a black sociologist, to show that communication problems go both ways. Since this test was devised in 1968, it also demonstrates that tests should not use items that get dated rapidly. Even a very informed black child currently might not be able to identify the Hully Gully or the Dixie Hummingbirds.

Although the Chitling Test is presented as a humorous example of the problems in controlling experiential factors in the selection of test items, it leads us to a critical problem in the development of culture-free tests. It seems probable that performance on this test will not predict academic success even for black children. As long as one of the aims of intelligence tests is to predict academic performance in schools whose goals are largely defined by white middle-class values, and as long as school grades or other intelligence tests are used as validating criteria, differences among subcultures at least partly attributable to experience are likely to occur.

IQ tests can predict the academic success of all groups equally well, which is the original goal of these tests. But can they predict *intelligent adaptive behavior outside of the classroom*? Since most attempts to develop completely new culture-free tests or to modify the content of tests have not been successful in eliminating the association between social class, ethnicity, and test performance, some psychologists have attempted to develop measures which sample the child's performance on practical learning problems within the child's own environment. The study by Mercer presented in Box 11-3 represents an attempt to distinguish between IQ scores and adaptive ability. It demonstrates that for lower-class and minority groups a standard intelligence test does not accurately distinguish individuals who cannot cope with practical problems in their environment from those who function well in the community. This is particularly important since the American Association on Mental Deficiency defines mental retardation as subaverage general intellectual functioning associated with impair-

BOX 11-2
THE CHITLING TEST

 It doesn't take a high IQ to recognize that intelligence tests have a built-in cultural bias that discriminates against black children. Tests designed to measure how logically a child can reason often use concepts foreign to the ghetto: a Harlem child who has never handled money or seen a farm animal, for example, might be asked a question that assumes knowledge of quarters and cows.

Adrian Dove, a sociologist and a Negro, for one, knows that black children have their own culture and language that "white" tests don't take into account. He saw this clearly when he worked with white civic and business leaders after the Watts riots. "I was talking Watts language by day," he says, "and then translating it so the guys in the corporations could understand it at night." Dove then designed his own exam, the Dove Counterbalance General Intelligence Test (the "Chitling Test") with 30 multiple-choice questions, "as a half-serious idea to show that we're just not talking the same language." The test has appeared in the Negro weekly Jet as well as in white newspapers, but mostly, says the 32 year-old Dove, "it has been floating around underground." Some samples (see end of story for the correct answers):

1. A "handkerchief head" is: (a) a cool cat, (b) a porter, (c) an Uncle Tom, (d) a hoddi, (e) a preacher.

2. Which word is most out of place here? (a) splib, (b) blood, (c) gray, (d) spook, (e) black.

3. A "gas head" is a person who has a: (a) fast moving car, (b) stable of "lace," (c) "process," (d) habit of stealing cars, (e) long jail record for arson.

4. "Down-home" (the South) today, for the average "soul brother" who is picking cotton from sunup until sundown, what is the average earning (take home) for one full day? (a) $.75, (b) $1.65, (c) $3.50, (d) $5, (e) $12.

5. "Bo Diddley" is a: (a) game for children, (b) down-home cheap wine, (c) down-home sinter, (d) new dance, (e) Moejoe call.

6. If a pimp is up tight with a woman who gets state aid, what does he mean when he talks about "Mother's Day?" (a) second Sunday in May, (b) third Sunday in June, (c) first of every month, (d) none of these, (e) first and fifteenth of every month.

7. "Hully Gully" came from: (a) East Oakland, (b) Fillmore, (c) Watts, (d) Harlem, (e) MotorCity.

8. If a man is called a "blood," then he is a (a) fighter, (b) Mexican-American, (c) Negro, (d) hungry hemophile, (e) Redman or Indian.

9. Cheap chitlings (not the kind you purchase at a frozen-food counter) will taste rubbery unless they are cooked long enough. How soon can you quit cooking them to eat and enjoy them? (a) 45 minutes, (b) two hours, (c) 24 hours, (d) one week (on a low flame), (e) one hour.

10. What are the "Dixie Hummingbirds?" (a) part of the KKK, (b) a swamp disease, (c) a modern gospel group, (d) a Mississippi Negro paramilitary group, (e) Deacons.

11. If you throw the dice and seven is showing on the top, what is facing down? (a) seven, (b) snake eyes, (c) boxcars, (d) little Joes, (e) 11.

12. "Jet" is: (a) an East Oakland motorcycle club, (b) one of the gangs in "West Side Story," (c) a news and gossip magazine, (d) a way of life for the very rich.

13. T-Bone Walker got famous for playing what? (a) a trombone, (b) piano, (c) "T-flute," (d) guitar, (e) "Hambone".

Those who are not "culturally deprived" will recognize the correct answers are 1. (c), 2. (c), 3. (c) 4. (d), 5. (c), 6. (e), 7. (c), 8. (c), 9. (c), 10. (c), 11. (a), 12. (c), 13. (d). ∎

Source: Dove, A. "The Chitling Test." In "Taking the Chitling Test." *Newsweek*, July 15, 1968. Copyright Newsweek, Inc., 1968, reprinted by permission.

ment in adaptive behavior. It involves both IQ (usually an IQ score of 84 or lower, or the bottom 16 percent of the population) and adaptive ability. Many schools use only the criteria of the lowest 7 percent, or a score of 75 to 79 or lower on a standard IQ test, whereas many test constructors suggest using an even more lenient criterion of only the bottom 3 percent, or an IQ of 70 or lower.

The investigator, Jane Mercer, attempted to deal with three issues:

How is mental retardation defined and how do variations in its definition affect the labeling of minority groups?

Is a retarded IQ on a standard intelligence test associated with an inability to get along socially and deal with problems in the environment?

Is the lower average IQ scores of blacks and Chicanos related to variations in their cultural background?

The problem of labeling a child as retarded is a critical one: it influences his academic placement; it influences attitudes toward him in the classroom, in his peer group, and in the community; and it may even result in institutionalization. Once a child has been labeled retarded, the label follows him and plays a pervasive role in shaping his life experiences and the expectancies of others about him.

In addition to bias in the test content, it has been proposed that the testing conditions themselves are deleterious to the performance of low socioeconomic status and minority-group children. Labov (1970) argues that the poor performance of black children on IQ tests is due to suspicion and hostility elicited by the test situation. The test is usually administered by a middle-class white psychologist, and lower-class children are less familiar with test stiuations and may be less likely to be motivated to perform well on tests. They also frequently bring in expectancies of failure based on past academic experience.

Some investigators have attempted to manipulate the race of the tester and others the motivation of the subjects. Under conditions which are not stressful, black children may actually perform better with white testers than black testers (Bucky & Banta, 1972). However, under anxiety-provoking situations where black subjects think they are not doing well or that their performance is to be compared to white norms, their performance improves with a black tester (Katz & Greenbaum, 1963; Katz, Robinson, Epps, & Waly, 1964; Katz, Roberts, & Robinson, 1965).

Attempts to elicit the best possible performance in children by familiarizing them with the test situation and test materials and through encouragement and the use of material rewards such as candy for motivation have been successful in improving the performance on intelligence tests of some lower-class and minority-group children (Golden & Birns, 1971).

Zigler and Butterfield (1968) studied differences in IQs of lower-class nursery school children tested on the Stanford-Binet Intelligence Test under

BOX 11-3
THE LETHAL LABELING OF LOW-IQ INDIVIDUALS

 The investigator devised a test of adaptive ability involving the person's increasing ability to cope with more complex roles and practical problems as he matures. The scale consisted of a series of twenty-eight age-graded skills ranging from such things in younger children as self-care items (dressing, feeding, etc) to more complex items in adults, such as being able to travel alone, hold a job, shop, and so on.

She compared the performance of 664 black, Mexican-American, or white persons on her adaptive behavior scale and on a standard intelligence test, usually the Standford-Binet or the Kuhlman-Binet. It was found that if an IQ of either 84 or 75 was used as the criterion to define retardation, many adults labeled as retarded were functioning competently in their social roles as measured by the adaptive behavior scale. Almost 100 percent could shop or travel alone, 84 percent had completed at least eight grades in school, 83 percent had held jobs, and 65 percent had semiskilled or skilled occupations. In contrast, most subjects who scored with an IQ below 70 were likely to be functioning inadequately in their environment. The investigator concludes that the cutoff level for retardation should be the lowest 3 percent (IQ below 70).

She then went on to compare quasi-retarded subjects, those who failed the IQ test but passed the test of adaptive behavior, with clinically retarded individuals, those who failed both tests at the 3 percent level.

She found that clinically retarded children had a more consistent history of learning problems, have had to repeat grades, and are likely to be in special programs. Quasi-retarded children are less likely to lag behind their age-mates or be in special classes although they too have low IQ scores.

Using the two tests to define retardation did not affect the Anglo-American children; every child who had an IQ below 70 also was in the bottom 3 percent on the test of adaptive behavior. However, 90 percent of the blacks and 60 percent of the Chicanos who had IQs below 70 passed the behavior test. Thus minority-group children of low socioeconomic status are most likely to suffer from the use of an IQ score alone as a definition of retardation.

Finally, the investigator found that the more similar the black and Chicano children's homes and families were to middle-class Anglo-American homes in such things as socioeconomic status, education, family size, size of the house, home ownership, English spoken in the home, and so on, the better were their scores on IQ tests.

She concluded that the content of IQ tests is heavily biased in favor of the middle-class white cultural background, and that because of this, the dual classification system using both a standard IQ test and the test of adaptive behavior should be used in defining retardation. ■

Source: Mercer, J. R. IQ: The lethal label, *Psychology Today*, September 1972, p. 44; and Mercer, J. R. Sociocultural factors in labeling mental retardates. *The Peabody Journal of Education*, 1971, **48**, 188–203.

motivating and standard test conditions. Each child was tested on two different forms of the test under the two motivating conditions in the fall of one year and the spring of the following year. In the intervening period half of the subjects had nursery school experience and half did not. The motivating testing condition was one in which items were administered in such a way that easy items on which the child was likely to be successful were given early. In addition the child was not permitted to experience a sustained series of failures. Whenever the child missed two items, an easy one which he or she could answer was interpolated. The child was gently encouraged to respond to all items. It was found that these lower-class children performed much better on intelligence tests under encouraging, supportive testing conditions than under standard conditions. In addition they showed marked improvement on IQ scores obtained under standard conditions if they had attended nursery school between the fall and spring sessions. The investigators propose that the change in IQ as a result of nursery school experience was due to a reduction in negative motivational factors in the test situation rather than an increase in intellectual competence. The children's wariness toward the adult examiner seemed to have decreased as a result of preschool experience. These results are presented in Figure 11-4.

Heredity and IQ   The second position that has been advanced to explain variations among social and racial groups in IQ is that these differences are based on genetic factors. One variant on this theme is that in a mobile society the brighter members of the lower class move upward and become middle class, and also that there is a tendency for people to marry within their class. This selective migration and assortative mating will tend to increase the difference between average IQ scores of the lower and middle classes over time (Herrenstein, 1971).

   The most articulate exponent of the genetic position is Arthur Jensen (1969, 1973). He proposes that there are two genetically independent types of learning: *associative learning*, or level I learning, involving short-term memory, rote

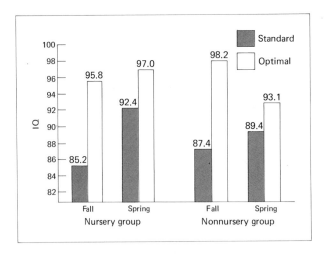

FIGURE 11-4   Mean IQs of combined nursery and nonnursery groups for standard and optimal fall and spring testings. *(From Zigler & Butterfield, 1968.)*

Stimulating preschool programs can have positive effects on the development of children. (Bruce Roberts, Photo Researchers, Inc.)

learning, attention, and simple associative skills; and *cognitive learning,* or level II learning, which involves abstract thinking, symbolic processes, conceptual learning, and the use of language in problem solving. The latter is clearly manifested in the ability to see relationships in such problems as:

Which number goes in the following series?

2, 3, 5, 8, 12, 17, ----.

How are an apple and a banana alike?

Most intelligence tests measure predominantly level II abilities. Some simple experimental tests, such as recalling a group of familiar objects or memory for numbers, measure level I abilities. Level I associative intelligence does not correlate with school performance. These abilities are not very important in academic learning, whereas level II intelligence as measured by IQ tests is predictive of achievement in school. Jensen suggests that level I abilities are equally distributed across social class and ethnic groups but that level II abilities are more concentrated in middle-class and Anglo-American than in lower-class or black American groups.

He further argues that on the basis of twin studies, estimates can be made that 70 to 80 percent of the contribution to intelligence is due to heredity and the remainder to environment. However, not all agree with Jensen, and next we turn to the environmental viewpoint.

Environment and IQ Psychologists who emphasize environmental factors point to the fact that the conditions of physical and cultural deprivation imposed by poverty are adequate to explain the social-class differences in cognitive performance without invoking genetic factors or systematic selection for IQ through social mobility. Poverty is associated with poor nutrition, poor health care, inadequate living conditions, and limited education. The effects of discrimination and lack of opportunity may lead to lack of motivation, low self-esteem, and feelings of helplessness, which will also influence performance on intelligence tests.

What happens if black children are adopted by white parents and raised in economically advantaged families that have an intellectual climate similar to that of white middle-class children? These adopted black children would be reared in environments relevant to the culture of IQ tests and the schools. If the racial differences usually obtained on IQ are attributable to such experiential differences, the IQs of these adopted black children should more closely resemble those of white children. In Box 11-4 a study which examines these effects is presented.

In addition to pointing to physical, emotional, and social factors which vary among social class and racial groups and would affect IQ, environmentalists seek evidence for their position in the late emergence of intellectual differences among such groups. In rebutting a genetic position they point out that no social class or racial differences are found on infant intelligence tests, but that these differences gradually emerge over the preschool years and therefore are attributable to cumulative effects of adverse experience. Jensen argues that infant intelligence tests use fewer items that involve level II abilities than do tests for older children such as the Stanford-Binet, and that the differential genetic salience of level II cognitive skills emerges only with age. He is arguing that it is not necessary for a genetically based trait to be present at birth in order to conclude that it is hereditary, and that the phenotypical manifestations may vary over age and may only appear in certain stages of development.

Environmentalists also argue that Jensen's estimate of a 70 to 80 percent heritability factor in IQ is not valid, and that the contribution of genetic factors to intelligence will vary with the population being studied and the environmental conditions under which they develop. Jerome Kagan (1969) uses the example of stature to illustrate this point. In the United States under conditions of reasonable nutrition and immunization against disease, height is largely genetically determined. Because the majority of Americans are well-nourished, the genes associated with height express themselves fairly directly in phenotypical (actual) height. However, the differences in height between these well-nourished American children and children suffering from disease and malnutrition in another, less affluent culture are not mainly genetically determined. Extremely adverse health and nutritional factors overwhelm and minimize genetic contributions to stature. Most starving children remain small in stature. Since the contribution of heritability to height in the two cultures is not the same, it is

BOX 11-4
WHEN BLACK CHILDREN GROW UP IN WHITE HOMES

 What happens to the IQs of children who are adopted and raised by white parents? Scarr and Weinberg studied 101 white families who adopted black children. The parents in these families were above average in intelligence, education, and socioeconomic status. All members over age 4 of the adoptive families, including the parents, adopted child, and biological offspring of the adoptive parents, were given age-appropriate IQ tests. The parents also were interviewed about experiences associated with the adoption, about being an interracial family, and about their lifestyle. The study involved 145 biological offspring of the adoptive parents, 130 adopted black children, and a small group of adopted white, Asian, and North and South American Indian children. Two-thirds of the adopted children were in the adoptive homes before their first birthday.

Figure 11-5 presents the IQ scores of the black and white adopted children and of the natural biological children of the adoptive parents. It can be seen that these children tend to score above the national average IQ of 100. It can also be seen that the earlier a child is placed, the more the child benefits from his or her home experiences. The white adopted children tended to be placed at a younger age than were other children and had the highest IQs, averaging 111. The Asian and Indian children who had endured longer periods of institutionalization and were the latest group to be placed had IQs at the national average of 100. In fact only three Asian and Indian children were adopted early, and therefore they are not included in the early adopted groups in Figure 11-5. The black children who were intermediate in age of placement are also intermediate in terms of test scores with an IQ of 106. It should

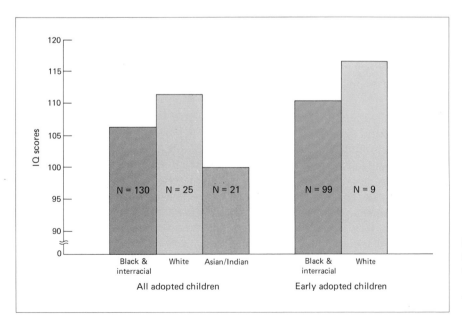

FIGURE 11-5 IQ scores for adopted children of different races. *(Adapted from Scarr & Weinberg, 1976, p. 732.)*

be noted that these black adopted children, especially the early placed children, score about 20 points above the national averages for black children and are performing much better than would have been predicted on the basis of the educational level and occupations of their natural parents. In addition, the range of scores for black and white adopted children was similar. That is, the top-scoring black children scored as high as the top-scoring white children, and this similarity was also found for the lowest-scoring children. The effects of the adoptive environment enhanced not only the IQ scores of the black children, but also their performance at school and scores on standardized achievement tests which were again above the national average. The natural children who have lived in these middle-class educated environments since birth score higher than any of the adopted children. It is unfortunate that the race of a child is confounded with the time of placement. However, there is a trend for early adoption to increase the scores of white as well as nonwhite children. The results of this study certainly show that social environment plays an important role in determining IQ scores and that the deficits in performance on IQ tests by black children can be reduced with placement in educated middle-class environments. This suggests that middle-class white environments facilitate the development of the skills necessary for good per-

formance on intelligence tests rather than that there are innate racial differences in intellectual ability.

Before we rush off and start placing black children in white adoptive homes, let us keep in mind a precautionary note advanced by the investigators.

Our emphasis on IQ scores in this study is not an endorsement of IQ as the ultimate human value. Although important for functioning in middle-class educational environments, IQ tests do not sample a huge spectrum of human characteristics that are requisite for social adjustment. Empathy, sociability, and altruism, to name a few, are important human attributes that are not guaranteed by a high IQ. Furthermore, successful adaptation within ethnic subgroups may be less dependent on the intellectual skills tapped by IQ measures than is adaptation in middle-class white settings. . . . The major findings of the study support the view that the social environment plays a dominant role in determining the average IQ level of black children and that both social and genetic variables contribute to individual variation among them. (Scarr & Weinberg p. 739) ■

Source: Scarr, S., & Weinberg, R. A. IQ test performance of black children adopted by white families. *American Psychologist*, 1976, *31*, 726–739.

inappropriate to use heritability indexes calculated on the basis of studies in one population and generalize these findings to different populations.

In a twin study Sandra Scarr-Salapatek investigated this problem directly by looking at the relationship between heritability and IQ in black and white lower- and middle-class children (Scarr-Salapatek, 1971). The investigator assumed that lower-class children and most blacks have limited experiences with environmental factors relevant to the development of academic skills or performance on intelligence tests. Therefore, just as the range of stature is smaller under conditions of extreme malnutrition, variability in scores on cognitive tests will be less for these groups than for white middle- or upper-class children. This was found to be the case. Genetic intellectual variations are more directly expressed in the performance on cognitive tests of white middle- or upper-class children than in lower-class or black children.

Social-class differences in parent-child interaction   It has been suggested that differences in parental behavior may mediate some of the relationships between IQ and social class. Because of this many investigators have studied differences in middle- and lower-class parent-child interactions which may influence the development of verbal and cognitive skills. Social-class differences in parent-child interaction have been found even in infancy. These social-class differences in family interaction are found within races and are not attributable to racial differences. The pattern of social-class differences between middle- and lower-class blacks and between middle- and lower-class whites is very similar.

The greatest differences between middle- and lower-class mothers are in their use of language. Middle-class mothers are more likely than lower-class mothers to talk in response to vocalizations by their infants. However, lower-class mothers touch and hold their infants more (Lewis & Wilson, 1972; Tulkin & Kagan, 1972). In addition, there are differences in the way lower- and middle-class babies respond to their mothers' vocalizations. Lower-class children are more likely to continue vocalizing when their mothers are speaking, whereas middle-class babies tend to cease vocalizing and listen (Lewis & Freedle, 1973). It has been suggested that these early social-class differences in the way infants attend to their mothers' speech may be related to later social-class differences in the ease with which children use verbal information for learning (Golden & Birns, 1976).

Robert Hess and Virginia Shipman (1967) studied the interaction between maternal control techniques, teaching styles, and language and the child's cognitive development. They differentiated individualistic, person-oriented control procedures from status, role-oriented maternal approaches to control of the child. The individualistic approach used by middle-class mothers emphasizes the child's feelings, characteristics, and reasons for actions and orients the child toward attending to relevant cues in problem-solving situations in the environment. The mother makes the child aware of the complexities of his or her social and physical environment. She organizes information for her child and uses a more complex linguistic code to do so. In contrast, the lower-class mother who uses status-oriented control is less likely to individualize responses and uses a simplistic stereotyped restrictive form of language. This type of maternal communication is less likely to facilitate the kinds of discriminations and classifications necessary for later problem-solving skills in the child.

Studies of social-class differences in parent-child interactions have been criticized for some of the same reasons as have reports of race and class differences in IQ. It is frequently said that the laboratory situations in which many of the studies are conducted are more unfamiliar and anxiety-provoking for lower-class or minority-group mothers than middle-class white mothers. Resentment or apprehension in the situation may cause lower-class minority-group mothers to interact with their children in a manner which is not representative of their behavior in the home or more familiar situations. In addition, it is argued that the teaching situations used in many interaction studies where the mother must teach the child to solve a problem, build a house of blocks, or put together a puzzle are biased toward the experiences of middle-class mothers who already are probably doing this kind of thing at home with their children.

A study of mother-child interaction comparing mothers having high school education or less to mothers with college education or more indicates that the interaction task is important (Streissguth & Bee, 1972). When a play situation where the child was allowed to play freely with toys was used, interaction differences between the two groups of mothers were less than when a teaching situation was used. The teaching situation involved having the mother teach the child selected motor items from an infant intelligence test, such as putting blocks in a cup or completing a form board.

The patterns of evaluative comments which differed for the two groups of mothers and varied in the two situations are presented in Figure 11-6. The results are summarized by the investigators as follows:

All mothers were much more active with their infants in the teaching situation than in the free play, apparently perceiving the teaching situation as requiring more active intervention. However, the two groups of mothers differed significantly in their teaching styles, particularly in their differential use of feedback to the infant about his performance. In free play, both groups used about the same amount of positive reinforcement (statements of approval and praise [such as "good girl"]) but the mothers with lower education used much more negative reinforcement (statements of disapproval and criticism [such as "not that way"]). These differences were intensified when the mothers were asked to teach their infants to solve a problem. Although the two groups of mothers gave their infants the same amount of overall feedback in the teaching situation, the higher education mothers used four times as much positive as negative reinforcement while the lower education mothers used almost the same amounts of negative and positive reinforcement. These same feedback patterns held for mothers of infants of each age: 9-, 12-, 15 and 18-months. It also appears that mothers with lower education used more demonstrations

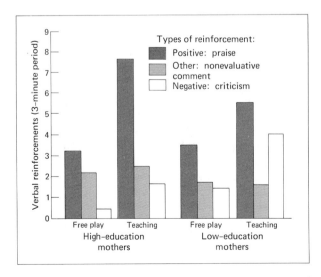

FIGURE 11-6 Average number of verbal reinforcements used by mothers with high school education or less compared with mothers will college education or more interacting with their infants in a free-play and a teaching situation. *(From Streissguth & Bee, 1972.)*

in teaching the task and were generally more specific in the type of help and suggestions they gave their infants, while mothers with higher education used teaching strategies that were aimed at maintaining the infant's attention and focusing him on the task, but did not give as much specific instruction on how to solve the problem. (Streissguth & Bee, 1972, pp. 172–173)

The finding of the more frequent use of praise for problem-solving performance by middle-class mothers has been related to the greater emphasis these mothers place on achievement and to the subsequent motivation their children may have to do well on intellectual tasks. In addition, the finding that the teaching style of lower-class parents, particularly black lower-class mothers, involves the use of a higher proportion of negative rather than positive reinforcement compared to that of middle-class mothers in the teaching of laboratory tasks has led some investigators to conclude that lower-class children are exposed to a particularly stressful learning environment (Feshbach, 1973).

This emphasis on parent-child interaction playing a critical mediating function in the association between social class and cognition has led many psychologists to include modification of such interactions as a component of intervention programs designed to improve the cognitive skills of children.

Family Influence on Cognitive Development

Parent-Child Relations We have discussed how social-class differences in parent-child relations affect cognitive development. However, specific aspects of family interaction have been found to influence cognitive development regardless of social class. Parental practices which engender emotional security and low anxiety, independence, and high internalized goals for achievement are associated with accelerated cognitive development. Mothers who value achievement, set high achievement standards, and reward their children for satisfactory performance and punish them for substandard performance have boys and girls who have high achievement motivation and effort (Crandall, Preston, & Rabson, 1960; Rosen & D'Andrade, 1959).

In addition, a supportive, warm home environment which encourages exploration, curiosity, and self-reliance leads to high achievement (Kelly & Worell, 1977). In malevolent homes characterized by extreme punitiveness and rejection, or in homes where the father is extremely authoritarian and enmeshes the child in rigid rules and regulations, low achievement results (Radin, 1976; Bradley, Caldwell, & Elardo, 1977). Such restrictiveness may inhibit early exploration and curiosity in children. It also seems probable that such parental behaviors lead to insecurity and high anxiety in children, which play an increasingly salient role in interfering with intellectual performance and academic achievement over the school years (Ferguson, 1970; Hill & Eaton, 1977).

There is some evidence that interactions between the sex of the parent and sex of the child must be considered in evaluating other parental influences on cognition. Some of the findings suggest that although mothers may be more important in stimulating intellectual development and achievement needs in both boys and girls, fathers may have relatively more influence on cognitive growth in daughters than in sons.

It may be that because children spend more time with their mothers than

Reading to children is associated with cognitive development. (Ken Heyman)

fathers in our culture, the mother is most important in determining the intellectual level of the home environment. The intelligence of mothers has been found to influence the expression of genetic predisposition for mental retardation in children. In homes in which the father is of average intelligence but the mother is retarded, retardation is $2^{1}/_{2}$ times more frequent among the children than in homes with equally retarded fathers and normal IQ mothers (Reed & Reed, 1965).

Mothers also seem to be more important than fathers in shaping the aptitudes of their children. When university students have fathers who are less educated than their mothers, their aptitude scores are higher than those of students with more educated fathers than mothers. This occurs in spite of the fact that homes with the more educated fathers were of higher socioeconomic status. Variations in the mothers' education seemed to counteract the commonly found effect of social-class factors on children's aptitudes (Willerman & Stafford, 1972).

In the Fels Institute Study (Kagan & Moss, 1962; Crandall & Battle, 1970) high achievement in boys was associated with high maternal protection and little hostility during the first three years of life followed by reinforcement and encouragement for acceleration of the boys' striving for achievement and independence from 3 to 10. In contrast, mothers of high intellectually achieving girls were less warm and lacking in protectiveness in the first three years of life, which may have encouraged early independence in the girls. This was accompanied by sustained emphasis on accelerating daughters' intellectual achievement by both mother and father. Such high-achieving daughters had fathers who were affectionate and nurturant and generally satisfied with their daughters' achievement striving. However, they did not hesitate to use both appropriate praise and criticism of their daughters' achievement performance.

This suggests that factors which might lead to some alienation from the mother and a closer relationship with the father facilitate achievement in girls. It would be interesting to know how this relationship would differ if daughters with high-achieving, career-oriented mothers were compared to daughters of low-achieving mothers. It could be that with a high-achieving mother, maternal warmth would encourage the daughter to identify with the mother and emulate her achievement attitudes and performance. The student should keep in mind that although parental behaviors are related to achievement in children, other factors such as social class, education, and social opportunities set important limits on the attainments of children.

Birth Order It has been proposed that family configuration, that is, the order, number, and spacing of children and the number of parents in the home, is associated with intellectual performance (Zajonc & Markus, 1975; Zajonc, 1976). Children born early in the birth order generally have higher IQs than later-born children. This can be seen in Figure 11-7, where the pattern of decreasing test scores with birth order and family size found in an extensive Dutch study of almost 400,000 men is presented (Belmont & Marolla, 1973). However, wide spacing in the intervals between siblings has been found to eliminate the adverse effects of being later-born. Why should this be? It has been suggested that the intellectual environment in a family changes with different family configurations. The cognitive level of the family can be viewed as being the average of the cognitive levels of each family member. Parents have higher mental ages and are more cognitively advanced than children and raise the cognitive level of the family. Younger children are less cognitively advanced than their older siblings and dilute the environment and bring down its mean level. In addition, early-born children are likely to experience more individual contacts with parents, especially in the early years. Parents have a limited amount of time available for their children. It follows that as the family increases in size, each child will have less parental time spent in such things as reading, playing, and individual face-to-face interactions.

Long birth intervals therefore give older children the benefits of being in a small family for a longer period of time and during an early phase of growth which is sensitive to

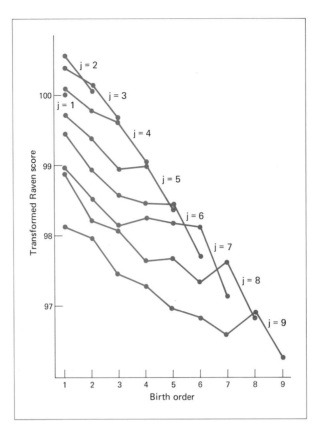

FIGURE 11-7 Scores on a nonverbal measure of intelligence according to birth order in families of different size. *(From Zajonc & Markus, 1975.)*

environmental effects. It is also to the advantage of the younger child to postpone its birth, because the later it arrives the more mature will be the environment which it enters at birth and in which it will develop. (Zajonc, 1976)

Further support for the notion of level of intellectual environment being established by the joint contribution of family members is supported in studies of multiple births. If twin neonates are present in the family, this would greatly depress the average intellectual level of the home. If we compare the intellectual level of children in two-children families in which there are twins versus those in which there are two singletons, and hence spaced births, the twins score lower on cognitive tests than the singletons. We might speculate that this is attributable to other aspects of multiple births such as lower birth weight, oxygen deficiencies, or delivery problems. However, twins whose co-twin died in the first month of life show cognitive scores comparable to those of singletons. The frequently reported finding of poor intellectual performance in twins is found only if both twins are present to dilute the intellectual level of the home (Record, McKeown, & Edwards, 1970).

Finally, early-born children have more opportunity to play the role of tutor to their younger siblings, and this teaching role may facilitate their cognitive development.

Cognitive Intervention Studies

In the past two decades a great many preschool compensatory education programs aimed at modifying the development of economically deprived children have been initiated. At first investigators were discouraged with the impact of these programs since the effects on cognitive development seemed to be modest or of short duration. When investigators did follow-up studies of these programs two or three years after termination of the projects, when the children were in their early elementary school years, the children seemed to be showing little sustained academic advantage resulting from the intervention. However, in contrast to the results of short-term follow-up studies, a recent survey of ten long-term follow-up studies of children who were involved in preschool intervention projects in the 1960s indicates that there may be positive, but delayed, effects of intervention. When these children are in later elementary grades or junior high school, in contrast to children from similar backgrounds who did not participate in intervention projects, they score higher on arithmetic and reading achievement and on IQ tests. In addition, they are less likely to have been retained in a grade or to have been assigned to special education classes (Palmer, 1977). It seems probable that the child who is progressing well in school is also experiencing more socioemotional satisfaction and greater self-esteem. There is much evidence of the destructive effects to self-esteem and motivation of a child with learning difficulties being labeled "dumb" by teachers or peers. Although teachers try to avert such labeling by calling special classes or programs by cunning names such as the Wolves or Badgers, or by keeping children in regular classes and taking them out for special tutoring for only a portion of the day, it is astonishing how rapidly children learn who the problem learners are. It may be the feelings of helplessness, anxiety, and incompetence engendered by such labeling that lead to negative or actively hostile attitudes toward learning and the school situation.

Many of the most successful intervention programs have been those that were begun early and involved the parents in the training of their children. It is difficult to maintain gains if children are put in a cognitively stimulating school environment but return to the unchanged home situation which has previously shaped their cognitive performance.

Programs in which the focus is on the parent-child relation and on improving the natural support systems of the family rather than only on placing the child in an educationally stimulating program are sometimes called home-based as contrasted to center-based programs.

One of the most successful intervention programs, that of the Milwaukee project carried out by Rick Heber and his colleagues, involved both family and infant intervention. It is presented in Box 11-5. One of the unique aspects of this project is that it undertook to prevent retardation by intervening early in life. It was not designed to raise IQ levels, but to allow normal intellectual development

BOX 11-5
THE MILWAUKEE PROJECT: EARLY INTERVENTION AS A TECHNIQUE TO PREVENT MENTAL RETARDATION

 How can declines in intelligence in children at high risk for intellectual deficts be averted? Rich Heber and his colleagues at the University of Wisconsin found that a combination of being from a low-socioeconomic-status home in the inner core of Milwaukee and of having a mother with a low IQ was associated with a progressive decline in intellectual level in children. In a preliminary study, 78 percent of the children with IQs below 80 had mothers with IQs below 80.

Forty lower-class black mothers with IQs below 75 and their newborn infants were randomly assigned to either an experimental or a control condition. The mothers and infants in the experimental group participated in a comprehensive six-year intervention program beginning when the infants were about 3 months of age. The program involved a maternal rehabilitation program and an infant stimulation program. The control group received no intervention, but was assessed at the same intervals as the experimental children. The maternal rehabilitation program consisted of two parts: a vocational rehabilitation program which improved job opportunities for the mothers and modified attitudes about their competence and a program to increase homemaking and childrearing skills.

The children's intervention program involved an intensive day-care program, five days a week, in which younger children were trained in perceptual-motor and cognitive language skills. The program for the children as they grew older emphasized language, reading, mathematics, and problem-solving skills. The social and emotional development of the children was encouraged through the interpersonal relationships developed between the teachers and the children and their families.

Figure 11-8 presents the IQ scores of the experimental and control groups and of the group of children involved in the preliminary study of IQs in children from this population. The last group is labeled the contrast group and shows the decline in scores with age that might be expected for

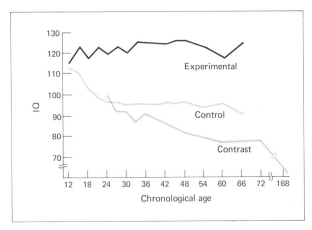

FIGURE 11-8 Mean IQ performance with increasing age for the experimental and control groups in comparison to the high-risk survey contrast group. *(From Garber & Heber, 1973.)*

children of mentally retarded mothers living in an economically depressed urban area who had not been repeatedly tested on IQ tests.

The IQs of the control and experimental groups are comparable for the first 18 months, but the IQs diverge steadily from that time. At 66 months the control group had an average IQ of 94 and the experimental group had an average IQ of 124—a 30-point difference. It might be asked why the IQ of the control group was not lower. Both experimental and control children were tested every four months during the first year of life and every six months thereafter. It appears that the repeated testing contributed to improved performance. This is evidenced in the significantly lower test scores of siblings of both experimental and control children who did not receive repeated testing. The IQs of older siblings of children in the experimental group average 39 points lower than those of the children in the program.

The improved performance of the children in the experimental program was not confined to intelligence tests, but was found on an array of learning, language, and problem-solving tasks and several measures of personality and social development. In addition, observations of the children interacting with their mothers showed that the experimental children exchanged and elicited more information from their mothers which led to improved learning. The children apparently were acquiring effective interpersonal strategies to facilitate learning.

This study showed that even in a population which is under extremely high risk for mental retardation, intensive intervention can successfully halt the cumulative decline in cognitive performance usually found in these children in the first six years of life. ■

Source: Garber, H., and Heber, R. The Milwaukee project: Early intervention as a technique to prevent mental retardation. University of Connecticut Technical Paper, March 1973.

---

in the offspring of mentally retarded mothers by altering adverse environmental circumstances.

Projects which have attempted to use parent education programs in neighborhood or child-care centers have not been very successful in either changing parental attitudes or affecting parental behavior (Chilman, 1973). One of the difficulties in such projects is in maintaining the involvement, interest, and attendance at meetings of the parents, especially of the fathers. Many lower-class parents see child-care workers' attempts to teach them how to be good parents as condescending and offensive. Others have reported that there are too many adverse reality factors in their lives, such as crowded or inadequate housing, lack of money, unemployment, and so on, to make concerns like improving child-care practices important (Horowitz & Paden, 1973).

The most successful programs seem to be those in which low-income parents are actively involved in the education of their children. In some cases the mothers are employed as teaching aids in the preschool centers; in other studies mothers are visited in their homes and instructed and supported in their educational activities with the child. The educational activities themselves vary widely in different studies; reading, demonstration of educational toys, exercises aimed at improving cognitive development, and even play have been used. The wide range of types of parent-child activities that have been successful in modifying the child's intellectual performance suggests that it may be increased positive interaction between mother and child rather than the specific content of the tasks that is leading to the changes. The description of a toy program

BOX 11-6
MOTHERS' TRAINING PROGRAM

In the home training sessions, the child's curiosity and growth are encouraged by the use of various simple educational materials and toys, many of which the mothers learn not only to use effectively with their babies, but also to make by themselves from inexpensive materials. Within a budget of $50 per child, the following materials are provided for each of the children in the program: (1) a table and chair set; (2) 11 educational toys; (3) crayons, scissors, play dough, slate and chalk; (4) four inexpensive books; and (5) a plastic laundry basket for storage of materials. A lending library of 30 wooden inlay puzzles and simple object lotto games is available for all children.

The most seemingly ordinary objects, such as the table and chair and the laundry basket, play a central role in revolutionizing the environment of mother and child. These objects help to establish an order in the home and to define the pattern of roles and behavior which is maintained in every training session. During these sessions the child always works sitting at his table, on his chair. Each day, the mother takes the training toys from the laundry basket, and at the end of each session she returns them to the basket for safe storage.

Working with the toys, the child learns finger coordination and gross motor skills, concepts of relative size, basic shapes, and verbal skills. One training session might find mother and child playing with a set of five nested cans which the mother has collected herself. Starting with two, she teaches the baby to stack them, saying "Put the *little* one *on top of* the *big* one. Put the *little* one *in* the *big* one." Later, the mother teaches him body parts, antonyms and prepositions, and visual matching. Scrapbook making and dramatic storytelling are also included in the training ses-

sions at a later stage. Often older brothers and sisters help in making the scrapbook, which the mother and baby "read" together, and the scrapbooks become a source of pride to both mother and child. For most of the mothers it comes as a surprise that these scrapbooks and simple toys, which encourage the child to manipulate and explore, are better than expensive electrical toys which he merely watches. They learn that the best kind of toy is often one that they can make themselves.

In addition to the regular program toys, there are several "fun toys" such as pounding bench and busy box—again, these are toys that will help the baby develop new skills or concepts. They are to be played with any time, not just during training sessions; and since a number of mothers have reported that their babies do not want to stop when the training session is ended, these "fun toys" are suggested as "transfer toys." The mother simply hands the child one of these toys as a substitute for those she is taking away and lets him play independently. For many of the mothers, this brings a new revelation. The baby does not accept the transfer toy; it is the end of his time with mother that upsets him, not the absence of the toys. The babies are learning, and the mothers are learning too—learning that time spent together and nurturing, affectionate behavior are not only the most important things they can give their babies but also the prerequisities for effective training. ■

Source: Reprinted from Model programs: Mothers' training program, Government Printing Office, 1970 (Pamphlet of the National Center for Educational Communication, Department of Health, Education, and Welfare.

developed by Merle B. Karnes, which is used to facilitate mother-child interaction, is presented in Box 11-6.

The effects of such programs are not restricted to the target child. In one of both mother and child in a preschool center, one-third of the mothers subsequently enrolled in school to finish their high school work (Miller, 1967). The experience of actively participating in their child's education and of feeling responsible for instigating changes in the child may help develop a sense of competence and initiative in the mother which partially mitigates the feelings of helplessness and of being externally controlled that are frequently found in lower-class people.

The effects also extend to younger siblings of the children receiving the enrichment program. Younger siblings of the children involved in such activities show superior test performance to those in homes where the older child is not in an enrichment program (Klaus & Gray, 1968; Miller, 1967).

We have been discussing intervention programs as if they were only appropriate for the poor. However, in the few studies in which middle-class children were included, these children and their mothers also benefited from the experience of early intervention. One investigator comments, "Middle-class children respond beautifully. . . . most of them literally soar in it" (Caldwell, 1973, p. 31). Although middle-class homes are more likely than lower-class homes to provide children with a milieu which promotes positive academic attitudes and achievement in school, they are by no means providing ideal environments for cognitive development.

One of the critical questions about intervention programs which remains unanswered is that of how early intervention must be in order to be effective. In the few studies in which intervention with preschool children was begun at different ages, no support for earlier intervention being more effective than later intervention within the preschool range was found (Palmer, 1977). However, it may be that intervention becomes more difficult in the school years when attitudes, values, and motivational patterns destructive to cognitive development may be more firmly fixed. Children seem to be more malleable and able to reverse the effects of early experience than are the young of some lower animals where the effects of adverse environments in infancy may result in irreversible deficits in problem solving (Clarke & Clarke, 1976).

Summary

Intelligence tests were orginally constructed to predict academic success, and they remain one of our best instruments for doing so. However, test scores show considerable variability over time, and IQ cannot be considered a stable measure of intellectual capacity. Intelligence test scores should always be viewed as a measure of performance rather than ability. Under different circumstances on different measures children who have not done well on one test may be able to demonstrate their cognitive skills. In some ways this distinction between capacity and performance is similar to that encountered in the discussion of Piagetian tasks in the previous chapter. Since under the right situation or with certain kinds of training children who previously have been unable to solve a conservation task now can, it is suggested that these tasks are not measuring the capacity to perform these operations. In a parallel fashion, training given to young children which results in their performing more adequately on intelligence tests and in school is not changing their intellectual capacity. It may be changing their ability to manifest a capacity which already existed.

Binet and Simon were the first people to attempt to construct a test of intelligence which would measure children's ability to solve a broad array of complex cognitive tasks. In this scale, as in most subsequent intelligence tests, the goal was to be able to predict successful academic performance. Binet and Simon were concerned with the same issues of test standardization, use of appropriate norms, reliability, and validity which still interest modern psychometricians. A contemporary revision of the Stanford Binet is still one of the most widely used intelligence tests. However, the Wechsler scales, which yield separate performance and verbal IQs, are also widely used.

The IQ is best regarded as a measure reflecting the interaction of genetic and environmental factors. Heredity, environmental stimulation, and deprivation; home and cultural factors; and characteristics of the test situation influence performance on intelligence tests.

Marked differences in amount and patterns of cognitive skills are related to social class, ethnic group, and sex. Low-socioeconomic-class children score lower on almost all tests of cognitive skills; however, the patterns of skills are influenced by ethnicity. Blacks and Jews score relatively higher on tests of language skills and low on spatial skills, whereas this pattern is reversed for Chinese and Puerto Ricans.

Many hypotheses have been advanced to explain the relatively poorer performance of low-socioeconomic-class and black children. Some investigators have argued that the tests used are culturally biased toward white middle-class experience and information and thus other groups are penalized. The test situation itself is regarded as stressful and unfamiliar to lower-class children.

A controversy now rages over whether the differences in test performance are partly based on genetic differences in social classes and ethnic groups or whether the differences can be explained entirely by experiential factors. Cultural factors associated with isolation and poverty do seem to have a marked effect on IQ.

Parental factors are important in shaping cognitive development. Parents who have high-achievement standards and both reward and criticize their children's performance have intellectually achieving children. Maternal affection with boys and more maternal distance and paternal warmth for girls are also associated with achievement. Malevolent, punitive, rejecting parents interfere with the cognitive development of both boys and girls. There is some evidence that mothers play a more salient role than fathers in the intellectual development of their children.

Some intervention programs which have taught and encouraged mothers to interact with their children in ways thought to facilitate cognitive growth have successfully raised the IQs of both parents and children. Although the impact of these programs on the academic performance of children's early school years has not been marked, there seem to be delayed positive effects of such programs.

In conclusion, it can be seen that cognitive development is a complex process influenced by a myriad of genetic, constitutional, environmental, and experiential factors.

References

Bayley, N. Development of mental abilities. In P. H. Mussen (Ed.), *Carmichael's manual of child psychology* (Vol. 1). New York: Wiley, 1970, pp. 1163–1210.

Bell, R. Q., Weller, G. M., & Waldrop, M. F. Newborn and preschooler: Organization of behavior and relations between periods. *Monographs of the Society for Research in Child Development*, 1971, **36** (4, Serial No. 142),1–145.

Belmont, L., & Marolla, F. A. Birth order, family size and intelligence. *Science*, 1973, **182,** 1096–1101.

Bradley, R. H., Caldwell, B. M., & Elardo, R. Home environment, social status and mental test performance. *Journal of Educational Psychology*, 1977, **69,** 697–701.

Bucky, S. F., & Banta, T. J. Racial factors in test performance. *Developmental Psychology*, 1972, **6,** 7–13.

Burnett, A., Beach, H. D., & Sullivan, A. M. Intelligence in a restricted environment. *Canadian Psychologist*, 1963, **4,** 126–136.

Burt, C. The evidence for the concept of intelligence. *British Journal of Educational Psychology*, 1955, **25,** 158–177.

Caldwell, B. M. Infant day care—the outcast gains respectability. In P. Robey (Ed.), *Child care—who cares?: Foreign & domestic infant and early child development policies.* New York: Basic Books, 1973.

Cameron, J., Livson, T. V., & Bayley, N. Infant vocalizations and their relationship to mature intelligence. *Science*, 1967, **157,** 331–333.

Chilman, C. S. Programs for disadvantaged parents: Some major trends and related research. In B. Caldwell & H. Riccuiti (Eds.), *Review of child development research* (Vol. 3). Chicago: University of Chicago Press, pp. 403–466.

Clarke, A. M., & Clarke, A. D. B. *Early experience: Myth & evidence.* New York: Free Press, 1976.

Crandall, P., Preston, A., & Rabson, A. Maternal reactions and the development of independence and achievement behavior in young children. *Child Development*, 1960, **31,** 243–251.

Crandall, V. C., & Battle, E. S. The antecedents and adult correlates of academic and intellectual achievement effort. In J. Hill (Ed.), *Minnesota symposia on child development* (Vol. 4). Minneapolis: University of Minnesota Press, 1970, pp. 60–73.

Dove, A. Taking the chitling test. *Newsweek*, July 15, 1968, pp. 51–52.

Dreger, R. M., & Miller, S. K. Comparative psychological studies of Negroes and whites in the United States. *Psychological Bulletin*, 1960, **57,** 361–402.

Dreger, R. M., & Miller, S. K. Comparative psychological studies of Negroes and whites in the United States: 1959–1965. *Psychological Bulletin Monograph Supplement*, 1968, **70** (3, Part 2) 1–58.

Dye, V. A., & Very, P. S. Developmental changes in adolescent mental structure. *Genetic Psychology Monographs*, 1968, **78,** 55–88.

Ferguson, L. R. *Personality development.* Belmont, Calif.: Brooks/Cole, 1970.

Feshbach, N. D. Cross-cultural studies of teaching styles in four-year-olds and their mothers. In A. Pick (Ed.), *Minnesota Symposia in Child Psychology* (Vol.

7). Minneapolis: University of Minnesota Press, 1973.

Garber, H., & Heber, R. The Milwaukee project: Early intervention as a technique to prevent mental retardation. University of Connecticut Technical Paper, March 1973.

Garrett, H. E. A developmental theory of intelligence. *American Psychologist*, 1946, **1**, 372–382.

Gladwin, T. *East is a big bird: Navigation and logic on Pulawat Atoll.* Cambridge, Mass.: Harvard University Press, 1970.

Golden, M., & Birns, B. Social class, intelligence, and cognitive style in infancy. *Child Development*, 1971, **42**, 2114–2116.

Golden, M., & Birns, B. Social class and infant intelligence. In M. Lewis (Ed.), *Origins of intelligence.* New York: Plenum, 1976.

Guilford, J. P. Intelligence: 1965 model. *American Psychologist*, 1966, **21**, 20–26.

Haan, N. Proposed model of ego functioning: Coping and defense mechanisms in relationship to IQ change. *Psychological Monographs*, 1963, **77**, 1–23.

Halverson, C. F., & Waldrop, M. F. Relations between preschool activity and aspects of intellectual and social behavior at age 7^1/$_2$. *Developmental Psychology*, 1976, **12**, 107–112.

Hayes, K. J. Genes, drives and intellect. *Psychological Reports*, 1962, **10**, 299–342.

Herrenstein, R. I.Q. *Atlantic*, 1971, **228**, 44–64.

Hess, R. & Shipman V. Cognitive elements in maternal behavior. Minnesota symposium on child psychology. Vol. 1. Minneapolis. University of Minnesota Press. 1967.

Hill, K. T., & Eaton, W. O. The interaction of test anxiety and success-failure experiences in determining children's arithmetic performance. *Developmental Psychology*, 1977, **13**, 205–211.

Honzik, M. P. Value and limitations of infant tests: An overview. In M. Lewis (Ed.), *Origins of intelligence.* New York: Plenum, 1976.

Honzik, M. P., & MacFarlane, J. W. Personality development and intellectual functioning from 21 months to 40 years. Paper presented at the meeting of the American Psychological Association, Washington, D.C., September 1970.

Horn, J. L., & Cattell, R. B. Refinement and test of the theory of fluid and crystallized general intelligences. *Journal of Educational Psychology*, 1966, **57**, 253–270.

Horowitz, F. D., & Paden, L. Y. The effectiveness of environmental intervention programs. In B. Caldwell & H. Riccuiti (Eds.), *Review of child development research* (Vol. 3). Chicago: University of Chicago Press, 1973, pp. 331–402.

Humphreys, L. G. The organization of human abilities. *American Psychologist*, 1962, **17**(7), 475–483.

Hunt, J. M. The role of experience in the development of competence. In J. M. Hunt (Ed.), *Human intelligence.* New Brunswick, N.J.: Transaction Books, 1972.

Jensen, A. R. How much can we boost IQ and scholastic achievement? *Harvard Educational Review*, 1969, **39**, 1–123.

Jensen, A. R. *Genetic, educability and subpopulation differences.* London: Methuen, 1973.

Jensen, A. R. Cumulative deficit in IQ of blacks in the rural south. *Developmental Psychology*, 1977, **13**, 184–191.

Kagan, J. S. Inadequate evidence and illogical conclusions. *Harvard Educational Review*, 1969, **39**, 274–277.

Kagan, J. S., & Moss, H. A. *Birth to maturity: A study in psychological development.* New York: Wiley, 1962.

Katz, I., & Greenbaum, C. Effects of anxiety, threat and racial environment on task performance of Negro college students. *Journal of Abnormal and Social*

Psychology, 1963, **66,** 562–567.

Katz, I., Roberts, S. O., & Robinson, J. M. Effects of difficulty, race of administrator and instructions on Negro digit-symbol performance. *Journal of Personality and Social Psychology*, 1965, **70,** 53–59.

Katz, I., Robinson, J. M., Epps, E. G., & Waly, P. Effects of race of experimenter and tests vs. neutral instructions on expression of hostility in Negro boys. *Journal of Social Issues*, 1964, **20,** 54–59.

Kelly, J. A., & Worrell, L. The joint and differential perceived contribution of parents to adolescents' cognitive functioning. *Developmental Psychology*, 1977, **13,** 282–283.

Kennedy, W. A. A follow-up normative study of Negro intelligence and achievement. *Monographs of the Society for Research in Child Development*, 1969, **34**(2, serial No. 126).

Kennedy, W. A., VanDeRiet, V., & White, J. C. A normative sample of intelligence and achievement of Negro elementary school children in the southeastern United States. *Monographs of the Society for Research in Child Development*, 1963, **28**(6, Serial No. 90), 13–112.

Klaus, R. A., & Gray, S. W. The early training project for disadvantaged children: A report after five years. *Monographs of the Society for Research in Child Development*, 1968, **33**(4, serial No. 120).

Labov, W. The logic of nonstandard English. In F. Williams (Ed.), *Language and poverty*. Chicago: Markham, 1970, pp. 153–189.

Lesser, G. S., Fifer, G., & Clark, D. H. Mental abilities of children from different social class and cultural groups. *Monographs of the Society for Research in Child Development*, 1965, **30**(4, Serial No. 102), 1–115.

Lewis, M. What do we mean when we say "infant intelligence scores"? A sociopolitical question. In M. Lewis (Ed.), *Origins of intelligence*. New York: Plenum, 1976.

Lewis, M., & Freedle, R. The mother-infant dyad. In P. Pliner, L. Kranes, & T. Alloway (Eds.), *Communication and affect: Language and thought*. New York: Academic, 1973.

Lewis, M., & Wilson, C. D. Infant development in lower-class American families. *Human Development*, 1972, **15,** 112–127.

McCall, R. B., Appelbaum, M. I., & Hogarty, P. S. Developmental changes in mental performance. *Monographs of the Society for Research in Child Development*, 1973, **38**(3, Serial No. 150), 1–84.

McCall, R. B., Hogarty, P. S., & Hurlburt, N. Transitions in infant sensorimotor development and the prediction of childhood IQ. *American Psychologist*, 1972, **27,** 728–748.

McNemar, Q. Lost our intelligence? Why? *American Psychologist*, 1964, **19**(17), 871–883.

Mercer, J. R. Sociocultural factors in labeling mental retardates. *The Peabody Journal of Education*, 1971, **48,** 188–203.

Mercer, J. R. IQ: The lethal label. *Psychology Today*, September 1972, p. 44.

Miller, J. Research, change and social responsibility: Intervention research with young disadvantaged children and their parents. *In DARCEE papers and reports*, Nos. 2 and 3. Nashville: George Peabody College for Teachers, 1967.

Model programs: Mothers' training program. Government Printing Office, 1970 (Pamphlet of the National Center for Educational Communication, Department of Health, Education, and Welfare).

Moore, T. Language and intelligence: A longitudinal study of the first eight years. Part I: Patterns of development in boys and girls. *Human Development*, 1967, **10,** 88–106.

Osborne, R. T. Racial differences in mental growth and school achievement: A longitudinal study. *Psychological Reports*, 1960, **7,** 233–239.

Palmer, F. H. The effects of early childhood educational intervention on school performance. Paper prepared for the President's Commission on Mental Health, 1977.

Radin, N. The role of the father in cognitive academic and intellectual development. In M. E. Lamb (Ed.), *The role of the father in child development.* New York: Wiley Interscience, 1976.

Record, R. G., McKeown, T., & Edwards, J. E. An investigation of the difference in measured intelligence between twins and single births. *Annals of Human Genetics,* 1970, **34,** 11–20.

Reed, E. W., & Reed, S. C. *Mental retardation: A family study.* Philadelphia: Saunders, 1965.

Rees, A. H., & Palmer, F. H. Factors related to change in mental test performance. *Developmental Psychology Monograph,* 1970, **3**(2).

Rosen, B. C., & D'Andrade, R. The psychological origins of achievement motivation. *Sociometry,* 1959, **22,** 185–218.

Scarr, S., & Weinberg, R. A. IQ test performance of black children adopted by white families. *American Psychologist,* 1976, **31,** 726–739.

Scarr-Salapatek, S. Race, social class and IQ. *Science,* 1971, **174,** 1285–1292.

Sherman, M., & Key, C. B. The intelligence of isolated mountain children. *Child Development,* 1932, **3,** 279–290.

Shuey, A. M. *The testing of Negro intelligence* (2d ed.). New York: Social Science Press, 1966.

Sontag, L. W., Baker, C. T., & Nelsen, V. L. Mental growth and personality: A longitudinal study. *Monographs of the Society for Research in Child Development,* 1958, **23** (No. 68), 1–143.

Spearman, C. *The abilities of man.* New York: Macmillan, 1927.

St. Clair, K. L. Neonatal assessment procedures: An historical review. *Child Development,* in press.

Streissguth, A. P., & Bee, H. L. Mother-child interactions and cognitive development in children. In W. W. Hartup (Ed.), *The young child: Reviews of research.* Washington, D.C.: National Association for the Education of Young Children, 1972.

Terman, L. M. *Genetic studies of genius* (Vol. 1) *The mental and physical traits of a thousand gifted children.* Stanford, Calif.: Stanford University Press, 1925.

Thurstone, L. L. *Primary mental abilities.* Chicago: University of Chicago Press, 1938.

Thurstone, L. L. Multiple factor analysis: *A development and expansion of "the vectors of the mind."* Chicago: University of Chicago Press, 1974.

Tulkin, S. R., & Kagan, J. Mother-child interaction in the first year of life. *Child Development,* 1972, **43,** 31–41.

Vernon, P. E. Ability factors and environmental influences. *American Psychologist,* 1965, **20**(9), 723–733.

Wechsler, D. *Wechsler Intelligence Scale for Children.* New York: Psychological Corporation, 1952.

Wechsler, D. *The measurement and appraisal of adult intelligence* (4th ed.). Baltimore: Williams & Wilkins, 1958.

Willerman, L., & Stafford, R. E. Maternal effects on intellectual functioning. *Behavior Genetics,* 1972, **2,** 321–325.

Williams, R. L. Black pride, academic relevance and individual achievement. *Counseling Psychologist,* 1970, **2,** 18–22.

Zajonc, R. B. Family configuration and intelligence. *Science,* 1976, **192,** 227–236.

Zajonc, R. B., & Markus, G. B. Birth order and intellectual development. *Psychological Review,* 1975, **82,** 74–88.

Zigler, E., & Butterfield, E. C. Motivational aspects of changes in IQ test performance of culturally deprived nursery school children. *Child Development,* 1968, **39,** 1–14.

Socialization is the process whereby an individual's standards, skills, motives, attitudes, and behaviors are shaped to conform to those regarded as desirable and appropriate for his or her present or future role in society. "From the moment of birth when the child is wrapped in a pink or blue blanket, swaddled and placed on a cradleboard, or nestled in a mobile, festooned bassinet, indulged by a tender mother or left to cry it out by a mother who fears spoiling the child, socialization has begun" (Hetherington and Morris, 1978, p. 3).

Certain groups and organizations within society play key roles in socialization. Parents, siblings, peers, and teachers spend a great deal of their time communicating values and

415

directing and modifying children's behavior. Some organizations, such as the school, the church, and legal institutions, have evolved with the specific mission of transmitting the culture's knowledge and its social and ethical standards and development, and maintaining culturally valued behaviors.

Socialization can therefore be viewed as the process whereby new members of society are taught the "rules of the game." In most cases, socializing agents have a vested interest in getting new members to adopt the "rules," to play the game in roughly the same manner as they do, to observe the social contract. The developing child doesn't always see it that way. The rules often seem arbitrary to him or, worse yet, deprive him of gratification. Eating with fingers seems more efficient than with cumbersome utensils. Toilet training seems an unnecessary refinement. The notion of private property quite readily translates into "that's mine" but much more slowly into "that's his." Sharing with peers may at first seem a fool-hardy and self-punishing act. The need to be quiet when the teacher is addressing the class may not be high on a child's priority list, especially since the teacher is obviously not talking to him. (Hetherington and Morris, 1978, p. 6)

Since socialization often seems to involve the sacrifice or delay of pleasures, the acceptance of arbitrary, sometimes irrational, standards, and a concern with the welfare of others rather than with the self, how is the child induced to play according to the rules of society's game?

In the following chapters there will be a discussion of some of the processes involved as families, peers, and teachers participate in the intricate task of socialization. Although these groups may seem to play very different roles in their relationship to the child, they share common processes in shaping the child's values, beliefs, and behavior. Each group influences the child through direct tuition, that is, by putting forth rules or standards of behavior and trying to maintain them through rewards and punishments. Each group exhibits behavior which the child may acquire through observational learning. Finally the home, school, and peer group provide settings in which the child has the opportunity to practice his or her new-found social skills.

In our presentation, the impact of these groups on the development of morality and self-control, on the inhibition of aggression and encouragement of positive social behavior, on achievement, and on behaviors regarded as appropriate for males or females within our culture will be emphasized particularly.

Although many social factors and groups affect the process of socialization, the family is frequently regarded as the most influential agency in the socialization of the child. This chapter will deal with the processes and problems of socialization within the family. Socialization has frequently been viewed as a process by which parents shape the behavior of children. However, it would be more accurate to think of it as a process of mutual shaping. The family is best conceived of as a complex system involving interdependent functioning among members. This functioning of the family system may be modified by changes in structure or by the behavior of a single family member. We will examine some of the changes in contemporary families, such as the increase in single-parent families and in maternal employment, which may modify the functioning of the family system.

Variations in Patterns of Socialization

The standards, goals, and methods of socialization vary among societies, within subgroups in the same society, and within a society over time. Behavior regarded as desirable and encouraged in one society would be regarded as undesirable or even pathological in another. The grandiose boasting accepted by the Kwakiutl Indians as an appropriate means of establishing status might seem more like a paranoid delusional system to other segments of the American population. The handling of poisonous snakes to demonstrate devoutness, a practice of some fundamentalist religious groups in the Appalachians and in the Southwest, might seem a trifle excessive to others. The confinement of infants in some Guatemalan villages to a small, dark, windowless, toyless hut for the first year of life because of the belief that outside fresh air, sunlight, and dirt are harmful would be viewed as the grossest deprivation by American middle-class mothers, who surround their children with educational toys, festoon cribs with spinning mobiles and busy boxes, and involve their children in a regular routine of daily sunbaths and walks in the park.

Even within the same culture, dramatic changes over time occur in the goals of socialization and the methods used to mold the values and behavior of children. In the years between 1910 and 1930, which were the heyday of American behaviorism led by John B. Watson, childrearing experts regarded the infant as an object for systematic shaping and conditioning. Little attention was paid to the needs and feelings of the child or the parent, or possible variations in genetic predispositions or temperamental characteristics of the child. Behaviorists of this era maintained an extreme environmentalist position and believed that desirable social behavior could be shaped in almost any child. Desirable social behavior could be attained if the child's antisocial behaviors were always punished and never indulged, and if positive behaviors were carefully conditioned and rewarded in a highly controlled and structured childrearing regime. The goal of the parents was to "shape in" good habits and avoid the development of, or "stamp out," bad habits. Watson advocated that the parents not indulge themselves by hugging and kissing the child, but treat children in a sensible way like young adults. He assured parents that if they behaved in an objective, unemotional way for only one week that they would be utterly ashamed of the mawkish, sentimental way they had been dealing with their child. Watson suggested:

Won't you then remember when you are tempted to pet your child that mother love is a dangerous instrument? An instrument which may inflict a never healing wound, a wound which may make infancy unhappy, adolescence a nightmare, an instrument which may wreck your adult son or daughter's vocational future and their chances for marital happiness. (Watson, 1928, p. 87)

Watson's vast influence was reflected in some of the popular childrearing literature of the day, even in the official government booklet for parents published by the U.S. Children's Bureau entitled "Infant Care." This booklet advocated never permitting the child to suck his thumb, and if necessary, restraining the child by tying his hands to the crib at night and painting his fingers with foul-tasting liquids or making him wear mittens during the day. It was recommended that feeding and toilet training be carefully scheduled. Daytime feeding sessions were at fixed four-hour intervals. Children were punished for soiling themselves and were seated on the toilet at prescribed times of the day and remained there until they urinated or defecated, at which time they were praised or rewarded. Parents were advised to let infants "cry themselves out" rather than reinforce this unacceptable behavior by picking them up and rocking and soothing them. This position seemed to emphasize all of the anxieties and drudgery and none of the joys of the parent-child relationship.

However, in the following years from the early 1930s until the mid-1960s, a more permissive attitude in which the parent was advised to be concerned with the feelings and capacities of the child emerged. This shift was due in part to the influence of Freudian psychology and its focus on the role of early deprivation and restrictions in the development of inhibitions which could serve as the foundation of many emotional problems. Another influence was the maturationally oriented child psychologists, such as Arnold Gesell, who stressed the importance of the "readiness" of the child in socialization. When the child was maturationally ready and at the appropriate stage for training, then weaning, toilet training, and other forms of self-control would proceed with greater ease and less stress for both mother and child. When the child was biologically ready, he would almost train himself with a little encouragement from the parent if there was a positive relationship between the parent and child.

This more relaxed attitude toward childrearing was given added impetus by the continuing influence of progressive educators, such as John Dewey, and the writings of humanistic psychologists, such as A. H. Maslow and Carl Rogers, which began to appear in the 1940s. Both of these groups believed that individuals have an innate capacity to learn and develop in a constructive and creative way and to realize their potential abilities if they are free to explore and develop in an open, accepting environment.

It became fashionable during the travails of the sixties, that is, during the sit-ins, protests, and riots, to blame the obstreperous, unconventional, and antiestablishment behavior of the young on their failure to be adequately socialized due to the widespread use by their parents of Benjamin Spock's book, *Baby and Child Care*. This influential book was first published in 1946, and since then over 21 million copies have been sold in the United States alone, in addition to a wide circulation in its many translated foreign editions. Spock's book became the parents' security blanket in dealing with everything from protruding navels to discipline. The students in this course may not have read Dr. Spock, but many will have been reared according to his precepts. Dr. Spock was not purveying a radical new doctrine; he was synthesizing and communicating in a jargon-free, highly readable style the beliefs and findings of the medical and social scientists of the era. Contrary to the statements of many of his critics, Spock did not advocate a completely indulgent and permissive approach to childrearing. He emphasized the importance of a warm parent-child relationship in the child's responsiveness to discipline. A child responds to the demands of loving parents more readily than to parents who are disliked and feared. If the parents are responsive to the capacities, needs, and feelings of the child, Spock thought they should seldom have to use discipline more severe than distracting, guiding, reasoning, and explaining. Even for parents things looked better with Dr. Spock, for his frequent cry was "Enjoy your baby!"

Since the mid-1960s there has been a continued emphasis on the role of parental love in the socialization of the child; however, experts now advise the parents to play a less permissive and more active role in shaping the child's behavior. The virtues of the "authoritative" versus the "authoritarian" parent are extolled. Parents should set limits and be authoritative in making decisions in areas where the child is not capable of making a reasonable judgment. However, they should listen and adapt to the child's point of view, should explain their restrictions and discipline, and should never be authoritarian; that is, they should never use their greater power to control the child in an unreasonable or hostilely punitive manner. The research findings which have led to this position will be discussed at length in the following chapters.

The Family and the Tasks of Socialization

Among the many social agencies that contribute to the socialization of the child, the family is clearly of central importance. But why is this the case? This emphasis on the great power of the family is largely attributable to the fact that family members are the first and often almost the only social contacts the child has in the early years which are critical in social development. The interaction and emotional relationship between the infant and parents will shape the child's expectancies and responses in subsequent social relationships.

In addition, note that the beliefs, values, and attitudes of the culture are filtered through the parents and presented to the child in a highly personalized, selective fashion. The personality, attitudes, socioeconomic class, religious affiliation, education, and sex of the parent will influence his presentation of cultural values and standards to his offspring. The desired and appropriate standards, beliefs, and role behavior shaped in a daughter by a lower-class, Baptist, authoritarian father would be quite different from those presented by an educated, middle-class, atheistic, feminist mother.

Specific norms and means of attaining socialization goals vary among cultures, but some tasks of childhood socialization seem to be almost universal. Children are expected to attain certain goals or master similar tasks if they are going to be successful and accepted individuals in a variety of societies. However, the specific techniques used by parents in helping their children master these apparently universal tasks and the expression of this mastery may be highly idiosyncratic.

Clausen (1968) has proposed the relationships between parental aims and activities and the socialization tasks or achievement of the child; these are presented in Table 12-1. This obviously is not a complete list, but serves as a kind of sampler of parental aims and children's tasks.

The Family as a System

Nowhere in the field of child development are greater methodological problems encountered than in the study of parent-child relations. To some extent this has been because of conceptual problems in thinking of socialization as a process whereby parents shape children rather than of the family members as an interacting system. To some extent it is because the statistical methods available to investigators have not been adequate to describe a transactional family model.

In most of the studies we will describe, the investigator has attempted to determine the relationship between parental characteristics, attitudes, and childrearing practices and the personality, cognitive, and social development of the child. As we noted, the assumption is often made that the behavior of the parent determines the behavior of the child. However, since most childrearing studies are correlational, such cause-and-effect relationships cannot be inferred (Bell, 1968). The frequently reported finding of a correlation between physical punishment, rejection, and inconsistent discipline in parents and aggression or delinquency in sons does not necessarily mean that these discipline practices led to the deviant behavior in the children. It may well be that a constitutionally active, irritable, demanding son causes parents to use increasingly more severe methods of control. A parent may begin by reasoning with or lecturing the child. If this is ineffective, mild deprivation of privileges, such as no TV for a week, may be used; this measure may also be ineffective. Then the parent may begin spanking the child. Finally, if these measures are unsuccessful, the parent becomes more frustrated, punitive, and erratic in discipline and desperately tries a variety of methods to cope with the recalcitrant child's aggression; finally the parent rejects the child. Thus, constitutional predispositions in the child may cause the parents' childrearing practices. This is obviously an extreme example. It is more accurate to view the family in terms of an interacting unit in which the characteristics and behavior of each family member interact with and shape the responses of all other members. However, no parent who has yielded to the relentless cries of an infant at three o'clock in the morning, in spite of a firm resolve to let him "cry himself out," ever doubts that the infant plays an active role in socializing the parents.

In the case of battered children, where the child is severely injured or even killed by parental mistreatment, the behavior of the child sometimes seems to contribute to the parental violence. Although the parents of battered children are frequently emotionally immature, unstable, frustrated individuals, their abused children are often reported to be difficult children (Gil, 1970). A higher than normal incidence of birth anomalies, physical and intellectual deviations, irritability, excessive crying with a peculiar and extremely irritating cry, fussiness,

TABLE 12-1 ,TYPES OF TASKS OF EARLY CHILDHOOD SOCIALIZATION IN THE FAMILY

Parental aim or activity	Child's task or achievement
1 Provision of nurturance and physical care	Acceptance of nurturance (development of trust)
2 Training and channeling of physiological needs in toilet training, weaning, provision of solid foods, etc.	Controlling the expression of biological impulses; learning acceptable channels and times of gratification
3 Teaching and skill-training in language, perceptual skills, physical skills, self-care skills in order to facilitate care, ensure safety, etc.	Learning to recognize objects and cues; language learning; learning to walk, negotiate obstacles, dress, feed self, etc.
4 Orienting the child to her immediate world of kin, neighborhood, community, and society, and to her own feelings	Developing a cognitive map of one's social world; learning to fit behavior to situational demands
5 Transmitting cultural and subcultural goals and values and motivating the child to accept them for her own	Developing a sense of right and wrong; developing goals and criteria for choices; investment of effort for the common good
6 Promoting interpersonal skills, motives, and modes of feeling and behaving in relation to others	Learning to take the perspective of another person; responding selectively to the expectations of others
7 Guiding, correcting, helping the child to formulate her own goals, plan her own activities	Achieving a measure of self-regulation and criteria for evaluating own performance

Source: Clausen, J. Perspectives on childhood socialization. In J. A. Clausen (Ed.), *Socialization and society.* Boston: Little, Brown, 1968, p. 141.

negativism, and other behaviors that exasperate the parents are found in many of these children. The parents feel they are being abused by the abused child. This negative perception of the battered child by her parents could be regarded as a means of their justifying their own cruelty. However, it is commonly found that other children in the families of battered children are not abused. In addition, in some cases, when abused children have been removed from their own homes and placed in foster homes, foster-parents who have not previously been harsh with other children have severely mistreated and abused the "battered child."

Although it would be unfair to say the battered child always "brought it on herself," in the case of child abuse as in other parent-child interactions the child is often an active participant in shaping her parents' responses.

Although in our examples we view socialization as a two-way street, rather than a one-way street, it might be more accurate to view it as a busy

It is said that the typical American family consists of a mother, a father, 2 1/3 children, a dog, and two cars. Here is an almost typical American family. (Erika Stone)

superhighway cloverleaf. Interaction in families does not just occur in parent-child dyads; it occurs among all family members.

Finally, it must be remembered that families exist within a larger milieu. An ecology of poverty, starvation, social disorder, and disease will influence the functioning of families in a different way than one characterized by affluence and social privilege. The same family will function differently in different situations and under varied circumstances.

Methods in the Study of Family Relations

Questionnaires and Interviews

The methods used to investigate family relations include parental questionnaires and interviews, direct observation, and laboratory analogue studies. Questionnaires and interviews often provide unreliable, inaccurate, and systematically distorted data. The task which the parent is being asked to perform during an interview or questionnaire is a difficult one. The parent is being asked to recall details which have occurred in the past, to rate himself or herself and the child in relation to dimensions of childrearing which are meaningful to psychologists but may have little to do with the way the parent thinks about parenthood, and to formulate attitudes or principles which determine his or her behavior toward the child. In the face of such a challenge, it is not surprising to find little agreement of reports over time or between different sources of information, and distortion in the direction of idealized expectations, precocity, and cultural stereotypes. Unless their child is grossly retarded, few parents report their child's development as slow. Instead the child is recalled as having walked and talked a little earlier and as having attained better grades in school than was actually the case and may be described as active and playful, a "real boy," rather than more aptly as the scourge of the neighborhood. In a 1963 study by Robbins, the retrospective reports of childrearing practices of parents of 3-year-old children were compared with those that had previously been gathered over the course of the first three years as part of a longitudinal study. It was found that parental distortions in recall which occurred were in the direction of greater agreement with the opinions of experts and the writings of Dr. Spock. For example, Dr. Spock in his 1957 book, *Baby and Child Care*, approves of use of a pacifier and disapproves of thumbsucking. In this study all mothers who were inaccurate in their reports of thumbsucking, and even those who at the time were recorded as having reported their concern to their physicians about their children's thumbsucking, denied that their children had ever sucked their thumbs. In contrast, most of the mothers who inaccurately recalled their use of pacifiers reported that they had used one when the actual records showed that they had not.

Parents with more than one child are also likely to have their memories of their children's past behaviors confused. On being asked to describe an

Bushman family. (Margorie Shostak/Nancy DeVore Photo Agency)

individual child, often what the parent produces is a composite child. Just as parents sometimes confuse their children and call them by each other's names, they confuse who did what, and to whom. Although parent attitude questionnaires and reports of early child-training practices are seldom able to predict independently assessed child behavior (Becker & Krug, 1964; Yarrow, Campbell, & Burton, 1968), some improvement in such predictions is obtained by focusing on specific current practices rather than broad retrospective attitudes (Winder & Rau, 1962; Bell, 1964; Kagan & Moss, 1962).

For example, rather than asking a mother to respond to the broad question, "Do you believe that children should not be permitted to defy or aggress against their parents?" an interviewer might begin with a general statement followed by increasingly specific probes such as:

Most parents encounter times when their child talks back to them, or gets angry at them or uses physical aggression towards them.

When_____gets angry at you, what does he (she) do?

a. Does_____ever shout at you? Answer back? How often?
b. Has_____ever struck you? Thrown things around the house? How often?
c. Stamped out of the house? Slammed doors? How often?
d. How much of this sort of thing have you allowed? What do you do?
e. (If this doesn't happen) How have you taught him (her) not to do these things?

Can you remember the most recent occasion when _____was angry or put out with you? Try and remember as many details as you can: When _____did, what was your reaction, how did_____react to any attempt on your part to discipline him (her)? In general let's try and reconstruct the actual sequence of who did what and the feelings that the two of you had.

The behavioral scientist is interested in quantifying data; therefore independent raters later would rate this section of the interview on 4-point scales specifically constructed to assess permissiveness and severity of punishment for disobedience and anger at the parent. For example:

Rating I

Permissive with respect to talking back, deliberate disobedience, shouting at parent, or other forms of showing anger at parent.

1. Not at all permissive. Would stop immediately. Would never ignore. Not permitted under any circumstances.
2. Would discourage rather firmly, but would expect some expression of anger toward parent to occur occasionally.
3. Moderately permissive. Sometime overlook, sometimes restrain, depending on circumstances.
4. Very permissive. Would not restrain child, unless he (she) likely to hurt parent.

Rating II

Punishment for talking back, or other forms of expressing anger at parent.

1. No punishment. Might talk to child, distract him (her) in some way, or explain why he (she) should not aggress toward me.
2. Mild punishment, consisting of "talking to" or mild reprimand, or withdrawing some small privilege.
3. Moderate punishment, consisting of scolding, or withdrawal of more important privileges, a mild spanking or slap, or warnings of even more severe punishment. You feel some irritation or anger as you give punishment.
4. Strong punishment. Severe scolding, perhaps shouting, or spanking or other physical punishment. Parent feels very angry with child.

This gives the psychologist a means of comparing the responses of different parents or groups of parents to similar children's behavior. It should be noted that the interview questions and the scales are structured to assess the parents' behaviors in the specific situation involving anger at the parent. There is no assumption that the parent would be similarly permissive or punitive in situations involving aggression against peers or other forms of misbehavior around the house. Different questions must be used to assess parental responses to those situations.

Another strategy is to use children's reports of parents' behavior rather than parents' reports of their own attitudes and behaviors. It can be argued rather convincingly that children's perception of their parents' attitudes are more important in their development than what the parents true feelings may be. A son may feel rejected by a father who really loves him but believes that men don't show emotion and that high standards and strict discipline are necessary to develop strong moral character in the young. The child's belief that his father does not find him worthy of love rather than the father's real attitude might result in the development of feelings of inadequacy and low self-esteem in the son.

In spite of the limited usefulness of self-report data in predicting the behavior of parents or children, it should be remembered that some kinds of information are difficult to obtain other than through self-reports. Measures of such things as the image family members have of each other and of how the family functions can be used to differentiate problem families from families which are functioning well. If family members perceive the family and each other in very different ways, these discrepancies tend to be associated with conflict and distress (Gottman, Markman, & Notarius, 1977). This might be expected since each family member is perceiving and responding to his or her individualistic view of the family. Many family therapists focus on helping families discover the distortions and discrepancies in their perceptions of each other and their communication as a way of reducing family conflict.

Direct Observation   In order to circumvent some of the problems in interviews and questionnaires, experimenters have resorted to the use of direct observation of parents and children in a variety of situations ranging from naturalistic home settings to highly structured tasks in the laboratory. Of course, those observational data are valid only to the extent that representative patterns of interaction have not been disrupted or distorted by the presence of the observer or the demands of the situation.

Studies suggest that when families are shifted from familiar to unfamiliar settings, from the home to the laboratory, or from unstructured to structured situations, there is a tendency for family members to express less negative emotion, exhibit more socially desirable responses, and assume socially pre-scribed behavior. Mothers are more directive and less passively attentive in the home than in the laboratory (Moustakas, Sigel, & Schalock, 1956). Similarly with a shift from the laboratory to the home, there is a change from stereotyped sex-role behavior to an increase in the expression of emotion by fathers and more active participation in decision making by mothers (O'Rourke, 1963).

Many investigators have expressed concern that when parents are being observed, they may attempt to appear in a more socially acceptable way than that in which they ordinarily behave. Most of us tend to exhibit more of our Dr. Jekyll side in public and our Mr. Hyde side in private. It has been found that mothers do behave in a warmer, more involved style with their children when they know they are being observed than when they are unaware that they are being observed (Zegoib, Arnold, & Forehand, 1975).

Most parents like to "show off" their children to reveal them in the best possible light. How successful are parents in doing this? Parents seem to be able to change their own behavior more readily than that of their children. Studies in which parents have been directed to make their children appear "good" or "bad" have found that parents are able to manipulate their child to appear socially undesirable, but not to appear more socially desirable (Lobitz & Johnson, 1975).

Attempts to minimize such distortions have been made by observing families in familiar situations, permitting a long period of adaptation through frequent sustained observations, and using unobtrusive measures. Some experi-menters have monitored homes by television or tape recorder during the entire waking hours of the family for periods as long as a month. Other studies have had observers appear at each dinner hour over a period of several weeks. Although it seems anyone would be a little disconcerted when an observer, wearing dark glasses to conceal the direction of his gaze and making notes on a clipboard, appeared regularly with the entreé, families report that they gradually almost become unaware of the observation. This is reflected in increases in less socially accepted behaviors, such as quarreling, criticizing, punishing, and using obscene language.

There are many ways of recording observations. In some cases the observer uses a specimen record, in which a description of everything the family is doing is written down. In other cases the observer may be interested only in studying a particular type of behavior such as how the child responds to commands by parents. The observer then might use event sampling, in which he or she only begins recording when a particular event occurs. The observer would start when the parent issues a command and terminate when the child has clearly obeyed or disobeyed the parent's directive. Finally the observer may use a sheet containing a list of behaviors; on this sheet the observer checks off which behaviors are occurring in a predetermined period of time. For example, if the family was going to be observed for an hour, the observer might divide the hour into 120 thirty-second units. Each time any of the behaviors on the list occurred in a single thirty-second time period, the observer would put a check beside the behavior on the list. This yields the frequency of different kinds of behaviors of family members in the hour session. In addition, by looking at the sequence of behaviors over successive thirty-second time units, a good picture of the interactions between family members emerges. If in the first thirty-second unit the baby throws his cereal, in the next the mother slaps the baby, in the third the baby cries, and in the fourth the mother picks the baby up and cuddles and pats him, a clear stream of behavior is apparent. The analysis of such behavioral sequences allows the psychologist to answer such questions as the following: When the mother criticizes her son, what is the most frequent response of the son? Does he ignore her? Argue with her? Yield and accept her criticism and show signs of remorse?

What do we do when we are interested in behavior that occurs infrequently and which we have only a slight chance of picking up in naturalistic observations? We can wait around for a long time before a child sets a fire, steals from her mother's purse, wets her bed, or has a temper tantrum. A number of techniques have been used to cope with infrequently occurring behaviors. One method is to structure situations in such a way that these behaviors are likely to occur. For example, if we are interested in parents' responses to their children's help-seeking behavior, we might increase the chance of children asking for help by giving them tasks or problems which are very difficult to solve. Another method used to obtain infrequent behavior is to have one of the family members serve as the observer. Thus the mother might keep a diary or checklist of the behaviors which occur in her interactions with her child or might be asked to keep a daily record of the child's behavior.

Laboratory Analogue Studies

Finally, there has been frequent use of laboratory analogue studies of family interaction over the past decade. In such studies a strange adult in the laboratory behaves in some manner assumed to be analogous to important parental behaviors or disciplinary practices. For example, the adult in the laboratory may be affectionate or withdraw attention and warmth, or be actively critical and punitive. The effects of these adult behaviors on the child's subsequent behaviors, such as responsiveness to rewards by the adult, attention seeking, resistance to temptation, or aggression, are then observed. Such controlled, experimental procedures permit greater inferences of cause-and-effect relationships within the specific laboratory setting. However, can it be assumed that these simplistic, restricted laboratory interactions of extremely short duration with strangers parallel the experience in intense, sustained, complex parent-child relations? It can be argued persuasively that an experimenter's giving children candy, praising them, and smiling differ qualitatively from the nurturance and warmth of a loving parent, or that a periodic criticism and removal of reward by a stranger are in no way similar to the overwhelming, inescapable, unpredictable threat of an erratic, punitive, rejecting parent.

Because of the limitations in all the methods used to study family interaction, many investigators have recently begun using multiple measures of family relations, with the hope that convergence of the findings based on different assessment techniques implies greater validity of the results.

Parent-Child Interaction

Most parents have some beliefs about the kinds of characteristics they would like to see in their children and the childrearing methods that should be used to attain them. However, it should be remembered that there are many paths to the development of positive social behaviors, just as there are many paths to the development of antisocial behaviors. There is no magically effective childrearing formula. Parental practices must be adapted to the temperament and needs of the individual child. Often very similar family situations are associated with divergent development in different children, and some children seem to be relatively invulnerable to the possible deleterious effects of adverse environments (Garmezy, 1975). With these limitations in mind, let us move on to examine the role of the parent in teaching and modeling social standards and behaviors, and of the home situation as an arena in which the child may practice some of these social skills.

The Parent as a Teacher

Early attachment of the parent to the child and the child to the parent in infancy serves as the foundation for later family relationships. Although socialization is certainly occurring in the first year of life, it seems to become more conscious and systematic with the occurrence of greater mobility and the beginning of language in the second year. Behaviors that previously were accepted, indulged, or regarded as "cute" start to be limited. Feet are no longer permitted on the high chair tray, smearing food is frowned on, exploration is restrained by playpen bars, and serious attempts at toilet training begin. As the child is practicing his new-found motor skills and exploring the world about him, climbing out of his crib, tottering to the head of the stairs, discovering the delights of the pot and pan cupboard, or eating cigarette butts, the air may be ringing with "Nos!" "Don'ts!" and "Stops!" The child will also be cuddled, petted, and praised for his achievements, for learning to use a spoon, for naming objects, for repeating words, for dry diapers, for the many behaviors that parents and society regard as desirable. The process of socialization has begun in earnest. The parent teaches the child the rules of the society in which he must live by telling the child what the rules are and by disciplining him as he conforms to or violates acceptable standards of behavior. In addition, parents will modify their children's behavior by serving as models for the child to imitate. The effectiveness of parents as teachers depends to some extent on their emotional relationship with the child and on the number and type of controls they attempt to exert.

Aspects of Parental Behavior   Parents' relationships with their children have frequently been conceptualized in terms of the interaction between two sets of parental attributes which are assumed to be relatively independent: warmth-hostility and restrictiveness-permissiveness. In a variety of studies based on both self-report and observational measures of parental attitudes and practices these key dimensions have emerged, sometimes in conjunction with less significant factors. The first factor deals with the emotional relationship of the parent with the child; the second with controls and restrictions placed upon the child's behavior. In general the parent's love dimension is more stable over time than the control dimensions.

In addition to these dimensions of parental behaviors, investigators have focused on the specific disciplinary techniques imposed by parents and the consistency with which discipline is applied. These disciplinary characteristics include such things as the use of reasoning and explanation versus physical forms of discipline, or the use of affection and threats of withdrawal of love versus material rewards and the withdrawal of privileges. These types of parental discipline are not independent of the dimensions of parental affection and control previously described. Hostile restrictiveness is associated with the frequent use of power-assertive techniques, and warmth is associated with induction in both mothers and fathers (Becker, Peterson, Luria, Shoemaker, & Hellmer, 1962).

The use of reasoning and explanation in discipline has positive effects on the social development of children. (Erika Stone)

The critical question must now be answered: Do these variations in parental behavior relate in any systematic way to differences in social and cognitive development in their children?

Parental Warmth or Hostility   Parental warmth is regarded as important in the socialization process for several reasons. First, the child is likely to wish to maintain the approval and be distressed at any prospect of the loss of love of a warm parent, and therefore the need for harsh forms of discipline to gain compliance is often unnecessary. In contrast, the threat of withdrawal of love is unlikely to be an effective mechanism of socialization when used by hostile parents who have little demonstrable affection to rescind. What has the child to lose?

Second, the frequent use by warm parents of reasoning and explanation permits the child to internalize social rules and identify and discriminate situations in which a given behavior is appropriate. It is easier to learn the rules of the game if someone tells you what they are and why you should play them that way. If the child reaches for a second piece of cake and her mother says, "No, you can't have another because your brother hasn't had one yet and there's only one piece left," it tells the child the circumstances under which she cannot have cake. At a future time she might anticipate that if everyone in the family had had cake, or if there were many pieces left, she would be permitted a second. If the parent uses inductive reasoning by adding "Brother would feel unfairly treated because he did not get his share," then the child becomes aware of how others feel in this situation, and as we will see in the chapter on self-control, this may lead to more concern with the well-being of others. This is in marked contrast to the effects of a peremptory parental "No!" where the child doesn't know if eating cake is bad, eating cake with hands is not permitted, she is bad, or the parent is mad. Even on those occasions when physical punishment is utilized by warm parents, they report it is more effective in limiting their child's behavior than do hostile parents. Again, this is probably both because the child wishes to conform to the standards of warm parents and because these parents are more likely to provide information about alternative socially desirable responses available to the child. These findings are consistent with the results of the laboratory studies of punishment and reasoning that were discussed earlier in the chapter on learning.

Third, warmth and nurturance by parents are likely to be associated with security, low anxiety, and self-esteem. Such attitudes and emotions are more likely to be conducive to learning than the high anxiety and tension associated with hostility or physical punishment in parents. The high stress associated with a punitive family situation may interfere with the child learning the "rules of the socialization game" which the parent is attempting to teach.

There are other reasons why warm parents may be more effective than hostile parents in inhibiting their children's behavior, particularly aggressive behavior, as was noted in the chapter on learning. When power-assertive methods such as physical punishment are used to control aggression, the hostile parent is also in the anomalous situation both of frustrating the child, which may lead to greater arousal of anger, and of offering an aggressive model to the child. In addition, the child may attempt to avoid contact with the punishing parent, which gives the parent less opportunity to socialize the child. As might be expected under such circumstances, the child usually exhibits little overt aggression in the home toward the threatening parents, but displaces it to others outside the home where he is less fearful of retaliation.

Child abuse   In some cases parental hostility and aggression become extreme, and severe abuse of the child occurs. Although it is difficult to get reliable estimates of how many children in the United States are abused, tens of thousands are brought to the attention of physicians, courts, and social service agencies each year. Many of these children have been sexually molested, starved, burned, beaten, cut, chained to furniture, or kept in isolation.

What circumstances contribute to this disastrous treatment of children? Most students reading this book probably think no one they know would ever abuse a child or that only someone who is really mentally ill would inflict such grievious physical harm on defenseless children. However, child abusers are found in all social classes and all religious, racial, and ethnic groups. In addition, there is no evidence of severe mental illness as a major contributing factor in child abuse.

Parents who abuse their children are frequently unemployed, poorly educated, and economically deprived (Garbarino & Grouter, 1978). In interpreting these findings on the greater incidence of abuse in lower-class parents, it should be kept in mind that middle- and upper-class parents may be less likely to have their abuse reported by their private physicians than are lower-class parents, who usually must go to public clinics or hospitals, the police, or social welfare agencies in seeking aid. In all economic levels the target of abuse seems more likely to be a child under the age of 3, whose mother had had a difficult pregnancy or labor, who had been premature or who have other physical and emotional problems, or who have a greater than average number of siblings. These factors may all contribute to the mother feeling antagonistic to the child and feeling that the child is different. It should not be thought that all abused children have such characteristics. It is just that they are found more often in abused than nonabused children. It may be that such problems in children are enough to tip the balance in already stressed families. Parents in these families often have conflicts with each other and are socially isolated. They seem to have fewer friends, relatives, or neighbors they can turn to in times of duress. The isolation may contribute in part to the fact that these parents often do not seem to recognize the seriousness of their behavior and blame the child rather than themselves for what is occurring. In addition, abusive parents seem to have unrealistic beliefs about parent-child relations. They often expect their children to perform in an impossibly developmentally advanced way or to exhibit levels of independence and self-control which would be unlikely in children of that age. These parents also frequently use the child for satisfaction of their own emotional needs. It is not surprising that mothers are most often the persons who abuse the child. They are locked into a stressful family situation and spend more time with the child than do other family members (Martin, 1976; Schmidt & Kempe, 1975; Parke & Collmer, 1975). How family tensions can interact to produce child abuse is vividly demonstrated in the case of Rachael, presented in Box 12-1. Note that it is not just one factor, but a series of interrelated stressful events, that leads up to the final catastrophe.

It has been proposed that there may be a generational effect of violence in families. Parents who abuse their children often themselves have been abused or emotionally deprived as children. In addition, the high incidence of child abuse may be supported by the general acceptance of physical punishment of children in the American culture (Gelles, 1976). In groups in which physical punishment of children is not accepted, such as in the American Indian, battered children are rarely found. Thus, it may be the cultural approval of violence in childrearing combined with the lack of social, economic, and emotional resources of caretakers which results in child abuse.

How can we help abusive parents and their children? Interventions should be oriented toward rapid responses to the first signs and cries for help and toward modifying the network of debilitating environmental circumstances associated with violence in the family. Emergency counseling services, twenty-four-hour-a-day hot lines which the parent can call for advice or assistance, crisis nurseries in which the parent can leave the child when he or she is under particular stress, therapeutic preschools, and involvement in parent groups similar to Alcoholics Anonymous have all been found useful in dealing with violence in the family (Lystad, 1975). Methods should be oriented not only toward protecting and helping the child, but toward reducing the parents' sense of isolation and the intensity and distortion in the stressful parent-child interaction. Aid for these parents does not have to come from highly trained professionals. Lay home visitors who show concern for the family and come into the home regularly to chat about the everyday problems of living encountered by the family can play an important role.

Finally, in child abuse cases, more than in most situations, it is difficult to strike a balance between the rights of parents and of children. Most of these parents do not want their children to be placed in substitute child-care facilities or foster homes. Many are genuinely attached to their children, and the children are surprisingly often very attached to the abusive parents. Courts and welfare agencies hesitate to break up families, especially since the alternative to the natural family is usually not a single foster home, but a series of foster homes which provide unstable relationships for the child. However, the reality of the situation is that what we may be dealing with is not just the rights of parents and children, but actual survival of the child. Half of the abused children who are returned to their homes ultimately die of neglect or abuse (Fontana, 1974). There is no way of accurately predicting which parents will continue to be violent. Careful attention and continuous support for the families should be available. However, it should be recognized that the parent's needs and the child's needs are not necessarily synonymous. In the case of battered children

BOX 12-1
A BATTERED CHILD: THE CASE OF RACHAEL

 At 11 weeks of age Rachael was admitted to the hospital hemorrhaging and covered with bruises, with a recent fracture of her leg and a new fracture of the arm. She had been severely beaten by her mother. What would lead a mother to so callously brutalize a tiny infant?

The father had an ordinary upbringing, but mother, the dominant partner, came from a notorious problem family. When her parents finally separated in her early teens she became the "Cinderella" of the household, staying home from school to care for younger siblings. She met her husband when she was fifteen years old, and after a two and a half year courtship they married. A pregnancy quickly followed. They were living amid hostility in the maternal grandmother's house. However, the baby, born after a pregnancy in which mother was physically fit, was "happy and contented." They moved to a distant town but because of unemployment soon were forced to return to maternal grandmother. A second pregnancy occurred. Mother became very ill with raised blood pressure and required hospitalization for six weeks, something she resented and blamed on the unborn child. There was great anxiety, among the obstetricians, over the fetal growth rate. Many investigations were performed culminating, at 34 weeks, in an amniocentesis which pierced the umbilical cord. Emergency Caesarean section had to be carried out to save the baby. Mother was horrified at being "cut open." The baby, Rachael, weighing five pounds six ounces, developed respiratory distress syndrome and remained in the special care nursery for five weeks. Mother felt strongly that the baby did not belong to her—"Just flesh and bone—with wires hanging out everywhere," (Mother's words). Ten days after mother had left hospital without her baby, she had the additional stress of moving into her own house. Her husband was now in regular work, but this entailed night shifts. It was difficult to visit the baby. When Rachael came home, no bond had formed between parents and child. She was difficult to feed, cried all the time and always had a cold. Her smile appeared late and was difficult to elicit. Advice with feeding and handling was regarded as interference by this defensive, isolated mother. However, on one occasion during a feeding battle, she bruised the buttocks and immediately called the family doctor. This open warning was not read, mother receiving only reassurance. Two and a half weeks later the child was admitted almost dead to the hospital. (Martin, 1976, pp. 43–44)

Each of the sequentially occurring stressful events put this baby at increased risk of abuse. The mother, unable to cope any longer, violently exploded against the infant. ■

Source: Martin, H. *The abused child.* Cambridge, Mass.: Ballinger, 1976.

the survival of the child and the child's psychological, emotional, and physical needs should be the primary concern (Fraser & Martin, 1976).

Parental Control   Parental love alone is not enough to lead to positive social development in children. Some degree of parental control is necessary if children are to develop into socially and intellectually competent individuals.

Either extreme of parental restrictiveness or permissiveness leads to deficient development. Baumrind (1967) suggests that *authoritative* rather than *authoritarian* parental control is desirable; in the former, parents are not intrusive and do permit their children considerable freedom within reasonable limits, but are willing to impose restrictions in areas in which they have greater knowledge or insight. Such discipline gives children the opportunity to explore their environment and gain interpersonal competence without the anxiety and neurotic inhibition associated with hostile, restrictive, power-assertive discipline practices, or the inexperience in conforming to the demands and needs of others associated with extreme permissiveness. In general, high warmth and moderate restrictiveness with the parents setting reasonable limits but being responsive and attentive to their children's needs are associated with the development of self-esteem, adaptability, competence, internalized control, and popularity with peers. This relationship is illustrated in a well-designed study by Baumrind (1967), which is presented in Box 12-2. She identified three groups of children having various characteristics and found that authoritative but not authoritarian or overly permissive behavior by parents led to positive emotional, social, and cognitive development in children.

In a subsequent study Baumrind (1971) used a reverse strategy and rather than initially finding the groups of children and then studying their parents, she first identified groups of parents having clusters of different attributes and then related these to the behavior of their children. The results confirmed many findings of the previous study. Sons of authoritative parents were more friendly, cooperative, and achievement-oriented than those of any other parent groups, and daughters of authoritative parents were more dominant, achievement-oriented, and independent.

Parental Conflict and Inconsistency in Discipline   A third characteristic of parental discipline which influences children's behavior is the consistency with which discipline is administered. Parental conflict and inconsistency are associated with maladjusted behavior in children, most often in the form of aggressive or delinquent behavior (Glueck & Glueck, 1950; Hetherington, Cox, & Cox, 1978a; Garmezy, 1975; McCord, McCord, & Zola, 1959; Martin & Hetherington, 1971; Patterson, 1977, 1978). Boys are much more susceptible to the negative effects of marital disharmony than are girls (Hetherington, Cox, & Cox, 1978e; Rutter, 1977).

It may be particularly important to study configurations of parent relations rather than the attributes of either parent singly. Even in homes with a criminal parent, when both the mothers and fathers are consistent in discipline, a low incidence of delinquency occurs in the children. In fact, the lowest rates of delinquency have been found in homes in which both parents were *either* consistently punitive or consistently warm in their discipline practices. When they were consistent, the particular form of discipline did not matter. It has been suggested that extremely restrictive, power-assertive discipline, especially in a hostile family atmosphere, results in frustration of dependency needs and an increased predisposition to respond aggressively. If the opportunity to express

BOX 12-2
PARENTAL BEHAVIORS AND THE DEVELOPMENT OF SOCIAL COMPETENCE IN CHILDREN

 What parental behaviors are associated with the development of social competence or maladaptive behaviors in children? In this study, on the basis of fourteen weeks of behavioral observation of nursery school children, three groups of children exhibiting markedly different behavior were identified. Group I (energetic-friendly) children were rated higher on the following characteristics than were the other two groups: interest and curiosity in approaching novel or stressful situations, self-reliance, self-control, energy level, cheerfulness, and friendly relations with peers. Group II (conflicted-irritable) children were less cheerful and more moody, apprehensive, unhappy, easily annoyed, passively hostile and guileful, and vulnerable to stress than were the energetic-friendly children. In interpersonal relations they alternated between aggressive, unfriendly interactions and withdrawal. Group III (impulsive-aggressive) children were even less self-reliant and controlled than group II conflicted-irritable children and seemed to be almost entirely impulsive and lacking in self-control. However, they were more cheerful and recovered more readily from irritations than did the conflicted-irritable children. Parent behavior was assessed by interview and by observations in the home and both in a structured observation procedure involving the mother teaching the child some simple mathematical concepts and in a free-play period in the laboratory. Data on parental behavior from all procedures tended to be congruent.

The parent scores on control, maturity demands, communication, and nurturance in the structured observation and home visit observations are graphed in Figure 12-1. Parents of the energetic-friendly child were more nurturant than parents in the other groups, as measured by high use of positive reinforcement and low use of

punishment, and responsiveness to the child's request for support and attention. However, they were not indulgent; they were willing to direct and control the child and were less likely to yield to unpleasant, coercive demands by the child based on crying, whining, and nagging. Baumrind describes their control as *authoritative* rather than *authoritarian* since it was not necessarily extremely restrictive, punitive, rigid, or intrusive. Although these parents did not yield to the child's coercive demands, they more often explicitly altered their position on the basis of specific arguments advanced by the child. They also demanded more mature, independent behavior from their children and explained to their children the reason for their position.

Parents of the conflicted-irritable children and the impulsive-aggressive children seemed to be inept parents for different reasons. The parents of the conflicted-irritable children viewed their children as dominated by impulsive antisocial forces which needed to be suppressed. They did not listen to the child's concerns or needs and did not respond in a manner appropriate to their children's developmental level. They were more persistent in enforcing their demands in the face of opposition and coercive techniques by the child than were the parents of the impulsive-aggressive children. In their rigid enforcement of rules they were likely to be more harsh in discipline than the other parents, and the fathers used more corporal punishment than the fathers in the other groups of children. These parents were labeled *authoritarian* parents. It may be that the parents' inflexible, frustrating responses, which may be aggression-producing, in combination with punitive responses, which may be aggression-inhibiting, could well be resulting in the neuroticlike conflict of these children.

Finally, the parents in the impulsive-aggressive group were more nurturant than those of the conflicted-irritable children. However, they were also excessively lax and inconsistent in discipline, were unable to direct their children's behavior, and made fewer demands for appropriately mature or independent behavior from their children. This was associated with a lack of self-control and lack of internalization of social standards in their children. ■

Source: Baumrind, D. Child care practices anteceding three patterns of preschool behavior. *Genetic Psychology Monographs*, 1967, **75**, 43–88.

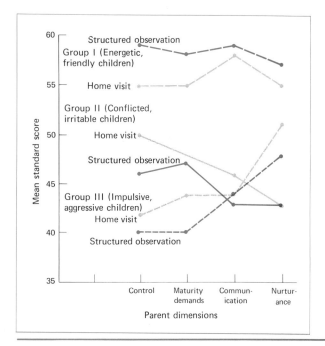

FIGURE 12-1 Profile of composited parent dimension scores from the summary ratings for the structured observation (SRSO) and the home visit sequence analysis (HVSA) for each pattern. *(From Baumrind, 1967, p. 73.)*

this aggression occurs through inconsistent discipline, laxity in one parent, or actual encouragement of aggressive behavior outside the home, this may increase the probability of antisocial, aggressive responses by the child.

The Parent as a Model

In addition to playing an important role in socialization by verbalizing the values of the culture and rewarding or punishing the child's behavior in relation to these cultural standards, the parent socializes the child by serving as a model for the child to imitate. Although the process is called by many names, all psychologists recognize that children emulate other persons or groups and that this process leads to increased actual or perceived similarity between the child and these persons. Psychoanalysts have called this process *identification*, learning theorists

Modeling is an important process in the learning of social roles and the acquisition of skills. (Hella Hammid, Photo Researchers, Inc.)

have called it *imitation* or *modeling*, and sociologists have called it the *adoption of roles*.

The question of which characteristics of a model are acquired and the specific processes involved in the acquisition of such similarities is a controversial one. If the people with whom the child comes in contact exhibit attributes valued by society, socialization is facilitated; if the child is surrounded by deviant models, culturally approved behaviors are less likely to be acquired. Children with emotionally unstable or criminal parents are more likely to develop maladaptive or delinquent patterns of behavior. The child who comes from a family with affectionate, honest, hard-working parents is more likely to demonstrate ethical behavior, a concern for others, and a need to achieve than is a child who has a viciously punitive father and an alcoholic mother and was reared in a slum populated by drug pushers, prostitutes, and pimps.

It is apparent that in most cases children identify with different attributes of a variety of models. A child may exhibit his mother's fear of dogs, his father's sense of humor, his older brother's enthusiasm for Paul Simon, and his scout master's interest in Indian lore. The characteristics on which individuals can resemble each other seem to range from generalized attitudes, aspirations, and interests to very specific mannerisms and behaviors. Sometimes similarities are manifested as broad cognitive, personality, or social styles which will influence behavior in a variety of situations. Both child and parent may be cautious and systematic in problem solving or concerned about social approval in interpersonal relations. In some cases such shared values or styles of relating to people may cause parent and child to behave alike even in new situations where the child has had no opportunity to observe the responses of his parent. Some of the most important behaviors in which imitation is assumed to play a key role are in moral development and self-control and in the development of behaviors viewed as appropriate for males or females. The development of these behaviors will be presented in later chapters.

Since imitation begins early and since the child's major social contacts are largely limited to the family in the preschool years, the role of the parents is critical in the process of identification. Even in the first year of life the child's imitation and the parents' encouragement of imitative behaviors can be seen. The child and parent repeatedly play imitative games such as "peek-a-boo" and "waving bye-bye." The parent echoes the baby's vocalizations and encourages the infant to repeat words after her. Mothers spend hours pointing to objects, naming them, and encouraging the child to repeat the names. Although the parents are the crucial models early in life, as the child gains greater social mobility with age, the roles of siblings, peers, social institutions, and mass media become increasingly important.

Various theorists have emphasized different aspects of the parent-child relationship as being most important in the process of identification. The dimensions of parental behavior that have been found to facilitate imitation by the child are presented in Box 12-3.

There are a number of reasons why a child may be motivated to acquire her parents' behaviors and values. The child maintains parental affection by behaving in a similar fashion to the parent, and also the child gains a sense of mastery over the environment by emulating the responses of a warm, competent, powerful parent (Kagan, 1964). In addition, as children gain some sense of self-identity, they begin to make what might be called "we-they" discriminations (Parsons, 1955). That is, the child gradually identifies persons or groups with whom she shares common characteristics (we) and those from whom she differs (they). She learns that "we" family members are different than "those" outsiders. She learns that "we" females (mothers, daughters, girls, and women) are different from "those" males (fathers, sons, boys, and men). It might be expected that some "we-they" categorizations would be more important in some cultures than in others. In Northern Ireland "we" Catholics versus "those" Protestants would be an early developed and influential differentiation. In this country "we" blacks versus "those" whites might be more salient. As the child perceives that she is similar to certain people or groups, it may become rewarding to emulate their behavior.

An important distinction should be noted between observational learning or imitation and tuition, reward, and punishment as processes of socialization. Parents in verbalizing standards and trying to enforce them through rewards and punishment usually are knowingly trying to shape the child's behavior. In contrast, imitation often occurs without the parent having intended to influence the child. Many parents verbalize one set of values and exhibit quite another.

BOX 12-3
CHARACTERISTICS OF MODELS
WHICH FACILITATE IMITATION

1   Fear of punishment—This is sometimes called identification with the aggressor or defensive identification. A threatening model is selected because of an individual's fear of injury or punishment from the model.

2   Secondary reinforcement—A model is selected because he or she has behaved in a nurturant or rewarding way to the child.

3   Fear of loss of love—A model is selected because the child is afraid that the model will withdraw love and approval.

4   Vicarious reinforcement—A model is selected because the model receives rewards, suggesting that observers who imitate the model's behavior may also be rewarded. In this case, in contrast to secondary reinforcement, it is the model rather than the child who is being directly rewarded.

5   Status envy—A model is selected because he or she is envied as a possessor, recipient, or consumer of rewards.

6   Social dominance—A model is selected because he or she is powerful in coping with the environment and in making decisions to reward or punish others.

7   Similarity—A model is selected because the child perceives that the model has characteristics similar to his or her own. ■

Source: Secord, P. R., & Backman, C. W. *Social psychology.* New York: McGraw-Hill, 1964.

A "do as I say, not as I do" approach to socialization is ineffective. If the child sees a church-going, platitude-spouting, moralizing parent lie about his golf score, cheat on his income tax, bully his children, and pay substandard wages to his help, the child may emulate his parents' behaviors rather than his hypocritical words. (Hetherington & Morris, 1978, p. 9)

Studies of Imitation   Attempts to assess the relation between various parental behaviors and identification have been focused on three parental characteristics which have been of great theoretical interest: warmth, power, and punitiveness. Evidence from imitation studies supports the position that children tend to emulate nurturant or powerful models more than nonnurturant or nondominant models, whether the models are parents or strangers (Bandura & Huston, 1961; Bandura, Ross, & Ross, 1963; Hetherington, 1965; Hetherington & Frankie, 1967; Mischel & Grusec, 1966; Mussen & Parker, 1965). However, there is some variation in the effects of the models' warmth and power on children's imitation according to what specific behaviors are to be modeled and whether it is a boy or girl doing the imitating. Girls tend to be more responsive to the model's warmth and boys to the model's dominance. Warmth also facilitates the imitation of task-irrelevant responses, such as gestures, mannerisms, and comments, more than task-relevant or problem-solving responses (Hetherington, Cox, Thomas, & Hunt, 1974). Children may view the parent or model who makes decisions and seems to be in control of things as more competent and more likely to succeed in problem solving. In task-relevant or problem-solving imitation it may be a matter of "Who wants to imitate a loser, even a loving loser, when you are trying to solve a problem?"

In addition, warmth of the model facilitates imitation more when the model is a parent than when the model is a strange experimenter interacting with the child in an attentive, affectionate, approving way. It may be that nurturance is difficult to communicate in short-term interactions in the laboratory with strangers, or that being with a stranger in an unfamiliar situation is more stressful than being with a parent. Stress may reduce the effects of the model's nurturance while increasing the effects of power. In a stressful situation the child may want to go along with the "boss" in order to feel more secure.

Laboratory studies give considerable support to theories of imitation and identification which emphasize the importance of the dominance and warmth or nurturance of the model or parent in the child's imitation. In contrast, laboratory studies of imitation offer little support for the theory of defensive identification with a threatening parent proposed by Freud. Evidence for identification with the aggressor rests largely on clinical cases (Freud, 1923; Freud, 1946) and anecdotal reports (Bettelheim, 1969). Bettelheim reports that prisoners in Nazi concentration camps frequently adopted vocal and postural mannerisms and styles of dress resembling those of the punitive guards. They were often similarly physically and verbally abusive toward new prisoners and were brutally and irrationally cruel and authoritarian when supervising others.

It has been suggested that three conditions are essential in producing identification with the aggressor: a hostile person who directs his aggression toward another person; a victim who is dependent upon the aggressor; and a situation involving stresses and limitations that prevent escape from the aggression (Sarnoff, 1951). The home situation which would seem to most adequately fulfill these criteria and lead to identification with a hostile, dominant parent would be one in which there is a stressful, conflictual atmosphere and both parents are cold. Such a home would offer the child no escape by seeking a closer relationship with a warm, nondominant parent, and the stressful family relationship should heighten his feelings of helplessness and anxiety and his tendency toward defensive identification with the aggressor.

In a study designed to test this position it was found that when both parents were hostile and there was high conflict in the home, boys and girls tended to imitate the dominant parent, whether it was the mother or the father. This effect was most marked with sons and dominant, hostile fathers. If either the nondominant parent was warm or conflict was reduced, there was less imitation of the aggressive, powerful parent. It appears that defensive identification with a dominant, punitive model occurs only under the extremely restrictive conditions of high stress and absence of a supportive, loving parent to whom the child may turn for protection and succor (Hetherington & Frankie, 1967).

The Thinking Child   The effects of parental tuition rewards, punishments, and modeling are not automatic. The parents are conveying complex information about social values and behavior to the child, and the way in which the child processes and interprets this information will determine her response. The child's cognitive level, to a large extent, will determine how the child processes socialization inputs. The developing child's changing conceptions of the world about her will have implications for how she interprets, remembers, and responds to rules, contingencies in parental reinforcement, and the behavior of models. Younger children will organize and view events in a different way than will older children because of their cognitive limitations.

We have said that socialization is the process whereby the child learns the rules of the social game. The child uses the information available from the observed actions of others, and responses of others to her own behavior, to make inferences about cause and effect in social behavior and to classify events and people in ways that facilitate the understanding and acquisition of social rules. If this is the case, what are the implications for a theory of socialization? Maccoby (1975) has suggested that the effectiveness of parents as agents of socialization will in large part depend on how their actions facilitate the rule-making processes in the child. Reasoning seems to facilitate rule making, and for a very young child predictibility of the environment may be particularly important. If the situation, events, or behavior of others is too rapidly changing or erratic, children may have difficulty in identifying consistencies in the social world. If the parent is sometimes responsive and sometimes neglecting, sometimes rocks the infant when she cries and occasionally spanks her, it may be difficult to learn the rules of the game.

Finally, parents should permit the child to take the initiative and assume responsibilities appropriate for her capabilities in social relations. The child needs the freedom to apply, test, and practice her social rules. She must learn by doing.

Husbands and Wives as a Mutual Support System

It is important to remember that parents have a relationship with each other as well as with their children. Parents serve as sources of mutual emotional and physical support and comfort. There is considerable evidence that nonworking mothers of young children are among the least satisfied and most depressed group of adults. This is in large part attributable to the task load, restrictions, and constant demands placed upon them in their caretaking role and is reflected in the mother-child interaction. High mother-infant involvement and sensitive, competent, affectionate mother-infant relationships have been found when fathers were supportive of mothers (Pederson, 1975; Pederson, Anderson, & Cain, 1977; Feiring & Taylor, 1977). Even successful maternal adaptation to pregnancy and low maternal distress during labor and delivery are related to the responsiveness and support of husbands. Dual participation in household chores and caretaking can free both parents for more playful and pleasurable interactions with their children and relieve some of the burdens often experienced by parents, especially mothers with young children.

In addition, high conflict between the parents is associated with negative feelings directed toward children (Pederson et al., 1977). Lack of satisfaction in the marital relationship seems to be reflected in poor parent-child relations. This suggests that the frequently employed strategy of having a baby as a means of solidifying an unstable marriage may have a disastrous outcome.

Again we must view these parental relations in terms of the total family system. At the same time as the relationship between the parents is affecting how they respond to their children, the child is influencing the marital relationship. Pregnancy and the birth of a first child, in particular, are associated with a shift toward a more traditional-type division of family roles (Cowan, Cowan, Coie, & Coie, 1976; Doering & Entwisle, 1977). It is particularly interesting that this shift toward more stereotyped masculine and feminine roles occurs whether or not the initial role division in the family before having children was traditional or egalitarian. In spite of the rhetoric concerning equality of roles for men and women, even in relatively untraditional homes there seems to be an implicit assumption that the role of the mother with young children is in the home and that of the father is to provide. Although many fathers take time from their work

Parents play important roles as mutual support systems in child rearing. (Erika Stone)

to be with their wife and newborn, it rarely exceeds two weeks, and then even in families where both parents have worked, it is the wife who is most likely to give up her occupation.

Children have an impact on the relationship between their parents in other ways. Temperamentally difficult, deviant, or handicapped children impose additional stresses on parents which may be reflected in marital conflict. The presence of a demanding, recalcitrant child may be enough to fragment a fragile marriage. It may be because the wife more often remains in the home with the children that mothers of problem children express more dissatisfaction with their marriage and family situation than do fathers.

Social Class and Socialization

No culture is entirely homogeneous. Subgroups within a culture may have different problems to cope with and divergent values. These may be reflected in different goals and methods in socialization.

Powerlessness and Poverty, Affluence and Alienation

Considerable concern has been focused on differences between the life situations of lower-working-class families and middle-class families in the American culture. Although the most obvious differences between these social groups are economic ones, other related pervasive features of their life may be more directly relevant to the process of socialization.

The critical importance of children having the opportunity of learning to control and shape their environment has been discussed previously. Without this growing sense of power based on the responsiveness of others, the child's feelings of helplessness, incompetence, and low self-esteem are reflected in disruptions in cognitive, emotional, and adaptive processes.

In an analogous manner, powerlessness is a basic problem of the poor. They have less influence over the society in which they live and are likely to be less adequately treated by social organizations than are members of the middle class. They receive poorer health and public services, and they are more likely to have their individual rights violated by agents of the law or social workers or educators or the medical profession. Their lack of power and prestige and lack of educational and economic resources restrict the availability of options in most areas of their lives. They have little control or choice of occupations or housing and little contact with other social groups; they are tragically vulnerable to disasters such as job loss, financial stress, and illness; and they are subject to impersonal bureaucratic decisions in the legal system and in social institutions, such as welfare agencies. In addition, the low educational level, restricted experience, and lack of information of the poor make it difficult for them to understand and avail themselves of the limited resources which are open to them.

However, it may be that the very stresses which engender an awareness of lack of social power in working-class families also result in the formation of extensive support networks of kin, friends, and neighbors by these families,

(a)

(b)

Children raised in afflu-
ence or in poverty con-
front different kinds of
stresses. (Photo (a) Burk
Uzzle, Magnum; photo
(b) United Press Interna-
tional)

particularly by economically deprived black families (McAdoo, 1978; Stack, 1974). These systems, which involve not only emotional support, but rendering of unpaid services, function as both a form of exchange and a type of insurance (Halbertsma, 1970). In the precarious financial situation of the poor, services cannot be purchased. Mutual assistance must be rendered in fulfilling not only emergency needs of the family in times of unemployment, childbirth, illness, and death, but also the day-to-day needs of family life.

It is when these networks break down, sometimes because of economically necessitated needs, such as adults having to move to a new location to obtain work, and sometimes because of change or destruction in neighborhoods, that working-class families are most vulnerable. Some of the policies which attempt to provide a higher standard of housing for working-class people through slum clearance or relocation to housing developments destroy the very support systems which are the mainstays of these families.

In the preceding discussion, middle-class family life appears much more desirable and less stressful than lower-class life. However, there is also considerable duress in middle-class families. The push toward academic, economic, and professional achievement and conformity with middle-class values and the social isolation of middle-class families all contribute to these tensions.

Very wealthy upper-class children often become anxious and alienated (Coles, 1978). They feel burdened by their possessions, their affluence, and their special position. They wonder whether they are valued for themselves or their status and become suspicious of, or detached from, their peers. Some of these children become distressed by the excess of choices open to them. Others feel oppressed because the options are sometimes less real than originally thought. Educational and vocational freedom for middle- and upper-class children often turns out to be a choice of going into business, going to graduate school for medicine or law, or going on for a graduate degree in some other subject. A decision not to go on to college precipitates disappointment or outrage in well-to-do parents. Seldom do middle- and upper-class parents view being a butcher, a baker, a candlestick maker, or a ski bum as reasonable career choices for their offspring. In addition, these economically privileged children often move from one home to another with increasing affluence or career opportunities for their parents. They also spend much of their vacation time in travel. This mobility sometimes results in a sense of rootlessness that is similar to that found in economically deprived migrant workers.

These pressures may result in middle- or upper-class children angrily or destructively rejecting their parents' values and life-styles. However, it also may result in a more constructive outcome involving concern with social justice and the plight of those who are less privileged.

In turn, the outcome for lower-class children may be positive in spite of their economic and social disadvantages. They may experience personal ties with a broader network of people in their neighborhoods and develop an ethic of mutual support and sharing. They may be more cynical but also more realistic in their view of how society operates. Their very awareness of their vulnerability and the threats in their world may make them more aware of and able to deal with interpersonal conflicts. Learning to cope with stress may be like any other learning situation; some practice helps. Although a situation where the child is overwhelmed by stress and completely restricted by a lack of social supports and options is likely to be harmful, the overprotected environment of the middle- or upper-class child may also offer the child few opportunities in which to learn to cope with difficult situations.

Social Class and Childrearing

In view of the wide discrepancy in life situations between the poor and the more economically privileged, it is surprising that there are not more differences found in values and childrearing. What few there are can best be conceptualized in terms of a dimension of power and self-direction versus helplessness and obedience to the demands of others. Lower-class parents place more emphasis on respectability and obedience to authority; middle-class parents put more emphasis on the development of curiosity, internal control, the ability to delay gratification and work for distant goals, and sensitivity in relations with others.

Social-class differences are found in the kind and timing of restrictions placed on children (Bronfenbrenner, 1961; Clausen & Williams, 1963; Hess, 1970). There is less restrictiveness among middle-class parents toward the infant and young child, but greater parental supervision and control in adolescence. Middle-class parents are more permissive in early feeding, toilet, sex, and aggression training. However, they also expect early development of responsibility and have higher achievement and academic goals for their children. The shift to greater permissiveness by the lower-class parents with older children may be attributable in part to the expectation of earlier attainment of economic independence by children in lower-class families. Most lower-class adolescents must of necessity help contribute financially to their own support, in contrast to middle-class children who usually expect to be supported through college and often graduate school, well into young adulthood.

Family Size, Siblings, and Socialization

Over 80 percent of the families in the United States have more than one child. The functioning of the family is influenced by the number, sex, and spacing of children. These factors must be considered not only in view of their effects on parent-child interaction, but also in terms of the influence siblings, that is, brothers and sisters, have on each other.

As family size increases, opportunities for extensive contact between the parents and the individual child decrease, but opportunities for a variety of interactions with siblings expand.

A parent's attitude toward childrearing and the circumstances under which a child is reared will change as more children are added to the family. With a large number of children, particularly in families with over six children, family roles tend to become more precisely defined, chores are assigned, and discipline is more authoritarian and severe (Bossard & Boll, 1960). Parents can't afford to be indulgent with a large number of children or chaos will result. There is little time for reasoning and extended explanations. More use of hostile, restrictive control by mothers, particularly in relation to daughters, occurs in large families (Nuttall & Nuttall, 1971). In addition, as family size increases, the mother exhibits not only less attention but less warmth toward individual children. Frequently older siblings are assigned the supervisory and disciplinary roles maintained by parents in smaller families.

Girls are more likely than boys to play an active caretaking and helping role with their siblings (Cicirelli, 1976). A firstborn girl of 12 in a large family may warm bottles, burp babies, change diapers, and soothe a squalling infant with

The birth of a new baby often leads to sibling rivalry. (Suzanne Szasz, Photo Researchers, Inc.)

the alacrity and skill of a young mother. Because the parents in large families cannot interact as closely with their children as those in smaller families, there is less opportunity for overprotection, infantalization, constant harassing, or close supervision of children. The results of this relationship are reflected in the greater independence but lower academic achievement of children from large families.

In addition to the changes in social relationships imposed by large family size, economic burdens and crowding may contribute to stresses within the family. When the large family is economically secure, many of the pressures on family members are alleviated and conflicts and authoritarianism are reduced. Since many lower-class families are large, some of the class differences in interaction patterns may be attributable to family size.

Parent-Child Interactions and Birth Order

When differences related to birth order have been obtained, these are usually attributed to variations in interaction with parents and siblings associated with the unique life experiences found in children with that position in the family.

This is particularly true in the unusual role of the firstborn child. The eldest child is the only one who, until he is dethroned by the birth of a subsequent child, does not have to share his parents' love and attention with other siblings. How distressing the dethroning of the firstborn child will be depends to a large extent on the responses of the parents. The birth of a new baby usually decreases the amount of interaction between spouses and between mothers and older children (Taylor & Kogan, 1973). However, increased involvement of the father with the firstborn child can to some extent counter the child's feelings of displacement and jealousy of the younger sibling (Legg, Sherick, & Wadland, 1974). In fact, since the demands on parents are increased by the birth of second or subsequent children, it has been proposed that a positive effect of the second birth may be that it requires greater participation in child care by fathers (Lamb, 1979).

In spite of the fact that a new infant or younger child necessitates more attention and care from parents than does an older child, there seems to be an especially intense and concerned involvement of parents and firstborn children which is maintained throughout life. Even when their children are infants, parents spend more time with, stimulate, and talk more to firstborn infants (Thoman, Liederman, & Olson, 1972). The difference in mothers' responsive affection to firstborns and secondborns is most marked if the secondborn child is a girl (Jacobs & Moss, 1976). This pattern of effects differs in interactions involving the mother or father. The father talks to and touches firstborn boys more than firstborn girls or later-born children (Parke & Sawin, 1975). In contrast, mothers smile and vocalize more to firstborn girls than to other children (Thoman, Liederman, & Olson, 1972). Parents pay more attention to the firstborn not only early in life; even after the birth of other children, parents tend to direct their comments toward and pitch their conversation at the level of the eldest child (Bossard & Boll, 1956; Koch, 1955). This may be one of the reasons firstborns show accelerated verbal development. The quality as well as the quantity of parent-child interaction varies with the birth order. Parents have higher expectations for, exert greater pressures toward achievement and acceptance of responsibility, and interfere more with the activities of firstborn than later-born children (Lasko, 1954; Cushna, 1966; Hilton, 1967; Rothbart, 1971). Firstborn children also have greater disciplinary friction with their parents. At any age more physical punishment is likely to be administered to a firstborn than to a later-born child. In contrast, parents are more consistent and relaxed in disciplinary functions with later-born children, perhaps as a result of self-confidence gained from practice in childrearing (Lasko, 1954). In a sense the firstborn is the "practice baby" on which the parent, through trial and error, learns parenting skills.

These divergent patterns of parent-child interaction for firstborn and later-born children are found in studies using both parental reports and direct observation. Hilton (1967) observed that mothers of only and firstborn 4-year-olds were more extreme, inconsistent, and interfering in their child's behavior on a puzzle-solving task in the laboratory than were mothers with their later-born children. Mothers of early-born children, in addition to giving their children more task-oriented instructions, were more likely to demonstrate love if the child was doing well and withdrawal of love and approval for poor performance.

There has been some suggestion that in such situations mothers are more exacting, critical, intrusive, and demanding of firstborn daughters than of sons (Cushna, 1966; Rothbart, 1971). Although there is insufficient evidence, it may be that both parents are more demanding of same-sexed eldest children.

Sibling Interaction and Birth Order

In addition to birth order being associated with differences in parent-child relations, it is associated with variations in sibling relations. The eldest child is frequently expected to assume some responsibility and self-control toward the younger sibling who has displaced him. When the eldest child feels jealousy or hostility, he is likely to be restrained or punished by his parents and the younger child is likely to be protected and defended. On the other hand, the eldest child is more dominant, competent, and able to bully or, conversely, to assist and teach the younger offspring.

Eldest children focus on parents as their main sources of social learning within the family, whereas younger children use both parents and siblings as models and teachers. Direct observational studies of the social interaction of siblings have confirmed that younger siblings, even infants as young as 12 months, tend to watch, follow, and imitate their older siblings (Lamb, 1977; Samuels, 1977). The fact that they take over toys recently abandoned by their older brothers and sisters and imitate their behavior suggests that older siblings may play an important role in facilitating the younger child's mastery over the inanimate environment (Lamb, 1977). It is noteworthy that no such reciprocal behavior of the older sibling toward the younger is found. Older siblings show relatively little interest in the activities of their younger brothers and sisters unless it interferes with their own pursuits.

This greater involvement of younger than older siblings is clearly seen in Figure 12-2. Figure 12-2 presents the relative amounts of behavior exhibited by infants 16 to 22 months of age and their siblings who were three years older, when they were interacting in pairs in a playroom. The impact of the older sibling is particularly apparent when we examine the differences in the effects of having an older brother or sister on the social behavior of younger children. Boys with older sisters in contrast to those with older brothers exhibit more feminine

FIGURE 12-2   Behaviors of infants and their older siblings interacting in a playroom. *(From Samuels, 1977.)*

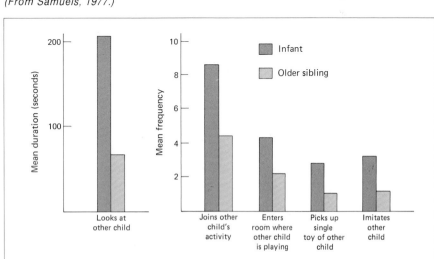

behavior (Brim, 1958), are less aggressive (Longstreth, Longstreth, Ramirez, & Fernandez, 1975), are more dependent and withdrawn, and are more likely to be underachievers in school (Hodges & Balow, 1961; Koch, 1960).

Characteristics of Firstborn Children

In view of the marked differences in family dynamics related to birth order it is not surprising that different characteristics are associated with firstborn and later-born children. Firstborn children remain more adult-oriented, helpful, self-controlled, conforming, anxious, and less aggressive than their siblings. The parental demands and high standards imposed on firstborns result in eldest children being more studious, conscientious, and serious. These children excel in academic and professional achievement. This is supported by their overrepresentation in *Who's Who* and among Rhodes scholars and eminent American men of letters and science.

Emotionally and socially firstborns show less self-confidence and social poise and greater fear of failure and guilt than later-borns. They are more apprehensive about pain and are more anxious than later-borns in stressful situations (Schacter, 1959). This is reflected in their avoidance of dangerous or competitive sports and of occupations or activities that may result in physical harm (Nisbett, 1968). Firstborns seem less able to cope with anxiety-producing situations. In situations involving danger, such as piloting a fighter plane in combat, firstborns are less effective than later-borns (Torrance, 1954). Under stressful conditions firstborns, especially firstborn girls, prefer to be with other people. In a laboratory situation where subjects expected to receive painful high-intensity shocks, firstborn females more often wished to wait in a room with another person in preference to being alone in the period preceding the experiment (Schacter, 1959).

The power failure in New York City on November 9 and 10, 1965, provided a naturalistic stress situation in which to test the generality of laboratory findings relating to anxiety and affiliation in firstborns. The blackout resulted in many people being stranded in the city and being physically uncomfortable and uncertain about what was going on. They were separated from families and friends, were often in unfamiliar situations, and were deprived of information. The experimenters collected information from people in a bus station and a hotel where there was some dim emergency lighting. Firstborns reported being more anxious than later-borns in this situation, and more firstborn than later-born women had been striking up casual acquaintances and talking or interacting with someone prior to the experimental interview (Zucker, Manosevitz, & Lanyon, 1968).

The greater pressures and anxiety of the primary birth order may also be a factor in the high frequency of admission of firstborns to child guidance clinics (Phillips, 1956; Rosenoer & Whyte, 1931) and of neurotic symptoms, such as oversensitivity, sleep disorders, and timidity (MacFarlane, Allen, & Honzik, 1954), in firstborns. Later-borns, on the other hand, tend to manifest conduct disorders such as aggression and hyperactivity.

The only child has frequently been regarded as a "spoiled brat," combining undesirable symptoms such as dependency, egotism, lack of self-control, and emotional disorders. However, research findings suggest that in many ways the only child has advantages over other children. Although exposed to the high parental demands and guidance of firstborns, an only child does not have to adapt to ultimate displacement and competition with siblings. As was the case with firstborns, this sustained close relationship with the parents is associated with dependency and high achievement; however, an only child is lower on anxiety, is more assertive, has higher self-esteem, and is socially more adaptable.

In social relations both outside and inside the home only children seem to make more positive adjustments than children distressed by sibling rivalry. The main disadvantages suffered by only children are the problems associated with too strong an identification with the opposite-sex parent. Sutton-Smith and Rosenberg state:

The most striking data on only children have to do with the sex role differences between male and female only children. Cushna's data (1966) show that mothers favor only boys to a much greater extent than only girls. There are other data to show that the only boy is more feminine than other males, and the only girl more masculine; moreover that the deviation in these opposite-sex directions leaves them with a greater general tendency toward sex deviation consonant with these tendencies. (Sutton-Smith & Rosenberg, 1970, p. 153)

Characteristics of Later-Born Children

The characteristics of the second or middle child in the family are less clearly defined. The middle child suffers from rivalry with a younger sibling, without the compensation of being in a power position comparable to that of the eldest. She also often experiences parental neglect since she is caught between the parents' intense relationship with the eldest sibling and nurturant, affectionate relation with the youngest. Middle children have poor achievement and short attention spans, are readily distractible, and are often characterized as flighty. They tend to be extroverted, frequently seeking the companionship and affection of others, and are more humorous and pleasure-oriented than their siblings (Altus, 1959; Cohen, 1951). Although these children are externally oriented, more middle-born children are regarded as extremely unpopular by their peers than are children in any other birth order (Elkins, 1958).

The last-born child is usually indulged by his parents and siblings and has a variety of sibling models available in addition to the parents. This state of security and sometimes benign neglect results in a set of characteristics which have many of the positive and few of the negative attributes of firstborns. The last child has similar assets in that he is striving, persevering, achievement-oriented, and popular; however, he is more optimistic, self-confident, and secure than firstborns.

The effects of birth order clearly are related to the interactions and role of that position within the family. The relationships of power and dependency, of attention or relative neglect, and of differential emotional bonds and the options for action and reaction within the family system all interact in shaping the characteristics associated with sibling position.

The Physical Environment of the Home

We have been discussing social interactions in families. It is apparent that the social interactions occur in and are modified by the physical setting of the home. There is a continuing interplay between the social and physical environment. A child growing up in a crowded, noisy, disorganized home with few objects with which to play, and a television set as a central member of the family, may be at some disadvantage for cognitive and social development. However, it should be noted that the way the parents or other caretakers organize the child's physical environment may be as important as the physical setting itself.

Amount of Stimulation and Organization of the Environment

Favorable cognitive development and social development have been associated with the predictability and regularity of home environments, that is, with homes where things have their time and place—where meals, bedtimes, and other routines are regular and where the child has a place for her belongings, a safe place in which to play, and a quiet place to study (Bradley & Caldwell, 1976). High levels of noise and stimulation from which the child cannot escape adversely affect cognitive development. If the home is noisy, small, and overcrowded, with the TV on most of the time and with too much stimulation from family members or visitors, the cognitive level of the child may be depressed. Such environments are associated not only with poor performance on standardized tests of intellectual development in infants and young children, but with lower teacher ratings of creativity and lower spelling and language achievement tests scores in school-aged children (Heft, cited in Wohlwill & Heft, 1977; Michelson, 1968). As can be seen in Box 12-4, it may be that noisy, disorganized homes lead to less efficient information processing and less focused attending in children (Heft, cited in Wohlwill & Heft, 1977). Some kind of stimulus shelter, such as a quiet situation or room to which children can escape, is a good predictor of positive cognitive development in children (Wachs, 1973).

The Effects of Television on Family Interaction

Nearly thirty years ago, a major change occurred in the organization of American and European home environments—the introduction of television. Although most interest in television has focused on the potentially beneficial effects of educational programming or on the deleterious effects of TV violence, its impact on the developing child can be viewed in another way. Television can be thought of as an environmental organizing event whose availability can affect children through altering social interaction patterns among family members (Parke, 1978).

What happens to family relations when television becomes a member of the household? Television increases the amount of time families spend together viewing TV, but decreases the amount of time families spend in non-TV-related joint family activities or with friends, relatives, and neighbors (Belson, 1959; Lyle, 1971; Maccoby, 1951; Robinson, 1971). Although it has been reported that TV can increase family conversation by stimulating discussion about programs and even commercials, it is often used in ways that intentionally

BOX 12-4
THE EFFECTS OF STIMULATION
IN THE HOME ON INFORMATION
PROCESSING BY CHILDREN

 We have discussed the importance of attention and effective information processing in the cognitive functioning of children. How does living in a home with a great deal of noise, movement, and visual stimulation affect the information processing of children? In a recent study using an interview-based home environment inventory, a measure of *background noise level* was determined from a variety of measures including noise level from TV, radio, record players, appliances, and exterior sources. The level of general activity and the frequency of interruptions in the child's solitary play by other family members were used to measure *general activity level* in the home. To generate an *overall measure of background stimulation*, the noise- and activity-level scales were combined with two other measures—presence of distinctive versus overlapping sounds and frequency of sudden unexpected sounds.

In order to assess the links between home environment measures and selective attention, 5-year-olds were presented with two tasks. The first was a search task which required the child to match a stimulus card picturing a familiar object with a similar card in an array of 20 cards. Total time spent in searching for the target stimulus was recorded, as well as incidental learning, which was measured by the number of nontarget

items the child recognized when they were interspersed among new pictures. Children from noisier homes or homes in which there was more general background stimulation took longer to locate the correct pictures and recognized fewer of the nontarget stimuli. In short, performance on the central task was slower and incidental learning was lower.

The second task was an auditory distraction task. Children performed a cognitive task under quiet conditions or a condition with a noisy distractor. Children from quiet home settings performed better than those from noisy home environments under both conditions. However, the drop in efficiency under the auditory distraction was most marked for children who were accustomed to quiet home environments. As Wohlwill and Heft note:

For the children from the noisier homes, it appears that their ability to selectively attend to the relevant stimulus features in each situation was adversely affected by the high noise levels in their homes in spite of their apparent adaptation to these conditions. (1977, p. 132) ■

Source: Wohlwill, J. F., and Heft, H. Environments fit for the developing child. In H. McGurk (Ed.), *Ecological factors in human development*. Amsterdam: North-Holland, 1977.

reduce family interaction. A national survey (Steiner, 1963) found that one-third of parents rated "baby sitting as one of the main advantages of TV."

The potential problem of this attitude is nicely summarized by the parent who noted that, "it takes some of the burden off me teaching them games." Parents may interact less with their children and specifically may feel less pressure to provide specific education experiences for their children. TV can do it for them! Moreover, the use of TV as a "babysitter" varies with the education of the parents: 53% of the mothers and 44% of the

In many families television is used as a baby-sitter. (Vivienne, Photo Researchers, Inc.)

fathers with only grade school education mention this function of TV, in contrast to 21% and 19% of the college educated mothers and fathers. The utilization of TV clearly should not be viewed independently of other aspects of the household organization and similarly should not alone be viewed as a causative factor in accounting for social class differences in cognitive development. (Parke, 1978, p. 29)

This is illustrated in studies of the relationship between family tension and amount of TV viewing in crowded and uncrowded homes. It has been found that in crowded home situations families who spend a great deal of time in television viewing report a high level of family tension (Rosenblatt & Cunningham, 1976). This was not found in uncrowded home situations. Although these results could be interpreted to mean that TV viewing may increase family tension, it could also mean that TV viewing serves as a tension control technique in crowded households. Stressed families may avoid fighting by focusing on the TV set instead of each other. Some support for this is found in reports that TV breakdowns are associated with increased tension levels and conflicts in families (Steiner, 1963). When the TV goes off, the fights come on.

In spite of the scattered findings on the positive effects of TV, some modern critics remain concerned:

Like the sorcerer of old the television set casts its magic spell, freezing speech, and action, turning the living into silent statues so long as the enchantment lasts. The primary danger

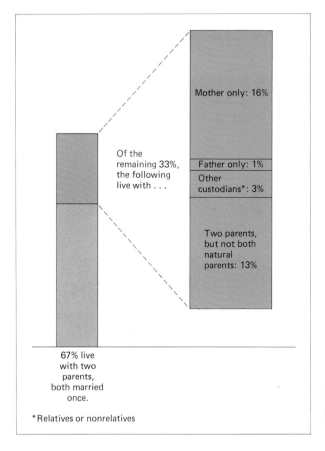

Of the remaining 33%, the following live with . . .

Mother only: 16%

Father only: 1%

Other custodians*: 3%

Two parents, but not both natural parents: 13%

67% live with two parents, both married once.

*Relatives or nonrelatives

FIGURE 12-3 Living arrangements for children under 18. *(From Nordheimer, 1977.)*

of the television screen lies not so much in the behavior it produces—although there is danger there—as in the behavior that it prevents: the talks, the games, the family festivities and arguments through which much of the child's learning takes place and through which his character is formed. Turning on the television set can turn off the process that transforms children into people. (Bronfenbrenner, 1970)

The Changing American Family

It is difficult to escape from modern prophets of doom predicting the demise of the nuclear family. Their gloomy prognostications often begin with "We view with alarm" and end with dire references to the Equal Rights Amendment, working mothers, teenaged pregnancies, abortion, the rising divorce rates, or the ominous threat of state-supported day-care centers. The American family is changing just as society is changing, but is it dying? It seems more accurate to say that family roles and forms are becoming more varied. It can be seen in Figure 12-3 that most children still live in families with two parents who have only been married once. However, the proportion of traditional nuclear families composed of two parents and children, with the father as the sole breadwinner, is declining as other family forms are increasing. What are some of the main changes in family structure and functioning which are occurring?

Families are decreasing in size. The average household size in 1976 was 2.9 people compared to 4.1 in 1890 and 5.8 in 1790. This is largely attributable to the declining birthrate and to the fact that fewer adult relatives such as grandparents or aunts and uncles are living in the family.

There has been an increase in single-parent households largely because of the rising divorce rate and to a lesser extent because of a rise in pregnancies of unwed teenagers. The divorce rate has doubled in the last decade, and more divorces now involve families with children than ever before. In the period from 1910 to 1960 only 25 percent of children lost a parent through divorce or death. It is now estimated that 40 to 50 percent of children born during the 1970s will suffer such a disruption during childhood and spend some time in a single-parent household.

The number of working mothers has also increased. Over one-half of all mothers with school-aged children now are employed, and more than a third of mothers with children under the age of 3 work. Young mothers, poor mothers, and mothers from single-parent families are most likely to enter the labor force because of economic need. Two-thirds of mothers in single-parent families work. This is to a large extent attributable to their dire financial situation.

Since the largest amount of research on the changing American family has been done on single-parent mother-headed families and on families with working mothers, we will focus our discussion on these two topics. In addition, since only 8.4 percent of single-parent families are those in which the mother is absent and since there is little research on these families, in our presentation we will be referring to mother-headed families.

Single-Parent Mother-Headed Families

It has been proposed that the state of being a single-parent family should be regarded as a time of transition since most single parents or members of divorced couples marry fairly rapidly (Ross & Sawhill, 1975). One out of every five divorced adults remarries within the first year after divorce, and the average interval between divorce and remarriage is about five to six years. Thus the experience of living in a single-parent family is one that parents and children pass in and out of, sometimes several times during the course of development.

Most transitions are stressful, and transitions, such as divorce, which involve losing family members, restructuring the family, and finding new patterns of family functioning, are frequently distressing to both parents and children. In spite of the fact that divorce may be a positive solution to destructive conflictual family functioning and the eventual outcome may be a constructive one, for many family members the transition period following separation and divorce is stressful. In fact, there is some evidence that feelings of distress and unhappiness in parents, poor parent-child relations, and the social and emotional adjustment of children actually get worse during the first year following divorce. However,

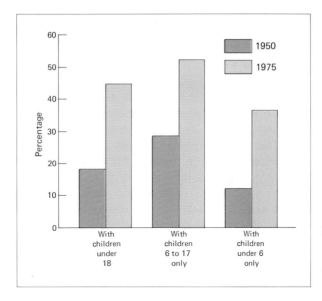

FIGURE 12-4   Percentage of mothers holding or looking for outside employment. *(From Nordheimer, 1977.)*

for many parents there is a dramatic increase in the sense of personal well-being, interpersonal functioning, and family relations in the second year following divorce when families are adapting to their new single-parent status. In the long run, children in single-parent families are better adjusted than children in conflict-ridden nuclear families. In the short run, in the first year following divorce, the children in single-parent families are more disturbed (Hetherington, Cox, & Cox, 1978a, 1978e).

Stresses in Single-Parent Families   How do the life-style and functioning of mothers and children in single-parent families differ from those in nuclear families? What stresses and patterns of coping and adjustment are more likely to be encountered in single-parent families?

First, mothers in single-parent families suffer from task overload. The single parent is dealing with family tasks and needs that are regarded as a full-time job for two adults in a nuclear family (Hetherington, Cox, & Cox, 1978c).

Second, single-parent mother-headed families often experience financial duress. In 1974 the mean family income of mother-headed-families was $6,413, in contrast to a mean income of $13,788 for male-headed families. Female-headed families with children experience more economic deprivation than those without children. In 1974, 51.5 percent of children under 18 in female-headed families were in families with income below the poverty level (Bane, 1976).

Third, mothers in single-parent families are often socially isolated and lacking in social and emotional support. It might be thought that the presence of children would attenuate this sense of loneliness; however, recent studies (Hetherington, Cox, & Cox, 1978a) suggest that the presence of children may actually make mothers feel more unhappy, frustrated, helpless, anxious, and incompetent. This was particularly true of divorced mothers with noncompliant, acting-out young sons. These mothers often complained of being prisoners, of being trapped, or of being locked in a child's world. One mother stated it cogently when she said, "There's no time outs in the parenting game in one parent families."

In a single-parent family only one parental figure serves as the agent of socialization through discipline or direct tuition or by acting as a model. Thus, the remaining parent is likely to become more salient in the development of the child. There is not a spouse to serve as a buffer between parent and child in a single-parent family. In nuclear families a loving, competent, or well-adjusted parent can help counteract the effects of a rejecting, incompetent, emotionally unstable parent. In a single-parent mother-headed family, adjustment of the mother and the quality of the mother-child relationship are more directly reflected in the adjustment of the child than they are in nuclear families (Hetherington, Cox, & Cox, 1978e).

The single mother may confront specific problems of authority in discipline. Children view fathers as more powerful and threatening than mothers. In nuclear families children exhibit less noncompliant and deviant behavior toward their fathers than their mothers, and when undesirable behavior occurs, the father can terminate it more readily than the mother can (Hetherington, Cox, & Cox, 1978a). The single mother may have to be supermother to counter the image of greater authority and power vested in males in our culture.

This leads to the final way in which single-parent families differ from nuclear families. The single parent offers the child a more restricted array of positive characteristics to model. A mother and father are likely to exhibit wider-ranging interests, skills, and attributes than a single parent.

The Development of Children in Single-Parent Families   The aspects of development of children in single-parent families on which there has been the most extensive research have been in intellectual development, sex-role typing, and the development of self-control (Hetherington, Cox, & Cox, 1978b). We will deal with sex-role typing in children from single-parent families in Chapter 15, where processes associated with the development of attributes considered to be masculine or feminine will be presented. In this section we will focus on the intellectual development and the development of self-control in children in single-parent families.

Intellectual development   Studies of the intellectual development of children from single-parent families have investigated both the overall level of intellectual performance and achievement and the patterning of intellectual abilities. Two recent reviews of this research have concluded that children growing up in mother-headed families show deficits on cognitive performance as assessed by standardized intelligence and achievement tests and as judged from school performance (Biller, 1974; Shinn, 1978). In her survey of this literature Shinn (1978) reports that the differences in cognitive performance between children from nuclear and single-parent families are considerable: "from 0.2 to 1.6 years in achievement, 0.2 to 0.9 standard deviation units in I.Q. and aptitude, and 0.8 of the difference between 'B' and 'C' in grade point average" (Shinn, 1978, p. 312).

What factors may be related to these differences? Since single-parent families are more frequent among black and economically deprived children and since such children perform less well than middle-class white children on tests of intelligence and achievement, it is essential to control for social class and race in evaluating differences in cognitive performance. However, even when appropriate controls are instituted, these differences remain, although as will be seen, the pattern of test scores may differ for lower- and middle-class children.

In general, although the effects are most marked for boys, they are found in both sexes. In addition, some studies find that early loss of the father is more deleterious than later separation and that the effects may be late-appearing and cumulative. Differences in the intellectual performance of children from single-parent and nuclear homes are rarely found in the preschool years; they emerge and increase over the course of development in the school years (Deutsch & Brown, 1964; Hess, Shipman, Brophy, Bear, & Adelberger, 1969; Hetherington, Cox, & Cox, 1978e; Rees & Palmer, 1970).

Variations in the availability of fathers occur not only between mother-headed and nuclear families but within nuclear families. Some fathers because of occupational demands or rejection and lack of involvement in the family are not available to their children. Children in nuclear families with unavailable fathers show decrements in achievement similar to those in mother-headed families. Blanchard and Biller (1971) studied the effects on third-grade boys of early (before age 5) versus late father absence and low father availability (less than six hours a week) versus high father availability in nuclear homes. They found that boys with highly available fathers surpassed the other three groups on achievement test scores and classroom grades. The early father-absent boys were also found to be underachievers. The boys from nuclear families with relatively unavailable fathers and the late father-absent boys were also found to be below grade-level expectations, although not as severely as boys who had been separated from their fathers before the age of 5. Other studies have found that children whose fathers have been temporarily absent for two years or less and children whose fathers were in the military or worked on nightshift and presumably were less available to their children have lower scores on achievement tests. These deficits are found even in young adulthood on the American College Entrance Examination.

The father with low participation in the family or with low warmth in his relationship with his family may be just as detrimental to the child's intellectual growth as one who is totally absent. This may in part account for the frequently reported finding of greater negative effects of divorce when compared to death of the father. It seems possible that in many cases the divorce may have been preceded by psychological or actual withdrawal of the father from the family setting. Clearly, in nuclear families, the presence of the father is not the important variable; the important variable is the participation of a good father.

The point has been made that in some cases father absence caused by divorce may in fact enhance the child's development (Lamb, 1977). If the child's loss of a disinterested father results in the acquisition of, or association with, a more accessible and suitable father figure, the child may benefit from the results of this transition. In support of this, several investigators have reported that the cognitive performance of children living with father surrogates, such as step-fathers, is superior or is not different than that of children in other nuclear families and is superior to those in single-parent families (Lessing, Zagorin, & Nelson, 1970; Santrock, 1972; Solomon, Hirsch, Scheinfeld, & Jackson, 1972).

In addition to studies of the overall level of cognitive performance, many investigators have studied the patterning of cognitive abilities. Aptitude and achievement tests in the general population have shown that females are usually superior to males in verbal areas, whereas males are superior to females on quantitative tasks. In single-parent families both male and female children are more likely to show the female pattern of higher verbal than quantitative scores. In most cases, this is associated with a decrement in quantitative scores; however, in middle-class, relatively elite samples such as college students from Harvard, Stanford, or Carleton, or in children from upper-middle-class families, being raised in a single-parent family may actually enhance verbal scores (Carlsmith, 1964; Funkenstein, 1963; Oshman, 1975; Lessing et al., 1970). This enhancement has never been found in children from lower socioeconomic levels.

Several explanations have been advanced to account for these differences in cognitive development. First it has been suggested that overall cognitive decrements may be associated with the fact that children in single-parent families receive less adult attention and interact less with adults than do children in nuclear families (Shinn, 1978; Zajonc, 1976). There is some evidence that many mothers in divorced families are less likely to read to their children at bedtime, prolong child-care routines in a playful way, or eat with their children (Hetherington, Cox, & Cox, 1978a). However, in some homes, single mothers, especially single middle-class mothers, may attempt to compensate for loss of a father. Shinn proposes that "single mothers who are coping with adverse economic circumstances may have little left over for their children, while single mothers who are financially better off may spend additional time with their children which they would otherwise have devoted to their husband." She goes on to say that with a highly verbal middle-class mother these interactions are likely to be of the kind to promote verbal development. This could explain the enhancement effects of verbal test scores in mother-headed families which were found only in relatively elite populations and never in economically deprived samples. Second, the higher verbal than quantitative scores in children from mother-headed single-parent families have been attributed to lack of a paternal male model with quantitative problem-solving skills with whom the child can identify. Third it has been suggested that considerable anxiety-provoking stress occurs in single-parent families and that anxiety is more likely to interfere with problem-solving skills than with verbal skills (Nelson & Maccoby, 1966).

A fourth interpretation can also be offered. In a longitudinal study of the two years following divorce by Hetherington, Cox, and Cox (1978a, 1978e) it was found that lack of parental control and fewer demands for mature, independent behavior led to short attention spans and distractibility in children, which resulted in a drop in scores on certain types of problem-solving and quantitative tasks that require sustained attention. What is being proposed is that parental control must precede self-control in children and that self-control and the ability to concentrate and persist are necessary in problem solving and academic success.

The development of self-control   The development of self-control is a second area in which there has been extensive study of children in single-parent families. There are two notable findings in the studies of the development of self-control in children from nuclear and single-parent families. The first is that differences in self-control and antisocial behavior between children in nuclear and single-parent families are found for boys, but are less marked or are not obtained for girls (Gurin, Veroff, & Feld, 1960; Langner & Michael, 1963; Hetherington, Cox, & Cox, 1978a, 1978d, 1978e; Hoffman, 1970; Nye, 1957; Rosenberg, 1965; Santrock, 1975). The second is that when differences in self-control occur between children in single-parent and nuclear homes, they are most likely to be found in children whose parents have been divorced rather than those in which the father has died.

Boys in mother-headed families have been found to be more antisocial, impulsive, and delinquent; less self-controlled and less able to delay immediate gratification; and more rebellious against adult authority figures than are boys in nuclear families (Douvan & Adelson, 1966; Hetherington, Cox, & Cox, 1978a, 1978e; Hoffman, 1970; Mischel, 1961; Santrock & Wohlford, 1970). These characteristics are manifested in a wide range of populations and situations.

Similar results have been found with older subjects. Siegman (1966), in a study of first-year law and medical students, found that males who were without a father for at least one year from age 1 to 4 scored higher on self-reported antisocial behaviors, such as parental disobedience, property damage, and drinking, than did boys from nuclear families. Suedfeld (1967) found that Peace Corps volunteers who were without a father for at least five years before their fifteenth birthday tended to be among those volunteers who returned prematurely because of adjustment or conduct problems.

Why is an increase in antisocial, aggressive behavior found in boys but not girls from divorced families? It may be that the greater aggressiveness frequently observed in boys and the greater assertiveness in the culturally prescribed male role necessitate the use of firmer, more consistent discipline practices in the control of boys than girls. Boys in nuclear families are less compliant than girls, and children are less compliant to mothers than fathers. It could be argued that it is more essential for boys that they have a male model to imitate who exhibits self-controlled ethical behavior, or that the image of greater power and authority vested in the father is more critical in the control of boys, who are socialized to be more aggressive. Is this the main factor in the greater aggressive, antisocial behavior in boys in divorced families? The longitudinal study by Hetherington, Cox, & Cox (1978a, 1978d, 1978e) of the two years following divorce found that the parenting practices and control of the divorced mothers deteriorated over the course of the first year following divorce, although they dramatically improved during the second year. Poor parenting was most apparent when divorced parents, particularly divorced mothers, were interacting with their sons. They exhibited less positive behavior, affection, and affiliation with their sons than daughters. In addition, they gave more threatening commands that they didn't systematically enforce with sons. Divorced mothers were barking out orders like a general in the field, but were not following through and responding appropriately to either their sons' negative or positive behavior.

Divorced mothers may have given their children a hard time, but mothers, especially divorced mothers, got rough treatment from their children, particularly their sons. In comparison with fathers and mothers in nuclear families, the divorced mother's children in the first year didn't obey, affiliate, or attend to her. They nagged and whined, made more dependency demands, and were more likely to ignore her. The aggression of boys with divorced mothers peaked at one year following divorce, then dropped significantly, but was still higher than that of boys in nuclear families two years after divorce. Some desperate divorced mothers described their relationship with their children one year after divorce as "declared war," a "struggle for survival," "the old Chinese water torture," or "like getting bitten to death by ducks." As was found in the divorced parents' behavior, one year following divorce seemed to be the period of maximum negative behaviors for children, and great improvement occurred by two years, although the negative behaviors were more sustained in boys than in girls. The second year appears to be a period of marked recovery and constructive adaptation for both divorced mothers and children.

Poor parenting was associated with aggression, impulsivity, and lack of control in boys both in the home and in a preschool setting. The importance of the maternal parenting practices relative to paternal practices increased markedly over the two-year period.

Who is doing what to whom? Mothers and sons seemed to be involved in a *coercive cycle.* Immediately following divorce, most divorced mothers and their children were expressing considerable emotional distress which often was reflected in more erratic, unaffectionate demanding behavior. It is difficult for parents to be consistently warm and supportive when they are themselves in need of support. Many mothers, following divorce, feel powerless and as if they cannot control the people or events around them. This is reflected in their relationship with their children, and since boys respond particularly intensely to conflict and divorce, it is most clearly found in the mother-son relationship. The inept parenting or lack of management skills of the mother accelerated the son's aversive behavior, for which she was both the main instigator and target. This led to increased feelings of helplessness, anxiety, depression, and incompetence in the mothers, which was associated with increased use of coercion in her parenting skills, and the cycle continued. In a subgroup of these divorced mothers who were involved in programs focused on the improvement of parenting skills and in which twenty-four-hour telephone contact with the parent trainer was available, both the divorced mother and child demonstrated improved adjustment. Such behaviorally oriented parenting programs often lead

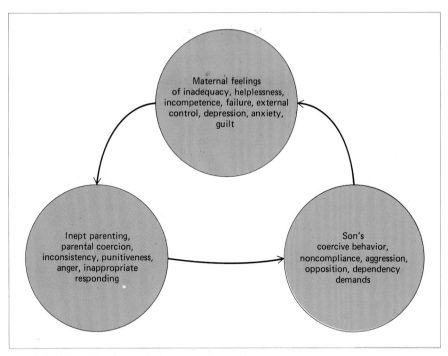

FIGURE 12-5 Coercive cycle between divorced mothers and sons.

to rapid changes in children's behavior. Once the mother saw that she was not helpless, that she could gain control over her child's behavior, she showed increases in self-confidence, self-esteem, happiness, and feelings of competence. These were in turn reflected in more able parenting, which continued to lead to more positive behavior on the part of the sons. The coercive cycle was broken! Throughout this book we have frequently discussed the importance of the development of a sense of personal control in children. It can be seen that this same sense of internal control is very important for parents as well (Hetherington, Cox, & Cox, 1978a).

Although we have emphasized the increasing salience of the mother in the development of children following divorce or separation, it should not be thought that divorced fathers cannot play a significant role in their children's development.

In the longitudinal study we have been discussing, when there was agreement in childrearing, a positive attitude toward the spouse, and low conflict between parents and when the father was emotionally stable, frequent visitation by the father was associated with more positive adjustment and self-control in the child. When there was disagreement and inconsistency in attitudes toward the child or when the father was poorly adjusted, frequent contact of the father and the child was associated with poor mother-child functioning and disruptions in the child's behavior. Again we see that it is not a simple matter of father or mother availability and amount of contact, but it is the quality of the parental contact that counts.

Maternal Employment and Child Development

Over the past decade there has been a steady increase in the number of mothers who are employed. This increase has been most marked in the mothers of preschool children. Mothers no longer feel compelled to remain in the home when their children are infants or toddlers. It seems likely that as mothers spend more time in their places of employment and less time in the home, family roles and patterns of family functioning will change. What are some of these changes in family roles and interaction that have already occurred and how do they influence childrens' behavior?

Lois Hoffman (1974, 1977) has suggested that there are five ways in which maternal employment affects the development of children. First, the role models provided by working and nonworking mothers and their husbands differ. If both parents work, their roles may be perceived as similar not only because the mother works, but also because the father participates more actively in family and childrearing tasks, often regarded as part of the maternal role. Children with employed mothers therefore are exposed to less stereotypical models of the father as breadwinner and mother as housekeeper and caregiver. It is thus not surprising that maternal employment is associated with more egalitarian views of sex roles by their children, particularly by daughters (Gold & Andres, 1978; Hoffman, 1974, 1977).

In middle-class families maternal employment is related to higher educational and occupational goals in children (Banducci, 1967; Nye & Hoffman, 1963; Stein, 1973). In addition, daughters of working as compared to nonworking mothers more often perceive the woman's role as involving freedom of choice, satisfaction, and competence (Broverman, Vogel, Broverman, Clarkson, & Rosenkrantz, 1972), and these daughters have higher self-esteem and intentions of working after marriage (Baruch, 1972; Hartley, 1966). Finally, maternal employment is associated with fewer traditional feminine interests and characteristics in daughters (Douvan & Adelson, 1966; Stein, 1973). Female college students with working mothers have fewer passive feminine characteristics and have high achievement motivation, endurance, and dominance.

Sons of working mothers, in contrast to sons of unemployed mothers, not only perceive the female role as more competent, but also view men as warmer and more expressive.

Second, the mother's emotional state and attitude toward her work will modify the effects of maternal employment on children. If the working mother obtains personal satisfaction from employment, if she does not experience excessive guilt about not being with her children, and if she has adequate household arrangements to prevent her from being stressed by dual-role demands, she is likely to perform as well or better than the nonworking mother.

When the mother works because she enjoys her occupation or in order to help out the family finances, there is less familial disruption than when maternal employment is motivated by a desire to escape from family responsibilities and from contact with her children. Nonworking mothers who have a sense of satisfaction and competence in their homemaking role and working mothers who enjoy their employment both show more positive relations with their children than unhappy nonworking mothers who would like to be employed (Hartley, 1966; Hoffman, 1961; Yarrow, Scott, DeLeeuw, & Heineg, 1962).

Third, there is some evidence that the childrearing practices of working mothers may differ from those of nonemployed mothers, particularly in the area of independence training. Except in cases where mothers feel guilty about leaving their children to work, employed mothers encourage their children to become self-sufficient and independent at an earlier age (Hock, 1978). These children are able to care for themselves and their belongings and as adolescents are able to participate in household tasks with more ease than are children in families with nonworking mothers. This early independence training is particularly beneficial in leading to high achievement motivation, achievement behavior, and competence in both sons and daughters (Woods, 1972).

Working mothers do tend to spend less time with their children than nonworking mothers do (Walker & Woods, 1972). However, there is evidence that many working mothers, particularly middle-class mothers, try to compensate for their time away by keeping regular times available and planning special activities with their children. Whether a difference in the quality of interaction makes up for the decreased quantity of interaction is not known. There is some evidence that working mothers are more relaxed and less concerned about separation from their infants than are nonworking mothers. In addition, working middle-class mothers are reported to be more helpful, warm, and satisfied in a family situation (Hoffman, 1961).

Fourth, it has been suggested that children of working mothers receive less adequate supervision than those of nonemployed mothers and that this may be related to juvenile delinquency. This link of maternal employment to delinquency has not been clearly established. However, the quality of substitute caregiving appears particularly important for the children of working mothers. About 10 percent of American children have no supervision when their parents are absent from the home. When there is no supervision or when there is inadequate care, household routines break down, meals are irregular, there is less attention to grooming, and there are fewer opportunities for organized social interaction and recreation. Lack of supervision in children of working mothers is associated with difficulties in school relations as well as lower achievement and intelligence test scores. In addition, rather than being more self-sufficient, unsupervised children are less self-reliant and have a decreased sense of personal freedom compared to their supervised peers (Woods, 1972). With adequate supervision and a warm mother-child relationship, there is no evidence of adverse effects of maternal employment.

Fifth, it has sometimes been suggested that when the mother works, the child receives less cognitive and social stimulation. This remains an open question since most of the work on maternal employment has dealt with school-aged children and we have little information on the interaction of employed mothers and their infants.

In summary, in spite of dire predictions to the contrary, the results of studies of maternal employment suggest that it does not usually have detrimental effects on children; in fact, in many studies positive consequences have been obtained. The effects of maternal employment can only be evaluated in relation to other factors, such as the reason why the mother is working, the mother's satisfaction with her role, the demands placed on other family members, the attitudes of the other family members toward the mothers' employment, and the adequacy of substitute care provided for the children.

Summary

The family plays a critical role in the socialization of the child. The early parent-child relationships are important because they serve as the initial social relationships which will shape the child's expectancies and responses in subsequent social encounters, and because the values and attitudes of the culture are filtered through the parents in their presentation to their offspring.

In the course of socialization parents serve important roles as teachers and models for their children. Two basic dimensions of parental behavior in relation to their children are warmth-hostility and permissiveness-control. The interaction of these two variables is associated with different clusters of behavior in children. In general, warm parents who are moderately restrictive and use consistent love-oriented discipline practices, such as explanation, reasoning, and withdrawal of affection, have children who exhibit many behaviors regarded as socially desirable, such as adaptability, self-esteem, competence, self-control, and popularity with peers.

Children imitate a wide range of behaviors in parents. Warmth or dominance in the parents will facilitate the child's imitation. Dominance plays the most significant role in task-relevant and problem-solving imitation. Warmth of the parent is more important for girls and dominance for boys.

Parents in different social classes have different values which may influence their socialization practices. Lower-class parents value respectability, obedience, conformity, neatness, and politeness. They are concerned more about the immediate consequences of their children's behavior rather than about the motives underlying their behavior. In shaping their children toward these goals, they tend to be more power-assertive and restrictive with young children, although they are permissive with older children. In contrast, middle-class parents focus on their children's "inner development" and are concerned with the development of responsibility, internalized controls, and achievement motivation.

Structural factors such as family size, sex, and number of siblings and birth order also play an important role in child development. The relationship of the firstborn child and parents seems to be a particularly close and demanding one which may mediate the later greater achievement orientation and anxiety in firstborn children.

The family appears to be in a period of marked change. Two of the most notable changes are in the increase in single-parent mother-headed families and in working mothers. Although most children in single-parent families show normal patterns of cognitive and social development, when adverse effects of divorce or of being raised in a single-parent family do occur, they are most extreme and enduring in boys. Some deficits in cognitive development and a pattern of higher verbal than quantitative scores have been reported for children in single-parent homes. In addition, a lack of self-control in boys is sometimes found, which seems to be associated with poor maternal parenting behaviors and a coercive cycle which develops between mothers and sons in some single-parent families.

No general conclusions can be drawn about the constructive or detrimental results of maternal employment. The effects seem to be closely linked to the characteristics and attitudes of the family members and the specific social and home situation involved. The clearest impact of maternal employment on child development has been in the development of independence and of less traditionally sex-stereotyped views of males and females.

References

Altus, W. D. Birth order, intelligence and adjustment. *Psychological Reports*, 1959, **5**, 502.

Banducci, R. The effect of mother's employment on the achievement, aspirations and expectations of the child. *Personnel and Guidance Journal*, 1967, **46**, 263–267.

Bandura, A., & Huston, A. C. Identification as a process of incidental learning. *Journal of Abnormal and Social Psychology*, 1961, **63**, 311–318.

Bandura, A., Ross, D., & Ross, S. A. A comparative test of the status envy, social power and secondary reinforcement theories of identificatory learning. *Journal of Abnormal and Social Psychology*, 1963, **67**, 527–534.

Bane, M. J. Marital disruption and the lives of children. *Journal of Social Issues*, 1976, **32**, 103–117.

Baruch, G. K. Maternal influences upon college women's attitudes toward women and work. *Developmental Psychology*, 1972, **6**, 32–37.

Baumrind, D. Child care practices anteceding three patterns of preschool behavior. *Genetic Psychology Monographs*, 1967, **75**, 43–88.

Baumrind, D. Current patterns of parental authority. *Developmental Psychology Monograph*, 1971, **4** (No. 4, Part 2).

Becker, W. C. & Krug, R. S. A comparison of the ability of the PAS, PARI, parent self ratings and empirically keyed questionnaire scales to predict ratings of child behavio . Mimeographed report, University of Illinois, Urbana, 1964.

Becker, W. C., Peterson, D. R., Luria, Z., Shoemaker, D. J., & Hellman, K. Relations of factors derived from parent interview ratings to behavior problems of five-year-olds. *Child Development*, 1962, **33**, 509–535.

Bell, R. Q. Structuring parent-child interaction situations for direct observation. *Child Development*, 1964, **35**, 1009–1021.

Bell, R. W. A reinterpretation of the direction of effects in studies of socialization. *Psychological Review*, 1968, **75**, 81–95.

Belson, W. A. *Television and the family*. London: British Broadcasting Corporation, 1959.

Bettelheim, B. *The children of the dream*. New York: Macmillan, 1969.

Biller, H. B. *Paternal deprivation: Family, school, sexuality, and society.* Lexington, Mass.: Heath, 1974.

Blanchard, R. W., & Biller, H. B. Father availability and academic performance among 3rd grade boys. *Developmental Psychology*, 1971, **4**, 301–305.

Bossard, J. H. S., & Boll, E. *The large family system.* Philadelphia: University of Pennsylvania Press, 1956.

Bossard, J. H. S., & Boll, E. *The sociology of child development.* New York: Harper & Row, 1960.

Bradley, R. H., & Caldwell, B. M. Early home environment and changes in mental test performance in children from 6 to 36 months. *Developmental Psychology*, 1976, **12**, 93–97.

Brim, O. G. Family structure and sex role learning by children: A further analysis of Helen Koch's data. *Sociometry*, 1958, **21**, 1–16.

Bronfenbrenner, U. Some familial antecedents of responsibility and leadership. In L. Petrullo & B. M. Bass (Eds.), *Adolescents in leadership and interpersonal behavior.* New York: Holt, 1961.

Bronfenbrenner, U. Who cares for America's children? Address presented at the Conference of the National Association for the Education of Young Children, 1970.

Broverman, I. K., Vogel, S. R., Broverman, D. M., Clarkson, F. E., & Rosenkrantz, P. S. Sex-role stereotypes: A current appraisal. *Journal of Social Issues*, 1972, **28**, 59–78.

Carlsmith, L. Effect of early father absence on scholastic aptitude. *Harvard Educational Review*, 1964, **34**, 3–21.

Cicirelli, V. G. Siblings helping siblings. In V. L. Allen (Ed.), *Children as tutors.* New York: Academic, 1976.

Clausen, J. A. Perspectives on childhood socialization. In J. Clausen (Ed.), *Socialization and society.* Boston: Little, Brown, 1968.

Clausen, J. A., & Williams, J. R. Sociological correlates of child behavior. In *Yearbook: National Society of Education, Part I.* Chicago: University of Chicago Press, 1963.

Cohen, F. Psychological characteristics of the second child as compared with the first. *Indian Journal of Psychology*, 1951, **26**, 79–84.

Coles, R. Privileged ones: The well-off and the rich in America (Children of Crisis Series, Vol. 5). Waltham, Mass.: Little, Brown, 1978.

Cowan, C., Cowan, P. A., Coie, L., & Coie, J. D. Becoming a family: The impact of a first child's birth on the couple's relationship. In L. Newman & W. Miller (Eds.), *The first child and family formation*, 1977, in press.

Cushna, B. Agency and birth order differences in very early childhood. Paper presented at the meeting of the American Psychological Association, New York, 1966.

Deutsch, M., & Brown, B. Social influences in Negro-White intelligence differences. *Journal of Social Issues*, 1964, **20**, 24–35.

Doering, S. C., & Entwisle. *The first birth.* Baltimore: Johns Hopkins, 1977.

Douvan, E., & Adelson, J. *The adolescent experience.* New York: Wiley, 1966.

Elkins, D. Some factors related to the choice status of ninety eighth grade children in a school society. *Genetic Psychology Monographs*, 1958, **58**, 207–272.

Feiring, C., & Taylor, J. The influence of the infant and secondary parent on maternal behavior: Toward a social systems view of infant attachment. *Merrill-Palmer Quarterly*, 1977, in press.

Fontana, V. J. *The maltreated child,* Springfield, Ill.: Charles C Thomas, 1974.

Fraser, B., & Martin, H. P. An advocate for the abused child. In H. P. Martin (Ed.), *The abused child: A multidisciplinary approach to developmental issues and treatment.* Cambridge, Mass.: Ballinger, 1976.

Freud, A. *The ego and the mechanisms of defense*. New York: International Universities Press, 1946.

Freud, S. *The ego and id*. London: Hogarth, 1923.

Funkenstein, D. H. Mathematics, quantitative aptitudes, and the masculine role. *Diseases of the Nervous System*, 1963, **24**, 140–146.

Garbarino, J., & Crouter, A. Defining the community context for parent-child relations: The correlates of child maltreatment. *Child Development*, 1978, in press, 49.

Garmezy, N. The study of competence in children at risk for severe psychopathology. In J. F. Anthony & C. Koupernik (Eds.), *The child in his family at psychiatric risk*. New York: Wiley, 1975.

Gelles, R. J. *The violent home: A study of physical aggression between husbands and wives*. Beverly Hills, Calif.: Sage, 1974.

Gelles, R. J. Abused wives: Why do they stay? *Journal of Marriage and the Family*, 1976, **38**, 659–668.

Gil, D. G. *Violence against children: Physical child abuse in the United States*. Cambridge, Mass.: Harvard University Press, 1970.

Glueck, S., & Glueck, E. T. *Unraveling juvenile delinquency*. Cambridge, Mass.: Harvard University Press, 1950.

Gold, D., & Andres, D. Developmental comparisons between 10-year-old children with employed and nonemployed mothers. *Child Development*, 1978, **49**, in press.

Gottman, J., Markman, H., & Notarius, C. The topography of marital conflict: A sequential analyses of verbal and nonverbal behavior. *Journal of Marriage and the Family*, 1977, **9**, 461–477.

Gurin, G., Veroff, J., & Feld, S. *Americans view their mental health*. New York: Basic Books, 1960.

Halbertsma, H. A. Working-class systems of mutual assistance in case of childbirth, illness and death. *Social Science and Medicine*, 1970, **3**, 321–330.

Hartley, R. E. Sex-roles from a child's viewpoint. Paper presented at the annual meeting of the American Orthopsychiatric Association, San Francisco, 1966.

Hetherington, E. M. A developmental study of the effects of sex of the dominant parent on sex-role preference, identification and imitation in children. *Journal of Personality and Social Psychology*, 1965, **2**, 188–194.

Hetherington, E. M., Cox, M., & Cox, R. The aftermath of divorce. In J. H. Stevens, Jr., & M. Matthew (Eds.), *Mother-child, father-child relations*, Washington, D.C.: National Association for the Education of Young Children, 1978. (a)

Hetherington, E. M., Cox, M., & Cox, R. The development of children in mother headed families. In H. Hoffman & D. Reiss (Eds.), *The American family: Dying or developing?* New York: Plenum, 1978. (b)

Hetherington, E. M., Cox, M., & Cox, R. Stress and coping in divorce: A focus on women. In J. Gullahorn (Ed.), *Psychology and transition*. B. H. Winston & Sons, 1978, in press. (c)

Hetherington, E. M., Cox, M., & Cox, R. Play and social interaction in children following divorce. National Institute of Mental Health Divorce Conference, 1978. (d)

Hetherington, E. M., Cox, M., & Cox, R. Family interaction and the social, emotional and cognitive development of children following divorce. Johnson and Johnson Conference on the Family, Washington D.C., May 1978. (e)

Hetherington, E. M., Cox, M., Thomas, J., & Hunt, L. The generalizability of laboratory analogue studies of imitation. Unpublished manuscript, 1974.

Hetherington, E. M., & Frankie, G. Effects of parental dominance, warmth and conflict on imitation in children. *Journal of Personality and Social Psychology*, 1967, **6**, 119–125.

Hetherington, E. M., & Morris. W. N. The family and primary groups. In W. H. Holtzman (Ed.), *Introductory psychology in depth: Developmental topics.* New York: Harper & Row, 1978.

Hess, R. D. Class and ethnic influences upon socialization. In P. Mussen (Ed.), *Carmichael's manual of child psychology* (Vol. 2). New York: Wiley, 1970.

Hess, R. D., Shipman, V. C., Brophy, J. E., & Bear, R. M. *The cognitive environments of urban preschool children.* Chicago: Graduate School of Education, University of Chicago, 1968 (ERIC Document Reproduction Service No. ED 039 264).

Hess, R. D., Shipman, V. C., Brophy, J. E., Bear, R. M., & Adelberger, A. B. *The cognitive environments of urban preschool children: Follow-up phase.* Chicago: Graduate School of Education, University of Chicago, 1969 (ERIC Document Reproduction Service No. ED 039 270).

Hilton, I. Differences in the behavior of mothers toward first- and later-born children. *Journal of Personality and Social Psychology*, 1967, **7**, 282–290.

Hock, E. Working and nonworking mothers with infants: Perceptions of their careers, their infants' needs, and satisfaction with mothering. *Developmental Psychology*, 1978, **4**, 37–43.

Hodges, A., & Balow, B. Learning disability in relation to family constellation. *Journal of Educational Research*, 1961, **55**, 4–42.

Hoffman, L. W. Mothers' enjoyment of work and effects on the child. *Child Development*, 1961, **32**, 187–197.

Hoffman, L. W. Moral development. In P. Mussen (Ed.), *Handbook of child psychology.* New York: Wiley, 1970.

Hoffman, L. W. Effects of maternal employment on the child. A review of the research. *Developmental Psychology*, 1974, **10**, 204–228.

Hoffman, L. W. Changes in family roles, socialization, and sex differences. *American Psychologist*, 1977, **32**, 644–657.

Jacobs, B. S., & Moss, H. A. Birth order and sex of sibling as determinants of mother-infant interaction. *Child Development*, 1976, **47**, 315–322.

Kagan, J. Acquisition and significance of sex typing and sex role identity. In M. L. Hoffman & L. W. Hoffman (Eds.), *Review of child development research* (Vol. 2). New York: Russell Sage, 1964, pp. 137–167.

Kagan, J., & Moss, H. A. *Birth to maturity: A study in psychological development.* New York: Wiley, 1962.

Koch, H. L. The relation of "primary mental abilities" in five and six year olds to sex of child and characteristics of his siblings. *Child Development*, 1955, **26**, 13–40.

Koch, H. L. The relation of certain formal attributes of siblings to attitudes held toward each other and toward their parents. *Monographs of the Society for Research in Child Development*, 1960, **25** (4, Whole No. 78), 1–134.

Lamb, M. E. The relationships between mothers, fathers, infants and siblings in the first two years of life. Paper presented to the biennial conference of the International Society for the Study of Behavioral Development, Pavia, Italy, 1977.

Lamb, M. E. Influence of the child on marital quality and family interaction during the prenatal, perinatal and infancy period. In R. M. Lerner & G. D. Spanier (Eds.), *Contributions of the child to marital quality and family interaction through the life span.* New York: Academic, 1979, in press.

Langner, G. S., & Michael, S. T. *Life stresses and mental health.* New York: Free Press, 1963.

Lasko, J. K. Parent behavior towards first and second children. *Genetic Psychology Monographs*, 1954, **49**, 96–137.

Legg, C., Sherick, I., & Wadland, W. Reactions of preschool children to the birth of a sibling. *Child Psychiatry and Human Development*, 1974, **5**, 5–39.

Lessing, E. E., Zagorin, S. W., & Nelson, D. WISC subtest and IQ score correlates of father absence. *Journal of Genetic Psychology*, 1970, **117**, 181–195.

Lobitz, G. R., & Johnson, S. M. Parental manipulation of the behavior of normal and deviant children. *Child Development*, 1975, **46**, 719–726.

Longstreth, L. E., Longstreth, G. V., Ramirez, C., & Fernandez, G. The ubiquity of Big Brother. *Child Development*, 1975, **46**, 769–772.

Lyle, J. Television in daily life: Patterns of use (overview). In *Television and social behavior* (Vol. 4). Washington, D.C.: U.S. Government Printing Office, 1971, pp. 1–33.

Lystad, M. H. Violence at home: A review of the literature. *American Journal of Orthopsychiatry*, 1975, **45**, 328–345.

Maccoby, E. E. Television: Its impact on school children. *Public Opinion Quarterly*, 1951, **15**, 421–444.

Maccoby, E. E. Socialization theory: Where do we go from here? Paper presented at the Western Psychological Association Meeting, April 1975.

MacFarlane, J. W., Allen, L., & Honzik, M. P. A developmental study of the behavior problems of normal children between twenty-one months and fourteen years. *University of California Publications in Child Development*, 1954, **2**.

McAdoo, H. R. The impact of extended family variables upon the upward mobility of black families. Families Research Project. Unpublished manuscript, 1978.

McCord, W., McCord, I., & Zola, T. K. *Origins of crime*. New York: Columbia University Press, 1959.

Martin, B., & Hetherington, E. M. Family interaction and aggression, withdrawal and nondeviancy in children. *Progress Report*, 1971, University of Wisconsin, Project NIMH 12474, National Institute of Mental Health.

Martin, H. *The abused child*. Cambridge, Mass.: Ballinger, 1976.

Michelson, W. The physical environment as a mediating factor in school achievement. Paper presented at the annual meeting of the Canadian Sociology and Anthropology Association, Calgary, 1968.

Mischel, W. Father-absence and delay of gratification. *Journal of Abnormal and Social Psychology*, 1961, **62**, 116–124.

Mischel, W. A., & Grusec, J. Determinants of the rehearsal and transmission of neutral and aversive behaviors. *Journal of Personality and Social Psychology*, 1966, **2**, 197–205.

Moustakas, C. E., Sigel, I. E., & Schalock, N. D. An objective method for the measurement and analysis of child-adult interaction. *Child Development*, 1956, **27**, 109–134.

Mussen, P. H., & Parker, A. L. Mother nurturance and girls' incidental imitative learning. *Journal of Personality and Social Psychology*, 1965, **2**, 94–97.

Nelson, E. A., & Maccoby, E. E. The relationship between social development and differential abilities on the scholastic aptitude test. *Merrill-Palmer Quarterly*, 1966, **12**, 269–289.

Nisbett, R. E. Birth order and participation in dangerous sports. *Journal of Personality and Social Psychology*, 1968, **8**, 351–353.

Nordheimer, J. The family in transition: A challenge from within. *New York Times*, Nov. 27, 1977.

Nuttall, E., & Nuttall, R. The effects of size of family on parent-child relationships. *Proceedings of the American Psychological Association*, 1971, **6**, 267–268.

Nye, F. I. Child adjustment in broken and in unhappy unbroken homes. *Marriage and Family Living*, 1957, **19**, 356–360.

Nye, F. I., & Hoffman, L. W. *The employed mother in America*. Chicago: Rand McNally, 1963.

O'Rourke, J. F. Field and laboratory: The decision making behavior of family groups in two experimental conditions. *Sociometry*, 1963, **26**, 422–435.

Oshman, H. P. Some effects of father absence upon the psychological development of male and female late adolescents: Theoretical and empirical considerations (doctoral dissertation, University of Texas at Austin, 1975). *Dissertation Abstracts International*, 1975, **36**, 919B–920B (University Microfilms No. 75-16, 719).

Parke, R. D. Children's home environments: Social and cognitive effects. In I. Altman & J. F. Wohlwill (Eds.), *Children and the environment*. New York: Plenum, 1978.

Parke, R. D., & Collmer, W. C. Child abuse: An interdisciplinary analysis. In E. M. Hetherington (Ed.), *Review of child development research* (Vol. 5). Chicago: University of Chicago Press, 1975, pp. 509–590.

Parke, R. D., & Sawin, D. Infant characteristics and behavior as elicitors of maternal and paternal responsibility in the newborn period. Paper presented at the biennial meeting of the Society for Research in Child Development, Denver 1975.

Parsons, T. Family structure and the socialization of the child. In T. Parsons & R. Bales (Eds.), *Family, socialization and interaction process*. Glencoe, Ill.: Free Press, 1955, pp. 35–131.

Patterson, G. Mothers: The unacknowledged victims. In T. H. Stevens & R. V. Matthews (Eds.), *Mother-child, father-child relations*. Washington, D.C.: National Association for the Education of Young Children, 1978.

Patterson, G. R. The aggressive child: Victim and architect of a coercive system. In E. Mash, L. Hamerlynck, & L. Hangy (Eds.), *Behavior modification and families I. Theory and research*. New York: Brunner/Mazel, 1977.

Pederson, F. A. Mother, father and infant as an interactive system. Paper presented at the annual convention of the American Psychological Association, Chicago, 1975.

Pederson, F. A., Anderson, B. T., & Cain, R. L. An approach to understanding linkages between the parent-infant and spouse relationships. Paper presented at the Society for Research in Child Development, New Orleans, 1977.

Phillips, E. L. Cultural vs. interpsychic factors in childhood. *Journal of Clinical Psychiatry*, 1956, **12**, 400–401.

Rees, A. H., & Palmer, F. H. Factors related to change in mental test performance. *Developmental Psychology Monograph*, 1970, **3**, 1–57.

Robinson, J. P. Television's impact on everyday life: Some cross-national evidence. In *Television and social behavior* (Vol. 4). Washington, D.C.: U.S. Government Printing Office, 1971, pp. 410–432.

Rosenberg, M. *Society and the adolescent self-image*. Princeton, N.J.: Princeton University Press, 1965.

Rosenblatt, P. C., & Cunningham, M. R. Television watching and family tensions. *Journal of Marriage and Family*, 1976, **38**, 105–110.

Rosenoer, C., & Whyte, A. H. The ordinal position of problem children. *American Journal of Orthopsychiatry*, 1931, **1**, 430–434.

Ross, H. L., & Sawhill, I. V. Time of transition: The growth of families headed by women. The Urban Institute, Washington D.C., 1975.

Rothbart, M. K. Birth order and mother-child interaction in an achievement situation. *Journal of Personality and Social Psychology*, 1971, **17**, 113–120.

Rutter, M. Maternal deprivation, 1972–1977: New findings, new concepts, new approaches. Invited address presented at the biennial meeting of the Society for Research in Child Development, New Orleans, 1977.

Samuels, H. R. The role of the sibling in the infant's social environment. Paper presented at the biennial meeting of the Society for Research in Child Development, New Orleans, 1977.

Santrock, J. W. Relation of type and onset of father-absence on cognitive development. *Child Development*, 1972, **43**, 455–469.

Santrock, J. W. Father absence, perceived maternal behavior, and moral development in boys. *Child Development*, 1975, **46**, 753–757.

Santrock, J. W., & Wohlford, P. Effects of father absence: Influences of, reason for, and onset of absence. *Proceedings of the 78th Annual Convention of the American Psychological Association*, 1970, **5**, 265–266.

Sarnoff, I. Identification with the aggressor: Some personality correlates of anti-Semitism among Jews. *Journal of Personality*, 1951, **20**, 199–218.

Schacter, S. *The psychology of affiliation.* Stanford, Calif.: Stanford University Press, 1959.

Schmidt, B., & Kempe, C. H. The pediatrician's role in child abuse and neglect. *Current problems in pediatrics monograph* (Vol. 5). Chicago: Yearbook Medical Publishers, 1975.

Secord, P. R., & Backman, C. W. *Social psychology.* New York: McGraw-Hill, 1964.

Shinn, M. Father absence and children's cognitive development. *Psychology Bulletin*, 1978, **85**, 295–324.

Siegman, A. W. Father-absence during childhood and antisocial behavior. *Journal of Abnormal Psychology*, 1966, **71**, 71–74.

Solomon, D., Hirsch, J. G., Scheinfeld, D. R., & Jackson, J. C. Family characteristics and elementary school achievement in an urban ghetto. *Journal of Consulting and Clinical Psychology*, 1972, **39**, 462–466.

Stack, C. B. *All our kin.* New York: Harper & Row, 1974.

Staub, E. *Positive social behavior and morality.* 1978, in press.

Stein, A. H. The effects of maternal employment and educational attainment on the sex-typed attributes of college females. *Social Behavior and Personality*, 1973, **1**, 111–114.

Steiner, G. *The people look at television.* New York: Knopf, 1963.

Suedfield, P. Paternal absence and overseas success of Peace Corps volunteers. *Journal of Consulting Psychology*, 1967, **31**, 424–425.

Sutton-Smith, B., & Rosenberg, B. G. *The sibling.* New York: Holt, 1970.

Taylor, N. K., & Kogan, K. L. Effects of birth of a sibling on mother-child interactions. *Child Psychiatry and Human Development*, 1973, **4**, 53–58.

Thoman, E. B., Liederman, P. H., & Olson, J. P. Neonate-mother interaction during breast feeding. *Developmental Psychology*, 1972, **6**, 110–118.

Torrance, E. B. A psychological study of American jet aces. Paper presented at the meeting of the Western Psychological Association, Long Beach, Calif., 1954.

Wachs, T. The measurement of early intellectual functioning. In C. Meyers, R. Eyman, & G. Tarjan (Eds.), *Socio-behavioral studies in mental retardation.* Washington, D.C.: American Association on Mental Deficiency, 1973.

Walker, K. E., & Woods, M. E. Time used for care of family members. Unpublished manuscript, Cornell University, 1972.

Watson, J. B. *Psychological care of infant and child.* New York: Norton, 1928.

Winder, C. L., & Rau, L. Parental attitudes associated with social deviance in preadolescent boys. *Journal of Abnormal and Social Psychology*, 1962, **64**, 418–424.

Wohlwill, J. F., & Heft, H. Environment fit for the developing child. In H. McGurk (Ed.), *Ecological factors in human development.* Amsterdam: North-Holland, 1977.

Woods, N. B. The unsupervised child of the working mother. *Developmental Psychology*, 1972, **6**, 14–25.

Yarrow, M. R., Campbell, J. D., & Burton, R. V. *Child rearing.* San Francisco: Jossey-Bass, 1968.

Yarrow, M. R., Scott, P., DeLeeuw, L., & Heineg, C. Child rearing in families of working and non-working mothers. *Sociometry*, 1962, **25**, 122–140.

Zajonc, R. B. Family configuration and intelligence. *Science*, 1976, **192**, 227–236.

Zegoib, L. E., Arnold, S., & Forehand, R. An examination of observer effects in parent-child interactions. *Child Development*, 1975, **46**, 509–512.

Zucker, R. A., Manosevitz, M., & Lanyon, R. D. Birth order, anxiety and affiliation during a crisis. *Journal of Personality and Social Psychology*, 1968, **8**, 354–359.

13

The Peer
Group as a
Socialization
Agency

In recent years there has been increasing recognition of the importance of extra-familial agents in the socialization process. With the rise in maternal employment and the increase in the availability of preschool education, the role of peers and teachers has been brought into sharp focus. The purpose of this chapter and the next will be to examine the contribution of the peer group and the school to childhood socialization.

The term "peers" usually refers to children who are social equals, and who are similar on characteristics such as age. However, recently it has been suggested that classifying children who interact at about the same level of behavioral complexity as peers might be more appropriate than just focusing on equal ages (Lewis & Rosenblum, 1975). It is frequently stated that the relationship with peers is qualitatively different from that with family members, that the child's relationship with parents is more intense and enduring than that with friends. Some investigators have noted that the more free and egalitarian relationship with peers permits a new kind of interpersonal experimentation and exploration, and most particularly a new kind of sensitivity, which will serve as one of the cornerstones for the development of social competence and the capacity to love (Piaget, 1932; Sullivan, 1953). This position is cogently stated by Harry Stack Sullivan:

All of you who have children are sure that your children love you; when you say that, you are expressing a pleasant illusion. But if you will look very closely at one of your children when he finally finds a chum—somewhere between eight-and-a-half and ten—you will discover something very different in the relationship—namely, that your child begins to develop a real sensitivity to what matters to another person. And this is not in the sense of "what should I do to contribute to the happiness or to support the prestige and feeling of worthwhileness of my chum." So far as I have ever been able to discover, nothing remotely like this appears before. . . . The developmental epoch of preadolescence is marked by the coming of the integrating tendecies which, when they are completely developed, we call love, or, to say it another way, by the manifestation of the need for interpersonal intimacy. . . . (Sullivan, 1953, pp. 245–246)

Although Sullivan has pointed to the importance of peer relations in the preadolescent period, we will see that interactions with peers begin to shape children's behavior at a much earlier age. These peer interactions are important factors in the development of social and cognitive competence in children.

Developmental Trends in Peer Interaction

As early as the first year of life infants are responsive to their peers. Babies in the first six months of life touch and look at each other and even cry in response to the other's crying. However, it is unlikely that these early responses are really social in the sense of the infant seeking and expecting a social response from the other child. It is not until the second half of the first year that truly social behaviors begin to appear.

It is difficult to think of infants as popular or unpopular, but even in the first year of life there are marked individual differences in the social style and social acceptance of infants. In a study of 8- to 10-month-old infants in a day-care center, it was observed that one child was avoided by his peers and another child was sought out and appeared to be unusually well liked (Lee, 1973). What variations in the behavior of the two children might explain the difference in their popularity? Jenny, the popular child, made fewer social initiations than Patrick, the unpopular child, but she began her initiations by looking at or approaching another child. In contrast, Patrick was likely to be highly assertive and initiated exchanges by grabbing the other child or the child's toy, not behaviors likely to rate highly in a preschool popularity poll. When other children made social overtures, Jenny responded positively whereas Patrick would ignore or respond to the overture inappropriately. Even 10-month-old infants don't like children who are aggressive or who do not reciprocate their friendly overtures. This is a pattern we will see extends throughout the life span. It seems likely that these variations in early social competence with peers are based on both temperament and experiences within the family. A secure attachment with parents has been discussed earlier as an important factor in later social relations. In addition, early interactions with siblings seem to be related to social acceptance. Infants who have older siblings are more likely than those with no brothers or sisters to both initiate and respond to social advances (Kelly, 1976).

It has been suggested that the changes in infant interactions which begin in the first year and continue over the course of the second year progress in a fixed sequence (Mueller & Lucas, 1975; Mueller & Vandell, in press). In the first stage, *the object-centered stage*, although children are interacting, they are usually directing most of their attention toward a toy or object rather than toward each other. In the second stage, *the simple interactive stage*, children respond to the behavior of peers and often try to regulate the behavior of the other child. Here is an example of a simple interchange

Larry sits on the floor and Bernie turns and looks toward him. Bernie waves his hand and

As infants grow older, not only positive social exchanges but also negative interactions increase. (Vivian Rodvogin, Black Star)

BOX 13-1
I LOVE MY MOM, BUT OH YOU KID!

We know that children enjoy playing with their parents, but given a choice would they rather play with their mother, a peer, or a strange adult? In order to answer this question, children of three different age groups (10 to 12, 16 to 18, and 22 to 24 months) and their mothers were observed for 20 minutes in a play room with another mother-child pair. As can be seen in Figure 13-1, older children, in contrast to the younger children, spent more time in social than in solitary play, and with increasing age children showed a marked preference for playing with each other, rather than with their mothers. At no time did children prefer to play with the unfamiliar adult, that is the other mother. ■

Source: Eckerman, C. O. Whatley, J. L., & Kutz, S. L. Growth of social play with peers during the second year of life. *Developmental Psychology*, 1975, **11**, 42–49.

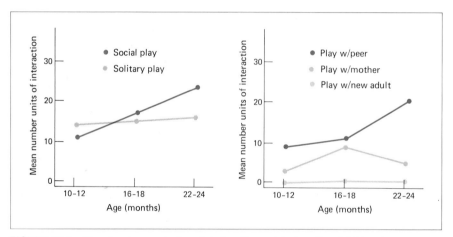

FIGURE 13-1   The development of social play. (In social play, the child involves others—peer, mother, or new adult—in his activities with nonsocial objects.) *(From Eckerman, Whatley, & Kutz, 1975, p. 47.)*

says "da," still looking at Larry. He repeats the vocalization three more times before Larry laughs. Bernie vocalizes again and Larry laughs again. Then the same sequence of one child saying "da" and the other laughing is repeated twelve more times before Bernie turns away from Larry and walks off. Bernie and Larry become distracted at times during the interchange. Yet when this happens the partner reattracts attention either by repeating his socially directed action or by modifying it, as when Bernie both waves and says "da," reengaging Larry. (Mueller & Lucas, 1975, p. 241)

In the third stage, *the complementary interactive stage*, more complex

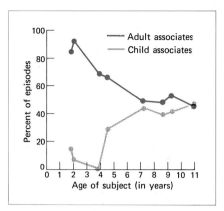

FIGURE 13-2 Amount of contact with parents, teachers, and peers during childhood. *(From Wright, 1967.)*

sequences of social interchanges are occurring. Imitation becomes more common. Reciprocal or complementary role relationships are seen, such as "chaser" and "chased," "hider" and "seeker," or "giver" and "receiver." Now when positive social interactions occur, they are more likely to be accompanied with a smile or laugh or other displays of appropriate positive affect (Mueller & Brenner, 1977; Mueller & Rich, 1976). However, all is not sweetness and light in the nursery set! As social exchanges become more complex and likely to be accompanied by vocal or emotional responses, negative as well as positive exchanges are increasing. During the second year fights over toys, hitting, hair pulling, and biting become more frequent (Eckerman, Whatley, & Kutz, 1975; Mueller & Vandell, in press). The shift toward increased social play and a greater preference for playing with peers rather than adults, even with the mother, are clearly illustrated in the study by Eckerman and her colleagues presented in Box 13-1.

These trends continue throughout the preschool and early school years. In one investigation, a group of children ranging from 2 to 11 years of age was "tracked" by an observer for a full day with the aim of providing as complete a record as possible of the child's activities. This record of the child's "stream of behavior" was divided into discrete "episodes" (behavioral units with clear-cut beginning and termination points, such as eating dinner and combing hair), and the frequency with which parents, teachers, and peers were involved in each behavioral episode was plotted (Barker & Wright, 1955; Wright, 1967). It was found that not only parent-child interaction decreases markedly as the child grows older, but interactions with teachers decrease. In fact, the number of episodes in which the child is involved with any adult associates is just about equal to those involving peers by age 11, as can be seen in Figure 13-2.

The classic description of the developmental course of peer interaction in the later preschool years was provided many years ago by Parten and Newhall (1943). Basing their study on observations of children from 2 to 5 years of age, these investigators offered a three-phase sequence of peer play patterns: a solitary phase in which the child plays by himself; a period of parallel play in which children play beside but do not interact directly with other children; and finally, the advent of cooperative play, by the time the child is ready to enter elementary school. A recent replication of Parten's study (Barnes, 1971) shows that the play behavior of preschoolers has changed somewhat in the past forty years. Modern 3- and 4-year-olds spend less time in social play than did those in the original study. This was attributed to the amount of time today's children spend in noninteractive, passive activities, such as watching television, and to the greater complexity and attractiveness of modern toys, which do not require interaction to be interesting. It may also be related to the decrease in family size. You will recall that experience with siblings facilitates competent social play. However, as the studies of infants that we discussed earlier and some other recent research indicates, Parten's classic description probably underestimates the complexity of early peer interaction.

Garvey (1977) discovered that by the age of 3 children are involved in highly ritualized social exchanges which she refers to as *turns* and *rounds*. Each child's verbal or nonverbal contribution is a *turn*. The response of one child to the other may be the same, for example, echoing speech or imitating gestures, or it may be complementary. The total pattern of alternating turns forms a rhythmic ritual called a *round*. If one child fails to take her turn and breaks the rhythm of echoings, the other may prompt her by saying "you go next" or "your turn." Here is an example of a round between a 5-year-old boy and girl.

Boy	Girl
Can you carry this? (shows girl toy fish)	
	Yeah, if I weighed 50 pounds.
You can't even carry it.	
Can you carry it by the string?	
	Yeah. Yes I can. (lifts fish overhead by string)
Can you carry it by the nose?	
	(carries it by the eye)
	Where's the nose?
That yellow one.	
	This? (carries it by nose)
Can you carry it by its tail?	
	Yeah. (carries it by tail)
Can you carry it by its fur?	
	(carries it by fur)
Can you carry it by its body?	
	(carries it by body)

Can you carry it like this?
(shows how to carry it by fin)

(carries it by fin)
I weigh 50 pounds almost, right?

Right. (Garvey, 1977, pp. 118–119)

In early elementary school such rituals become much more formalized in the verbal exchanges and chants, rhymes, and signal calls found in games such as jump rope, red rover, and ships and sailors.

Play

Most of the social interchanges of peers occur in the setting of play, and as can be seen in Figure 13-3, children spend more of their time outside of school playing with friends than involved in any other activity. What is play? We would all agree that when children are chasing each other around the school grounds, swinging on swings, climbing trees, or engaging in a game of chess, Monopoly, or baseball that they are playing. What distinguishes play from other types of activity? It seems to be the freedom of choice to become engaged in play and to structure or respond to play activities in a highly individual way. Dearden's (1967) definition of play as a nonserious and self-contained activity engaged in for the sheer satisfaction it brings seems as adequate as any available.

The Function of Play

What are the functions that play serves in the development of competence in children? First, play facilitates the cognitive development of children. It permits them to explore their environment, to learn about objects, and to solve problems. Second, play advances the social development of the child. Particularly in fantasy play through acting out roles, the child learns to understand

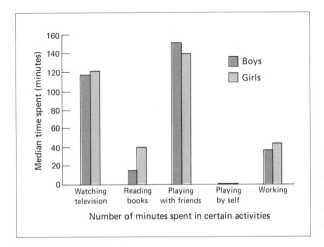

FIGURE 13-3 Parents' reports of 6- to 11-year-old children's use of time outside of school, United States. *(From Roberts & Baird, 1971.)*

others and to practice roles she will assume as she grows older. Finally, play permits the child to solve some of her emotional problems, to learn to cope with anxiety and inner conflicts in a nonthreatening situation.

Play and Cognitive Development Berlyne (1966) has proposed that play is stimulating and pleasurable because it is a way of satisfying an *exploratory drive*. The exploratory drive involves a need for new experiences and information and a curiosity about objects and events. The style of exploration, objects, and modes of play which help children to gratify their exploratory needs and to solve problems vary with the age of the children. Hunt (1965) has spoken of the "problem of match" between the cognitive level and knowledge of the child and the complexity of the stimulus. As children grow older and are able to process information more effectively, they enjoy increasingly complex, novel, and incongruous objects and situations for play. If an object is too simple or too familiar, it does not invoke in the child a sense of discovery and he becomes bored. If it is too difficult, he becomes frustrated and stressed, and learning is not facilitated (Switzky, Haywood, & Isett, 1974). It seems to be the unique opportunity for experimenting with objects in play without the pressure of evaluation that promotes the cognitive development of children. The role of play in facilitating problem solving can be seen in a recent study by Sylva, Bruner, and Genova (1976). Children aged 3 to 5 were asked to obtain a piece of chalk from a box that lay out of their reach. In order to solve the problem they needed to clamp two sticks together and extend them into the box. It was found that children who had seen the solution demonstrated by an adult were no more successful in solving the problem than those who were just allowed to play with the materials. In addition, the children who had played solved the problem more often than those who had seen only part of the solution modeled by an adult.

Early differences in exploration and curiosity in play are also associated with long-term differences in cognitive and personality development. Preschool boys who are active explorers later are curious, venturesome, independent, and creative in the elementary school years. Girls who as toddlers are restrained and do not explore or experiment with objects in their environment subsequently tend to exhibit poor social relations and personality problems (Hutt & Bhavnani, 1972).

Play and Social Competence

Within the context of play, children are granted opportunities for discovery without risk. For example, in make-believe play, children can experiment with dominant and submissive roles with few adverse consequences. The child learns to recognize and to act in his or her own fantasies, as well as in those of others. One play session may find the child taking a variety of roles, ranging from cowhand to lion to baby. Children can learn behaviors appropriate to each play situation in a relatively risk free setting. They can test without fear the outer limits of what is acceptable. Later on in life, failure to abide by social hierarchies may prove more costly. (Fein, 1978, p. 269)

Imaginative play seems particularly important in the development of social competence. It permits children to practice their own future roles as well as to playfully experience the roles and feelings of others. It teaches children to function as part of the social group and to coordinate their activities and roles with those of other children.

Imaginative play initially appears about halfway through the second year. This usually involves solitary symbolic activities such as feeding a doll with make-believe food. By age 3 not only solitary make-believe play is occurring, but complex cooperative dramatic play is emerging. This often takes a fanciful, exaggerated, roughhousing form that has been called "galumphing" (Miller, 1973). In aggressive play children may have slow-motion fistfights and gun battles or prolonged, staggering, agonized death throes that would do merit to a diva in the Metropolitan Opera. The gestures are broad caricatures. The mock blows are telegraphed. Imaginative play peaks around 6 years of age when it involves highly coordinated fantasies, rapid transitions between multiple roles, and unique transformations of objects and situations. Fantasy play then begins to decline in the school years as the child engages in structured games. Why does fantasy decline? No one is really sure. Piaget (1951) has suggested that as the individual recognizes the realities and logic of the world, it is incompatible

A frequent form of girls' fantasy play is playing "dress-up." (Yan Lukas, Photo Researchers, Inc.)

with fantasy. However, Singer (1977) has proposed that imagination doesn't really disappear but is expressed in different ways—through daydreaming, reading, or watching television.

Play, Peers, and Pathology   Children's peer interactions and play not only provide a critical opportunity in which to acquire certain social competencies, but also have been found to play an important role in the development of self-control and in working through or modifying problem behavior in children (Hartup, 1976, 1978).

An important feature of pretend play is that it again provides opportunities for expression and control of affect and the representation in miniaturized form of conflictual or frightening scenes or encounters. The child engaged in pretend play of adventurous or hostile encounters gains some sense of competence and power (Sutton-Smith, 1976) or empathy (Gould, 1972; Saltz and Johnson, 1974) and may in effect be establishing better organized schema or plans and subroutines for observing others' emotions and expressing or controlling its own. . . . Differentiating aggression or violence from adaptive assertiveness, impulsivity from means-end action, egocentricism from sharing, dependent demanding from sharing or helping, infantile sexuality from interpersonal intimacy—all these are demands we all must confront in the growth process. Make-believe play as child psychotherapists have long stressed is an important arena in which children can express and differentiate issues of this kind. (Singer, 1977)

Disruptions and rigidity in the play patterns of emotionally disturbed children have frequently been noted. Age-inappropriate play, deviations in play, and unpopularity with peers have consistently been found to be related to anxiety and emotional disturbance in children (Hartup, 1976; Roff, Sells, & Golden, 1972; Singer, 1977). Processes in imaginative play seem to be particularly vulnerable to the effects of psychological stress. It has been suggested that the failure to develop imaginative play is indicative of serious pathology, particularly of an aggressive, acting-out, impulsive type in children. Children who are undergoing psychological stress, such as those whose parents have recently gone through a divorce, show a marked rigidity in imaginative play (Hetherington, Cox, & Cox, 1978). They have fewer different characters involved in their fantasies, less frequently make different uses of the same objects in play, and are more bound to objects in play. They are less able to free themselves from reality. They need a stick to be a sword or a chair to be a castle. They rarely fantasize completely imaginary objects or people. They also show less reversibility in play. Once a stick is a sword, it is not subsequently transformed into a witch's broomstick or a magic wand or a horse. In addition, they show less diversity in both themes and affect. Another characteristic which is revealed in their play is one which is frequently reported in disturbed children: a preoccupation with aggression and an inability to assume the role of providing or caring for others in imaginative play. In addition, they seem to have great difficulty in moving from "I" to the assumption of another's role in fantasy play, in moving out of the self. Gould (1972) has remarked that the transition from the consistent use of "I" in play to play in which the child is able to assume or

BOX 13-2
TRAINING CHILDREN IN FANTASY

Since low frequencies of imaginative sociodramatic play are associated with problems in personality and cognitive functioning, would training in sociodramatic play improve functioning in these areas?

Economically disadvantaged preschool children were trained in one of three types of fantasy activities over a school year. One group of children listened to fairy tales, such as *The Three Billy Goats Gruff* or *The Three Little Pigs*, and then acted them out. The children would pantomime such things as the wolf blowing the pigs' houses down, or the pigs running and screaming with the wolf in hot pursuit. The children were encouraged to trade roles from session to session. Another group of children acted out common experiences, such as visits to the doctor or grocery store, or outings to the zoo, a fire station, etc. The stories acted out were thus closer to the children's actual experience and involved less fantasy than those of the first group. A third group of children were read fairy tales, but they did not act them out. After hearing the stories, the children would discuss them. In addition to these three groups, a fourth group of children acted as a control group who had interaction sessions with the staff involving such typical preschool activities as finger painting, cutting and pasting, and identifying animals in picture books.

It was found that the physical enactment of fantasy experiences markedly improved children's performance on a variety of measures of intellectual functioning, empathy, length of resistance before touching an attractive but forbidden toy, and other measures of impulse control. Simply listening to and discussing the stories was usually no more effective than the control situation. In addition, the results suggested that fantasy play, which was farther removed from reality, such as that involving fairy tales, had more positive consequences than sociodramatic play dealing with more common experiences. Imaginative sociodramatic play can be used successfully as a means of facilitating cognitive development and self-control in young children. ■

Source: Saltz, E., Dixon, D., & Johnson, J. Training disadvantaged preschoolers on various fantasy activities: Effects on cognitive functioning and impulse control. Technical Report 8, May 1976, Wayne State University.

alternate in playing another's role ("I'm R2 D2" or "I'll play Batman") occurs between the ages of 3½ and 4. She notes that continued focusing on the "I" in fantasy play in children beyond this age tends to be associated with psychopathology and a lack of self-control. Similar constriction and lack of flexibility in imaginative play have been found in economically disadvantaged children. In fact economically deprived children spend little time involved in imaginative, sociodramatic play (Rosen, 1974). In a study involving direct observation of free play of kindergarten children, it was reported that imaginative sociodramatic play occurred about 78 percent of the time with affluent children, but only 10 percent of the time with poor children (Smilansky, 1968).

If the frequency of sociodramatic "pretend" play could be increased, would it have any effect on the cognitive development and impulse control of disadvantaged children? The results of the study presented in Box 13-2 suggest that training in imaginative play can have a positive impact on the development of children.

Imaginativeness in play is associated not only with self-control, low impulsivity, and low aggression, but also with sharing, cooperativeness, independence (Singer, 1977), and social maturity (Rubin, Maione, & Hornug, 1976). In addition, children who show spontaneous imaginativeness in play are likely to show a broader range of emotions and more positive emotions than less imaginative children. They are more likely to smile, be curious and interested in new experiences, and express joy in play and in peer relations (Singer, 1977).

The Function of Peers

We have spoken of socialization as learning to play by the rules of the social game. Peers are a source of information about these rules, and about how well the child is playing the game, from a different perspective than that of the family. It is the perspective of equals with common problems, goals, status, and abilities. How does the peer group influence the development of the child? In many of the same ways that parents do, through reinforcement and through modeling. However, there is another way in which they may play an even more important role, and that is through serving as standards against which the child evaluates herself. Since there are few objective ways in which the child can evaluate her characteristics, values, and abilities, she turns to other people, particularly to peers. She uses others as a yardstick with which to compare herself. This process of social comparison is the basis of the child's self-image and self-esteem.

Peers as Reinforcers

As children grow older, the salience of peers as reinforcing agents and as models increases. Many parents, particularly of adolescents, bemoan the fact that their children ignore their wise advice while listening to and emulating their peers. Even throughout the preschool years, the frequency with which peers reinforce each other increases.

A study by Charlesworth and Hartup (1967) has documented the shift in the reinforcing capacity of peers that occurs in 3- and 4-year-olds. These investigators gathered normative information on the amount and kinds of positive social reinforcement dispensed by 3- and 4-year-old children to each other in a nursery school setting. The following kinds of social categories were scored:

1 *Giving positive attention and approval:* attending, offering praise and approval, offering help, smiling, informing someone of another child's needs, general conversation.

2 *Giving affection and personal acceptance:* physical and verbal.

3 *Submission:* passive acceptance, imitation, sharing, accepting another's idea or help, allowing another child to play, compromise, following an order or request with pleasure and cooperation.

Four-year-olds socially reinforced their peers at a higher rate than did three-year-old children. Moreover, older children tended to distribute their reinforcements over a larger number of recipients than did younger children. Regardless of age, however, there was a marked tendency for boys to direct their reinforcement to boys, while girls gave more reinforcements to other girls than to opposite-sexed peers. This is consistent with numerous findings (Moore, 1967) that young children tend to prefer to interact with peers of the same sex. Another issue concerns the development of reciprocity: Do young children tend to reinforce the same individuals who reinforce them? The relationship between giving and receiving of positive reinforcement was large ($r = .79$). Similarly the child who tended to reinforce a large number of different peers received reinforcement from many children. Even by 3 and 4 years of age, therefore, giving and receiving have developed into reciprocal activities.

Although reciprocity is the most common pattern of interchanges among children, a recent study by Leiter (1977) of peers' responses to children's social initiations reveals that complementary interchanges also sometimes occur. Children have many different ways of starting social interchanges. Some children are friendly and join in or suggest activities in a smiling, affable manner. Other children are demanding and yell and try to command or physically force participation by other children. Still others are whiny and beg, cry, or watch timorously rather than actively joining in play. How are peers likely to respond to these different types of initiations? Peers were more likely to comply with and include the friendly child in play. The whiny child was most often greeted by ignoring, and the demanding child usually met with a coercive often physical threatening response such as a hit, shove, or command. However, peers

Peer reactions can reinforce aggressive behavior in children. (Chester Missins, Rapho/ Photo Researchers, Inc.)

sometimes responded to demands with high-intensity levity where joshing and teasing roughhousing occurs or with submissive responses such as pleading, leaving the situation, or asking the teacher or another child for help. It thus seems that although reciprocity usually occurs, this is not always the case, and as the study in Box 13-3 illustrates, the reactions of other children during social exchanges, such as an aggressive encounter, are an important form of control in peer-peer interaction.

There is no doubt that peer reinforcement in the form of attention and approval affects the behavior patterns of the peer recipient. A study by Wahler (1967) will illustrate this effect. Instead of merely observing peer interactions, Wahler directly intervened and trained a group of youngsters to serve as experimenter confederates. Wahler instructed the peers of five children to attend to only certain behaviors and to ignore other social responses. Eddie, a 5-year-old boy, will illustrate the procedures used. First, the aspects of Eddie's behavior that were consistent and stable parts of his response repertoires were noted, namely cooperative behavior (playing a game initiated by peers), solitary play (playing alone), and shouting. Two other 5-year-old boys were selected to "shape" Eddie's behavior. They were taught to ignore the boy whenever he made a cooperative overture; as expected, ignoring this class of responses produced a marked reduction of cooperative behaviors. At the same time, solitary play and shouting increased in rate during this period. To demonstrate that Eddie's behavior was under peer reinforcement control, Wahler next instructed his young assistants to resume their attention to Eddie's cooperative behavior. The result was more cooperative responses from Eddie. Using other 5-year-olds, Wahler was able to demonstrate similar effects for a variety of other social responses, including speech, aggression, and play behavior.

Home and background factors may also contribute to the patterns of reinforcement used by preschool children in peer interactions. Recall from the chapter on the assessment of intelligence that middle-class parents use more praise and less punishment in interaction with their children than do lower-class parents.

On the basis of these findings, Feshbach and Devor argued that "if a child duplicates in his social transactions with peers, modal patterns of reinforcement observed at home, then peer interaction and influences may vary with social class" (1969, p. 1). Specifically, these investigators predicted that middle-class Caucasian children would make greater use of positive reinforcement, while children from more deprived backgrounds would manifest greater instances of negative reinforcement. Rather than assess spontaneous occurrences of positive and negative social reinforcement, Feshbach and Devor experimentally arranged the 4-year-olds in the study to teach a younger child how to solve a simple wooden puzzle. The extent to which the child-teacher used positive and negative reinforcements in carrying out the instructional task was recorded by observers. The positive category included statements of praise, encouragement, and affirmation, such as "that's a girl" or "she did it," while the negative category included criticism, negations, and derogatory comments, such as "wrong way" or "you skipped." Although all "teachers" were equally effective,

BOX 13-3
PEER REACTIONS AS REINFORCERS OF AGGRESSIVE BEHAVIOR

 The aim of the Patterson, Littman, and Bricker (1967) research was to demonstrate the important role that peer-group reactions play in reinforcing aggressive behavior in nursery school children. To investigate the problem of how the peer group contributes to aggression development, these investigators trained a group of students to make observations of the aggressive exchanges between children in a nursery school setting. The eighteen boys and eighteen girls participating in the study were observed for thirty-three 2½-hour sessions. By gathering detailed information they were able to assess how the reaction of the target or victim of an aggressive attack affected the subsequent behavior of the aggressor. What happens when one child rushes up, pushes, and grabs another child's teddy bear? When the target child responded by withdrawing, by acquiescing, or by crying, the attacker in subsequent interactions was likely to perform the same aggressive act (pushing and grabbing toys) toward the same victim. In other words, these reactions functioned as positive reinforcers for the aggressor.

In contrast, if the aggressive behavior was followed by negative reinforcement, such as teacher intervention, attempts at recovery of property (for example, the teddy bear), or retaliation (for example, hitting the aggressor), then the aggressive child had a high probability of either choosing a new victim or altering the form of aggression.

Not only is aggression controlled by peer feedback, but nonaggressive children may learn to behave aggressively, particularly if they are frequently the victims of an aggressive attack. The best way to understand how this type of learning occurs is to examine closely what happens to a typical victim. First, children who are victimized by peers are provided with many opportunities to counterattack their aggressors. After frequent attacks, even a passive victim will finally strike back, and by counterattacking, the number of future attacks is often decreased—a highly reinforcing outcome for the victim. In addition, aggression is a highly successful response in the nursery school set. If the child fights back, he has about a 68 percent chance of successfully fending off his aggressor. Over repeated occasions, the victim's aggressive responses are therefore strengthened, thus making it more probable that he will *initiate* aggressive attacks in future situations. In fact, this is precisely the pattern that these investigators discovered. Over the period of the study they found a striking association between the frequency with which children were victimized by aggressive acts of peers, the frequency of their successful counterattacks, and increases in their aggressive behavior. Even Charlie Brown could eventually learn to be aggressive—in self-defense! The study suggests that peers as well as adults are important reinforcing agents and that the reactions or feedback provided by the victim constitute an important class of reinforcing events for both controlling and developing aggressive and assertive behaviors. ■

Source: Patterson, G. R., Littman, R. A., and Bricker, W. Assertive behavior in children: A step toward a theory of aggression. *Monographs of the Society for Research in Child Development*, 1967, **32** (Serial No. 113).

the children differed in their relative use of positive and negative reinforcers. Middle-class Caucasian children used a greater number of positive reinforcers than the lower-class group. There was a slight tendency for the lower-class subjects to use more negative reinforcements in instructing a younger child than the middle-class children; however, the effect was less marked than in the case of positive reinforcement. More recently, Feshbach (1973) has reported similar results for middle- and lower-class children in England and Israel. Differences previously reported in relation to parental reinforcement patterns across social class appear to be reflected, at least in part, in peer behavior. The differential encouragement and positive support that the middle-class Caucasian child receives from his or her peer group may contribute to greater school achievement - and intellectual accomplishment. Moreover, it is clear that no typical reinforcement pattern can be described; the social class of the child required consideration.

Peers as Models

Peers influence each other by serving not only as reinforcers, but also as social models. Children acquire a wide range of knowledge and a variety of responses by observing the behavior of their peers.

Imagine the situation of the new child at school. Through observation he may rapidly learn that the children are expected to stand when the teacher enters the room, that it is risky to shoot spitballs, that the game of marbles is played with different rules in this school, and that contact with the big red-headed kid in the corner should be avoided because he is the class bully.

Some of the things children learn through exposure to peers are positive, such as to make mature moral judgements (Bandura & McDonald, 1963), to resist temptation (Walters & Parke, 1964), to become more successful in peer interactions (O'Connor, 1969), and to become less fearful (Bandura, Grusec, & Menlove, 1967). Others involve socially undesirable behaviors such as disobedience, selfishness, and aggression (Hicks, 1965). Some of these studies are discussed in detail in other chapters.

The characteristics of children which facilitate their being imitated by their peers are similar to those we discussed in adult models. Children are more likely to imitate peers who are warm and rewarding, who are powerful, who are in control of resources, who are rewarded by others, and whom they perceive as being similar to themselves.

The nature of the child's typical interactions with her peer group is one important determinant of peer imitation. Hartup and Coates (1967) classified children as those who often received social reinforcement from their peers, that is, they were relatively popular, and as those who were less popular and seldom received reinforcement from their peers. The children were then put in an experimental modeling situation where they had the opportunity of imitating the sharing behaviors of peers in a maze game. Half of the children in each group were exposed to children who frequently interacted with their peers and had often reinforced other children in the past. The other half were exposed to children who were low in their amount of peer interaction and the frequency with which they reinforced their peers. Thus, half of the children in each group were paired with someone similar to themselves in terms of how they interacted with peers and half were paired with someone who was dissimilar. As Figure 13-4 shows, both the children's past history of reinforcement and their prior relationship with the model were important determinants of peer imitation. The popular children tended to imitate the altruistic behavior of a peer who had frequently rewarded them in the past. In contrast, the less popular children were more likely to imitate a peer when that peer had never reinforced them. What can be causing this difference? We have stated that children tend to imitate rewarding models, but in this study only the popular children preferred to model a rewarding peer. Why are the less popular children opting to imitate the behavior of peers who seldom or never have reinforced them? The investigators suggest that the children are imitating peers they view as similar to themselves. The popular children, who themselves often reward their peers, imitate children who also frequently interact and dispense rewards. The unpopular children and the children they imitate resemble each other in their low levels of peer interaction and reinforcement.

Most studies of modeling among peers have focused on the effects of the model's behavior or characteristics on the child doing the imitating. Is there any effect on the model of being imitated?

Most children like to be imitated. In fact, there is some evidence that cycles of *reciprocal imitation* occur. If an adult imitates a child's behavior, the child prefers that adult over a nonimitating person, and is likely to model the imitating adult's behavior (Thelen, Dollinger, & Roberts, 1975). However, keep in mind that these results are being obtained with adults doing the imitating. It may be

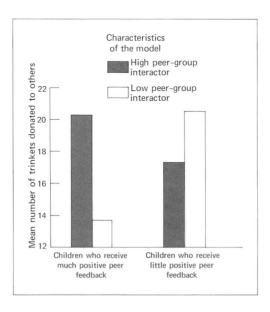

FIGURE 13-4 Peer imitation: Subject and model characteristics. *(Adapted from Hartup & Coates, 1967.)*

flattering for a child to be imitated by a high-status adult. Further research suggests that the response to being imitated depends on the status of the imitator. The study presented in Box 13-4 shows that children respond positively to imitation by older (high-status) children, but not to younger (low-status) children.

These results are congruent with the finding we reported earlier that younger siblings attend to and imitate older siblings, but that the reverse seldom occurs.

It is interesting to speculate on how the rigid age grading of organizations and activities dealing with children, such as schools, team sports, Sunday school classes, and so on, may be limiting, or at least altering, their opportunities to learn from peers of different status.

Peers and the Social Comparison Process

To whom do we turn when we engage in social comparison? Festinger (1954) persuasively claims that we seek people who are similar to ourselves as the comparison group. If a child wants to know how good a fighter he is, he doesn't dwell on how he'd do against Muhammed Ali, but, instead, is more likely to take into account the outcomes of neighborhood scuffles he's been in together with his impression of how "tough" his peers see him as being. How good a reader the child thinks he is is affected little by the fact that his mother can read many more words faster than he can, but much by his opportunity to observe other children in his class. Thus, the answer to the question of whom we turn to is the peer group. If you will excuse the pun, in matters of self-definition, the peer group has no peer. . . . The emerging power of the peer group to shape the attitudes, behaviors, and self-concepts of its members is a by-product of the interaction that goes on within it, rather than the reason for the interaction. We should not forget that children spend more and more time in peer groups because it is fun. There the child finds relatively like-minded people with similar problems, interests, and skills, and he can interact with them in a more democratic atmosphere than he is probably used to at home. Your friends don't tell you to wash your hands all the time, clean up your room, or apologize to your little brother. (Hetherington & Morris, 1978, p. 60)

It has been found that the use of social comparison with the peer group as a means of self-evaluation in children increases markedly in the early elementary school years (Dinner, 1976; Pepitone, 1972; Ruble, Feldman, & Boggiano, 1976). The child's self-image and self-acceptance are closely associated with how he or she is received by peers.

Determinants of Peer Acceptance: Children and Their Friends

What kinds of characteristics are related to acceptance or rejection by the peer group? This to some extent depends on the particular peer group. However, there seem to be certain expectations which children have about relationships with friends which run across groups. In addition, these expectations about friends seem to progress in three stages (Bigelow, 1977; Bigelow & LaGaipa, 1975).

BOX 13-4
ON STATUS AND BEING IMITATED: EFFECTS ON RECIPROCAL IMITATION AND ATTRACTION

Is it always pleasurable to be imitated by a peer? In an experimental situation, 8- and 9-year-old children's problem-solving behavior was imitated by one peer and not by the other peer. Half of the imitators and nonimitators were older children (high-status peers), and half were younger children (low-status peers). The subjects were then given the opportunity to model the responses of the imitating or nonimitating peers when performing new problem-solving tasks. It appears that being imitated is not always regarded positively by children. Only if the imitating peers had been of high status did the children subsequently imitate them and say that they had enjoyed being imitated. They neither imitated their low-status imitators, nor regarded them positively. Children often said they did not like to be imitated by low-status imitators, and that these younger children had modeled their problem-solving choices because they were unable to solve problems or could not decide for themselves. In the case of the low-status peers, imitation was viewed as a further sign of inadequacy. ∎

Source: Thelen, M. H., & Kirkland, K. D. On status and being imitated: Effects on reciprocal imitation and attraction. *Journal of Personality and Social Psychology*, 1976, **33**, 691–697.

1 *A reward-cost stage.* This stage emerges at about grades 2 or 3 and is characterized by similar expectations, common activities, and propinquity (nearness).

2 *A normative stage.* At about grades 4 and 5, similar values and attitudes toward rules and sanctions appear.

3 *An empathic stage.* In this stage, which emerges about grades 6 and 7, self-disclosure, understanding, and shared interests occur. This is the relationship Sullivan has so poignantly described as "chumship" in the quote in the introduction to this chapter and which represents a unique kind of intimacy in the development of children.

The progression of these stages and attributes associated with them are presented in more detail in Table 13-1. The expectations about friendship that emerge at each stage do not disappear with the next stage; in fact, those marked with asterisks tend to increase with age.

Children have expectations about how friends should behave, but are these expectations the main basis for acceptance or rejection by the peer group? Let us examine some of the personal characteristics and social skills associated with being well received by peers.

It would be pleasant to believe that children select friends on the basis of

TABLE 13-1 ONSET GRADES FOR AGE-INCREASING FRIENDSHIP EXPECTATIONS

Dimension	Onset grade
Friend as help-giver*	2
Share common activities*	2
Propinquity*	3
Stimulation value	3
Organized play	3
Demographic similarity	3
Evaluation*	3
Acceptance*	4
Admiration*	4
Increasing prior interaction*	4
Loyalty and commitment*	5
Genuineness*	6
Friend as receiver of help	6
Intimacy potential*	7
Common interests*	7
Similarity in attitudes and values	7

Source: Bigelow, B. J., and LaGaipa, J. J. Children's written descriptions of friendship: A multidimensional analysis. *Developmental Psychology,* 1975, **11**, 857–858.

desirable personal attributes such as altruism, honesty, and sensitivity and that such factors may play a role in friendship formation. However, a number of characteristics associated with peer acceptance are enduring, are difficult to change, and have little to do with the personal merits of the individual child. Children cannot readily modify their appearance, race, sex, age, or name, but these attributes are correlated with how warmly they are accepted by their peers.

Names and Peer Acceptance   Children seem to respond adversely to unfamiliar or strange names. As can be seen in Box 13-5, Sam, Karen, Michael, or Steven are going to be greeted more cordially by the peer group than are Dwayne, Darcy, Lana, or Shureen. However, a precautionary note is in order. It is important not to overestimate the importance of names. It is only one of the many variables that influence social acceptance. United States Presidents in the twentieth century have included a Theodore, Woodrow, Warren, Calvin, Herbert, Franklin, Dwight, Lyndon, and Gerald. The last five Vice Presidents have included an Alben, Hubert, and Spiro. It may be that many Americans will vote for a man they wouldn't want as a friend; a more plausible interpretation is that names are not everything (Asher, R., Gaen, S., & Gottman, M, 1976, p. 3).

Appearance and Peer Acceptance   Although everyone has heard the maxim "Beauty is only skin deep," most people don't respond as if beauty is such a negligible attribute. Physical attractiveness plays an important role in the responses and evaluations of children and adults.

BOX 13-5
WHAT'S IN A NAME?

"What's in a name? That which we call a rose
By any other name would smell as sweet."
Romeo and Juliet, Act II, Scene ii

 Although Shakespeare's famous lines may be good poetry and good horticulture, it doesn't apply to children's names. At least this is the implication of the study of McDavid and Harari (1966) of the relation between the social desirability of children's names and peer popularity. Ten- to twelve-year-old boys and girls who were members of four different youth groups at an urban community center were asked to rate the attractiveness of a list of first names. In making their ratings, the children were told to concentrate on the names and not on people bearing these names. Two sets of scores were derived; first, the desirability of names occurring in their own group; and second, a rating of the attractiveness of names that were not associated with anyone in their own group. This latter index provided a rating that was relatively free of contamination from direct familiarity with a particular person. Is there any relationship between peer popularity and children's names? To find out, a month later the investigators asked the children in each of the four groups to pick the three most popular and three least popular members of their own group. When the attractiveness rankings of the names were correlated with the popularity scores, those that had the more attractive names were rated as more popular. However, this may simply mean that children rated the names of people that they already liked as more attractive. A better test involved relating the child's popularity score with the rating of his name by another group of children who didn't know him. If names per se are really important determinants of popularity, children who are well liked by their peers should have names that even strangers find attractive. This approach involves relating the peer popularity scores of one class with the attractiveness scores that these names received from children in a different class who didn't know children with those names. Again, the popular children were found to have the most attractive names. The implication is clear: "The child who bears a generally unpopular or unattractive name may be handicapped in his social interactions with peers" (McDavid & Harari, 1966, p. 458). Naming a child a relatively rare and unusual name, such as Thelonius or Tondeleyo, may provide a child increased distinctiveness and individuality, but the price may be peer rejection. We have to be careful in generalizing, however, since different subcultures in our society value different kinds of names. Many blacks, for example, have chosen unusual Moslem names, such as "Ali" and "Kahil," as a way of emphasizing their cultural distinctiveness. Depending on the reference group, names may be popular or unpopular and, hence, so may the bearers of these names. However, the basis for this link between names and popularity still remains a mystery. For example, is the actual behavior of children with odd names clearly distinguished from the behavior of children with names like Bob and Susan? If so, how early do these patterns develop? Moreover, is the unpopularity of these children a result of early rejection by peers who discriminate against them because of their names, or are parents who choose peculiar names for their children likely to encourage atypical behaviors in their offspring, thus contributing directly to their subsequent unpopularity? In any case (with apologies to Gertrude Stein), "a name is not a name is not a name." ■

Source: McDavid, J. W., & Harari, H. Stereotyping of names and popularity in grade school children. *Child Development,* 1966, **37,** 453–459.

Body build   Are children with various types of body builds treated differently by their peers? Is it true that fat, chubby children have a tougher time gaining peer acceptance than more muscular children? To answer these questions Staffieri (1967) asked children to rate different body types and then related these evaluations to peer popularity scores. Three common body types, distinguished earlier by Sheldon, Stevens, and Tucker (1940), were used. One type, the *endomorph*, is characterized by a softness and spherical appearance and an underdevelopment of muscle and bone. The *mesomorph* individual has an athletic build, muscular, broad-shouldered, and large-boned. The third type, the *ectomorph*, is thin and has poor muscular development. Six- to ten-year-old boys exposed to full body silhouettes of either child or adult endomorphs, mesomorphs, or ectomorphs were asked to assign a list of descriptive adjectives to the types as well as to designate their preferred body type. The results were clear: all the adjectives assigned to the mesomorph image were favorable. For example, the children expected a person with this muscular, athletic build to be brave, happy, good-looking, strong, helpful, and intelligent—a clearly positive set of traits; the adjectives assigned to the endomorph, primarily a socially aggressive type, were unfavorable, such as argumentative, dishonest, and stupid; finally, the ectomorph, a generally socially submissive type, was described as weak, quiet, and worried. Similar results have been found for older boys (10 to 20 years of age) (Lerner, 1969) and for adults (Brodsky, 1954). As would be expected, by age 7 the boys showed a clear preference for looking like the mesomorph. Girls tend to be more favorably disposed than boys toward ectomorphs, perhaps because of their resemblance to "high-fashion" models.

Is there a link between these stereotypes of body builds and peer acceptance? Staffieri (1967) found that mesomorphs were selected by classmates as one of "five best friends" more often than endomorphic or ectomorphic children. In fact, the endomorphic boys were the least popular of the three body types.

Physically disabled children are also viewed as low in physical attractiveness by children from a wide range of ethnic groups, area of the country, and social class. A rank ordering of pictures of children from most to least liked by 10- to 11-year-old children was the nonhandicapped child, a child with crutches and a brace, a child in a wheelchair, a child with a left hand missing, a child with a facial disfigurement, and last, an obese child (Richardson, Goodman, Hastorf, & Dornbusch, 1961). If there is such a thing as the stereotyped "jolly fat person," it is obviously not a result of their reception by peers.

Why should children respond so negatively to disabled persons? It may be for the same reasons they respond negatively to people who differ from them in other ways such as in race or ethnicity. They perceive these children as different from themselves and attribute dissimilar values, attitudes, and personality characteristics to them.

Facial attractiveness and peer acceptance   Children as young as 3 to 5 years old can differentiate attractive from unattractive children and seem to judge these children on the basis of the same physical attributes as adults do

(Dion, 1973; Styczynski & Langlois, 1977). More desirable characteristics are attributed by both children and adults to attractive than unattractive children, even to photographs of attractive or unattractive children whom the evaluators have never met (Dion & Berscheid, 1974; Lerner & Lerner, 1977; Styczynski & Langlois, 1977). Aggressive, antisocial behavior and meanness are regarded as more characteristic of unattractive children, while behaviors such as independence, fearlessness, friendliness, sharing, and self-sufficiency are attributed to attractive children (Langlois & Stephan, 1977). In addition, female adults and teachers view the same undesirable behaviors in attractive children as less serious than those in unattractive children, and they are less likely to make ominous predictions about the attractive children becoming chronically antisocial and requiring severe punishment (Dion, 1972, 1974; Dion, Berscheid, & Walster, 1972). Thus the prevailing perception appears to be that what is beautiful is good. Since adults and peers both view unattractive children so adversely, it is not surprising that they are rated as less popular by the peer group.

Are these negative views of unattractive children all in the eye of the beholder, or are they based in behavioral reality? A recent study by Langlois and Downs (1978) found no differences in the social behavior of attractive or unattractive 3-year-olds. However unattractive, in contrast to attractive, 5-year-olds were more likely to be aggressive, hit peers, play in an active, boisterous manner, and play with masculine toys. This age trend suggests that the aggressive behavior may be a response to being perceived as unattractive by others.

There is further evidence that helps us understand what developmental processes may be at work. Not only are unattractive children perceived by peers, adults, and teachers to be poorly adjusted, and by teachers as having poorer academic ability, but they score less well on personality tests, on grade point averages, and on self-ratings of self-esteem (Lerner & Lerner, 1977). This suggests that the negative expectations and perceptions peers and adults have of children with unattractive body builds or faces may foster the emergence of the very characteristics attributed to these children. Individuals do behave to some extent in a manner consistent with others' expectations. In addition, if children are expected to behave aversively and if they are not accepted by others, social interactions become frustrating and self-esteem drops, and this may be reflected in poor cognitive performance or antisocial behavior. A self-fulfilling prophecy may be occurring.

Rate of maturation and peer acceptance   Another way of approaching the issue of physical characteristics and peer acceptance is by examining the effects of the *rate* of physical growth. Although norms can be described for the rate at which individuals reach physical maturity, there are sufficiently wide individual differences to warrant a distinction between early- and late-maturing individuals. Physical maturity has been indexed in a variety of ways. Among the common measures are appearance of pubic hair for boys and the onset of menarche for girls. The rate of skeletal growth is another popular and reliable index of physical maturity. Studies carried out at the University of California indicate clearly that the rate of physical maturation can affect the child's social and emotional adjustment. However, not only do boys and girls differ in the speed of reaching physical maturity, with girls ahead of boys, but the sex of the child determines the advantages and disadvantages of being an early or late maturer as well. For boys, it appears to be advantageous to peer acceptance to reach the developmental milestone of pubescence early, but for girls late maturity may be advantageous. Let us examine the evidence in more detail.

Jones and Bayley (1950), in their pioneering study in this area, selected sixteen early-maturing and sixteen late-maturing boys from the extremes of a normal public school population and tracked their development over the six-year period of adolescence. Observations made in a number of free-play settings indicated that the boys who were slower in their physical development were rated lower in physical attractiveness, masculinity, and grooming than were

Rate of maturation is related to peer popularity. Here are early- and late-maturing 12-year-old girls and 13-year-old boys. The individuals on the right have gone through their growth spurts. (Photo (a) Alice Kandell, Photo Researchers, Inc.; Photo (b) Mini Forsyth/Monkmeyer)

(a)

(b)

their faster-developing peers. Behavioral ratings indicated that the late matures were more childish, more eager, less relaxed, and generally higher in attention-seeking behaviors. Peer evaluations generally confirmed this profile; the late maturer is regarded as restless, bossy, talkative, attention-seeking, and less likely to have older friends.

Moreover, the early maturers were overrepresented in terms of both athletic honors and election to important student offices, which suggests that the early maturer is accorded greater peer acceptance. Other investigators (Ames, 1956) found that both sociability and popularity are positively correlated with the rate of maturity.

The differences in appearance between early and late maturers tend to diminish as the child grows older, and by young adulthood height, weight, and body build distinctions have disappeared. However, reaching maturity at different rates seems to have long-lasting effects on social behavior. Jones (1957), for example, found that the early and late maturers in their early thirties possess many of the same characteristics that distinguished them during adolescence. In adulthood, the male early maturer still has a clear social advantage; he is more sociable and more likely to be accorded prestige, popularity, and recognition by his peers.

For girls, a very different and less consistent picture emerges. The California research (Everett, 1943) suggests that the late-maturing girl, unlike her male counterpart, is likely to have the social advantage. Adult ratings indicated that the late maturer was more sociable and more likely to be allotted a prominent position in her peer group. Similarly, Ames (1956) found a negative correlation between rate of maturing and peer popularity. However, later research by Faust (1960) suggested that peer prestige may not be accorded consistently to the late-maturing girl. It depends on the age level of the peers and their resulting value system. Studying girls in the sixth through ninth grades, this investigator classified her subjects as prepuberal, puberal, or postpuberal and then had peers rate one another on a number of prestige dimensions. While the late maturers were the most prestigeful in the sixth grade, they lost their advantage in the later grades. In the seventh- and ninth-grade levels, the early maturers were accorded more peer prestige. Probably the shift is due to the awakening interest in heterosexual relationships; the greater popularity of the faster-maturing girls among members of the opposite sex undoubtedly enhanced their standing among their female peers. Clearly, the values of the age group are important such that "for girls neither physical acceleration nor physical retardation is consistently advantageous" (Faust, 1960, p. 181). Finally, rate of maturation is a poor long-term predictor in the case of girls, with few relationships existing between adult status and adolescent growth rate.

Age, Race, and Sex Peer Acceptance   Children tend to select friends who are similar to themselves in age, race, and sex.

Age   To some extent the relation between age and friendship choice may be related to the fact that for small children groups in Western societies tend to be age-graded. In many other cultures, particularly those where older children are responsible for the care of younger children, multiage play groups are more common (Konner, 1975). Peers of different ages seem to serve different functions for children. Peers may facilitate social learning, be more effective models, and be preferred as tutors by younger children (Allen & Feldman, 1976).

Younger peers may provide an opportunity to acquire caretaking skills or to acquire social skills in children who are socially isolated or poorly adjusted. Children with emotional or social problems may actually be driven out of their same-aged peer groups and find acceptance easier to gain with younger children (Hetherington et al., 1978). In addition, younger children may be less threatening and exhibit social skills at a more comparable level to those of a disturbed or socially immature child. Interaction with younger peers may actually play a therapeutic role. In Harlow's famous studies, the adverse social effects of prolonged isolation on rhesus monkeys were reversed by a program of sustained contact with younger monkeys (Suomi & Harlow, 1972).

In a recent study by Furman, Rahe, and Hartup (1978), presented in Box 13-6, great changes in sociability in socially withdrawn 4- and 5-year-old children resulted from interaction with younger peers.

In adolescence, interaction of mixed-sex peer groups increases. (Erika Stone)

BOX 13-6
SOCIAL REHABILITATION OF LOW-INTERACTIVE PRESCHOOL CHILDREN BY PEER INTERVENTION

Does play with younger children possess therapeutic potential for rehabilitating socially withdrawn children?

One research team (Furman, Rahe, & Hartup, 1977) located 24 socially-withdrawn children in five child care centers by means of observations conducted over 2-week periods. (These children may be considered social isolates but were not autistic or emotionally disturbed.) For 8 children, an intervention was devised consisting of 15 daily play sessions involving a second child who was 18 months younger than the subject. Another 8 children participated in daily play sessions with a child who was within 4 months of the subject's own age. The remaining children received no

treatment. Significant improvement in sociability occurred in both experimental groups as contrasted to the no-treatment group (which did not change), but greater increases in sociability occurred among the children exposed to younger "therapists" than among those exposed to same-age "therapists." Nonprogrammed interaction with younger children, indeed, promotes social competence in some situations more effectively than experience with agemates (Furman, Rahe, & Hartup, 1978). ■

Source: Furman, W., Rahe, D., & Hartup, W. W. Social rehabilitation of low-interactive preschool children by peer intervention. Unpublished paper, 1978.

In spite of the contributions of older and younger peers, Hartup has concluded that the preference for same-aged friends and interaction with same-aged peers serve a very special role in social development.

I am convinced that age-grading would occur even if our schools were not age graded and children were left alone to determine the composition of their own societies. After all, one can only learn to be a good fighter among agemates: the bigger guys will kill you, and the little ones are no challenge. Sexual experience at pubescence with bigger people is too anxiety-laden and sexual experience with littler ones is really not very interesting. (Hartup, 1976, p. 10)

Race and peer acceptance   Most children develop racial awareness and can identify their own racial group as early as 3 years of age (Durrett & Davy, 1970; Hraba & Grant, 1970). Racial similarity is one factor used in selecting friends. Although children prefer friends of their own race, many cross-race friendships are found in preschool and elementary school children (Asher, 1973; Shaw, 1974). The pattern in high schools is less positive. A recent study of high school students found that less than 3 percent of social interactions occurred between black and white peers (Silverman & Shaw, 1973). If students have always been exposed to an integrated educational system or if children have contact with another racial group having similar status, there are increases in cross-race

Although rough and tumble play is more common in boys, it also occurs in girls. (Michael Hyman, Black Star)

friendships (Asher, 1975; Clore, Bray, Itkin, & Murphy, 1978; Singleton & Asher, 1977). To the extent that children share the same life-style, attitudes, interests, social class, and educational level, interracial acceptance will occur. Contact with children of another race who are viewed as very dissimilar or of lower status has been found to have no effects or negative effects on evaluation and friendship formation.

Sex and peer acceptance Sex of a child has a much more marked effect on friendship formation than does race. Even in the preschool years same-sexed peers prefer to play together, and this tendency increases throughout the elementary school years. When cross-sex friendships occur, they are extremely short-lived, and friendships between males tend to be more enduring than those between females (Gronlund, 1955). It is not until early adolescence when dating begins that this pattern changes.

What might be causing this self-imposed segregation and lack of acceptance between boys and girls? It seems to be related to differences in the interests and play patterns of girls and boys (Markell & Asher, 1974). Boys tend to maintain a broader network of friends and to be involved in rough-and-tumble play, in group activities, and in games. Girls' friendships tend to be more narrowly focused on a single best friend, and their play is in smaller groups often involved with art, books, or dolls (Eder & Hallinan, 1977; Shure, 1963; Waldrop & Halverson, 1975). It seems possible that as traditional sex roles break down, more shared interests will emerge and boys and girls will accept and interact with each other more.

Personality, Social Skills, and Peer Acceptance   It is more difficult to make generalizations about the relationship between personality and social behavior and peer acceptance than about the previous characteristics we have discussed. This is because these relationships will differ somewhat among various social-class, ethnic, racial, sex, and age groups. Popular children are those who have attributes valued in any given subgroup. If the group values toughness in males, a boy who is competently aggressive will be popular; if it values athletic prowess or intellectual achievement, competence in those areas will be associated with popularity. However, there are some characteristics that seem to facilitate social acceptance in most groups. Good adjustment, friendliness, low anxiety, a reasonable level of self-esteem, kindness, and some responsiveness and sensitivity to the needs and feelings of other members of the group are related to popularity across a wide array of populations (Hartup, 1978; Mannarino, 1976). In addition, social skills such as reinforcing others and being able to communicate well and initiate interactions effectively play an important role in social acceptance (Gottman, Gonso, & Rasmussen, 1975; Asher, 1978). The new

In the elementary school years, same-sex play groups are most common. (Helen Nestor/Monkmeyer)

child in school who tries to initiate a relationship by hovering silently or making aggressive or inappropriate responses is behind before she gets started. In contrast, the young child who asks for information (for example, "Where do you live?"), gives information (for example, "My favorite sport is basketball."), or tries to include the child in a mutual activity (for example, "Wanna help me build this sand castle?") is well on the way to being accepted by the group (Gottman et al., 1975).

What can we do to help socially isolated or unpopular children become more accepted? Social acceptance can be facilitated by shaping socially desirable behavior through reinforcement or modeling and by directly coaching improved social skills. In addition, pairing isolated children with popular children in the classroom in working on a joint project, such as planning a party, increases the isolates' popularity.

Group Formation

Children not only interact more as they develop, but form groups that possess common goals and aims and rules of conduct. In addition, groups usually develop a hierarchical organization or structure that identifies each member's relationship to other members of the group and that facilitates the interaction among its members. Some group members are identified as dominant or as leaders, and their roles are quite different from those of the less dominant children in the group.

What are the conditions that influence group formation? In order to answer this question we will turn to a description of a classic study by Sherif (1956) in which the formation of groups in a boys summer camp was observed.

Factors Which Facilitate Group Formation

When the twenty-two 11-year-old boys who participated in the project arrived at the camp, they were divided into two sets. Both how close the children lived in camp and the sharing of enjoyable activities (for example, hiking and crafts) facilitated group formation. In addition, if the activities required cooperation and a division of labor among the members of the group for their attainment, a group structure emerged more readily. Sherif tried to structure opportunities for such interactions in the group. For example, the boys appeared for their dinner at the end of the day and found to their dismay that the staff had not prepared their dinner. However, the raw ingredients for a meal were available. What did the boys do? They began to cooperate and assume responsibilities; some mixed Kool-Aid, some cooked the meat, and others sliced watermelon or served. This and similar cooperative activities led to the formation of two groups with their own rules of conduct and special interests. One group named itself the "Eagles," and the other the "Rattlers."

Intergroup Conflict

While participating together may promote group formation, other factors, such as competition with other groups, are extremely influential in increasing group solidarity and group pride. However, competition may also increase hostility between groups. A tournament of competitive games such as baseball, tug-of-war, and a treasure hunt was arranged. As it progressed, children on the rival teams began to taunt each other (for example, "You're not Eagles, you're pigeons") or call each other names. Friendships broke up between children on differing teams. Rival groups made threatening posters and planned raids with green apples for ammunition. After losing a game the Eagles burned a Rattler's flag, and the Rattlers retaliated by raiding an Eagle's cabin and stealing comic books and a pair of jeans belong to the Eagles' leader. The jeans were painted orange and triumphantly flown as a flag by the Rattlers. The counselors intervened just in time to avert real mayhem as the Eagles were arming themselves with rocks for a retaliatory mission. Competition was clearly effective in increasing hostility, rivalry, and conflict although it enhanced in-group identification and strengthened group solidarity. These findings offer little support to advocates of competitive sports as a safe outlet for reducing aggression (Lorenz, 1966). Rather, competition either between groups or between individuals (Nelson, Gelfand, & Hartmann, 1969) is likely to increase, not decrease, aggression.

Reduction in Intergroup Hostility

What could the experimenter do to reduce the conflict the he had so cleverly engineered? First, Sherif gave the members of the conflicting groups opportunities for noncompetitive, highly pleasant social contacts, such as going to the movies or sharing the same dining room. The results were disastrous: the boys simply took advantage of these occasions to vent their hostilities against one another; if anything, the conflict was heightened rather than reduced by this approach. Next, Sherif provided the groups with a series of tasks that required their cooperative effort to solve. This tactic was much more successful. Sherif cites the following examples of the kinds of experimentally produced crises that forced the rivals to "pull together":

One was a breakdown in the water supply. Water came to our camp in pipes from a tank about a mile away. We arranged to interrupt it and then called the boys together to inform them of the crisis. Both groups promptly volunteered to search the water line for trouble. They worked together harmoniously, and before the end of the afternoon they had located and corrected the difficulty. . . . On another occasion, just when everyone was hungry and the camp truck was about to go to town for food, it developed that the engine wouldn't start, and the boys had to pull together to get the vehicle going. (Sherif, 1956, p. 5)

Figure 13-5 illustrates how the provision of these "superordinate" goals restored positive intergroup attitudes and feelings. When groups work together to achieve meaningful overriding goals, intergroup tensions can be resolved.

Group Hierarchies

Children very early become aware of group hierarchies. Although preschool children's perception of their own position of relative dominance may be

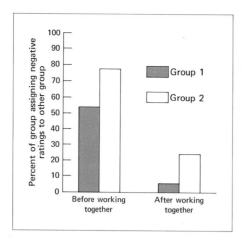

FIGURE 13-5 Ratings of opposing groups before and after working together on a common task. *(Adapted from Sherif, 1956.)*

somewhat aggrandized, their accuracy in perceiving their own status increases rapidly in the early school years. Preschool children when asked "Who is the toughest?" often respond "me." In contrast, by second grade there is over 70 percent agreement on the relative toughness of students in their class (Edelman & Omark, 1973). Although preschool children's dominance hierarchies are simpler and more loosely differentiated than those of older children, older preschool children show considerable agreement in indentifying group status structures (Sluckin & Smith, 1977; Strayer & Strayer, 1976). It is not surprising that children's ability to order their peers from highest to lowest in dominance seems to be related to their ability to perform cognitive seriation tasks. Children who are able to do such things as order a series of sticks of varying length from the shortest to the longest are also able to order peers in terms of dominance. Again, we see the close relationship between the child's cognitive and social development.

Young children seem to differentiate the power of peers on the basis of toughness, the ability to direct the behavior of others, leadership in play, and physical coercion. In contrast, in older children such status structures are more likely to be based on appearance, leadership skills, pubertal development, athletic prowess, and academic performance (Savin-Williams, 1978). Dominant children may play a particularly influential role in shaping the behavior of others. A recent study in which children were observed in a free-play session found that dominant children were looked at and imitated more than nondominant children (Abramovitch & Grusec, 1978). In addition, as will be discussed in the next section, children are more likely to conform to the opinions and behavior of high-status peers.

Conformity to the Peer Group

With the formation of peer groups comes pressure for children to conform to the beliefs and norms of conduct viewed as desirable by the peer group. Conformity is one way of gaining the approval of the group, and nonconformity usually

Peer groups develop their own set of norms. (Ed Lettau, Photo Researchers, Inc.)

leads to rejection and punishment, often by being labeled such things as an "oddball" or "weirdo." What are the personal and situational factors associated with conformity?

There is a common belief that children become more conforming with age and that adolescents in particular adhere closely to the standards of the peer group. However, research findings suggest that this is too simplistic a view of developmental trends in conformity. Little conformity is exhibited in the behavior of preschool children, and the conformity of elementary school children and adolescents varies with the ambiguity of the task. When tasks are easy or unambiguous, agreement with the responses of a peer decreases with age. Adolescents express deviant opinions when they are in situations where they are more certain that their own responses are correct. However, on hard or ambiguous tasks where children are uncertain of the correct response, there is an increasing tendency with age to agree with the response of a peer (Hoving, Hamm, & Galvin, 1969).

Age, of course, is only one of a host of individual difference factors that determine children's conformity. Sex of the child frequently has been found to be important, with girls typically conforming more than boys (Iscoe, Williams & Harvey, 1963). While this finding is consistent with cultural sex-role expectations of the passive, dependent female and the assertive, independent male, one cannot legitimately conclude that girls are *always* more conforming than boys. Situational variables require consideration as well. If the conformity task is presented as an "achievement" task, boys, who are more achievement-oriented than girls, are likely to show greater peer compliance (Sampson & Hancock, 1967). On the other hand, if the conformity context makes salient feminine sex-typed motivations, such as affiliative and social acceptance tendencies, girls show greater susceptibility to social influence than boys (Patel & Gordon, 1960). In addition, conformity to peer-advocated misbehavior is more likely to occur in males (Bixenstine, DeCorte, & Bixenstine, 1976). Since males show acting-out, antisocial behaviors more often than do females, this too might be viewed as behavioral conformity with sex-role values. The extent to which conformity is viewed as congruent with sex-role standards, then, must be considered before sex differences in peer conformity can be predicted.

What about the peer-group status of the child being pressured to conform? One might think that the lower the child is in the group hierarchy the more compliant he would be. However, Harvey and Consalvi (1960) suggest otherwise. In fact, in their studies of cliques of delinquent adolescent boys, they found the least conformity among the very high and the very low status members. Most conforming were the middle-ranking adolescents, who may have aspirations to become more popular and therefore may have been using conformity to group norms as a technique to improve their status with their peers.

In addition, the characteristics of the influence source, the nature of the group, and the characteristics of the task also influence conformity. Children are more likely to yield to the opinions of a prestigious competent peer (Gelfand, 1962) and to conform when faced with a difficult, rather than an easy, problem-solving situation (Berenda, 1950). This seems to parallel the findings in imitation studies that power and competence of the model and task difficulty affect modeling. The importance of status of the peer in promoting conformity is clearly illustrated in the study in Box 13-7. In addition, group size, the relationship among the members, the degree of agreement with the group, and the importance of the issue to the group also affect conformity responses (Hartup, 1970).

Peer versus Adult Influences on the Child

Many behavioral scientists and parents view preadolescence and adolescence as particularly stressful periods where the child is being pulled and buffeted by the often conflicting standards of parents and peers. However, other authors have argued that the conflict between these two sets of standards is not as extreme as is believed and that there is often remarkable agreement between the values of peers and adults (Hartup, 1970; Douvan & Adelson, 1966). A better question than whether peers or adults are more influential is under what conditions and with what behaviors are peers or adults influential? Peers are more influential in situations involving friendship choices, challenges to authority, interpersonal behavior, and personal or group identity (Brittain, 1963). Parents are more influential in job preferences, academic choices, future aspirations, and moral development. Although in the previous chapter we stressed the importance of the family in the social development of the child, a recent cross-cultural study suggests that across a wide range of cultures aggressiveness, sociable behavior,

BOX 13-7
TO FINK OR NOT TO FINK—THAT IS THE QUESTION

When will children report the transgressions of their peers to adult authorities? In order to study this question Harari and McDavid (1969) examined the responses of junior high school students in two classes viewing either a low-status peer or a high-status peer stealing money from the teacher's desk while she was out of the room. The student "thieves" were accomplices of the experimenters.

Children were then questioned either alone or in the company of another innocent peer about their knowledge of the theft. Under which conditions do children "fink" and identify the culprit?

The identity of the low-status-peer thief was revealed in all conditions. However, the high-status-peer thief was identified only when the children were interviewed alone. When another innocent peer was present, the child did not betray the identity of the high-status peer. This may occur because the child is afraid of reprisal from the peer group or because the children pairs assume the other child present is responsible for doing the "finking." ∎

Source: Harari, H., & McDavid, J. W. Situational influence on moral justice: A study of "finking." *Journal of Personality and Social Psychology*, 1969, **11**, 240–244.

and prosocial activity are markedly influenced by peer relations (Whiting & Whiting, 1975). It seems likely that peer relations offer more opportunities to practice certain behaviors. Aggression against a parent is likely to have more adverse consequences than aggression against a peer. Sexual behavior can be discussed by parents, but is practiced with peers.

In most cases, a child's behavior is a result of both peer and parental influence (Siman, 1977). Kandel (1973) studied marijuana use by adolescents whose parents either used or did not use psychoactive drugs and whose best friends either used or did not use marijuana. Among teenagers whose best friends were nonusers but whose parents were users, only 17 percent smoked marijuana. If friends only used drugs, 56 percent of the adolescents reported using marijuana. However, 67 percent of the subjects used marijuana when both parents and peers were users. Thus, there was a combined impact of drug usage by parents and peers on marijuana use by adolescents.

Family relations and attitudes toward adults play an important role in children's conformity to the peer group (Devereux, 1970; Bixenstine et al., 1976). When families are warm and supportive and neither highly punitive nor highly permissive, children are less likely to become inaccessible to adult influence. It has been suggested that early adolescents who become overly susceptible to antisocial peer influences are not so much involved in an increased regard and loyalty to peers as in disillusionment with adult justice, wisdom, status, and goodwill. This disillusionment in highly peer-oriented children seems particularly associated with perceived vulnerability and shortcomings in the father (Bixenstine, et al., 1976).

The Peer Group in Cross-Cultural Perspective

So far we have cited only American research on the role of peers in socialization. A question can legitimately be raised, therefore, concerning the generality of this review. Are peers equally important in all cultures or in all parts of one culture? Is America a uniquely peer-oriented culture? Even within cultures, patterns of peer interaction may differ; for example, comparison of urban and rural peers indicates that Israeli children reared in rural kibbutzim are more cooperative than city-reared children (Shapira & Madsen, 1969). Therefore, it is not surprising that there are cross-cultural variations that deviate in both directions from the American pattern; in some countries, peers play an even more influential role, while in others the family and adult agents are more important. For example, Maslow and Diaz-Guerrero (1960) suggest that Mexican, in contrast to American, children are more family-oriented and less under the influence of peers. In Mexico, as well as in most European countries, this family orientation often is maintained by the parents' direct discouragement of peer interaction.

This attitude of the greater role and inclusiveness of the family is also reflected in European attitudes toward education. The family is expected to assume much more responsibility for "character education" or social skill development in Europe; the school is directly concerned with traditional academic learning and knowledge (Boehm, 1957). Consequently one would expect more opportunities for and encouragement of peer-peer interactions in American schools. In fact, this is the case. In Europe the child works alone, while in the United States children are encouraged to work together and to help each other. Cooperative class projects tend to be more common in American than in European schools, where individual products are more highly valued. In fact, as Reisman (1950) suggests in *The Lonely Crowd*, the American teacher has become a "peer group facilitator and mediator" (p. 91.

As a result of this combination of family and school influences, one would expect European children to be less susceptible to peer influence than their American counterparts. Boehm (1957) tested this hypothesis in a comparative study of twenty-nine Swiss children and forty American elementary-school-age children. To assess the relative impact of peer versus adult influence, subjects were asked to respond to stories involving children their own age. For example: "A group of children want to give a surprise birthday party for their scout leader. One boy has accepted the responsibility of decorating the room. He wonders whom he could ask for advice" (Boehm, 1957, p. 89). The results clearly supported the hypothesis: 69.5 percent of the twenty-three Swiss subjects insisted that teachers and parents always give the best advice, even in matters requiring special talent. The American children's greater reliance on the peer group was obvious: only three out of forty children, or 7.5 percent, preferred the teacher's advice to that of the gifted child. Moreover, all three of these children were quite young, 6 years of age. The Swiss children (91 percent) expected that the teacher would express anger if his advice was ignored, while only 6 percent of the American sample expressed this view. These data suggest that emancipation from adults comes earlier for American than Swiss children; on the other hand, American children appear to have greater confidence in their peers and are more dependent on their age-mates than Swiss children.

Other cross-cultural research suggests that this difference in peer and adult orientations observed in the American-Swiss comparison is not unique. Children in the Soviet Union are particularly resistant to peer pressures which conflict with adult societal values. This finding comes from the Cornell University cross-cultural programs (Devereux, 1970; Bronfenbrenner, Devereux, Suci, & Rogers, 1965; Bronfenbrenner, 1967) in which sixth-grade children in England, Germany, the Soviet Union, and the United States participated. In order to assess the responsiveness of these children to conflicting peer and adult pressures, a "dilemmas test" was devised which consisted of thirty hypothetical conflict situations; each situation pitted an adult-endorsed norm against peer pressure to violate the adult standard. Items dealt with such situations as going to a movie recommended by friends but disapproved of by parents, neglecting homework to join friends, standing guard while friends put a rubber snake in the teacher's desk, leaving a sick friend to go to a movie with the gang, joining friends in pilfering fruit from an orchard with a "no trespassing" sign, wearing styles approved by peers but not by parents, running away after breaking a window accidentally while playing ball, etc.

The Russian children were most resistant to peer influence, with significantly less resistance being demonstrated by both the American and German children. The English children showed the greatest responsiveness to peer-group pressure. As in the case of the Boehm data, opportunity for peer contact and interaction is probably important. Both cross-cultural and within-cultural comparisons point in this direction. For example, the English children spent more time with their peers and less time with the parents than did Russian children. Similarly the American children yielded more readily to peer pressure, while level of association with parents, particularly with the mother, was positively related to the ability to resist deviant peer pressure. The kind of peer group, however, must be considered as well. Children who were members of groups with a high record of actual misconduct were less able to remain adult-oriented than children who were in less deviant groups. Apparently "most any gang corrupts, and a bad gang corrupts absolutely" (Devereux, 1970, p. 24).

Let us examine the Russian-American differences more closely, for the contrasts are shown even more clearly in a study by Bronfenbrenner (1967). Groups of Russian children and groups of American children were asked to respond to the dilemmas test under three different conditions: a neutral condition in which they were told that their answers would be kept strictly confidential; an adult-exposure condition in which they were informed that their answers would be posted on a chart for parents and teachers; and a peer-exposure condition in which the answers would later be shown to the class. The results revealed a number of cross-cultural differences. First, the Russian children showed less inclination to engage in antisocial activity, which attests to their greater acceptance of adult social values. Although the exposure-to-adult condition tended to increase the adherence to socially acceptable behavior in

Russian children are trained early to participate in group activities. (Boris Erwitt, Photo Researchers, Inc.)

both cultures, the peer condition had opposite effects on the Soviet and American children. In the case of the Russian children, anticipation that classmates will eventually see their answers had the same effect as the adult-exposure manipulation: adherence to the social norms increased. American children, on the other hand, were more likely to violate the socially appropriate norms in the peer condition. Clearly, in the Russian culture the peer group operates to enforce and uphold social norms, while in the United States the evidence suggests greater norm conflict under peer influence.

The reason for this cross-national difference in the role played by the peer group becomes apparent upon examination of Soviet socialization practices. Bronfenbrenner has provided a detailed account of the role played by peers in the Soviet education system. According to this review, from the earliest years in school the peer group is employed to assist adult authorities teach and enforce the dominant social values of the society. The social group or collective, rather than the individual, is the main unit of concern; evaluation of the individual's behavior is mainly in terms of its relevance to the goals and aims of the collective. The allegiance to the group is further strengthened by awarding group rewards or administering group punishment; the group, in short, is held responsible for the actions of its individual members. To promote group identification and pride, interclass and interschool competitions are frequently held. In the school the social unit may be the row of pupils in a classroom and later the "cell" of the Communist youth organization. Bronfenbrenner suggests that this peer collective rivals and, at an early age, surpasses the family as the principal agent of socialization. From the earliest grades, peer monitors are selected to keep records of their group's progress and to evaluate and criticize deviant behaviors. In fact, one of the principal methods of social control is public recognition and criticism. Children are taught that it is their civic responsibility to observe and report on the behavior of their peers. The following excerpts of conversation from a third-grade class (or link) illustrate some of these processes:

"What are you fooling around for? You're holding up the whole link" whispers Kolya to his neighbor during the preparation period for the lesson. And during the break he teaches her how to better organize her books and pads in her knapsack.

"Count more carefully" says Olga to her girlfriend. "See, on account of you our link got behind today. You come to me and we'll count together at home." (Bronfenbrenner, 1970, p. 70).

These examples illuminate some of the techniques typically employed by the peer group to enforce the social norms. In light of this description, with the emphasis on congruence between peer and adult norms, Bronfenbrenner's cross-cultural finding of the contrasting roles played by Soviet and American peers is understandable. In the Soviet Union the peer group is a mechanism for maintaining the adult system; in America, at least in adolescence, the peer group is often in the vanguard of efforts to alter the existing system.

Summary

In this chapter the peer group, one important extrafamilial socialization agent, was examined.

Although even infants are responsive to their age-mates, the importance of peers increases rapidly and markedly in the preschool years. A shift from isolated play toward social play occurs and there is a greater preference for playing with peers than adults.

Play serves an important role in facilitating the cognitive development of children, in satisfying exploratory and curiosity needs, and in developing social competence. Imaginative play seems particularly important, and disruptions in the development of imaginative play have been associated with antisocial behavior, dependency, and social immaturity.

Peer relations serve a number of functions in helping children learn to play by the rules of the social game. They serve as sources of information, reinforcers, models, and standards of social comparison. Reciprocity and similarity seem to play an important role in both reinforcement and imitation. Children who dispense many rewards receive many rewards. Children who are modeled by a high-status peer are likely to imitate a high-status peer. In addition, children are likely to imitate and respond to reinforcements from peers they perceive as similar to themselves.

What determines peer popularity? No simple answer is possible. First, children of different social strata value different characteristics in their age-mates. Aggressive behavior, for example, may lead to popularity and prestige among lower-class males, while this same behavior may lead to rejection in middle-class boys. Children's names, physical characteristics, and attractiveness are related to peer acceptance. Boys with muscular body builds are more likely to be popular than their thin or chubby peers. Similarly the rate of maturation is an important factor in peer acceptance. Boys who mature early tend to have a social advantage over late-maturing males. For girls, on the other hand, rate of maturation tends not to be reliable as a predictor of popularity and prestige. In addition, physically attractive children are more accepted and viewed more positively by peers and adults. They behave in a more socially competent fashion than their less attractive peers.

Conditions that promote group formation, such as the cooperative participation in achieving shared goals, were discussed. Intergroup competition is a factor that heightens group solidarity although it increases hostility and conflict between groups. When conflicting groups work together to achieve a common aim, hostility is often reduced. Group hierarchies are developed early and define roles within groups.

A number of factors that affect the degree to which children conform to their peer group were examined. For example, the age of the child must be considered since children of all ages are not equally susceptible to peer pressure. In uncertain situations, peers tend to conform more as they mature, while peer influence tends to decline with age in situations where the correct response is clear. Also, the sex of the child as well as his or her group status is important. The prestige and competence of the influence source must be considered, with children being more influenced by a high-prestige peer than by a low-status individual. Situation factors, such as the nature of the pressure group, the task, and consensus within the group, are other determinants of peer-group conformity. Both peers and adults play an important role in shaping the responses of children, and it is important to consider their interaction in influencing children's behavior.

In the final section of the chapter, the role of peers in other cultures was examined. In some societies, peers play an even more influential role than in our culture, while in others the family and adult socializing agencies are more important. Particular attention was paid to a comparison of American and Russian children. Unlike our culture, where peer and adult values often clash, in Russia the peer and adult norms are more usually congruent, with peers serving to enforce rather than change adult social values.

References

Abramovitch, R., & Grusec, J. E. Peer imitation in a natural setting. *Child Development*, 1978, **49,** 167–180.

Allen, V. L., & Feldman, R. S. Studies on the role of tutors. In V. L. Allen (Ed.), *Children as tutors.* New York: Academic, 1976.

Ames, R. A longitudinal study of social participation. Unpublished doctoral dissertation, University of California, 1956.

Asher, S. R. The influence of race and sex on children's sociometric choices across the school year. Unpublished manuscript, 1973.

Asher, S. R. The effect of interest on reading comprehension for black children and white children. Unpublished manuscript, 1975.

Asher, S. R. Children's peer relations. In M. E. Lamb (Ed.), *Sociopersonality development*. New York: Holt, 1978, in press.

Asher, S. R., Oden, S. L., & Gottman, J. M. Children's friendships in school settings. *Quarterly Review of Early Childhood Education*, 1976, **1**, 1–17.

Bandura, A., Grusec, J., & Menlove, F. L. Observational learning as a function of symbolization and incentive set. *Child Development*. 1967, **37**, 499–506.

Bandura, A., & McDonald, F. J. The influence of social reinforcement and the behavior of models in shaping children's moral judgments. *Journal of Abnormal and Social Psychology*, 1963, **67**, 274–281.

Barker, R. G. & Wright, H. F. *Midwest and its children*. New York: Harper, 1955.

Barnes, K. E. Preschool play norms: A replication. *Developmental Psychology*, 1971, **5**, 99–103.

Berenda, R. W. *The influence of the group on the judgements of children*. New York: Columbia University, Kings Crown Press, 1950.

Berlyne, D. E. Curiosity and exploration. *Science*, 1966, **153**, 25–33.

Bigelow, B. J. Children's friendship expectations: A cognitive-developmental study. *Child Development*, 1977, **48**, 246–253.

Bigelow, B. J., & LaGaipa, J. J. Children's written descriptions of friendship: A multidimensional analysis. *Developmental Psychology*, 1975, **11**, 857–858.

Bixenstine, V. E., De Corte, M. S., & Bixenstine, B. A. Conformity to peer-sponsored misconduct at four grade levels. *Developmental Psychology*, 1976, **12**, 226–236.

Boehm, L. The development of independence: A comparative study. *Child Development*, 1957, **28**, 85–92.

Brodsky, C. M. A study of norms for body form-behavior relationships. Washington, D.C.: Catholic University of America Press, 1954.

Bronfenbrenner, U. Response to pressure from peers versus adults among Soviet and American school children. *International Journal of Psychology*, 1967, **2**, 199–207.

Bronfenbrenner, U. *Two worlds of childhood: U.S. and U.S.S.R.* New York: Russell Sage, 1970.

Bronfenbrenner, U., Devereux, E. C., Suci, G., & Rogers, R. R. Adults and peers as sources of conformity and autonomy. Paper presented at the Conference for Socialization for Competence, Social Science Research Council, Puerto Rico, 1965.

Charlesworth, R., & Hartup, W. W. Positive social reinforcement in the nursery school peer group. *Child Development*, 1967, **38**, 993–1002.

Clore, G. L., Bray, R. M., Itkin, S. M., & Murphy, P. Interracial attitudes and behavior at a summer camp. *Journal of Personality and Social Psychology*, 1978, **36**, 107–116.

Dearden, R. F. The concept of play. In R. S. Peter (Ed.), *The concept of education*. London: Routledge, 1967.

Devereux, E. C. The role of peer-group experience in moral development. In J. P. Hill (Ed.), *Minnesota symposium on child psychology* (Vol. 4). Minneapolis: University of Minnesota Press, 1970, pp. 94–140.

Dion, K. K. Physical attractiveness and evaluations of children's transgressions. *Journal of Personality and Social Psychology*, 1972, **24**, 207–213.

Dion, K. K. Young children's stereotyping of facial attractiveness. *Developmental Psychology*, 1973, **9**, 183–188.

Dion, K. K., & Berscheid, E. Physical attractiveness and peer perception among children. *Sociometry*, 1974, **37,** 1–12.

Dion, K. K., Berscheid, E., & Walster, E. What is beautiful is good. *Journal of Personality and Social Psychology*, 1972, **24,** 285–290.

Dinner, S. H. Social comparison and self-evaluation in children. Unpublished doctoral dissertation, Princeton University, 1976.

Douvan, E., & Adelson, J. *The adolescent experience.* New York: Wiley, 1966.

Durrett, N. E., & Davy, A. I. Racial awareness in young Mexican-American, Negro and Anglo children. *Young Children*, 1970, **26,** 16–24.

Eckerman, C. O., Whatley, J. L., & Kutz, S. L. Growth of social play with peers during the second year of life. *Developmental Psychology*, 1975, **11,** 42–49.

Edelman, M. S., & Omark, D. R. Dominance hierarchies in young children. *Social Science Information*, 1973, **12,** 1.

Eder, D., & Hallinan, M. T. Sex differences in children's friendships. Unpublished manuscript, 1977.

Everett, E. G. Behavioral characteristics of early and late maturing girls. Unpublished master's thesis, University of California, 1943.

Faust, M. S. Developmental maturity as a determinant of prestige in adolescent girls. *Child Development*, 1960, **31,** 173–184.

Fein, G. *Child Development.* Englewood Cliffs, N. J.: Prentice-Hall, 1978.

Feshbach, N. D. Reinforcement patterns of children. In A. Pick (Ed.), *Minnesota symposium on child psychology* (Vol. 7). Minneapolis: University of Minnesota Press, 1973, pp. 87–116.

Feshbach, N. D., & Devor, G. Teaching styles in four-year-olds. *Child Development*, 1969, **40,** 183–190.

Festinger, L. A theory of social comparison. *Human Relations*, 1954, **7,** 117–140.

Furman, W., Rahe, D., & Hartup, W. W. Social rehabilitation of low-interactive preschool children by peer intervention. Unpublished manuscript, 1978.

Garvey, C. *Play.* Cambridge, Mass.: Harvard University Press, 1977.

Gelfand, D. The influence of self-esteem on rate of verbal conditioning and social matching behavior. *Journal of Abnormal Social Psychology*, 1962, **65,** 259–265.

Gottman, J., Gonso, J., & Rasmussen, B. Social interaction, social competence and friendship in children. *Child Development*, 1975, **46,** 709–718.

Gould, R. *Child studies through fantasy.* New York: Quadrangle, 1972.

Gronlund, N. W. The relative stability of classroom social status with unweighted and weighted sociometric choice. *Journal of Educational Psychology*, 1955, **46,** 345–354.

Harari, H., & McDavid, J. W. Situational influence on moral justice: A study of "finking." *Journal of Personality and Social Psychology*, 1969, **11,** 240–244.

Hartup, W. W. Peer interaction and social organization. In P.H. Mussen (Ed.), *Manual of child psychology.* New York: Wiley, 1970, pp. 361–456.

Hartup, W. W. Peer interaction and behavioral development of the individual child. In E. Shopler & R. L. Reichler (Eds.), *Psychopathology and child development.* New York: Plenum, 1976.

Hartup, W. W. Children and their friends. In H. McGurk (Ed.), *Child social development.* London: Methuen, 1978, in press.

Hartup, W. W., & Coates, B. Imitation of a peer as a function of reinforcement from the peer group and rewardingness of the model. *Child Development*, 1967, **38,** 1003–1016.

Harvey, O. J., & Consalvi, C. Status and conformity to pressures in informal groups. *Journal of Abnormal Social Psychology*, 1960, **60,** 182–187.

Hetherington, E. M., Cox, M., & Cox, R. Play and social interaction in children following divorce. Paper presented at the NIMH Conference on Divorce, 1978.

Hetherington, E. M., & Morris, W. N. The family and primary groups. In W. H.

Holtzman (Ed.), *Introductory psychology in depth: Developmental topics.* New York: Harper's College Press, 1978.

Hicks, D. Imitation and retention of film mediated aggressive peer and adult models. *Journal of Personality and Social Psychology*, 1965, **2**, 97–100.

Hoving, K. I., Hamm, M., & Galvin, P. Social influence as a function of stimulus ambiguity at three age levels. *Developmental Psychology*, 1969, **1**, 631–636.

Hraba, J., & Grant, G. Black is beautiful: A reexamination of racial preference and identification. *Journal of Personality and Social Psychology*, 1970, **16**, 398–402.

Hunt, J. M. Intrinsic motivation and its role in psychological development. In D. Levine (Ed.), *Nebraska symposium on motivation* (Vol. 13). Lincoln: University of Nebraska Press, 1965.

Hutt, C., & Bhavnani, R. Predictions from play. *Nature*, 1972, **237**, 171–172.

Iscoe, I., Williams, M., & Harvey, J. Modifaction of children's judgments by a simulated group technique: A normative developmental study. *Child Development*, 1963, **34**, 963–978.

Jones, M. C. The later careers of boys who were early or late maturing. *Child Development*, 1957, **28**, 113–128.

Jones, M. C., & Bayley, N. Physical maturing among boys as related to behavior. *Journal of Educational Psychology*, 1950, **41**, 129–148.

Kelly, K. R. The effects of peer and sibling exposure on social development in young children. Unpublished manuscript, 1976.

Konner, N. Relations among infants and juveniles in comparative perspective. In M. Lewis & L. H. Rosenblum (Eds.), *Friendship and peer relations.* New York: Wiley, 1975.

Langlois, J. H., & Downs, C. A. Peer relations as a function of physical attractiveness: The eye of the beholder or behavioral reality? *Child Development*, 1978, in press.

Langlois, J. H., & Stephan, C. The effects of physical attractiveness and ethnicity on children's behavioral attributions and peer preferences. *Child Development*, 1977, **48**, 1694–1698.

Lee, C. L. Social encounters of infants: The beginnings of popularity. Paper presented at the meeting of the International Society for the Study of Behavioral Development, Ann Arbor, Mich., August 1973.

Leiter, M. P. A study of reciprocity in preschool play groups. *Child Development*, 1977, **48**, 1288–1295.

Lerner, R. M. The development of stereotyped expectancies of body build relations. *Child Development*, 1969, **40**, 137–141.

Lerner, R. M., & Lerner, J. Effects of age, sex and physical attractiveness on child-peer relations, academic performance, and elementary school adjustment. *Developmental Psychology*, 1977, **13**, 585–590.

Lewis, M., & Rosenblum, L. A. (Eds.). *Friendship and peer relations.* New York: Wiley, 1975.

Lorenz, K. *On aggression.* London: Methuen, 1966.

Mannerino, A. P. Friendship patterns and altruistic behavior in pre-adolescent males. *Developmental Psychology*, 1976, **12**, 555–556.

Markell, R. A., & Asher, S. R. The relationship of children's interests to perceived masculinity and feminity. Paper presented at the annual meeting of the American Educational Research Association, 1974.

Maslow, A. H., & Diaz-Guerrero, R. Delinquency as a value disturbance. In J. G. Peatman and E. L. Hartley (Eds.), *Fertschrift for Gardner Murphy.* New York: Harper & Row, 1960, pp. 228–240.

McDavid, J. W., & Harari, H. Stereotyping of names and popularity in grade school children. *Child Development*, 1966, **37**, 453–459.

Miller, S. Ends, means and galumphing. Some leitmotifs of play. *American Anthropologist*, 1973, **75**, 87–98.

Moore, S. G. Correlates of peer acceptance in nursery school children. In W. W. Hartup & N. L. Smothergill (Eds.), *The young child.* Washington, D.C.: National Association for the Education of Young Children, 1967, pp. 229–247.

Mueller, E., & Brenner, J. The origin of facial skill as interaction among play group toddlers. *Child Development*, 1977, **48**, 854–867.

Mueller, E., & Lucas, T. A developmental analysis of peer interaction among toddlers. In M. Lewis & L. A. Rosenblum (Eds.), *Friendship and peer relations.* New York: Wiley, 1975.

Mueller, E., & Rich, A. Clustering and socially directed behaviors in a play group of 1-year-old boys. *Journal of Child Psychology and Psychiatry*, 1976, **17**, 315–322.

Mueller, E., & Vandell, D. Infant-infant interaction. In J. Asofsky (Ed.), *Handbook of infant development.* New York: Wiley, in press.

Nelson, J. D., Gelfand, D., & Hartmann, D. P. Children's aggression following competition and exposure to an aggressive model. *Child Development,* 1969, **40**, 1085–1097.

O'Connor, R. D. Modification of social withdrawal through symbolic modeling. *Journal of Applied Behavior Analysis*, 1969, **2**, 15–22.

Parten, M., & Newhall, S. W. Social behavior of preschool children. In R. G. Barker, J. S. Kounin, & H. F. Wright (Eds.), *Child behavior and development.* New York: McGraw-Hill, 1943, pp. 509–525.

Patel, H. S., & Gordon, J. E. Some personal and situational determinants of yielding to influence. *Journal of Abnormal Social Psychology*, 1960, **61**, 411–418.

Patterson, G. R., Littman, R. A., & Bricker, W. Assertive behavior in children: A step toward a theory of aggression. *Monographs of the Society for Research in Child Development,* 1967, **32** (Serial No. 113).

Pepitone, E. A. Comparison behavior in elementary school children. *American Educational Research Journal*, 1972, **9**, 45–63.

Piaget, J. *The moral judgement of the child.* London: Kegan Paul, 1932.

Piaget, J. *Play, dreams and imitation in childhood* (C. Gallengno & F. M. Hodgsons, trans.). New York: Norton, 1951.

Reisman, D. *The lonely crowd.* New York: Anchor, 1950.

Richardson, S. A., Goodman, U., Hastorf, A. H., & Dornbusch, S. A. Cultural uniformity in reaction to physical disabilities. *American Sociological Review*, 1961, **26**, 241–247.

Roberts, J., & Baird, J. L., Jr. Parent ratings of behavioral patterns of children. *Vital and Health Statistics. Data from the National Health Survey* (Ser. 11, No. 108). Washington, D.C.: U.S. Government Printing Office, 1971.

Roff, N., Sells, S. B., & Golden, N. N. *Social adjustment and personality development in children.* Minneapolis: University of Minnesota Press, 1972.

Rosen, C. E. The effects of socio-dramatic play on problem solving behavior among culturally disadvantaged preschool children. *Child Development*, 1974, **45**, 920–927.

Rubin, K. H., Maione, T. L., & Hornug, M. Free play behaviors in middle and lower-class preschoolers: Parten and Piaget revisited. *Child Development*, 1976, **47**, 414–419.

Ruble, D. N., Feldman, N. S., & Boggiano, A. K. Social comparison between young children in achievement situations. *Developmental Psychology*, 1976, **12**, 192–197.

Saltz, E., Dixon, D., & Johnson, J. Training disadvantaged preschoolers on various fantasy activities: Effects on cognitive functioning and impulse control. Technical report 8, May 1978, Wayne State University.

Sampson, E. E., & Hancock, T. An examination of the relationship between ordinal position, personality, and conformity: An extension, replication, and partial verification. *Journal of Personality and Social Psychology*, 1967, **5,** 398–407.

Savin-Williams, R. C. Dominance-submission behaviors and hierarchies in young adolescents: Sex similarities and differences. *Child Development*, 1978, in press.

Shapira, A., & Madsen, M. C. Cooperative and competitive behavior of kibbutz and urban children in Israel. *Child Development*, 1969, **40,** 609–617.

Shaw, M. E. Changes in sociometric choices following forced integration of an elementary school. *Journal of Social Issues*, 1974, **29,** 143–157.

Sheldon, W. H., Stevens, S. S., & Tucker, W. B. *The varieties of human physique.* New York: Harper, 1940.

Sherif, M. Experiments in group conflict. *Scientific American*, 1956, 54–58.

Shure, N. B. Psychological ecology of a nursery school. *Child Development*, 1963, **34,** 979–992.

Silverman, I., & Shaw, M. E. Effects of sudden mass desegregation of interracial interactions and attitudes in one southern city. *Journal of Social Issues*, 1973, **29,** 133–142.

Siman, M. L. Application of a new model of peer group influence to naturally existing adolescent friendship groups. *Child Development*, 1977, **48,** 270–274.

Singer, J. L. Television, imaginative play and cognitive development: Some problems and possibilities. Paper presented at the American Psychological Association Meeting, San Francisco, August 1977.

Singleton, L. C., & Asher, S. R. Peer preferences and social interaction among third grade children in an integrated school district. *Journal of Educational Psychology*, 1977, **69,** 330–336.

Sluckin, A. M., & Smith, R. K. Two approaches to the concept of dominance in preschool children. *Child Development*, 1977, **48,** 917–923.

Smilansky, S. *The effects of sociodramatic play on disadvantaged children: Preschool children.* New York: Wiley, 1968.

Staffieri, J. R. A study of social stereotype of body image in children. *Journal of Personality and Social Psychology*, 1967, **7,** 101–104.

Strayer, F. F., & Strayer, J. An ethological analysis of social agonism and dominance relations among preschool children. *Child Development*, 1976, **47,** 980–989.

Switzky, H. N., Haywood, H. C., & Isett, R. Exploration, curiosity and play in young children. Effects of stimulus complexity. *Developmental Psychology*, 1974, **10,** 321–329.

Styczynski, L. E., & Langlois, J. H. The effects of familiarity on behavioral stereotypes associated with physical attractiveness in young children. *Child Development*, 1977, **48,** 1137–1141.

Sullivan, H. S. *The interpersonal theory of psychiatry.* New York: Norton, 1953.

Suomi, S. J., & Harlow, H. F. Social rehabilitation of isolate-reared monkeys. *Developmental Psychology*, 1972, **6,** 487–496.

Sylva, K., Bruner, J. S., & Genova, P. The role of play in the problem-solving of children 3–5 years old. In J. S. Bruner, A. Jolly, & K. Sylva (Eds.), *Play: Its role in development and evolution.* London: Penguin, 1976, pp. 244–257.

Thelen, M. H., & Kirkland, K. D. On status and being imitated: Effects on reciprocal imitation and attraction. *Journal of Personality and Social Psychology*, 1976, **33,** 691–697.

Thelen, M. H., Dollinger, S. J., & Roberts, M. C. On being imitated: Its effects on attraction and reciprocal imitation. *Journal of Personality and Social Psychology*, 1975, **31,** 467–472.

Wahler, R. G. Child-child interactions in free field settings: Some experimental analyses. *Journal of Experimental Child Psychology*, 1967, **5,** 278–293.

Waldrop, M. F., & Halverson, C. F. Intensive and extensive peer behavior:

Longitudinal and cross-sectional analyses. *Child Development*, 1975, **46,** 19–26.

Walters, R. H., & Parke, R. D. Influence of response consequences to a social model on resistance to deviation. *Journal of Experimental Child Psychology*, 1964, **1,** 269–280.

Whiting, B. B., & Whiting, J. W. M. *Children of six cultures: A psycho-cultural analysis.* Cambridge, Mass.: Harvard University Press, 1975.

Wright, H. F. *Recording and analyzing child behavior.* New York: Harper & Row, 1967,

14

The School
as a
Socialization
Agency

Most psychological theories of child development under the influence of Freud stress the early experiences of the child in the family as the main determinants of future social, emotional, and even intellectual development. As we have seen, a second major force in the socialization process is the peer group. A third and often neglected agent is the school. Probably no other institution has as much opportunity as the school to shape the developing child. After a child enters the first grade, an increasingly large proportion of her life will be dominated by the school. Even if she is not there, the demands of the school through home assignments and the social obligations and ties of school clubs and activities make the school a salient force in the child's daily existence. In this chapter we will focus on the ways in which the school exerts its socializing influence. The importance of school will be discussed, and then some of the structural features of schools will be considered, such as school size, classroom size, and seating arrangements.

Second, we will examine the effects of open- versus traditional-classroom organization on children's development. Next, the effects of the central character in the school drama, the teacher, will be examined. Do variations in teaching styles affect the child's progress in school? How important are textbooks? Do they mislead and misinform young children as some experts claim, or has the influence of texts been exaggerated. Next, the issue of special classes for special children such as the retarded and the gifted will be explored. Then, the relationship of the lower-class child and the school system will be considered. Finally, desegregation is discussed.

The Importance of the School

Children attend school for more hours each day and more days each year than ever before. Children now go to school an average of 5 hours a day, 180 days a year. In 1880, the average pupil attended school about 80 days each year. Not only are children attending school more often, for longer periods of time, but a larger proportion of the population go to school. And they start school earlier and stay in school longer. Even in the last few decades there have been dramatic shifts. In 1965, 27 percent of all 3- to 5-year-olds were enrolled in school; by 1973 41 percent of this age group attended school (Bane, 1976).

Although impressive, merely underlining the increasingly large amount of time children spend in the classroom is hardly convincing evidence that the school has an impact on the child's development. More substantial documentation is necessary. One influential kind of evidence concerning the importance of the school as a socializing force has come from studies of the impact of schools on children's values and aspirations. These studies show that schools, along with the family and the peer group, can influence the child's moral value orientation (Bronfenbrenner, Devereux, Suci, & Rodgers, 1965) as well as his or her achievement and occupational aspirations (Walberg & Rasher, 1977). Moreover, as cross-cultural studies have demonstrated, schooling has a major impact on the way in which children organize their thoughts and cognitions (Cole, Gay, Glick, & Sharp, 1971; Glick, 1975). Schooling teaches an abstract symbolic orientation to the world which allows children to develop the capacity to think in terms of general concepts, rules, and hypothetical events. Schools do not simply teach children more knowledge; schools teach children to think about the world in different ways. These diverse impacts of schooling underline the important and unique role that the school plays in modifying children's social and cognitive development.

Variations within the school setting have an important impact on children's emotional and social adjustment as well as on their academic progress. In order to explore this impact, the effects of the physical structure of the school environment need to be examined.

The Effects of the Physical Structure
of the School Environment

Although most discussions of the school concentrate on teachers, tactics, and texts, the structural features of the school environment merit consideration. Does the size of the school that a child attends make any difference? Similarly, do such factors as seating arrangements, class size, wall color, and ventilation affect the child's scholastic achievement, his attitudes toward school, or the degree to which he actively participates in class and extracurricular functions? Although it is impossible to answer all these questions, recent research has given us answers to at least some of them.

Big School, Small School: The Effect of School Size

The large school has authority: its grand exterior dimensions, its long halls and myriad rooms and its tides of students all carry an implication of power and rightness. The small school lacks such certainty: its modest building, its short halls and few rooms and its students, who move more in trickles than in tides, give an impression of a casual or not quite decisive educational environment. (Barker & Gump, 1964, p. 195)

But that is only an outside view. And apperances are often deceiving. To find out how schools of different sizes look from the inside was the aim of a research project conducted by Roger Barker and Paul Gump of the University of Kansas. These investigators were concerned with the extent of student participation in extracurricular functions in small and large schools. They wanted to learn whether or not large schools offer more, and more varied, activities for their students than smaller schools and whether this meant that the student in the large school has a richer experience. High schools ranging in size from 35 to 2,287 students participated in the study; all were located in an economically, culturally, and politically homogeneous region of eastern Kansas, and all were controlled by the same state authority. The results were surprising. Although the largest school had twenty times as many students as a small school in a nearby county, there were only five times as many extracurricular activities. More importantly, the large and small school do not differ greatly in terms of the variety of activities that they offer. The small school is small in enrollment but not necessarily limited in opportunities for activity and participation. Barker and Gump compare it to a small engine in that "it possesses the essential parts of a large entity but has fewer replications and differentiations of some of the parts" (Barker & Gump, 1964, p. 195). With fewer students but nearly as many participation opportunities, one would expect that more students would be more involved in more activities in more important ways in the smaller setting. This is precisely what the researchers found. The proportion of students who participated in district music festivals and dramatic, journalistic, and student government competitions was three to twenty times as great in the small, as contrasted with the large, instituion. Figure 14-1 presents a graphic picture of this relationship. Students at a small school would participate in twice as many activities over their high school career. Moreover, there would be greater variety in their activities if they attended a small school. The kinds of positions occupied by students at

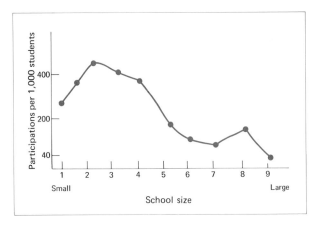

FIGURE 14-1 Partici-
pation of high school
students in extracurricu-
lar district activities.
*(From Barker & Gump,
1964.)*

large and small schools differed as well. Small-school adolescents were more likely to hold positions of importance and responsibility than their peers at a large school. In light of these findings, it was not surprising to learn that the rewards and satisfactions derived from participation differed for students in these two types of environments. Students from the small schools reported

. . . more satisfaction relating to the development of competence, to being challenged, to engaging in important actions, to being involved in group activities and to achieving moral and cultural values [while large school students reported] more satisfaction dealing with vicarious enjoyment, with large entity affiliation, with learning about their school's persons and affairs and with gaining "points" via participation. (Barker & Gump, 1964, p. 197).

Further analysis revealed that these differences were largely due to the fact that a greater number of pupils held responsible positions in small schools.

There is one other way in which the two types of institutions differed. In the small-school setting there were many more pressures to participate; students themselves felt more obligation and responsibility to play an active role in their school functions, and they felt that their peers expected them to participate more. One outcome is that there were fewer "outsiders," that is, students who were left out of most extracurricular activities, in the smaller schools. Compari-sions of marginal students, or potential dropouts, with regular students indicated that the marginal students felt few pressures to participate in large schools. On the other hand, in small settings the two types of students felt similar pressures to participate in extracurricular affairs. This greater sense of identification and involvement of the marginal students in the smaller school may be part of the reason that dropout rates are lower in small schools.

The question of whether or not school size affects academic progress is, unfortunately, left unanswered. Class size rather than institution size probably would be a better predictor in this realm. However, if we view the school as a socialization agency, it is clear that much of the school's influence in transmitting

The one-room school-
house: an endangered
species. (Guy Gillette,
Photo Researchers, Inc.)

social and cultural values comes through these extracurricular functions. Not
only does the research of Barker and Gump provide important information
about the impact of school size on student behaviors, but it also serves as a
remainder that much of the learning taking place in school is not in the
classroom. The main implication of this study lies in the answer to the question
that guided their research: "What size should a school be? . . . sufficiently small
that all of its students are needed for its enterprises. A school should be small
enough that students are not redundant" (Barker & Gump, 1964, p. 202).

**The Spatial
Arrangement
of the Classroom**

One of the most obvious features of the learning environment is the *rectangular*
classroom. Why not a round class or a square one? Or does it matter anyway?
According to one design expert:

The present rectangular room with its straight row of chairs and wide windows was
intended to provide for ventilation, light, quick depature, ease of surveillance and a host
of other legitimate needs as they existed in the early 1900's. . . . The typical long narrow
shape resulted from a desire to get light across the room. The front of each room was
determined by window location, since pupils had to be seated so that window light came
over the left shoulder. Despite new developments in lighting, acoustics and structures,

most schools are still boxes filled with cubes each containing a specified number of chairs in straight rows. There have been attempts to break away from this rigid pattern, but experimental schools are the exception rather than the rule. (Sommer, 1969, pp. 98-99).

Maria Montessori once described the children who have to exist in these traditional classrooms as "butterflies mounted on pins, fastened each to a desk, spreading the useless wings of barren and meaningless knowledge they have acquired" (Montessori, 1964, p. 81).

Does a pupil's location within the classroom make a difference? Are individuals in front more active than those in the rear? Are those in the center more active than those at the aisles, regardless of the type of room? Consider the seminar room first. Sommer (1969) compared the participation of college students at the side tables with those sitting directly opposite the instructor. Students sitting opposite the teacher participated most, while those at the side tables talked very little. Finally, while students tended to avoid chairs adjacent to the teacher, when they were "stuck" in these positions they pretended that they weren't there by being silent.

Participation in straight-row arrangements seems to be determined by location as well. Sommer found that first-row students participate more than students near the rear and centrally located students participate more than the fringe dwellers. This location-participation relationship is a very common one and by no means restricted to college students. In a study of elementary and high school classes, it was reported that the center-front pattern emerged regardless of grade level (first, sixth, and eleventh), sex or age of teacher, or subject matter (mathematics or social studies) (Adams & Biddle, 1970). The effect was so consistent that this spatial location was termed the *action zone* of the classroom. Figure 14-2 illustrates the relationship. The reasons for the effect are unclear. Do interested students sit closer to the teacher, or do students take a greater interest if they do sit closer to the teacher?

Seat choices may have psychological implications. Levinger and Gunner

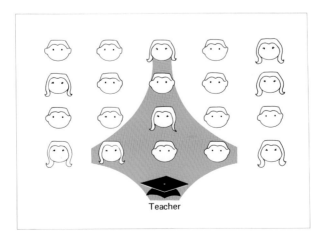

Teacher

FIGURE 14-2   Area of maximum amount of teacher-pupil inter-action (shaded area) in classroom. *(From Adams & Biddle, 1970.)*

(1967) found that students who typically sat at the rear of a classroom placed greater psychological distance between themselves and the teacher; these investigators had used a projective test in which students arranged geometric forms and silhouettes on a felt background to index psychological distance in their study. How such "distance" develops is not clear. Children may sit near the back of the class because of some fear of or alienation from the teacher; on the other hand, the psychological barrier may develop out of the spatial arrangements themselves.

Finally, what about class size? In spite of the frequency of discussion and debate concerning the "optimal" class size, there is a surprising paucity of relevant investigations. An exception is an early study by Dawe (1934), in which she examined the effects of kindergarten size on pupil participation. In classes ranging in size from fifteen to forty-six children, the number of comments made by each child during a controlled discussion period was recorded. As class size increased, not only did the total amount of discussion decrease, but a smaller percent of the children participated; when they did talk, their average amount of participation was likely to be less. Nearly forty years later, Tuana (1969) found a similar inverse relationship between participation and class size at the college level. It will come as no surprise to college students to learn that a mere 2.3 questions per class was typical in the large lecture class. As in the earlier classroom studies, those students in the two front rows of the center section of a lecture hall asked almost half of the questions. Another third of the questions came from students sitting along the side aisles. The "faceless mass" in the middle, to use Sommer's description, participated very little. This suggests that the location-participation link may be even stronger as class size increases. The result, of course, is an increasingly large proportion of children being excluded systematically from an active role in their education. If children do learn more by participating more, then the data are clear: smaller classes are preferable.

The findings concerning participation, size, and seating are consistent with a more general proposition governing social interaction, namely, that verbal communication is more likely when the potential conversationalists have eye-to-eye contact. In general, if you sit closer, you will participate more.

Size alone is not the only important factor; density, or the amount of space per pupil, makes a difference. In one recent study, preschoolers listened to a story or watched a teacher demonstration under crowded or uncrowded conditions. Visual attention to the teacher and to the educational materials was less when the children were spatially crowded than when the children listened in an uncrowded setting (Krantz & Risley, 1977).

In light of these findings, it is encouraging to see trends toward greater flexibility in arranging classroom space. Movable furniture is becoming increasingly popular, as in the "school without walls," an open-plan architecture designed for team teaching in which several grades share a large open space (Gump & Ross, 1977). However, merely providing flexible space and movable furniture does not guarantee that innovative teaching will necessarily follow. In one Texas experiment involving fully portable furniture, Sanders (1958) found that the equipment rarely moved in actual practice. This failure to take advantage of the flexible facilities is even more surprising in light of the fact that only 1.4 minutes were required to make a major rearrangement of the furniture. Other investigators have found similar results. For example, in one comparison of traditional and modern classrooms the teachers were "quick to emphasize that the large classroom had not changed their teaching methods" (Rolfe, 1961, p. 192, cited by Sommer, 1969). Clearly, teachers must learn to use space and facilities; without direct instruction concerning the possibilities offered by new classroom arrangements, it is unlikely that few substantial changes in individual class activities or teaching techniques will actually take place. As Sommer wryly commented, "If the school traditions make straight row arrangements immutable, even though the chairs are portable, portable chairs serve only to increase the workload of the janitors who have to straighten the rows every evening" (Sommer, 1969, p. 104).

The Organization and Structure of the Classroom

The teacher can organize her classroom in a multitude of ways. For example, she can arrange to have students participate in the decision making; she can organize her class into small groups; she can arrange for students to help each other; or she can organize classroom activities in the traditional manner. In this section we will focus on the consequences of different types of classroom organization.

The classic study of differing leadership styles on classroom climate was that of Kurt Lewin and his colleagues (Lewin, Lippitt, & White, 1939). Groups of five 10-year-old boys, organized into clubs for recreational purposes, were assigned leaders who had been instructed to be either "authoritarian," "democratic," or "laissez-faire" (permissive) in their orientation. Table 14-1 presents descriptions of these leadership styles. The democratic leadership style was superior to the other two leadership approaches in a variety of ways. The boys in the democratic groups were more productive (even in the leader's absence), happier with both their leader and their group, and less hostile toward each other. The laissez-faire leadership produced disorganization, boredom, inefficiency, and quarrels, while the boys in the authoritarian groups were either passive or rebellious, were aggressive in their peer interaction, and showed little capacity to work efficiently in the leader's absence.

The Open versus Traditional Classroom

Many of these differences in teacher style that Lewin originally investigated have reappeared in more recent investigations of the effects of the open classroom versus the traditional classroom. Originally developed in Great Britain, the open-classroom philosophy is based on the assumption that children learn best by actively participating and becoming involved in their own learning rather than being passive recipients of knowledge. Here is a description of the open classroom:

In the open classroom, it is rare for all the children to be engaged in the same activity at the same time. They do not sit at rows of desks, dutifully listening (or pretending to listen) as their teacher lectures in front of the room. Instead, they tend to be scattered around the

TABLE 14-1 AUTHORITARIAN, DEMOCRATIC, AND LAISSEZ-FAIRE LEADERS

Authoritarian	Democratic	Laissez-Faire
1. All determination of policy by the leader.	1. All policies a matter of group discussion and decision, encouraged and assisted by the leader.	1. Complete freedom for group or individual decision, without any leader participation.
2. Techniques and activity steps dictated by the authority, one at a time, so that future steps were always uncertain to a large degree.	2. Activity perspective gained during first discussion period. General steps to group goals sketched, and where technical advice was needed the leader suggested two or three alternative procedures from which choice could be made.	2. Various materials supplied by the leader, who made it clear that he would supply information when asked. He took no other part in work discussions.
3. The leader usually dictated the particular work task and work companions of each member.	3. The members were free to work with whomever they chose, and the division of tasks was left up to the group.	3. Complete nonparticipation by leader.
4. The dominator was "personal" in his praise and criticism of the work of each member, but remained aloof from active group participation except when demonstrating. He was friendly or impersonal rather than openly hostile.	4. The leader was "objective" or "fact-minded" in his praise and criticism, and tried to be a regular group member in spirit without doing too much of the work.	4. Very infrequent comments on member activities unless questioned, and no attempt to participate or interfere with the course of events.

Source: Lewin, K., Lippitt, R., & White, R. K. Patterns of aggressive behavior in experimentally created "social climates." *Journal of Social Psychology*, 1939, **10**, 271–299. © 1939 by the Journal Press. Reprinted by permission.

room—at tables, on couches, or on the floor—working individually or in small groups. A typical view of an open classroom might show us two youngsters stretched out on a rug reading books they have chosen from the classroom library. The teacher is at the math table, showing a small group of children how to use a set of scales to learn about relative weights. Two children in the writing corner are playing a word game. And one child is taking notes on the nursing behavior of the class guinea pig. Other children are working individually or in small groups at desks or tables. A sense of purpose pervades the room attesting to the children's interest in their various learning activities. (Papalia & Olds, 1975, p. 463)

But do children learn more and dislike it less in open classrooms? Problems plague attempts to evaluate the effects of open classrooms since the backgrounds of children in these two types of schools or classrooms tend to differ. However, some tentative conclusions can be suggested. Open-classroom children do not appear to learn more in terms of conventional achievement areas (Featherstone, 1971), but they do like school and their teachers more than children in formal or traditional schools (Groobman, Forward, & Peterson, 1976). Moreover, children in low-structure classes engage in more prosocial behavior and more imaginative play but are more aggressive than children in a more highly structured environment (Huston-Stein, Freidrich-Cofer, & Susman, 1977). There are other positive benefits as well. Harvey and his associates (Harvey, Prather, White, & Hoffmeister, 1968) found that children in open classrooms exhibited freer expression of feelings, more voluntary participation, higher independence, and a larger voice in classroom activities. Activitity level,

In this open classroom the activities are group-centered. (Larry Smith, Black Star)

as reflected in both the amount and diversity of goal-relevant activity, was higher in these classes. Novelty of their answers was higher, and there was less emphasis on rote answers and solutions. On the other hand, not all kinds of children fare well in open classrooms. Some children may perform better under a more structured type of classroom regime. In their study in Box 14-1, Grimes and Allinsmith (1961) illustrate the interdependence between the type of child and the kind of classroom organization.

It should come as no surprise that the open classroom so far seems to fall far short of being a panacea. Other widely acclaimed innovations in education such as Summerhill (Neill, 1960) have been similarly disappointing when you look carefully at their overall record of success (Bernstein, 1968). Even if most experiments in education do not survive intact, however, valuable aspects of their program may persist and eventually become absorbed by mainstream educational institutions. Thus, while it is unlikely that American public schools will convert to the open classroom model, many schools already offer both types of classrooms, the traditional and the open, attempting to assign students and teachers to the one which seems best suited to their own needs, predispositions, and abilities. (Hetherington & Morris, 1978, p. 321)

The Teacher

By far the most important figures in the school are the teachers. In this section we will examine who they are, what they do, and what effects they have on their pupils' academic progress and social and emotional adjustment. As we will see in our later discussion of sex roles (Chapter 15), teachers are usually female and tend to treat boys and girls differently in their classroom interactions. In this section, we focus on other aspects of the teacher's behavior. Do teachers' early impressions of how smart a child is make a difference? The teacher plays a variety of roles in the classroom as evaluator, disciplinarian, and social model. The way that she manages each of these roles can affect her pupils in a variety of ways. Even before teachers are acquainted with their pupils, teachers may have expectations that will affect the children's future academic performance.

Teacher Expectation and Academic Success

Although many teachers would probably deny it, most of them form impressions early in the school year concerning the probable performance of the incoming group of students. These expectations come from a variety of sources, such as the pupil's past academic record, achievement test scores, family background, appearance, and classroom conduct history. Do these prejudgments of the child's performance have an impact on the child's actual scholastic success or failure? It is possible to investigate the impact of these naturally developed expectations on the child's performance by soliciting predictions from teachers early in the year and then determining how closely the child's output conforms to the teacher's prediction. A more powerful technique involves experimentally planting an expectation concerning certain children in a classroom and then assessing to what degree the expectations will be fulfilled. Rosenthal

BOX 14-1
READING ACHIEVEMENT AND
CLASSROOM ORGANIZATION

Grimes and Allinsmith (1961) compared the reading achievement of highly anxious and highly compulsive children under two types of classroom regimes. Anxious children were characterized as restless, distractible, and fidgety, while compulsive children were defined as those who were upset by disorder and lack of organization. Under one regime, children learned to read under the phonics method, which is a highly structured, rulebound approach; in addition, the classroom using this structured approach tended to be more authoritarian than the comparison classroom, which employed the whole-word approach to reading, a less structured system of teaching. In this approach, the child is exposed to whole words from the outset and learns to read by experience in the reading process itself. The rule-bound, step-by-step character of the phonic

approach is absent. As Figures 14-3 and 14-4 indicate, children low in anxiety and compulsivity were relatively unaffected by the type of atmosphere. However, highly anxious children performed very poorly in the unstructured school and slightly better than their less anxious peers in the structured learning situation. On the other hand, the lack of structure did not affect the low-compulsive children; however, highly compulsive children performed markedly better under a structured classroom teaching regime. "The choice of instructional methods makes a big difference for certain kinds of people, and a search for the 'best' way to teach can suceed only when the learner's personality is taken into account" (Grimes & Allinsmith, 1961, p. 271). ■

Source: Grimes, J. W., & Allinsmith, W. Compulsivity, anxiety, and school achievement. *Merrill-Palmer Quarterly*, 1961, **7**, 247–269.

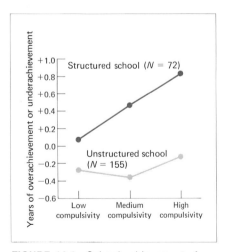

FIGURE 14-3 School achievement of compulsive children in two types of schools. *(From Grimes & Allinsmith, 1961.)*

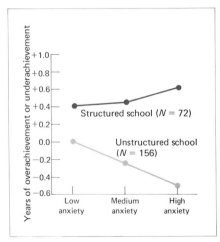

FIGURE 14-4 School achievement of anxious children in two types of schools. *(From Grimes & Allinsmith, 1961.)*

and Jacobsen of Harvard University (1966, 1968) have carried out such an experiment. In a number of elementary school classes, teachers were informed that 20 percent of their students were "intellectual bloomers who would show unusual intellectual gains during the academic year" (Rosenthal & Jacobsen, 1968, p. 66). The critical 20 percent was, of course, randomly chosen. In order to assess the impact of teacher expectations, the children were administered an IQ test before the experiment commenced and again after eight months of additional classroom experience with the "expectant" teacher. Would the children labeled as academic bloomers show a larger improvement than nonlabeled control children in the same classroom? For the school as a whole, those children for whom the teachers had been led to expect greater intellectual gain showed a signficantly greater increase in IQ scores than did the remaining students. However, the effect was most marked in the lower grade levels. In fact, the lower the grade level, the greater the effect.

But is the gain reflected in academic performance as well? To find out, the children's report cards were examined, and in one area, reading, there were marked effects. Children who were expected to do well were judged by their teachers to show greater advances in their reading ability. Again, the gains were most marked at the lower levels. Finally, classroom behavior was affected, as indicated by the fact that the "experimental" pupils were rated as higher in "intellectual curiosity" than the control children.

To determine whether these advantages would persist when contact with the expectant teacher was terminated, Rosenthal and Jacobsen retested the children after two full academic years. Before this final retest the children had spent a year with a teacher who had not been given favorable expecations. Although the younger children had been easier to influence initially, they had lost their advantage by the final follow-up evaluation. However, after the delay the older children, that is, those in the third to sixth grades, who had shown smaller gains in the early stages still showed the effect of the original expectancy manipulation. As the authors suggest, continued contact with the expectant teacher seems to be necessary for maintaining the effect in younger children, while older pupils are better able to maintain their advantage autonomously.

However, Rosenthal and his self-fulfilling prophecy in the classroom has met with severe methodological criticism (Elashoff & Snow, 1971; Jensen, 1969; Thorndike, 1968). In spite of some failures to find a Pygmalion effect, there has been corroboration of the central finding by other investigators for Head Start children, retardates, and institutionalized adolescent female offenders. Nor is the expectancy effect restricted to academic learning situations; Burham and Hartsough (1968) have demonstrated the expectancy effect with swimming ability in a group of children at a summer camp.

How can we explain the Pygmalion effect? Rosenthal (1973) has proposed four factors that may account for the effect. First, people who are led to expect good performance from a pupil may create a warmer social-emotional *climate* for their special students; research has indicated that when teachers think they are dealing with a bright student, they are more friendly and supportive than when they view their students as less capable.

Another factor is *feedback* for the student's performance; how often does the teacher respond to the child by rewarding her right answer or correcting her errors. A study by Brophy and Good (1970) illustrates that this may be a factor in the expectancy effect. After teachers named their high and low achievers, these investigators recorded the amount of feedback provided these two types of pupils. The teachers ignored only 3 percent of the high achiever's answers, but they ignored 15 percent of the low achiever's responses. Students that teachers view as high achievers may do better, in part, because they get more feedback from their teachers.

A third factor is *input*, or the amount of teaching that children may receive. Beez (1968) led some teachers in a Head Start program to expect poor performance from their "below-average" children while other teachers expected good performance from their "bright" children. Teachers taught the bright children more. For example, 87 percent of the teachers of the bright children taught eight or more words, while only 13 percent of the teachers of the below-average children tried to teach that number of words. Table 14-2 summarizes these teacher differences for the two groups of children. As a result, the teacher expectations were confirmed: over 75 percent of the bright children learned five or more words, while only 13 percent of the dull children learned five words.

Expectancies of good performance may not only translate into more teacher input but may also lead teachers to demand more *output* from students as well (Rubovitz & Maehr; 1973). As Rosenthal notes, teachers "call on such students more often, ask them harder questions, give them more time to answer and prompt them toward the correct answer" (1973, p. 62). In summary, at least four factors may aid in explaining the Pygmalion effect: the climate of the classroom; differences in teacher feedback; teacher input; and opportunities for student output. The case is not closed, but these studies do raise an important question: "How much of the improvement in intellectual performance attributed to the contemporary educational programs is due to the content and methods of the programs and how much is due to the favorable expect-

TABLE 14-2 TEACHING DIFFERENCES FOR ABOVE- AND BELOW-AVERAGE STUDENTS

Number of words taught	Teacher's expectation	
	Below average	Above average
11 or more	0%	47%
9 or 10	3.0%	33%
7 or 8	22.5%	10%
5 or 6	50.0%	3%
4 or less	22.5%	7%

Adapted from Beez, 1968.

ancies of the teachers and administrators involved?'' (Rosenthal & Jacobsen, 1966, p. 118).

The Teacher as an Evaluator

The dominant impression of students is that schools are first and foremost places of evaluation, not of learning. Nowhere else in society is the individual scrutinized for so long a time or as intensely as he is in school. This scrutiny usually takes the form of constant testing and examination. (Covington & Berry, 1976)

The way that teachers organize evaluation procedures makes an important difference to children's attitudes, motivation, and performance. Some children are typically anxious in test-taking situations, while other children are relaxed in these evaluation settings. Every teacher has heard students say, "I really knew the material, but I was so uptight in the exam my mind went blank" or "I just can't take exams; I get so tense." Are these just glib student rationalizations or can test-taking anxiety seriously affect academic performance?

High-anxious children do perform especially poorly on measures of academic skills, classroom learning, and verbal problem-solving ability, areas critical to a child's progress in school (Hill, 1972). However, these types of children are not less capable than their low-anxious peers, and it is the type of evaluation or test-taking setting that accounts, in part, for the poor performance of high-anxious children. To demonstrate the role of different types of evaluation procedures on children's performance, Hill and Eaton (1977) tested children's arithmetic performance under two conditions. In one case, time limits were imposed so that children could complete two-thirds of the problems they attempted, but failed to complete the remaining third. In an optimizing condition, the time limit was removed, which minimized the failure experience and permitted the children to complete all the problems they attempted. Under the time-pressure condition, the high-anxious fifth and sixth graders showed three times the errors, took twice as long on each problem, and cheated twice as often as low-anxious children. In contrast, in the optimizing condition in which the time pressure was removed high-anxious children caught up, going just as fast and performing just as accurately as their low-anxious peers. Nor is this general pattern restricted to "time pressure"; a number of other optimizing conditions have been identified that focus on the child's expectations for adult approval or disapproval based on performance. In a study by Williams and Hill (1976), children performed under one of four conditions: (1) a standard condition involving typical test instructions, (2) a diagnostic condition in which the examiner indicated that the information gained from the test would be used to help teach the children, (3) an expectancy-reassurance condition in which the examiner indicated that the problems are difficult, most children miss quite a few of them, and the children shouldn't worry if they miss some of them, and (4) a normative condition in which the examiner indicated he was interested in knowing how children go about doing problems and so the children shouldn't even put their names on the test booklets. As Figure 14-5 shows, under the

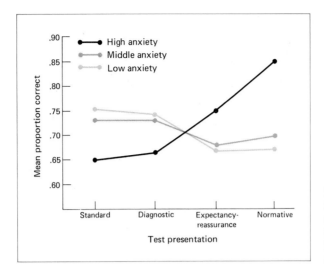

expectancy-reassurance condition and the normative condition, which were designed to minimize stress, the high-anxious children show gains in accuracy.

Together these studies suggest that "the performance deficits of the high-anxious children . . . were due to motivational and test-taking factors and not to learning deficits, since the deficits were removed by simply modifying the testing conditions" (Hill, 1978, p. 6). Evaluation is not going to disappear from the school scene, but it is clear that closer attention to the way in which evaluation is provided can help rather than hinder children's progress.

The Teacher as a Disciplinarian

Teachers not only are evaluators, but spend a good deal of their time as disciplinarians. How effective are different teacher-control techniques for achieving and maintaining classroom order, and what effect do teacher tactics have on children's motivation? Although it might be predicted intuitively that praise is more effective than disapproval, a systematic analysis of the use of praise is necessary before any conclusions concerning its effectiveness can be drawn legitmately. Other questions require consideration as well. How important are classmates in achieving classroom control? Can the power of the peer group be effectively harnessed by the teacher to achieve more effective discipline?

Operant Reinforcement in the Classroom   Recent attempts to apply operant reinforcement principles to classroom control have been very successful (O'Leary & O'Leary, 1977). In some cases, social reinforcement in the form of verbal approval is used whereby teachers are taught to praise appropriate behavior and ignore disruptive behavior.

However, in some cases ignoring disruptive behavior and praising appropriate responses is not powerful enough to establish control. This may be particularly likely in a classroom where a few individual children continue to be

"Token economies": use with care. (Professor Randy
Lee Williams, University of Kansas)

disruptive under a praise-and-ignore regime. When other children observe their
peers behaving disruptively without any negative consequence, they may
become disruptive themselves.

A technique that has proved effective in establishing classroom control is the
combination of material or token rewards and social reinforcements. This
approach was not used routinely until the 1960s but is certainly not new.

In 610 A.D., a monk formed the ends of left-over bread dough into strips which he folded
into a twisted loop to represent the folded arms of children in prayer. The baked treat,
called a "pretiola" (Latin for "little reward") was then offered to children as a reward for
learning their prayers. . . . (O'Leary & O'Leary, 1977, p. 257)

Under the modern version of these programs children accumulate points or
tokens for good behavior, which they can then exchange for material rewards
such as candy, peanuts, comics, or toys. Numerous studies have demonstrated
the effectiveness of this approach for controlling children in classrooms (O'Leary
& O'Leary, 1977).

But token economies may not always be necessary, and, in fact, may
undermine children's interest in their school activities—under some circumstances. As the study in Box 14-2 illustrates, activities that are intrinsically
interesting may lose their appeal if rewards are provided. While this study implies
that token economies should be introduced in classrooms only when necessary
and not as a routine practice, there are many classroom activities, such as
learning multiplication tables, that may be unappealing. In such cases, tokens or
extrinsic rewards can often increase children's interest in these classroom

BOX 14-2
WHEN TOKENS FAIL: LOSS OF INTEREST THROUGH UNNECESSARY REWARD

Token economies in classrooms are neither always necessary nor always desirable. There are many activities in school that are intrinsically interesting for children; solving math problems can be fun for a high school student, just as making a paper hat can be interesting for a preschooler. What happens if children are rewarded for already interesting activities? Will they simply become more interested, or will interest lag? To find out, Lepper, Greene, & Nisbett (1973) rewarded one group of preschoolers with a "Good Player Award"—a big gold star and a bright red ribbon—for drawing pictures with felt pens, an activity that these children already enjoyed a great deal. Other children were asked to draw pictures, but received no reward for their products. The amount of time that the children spent drawing during their free-play periods in

the nursery school was recorded by observers before and after the special drawing sessions. The results were dramatic: the children who were rewarded for drawing spent less time during free-play periods in this activity while the children who did not receive an "award" maintained their interest in drawing.

These findings suggest that token reinforcers may sometimes undermine the intrinsic interest in activities. Reinforcers can be effective in the classroom, but should be used in situations where intrinsic interest in the activity is low. Once the merits of the activity become clear to the child, tangible rewards may become unnecessary, or as this study shows, even undesirable. ∎

Source: Lepper, M., Greene, D., & Nisbett, R. Test of the "overjustification hypothesis." *Journal of Personality and Social Psychology*, 1973, **28**, 129–137.

activities (Feingold & Mahoney, 1975). Token economies have a place in the classroom, but care needs to be exercised in choosing the target activities.

Teachers are not the only control agents; peers can often achieve classroom control as well (McGee, Kauffman & Nussen, 1977). Two experimental studies will illustrate this point. In one study (Barrish, Sanders, & Wolf, 1969) a fourth-grade class was divided into two teams and any misbehavior (for example, talking in class or leaving your seat without permission) by any team member resulted in a loss of privileges for the whole team. The privileges were events which are available in almost every classroom, such as extra recess, first to line up for lunch, time for special projects, stars, and of course the fun of winning the contest. These investigators found that individual contingencies resulting in group consequences were very effective in reducing disruptive classrooms. However, the effect was present only in the class period (math) where the peer game was in effect; there was little generalization to other periods (for example, reading). Only when the game was introduced in the reading class did a drop in disruptive behavior occur. This suggests that " 'generalization' is no magical process, but rather a behavioral change which must be engineered like any other change [O'Leary et al., 1969, p. 13]."

A related study by Schmidt and Ulrich (1969) indicated that team competition may not be necessary. These investigators were able to lower the level of classroom noise by making any individual violation of a previously specified noise ceiling result in loss of privileges (extra time in gym period) not just for the individual but for the whole class. This procedure seemed to work just as well as the competition procedure used by Barrish and his colleagues and avoided some of the undesirable consequences that between-group competition may produce, such as increased intergroup hostility (Sherif & Sherif, 1953; *see* Chapter 13). As Bronfenbrenner notes in his recent *Two Worlds of Childhood: U.S. & U.S.S.R.* (1970), the technique of peer control is used regularly in Russian school classrooms.

Turning the Tables: Student Control of Teacher Behavior   Student control is not limited to their classmates; students can control their teachers as well. By applying the same operant principles that teachers have successfully used to control their pupils, children have been taught to modify their teachers' behavior. In one California classroom, a group of 12- to 15-year-olds were taught to reward positive teacher behavior by smiling. making eye contact, and sitting up straight (Gray, Graubard, & Rosenberg, 1974). At the same time they were taught to discourage negative teacher behavior with statements like "It's hard for me to do good work when you're cross with me." The results were striking: Over a five-week intervention period, there was a fourfold increase in the rate of positive teacher behavior, while negative teacher behavior was completely eliminated by the end of the intervention period. When these student behavior engineers were instructed to discontinue reinforcing their teachers, the rate of positive teacher behavior dropped. Other studies (Bates, 1975; Berberich, 1971) confirm these findings and underline the influential role that students can play in modifying teacher behavior. The same bidirectional principle that characterizes parent-child interaction clearly applies to teacher-student interchanges as well.

Self-monitoring: Power to the Pupil   Teachers and peers are not the only source of pupil control; children can exercise self-control. One of the most promising techniques for improving children's classroom conduct, concentration, and achievement is *self-monitoring*. Self-monitoring is a system by which students are taught to keep track of their own classroom behavior on a daily basis. Here is how it worked in one fifth- and sixth-grade classroom with an individualized mathematics instruction program (Sagotsky, Patterson, & Lepper, 1977). Children could proceed at their own speed in this program. Some of the students received self-monitoring instructions. These children were told that:

They should note from time to time whether or not they were actually working on their math units. If, when the child chose to monitor himself, he found himself working appropriately, he was asked to put a "+" in one of 12 blank boxes that were on the cover sheets. If, on the other hand, he was not working at this point, he was asked to put a "−"

in one of the boxes. . . . At the end of the math period each day, they were also instructed to mark the page and problem number where they had stopped working. (Sagotsky et al., 1977, p. 9)

Others were asked only to record the place that they stopped each day, but received no self-monitoring instructions. The treatment affected the children's behavior in two ways. First, the self-monitoring children studied more during their math sessions and engaged in less off-task behaviors, such as talking, walking around, or playing. Second, these students progressed faster through the math curriculum in the self-monitoring conditions. These are impressive results and are of practical importance due to the low cost of implementation in terms of money and teacher time. Moreover, teaching self-management skills may be a way to avoid the drop in classroom conduct that is often seen when adult approval or token programs are withdrawn. Most importantly, a child with self-management skills will be better able to learn when a teacher or other adult is completely absent. Self-monitoring can reduce the child's dependence on external supports.

The Peer-Teacher Approach

Not only can peers aid in controlling their classmates, but they can function as peer-teachers as well. Older children are cast in the role of assistant teachers and given responsibility for teaching younger children. Although the details of different programs vary, most involve some kind of instruction session for the "helpers" in which they learn the techniques of relating to and teaching younger

Students sometimes can more easily accept instruction and correction from other students than they can from adults. (Van Bucher, Photo Researchers, Inc.)

children. In addition, to coordinate the tutoring program with the younger child's regular classroom experience, assistants often meet with the teacher of the child that they are aiding. The results are encouraging and indicate that both tutor and pupil benefit in a variety of ways (Allen, 1976; Sheehan, Feldman, & Allen, 1976).

First, both participants showed greater academic progress in the tutorial subject. Cloward (1967) found significant changes in reading achievement over a five-month period: not only did the tutored pupils show a gain of 6.2 months in reading level in contrast to a gain of only 3.5 months for nontutored control children, but the tutors gained as well. In fact, over a seven-month period the tutors improved an average of nineteen months in reading level.

More recently, Allen and Feldman (1973) found that the experience of being a tutor can benefit low-achieving children. Children who are low achievers often have a record of failure and tend to be passive participants in any learning exchange. Motivation and involvement will increase in the tutoring situation, and so these investigators argued that low achievers would learn better when placed in the role of peer-teacher than when studying alone. Ten low-achieving fifth graders whose reading scores were at least one year below average grade level served as tutors; ten third graders were the tutees or learners. Subjects participated for ten consecutive weekdays for a two-week period; for every alternate day the fifth-grade tutor either taught a third grader for twenty minutes or studied the material alone. By the end of the two-week period, tutoring resulted in significantly better performance than studying alone for the low-achieving fifth-grade children. These gains were made in spite of the fact that the third graders learned equally with the tutor or studying alone. The tutoring effect in this case had more impact on the tutors than the tutees. While follow-up studies are necessary to determine the stability of these gains, these results point clearly to the effectiveness of the peer-teacher program.

Moreover, other benefits have been reported. Lippitt and Lippitt, for example, summarized some of these additional effects:

Teachers of younger children who receive help say that their youngsters show increased self-respect, self-confidence, and pride in their progress. They are less tense, can express themselves more clearly, are better groomed, and have improved attendance records.

As for the older students, working with their juniors provides valuable learning experiences in addition to giving them a chance to be appreciated by teachers and younger students. They learn how to help someone else learn. They learn to relate to a younger child. They get a chance to work through, at a safe emotional distance, some of the problems they have in relation to their own peers or younger siblings. Ordinarily, older children might not be interested in the social skills involved in getting along with people, but they are highly motivated to learn them when learning those skills enables them to do a better job of helping the younger children.

Academically, too, older students benefit from being crossage helpers. Children who might have had no interest in reviewing subject matter which they did not understand when they were in the lower grades make a tremendous effort to fill the gaps when they are responsible for helping someone else understand. (1968, p. 4)

Although other investigators have reported similar effects (Allen, 1976; Deering, 1968; Kuppel, 1964), systematic research is required to determine the critical factors that account for the effectiveness of these programs.

Children can clearly serve as effective helpers for their classmates and for younger pupils and may, in the process, help themselves.

The Teacher as a Social Model

Just as parents and peers serve as models for the developing child, recent evidence suggests that young children imitate their teachers as well. However, not all teachers are likely to be imitated, nor are all children equally likely to copy their teacher's actions. In a recent study Portuges and Feshbach (1971) have isolated some of the teacher and observer characteristics that affect the degree of teacher imitation. Groups of 8- to 10-year-old boys and girls were shown movies of a female teacher presenting a geography lesson, using either a rewarding or critical teaching style. The "positive" teacher responded approvingly to correct answers, while the negative model rebuked the pupils in the film for their errors. In addition, the models exhibited different distinctive incidental movements, such as cupping the ear or clasping the hands. To assess the extent to which the children would imitate the teacher-model's distinctive mannerisms, the children were required to "teach a geography lesson" to two life-sized dolls. The rewarding teacher was imitated more than the negative instructor. The use of a positive approach, then, apparently enhances teacher influence by making it more likely that the pupils will imitate the teacher's behavior. However, the strength of the effect varied with the sex and social class of the observing child. Girls imitated the female teacher-model more than the boys did; girls probably view the role of teacher as more sex-appropriate than do boys. Moreover, middle-class children imitated more of the teacher's gestures than did lower-class observers. It was the middle-class girls who imitated the model to the greatest degree, while lower-class boys were the least influenced by the teacher-model. The implications of this social class difference will be explored in detail in a later section. Other studies suggest that the children may imitate their teacher's typical problem-solving style. As we saw earlier in our discussion of cognitive style (see Chapter 9), impulsive children exposed to reflective teachers become more reflective in their problem-solving strategies (Yando & Kagan, 1968). Teachers as well as parents and peers serve as influential models for children. We have examined teachers and tactics; now we turn to an evaluation of texts.

Textbooks

What's Wrong with Primary Readers?

In the past decade there has been a reawakening of interest and concern with children's readers. Educators have recognized that children are influenced not only by their teachers and peers but also by the reading material to which they are exposed. Primers serve an important socializing function. Many of the attitudes and cultural values that are slowly emerging during the early school years are directly shaped by the content and themes of these textbooks. In addition, these readers play an important role in determining the child's attitudes toward the task of reading itself. Particularly for children who have had little encouragement to read before entering school and, therefore, have little appreciation of the value of books and the rewards of reading, primers with lively, interesting, and relevant content would seem to be necessary to interest them in books and reading.

However, most evaluators of available readers give these texts a failing grade. Here is one such evaluation of the current status of the American reader:

The reading textbooks used in the first grade were inappropriate in terms of interest value. They concealed the results of life in America, hiding not only its difficulties and problems, but also much of its excitement and joy. They featured Dick and Jane in the clean, Caucasian, correct suburbs, in houses surrounded by white fences, playing happily with happy peers and happy parents. They contained a dearth of moral content which could have high interest values. They presented a monstrous repetition of pollyanish family activities. They offered no new knowledge. They contradicted the everyday experiences of children in general since most American children seldom, if ever, experience the affect-less situations depicted in the books . . . the stories were so predictable in outcomes that little, if any, of a child's incentive to continue reading was derived from the story content. (Blom, Waite, & Zimet, 1970, p. 433)

Other surveys have unearthed further deficiencies. For example, Klineberg (1963) has pointed out that in addition to distorting the picture of current American society, these texts pay little attention to foreign nationalities. Maybe it is just as well, for when other national groups are depicted it is often in stereotyped terms or in an unfavorable light. It is not surprising that American children are markedly ethnocentric.

Moreover, textbooks carry hidden agendas to the young about sex-role mythologies in our society (Busby 1975). A recent analysis of first-, second-, and third-grade readers revealed evidence of a stereotypic portrayal of male and female roles (Saario, Jacklin, & Tittle, 1973). Boys were portrayed as demonstrating significantly higher amounts of aggression, physical exertion, and problem solving, while girls were often cast as characters engaged in fantasy, carrying out directions, and making statements about themselves. Nor were these rigid sex-role pictures restricted to child story characters. Adult males were portrayed more often as engaging in constructive and productive behaviors, physical activity, and more problem-solving behavior. On the other hand, adult females were presented as conforming and were usually found in home or school settings. Males were found more frequently outdoors or in business. Finally, young male characters significantly more often receive positive outcomes as a result of their *own* actions; girl characters receive positive outcomes, but they are more often because of circumstance. This kind of sex-role stereotyping, in fact, starts very early in children's literature: other studies of picture books for preschoolers reveal a very similar pattern (Weitzman, Eifler, Hokada, & Ross, 1972).

Direct evidence that the children themselves are dissatisfied with their classroom readers comes from a recent comparison of the content of first-grade primers and the library selections made by first graders when they had a free choice (Wiberg & Trost, 1970). The marked discrepancies between the two sets of books underlined the differences between children's reading interests and primer content. Unlike the play and Pollyannaish themes of the primers, the children's library choices emphasized folk tales, lessons from life, nature, and real-life events that had both sad and happy endings. Activities involving boys and older children were more frequent in the library books, as were stories about foreign countries. Moreover, although boys and girls read the same books in the classroom, clear sex differences in book preferences were evident when the children were given a choice. Boys preferred books with boy activity stories and prank and information themes. Girls, on the other hand, showed no preference in terms of the sex appropriateness of the activity, but did choose pet books frequently. These data suggest that if children's interest in reading is to be stimulated, some radical redesigning of primers is necessary. The children themselves can, in fact, point the way to more realistic and relevant texts. Not only do young children know what they want; what they want is probably better for them!

Some Implications of Traditional Readers

What are the implications of these elementary school readers for children's academic progress and for their emotional, social, and cultural development? One would expect that children would be much more involved and motivated if the content of the reading material were relevant to their own background, interests, and experience. It is likely that many children simply "tune out" at a very early age due to the perceived irrelevance of school as reflected in these primers. If this is the case, one would expect differences between reading ability of children exposed to the "Dick and Jane" stories and those taught to read with more sophisticated, realistic, and relevant materials. In fact, children do comprehend more when reading high- than low-interest material (Asher, Hymel, & Wigfield, 1976).

In related work, Asher and Markell (1974) have demonstrated that the reading scores of boys, even more than girls, are affected by the interest value of stories. Fifth graders were given passages to read that were of either high or low interest. When boys had the chance to read stories about astronauts and airplanes, they read much better than when they read low-interest stories. Moreover, the typical difference in reading level between boys and girls was not present when the material was interesting. Girls, on the other hand, tended to be less affected by the interest level of the stories (see Figure 14-6). Although there is no simple solution to the problem of lower reading achievement of boys in elementary school, this study suggests that more attention should be paid to motivational factors. Boys can read better if the material turns them on!

Settings may make a difference as well. When popular paperbacks were introduced into an elementary school library, the student use of the library did not change until the atmosphere also changed. To remove the drab classroom

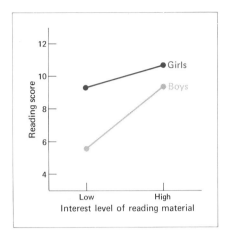

FIGURE 14-6 Reading level of boys and girls with low- and high-interest material. *(From Asher & Markell, 1974.)*

look of the library, one enterprising librarian added a large, shaggy, red carpet to the middle of the library, scattered colorful pillows around and removed most of the tables and chairs. "So many kids flocked in to sprawl on the carpet and read that she eventually had to ration the space" (Mehrabian, 1976, p. 155).

Nontraditional Readers

Do ethnic readers, that more realistically characterize ethnic and racial groups, make any difference to children's reading? Although the issue is far from settled, one early investigator (Whipple, 1963) did find differences in measures of word recognition and oral reading accuracy between children taught with traditional primers and those introduced to reading through a multiethnic reading text. The children using the new text, one which portrayed the diverse ethnic and racial groups in American society, had higher scores on both measures. Probably these effects would be particularly marked for non-Caucasian, non-middle-class children. Is it at all surprising that these children feel alienated from the school system when the system presents such a uniformly consistent but irrelevant and foreign set of values? Even for white middle-class children the misrepresentation of our society promoted in the typical primer has detrimental effects. Readers provide an excellent device for exposing these socially naive children to some of the other racial and ethnic groups that compose American society—a needed lesson in cultural learning. Possibly many of the stereotypes that often underlie current white middle-class prejudices would be eliminated by a more realistic presentation of the current American scene. In one study, the use of multiethnic readers increased the positive attitudes of white children to their black classmates (Litcher & Johnson, 1969).

Fortunately readers are changing, and a number of publishing firms are producing primers that include children of more than one ethnic background as story characters, and that represent boys and girls in less stereotyped fashion. In spite of these trends, many critics (Oliver, 1974) still contend that texts "have not kept pace with a changing society" (Graebner, 1972, p. 52).

A Closing Comment on Texts

Perhaps the most appropriate way to close this section is to offer the following plea that texts not only need to recognize differences in sex and race, but should be generally more aware that:

The real world is more varied than the one depicted in elementary readers. Boys and girls, and men and women, are fat and skinny, short and tall. Boys and men are sometimes gentle, sometimes dreamers. Artists, doctors, lawyers, and college professors are sometimes mothers as well. Rather than limiting possibilities, elementary texts should seek to maximize individual development and self-esteem by displaying a wide range of models and activities. If the average is the only model presented to a child and therefore assumed to be the child's goal, most children—and most adults—would probably be unable to match the model. (Saario, et al., 1973, p. 399)

Special Children, Special Needs?

Mainstreaming

Not all children learn at the same pace or in the same way. Some are slower to learn; others learn faster than their classmates; some are blind or deaf or in a wheelchair. A major issue of the 1970s has been the question of whether or not these "special" children should be placed in separate classes or whether they should be integrated into regular classrooms. In the world of special education, this shift toward including children of all abilities in regular classrooms is known as "mainstreaming" and in the mid-70s this became a law. Supporters of this new legislation cite some powerful arguments but few hard facts. They argue that mainstreaming will result in higher levels of achievement, both academically and socially. Second, they suggest that this move away from special isolated classes to a regular school setting "does a better job than a segregated setting of helping children adjust to and cope with the real world when they grow up." (Brenton, 1974, p. 23). Third, they assume that exposure to a wide range of children will help normal children understand individual differences in people and it will also help to diminish stereotyping of children with various types of handicaps or disabilities (Brenton, 1974). In spite of the legal fact of mainstreaming, there are skeptics.

The physical needs of severely and profoundly retarded children necessitate the employment of additional personnel and the use of specialized architectural arrangements, equipment and facilities which cannot be established in every overcrowded regular classroom. The centralization of these children in regional special classes allows a focus and concentration of therapeutic time and effort. In contrast, the distribution of these children across scattered regular classes would lead to a tremendous waste of theapy time lost in traveling to various schools. The regular classroom teacher serving 20 to 40 children cannot be expected to meet the educational, physical, social and emotional needs of children with severe deficits. . . . A token gesture of integration cannot replace an intensive, carefully planned developmental education program. (Smith & Akrans, 1974, p. 501)

Nor is it just academic progress that may sometimes suffer from mainstreaming. Integration of retarded children may lead to increased social rejection (Gottlieb, 1978) by their nonretarded peers. Elementary school children express less liking for retarded children than nonretarded children, and increased contact through integrated classrooms leads to increased rejection of the retarded (Goodman, Gottlieb, & Harrison, 1972). Other evidence indicates that in a school with no interior walls, retarded children were more rejected than in a school with walls and segregated children (Gottlieb & Budoff, 1973).

As long as people judge others by their abilities, increased contact with those who are relatively less expert may lead to less rather than more acceptance. (Asher, Oden, & Gottman, 1977, p. 42)

Perhaps the most reasonable view is one that encourages flexibility in response to the individual needs of the children in the schools. Hobbs summarizes this view:

In schools that are most responsive to individual differences in abilities, interests, and learning styles of children, the mainstream is actually many streams, sometimes as many streams as there are individual children, sometimes several streams as groups are formed for special purpose, sometimes one stream only as concerns of all converge. We see no advantage in dumping exceptional children into an undifferentiated mainstream; but we see great advantage to all children, exceptional children included, in an educational program modulated to the needs of individual children, singly, in small groups, or all together. Such a flexible arrangement may well result in functional separations of exceptional children from time to time, but the governing principle would apply to all children: school programs should be responsive to the learning requirements of individual children, and groupings should serve this end. (1975, p. 197)

The Gifted

"What number is that which, being divided by the product of its digits, the quotient is 3, and if 18 be added, the digits will be inverted? He flew out of his chair, whirled around rolled up his eyes and said in about a minute, 24. Multiply in your head 365,365,365,365,365,365 by 365,365,365,365,365,365. . . . in not more than one minute said he, 133,491,850,208,566,925,016,658,299, 583,255!" (mid-19th century child prodigy, Barlow, 1952, p. 43).

"I was standing at the front of the room explaining how the earth revolves and how, because of its huge size it is difficult for us to realize that it is actually round. All of a sudden, Spencer blurted out, 'The earth isn't round.' I curtly replied, 'Ha, do you think it's flat?' He matter-of-factly said, 'No, it's a truncated sphere.' I quickly changed the subject. Spencer said the darndest things" (Payne, Kauffman, Brown, & DeMott, 1974, p. 94).

Just as there are special problems in organizing the best type of education for retarded and handicapped children, similar problems exist for the exceptionally talented children. Should these extremely bright children be accelerated and be permitted to begin school early, skip grades, and graduate ahead of their age-mates? These are controversial issues. Some argue that acceleration is necessary to maintain interest and motivation. Critics retort that the accelerated child's intellectual needs may be met at the expense of the child's social and emotional development. Since the accelerated child is with older peers, he or she may be socially isolated. However, this is probably another "myth," since very bright children often seek out the company of older children and of adults. As Terman (1954), one of the earliest leaders in the study of the gifted child, noted, bright children are usually far ahead of their age-mates not just intellectually, but socially and physically as well.

Support for acceleration comes from a new program at Johns Hopkins University, called "Study of Mathematically Precocious Youth." In the program seventh and eighth graders with exceptional talent for mathematics are identified. These children are helped through a variety of special programs to move ahead at an accelerated pace in mathematics. The results have been spectacular.

By the end of the summer of 1976, 144 precollege youths had taken a total of 312 college courses with an overall gradepoint average of 3.57. In 1976, a young man graduated from Johns Hopkins at barely age 17 with a BA in mathematical sciences after only 5 semesters there, one year in senior high school and one year in junior high school. . . . Nor was he narrow in his interests. . . . His list of extracurricular activities is long, including a high school letter in wrestling and a varsity spot for two years on the college golf team. (Stanley, 1976, p. 41)

As the program so dramatically shows, talented children can be accelerated and

This 13-year-old is studying college-level calculus as part of an acceleration program for gifted children. (Editorial Photocolor Archives)

succeed extremely well. One wonders how much talent has been wasted by our reluctance to accelerate precocious pupils in the past.

Stanley makes an eloquent plea for acceleration:

A well-known quotation from Thomas Gray's famous elegy sums up the case for seeking talent and nurturing it:

Full many a gem of purest ray serene,
The dark unfathom'd caves of ocean bear:
Full many a flower is born to blush unseen,
And waste its sweetness on the desert air.

Another poet (Browning) tells us that ". . . a man's reach should exceed his grasp, Or what's a heaven for?"

It is our responsibility and opportunity to help prevent the potential Miltons, Einsteins, and Wieners from coming to the "mute inglorious" ends Gray viewed in that country churchyard long ago. The problem has changed little, but the prospects are much better now. Surely we can greatly extend both the reach and the grasp of our brilliant youths, or what's an educational system for? (Stanley, 1976, p. 41)

Other educational alternatives for gifted children include enrichment programs, which avoid accelerating the child's grade level. These include extra work on the same level of difficulty, but more of it. One critic termed this form of enrichment "busywork" (Stanley, 1976). A second type involves "irrelevant academic enrichment," which consists of setting up a special subject or activity meant to enrich the educational lives of some group of intellectually talented students. For example, a special class in science or social studies might be arranged as a supplement and diversion for the bored high-IQ students. Another form of enrichment is "cultural", which involves supplying aspects of the performing arts such as music, art, drama, dance, and creative writing or offering instruction in foreign language. Critics argue that these opportunities are often unrelated to the area of the child's talent and do not provide full opportunity for the development of these areas of unique talent. Although still controversial, the case for acceleration *versus* enrichment is gaining support.

Social Class, Race, and the School

It has been estimated that the school has a cumulative effect on the lower-class child such that "by the third grade he is approximately one year behind academically, by the sixth grade two years behind, by grade eight two and one half to three years retarded academically and by the ninth grade a top candidate for dropping out" (Rioux, 1968, p. 92). For the middle-class child the picture is very different; rather than dropping out, he is much more likely to go to college than his lower-class peer (DeLury, 1974).

Why the social-class difference? Many answers have been offered. Recall our earlier discussions of the cognitive and linguistic differences between lower- and middle-class children. At that time, it was noted that those differences are present and detectable before the child ever reaches the schoolroom. So it may not be entirely the school's fault; children of lower-class backgrounds are simply not as well prepared to fit into the middle-class culture of the classroom. But it is the aim of education presumably to teach children regardless of their background.

Children of lower-class backgrounds are not the only ones who have special difficulty with the school system. Children of different racial and ethnic backgrounds often fail to achieve their full potential in our schools. In this section, we examine the roles that parent and teacher attitudes and expectations play in the academic performance of children of different racial and ethnic backgrounds. Finally, we will critically evaluate one solution to the problem of poor progress in school among minority group children—desegregation.

The Middle-Class Bias of the School

First of all, the fact that the school is a middle-class institution, espousing middle-class values and staffed by middle-class teachers, puts the child from a lower-class background at a disadvantage from the outset.

The lower class child experiences the middle class oriented school as discontinuous with his home environment and further, comes to it unprepared in the basic skills on which the curriculum is founded. The school becomes a place which makes puzzling demands and where failure is frequent and feelings of competence are subsequently not generated. Motivation decreases and the school loses its effectiveness. . . . (Deutsch, 1964, p. 255)

In contrast, for the middle-class child,

The school is very central and is contiguous with the totality of his life experiences. As a result there are few incongruities between his school experiences and any others he is likely to have had and there are intrinsic motivating and molding properties in the school situation to which he has been sensitized. . . . faculty orientation with his family orientation. (Deutsch, 1964, p. 255)

Simply by virtue of their class membership, middle-class children have an advantage over their lower-class peers.

Parent Attitudes toward the School

Part of the reason for this feeling of discontinuity stems from the different orientation to the school system that middle- and lower-class parents provide their children. There are clear social class differences in the manner that children are introduced to the school. Hess and Shipman (1967) studied this problem by asking black middle- and lower-class mothers to indicate "what she would tell her child on the first day of school before he left the house" (p. 69). It was assumed that the answer to this inquiry would tap the parental attitude toward the school. The lower-class mothers tended to give their children unqualified commands concerning how to behave in school. Little or no rationale for thier

(King Features Syndicate)

directives were provided: "sit down," "don't holler," and "mind the teacher" were typical of the answers. On the other hand, the middle-class mothers tended to use a more cognitive, rational orientation which provided the child with some explanation for the rules that the school would impose on the children's behavior. For example, a middle-class mother might instruct her child: "You shouldn't talk in school because the teacher can't teach so well and you won't learn your lessons properly." Consider the implications of these different orientations for the child in the classroom. The child who is given the imperative orientation is likely to view the school as a rigid authoritarian institution governed by inflexible and unexplained rules and regulations. This attitude may lead to overzealous acceptance of absolute answers and less likelihood of inquiry, curiosity, and debate. The child's interest and involvement would probably be low. In contrast, the child given the rational, cognitive orientation will be more likely to expect that answers should have reasons underlying them. A spirit of inquiry is kindled in the middle-class child which probably delights the teacher and, in turn, aids the child's progress. In fact, if these motivational and attitudinal consequences are true, one would expect performance differences between the two groups. Hess and Shipman found a clear relationship between the mother's orientation and the child's mental performance; the use of an imperative approach was associated with low performance in several areas, including lower IQ scores among children of imperative mothers.

Moreover, the differences are not simply in the initial orientations but also in the amount and quality of home support for academic achievement. A number of studies have indicated that the child's perception of parental support and interest in his or her academic progress is significantly related to the child's actual school performance and the child's attitude toward school (Crandall, 1972). Class differences are clear: there is more likely to be support from middle-class parents than from lower-class parents for scholastic achievement and success (Katz, 1967).

Many lower-class parents are involved and interested in their children's school work. It has been found that when lower-class parents are more knowledgeable about the school system and have higher levels of aspiration for their children, it is associated with the achievement of good grades for their children (Greenberg & Davidson, 1972). Parental involvement can make a difference.

(King Features Syndicate)

Lower-class parents not only are less likely to provide encouragement, but are often less able to help the child in school tasks. Often their own education is limited, and as the child moves to higher grades, the parents are increasingly unable to assist their children or even appreciate the usefulness and relevance of the school's demands. Incidentally, the frustration experienced by many middle-class parents in trying to comprehend the "new math," for example, suggests that this problem is not restricted to lower-class parents. With increasing specialization and curriculum innovation it may be necessary to teach the parents as well.

The Problem of Appropriate Models

There are other problems encountered by lower-class children which tend to lessen their chances for scholastic success. While the middle-class children can adopt their parents as models of scholastic achievement, the lower-class children must look elsewhere. Their parents are simply inappropriate models from which to learn the attitudes and values necessary for school success. The teacher, of course, provides an alternative model, and if the child could identify with and emulate the actions and attitudes of the middle-class teacher, chances of succeeding in the school system would increase. However, as Portuges and Feshbach (1972) found in their study of social class differences in teacher imitation, middle-class white children imitated the teacher more than did the lower-class black children. This is consistent with other evidence that middle-class children are more likely to aspire to the teaching profession than are lower-class children. Whether or not these black students were rejecting the teaching role or merely the *white* teacher is left unanswered. One might expect that more black teachers with whom the disadvantaged black pupils could more readily identify would result in a more positive attitude toward school among black students. If the child does adopt the teacher as the primary model, this may emphasize further the discontinuity between the child's home life and the school.

Social Class and Racial Differences in Teacher Attitudes

How much of the blame should the teacher assume for the failures of the lower-class child? The teacher, of course, has been a favorite target; a number of investigators have blamed the white middle-class teacher's lack of appreciation of the problems of the disadvantaged as a primary cause of the lower-class child's scholastic plight. An angry and outspoken advocate of this view is Clark:

The clash of cultures in the classroom is essentially a class war, a socioeconomic and racial warfare being waged on the battleground of our schools with middle-class and middle-class aspiring teachers provided with a powerful arsenal of half-truths, prejudices and rationalizations arrayed against hopelessly outclassed working class youngsters. (Clark, 1965, p. 129)

Support for the claim that teachers fail to understand and appreciate the differences in background, experience, and values of lower-class children comes from a study by Groff (1963). In his search for the reasons for dissatisfactions in teaching the culturally disadvantaged child, he found that 40 percent of the 294 teachers interviewed cited the "peculiarities" in the personalities of the children as the major cause of dissatisfaction.

There is little doubt that this is due to the middle-class outlook of the teachers. In an investigation by Gottlieb (1964), the attitudes of white middle-class teachers and black teachers with lower-class origins were compared. When asked to indicate the factors that contributed to job dissatisfaction, the white teachers cited "clientele" factors, such as lack of parental interest and student behavior or discipline problems. In contrast, the black teachers tended to see such factors as lack of proper equipment and overcrowded conditions—rather than the students—as their major sources of discontent. Teacher race and background were related to their perceptions of their students as well. When asked to check those adjectives which came closest to describing the outstanding characteristics of their children, white teachers most frequently selected "talkative," "lazy," "fun-loving," "high-strung," and "rebellious" to describe their lower-class pupils. Black teachers, however, saw their pupils in a much more positive light and checked such adjectives as "happy," "cooperative," "fun-loving," "energetic," and "ambitious."

It would appear that the Negro teachers are less critical and less pessimistic in their evaluations of these students than the white teachers, probably because many of them have themselves come from backgrounds similar to that of their students and yet have managed to overcome social barriers and status. (Gottlieb, 1964, p. 353)

It is not just the failure to appreciate differences in customs, values, and background that leads to the lower-class or black child's lack of success. It has been proposed that biases of teachers may lead to these children being assigned lower grades than their middle-class or white peers. The correlation, however, between teachers' grades and a child's scores on standardized achievement tests, over which the teacher had no control, does not differ for black and white children (McCandless, Roberts, & Starnes, 1972). There is little evidence of bias in grading against black students. In fact, if anything, the reverse situation occurs. That is, while achievement scores of white children are higher than black children, their grades are not. Of course this study is not definitive in ruling out bias; it simply shows that it is not evident in grading practices. But discrimination comes in many forms. The finding that the black and white children's grades are similar in spite of achievement differences may suggest another kind of bias, unrealistic feedback. Do black children receive clear and realistic information

The physical environment of the classroom can often affect children's attitudes toward their school experience. (Burk Uzzle, Magnum)

about their performance, or do teachers give the black children good grades in spite of their performance? If so, this could seriously interfere with the children's progress toward mastering school tasks.

A recent large study in urban high schools by Massey, Scott, and Dornbusch (1975) is relevant. Black and Spanish-surname students, in comparison with Asian and "other white" groups, received lower grades and scored lower on math and verbal achievement tests, but these low-achieving black and Spanish students maintained generally *positive* conceptions of their skills in these academic subjects. What accounts for this discrepancy between academic self-concept and their actual performance? Half of these low-achieving black and Chicano students believed that they would not usually receive poor grades for inadequate work or low effort. Moreover, the low achievers, even more than their higher-achieving white or Asian classmates, viewed their teachers as warm, friendly, and dispensing more frequent praise. The authors summarize the implications of their findings as follows:

The academic standards and evaluation system found in the schools did affect the students' assessment of their effort and achievement. Low achievers, especially black students, were allowed to delude themselves into thinking they were doing well. . . . (Massey, Scott, & Dornbusch, 1975)

This is a pattern of institutional racism that perpetuates inequality. The aim of evaluation is to provide children, regardless of their social class or race, with accurate feedback, so that they can, in turn, set realistic goals. All children can achieve, but only by providing guides concerning their strengths and weaknesses can they reach their full potential.

Implications for the Lower-Class Child

What are the implications of middle class teachers' frequent failure to understand the lower-class child? Often resentment, dissatisfaction, and a sense of bewilderment characterize the middle-class teacher in ghetto schools. Attempts to teach are often abandoned in favor of primitive control tactics. In fact, Deutsch (1960) has estimated that lower-class children receive one-third less actual teaching than their middle-class peers. The teacher spends almost 80 percent of the school day disciplining students or engaging in noneducational duties, such as collecting milk money. The teacher then becomes redefined as a disciplinarian, and since the teacher spends less time in educating students, they learn less, become increasingly bored, and become even more disruptive. The result is a vicious circle: a tougher control policy and even less teaching. To the teacher in this situation:

School is not an enthusiastic learning center where everybody is academically alert, where people desire to learn something now because it is worth knowing. Instead it is a place where a major part of the teachers' time must be devoted to maintaining discipline among children who never before have known it. Thus, it is often felt that years of excellent preparation go for naught. (Cheyney, 1966, p. 79)

The upshot is that many teachers tend to regard being assigned to teach in lower-class schools not as a challenge but simply as a less desirable, less prestigious placement. For many it is merely a necessary first step to a "better" job; the aim is not to learn to adjust to the situation but to apply for transfers as soon as the system's regulations permit. This may contribute to the fact that one out of every two children from the bottom rung in society will drop out before completing high school (Cervantes, 1965).

Clearly any program aimed at improving the academic progress of lower-class children should not be restricted to content and curriculum innovations. Drastic alterations in teacher preparation and teacher attitudes are necessary. This education should include an extensive exposure to lower-class life and lower-class values. Once teachers decide that lower-class pupils can learn, maybe they will learn. One lesson that Head Start has taught us is that children of all backgrounds can learn. Next we turn to the final topic: desegregation, and examine whether this is a route to achievement of educational equality.

School Desegregation

Few topics have generated as much public concern in the last two decades as the desegregation of American schools. In 1954, the United States Supreme Court mandated an end to segregated education in a classic case entitled *Brown v. Board of Education.* Here is part of that landmark decision:

Does segregation of children in public schools solely on the basis of race, even though the physical facilities and other "tangible" factors may be equal, deprive the children of the minority group of equal educational opportunities? We believe that it does. . . . To separate them from others of similar age and qualifications solely because of their race generates a feeling of inferiority as to their status in the community that may affect their hearts and minds in a way unlikely ever to be undone. . . . We conclude that in the field of public education the doctrine "separate but equal" has no place. Separate educational facilities are inherently unequal. (*Brown v. Board of Education*)

Desegregation was expected to correct these ills, and recently there has been an evaluation of how successful desegregation efforts have been in achieving these goals. Here are the main expectations that emerged from the 1954 decision:

1 For whites, desegregation will lead to more positive attitudes toward blacks.

2 For blacks, desegregation will lead to more positive attitudes toward whites.

3 For blacks, desegregation will lead to increases in self-esteem.

4 For blacks, desegregation will lead to increases in achievement. (Stephan, 1978, p. 221)

How accurate were these early predictions?

First, are whites and blacks less prejudiced toward each other after going to school together? The evidence is mixed. Some studies (Singer, 1967) find that black and white children in *naturally* integrated schools are more accepting of each other than in segregated schools. Other investigations indicate that blacks and whites had more negative attitudes toward the other group in integrated schools—particularly if integration is forced rather than voluntary (St. John, 1975). The manner in which integration is reached makes a difference as well. Linney (1978) compared black children who were bused to achieve desegregation with those black children who remained in the same school and achieved integration by the addition of white students to their school. After desegregation, the black children who were bused were rated as more aggressive and less prosocial by both their new peers and teachers, while the nonbused black children were not viewed differently following integration. Modifying racial attitudes is complex, and merely placing black and white children in the same school does not mean that they will necessarily interact with each other. In their extensive four-year longitudinal study of the effects of desegregation in Riverside, California, Gerard and Miller (1975) conclude that the "data we have examined point unmistakably to the conclusion that with the exception of playground interaction, little or no real integration occurred during the relatively long-term contact situation represented by Riverside's desegregation program. If anything we found some evidence that ethnic cleavages became somewhat more pronounced over time" (p. 243). In recent years the rise of ethnic pride has meant that spontaneous cross-race mixing is less likely, and integration may foster this type of in-group orientation. To illustrate, black children in one city who were bused to achieve integration increased in black separatist ideology more than did nontransferred siblings (Armor, 1972).

How is self-esteem affected? Again, the findings are mixed and inconclusive. Some report increased self-esteem among black students, while others report either no effect or decreases in self-esteem, especially in academic self-concept (St. John, 1975). One difficulty with this area is the underlying assumption that the black child has low self-esteem and that desegregation will improve the black child's self-image. However, the assumption of the black child's low self-image has been challenged by several studies (Rosenberg & Simons, 1972; Soares & Soares, 1969), which have shown that black children's self-image is at least as positive as that of white students. Even when a gain in self-esteem is clear, the factors which account for this change are uncertain. Possibly such changes are "a by-product of improved achievement, increased attention by faculty to black educational needs, a greater sense of black unity, or still other factors" (Evans & McCandless, 1978, p. 485).

There is more support for the final prediction concerning increases in the achievement of black students in integrated schools. In only 3 percent of the studies does desegregation lead to a decrease in achievement, while in 29 percent of the studies, an increase occurs (Stephan, 1978). This means that in 68 percent of the studies, the achievement of black children was unaffected by integration. Moreover, even when there are changes, not all academic areas are equally affected: Increases in mathematical skills are reported more often than gains in verbal or reading skills (St. John, 1975; Weinberg, 1975). The most consistent effects concern the age of the child at the time of integration. In general the earlier the desegregation occurs, the more beneficial it is for students in terms of achievement-test performance. In one careful study, groups of black city children in kindergarten through the fifth grade were randomly chosen to be bused to suburban white schools (Mahan & Mahan, 1970). After two years the children transferred in kindergarten through the third grade gained significantly more than the nontransferred students on both intelligence and achievement measures. For those transferred in the fourth and fifth grades the gains favor the nontransferred control group on both measures. In spite of modest gains, the achievement gap between black and white children remains after integration (Gerard & Miller, 1975; Linney, 1978; St. John, 1975).

Finally, black children may sometimes pay a hidden price for shifting to integrated schools. These children may suffer a loss of academic status as a result of losing their place at the top of the class, in terms of performance, by being shifted to a class where white children more often occupy the top achievement slots (Linney, 1978). Combined with the fact that black children who are transferred to white schools are often less well accepted by their new peers and teachers has led one investigator to argue that "desegregation may be more detrimental to their academic and psychological development than the segregated situation" (Linney, 1978, p. 163).

Unraveling the complexities of desegregation is far from finished. Understanding desegregation will require investigation of a multitude of factors including busing, voluntary and mandatory integration, attitudes and values of teachers and families, and ethnic ratios. By considering these issues we may

In the integrated school, learning activities in the classroom may become the basis for discussion and socialization in the school cafeteria. (Photo (a) Larry Smith, Black Star; Photo (b) Bruce Roberts, Rapho/Photo Researchers, Inc.)

begin to ask not whether desegregation works, but under what conditions can it work.

Summary

The school is an extremely influential, although often neglected, socializing force. In this chapter several factors that affect the kind and extent of the school's influence were examined. First, the physical structure of the school environment came under scrutiny. School size, for example, determines the extent of involvement in extracurricular activities; children at small high schools are not only more likely to participate but also more likely to occupy positions of prestige and importance. One result is that there are few potential dropouts in small schools. Next, the impact of the size, shape, and seating arrangements of the classroom was examined. Both class size and the pupil's location in the class determine the extent to which he or she participates in classroom activities. While participation is higher in smaller classrooms, the child located in the front and center of the class, the action zone, participates more than children seated in other parts of the room.

In examining the effects of different classroom organizations it was found that students generally prefer a group-centered or open classroom in which they are allowed some opportunity to participate in the decision making. While conventional achievement does not appear to be affected, imaginative play and novelty of answers increase. However, this is still an unresolved issue, and in the final analysis, any conclusion about the advantages of a traditional, authoritarian regime over more pupil-oriented arrangements must take into account the kind of pupils involved. Different personalities apparently function better under different types of classroom organizational arrangements.

Teachers play a variety of roles, namely evaluators, disciplinarians, and models. Teachers' early impressions and expectations concerning a pupil's probable success can affect the child's academic progress. A self-fulfilling prophecy is evident: children succeed when teachers believe they will do well, while pupils are likely to perform poorly when instructors expect them to fail. The types of evaluation conditions that teachers arrange can affect student performance, and anxious children may improve their performance under optimal test-taking conditions.

Recent applications of behavior modification techniques for controlling children's classroom behavior were examined and found to be successful. This is particularly true when these programs have used material or token reinforcers for shaping appropriate behavior. Caution in the use of external rewards is necessary, since children's intrinsic interest in school activities, under some conditions, may be undermined by external reinforcers.

Finally, the teacher may influence students by serving as a social model. Evidence was presented indicating that a rewarding teacher tends to be imitated more than a negative instructor tends to be. Again, the sex and social class of the child observers must be considered. Middle-class girls, for example, tend to imitate a teacher-model to the greatest extent, while lower-class boys are influenced relatively little by a teacher-model. The impact of the teacher as model is not restricted to reinforcing style; the typical problem-solving style of the teacher is often imitated by students as well.

One promising technique in classroom organizations is the peer-teacher approach, where older children are cast in the role of assistant teachers and given responsibility for teaching younger peers. Evaluations indicate that both the tutor and the child who is assisted benefit from this arrangement.

After this discussion of teachers and their tactics, primary school textbooks were examined. Texts are important vehicles for learning and reinforcing attitudes and social values. Unfortunately, most current primers are grossly inadequate; rather than presenting a realistic picture of American culture, the typical text offers a Pollyannaish substitute. This is not merely an adult evaluation: children's library choices indicate that children themselves prefer very different kinds of books than those usually available as primary readers. Tentative evidence indicated that children provided with more reality-oriented interesting readers scored higher on a variety of reading and language measures. Although texts are changing, many of the white, middle-class, suburban biases still persist in more recent "new look" primers.

Special children, such as the retarded, often require special treatment. The controversy over mainstreaming, which involves placing children of varying abilities in regular classrooms rather than segregating low-ability children in special classes, was discussed. Next, another special group, gifted children, was considered, and recent evidence favoring academic acceleration was presented.

The impact of the schools on the academic progress of the lower-class child was examined. A number of factors militate against the success of the lower-class child. In this chapter, some of the reasons underlying the school's inability to effectively educate lower-class children were presented. The incongruity between the attitudes and motivations of the lower-class child and the middle-class school was seen as an important factor. The school is a strange and often hostile environment for lower-class children. Even if they do succeed, they are unlikely to receive either parental support or peer acceptance for their accomplishments. Some have blamed the teachers for their failure to appreciate the differences in background, experience, and values of the disadvantaged pupil. In fact, comparisons of middle-class white and lower-class black instructors suggests that this charge has validity; teachers from lower-class origins were more accepting and less pessimistic in their evaluations of their lower-class charges than were middle-class teachers. Clearly, any program aimed at solving the problems of the lower-class child's chronic academic failure must include alterations in teacher preparation. Curriculum and content changes are not enough; teacher attitudes toward children must change as well.

Desegregation was the final topic. Evidence indicates that desegregation does not affect prejudice or self-esteem, but may raise black achievement. In general, the effects of desegregation are not yet fully understood.

References

Adams, R. S., & Biddle, B. J. *Realities of teaching.* New York: Holt, 1970.

Allen, V. L. (Ed.). *Children as teachers: Theory and research on tutoring.* New York: Academic, 1976.

Allen, V. L., & Feldman, R. S. Learning through tutoring: Low achieving children as tutors. *Journal of Educational Psychology*, 1973, **42,** 1–5.

Armor, D. J. The evidence on busing. *Public Interest*, 1972, **28,** 90–126.

Asher, S. R., Hymel, S., & Wigfield, A. Children's comprehension of high and low interest material and a comparison of two scoring methods (Tech. Report No. 17). Urbana, Ill.: Center for the Study of Reading, University of Illinois, 1976.

Asher, S., & Markell, R. A. Sex differences in comprehension of high and low interest reading material. *Journal of Educational Psychology*, 1974, **66,** 680–687.

Asher, S. R., Oden, S. L., & Gottman, J. M. Children's friendships in school settings. In L. G. Katz (Ed.), *Current topics in early childhood education* (Vol. 1). Norwood, N.J.: Ablex, 1977.

Bane, M. J. *Here to stay: American families in the twentieth century.* New York: Basic Books, 1976.

Barker, R. G., & Gump, P. V. *Big school, small school*, Stanford, Calif.: Stanford University Press, 1964.

Bates, J. E. Effects of a child's imitation versus non-imitation on adults verbal and nonverbal positivity. *Journal of Personality and Social Psychology*, 1975, **31,** 840–851.

Barlow, F. *Mental prodigies.* New York: Greenwood, 1952.

Barrish, H. H., Saunders, M., & Wolf, M. M. Good behavior game: Effects of individual contingencies for group consequences on disruptive behavior in a classroom. *Journal of Applied Behavior Analysis*, 1969, **2,** 119–124.

Beez, W. V. Influence of biased psychological reports on teacher behavior and pupil performance. *Proceedings of the 76th Annual Convention of the American Psychological Association*, 1968, **4,** 605–606.

Berberich, J. P. Do the child's responses shape the teaching of an adult? *Journal of Experimental Research in Personality*, 1971, **5,** 92–97.

Blom, G. E., Waite, R. R., & Zimet, S. G. A motivational content analysis of children's primers. In P. H. Mussen, J. J. Conger, & J. Kagan (Eds.), *Readings in child development and personality.* New York: Harper & Row, 1970.

Brenton, M. Mainstreaming the handicapped. *Today's Education*, 1974, **63,** 20–25.

Bronfenbrenner, U. *Two worlds of childhood: U.S. & U.S.S.R.* New York: Russell Sage, 1970.

Bronfenbrenner, U., Devereux, E. C., Jr., Suci, G. J., & Rodgers, R. R. Adults and peers as sources of conformity and autonomy. Unpublished study, Cornell University, Dept. of Child Development and Family Relations, 1965.

Brophy, J. E., & Good, T. L. Teachers' communication of differential expectations for children's classroom performance: Some behavioral data. *Journal of Educational Psychology*, 1970, **61,** 365–374.

Burham, J. R., & Hartsough, D. M. Effects of experimenter's expectancies on children's ability to learn to swim. Paper presented at the meeting of the Midwestern Psychological Association, Chicago, May 1968.

Busby, L. J. Sex role research on the mass media. *Journal of Communication*, 1975, **25,** 107–131.

Cantor, N. L. & Gelfand, D. M. Effects of responsiveness and sex of children on adults' behavior. *Child Development*, 1977, **48,** 232–238.

Cervantes, L. F. Family background, primary relationships and the high school dropout. *Journal of Marriage and the Family*, 1965, **5,** 218–223.

Cheyney, A. B. Teachers of the culturally disadvantaged. *Exceptional Children*, 1966, **33,** 83–88.

Clark, K. B. *Dark ghetto: Dilemmas of social power.* New York: Harper & Row, 1965.

Cloward, R. D. Studies in tutoring, *Journal of Experimental Education*, 1967, **36,** 14–25.

Cole, M., Gay, J., Glick, J., & Sharp, D. *The cultural context of learning and thinking.* New York: Basic Books, 1971.

Covington, M. B., & Berry, R. G. *Self-worth and school learning.* New York: Holt, 1976.

Crandall, V. C. The Fels study: Some contributions to personality development and achievement in childhood and adulthood. *Seminars in Psychiatry*, 1972, **4,** 383–397.

Dawe, H. C. The influence of size of kindergarten group upon performance. *Child Development*, 1934, **5**, 295–303.

Deering, M. Youth tutoring youth. *Supervisor's Manual.* National Commission on Resources for Youth, Inc. New York, 1968.

DeLury, G. E. *World almanac.* Garden City, N.Y.: Doubleday, 1974.

Deutsch, M. Minority group and class status as related to social and personality factors in scholastic achievement. *Monographs of the Society for Applied Anthropology, 1960,* **2.**

Deutsch, M. Facilitating development in the preschool child: Social and psychological perspectives. *Merrill-Palmer Quarterly*, 1964, **10,** *249–263.*

Elashoff, J. D., & Snow, R. E. *Pygmalion reconsidered.* Worthington, Ohio: Charles A. Jones, 1971.

Evans, E. D., & McCandless, B. R. *Children and youth: Psychosocial development.* New York: Holt, 1978.

Featherstone, J. Open schools—the British and U.S. *The New Republic*, Sept. 11, 1971, 20–25.

Feingold, B. D. & Mahoney, M. J. Reinforcement effects on intrinsic interest: Undermining the overjustification hypothesis. *Behavior Therapy*, 1975, **6,** 367–377.

Gerard, H. B. & Miller, N. *School desegregation: A long-term study.* New York: Plenum Press, 1975.

Glick, J. Cognitive development in cross-cultural perspective. In F. D. Horowitz (Ed.), *Review of child development research* (Vol. 4). Chicago: University of Chicago Press, 1975.

Goodman, H., Gottlieb, J., & Harrison, R. H. Social acceptance of EMRs integrated into a nongraded elementary school. *American Journal of Mental Deficiency*, 1972, **76,** 412–417.

Gottlieb, D. Teaching and students: The views of Negro and white teachers. *Socioloy of Education*, 1966, **37,** 345–353.

Gottlieb, J. Observing social adaptation in schools. In G. P. Sackett (Ed.), *Observing behavior* (Vol. I). Baltimore: University Park Press, 1978.

Gottlieb, J., & Budoff, M. Social acceptability of retarded children in nongraded schools differing in architecture. *American Journal of Mental Deficiency*, 1973, **78,** 15–19.

Graebner, D. B. A decade of sexism in readers. *The Reading Teacher*, 1972 (October), **26.**

Gray, F. Graubard, P. S. Rosenberg, H. Little brother is changing you. *Psychology Today*, 1974, March, 42–46.

Greenberg, J. W., & Davidson, H. H. Home background and school achievement in black urban ghetto children. *American Journal of Orthopsychiatry*, 1972, **42,** 803–810.

Grimes, J. W., & Allinsmith, W. Compulsivity, anxiety, and school achievement. *Merrill-Palmer Quarterly*, 1961, **7,** 247–269.

Groff, P. J. Dissatisfactions in teaching the culturally deprived child. *Phi Delta Kappan*, 1963, **45,** 76.

Groobman, D. E., Forward, J. R., & Peterson, C. Attitudes, self-esteem and learning in formal and informal schools. *Journal of Educational Psychology*, 1976, **68,** 32–35.

Gump, P. V., & Ross, R. The fit of milieu and programme in school environments. In H. McGurk (Ed.), *Ecological factors in human development.* New York: North-Holland, 1977.

Harvey, O. J., Prather, M., White, B. J., & Hoffmeister, J. K. Teachers' beliefs, classroom atmosphere and student behavior. *American Educational Research Journal*, 1968, **5,** 151–166.

Hess, R., & Shipman, V. Cognitive elements in maternal behavior. In J. Hill (Ed.),

Minnesota Symposium on Child Psychology. Minneapolis: University of Minnesota Press, 1967, pp. 57–81.

Hetherington, E. M., & Morris, W. N. The family and primary groups. In W. H. Holtzman (Ed.), *Introductory psychology in depth: Developmental topics.* New York: Harper & Row, 1978.

Hill, K. T. Anxiety in an evaluative context. In W. W. Hartup (Ed.), *The young child* (Vol. 2). Washington, D.C.: National Association for the Education of Young Children, 1972.

Hill, K. T. Evaluative feedback in a broader perspective. Paper presented at the annual meeting of the American Educational Research Association, Toronto, March 1978.

Hill, K. T., & Eaton, W. O. The interaction of test anxiety and success-failure experiences in determining children's arithmetic performance. *Developmental Psychology*, 1977, **13,** 205–211.

Hobbs, N. *The futures of children.* San Francisco: Jossey-Bass, 1975.

Huston-Stein, A., Freidrich-Cofer, L., & Susman, E. J. The relation of classroom structure to social behavior, imaginative play and self-regulation of economically disadvantaged children. *Child Development*, 1977, **48,** 908–916.

Jensen, A. R. Review of Pygmalion in the classroom. *American Scientist*, 1969, **51,** 44A–45A.

Katz, I. The socialization of academic motivation in minority group children. *Nebraska Symposium on Motivation*, 1967, **15,** 133–191.

Klineberg, O. Life is fun in a smiling, fair skinned world. *Saturday Review*, 1963, **87,** 75–77.

Krantz, P. J., & Risley, T. R. Behavioral ecology in the classroom. In K. D. O'Leary & S. G. O'Leary (Eds.), *Classroom management.* New York: Pergamon, 1977.

Kuppel, H. Student tutors for floundering classmates. *School Activities*, 1964, **35,** 255–256.

Lepper, M., Greene, D., & Nisbett, R. Test of the "overjustification hypothesis." *Journal of Personality and Social Psychology*, 1973, **28,** 129–137.

Levinger, G., & Gunner, J. The interpersonal grid: Felt and tape techniques for the measurements of social relationships. *Psychonomic Science,*1967, **8,** 113–174.

Lewin, L., Lippitt, R., & White, R. K. Patterns of aggressive behavior in experimentally created "social climates." *Journal of Social Psychology*, 1939, **10,** 271–299.

Linney, J. A. A multivariable, multilevel analysis of a midwestern city: court ordered desegregation. Unpublished doctoral dissertation. University of Illinois, Champaign-Urbana, 1978.

Lippitt, P., & Lippitt, R. Cross-age helpers. *National Education Association*, March 1968, 1–6.

Litcher, J., & Johnson, D. Changes in attitudes toward negroes of white elementary students after use of multi-ethnic readers. *Journal of Educational Psychology*, 1969, **60,** 148–152.

Mahan, A. M. & Mahan, T. W. Changes in cognitive style: An analysis of the impact of white suburban schools on inner city children. *Integrated Education*, 1970, **8,** 58–61.

Massey, G. C., Scott, M. V., & Dornbusch, S. M. Racism without racists: Institutional racism in urban schools. *The Black Scholar*, 1975, **7,** 2–11.

McCandless, B. R., Roberts, A., & Starnes, T. Teachers' marks, achievement test scores and aptitude relations with respect to social class, race and sex. *Journal of Educational Psychology*, 1972, **63,** 153–159.

McGee, C. S., Kauffman, J. M., & Nussen, J. Children as therapeutic change agents: Reinforcement intervention paradigms. Unpublished manuscript, University of Virginia, 1977.

Mehrabian, A. *Public places and private spaces.* New York: Basic Books, 1976.

Montessori, M. *Spontaneous activity in education.* Cambridge, Mass.: Robert Bentley, 1964.

O'Leary, K. D., Becker, W. C., Evans, M. B., & Saudargas, R. A. A token reinforcement program in a public school: A replication and systematic analysis. *Journal of Applied Behavior Analysis,* 1969, **2,** 3–13.

O'Leary, K. D., & O'Leary, S. G. (Eds.). *Classroom management.* New York: Pergamon, 1977.

Oliver, L. Women in aprons: The female stereotype in children's readers. *Elementary School Journal,* 1974, **74,** 253–259.

Papalia, D., & Olds, S. *A child's world.* New York: McGraw-Hill, 1975.

Payne, J. S., Kauffman, J. M., Brown, G. B., & DeMott, R. M. *Exceptional children in focus.* Columbus: Merrill, 1974.

Portuges, S. H., & Feshbach, N. D. The influence of sex and social class upon imitation of teachers by elementary school children. *Child Development,* 1972, **43,** 981–989.

Rioux, J. W. The disadvantaged child in school. In J. Helmuth (Ed.), *The disadvantaged child.* New York: Brunner/Mazel, 1968.

Rosenberg, M. & Simmons, R. G. *Black and white self-esteem: The urban school child.* Washington: American Sociological Association, 1972.

Rosenthal, R. The pygmalion effect lives. *Psychology Today,* September 1973, 46–63.

Rosenthal, R., & Jacobsen, L. Teachers' expectancies: Determinants of pupils' IQ gains. *Psychological Reports,* 1966, **19,** 115–118.

Rosenthal, R., & Jacobsen, L. *Pygmalion in the classroom.* New York: Holt, 1968.

Rubovitz, P. C., & Maehr, M. L. Pygmalion black and white. *Journal of Personality and Social Psychology,* 1973, **25,** 210–218.

Saario, T. N., Jacklin, C. N., & Tittle, C. K. Sex role stereotyping in the public schools. *Harvard Educational Review,* 1973, **43,** 386–416.

Sagotsky, G., Patterson, C. J., & Lepper, M. R. Training children's self-control: A field experiment. Unpublished manuscript, Stanford University, 1977.

Sanders, D. C. Innovations in elementary school classroom seating. *Bureau of Laboratory Schools Publication No. 10.* Austin: University of Texas, 1958.

Schmidt, G. W., & Ulrich, R. E. Effects of group contingent events upon classroom noise. *Journal of Applied Behavior Analysis,* 1969, **2,** 171–179.

Sheehan, L., Feldman, R. S., & Allen, V. L. Research on children tutoring children: A critical review. *Review of Educational Research,* 1976, **46,** 355–385.

Sherif, M., & Sherif, C. W. *Groups in harmony and tension. An integration of studies on intergroup relations.* New York: Harper & Row, 2953.

Singer, D. Reading, writing and race relations. *Trans-Action,* 1967, **4**(7), 27–31.

Smith, J. O., & Akrans, J. R. Now more than ever: A case for the special class. *Exceptional Children,* 1974, **40,** 497–502.

Soares, A. T. & Soares, L. M. Self perceptions of culturally disadvantaged children. *American Educational Research Journal,* 1969, **6,** 31–45.

Sommer, R. *Personal space. Englewood Cliffs, N.J.: Prentice-Hall, 1969.*

Stanley, J. C. Concern for intellectually talented youths: How it originated and fluctuated. *Journal of Clinical Child Psychology,* 1976, **5,** 38–42.

Stephan, W. G. School desegregation: An evaluation of predictions made in *Brown v. Board of Education. Psychological Bulletin,* 1978, **85,** 217–238.

St. John, N. H. *School desegregation.* New York: Wiley, 1975.

Terman, L. M. The discovery and encouragement of exceptional talent. *American Psychologist,* 1954, **9,** 221–230.

Thorndike, R. L. Review of R. Rosenthal and L. Jacobsen, "Pygmalion in the classroom." *American Educational Research Journal,* 1968, **5,** 708–711.

Tuana, S. Unpublished research. In R. Sommer, *Personal space*. Englewood Cliffs, N.J.: Prentice-Hall, 1969, p. 118.

Walberg, H. J., & Rasher, S. P. The ways schooling makes a difference. *Phi Delta Kappa*, 1977, **58,** 703–707.

Weinberg, M. The relationship between school desegregation and academic achievement: A review of the research. *Law and Contemporary Problems*, 1975, **39,** 241–270.

Weitzman, L., Eifler, D., Hokada, E., & Ross, C. Sex-role socialization. *American Journal of Sociology*, 1972, **77,** 1125–1150.

Whipple, G. *Appraisal of the city schools reading program*. Detroit: Detroit Public Schools Division for Improvement of Instruction, Language Education Department, 1963.

Wiberg, J. L., & Trost, M. A comparison between the content of first grade primers and free choice library selections made by first grade students. *Elementary English*, 1970, **47,** 792–798.

Williams, J. P., & Hill, K. T. Performance on achievement test problems as a function of optimizing test presentation instructions and test anxiety. Unpublished manuscript, University of Illinois, Urbana-Champaign, 1976.

Yando, R. M., & Kagan, J. The effect of teacher tempo on the child. *Child Development*, 1968, **39,** 27–34.

15

The Development
of Sex Roles
and Sex
Differences

Sex-role typing is the process by which children acquire the values, motives, and behaviors viewed as appropriate to either males or females in a specific culture. Systematic attempts to communicate sex-role standards and to shape different behaviors in boys and girls begin in earliest infancy and have been described as follows:

Sex-role differentiation usually commences immediately after birth, when the baby is named and both the infant and the nursery are given the blue or pink treatment depending upon the sex of the child. Thereafter, indoctrination into masculinity and femininity is diligently promulgated by adorning children with distinctive clothes and hair styles, selecting sex-appropriate play materials and recreational activities, promoting associations with same-sex playmates, and through non-permissive parental reactions to deviant sex-role behavior. (Bandura, 1969, p. 215).

One investigator who was studying sex differences in infancy and did not want her observers to know whether they were watching boys or girls complained that even in the first few days of life some infant girls were brought to the laboratory with pink bows tied to their wisps of hair or taped to their little bald heads. Later when another attempt at concealment of sex was made by asking mothers to dress their infants in overalls, girls appeared in pink and boys in blue overalls, and as the frustrated experimenter said, "Would you believe overalls with ruffles?"

Sex-Role Standards

Considerable consistency in standards of appropriate sex-role behavior exists within and between cultures. In this chapter when we talk about sex-appropriate behavior or masculine or feminine behaviors, we will be talking about behavior viewed as more characteristic of males or females in our culture. The term "appropriate" is in no way meant to imply desirable. The male role is oriented toward controlling and manipulating the environment. Males are expected to be independent, assertive, dominant, and competitive in social and sexual relations. Females are expected to be more passive, loving, sensitive, and supportive in social relationships, especially in their family role as a wife and mother. Expression of warmth in personal relationships, anxiety under duress, and suppression of overt aggression and sexuality are regarded as more appropriate for women than men (Bennett & Cohen, 1959; Parsons, 1955). Although this may appear to be a rather outdated presentation of sex-role standards, studies have indicated that affection, nurturance, and passivity still are viewed as more characteristic of females and aggression, independence, competence, and dominance as characteristic of males by the majority of both elementary school children (Hartley, 1960) and adults (Hetherington, 1974; Jenkins & Vroegh, 1969; Broverman, Vogel, Broverman, Clarkson, & Rosenkrantz, 1972). Cross-cultural studies also find these stereotyped roles widespread not only in the American culture but in the majority of societies (Barry, Bacon, & Child, 1957; D'Andrade, 1966; Best, Williams, Cloud, Davis, Robertson, Edwards, Giles, & Fowles, 1977).

There is, however, some variation in culturally accepted sex-role standards. In the United States female students and college-educated women between the ages of 18 and 35 are more likely to perceive the feminine role as involving greater independence and achievement striving than do older or less educated females. Children with mothers who are employed in skilled occupations and professions also regard female educational and professional aspirations and the assumption of housekeeping and child-care tasks by males as more appropriate than do children whose mothers are unemployed. However, men, even young educated men, maintain more stereotyped sex-role standards than do women

(Hetherington, 1974). Although adults regard sex-role standards in preschool children as less clearly delineated than those in older children, more men than women rate the behaviors of toddlers as young as 18 months as sex-typed (Fagot, 1973). This clearer differentiation of sex roles by men is probably related to the frequently reported finding that fathers are more concerned than mothers about their children maintaining sexually appropriate behaviors, and that the father plays a more important role in the sex-role typing of children than does the mother. It is interesting that in spite of some variations in sex-role standards among groups in the United States, almost all groups regardless of sex, social class, and education still view aggression as more characteristic of men and interpersonal sensitivity as more frequent in women (Hetherington, 1974).

One of the most frequently cited reports of divergence among cultures in sex-role standards and behavior is Margaret Mead's study of social roles in three primitive tribes: the Arapesh, the Mundugumor, and the Tchambuli (Mead, 1935). Little sex-role differentiation was prescribed by the Mundugumor and the Arapesh. However, the Arapesh exhibited behaviors which in many societies would be regarded as feminine and the Mundugumor those traditionally thought of as masculine. The Arapesh were passive, cooperative, and unassertive, whereas both men and women in the Mundugumor tribe were hostile, aggressive, cruel, and restrictive. Both Arapesh mothers and fathers were actively involved in raising infants. In fact, Mead remarks, "If one comments upon a middle-aged Arapesh man as good-looking, the people answer: Good looking? Ye-e-e-s? But you should have seen him before he bore all those children" (Mead, 1935, p. 56).

In the Tchambuli a reversal of Parsons' traditional sex roles was found. The men were socially sensitive and concerned with the feelings of others, dependent, and interested in arts and crafts. The women were independent and aggressive and played the controlling role in decision making. Thus although the "traditional" sex roles are most common, there is enough variability within and across cultures to indicate that there is a great deal of plasticity in the development of masculine and feminine behaviors. If there are constitutionally based social and cognitive differences between males and females, they can be considerably modified by cultural forces.

Sex Differences in Development

How accurately do sex-role stereotypes reflect differences in the actual behaviors of males and females? Table 15-1 presents some characteristics on which sex differences have been found, some which are commonly assumed but are not true, and some attributes where evidence for sex differences is equivocal. That is, there are suggestive findings, but more research needs to be done before definite conclusions can be drawn. In examining this table and in our discussion of sex differences, it should be kept in mind that there is considerable overlap in the characteristics of males and females. Some males are more compliant, verbal, and interested in the arts than are some females.

TABLE 15-1   ACTUAL, MYTHICAL, AND EQUIVOCAL SEX DIFFERENCES

Actual Sex Differences

Physical, motor, and sensory	Girls are physically and neurologically more advanced at birth, and earlier in walking and attaining puberty. Boys have more mature muscular development, larger lungs and heart, and lower sensitivity to pain at birth. With increasing age boys become superior at activities involving strength and gross motor skills. Boys are miscarried more, have a higher rate of infant mortality, and are more vulnerable to disease, malnutrition, and many hereditary anomalies. Females are definitely not the weaker sex in terms of physical vulnerability.
Cognitive	Even in infancy girls are superior in verbal abilities, and this superiority increases markedly in the high school years. This includes vocabulary, reading comprehension, and verbal creativity. From about age 10 boys excel in visual-spatial ability, which is involved in such tasks as manipulating objects in two- or three-dimensional space, reading maps, or aiming at a target. Boys excel in mathematics beginning at about age 12. Almost all children labeled as exceptionally talented in mathematics by the junior high school level are male.
Social and emotional development	Boys are more often the aggressors and the victims of aggression, particularly of physical aggression, even in early social play. Girls are more compliant to the demands of parents and other adults as early as 2 years of age. Boys are more variable in their responses to adult directions. Sex differences in compliance are not consistently found in peer relations, although preschool boys are less compliant to the demands of girls than they are to boys, or than girls are with partners of either sex.
Sex differences in atypical development	Boys are more likely to have school problems, reading disabilities, speech defects, and emotional problems.

Equivocal Sex Differences

Activity Level	When differences in activity level are found, it is usually boys who are more active than girls. Many studies find no differences in activity level.
Dependency	There is no difference in dependency in younger children. However, older children and adult females tend to rate themselves as more dependent.

TABLE 15-1 continued

Fear, timidity, and anxiety	In young children consistent differences in timidity between boys and girls are not found. However, older girls and women report themselves as being more fearful, and males are more likely to involve themselves in physically risky recreations and occupations.
Exploratory activity	A number of studies of early exploratory activity have found boys to be more venturesome and curious and likely to attack barriers intervening between themselves and a desirable object. However, differences on these behaviors are not consistently found.
Vulnerability to stress	Recent findings suggest that males are more vulnerable to family disharmony and interpersonal stress. This is supported by the overrepresentation of boys in child guidance clinics. However, further research needs to be done before conclusions can be firmly drawn.
Orientation to social stimuli	There is some evidence that infant girls may orient to faces more than boys, and may recognize their mother's face at an earlier age.

Mythical Sex Differences	
	Boys are not less social than girls. Boys and girls spend as much time with others and are equally responsive to others.
	Girls are not more suggestible. Girls are not more likely to conform to standards of a peer group or to imitate the responses of others.
	Girls are not better at rote learning and simple repetitive tasks. Boys are not better at tasks involving the inhibition of previously learned responses or complex cognitive tasks.
	Boys are not more responsive to visual stimuli and girls to auditory stimuli.
	Boys do not have more achievement motivation than do girls. Differences in achievement motivation and behavior vary with the type of task and conditions involved. Under neutral conditions girls are often more achievement-oriented than boys. However, competition is more likely to increase the achievement motivation of boys than girls.
	Girls do not have lower self-esteem than boys. There are few sex differences in self-satisfaction. However, girls rate themselves as more competent in social skills, and boys view themselves as strong and powerful.

Source: Some of this material was taken from Maccoby, E. E., and Jacklin, C. N., 1974; however, additional material has been included based on Hetherington and Parke's interpretation of new studies.

Similarly, although males seem constitutionally predisposed to be stronger and better adapted to successful aggressive interactions, some women are pretty hardy types, as can be witnessed at women's roller derbies or wrestling matches. In addition in the area of intellectual and occupational achievement there are outstanding female architects, mathematicians, engineers, and scientists, although males receive more encouragement in these areas.

Developmental Patterns of Sex Typing

Developmental patterns of sex typing differ for boys and girls. Our culture is basically a male-oriented culture, with greater esteem, privileges, and status accorded to the masculine role (Brown, 1957; D'Andrade, 1966). The male role is more clearly defined, and there is greater pressure for boys than girls to conform to narrower sex-appropriate standards. Tomboys are tolerated, but sissies rejected. Parents and peers condemn boys for crying, retreating in the face of aggression, wearing feminine apparel, or playing with dolls. In contrast, an occasional temper tantrum, rough-and-tumble play, wearing jeans, or playing with trucks is at least moderately acceptable for girls. Mothers and fathers and other adults respond more negatively to opposite-sex behaviors by boys than by girls and are quick to discourage such behaviors in boys (Fling & Manosevitz, 1972; Lawsky, 1967: Fagot, 1977b). Studies suggested that fathers tend to respond more negatively to feminine behaviors in boys than do mothers. Such intense concern about inappropriate sex-typed behavior as is revealed by fathers may be a manifestation of their anxieties about their own masculinity (Goodenough, 1957), or may be due to a pervasive masculine concern in our culture (Seavey, Katz, & Zalk, 1975).

It has been speculated that sex-role behavior for boys is seldom defined positively as something the child should do, but more often negatively as something he should not do, and that these negative sanctions are frequently enforced by punishment (Hartley, 1959). Boys receive physical punishment more often than do girls. It even has been concluded that the basic developmental task of girls is learning how not to be a baby, and of boys is learning how not to be a girl (Emmerich, 1959). It has also been proposed that an additional difficulty in sex-role identification for boys is the necessary shift from their initial identification with the mother to identification with the father, whereas girls need only intensify their initial maternal identification. This difficult transition plus the greater demands for conformity and harsher prohibitions utilized in sex-role training of boys may make sex-role identification more stressful for boys than for girls (Lynn, 1969). All these factors seem to combine to make boys more aware of and responsive to sex-stereotyped beliefs (Fagot, 1974; Flerx, Fidler, & Rogers, 1976; Hartley & Hardesty, 1964). Many boys express great anxiety about maintaining their sex roles, and this anxiety verges on panic at being detected in the performance of feminine activities (Hartley, 1959). Such apprehension is rarely expressed by girls.

In view of the above factors it is not surprising that boys develop sex-appropriate behaviors earlier and more consistently than do girls. On measures

Boys are usually more physically aggressive than are girls. (Suzanne Szasz)

of sex-role preference such as the It Scale for Children, which asks a child to select preferred masculine or feminine toys or whether the child would like to grow up to be a mommy or a daddy, girls make masculine choices until about the age of 10, when a rapid shift toward femininity occurs. There is some evidence that feminine preferences increase rapidly from age 3 to 4 (Hartup & Zook, 1960), but that girls shift toward more masculine choices from age 4 to 10 (Brown, 1957; Ward, 1973). This might be attributed to the elementary-school-age girl's increasing awareness of the greater privileges and prestige of the male role, followed by her eventual capitulation to social pressures toward sexual conformity in the preadolescent period. In contrast, even in the preschool years most boys prefer and sustain a marked preference for the masculine role.

Observational studies of play patterns of boys and girls have obtained similar results in indicating that preschool and elementary school girls conform less strictly to sex-appropriate behaviors than do boys, in addition to voicing less culturally appropriate sex-role preferences. Girls are more likely to play with a truck than boys are to cuddle a doll.

The course of sex typing varies in the lower and middle classes (Nadelman, 1970, 1974). Lower-class boys clearly prefer sex-appropriate toys by age 4 or 5, middle-class boys and lower-class girls by about 7, and finally middle-class girls at age 9 (Rabban, 1950). Class differences in sex-role standards for males become particularly apparent in adolescence. In a study of forty early adolescents it was found that the aggressive playground bully was the undisputed leader among low-socioeconomic-class boys, while both the sissy and the classroom conformer were likely to be rejected by their peers. In contrast, aggressive, domineering behaviors at the high socioeconomic level made a boy unpopular not only with other boys but with girls as well. Skill and daring in competitive games were highly valued instead, and even the studious adult-conformer and classroom "intellectual" was accorded much more acceptance by his peers than in lower-social-class groups. The sissy, however, was rejected just as he was by lower-class children. Both lower- and middle-class girls accepted the "little lady" pattern of behavior, comprising friendliness, conformity, goodness, and tidiness in girls (Pope, 1953).

These differences have been attributed to the clearer delineation of sex roles, more rigid demands for conformity to sex standards, and more conventional masculine or feminine models offered by lower-class parents. The middle-class mother is less home-oriented and feels she has more control over what happens to her and her children than the lower-class mother. She has interests and activities outside the family and may be employed in a vocation which is not regarded as suitable solely for women. The main roles of lower-class women are often focused on sexual satisfaction, housekeeping, and child care. Their employment also frequently involves traditionally feminine activities, such as cooking, housework, and child care. Lower-class men usually work in occupations regarded as uniquely masculine, such as those involving heavy labor, and their function in childrearing is often limited to that of family provider and disciplinarian. In contrast, middle-class fathers spend more time with their children and participate more actively in the tasks of routine child and household care and family recreational activities.

Stability of Sex Typing

Masculinity or femininity appears to be a remarkably early developed and stable personality characteristic. The longitudinal Fels Institute study (Kagan & Moss, 1962), which studied the development of a group of middle-class children from birth to adulthood, found that adult heterosexual behavior could be predicted from sex-typed interests in elementary school. Figure 15-1 presents a summary of the relationship between some selected child behaviors and similar adult behaviors. Boys who were interested in competitive games, gross motor skills, and such things as mechanics and girls who were interested in cooking, sewing, reading, and noncompetitive games were involved in sex-typed activities in adulthood. A finding of greater stability for boys than girls on this characteristic is not unexpected in the light of the ambivalence toward the feminine role experienced by many females. The earlier sex typing of boys is again demonstrated since childhood sexuality and masculine play even in the preschool years is associated with adult sex-role interests and heterosexual activities in boys but not in girls. It was found that the stability of many of the personality characteris-

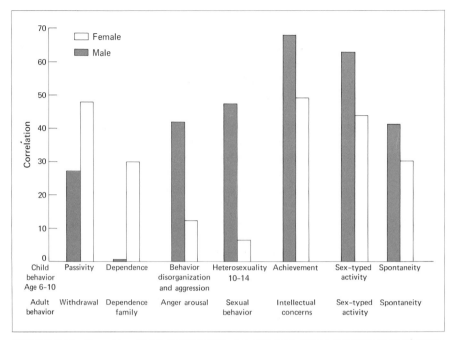

FIGURE 15-1 Summary of relationship between selected child behaviors (6 to 10 years of age) and functionally similar adult behaviors. *(From Kagan & Moss, 1962.)*

tics investigated was related to their appropriateness to culturally accepted sex-role standards. When a characteristic conflicted with sex-role standards, it led to some form of more socially acceptable substitute or derivative behavior in adulthood. When it was congruent with such standards, it tended to remain stable from childhood to maturity. Thus sex-typed interests, which are encouraged in both sexes, tend to remain stable in both males and females. In contrast, childhood sexuality and aggression are predictive of adult sexuality and anger arousal in males but not in females; and childhood passivity and dependency are predictive of these adult behaviors in females but not in males.

The sexually incongruent behaviors, which it may be assumed are eliminated through socialization practices, do emerge in derivative forms of behavior in adulthood. Anger and tantrums in girls are associated with intellectual competitiveness, masculine interests, and dependency conflict in women. Passivity in boys is related to social apprehension, noncompetitiveness, and sexual anxiety in men.

Factors Which Influence Sex Differences and the Development of Sex Roles

Biological, cognitive, and social factors interact to shape the development of sex roles and sex differences in behavior.

Biological Factors in Sex-Role Typing

Most of the interest in the influence of biological factors on sex-role typing has focused on two areas. The first is that of the effects of hormones on sex typing. The second is the relationship between sex differences in development and lateralization of brain function, that is, the relatively greater specialization of the two hemispheres of the brain in determining various behaviors.

The Effects of Hormones on Sex Differences in Social Behavior   Hormones are powerful and highly specialized chemical substances which interact with cells which are able to receive the hormonal message and respond to it. Androgens are male hormones, and testostrogen, which has been involved in many studies of sex differences, is a special type of androgen. Estrogens and progesterones are female hormones. However, both male and female hormones are found in differing concentrations in male and female infants, adolescents, and adults. The differences are less marked in preschool and elementary-school-aged children. It has been suggested that the prenatal and pubertal periods are critical periods in terms of the response of the organism to hormones (Goy, 1968). Hormones *organize* the psychological and biological predisposition to be masculine or feminine in the prenatal period, and the increase in hormones during puberty activates these early predispositions determined in the organization phase.

Most of the studies of the relation of hormones to behavior have been performed on animals or adults, or on individuals where deviations in hormonal functioning have occurred. Studies on infants and young children are rare because it takes a large amount of blood to perform an adequate hormonal assay. One recent study has tried to get around this problem by assessing hormones in the blood of the umbilical cord at birth and relating it to later social development in children.

Some writers have suggested that hormonal differences (Beach, 1958; Young, Goy, & Phoenix, 1964) experienced prenatally or during the subsequent course of development may contribute to differences in social behavior between sexes and within the same sex. Young et al. (1964) injected pregnant monkeys with testosterone (a male hormone) during the second quarter of pregnancy; this resulted in pseudohermaphroditic female offspring who exhibited not only genital alterations but also social behavior patterns which are characteristic of male monkeys. These infant female monkeys manifested masculine behaviors such as more threatening gestures, less withdrawal to approach or threat by other animals, more mounting behavior, and more rough-and-tumble play.

Subsequent studies have found that if male hormones are injected into normal female monkeys after birth but preceding puberty, the females also become much more assertive, sometimes even attaining the prime dominance status in the monkey troop. When this occurs, it is an evil day for the male monkeys in the troop. The tyrannical female restricts sexual and rough-and-tumble play between males and demands more restrained and docile behavior from her followers.

The relation between testosterone and aggression is a good one to demonstrate the complexities of interactions between biological and environmental factors. Not only are testosterone levels in young adult males associated with aggression, but stress in humans and repeated defeats in fights, or placing animals in situations in which they cannot be dominant, cause drops in testosterone (Lunde & Hamburg, 1972; Rose, Gordon, & Bernstein, 1972). Thus testosterone may be causing social responses, but social experiences are altering testosterone levels.

Another example of modification of the effects of hormonal factors by social experiences is dramatically demonstrated in the studies of Money and his colleagues (Money & Ehrhardt, 1972). These investigators studied prenatal hormonal anomalies, such as high levels of androgen, which result in masculinizing the female child and the subsequent mistaken sexual identity of the child. Many of the subjects in these studies were female infants who had the normal internal female reproduction system, but an enlarged clitoris which resembled a penis, and labial folds often fused and resembling a scrotum.

John Money's studies of androgenized girls found that if the reassignment of the child to her correct feminine gender role occurred after the first few years of life, inadequate sex typing and poor psychological adjustment occurred. If early reassignment occurred, normal psychosexual development in most of the subjects followed. This finding led the authors to conclude that there is a "critical period" for the establishment of gender role between 18 months and 3 years.

A study of twenty-five fetally androgenized girls who were raised as girls, and given corrective surgery if it was necessary, found that these girls were characterized by tomboyishness. Such girls enjoy vigorous athletic activities such as ball games. There is little rehersal of the maternal role early in life in such things as doll play, or at adolescence in baby-sitting or caring for younger children. These girls also prefer simple utilitarian clothing, such as slacks and shorts, and show little concern with cosmetics, jewelry, or hairstyle.

In addition to the play and grooming interests of these girls more closely resembling those of boys, their assertiveness and attitudes toward sexuality and achievement are similar to those more often found in males in our culture. These girls are assertive enough to be successful in establishing themselves in the dominance hierarchy of their male friends, although they do not compete for the top position in the hierarchy. They showed little concern in establishing a position in the dominance hierarchy of groups of girls, perhaps because of a lack of interest in traditional feminine games and activities.

Even in childhood the fantasies of these girls show a preference for success through achievement rather than marriage. They do show some interest in marriage and children but think in terms of a late marriage in conjunction with a career and few children. It should be noted that there is not an unusual incidence of lesbianism in these girls. Although their dating behavior tends to begin late and although their sexual fantasies tend to resemble those of males in specifically portraying the imagined sexual partner, they choose a male sexual partner in real life and in fantasy.

It has been suggested that their intense focus on achievement is based on the fact that these girls often have high IQs and perform unusually well on academic tasks. In fact, both males and females who have been exposed to high prenatal androgen levels show elevated scores on intelligence tests. However, it has been demonstrated that not only these androgenized girls, but their siblings and parents, have high IQs (Baker & Ehrhardt, 1974). The intellectual correlates may therefore be genetic or social rather than androgen-induced. The issue of the relation between prenatal exposure to androgen and intellectual level continues to be a controversial one.

It has also been suggested that progesterone may play a role in the development of the cerebral cortex and in cognitive development. Recently the children of mothers given progesterone during pregnancy to prevent miscarriage were studied, and these children had significantly higher than average IQs. In addition, in closely spaced births the mother seems to suffer a progesterone depletion as measured by progesterone levels in the umbilical cord. If children are born one or two years apart, the progesterone level is lower than if children are born four years apart (Maccoby, 1978). If progesterone is related to IQ, it would explain why later-born and closely born siblings perform less well on intelligence tests.

Hormones, Cerebral Lateralization, and Sex Differences in Cognition   Behavior is determined to some extent by how the two cerebral hemispheres are organized. In general, the right hemisphere is more involved in processing spatial information and the left hemisphere in processing verbal information. The functioning of the brain becomes increasingly more specialized and lateralized with age. There is some evidence that men are more lateralized than women in brain function (Bryden, 1978). Women who suffer damage to the left hemisphere are less likely than men to have verbal deficits, and right-hemisphere-damaged women show fewer spatial deficits than do men (McGlone, 1977). The greater bilaterality of brain functioning in girls can be seen in the study presented in Box 15-1.

It has been suggested that at a critical period in prenatal development sex hormones may determine the potentials for hemispheric lateralization and brain organization. This brain organization may in turn extend not only to differences in lateralization, but to sex differences in the effectiveness with which males and females develop verbal and spatial skills. That is, prenatal hormones may sensitize the brains of females to be more effective processors of verbal information and males to be more effective processors of spatial information. This more effective spatial processing of males may be associated with their superiority in mathematics. Why should spatial ability be associated with mathematical ability? The marked superiority of males over females is found in geometry, which requires spatial visualization. In areas of mathematics which are not solely based on spatial ability but where problems can be solved verbally, such as in algebra, no sex differences are found (Fennema, 1974).

Again it should be kept in mind that even if definitive evidence of a biological basis for sex differences in spatial abilities was established, it would not mean that these differences are not culturally influenced or modifiable. It has been suggested that boys are encouraged more often to play with toys such as models or motors that involve spatial abilities (Sherman, 1967), and are

BOX 15-1
THE ROLE OF CEREBRAL LATERALIZATION IN TOUCH PERCEPTION

 Are boys more lateralized in spatial perception than girls? In a study of 6- to 13-year-old children, the children by tactually exploring or touching alone were asked to recognize two different objects presented simultaneously one to each hand.

In order to study the relative contributions of the two hemispheres in nonverbal spatial tasks, the stimuli used were meaningless shapes. The child felt the concealed figures for 10 seconds with the index and middle fingers of each hand and then had to choose these two shapes from a visual array of six similar shapes. Then one may deter-mine whether the individual is more accurate in choosing objects presented to the right or the left hand. As indicated before, because the information from each hand is mainly transmitted to the contralateral (opposite) hemisphere, if the right hemisphere is better at this form perception task, then one might predict that left-hand objects would be recognized more accurately. And these results were obtained—but only for the boys studied. (Witelson, 1978, p. 302) ■

Source: Witelson, S. F. Sex differences in the neurology of cognition. Psychological, social, educational and clinical implications. In S. Sullerot (Ed.), *La Fait Feminin.* France: Fayard, 1978, 287–303.

encouraged in mathematical and scientific endeavors. Whatever the reason may be, girls enroll in increasingly fewer mathematics and science courses over the high school and college years, and it becomes more difficult to interest even girls with superior mathematical abilities to remain involved in the subject. However, a national study which involved over 400,000 children compared the cognitive skills of high school children in 1960 and 1975 and found a great improvement in the mechanical and spatial performance of girls, which may mean that changing sex-role standards are having some effects on the cognitive interests and abilities of girls (Flanagan, 1978).

Living in a Male or Female Body   Finally it has been proposed that the differ-ence between living in a male or female body in terms of such things as physical strength and the necessary roles in sexual intercourse, pregnancy, and the breast feeding of infants may have an important effect in shaping sex-role standards and in sex typing (La Barre, 1954). Particular interest has focused on whether females are in some way biologically programmed to be more responsive to the sight and signals of infants and children. Few sex differences are found in the responses of young children to babies. However, by adolescence, females are becoming more interested and responsive than males (Feldman, Nash, & Cutrona, 1978). These sex differences in adolescents and adults are less apparent under private conditions than in situations where the subjects are aware that they are being observed (Berman, 1976). When subtle measures of responsiveness to an infant's crying are used, such as changes in autonomic

There is no evidence to support the position that males are less predisposed biologically to be responsive to infants than are females. (Christa Armstrong, Rapho/Photo Researchers, Inc.)

nervous system responses, in blood pressure, or electrical skin conductance, no differences are found in the autonomic responses of mothers and fathers (Frodi, Lamb, Leavitt, & Donovan, 1978).

The particular life situation of young adult males—whether a cohabiting single, childless, or married, awaiting the first child, or a parent of an infant—does not affect their interest in or responsivity to a live baby in a waiting-room situation. However, young mothers of infants are more responsive to babies than are childless women (Feldman & Nash, 1978). These findings suggest that culturally proscribed sex roles are having considerable impact on overt responses to babies rather than that biological preprogramming is determining such differences.

Cognitive Factors in Sex-Role Typing

Kohlberg (1966) has presented a provocative cognitive theory of the development of sex typing. In contrast to the social learning position that sex typing is a result of reinforcement and modeling, he argues that the child's differentiation of gender roles and his perception of himself as more similiar to same-sexed models precedes, not follows, identification. His notion of the development of sex-role concepts is similar to Parsons' belief that children make "we males" and "those females" differentiations in learning social roles. When the child on the basis of physical and sex-role differences such as clothing, hair style, occupation, etc., categorizies himself as male or female, it then becomes rewarding to behave in a sex-appropriate manner and imitate same-sexed models. Thus the girl says, "I am a girl since I am more like my mother and other girls than boys; therefore I want to dress like a girl, play girl games, and feel and think like a girl." Consistency between the child's gender, self-categorization, and appropriate behaviors and values is critical in sustaining self-esteem.

Kohlberg thinks all children go through the following stages in gaining an understanding of gender:

1   *Basic gender identity.* In this stage the child recognizes that he is a boy or a girl.

2   *Gender stability.* In this stage the child accepts that males remain male and females remain female. Little boys no longer think they might grow up to be a mommy, and little girls give up their heady hopes of becoming Batman.

3   *Gender constancy.* In this stage children recognize that superficial changes in appearance or activities do not alter gender. When a girl wears jeans or plays football, or when a boy has long hair and a burning interest in needlepoint, their sex remains constant.

Children seem to understand gender labels such as boy and girl as early as age 3 (Slaby & Frey, 1975; Thompson, 1975). However, gender constancy does not develop until about 5 and becomes increasingly evident around 7 (DeVries, 1969; Emmerich & Goldman, 1972). Although older children perceive their own sex roles as much less stereotyped than those of their friends (Guttentag & Bray, 1977), children seem to understand gender constancy earlier when it applies to themselves than when it is applied to others. They are sure earlier that no matter how much they want to be transformed into a member of the opposite sex, it could not happen. But they are not so sure about that kid down the street. In addition, in support of a cognitive position, gender constancy is related to cognitive level and to performance on Piagetian tasks of physical conservation, which of course require the recognition of constancy of physical objects in spite of superficial transformations (LaVoie & Andrews, 1975; Marcus & Overton, 1978). However, contrary to what Kohlberg would predict, sex typing begins before the child has a stable concept of gender constancy, and children prefer sex-appropriate toys and activities as early as 2 or 3 years of age. In addition, there is no relation between development of gender constancy and sex-typed play and activity preferences (Marcus & Overton, 1978). This suggests that although cognitive factors may play a role in the development of sex-role typing, they alone are not adequate to explain the development of sex differences in behavior. We will now turn to social and situational factors in order to obtain a more complete view of the development of sex typing.

Sex-role standards and pressure to adopt sex-typed behavior patterns converge on the developing child from a variety of sources—from family, teachers, friends, television, and children's books.

The Family and Sex-Role Typing

Parents and infants From earliest infancy parents are likely to view their sons and daughters differently. Parents are more likely to describe their newborn daughter as smaller, softer, less attentive, cuter, more delicate, and finer featured than their sons. And fathers, even if they have seen but not yet handled their infants, are more extreme than mothers in emphasizing the size, strength, coordination, and alertness of their sons versus the fragility and beauty of daughters (Rubin, Provenzano, & Luria, 1974; Krieger, 1976). In view of such differences in parents' perceptions of their male and female infants, it is not surprising that from the earliest days of life boys and girls are treated differently and that this differential treatment of boys and girls is most marked for fathers.

Even before their child is born, fathers show a strong preference to have a son. After birth, especially with firstborn children, they are more likely to stimulate and talk to their sons. As children grow older, fathers with male toddlers spend more time in play and watch and touch their infants more. They indulge in rough-and-tumble antics or talk in a sort of "hail-baby-well-met" style saying such things as "Hello Tiger!" or "Come here, Dingbat" more than do fathers with daughters (Lamb, 1977; Parke & Sawin, 1977; Rendina & Dickerscheid, 1976; Shenker, 1971). Fathers are more likely to gently cuddle than actively stimulate their infant daughters. In addition, fathers seem more willing to persist in social activities with temperamentally difficult male infants than with troublesome daughters, from whom they are more likely to withdraw (Rendina & Dickerscheid, 1976).

In contrast, mothers' differential treatment of sons and daughters is less extreme and less consistently found. However, mothers seem to be more verbally responsive to firstborn girls and talk to them and echo their verbalizations more than those of their sons.

This pattern of differences in mother's and father's interactions with sons and daughters suggests that the social forces involved in sex-role typing may begin as early as the newborn period and that fathers play a more important role in the sex-typing process than do mothers.

Parental tuition of sex roles As children grow older, do parents actively encourage and reinforce them for behaving in a sex-appropriate manner? It can be seen in the study presented in Box 15-2 that such processes begin very early.

In general it has been found that parents are more apprehensive and protective about their daughters' physical well-being. This is associated with more encouragement of dependency and close family ties in girls and more emphasis on early exploration, achievement, independence, and competition in boys. Parents think boys should be able to play away from home without telling parents where they are, run errands in the neighborhood, cross the street alone, use sharp scissors, and indulge in other venturesome activities at an earlier age

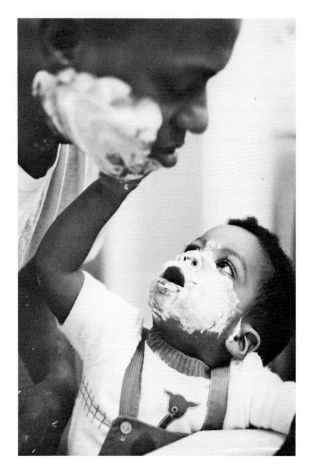

Sex-role typing begins
early. (Burk Uzzle, Mag-
num Photos, Inc.)

than should girls (Callard, 1964; Duncan, Schuman, & Duncan, 1973; Saegert
& Hart, 1976). No sex differences are expected by parents in independence and
maturity in such safe activities as tidying up rooms, putting away toys or clothes,
or getting dressed.

Many of the parents' sex-differentiated behaviors seem to be associated
with achievement, particularly in the attitudes and behavior of fathers. Parents,
especially fathers, are more likely to stress the importance of a career or
occupational success for sons than daughters (Block, 1978; Hoffman, 1975). In
teaching and problem-solving situations, fathers of boys are more attuned with
achievement and the cognitive aspects of the situation. Fathers of girls seem to
be less concerned with performance and more concerned with interpersonal
interactions with their daughters (Block, Block, & Harrington, 1974). In addition,
fathers, but not mothers, will respond to appropriate task-oriented questions and
requests for help from boys but are more likely to reinforce inappropriate
dependency bids from daughters (Osofsky & O'Connell, 1972; Cantor, Wood,
& Gelfand, 1977; Hetherington, 1978). This tendency of fathers to reinforce

BOX 15-2
MOTHERS AND FATHERS, SONS AND DAUGHTERS

Do parents encourage different types of behavior in their sons and daughters? Home observations were done on the interactions of parents with their 20- to 24-month-old infants. Boys were encouraged to play with masculine toys that required large-muscle activity such as pull toys, blocks, and trucks and were punished for activities such as playing with dolls or seeking help. In contrast, girls were encouraged to play with dolls, dress up as a woman, dance, ask for assistance, and follow the parents around. Parents tried to inhibit girls from very active play such as running, jumping, or climbing and discouraged them from manipulating objects. Boys were more often punished for feminine behavior than girls were for masculine play. Although parents viewed rough-and-tumble play and aggression as more suitable for boys, they did not reinforce either boys or girls who exhibited these behaviors. ■

Source: Fagot, B. Sex-determined parental reinforcing contingencies in toddler children. Paper presented at the biennial meeting of the Society for Research in Child Development, New Orleans, 1977.

---

inappropriate dependency in girls increases in the early elementary school years (Hetherington, 1978).

Before we leap to the conclusion that differential reinforcement of sex-typed behavior can explain all observable sex differences in behavior, it should be noted that boys do not get more reinforcement for aggressive behavior than girls. Physical aggression is the most consistently reported difference between boys and girls, and neither sex is encouraged to be aggressive (Fagot, 1977b).

Parental characteristics, modeling, and sex typing   Let us turn now to the role of parental characteristics and the possibility of imitation of the same-sexed parent as an explanation for the development of sex typing.

Although characteristics of mothers have some effect on the development of femininity in girls, they have little influence on the masculinity of sons. Nurturance and warmth in the same-sex parent increase appropriate sex-role learning for both boys and girls (Bronson, 1959; Helper, 1955; Mussen & Distler, 1959, 1960; Mussen & Rutherford, 1963; Payne & Mussen, 1956; Sears, 1953). However, where both maternal and paternal warmth increase femininity in girls, highly masculine boys perceive their fathers but not their mothers as more nurturant and rewarding than do boys who are lower in masculinity (Hetherington, 1967).

Great consistency is found in the evidence for the effects of parental power on sex typing in boys. In decision making, dominant mothers and passive fathers are particularly destructive in the identification of boys although they have no effect on femininity in girls. If a boy has a Caspar Milquetoast for a father and a Thurber woman for a mother, he is likely to exhibit feminine characteristics. Highly masculine boys have fathers who are decisive and dominant in setting limits and dispensing both rewards and punishments (Biller, 1968; Hetherington, 1965; Moulton, Liberty, Burnstein, & Altucher, 1966; Mussen & Distler, 1959). They play an active role in discipline of their sons. Paternal punishment seems to facilitate sex-role typing in boys only if the father is also nurturant and dominant. In contrast to the strong relationship with the development of masculinity in boys, parental power has little effect on the development of femininity in girls.

Parental characteristics other than warmth, power, and hostility might also be expected to affect sex typing. One might speculate that the masculinity or femininity of the parents and their encouragement of sex-typed behaviors should be particularly important for the child's delineation and discrimination of gender roles. However, sex typing of parents and encouragement of sex-typed activities by parents are not related to masculinity in boys (Angrilli, 1960; Mussen & Rutherford, 1963; Payne & Mussen, 1956). Again in girls we see the importance of the father in sex typing; femininity in daughters is related to father's masculinity, father's approval of the mother as a model, and father's reinforcement for participation in feminine activities. It is interesting that it is not related to femininity in mothers. More feminine mothers do not have more feminine daughters (Hetherington, 1967).

Even in adulthood sexual adjustment and marital relations are more influenced by earlier relations with fathers than mothers. A lack of involvement in family life and ineffectuality or hostility in fathers have been related to problems in forming lasting heterosexual relationships.

A woman's desire to get married and have children and even her sexual responsiveness and orgasmic satisfaction in intercourse are related to an affectionate, attentive, supportive relationship with her father (Fisher, 1973; Johnson, Stockard, Acker, & Naffziger, 1974).

A history of inadequate fathering, rather than inadequate mothering, often is found for homosexuals of both sexes. Fathers of male and female homosexuals are described as ineffectual, hostile, aloof, and not reinforcing of sex-appropriate activities (Apperson & McAdoo, 1968; Saghir & Robbins, 1973; West, 1967).

Father unavailability, single-parent families, and sex typing Since the father plays such a critical role in sex typing, it might be expected that children from homes in which the father is either permanently absent or away for long periods of time would show disruptions in sex typing. In some ways the home in which no father is present may resemble a mother-dominated, nuclear family since the mother must of necessity assume a more decisive role in rearing her children alone. The absence of a male model and lack of opportunity for interaction with a father may also contribute to difficulty in sex typing in such homes.

Permanent separation from a father due to death or divorce, temporary separation or unavailability due to war or occupational demands, and paternal disinterest have been shown to disrupt sex typing in young boys (Hetherington & Deur, 1971; Le Corgne & Laosa, 1976; Drake & McDougall, 1977). Disruptions in sex typing are most apparent in preadolescent boys. These effects are most severe if the separation has occurred before age 5. In girls disruptions in

Some adults, such as Renee Richards (formerly Dr. Richard H. Raskind), feel more psychologically similar to members of the opposite sex and go through sex-change operations to assume a new sexual identity. (Photo (a) Wide World Photos; photo (b) Norcia, Transworld Feature Syndicate, Inc.)

sex-typed behaviors seem to be largely limited to deviations in relationships with males which do not emerge until adolescence.

Preschool boys who are separated from their fathers early in life are found to be less aggressive and more dependent, to have more feminine self-concepts, and to exhibit more feminine patterns of play and social interactions involving such things as the use of high verbal aggression and low physical aggression. The importance of age of separation is apparent in a study by Hetherington (1966) which involved direct observations by male recreation directors of boys in a recreation center. Boys who were 6 years of age or older at the time of separation from fathers did not differ from children raised in nuclear families. However, if the father had left before the son was 5, the son scored as less masculine on the It Scale for Children, a measure of sex-role preference, was rated as more dependent on peers and less assertive, as engaged in fewer rough physical contact sports than father-present boys. They were demonstrating behaviors more characteristic of girls than of boys. This supports the premise that there is a sensitive period for sex typing in the preschool years.

Although preschool boys with absent fathers exhibit disruptions in sex typing, the results with older boys are less consistent. Some studies have reported no differences between adolescent boys with fathers absent and those with fathers present (Barclay & Cusumano, 1967), especially if the son was not deprived of his father until after age 5 (Biller & Bahm, 1971); others have found compensatory masculinity. Compensatory masculinity involves the exhibition of inconsistent patterns of both masculine and feminine behaviors. Such boys exhibit both excessively masculine, assertive forms of behavior and at times feminine behaviors such as dependency. Delinquents are often found to have this combination of flamboyant, swaggering toughness and sexuality, accompanied by dependency. This has been associated with the high rates of father absence found in the homes of delinquent children. With age, boys with absent fathers may gradually become more aware of the greater privileges and prestige of males and therefore prefer the masculine role. However, the lack of early identification with a masculine, paternal model may result in difficulty in developing a subtle, integrated repertoire of masculine behaviors.

With increasing age and wider social contacts, other models, such as teachers, peers, siblings, surrogate fathers, and those in the mass media, serve to partially mitigate the effects of father absence on sex-role adoption. Models other than parents have been demonstrated to affect sex typing. In two-child families, children who have siblings of the same sex rather than the opposite sex are rated as more appropriately sex-typed by teachers (Brim, 1958), and adolescents who report frequent childhood experiences with older members of the same sex exhibit more appropriate sex-typed interests (Steimel, 1960). In single-parent, mother-headed families, children who have older brothers are more aggressive and less dependent than children with no older male siblings (Wohlford, Santrock, Berger, & Leiberman, 1971).

Recent research suggests that it may be more than the unavailability of male models that is associated with early less masculine patterns of behavior in boys in single-parent families. Many mothers in single-parent families are overprotective, infantalizing, and apprehensive about adventurous, risk-taking activities in their sons. When these mothers do not exhibit such attitudes and behaviors and encourage independent exploratory and masculine behavior on the part of their sons and when they do not have a negative attitude toward the missing father, disruptions in sex-role typing are unlikely to occur (Hetherington, Cox, & Cox, 1978). The behaviors of the mother become more salient in the sex typing of boys in single-parent mother-headed families.

The effects of paternal absence on preadolescent girls appear to be minimal. Although a study by Lynn and Sawrey (1959) of 8- and 9-year-old children of Norwegian seamen whose fathers were away for extended periods of time found the daughters to show greater dependency on the mother, a current investigation (Santrock, 1970) found no effects of father absence on the dependency, aggression, and femininity of preschool black girls.

It is only evidence largely based on studies of adolescents that suggests paternal absence may have a delayed effect on the sex typing of girls. The study presented in Box 15-3 shows that father absence is associated with disruptions in relating to other males by adolescent daughters and that the form of this disruption differs for daughters of widows and divorcees.

BOX 15-3
THE EFFECTS OF FATHER ABSENCE ON PERSONALITY DEVELOPMENT IN ADOLESCENT DAUGHTERS

What are the effects on daughters of absence of a father? The subjects were three groups of twenty-four lower- and lower-middle-class first-born adolescent white girls with no male siblings. The first group came from families with both parents living in the home, the second group from families in which the father was absent due to divorce, and the third in which the father had died. Both groups of girls with fathers absent had no males living in the home.

The measures included the following: observations of the girls' behavior in a recreation center; interviews, personality tests, and tests of sex typing of mother and daughter; and observed measures of nonverbal communication, such as posture, gestures, and eye contact, when the girls were being interviewed by a male or female interviewer.

There were few differences among the three groups of girls on traditional measures of sex typing. The girls in all groups had feminine interests, activities, preferences, and behaviors. However, girls with fathers absent showed different patterns of heterosexual behavior than girls from nuclear families. A disruption in relationships with males in girls from mother-headed homes appeared either as excessive sexual anxiety, shyness, and discomfort around males or as sexually precocious and inappropriately assertive behavior with male peers and adults. The former syndrome was more common when separation had occurred because of the father's death, and the latter when separation was a result of divorce. These behaviors did not occur in interacting with females.

The behavior of these girls was observed in a recreation center they attended. In recreation

center dances, males tended to congregate at one end of the hall and females at the other. The behavior of the girls was recorded during these occasions. The first group, the daughters of widows, tended to remain in the cluster of other girls unless they were invited to dance. They more frequently positioned themselves in the back row than did the other group of father-absent or father-present girls. Some even spent over 90 percent of the evening hiding in the ladies' room. In contrast, the second group, the daughters of divorcees, spent more time at the boys' end of the hall, more frequently initiated encounters and asked male peers to dance, and more frequently touched the males in proximity to them. This was not related to differences in popularity since girls in all three groups were asked to dance equally often when they were in the hall.

Except for behaviors associated with proximity and attention seeking or avoidance of males there were few differences in sex-typed behaviors between girls with absent fathers or fathers present in the home.

In interviews in the laboratory where three chairs were available to the interviewees, daughters of widows tended to seat themselves on the most distant chair, daughters of divorcees on a chair immediately adjacent to the interviewer, and girls from nuclear families directly across the desk in what might be considered the most appropriate position for interactions in such situations. The daughters of widows spent the least time in mutual eye contact with the interviewer, most frequently were turned away from the interviewer, and had the most constricted body posture, often with arms tensely folded and legs crossed. The daughters of divorcees spent more time looking at the male interviewer, with their bodies oriented directly toward him. They also assumed a sprawling, open-body position with legs and arms apart, a position which some investigators of nonverbal communication would assume was a sexually receptive position. Girls from nuclear families tended to fall between the two father-absent groups on measures of nonverbal communication. The important finding was that these differences occurred only if the interviewer was a man. With a female interviewer the differences between groups were no greater than would be expected by chance.

It seems plausible that such differences in the daughters might be the result of differences in childrearing practices and attitudes of their mothers. However, the mothers of the different groups of girls were very similar in their childrearing practices. Until the girls reached adolescence, the mothers were equally loving, consistent, and permissive. Greater conflict, inconsistency, and punitiveness and restrictiveness about sex found in divorcees after their daughters were adolescents could well be a reaction to, rather than a precursor of, daughters' adolescent behavior.

The following are portions of representative interviews by mothers from each of the father-absent groups; the first is from the widowed group, and the second is from the divorced group.

_____is almost too good. She has lots of girl friends but doesn't date much. When she's with the girls she's gay and bouncy—quite a clown but she clams up when a man comes in. Even around my brother she never says much. When boys do phone she often puts them off even though she has nothing else to do. She says she has lots of time for that later, but she's sixteen now and very pretty, and all her friends have boy friends.

That kid is going to drive me over the hill. I'm at my wits' end. She was so good until the last few years then Pow! At eleven she really turned on. She went boy crazy. When she was only twelve I came home early from a movie and found her in bed with a young hood and she's been bouncing from bed to bed ever since. She doesn't seem to care who it is, she can't keep her hands off men. It

isn't just boys her own age; when I have men friends here she kisses them when they come in the door and sits on their knees all in a very playful fashion but it happens to them all. Her uncle is a 60-year-old priest and she even made a "ha ha" type pass at him. It almost scared him to death. I sometimes get so frantic I think I should turn her in to the cops but I remember what a good kid she used to be and I do love her. We still have a good time together when we're alone and I'm not nagging about her being a tramp. We both like to cook and get a lot of good laughs when we're puttering around in the kitchen. She's smart and good-looking—she should know she doesn't have to act like that. (Hetherington, 1972, p. 322)

All the mothers were equally feminine, reinforced their daughters for sex-appropriate behaviors, and surprisingly had equally positive attitudes toward men in general.

It was mainly in attitudes toward herself, her marriage, and her life that the divorced woman differed from the widow. The divorced woman was anxious and unhappy. Her attitude toward her spouse was hostile, and her memories of her marriage and life were negative. These attitudes were reflected in the critical attitude of her daughter toward the divorced father. Although she loved her daughter, she felt she had had little support from other people during her divorce and times of stress and with her difficulties in rearing a child alone. This is in marked contrast to the positive attitudes of the widows toward marriage, their lost husbands, the emotional support of friends and family at the loss of a husband, and the gratification of having children. These attitudes were reflected in the happy memories their daughters had of their fathers.

Both groups of girls from single-parent families reported feeling anxious around males but had apparently developed different ways of coping with this anxiety. It may be that daughters of divorced women viewed their mothers' separated lives as unsatisfying and felt that for happiness it was essential to secure a man. It may also be that life with a dissatisfied, anxious mother, even if she loves the daughter, is difficult, and that these daughters were more eager to leave home than daughters of widows living with relatively happy, secure mothers with support from the extended family. In contrast, daughters of widows with their aggrandized image of their father may have felt that few other males could compare favorably with him or alternatively may regard all males as superior and as objects of deference and appre-

hension. One can also speculate that after experiencing the sudden loss of a father, they were unwilling to make another deep emotional commitment to a male. ■

Source: Hetherington, E. M. Effects of father absence on personality development in adolescent daughters. *Developmental Psychology,* 1972, *7,* 303–326.

The studies of paternal absence again indicate the important role of the father in the social development of girls. Daughters learn to feel competent and to value and acquire the social skills necessary for effective heterosexual interactions by interacting with a warm, masculine, instrumental father who rewards and enjoys her femininity. However, the severity of the effects of father absence is moderated by maternal behavior. Mothers who present their husbands and their previous relationships with them in a positive manner and who are themselves stable lessen the deleterious effects of father absence.

A follow-up study was conducted on the girls in the study reported in Box 15-3 to see how long-lasting the effects of father absence on daughters' relationships with men are, as reflected in the girls' subsequent martial relationships. Not only did daughters of divorcees marry younger, but more of them were pregnant at the time of marriage and several are already separated or divorced. No differences in frequency of marital sexual intercourse were reported for the three groups, but orgasmic satisfaction was less in girls from single-parent families.

Freud has suggested that girls continue to relive their relationships with their fathers through subsequent interactions with men. Do girls marry men who resemble their image of their fathers? On an adjective checklist on which the girls checked adjectives which were most or least like their husband, father, or most men, both daughters of divorcees and widows reported more similarity between their husbands and fathers than did girls from intact families. Freud may be right, but only for father-absent girls. Girls from father-absent families may not have the opportunity to work through their feelings about their fathers as do girls with the father present, and may seek to resolve these feelings with their mates. Girls who have had a continuous relationship with a father may come to view them in a more balanced, realistic way, perceiving virtues and shortcomings. Girls with absent fathers maintain their childhood image of their fathers. Daughters of widows perceived both their husbands and fathers as having many more favorable characteristics than most men. Daughters of divorced parents viewed their fathers, husbands, and most men as having predominantly undesirable characteristics. Their attitude could be characterized as "Men are no damned good, they never have been, and they'll never change." In contrast, girls from nuclear families viewed men in general and their husbands and fathers as good but not perfect, as having a substantial number of favorable attributes but also some flaws.

The appraisals of the husbands on the basis of interviews, tests, and direct observations to some extent confirm the wives' opinions. The husbands of the daughters of divorced parents were less educated, had less stable employment records, and were more frequently involved in problems with the law than were the other two groups of husbands. In addition, they felt more ambivalent or hostile toward their wives and infants and were less emotionally mature and more impulsive and self-centered. In contrast, daughters of widows tended to marry husbands with more education or a higher vocational status than their parents had. These men were self-controlled almost to the point of being too inhibited. They were also nurturant, ambitious, concerned about social approval, and conventional, and they maintained stereotyped views of male and female roles. One interviewer characterized them as "repulsively straight." The results of this study indicated that the effects of fathers' absence on their daughter's interactions with males were long-lasting and extended even into their marital choices. These girls seemed to select mates who were similar to their images of their fathers, whereas girls from intact families were less constrained by their relationship with their father in their choice of a husband. These couples were studied in the first year following marriage. It might be questioned how long the marriages based on a father fantasy can be sustained for either of these groups of girls from mother-headed families.

Extrafamilial Influences on Sex-Role Typing   As children grow older, influences outside the family become increasingly important in shaping sex-role typing.

Television and sex roles   Male and female roles are portrayed in similarly sex-stereotyped ways on television and in children's stories. Males on television are more likely than females to be depicted as aggressive, decisive, professionally competent, rational, stable, powerful, and tolerant. In contrast, females are more often portrayed as unemployed or involved in housework and child care, warmer, more sociable, emotional, and happier. When women on television are aggressive, they are usually inept or unsuccessful aggressors, and women are more likely to be shown as victims than as initiators of violence. Females are less likely to be leading characters and are more likely to be in comedy roles, to be married or about to be married, and to be younger than males (Gerbner, 1972; Sternglanz & Serbin, 1974; Tedesco, 1974). Even in television commercials males are more often portrayed as the authorities and are used in the voice-over comments about the merits of products and women are usually the ones who are shown as believing demonstrations of a product's superiority (Courtney & Whipple, 1974). When women are shown as experts, it is likely to be in food products, laundry soap, or beauty aids.

The impact of such stereotypical presentations of male and female roles is suggested by findings that children who are heavy TV viewers are more likely to have stereotypical notions of sex and race and are more likely to show conformity to culturally appropriate sex-role preferences (Freuh & McGhee, 1975).

Teachers, peers, and sex roles   When children move out of the home and into the school and peer group, boys and girls continue to be treated differently. In many ways schools are feminine: they value quiet, obedience, and passivity, and these are many of the qualities, unfortunately, that the culture dictates as sex-role-appropriate for girls. The boisterous, assertive, competitive, and independent qualities which are encouraged in boys are often frowned upon in school. It is not surprising that in the early grades, at least, girls tend to like school more and perform better in their academic work than do boys. For boys, on the other hand, school is not a happy place. They view themselves as being less well liked than girls by their teachers (Dweck & Goetz, 1977). They have more difficulty in adjusting to school routines, create more problems for their teachers, are criticized more (Meyer & Thompson, 1966), and generally perform not only at a lower level than their female classmates but often well below their abilities.

Even in the preschool years boys and girls are responded to differently by teachers and peers. Although boys are encouraged to engage in quiet activities

rather than aggression and rough-and-tumble play, they receive more criticism from teachers and peers for cross-sexed behaviors such as dress-ups and doll play (Fagot & Patterson, 1969; Fagot, 1977a). However, preschool teachers are more likely to instruct and respond to boys than to girls who are involved in task-oriented activities (Fagot, 1977; Serbin, O'Leary, Kent, & Tonick, 1973). Girls are less likely to receive criticism from teachers and peers for engaging in cross-sexed play. Girls have more latitude in play interests. This pattern of greater tolerance for cross-sex activities of girls parallels the experiences children have within the family.

Even with male teachers, boys receive more criticism than do girls. However, male teachers are generally more approving of boys than female teachers are. In addition, male teachers are more likely to get involved in male-type activities and to assign leadership roles to boys. It is therefore not surprising that boys feel closer to and better liked by male than by female teachers (Lee & Wolinsky, 1973). The introduction of a male teacher into the classroom makes school a more congenial place for young boys. However, male teachers are still a rarity in preschool and elementray schools. In view of the experiences of boys in preschool combined with the usual female teacher, it is not surprising that children tend to perceive school and school-related objects and activities as feminine (Kagan, 1964).

More recent research (Stein, 1971; Stein & Pohly, 1973) has established a clear set of relationships between children's perception of the sex-role appropriateness of different activities (for example, mecahnical, artistic, reading, math) and their motivation to achieve in these tasks. Sixth and ninth graders rated how "boyish" or "girlish" a variety of activities were and then indicated the importance of accomplishment in each of these areas. In addition, the children indicated how well they thought they would perform and what minimum standard of performance they would be satisfied with. For activities that were viewed as sex-appropriate, the children attached more importance to achievement, set higher minimum standards, and expected to do better than on sex-role-inappropriate activities.

What are the implications of the young boy's perception of school as a sex-inappropriate institution? One of the obvious effects is that he is less likely to be as motivated and interested in school-related activities as girls, who, of course, view school as consistent with their own sex-role identity. It is not surprising, therefore, to find that girls outperform their opposite-sexed peers in the early grades. Sex ratios in reading problems range from 3:1 to as high as 6 boys to 1 girl in some surveys (Tyler, 1947; Bentzen, 1963). Although this difference in reading achievement may in part be due to the fact that boys' cognitive development is slower than girls, it is possible that boys simply fail to excel in the feminine environment of the early elementary school years.

Recent evidence from a Japanese study suggests that boys' reading difficulties could be lessened if the school were defeminized by the introduction of more male teachers in the early grades. On the island of Hokkaido in nothern Japan, approximately 60 percent of the teachers in the first and second grades are male. In this community boys do not have more frequent difficulties in reading; rather boys and girls are equally represented with about 9 percent of each sex experiencing reading problems (cited by Janis, Mahl, Kagan, & Holt, 1969). It is worth nothing that the presence of the male teacher does not appear to disrupt the learning progress of young girls, while it simultaneously increases the academic achievement of the boys.

Although not all investigations in North America have supported this finding, there is some American evidence to support the Japanese investigation. An American study by Shinedling and Pederson (1970) found that boys taught by male teachers did better in reading than boys taught by female teachers. In combination with the study of male teachers in nursery school that we discussed earlier, it suggests that the introduction of more male teachers into schools may be beneficial, but it is unlikely that this change alone will solve the problem of boys' reading.

Moreover, there is an apparent paradox which must be resolved. The school situation we have been describing certainly is not adequate to explain the greater eventual achievement of males in the late high school and college years. Up to this point, the argument has centered almost exclusively on the detrimental effects of the school environment on boys. What are the effects on girls? Girls may have an advantage in the early grades, but the advantage is short-lived. Girls' achievement levels decrease as they grow older, and by college the proportion of female underachievers exceeds the proportion of male underachievers (Ralph, Goldberg, & Passow, 1966). The kinds of passive and dependent behaviors that teachers accept and encourage in girls may, in the long run, be detrimental for later academic success. Intellectual achievement is negatively related to dependency. Independence, assertiveness, and nonconformity are more likely to lead to creative problem solving and high levels of achievement.

In addition, some recent work on how the type of teacher feedback is related to sex differences in response to failure may cast light on this issue (Dweck & Goetz, 1977). When girls have difficulty on a task, they are more likely to attribute their failure to lack of ability, whereas boys attribute failure to external factors or lack or motivation. In response to these attributions, girls are more likely than boys to show decreased persistence or poor performance under failure or increasing task difficulty. What might be contributing to these differences in response to failure? Teacher's negative criticism of boys is more often for conduct and nonintellectual aspects of work such as neatness, sloppy writing, or lack of motivation. In contrast, girls are more often graded on the accuracy and intellectual quality of their work. It has been proposed that boys see that teacher's responses are unrelated to their intellectual performance and begin to discount them, attribute them to external circumstances, and become less concerned about feedback from teachers and adults. Girls, in contrast, feel the evaluation is a valid indicator of their intellectual ability and become more distressed and disrupted by failure.

Finally males' and females' perceptions of the responses of others to their successful performance on different types of tasks alter their behavior. Females are likely to perform better on tasks they believe are sex-appropriate (feminine) rather than on those that they believe are sex-inappropriate (masculine) (Stein, Pohly, & Mueller, 1971). This may be why female achievement orientations are

Children in nontraditional schools, in which androgenous patterns of behavior are encouraged, show less sex-sterotyped play. (Suzanne Szasz)

likely to be manifested in social skills. Even on perceptual tests, if the task is made more person-oriented by using human figures instead of designs, and by saying the test is a test of empathy, rather than spatial skills, girls may actually score higher on some perceptual tests (Coates, 1974; Naditch, 1976).

Public achievement, particularly in competitive activities, is often threatening to females. Some girls cope with their conflict about achievement by concealing their ability, particularly from males. For example, they may tell male peers that they received lower grades than they really did (Horner, 1972). Another coping response is to decrease their efforts and intentionally perform less adequately (Weiss, 1962). Finally, a competent woman may counteract her achievement striving by being superfeminine in appearance and behavior. She may be warm, flirtatious, and submissive. She may even try to be supermother, superwife, and super-career woman by fulfilling all the demands of a conventional domestic role in addition to having a career (Stein & Bailey, 1973).

Androgyny

Many psychologists believe that traditional ideas of masculinity and feminity have been socially and psychologically destructive. We have been speaking

BOX 15-4
ANDROGYNY IN THE SCHOOLS

A psychologist overheard her 4-year-old son trying to explain her occupation to a young friend.

Son: My mother helps people. She's a doctor.

Friend: You mean a nurse.

Son: No. She's not that kind of doctor. She's a psychologist. She's a doctor of psychology.

Friend: I see. She's a nurse of psychology.

Such stereotypes abound. Can the schools help alter these stereotypes and help children become more androgynous? An intervention program oriented toward changing attitudes toward occupational, family, and socioemotional sex-role stereotypes in kindergarten, fifth-grade, and ninth-grade classes was initiated. Curriculum materials were introduced which showed flexible family roles, occupational competence without regard to sex, and enrichment of men and women's lives through more androgynous behavior. Teachers were also encouraged and trained to monitor their teaching styles to provide feedback to children on an individual basis regardless of sex. The aid of peers in breaking down stereotyped behaviors was also enlisted.

Children were less apt to stereotype themselves than others of either the same or opposite sex, although the male stereotype is most clearly defined.

Boys hold stereotypes more rigidly than girls. And fourteen year old boys were the most resistant to change. But even their attitudes can be changed in a well conducted, non-sexist school intervention. Girls' stereotypes become more flexible at every age after the intervention. Interestingly, one of the important side effects of the intervention with fourteen year-old girls, was that it made them feel, individually, more attractive and valuable. Change is quite possible.

Interventions are most needed at early adolescence, when stereotypes have a particularly limiting effect on both sexes. Interventions at that age seem more effective when teachers take active leadership roles, since same-sex peer groups tend to uphold traditional stereotypes. Ten-years-olds are the most open to change and the least rigid about stereotypes. Leisure time and family roles as well as occupational roles should be part of any non-sexist school interventions. Schools can be effectively used to promote androgynous attitudes—and all their intellectual and aspirational benefits—with children of both sexes. (Guttentag & Bray, 1977) ■

Source: Guttentag, M., & Bray, H. Androgyny in the schools. Unpublished manuscript, 1977.

almost as if people are either masculine or feminine in their interests, attitudes, and behaviors when we know in reality that most people have a combination of characteristics viewed as masculine or feminine. A person can be tender and nurturant with children, a competitive terror on the tennis court, professionally successful, and a good cook and be either a male or a female. Many people are *androgynous*; that is, they possess both masculine and feminine psychological characteristics (Bem, 1974; Bem & Lenney, 1976; Spence, Helmreich, & Stapp, 1974). It would seem constructive to facilitate the development of desirable characteristics such as social sensitivity, nurturance, open expression of positive feelings, appropriate assertiveness, and independence in both males and females. Some contemporary parents are working toward this goal, and as can be seen in Box 15-4, even adrogynous school programs have been developed.

Attitudes toward sex roles and acceptable behavior for males and females are slowly changing, and as suggested by Sandra Bem, it may be "that androgynous individuals will someday come to define a new and more human standard of psychological health" (1975, p. 643).

Summary

The development of sex-typed values, motives, and behaviors is influenced by a complex network of biological, cognitive, and social factors. None of these types of factors in isolation offers an adequate explanation of the development of sex-role typing.

Hormonal studies of both animals and humans suggest that hormones may play a role in sensitizing and organizing areas of the brain associated with certain sex-typed behaviors such as aggression, spatial relations, or verbal skills. In addition, sex differences in organization of the brain may be reflected in the greater lateralization of brain functioning in males than in females.

Even if biologically based sex differences in behavior occur, social and cognitive factors play a major role in modifying their expression. From the moment of birth boys and girls are exposed to different sex-role standards and treatment by the significant people around them. Fathers, in particular, seem concerned about their own sex roles and maintaining sex-appropriate behavior in their children. Fathers are more likely to be interested in, attend to, and play with firstborn sons more than daughters. In contrast, mothers are more likely to talk to daughters. Fathers play a more important role than mothers in sex typing of both boys and girls. This is reflected particularly in the more feminine behavior of boys from single-parent families in which the father was absent before the child reached 5 years of age. In girls the absence of a father is reflected in disruptions in heterosexual relations which do not appear until adolescence.

The male role is more rigidly defined and highly valued in our culture and in most cultures. When boys indulge in sex-inappropriate play, they are more likely to be greeted with disapproval or even punishment than are girls. Thus, more stress and anxiety are associated with maintaining the male role, and this may be why it is more difficult to shift male than female sex-type attitudes and behavior in intervention studies.

Many of the differences in standards and feedback for males and females are associated with independence training and achievement. The aspirations for achievement and occupational status that parents, again especially fathers, hold are higher for boys than for girls. There is some evidence that girls get more reinforcement by fathers for inappropriate dependency bids in problem-solving tasks. Although schools are in general a much more congenial and supportive place for girls than for boys, by the end of the high school years boys are pulling away from girls in achievement in such areas as mathematics and science. The different patterns of feedback on their schoolwork that boys and girls receive from teachers in the elementary school years may be related to attitudinal and motivational factors that funnel into sex differences in achievement. Teachers tend to give feedback for the academic performance of girls on the basis of the intellectual quality of their work. Boys, in contrast, are more likely to be evaluated on the basis of conduct or trival things like neatness. For boys, an intellectual jewel embedded in untidy handwriting may be underappreciated.

This leads boys not to rely on teacher's opinions when evaluating their performance, but to lean more heavily on their own judgments or those of peers whom they have found more useful. Thus when boys encounter failure or criticism which they have been experiencing in an untrustworthy way from teachers throughout their school life, they are less likely to be distressed or immobilized. Rather than blaming themselves and saying "I'm an academic idiot," they will blame the situation or their motivation and try harder. Girls, in contrast, blame their own inadequacies, become more anxious, and are more likely to give up in the face of failure.

In addition, as girls grow older, they may view achievement as incompatible with their socially approved feminine role and attempt to conceal it or compensate for it.

Recently emphasis has been placed on training children to become more androgynous, to develop socially desirable attributes without concern for their appropriateness to male or female roles. Some people have expressed concern that such a view will eliminate individual differences. This is not the case. A more androgynous society would free both male and female children to capitalize on their positive temperamental and intellectual differences without the constraints of stereotyped sex-role standards.

References

Angrilli, A. F. The psychosexual identification of preschool boys. *Journal of Genetic Psychology*, 1960, **97,** 329–340.

Apperson, L. B., & McAdoo, W. G. Parental factors in the childhood of homosexuals. *Journal of Abnormal Psychology*, 1968, **73,** 201–206.

Baker, S. W., & Ehrhardt, A. A. Prenatal androgen intelligence and cognitive sex differences. In R. C. Friedman, R. M. Richart, & R. L. Vande Wiele (Eds.), *Sex differences in behavior.* New York: Wiley, 1974.

Banducci, R. The effect of mother's employment on the achievement, aspirations and expectations of the child. *Personnel and Guidance Journal*, 1967, **46,** 263–267.

Bandura, A. Social learning theory and identificatory processes. In D. A. Goslin (Ed.), *Handbook of socialization theory and research.* Chicago: Rand McNally, 1969, pp. 213–262.

Barclay, A. G., & Cusumano, D. Father absence, cross-sex identity, and field dependent behavior in male adolescents. *Child Development*, 1967, **38,** 243–250.

Barry, H., Bacon, M., & Child, I. L. A cross cultural survey of some sex differences in socialization. *Journal of Abnormal and Social Psychology*, 1957, **55,** 327–332.

Beach, F. A. Neural and chemical regulation of behavior. In H. F. Harlow & C. N. Wolsey (Eds.), *Biological and biochemical bases of behavior.* Madison: University of Wisconsin Press, 1958.

Bem, S. L. The measurement of psychological androgyny. *Journal of Clinical and Consulting Psychology*, 1974, **42,** 155–162.

Bem. S. L. Sex-role adaptability: One consequence of psychological androgyny. *Journal of Personality and Social Psychology*, 1975, **31,** 634–643.

Bem, S. L., & Lenney, E. Sex typing and avoidance of cross-sex behavior. *Journal of Personality and Social Psychology*, 1976, **32,** 48–54.

Bennett, E. M., & Cohen, L. R. Men and women, personality patterns and contrasts. *Genetic Psychology Monographs*, 1959, **59**, 101–155.

Bentzen, F. Sex ratios in learning and behavior disorders. *American Journal of Orthopsychiatry*, 1963, **33**, 92–98.

Berman, P. W. Social content as a determinant of sex differences in adults' attraction to infants. *Developmental Psychology*, 1976, **12**, 365–366.

Best, D. L., Williams, J. E., Cloud, J. M., Davis, S. W., Robertson, L. S., Edwards, J. R., Giles, H., & Fowles, J. Development of sex-trait stereotypes among young children in the United States, England and Ireland. *Child Development*, 1977, **48**, 1375–1384.

Biller, H. B. A multiaspect investigation of masculine development in kindergarten age boys. *Genetic Psychology Monographs*, 1968, **76**, 89–139.

Biller, H. B., & Bahm, R. M. Father absence, perceived maternal behavior and masculinity of self-concept among junior high school boys. *Developmental Psychology*, 1971, **4**, 178–181.

Block, J. H. Another look at sex differentiation in the socialization behaviors of mothers and fathers. In F. Wenmark & J. Sherman (Eds.), *Psychology of women: Future direction of research.* New York: Psychological Dimensions, 1978.

Block, J. H., Block, J., & Harrington, D. M. The relationship of parental teaching strategies to ego-resiliency in preschool children. Paper presented at the meeting of the Western Psychological Association, San Francisco, 1974.

Brim, O. G. Family structure and sex role learning by children: A further analysis of Helen Koch's data. *Sociometry*, 1958, **21**, 1–16.

Bronson, W. C. Dimensions of ego and infantile identification. *Journal of Personality*, 1959, **27**, 532–545.

Broverman, I. K., Vogel, S. R., Broverman, D. M., Clarkson, F. E., & Rosenkrantz, P. S. Sex-role stereotypes: A current appraisal. *Journal of Social Issues*, 1972, **28**, 59–78.

Brown, D. G. Masculinity-femininity development in children. *Journal of Consulting Psychology*, 1957, **21**, 197–202.

Bryden, N. P. Evidence for sex differences in cerebral organization. In M. A. Wittig and A. C. Petersen (Eds.), *Sex-related differences in cognitive function. Developmental issues.* New York: Academic, 1978, in press.

Callard, E. Achievement motive in the four-year-old and its relationship to achievement expectancies of the mother. Unpublished doctoral dissertation, University of Michigan, 1964.

Cantor, N. L., Wood, D., & Gelfand, D. Effects of responsiveness and sex of children on adult males' behavior. *Child Development*, 1977, **48**, 1426–1430.

Coates, S. Sex differences in field-independence among preschool children. In R. C. Friedman, R. M. Richart, & R. L. Vande Wide (Eds.), *Sex differences in behavior.* New York: Wiley, 1974, pp. 259–274.

Courtney, A. E., & Whipple, T. W. Women in T.V. commercials. *Journal of Communication.* 1974, **24**, 110–118.

D'Andrade, R. Cross-cultural studies of sex differences in behavior. In E. Maccoby (Ed.), *The development of sex differences.* Stanford, Calif.: Stanford University Press, 1966, pp. 82–172.

DeVries, R. Constancy of generic identity in the years three to six. *Monographs of the Society for Research in Child Development*, 1969, **34** (3, Serial No. 127).

Drake, C. T., & McDougall, D. Effects of the absence of a father and other male models on the development of boys' sex roles. *Developmental Psychology*, 1977, **13**, 537–538.

Duncan, D., Schuman, H., & Duncan, *Social change in a metropolitan community.* New York: Russell Sage, 1973.

Dweck, C. S., & Goetz, F. E. Attributions and learned helplessness. In J. H.

Harvey, W. Ickes, & R. F. Kidd (Eds.), *New directions in attribution research* (Vol. 2). Hillsdale, N.J.: Lawrence Erlbaum, 1977.

Emmerich, W. Parental identification in young children. *Genetic Psychology Monographs*, 1959, **60**, 257–308.

Emmerich, W., & Goldman, K. S. Boy-girl identity task (technical report). In V. Shipman (Ed.), *Disadvantaged children and their first school experiences* (Technical Report PR-72-20). Educational Testing Service, 1972.

Fagot, B. I. Sex-related stereotyping of toddlers' behaviors. *Developmental Psychology*, 1973, **9**, 429.

Fagot, B. I. Sex differences in toddlers' behavior and parental reaction. *Developmental Psychology*, 1974, **10**, 554–558.

Fagot, B. I. Consequences of moderate cross-gender behavior in preschool children. *Child Development*, 1977, **48**, 902–907. (a)

Fagot, B. I. Sex-determined parental reinforcing contingencies in toddler children. Paper presented at the biennial meeting of the Society for Research in Child Development, New Orleans, 1977. (b)

Fagot, B. I., & Patterson, C. R. An in vivo analysis of reinforcing contingencies for sex role behaviors in the preschool child. *Developmental Psychology*, 1969, **1**, 563–568.

Feldman, S. S., & Nash, S. C. Interest in babies during young adulthood. *Developmental Psychology*, 1978, in press.

Feldman, S. S., Nash, S. C., & Cutrona, D. The influence of age and sex on responsiveness to babies. *Developmental Psychology*, 1978, in press.

Fennema, E. Mathematics, spatial ability and the sexes. Paper presented at the American Educational Research Association Annual Meeting, Chicago; 1974.

Fisher, S. F. *The female orgasm: Psychology, physiology, fantasy.* New York: Basic Books, 1973.

Flanagan, J. C. *Trends in male/female performance on cognitive ability measures.* American Institutes for Research, 1978.

Fling, S., & Manosevitz, M. Sex typing in nursery school children's play interests. *Developmental Psychology*, 1972, **7**, 146–152.

Frodi, A. M., Lamb, M. E., Leavitt, L. A., & Donovan, W. K. Father's and mother's responses to infant smiles and cries. *Infant Behavior and Development*, 1978, in press.

Frueh, T., & McGhee, P. E. Traditional sex-role development and the amount of time spent watching television. *Developmental Psychology*, 1975, **11**, 109.

Gerbner, G. Violence in television drama. Trends and symbolic functions. In G. A. Constick & E. A. Rubenstein (Eds.), *Television and social behavior* (Vol. 1). *Media content and control.* Washington, D.C.: U.S. Government Printing Office, 1972, pp. 28–187.

Goodenough, E. W. Interest in persons as an aspect of sex differences in the early years. *Genetic Psychology Monographs*, 1957, **55**, 287–323.

Goy, R. W. Organizing effects of androgen on the behavior of rhesus monkeys. In R. P. Michael (Ed.), *Endocrinology and human behavior.* New York: Oxford University Press, 1968.

Guttentag, M., & Bray, H. Androgyny in the schools. Unpublished manuscript, 1977.

Hartley, R. E. Sex-role pressures and socialization of the male child. *Psychological Reports*, 1959, **5**, 457–468.

Hartley, R. E. Children's concepts of male and female roles. *Merrill-Palmer Quarterly*, 1960, **6**, 83–91.

Hartley, R. E., & Hardesty, R. P. Children's perceptions of sex-roles in childhood. *Journal of Genetic Psychology*, 1964, **105**, 43–51.

Hartup, W. W., & Zook, E. A. Sex role preference in three- and four-year-old children. *Journal of Counsulting Psychology*, 1960, **24**, 420–426.

Helper, M. M. Learning theory and the self concept. *Journal of Abnormal and Social Psychology*, 1955, **51**, 184–194.

Hetherington, E. M. A developmental study of the effects of sex of the dominant parent on sex-role preference, identification and imitation in children. *Journal of Personality and Social Psychology*, 1965, **2**, 188–194.

Hetherington, E. M. Effects of paternal absence on sex-typed behaviors in Negro and white preadolescent males. *Journal of Personality and Social Psychology*, 1966, **4**, 87–91.

Hetherington, E. M. The effects of familial variables on sex typing, on parent-child similarity and on imitation in children. In J. P. Hill (Ed.), *Minnesota symposia on child psychology* (Vol. 1). Minneapolis: University of Minnesota Press, 1967, pp. 82–107.

Hetherington, E. M. Effects of father absence on personality development in adolescent daughters. *Developmental Psychology*, 1972, **7**, 313–326.

Hetherington, E. M. Changing sex role stereotypes. Unpublished manuscript, 1974.

Hetherington, E. M. Mothers' and fathers' responses to appropriate and inappropriate dependency in sons and daughters. Unpublished manuscript, 1978.

Hetherington, E. M., Cox, M., & Cox, R. Family interaction and the social, emotional and cognitive development of children following divorce. Paper presented at the Johnson and Johnson Conference on the Family, Washington, D.C., May 1978.

Hetherington, E. M., & Deur, J. The effects of father absence on child development. *Young Children*, 1971, **26**, 233–248.

Hoffman, L. W. The value of children to parents and the decrease in family size. *Proceedings of the American Philosophical Society*, 1975, **119**, 430–438.

Horner, M. S. Toward an understanding of achievement-related conflicts in women. *Journal of Social Issues*, 1972, **78**, 157–176.

Janis, I. L., Mahl, G. F., Kagan, J., & Holt, R. R. *Personality: dynamics, development and assessment.* New York: Harcourt, Brace & World, 1969.

Jenkins, N., & Vroegh, K. Contemporary concepts of masculinity and femininity. *Institute for Juvenile Research Reports*, 1969, 1.

Johnson, N. N., Stockard, J., Acker, J., & Naffziger, C. Expressiveness reevaluated. Paper presented at the meeting of the American Sociological Association, August 1974.

Kagan, J., & Moss, H. A. *Birth to maturity: A study in psychological development.* New York: Wiley, 1962.

Kohlberg, L. A cognitive-developmental analysis of children's sex-role concepts and attitudes. In E. E. Maccoby (Ed.), *The development of sex differences.* Stanford, Calif.: Stanford University Press, 1966, pp. 82–173.

Krieger, W. G. Infant influences and the parent sex by child sex interaction in the socialization process. *JSAS Catalogue of Selected Documents in Psychology*, 1976, **6**(1), 36 (Ms. No. 1234).

LaBarre, W. *The human animal.* Chicago: University of Chicago Press, 1954.

Lamb, M. E. The development of mother-infant and father-infant attachments in the second year of life. *Developmental Psychology*, 1977, in press.

Lansky, L. M. The family structure also affects the model sex role attitudes in parents of preschool children. *Merrill-Palmer Quarterly*, 1967, **13**, 139–150.

La Voie, J. C., & Andrews, R. Cognitive determinants of gender identity and constancy. Paper presented at the annual meeting of the American Psycal Association, Chicago, 1975.

Lee, P. C., & Wolinsky, A. L. Male teachers of young children. *Young Children*, 1973, **28**, 342–353.

Le Corgne, L. C., & Laosa, L. M. Father absence in low-income Mexican-American families: Childrens' social adjustment and conceptual differentiation of sex-role attributes. *Developmental Psychology*, 1976, **12**, 439–448.

Lunde, D. T., & Hamburg, D. A. Techniques for assessing the effects of sex hormones on affect, arousal, and aggression in humans. In B. Astwood (Ed.), *Recent progress in hormone research* (Vol. 28). New York: Academic, 1972.

Lynn, D. B. *Parental and sex-role identification.* Berkeley: McCutchan, 1969.

Lynn, D. B., & Sawrey, W. L. The effects of father-absence on Norwegian boys and girls. *Journal of Abnormal and Social Psychology*, 1959, **59**, 258–262.

Marcus, D. E., & Overton, W. F. The development of cognitive gender constancy and sex-role preferences. *Child Development*, 1978, in press.

Maccoby, E. E. Personal communication. 1978.

Maccoby, E. E., & Jacklin, C. N. *The psychology of sex differences.* Stanford, Calif.: Stanford University Press, 1974.

McGlone, J. Sex differences in functional brain asymmetry. *Cortex*, 1977, in press.

Mead, M. *Sex and temperament in three primitive societies.* New York: Morrow, 1935.

Meyer, W. T., & Thompson, G. G. Sex differences in the distribution of teacher approval and disapproval. *Journal of Educational Psychology*, 1966, **41**, 385–396.

Money, J., & Ehrhardt, A. A. *Man and woman, boy and girl.* Baltimore: Johns Hopkins, 1972.

Moulton, R. W., Liberty, P. G., Burnstein, E., & Altucher, N. Patterning of parental affection and disciplinary dominance as a determinant of guilt and sex typing. *Journal of Personality and Social Psychology*, 1966, **4**, 356–363.

Mussen, P. H., & Distler, L. Masculinity identity and father-son relationships. *Journal of Abnormal and Social Psychology*, 1959, **59**, 350–356.

Mussen, P. H., & Distler, L. Child rearing antecedents of masculine identity and kindergarten boys. *Child Development*, 1960, **31**, 89–100.

Mussen, P. H., & Rutherford, E. Parent-child relations and parental personality in relation to young children's sex role preferences. *Child Development*, 1963, **34**, 589–607.

Nadelman, L. Sex identity in London children: Memory, knowledge and sex preference tests. *Human Development*, 1970, **13**, 28–42.

Naditch, S. F. Experimental demand characteristics and sex differences on the rod and frame test. Paper presented at the annual meeting of the American Psychological Association, Washington, D.C., September 1976.

Osofsky, J. D., & O'Connell, E. J. Parent-child interaction: Daughters' affects upon mothers' and fathers' behavior. *Developmental Psychology*, 1972, **7**, 157–168.

Parke, R. D., & Sawin, D. B. The family in early infancy. Social interactional and attitudinal analysis. Paper presented at the Society for Research in Child Development, New Orleans, March 1977.

Parsons, T. Family structure and the socialization of the child. In T. Parsons & R. Bales (Eds.), *Family, socialization and interaction process.* Glencoe, Ill.: Free Press, 1955, pp. 35–131.

Payne, D. E., & Mussen, P. H. Parent-child relations and father identification among adolescent boys. *Journal of Abnormal and Social Psychology*, 1956, **52**, 358–362.

Pope, B. Socio-economic contrasts in children's peer culture prestige values. *Genetic Psychology Monographs*, 1953, **48**, 157–220.

Rabban, M. Sex role identity in young children in two diverse social groups. *Genetic Psychology Monographs*, 1950, **42**, 81–158.

Ralph, J. B., Goldberg, M. L., & Passow, A. H. *Bright Underachievers.* New York: Teachers College, 1966.

Rendina, I., & Dickerscheid, J. D. Father involvement with first-born infants. *Family Coordinator*, 1976, **25**, 373–379.

Rose, R. M., Gordon, T. P., & Bernstein, I. S. Plasma testosterone levels in the male rhesus: Influences of sexual and social stimuli. *Science*, 1972, **178,** 643–645.

Rubin, J. Z., Provenzano, F. J., & Luria, Z. The eye of the beholder: Parents' views on sex of newborns. *American Journal of Orthopsychiatry*, 1974, **43,** 720–731.

Saegert, S., & Hart, R. The development of sex differences in the environmental competence of children. In P. Burnett (Ed.), *Women in society.* Chicago: Maaroufa Press, 1976.

Santrock, J. W. Paternal absence, sex-typing and identification. *Developmental Psychology*, 1970, **2,** 264–272.

Saghir, M. T., & Robbins, F. *Male and female homosexuality.* Baltimore: Williams & Wilkins, 1973.

Sears, P. S. Child rearing factors related to playing of sex-typed roles. *American Psychologist*, 1953, **38,** 431 (Abstract).

Seavey, C. A., Katz, P. A., & Zalk, S. R. Baby X: The effect of gender labels on adult responses to infants. *Sex Roles*, 1975, **1,** 103–109.

Serbin, L. A., O'Leary, D. K., Kent, R. N., & Tonick, I. J. A comparison of teacher response to the preacademic and problem behavior of boys and girls. *Child Development*, 1973, **44,** 796–804.

Shenker, I. How do parents talk to their children? Two psychologists listened in. *New York Times*, Oct. 10, 1971.

Sherman, J. A. Problems of sex differences in space perception and aspects of intellectual functioning. *Psychological Review*, 1967, **74,** 290–299.

Shinedling, M. M., & Pederson, D. M. Effects of sex of teacher and student on children's gains in quantitative and verbal performance. *Journal of Psychology*, 1970, **76,** 79–84.

Slaby, R. G., & Frey, K. S. Development of gender constancy and selective attention to same-sex models. *Child Development*, 1975, **46,** 849–856.

Spence, J., Helmreich, R., & Stopp, J. The personal attributes questionnaire. *JSAS Catalogue of Selected Documents in Psychology*, 1974, **4,** 43.

Steimel, R. J. Childhood experiences and masculinity-femininity scores. *Journal of Counseling Psychology*, 1960, **7,** 212–217.

Stein, A. H., & Bailey, M. M. The socialization of achievement orientation in females. *Psychological Bulletin*, 1973, **80,** 345–366.

Stein, A. H., Pohly, S. R., & Mueller, E. The influence of masculine, feminine and neutral tasks on children's achievement behavior, expectancies of success and attainment of values. *Child Development*, 1971, **42,** 195–207.

Stern, G. G. Measuring noncognitive variables in research on teaching. In N. L. Gage (Ed.), *Handbook of research on teaching.* Chicago: Rand McNally, 1963, pp. 398–447.

Sternglanz, S. H., & Serbin, L. A. Sex-role stereotyping in children's television programs. *Developmental Psychology*, 1974, **10,** 710–715.

Tedesco, N. S. Patterns in prime time. *Journal of Communication*, 1974, **15,** 55–64.

Thompson, S. K. Gender labels and early sex-role development. *Child Development*, 1975, **46,** 339–347.

Tyler, L. E. *The psychology of human differences.* New York: Appleton-Century-Crofts, 1947.

Ward, W. D. Patterns of culturally defined sex-role preference and parental imitation. *Journal of Genetic Psychology*, 1973, **122,** 337–343.

Weiss, P. Some aspects of femininity. *Dissertation Abstracts*, 1962, **23,** 1083.

West, D. J. *Homosexuality.* Chicago: Aldine, 1967.

Witelson, S. F. Sex differences in the neurology of cognition. Psychological, social, educational and clinical implications. In S. Sullerot (Ed.), *La Fait Feminin.* France: Fayard, 1978.

Wohlford, P., Santrock, J. W., Berger, S. E., & Leiberman, D. Older brothers' influence on sex-typed aggressive and dependent behavior in father absent children. *Developmental Psychology*, 1971, **4,** 124–134.

Young, W. C., Goy, R. W., & Phoenix, C. H. Hormones and sexual behavior. *Science*, 1964, **143,** 212–218.

16

The Development
of Morality
and
Self-Control

How do moral values and behaviors develop? How does the child become capable of self-control, resistance to temptation, and personal sacrifices for the welfare of others? This chapter will trace the course of moral development. Theories of the development of moral judgment will be presented. The relationship of moral judgment, moral behavior, and guilt and their consistency across situations and over time will be discussed. In addition, the development of altruism and prosocial behavior will be examined. How early does altruism begin, how does it change, and what role do parents play in the emergence of prosocial behavior? Finally, aggression will be explored. How does aggression change in form and frequency? What are the ways in which family and mass media contribute to aggression? How can aggression be effectively controlled?

An Overview of Moral Development

A basic task of socialization in every culture is that of communicating ethical standards and shaping and enforcing the practice of "good" behaviors in the developing child. Although the specific values and behaviors regarded as desirable vary among cultures, all societies have a system of rules about the rightness and wrongness of certain behaviors. The child is expected to learn these rules and to experience emotional discomfort or guilt when violating them and satisfaction when conforming to them.

Initial control over the young child's behavior is maintained largely through immediate external social factors, such as the presence of authority figures or fear of punishment. However, with age the child's behavior seems to be increasingly maintained by internalized standards of conduct which lead to self-control in the absence of external restraints. This shift from external factors to personal feelings and ethical beliefs as the basis of moral behavior is called *internalization*; many psychologists believe internalization to be the basic process in the development of morality.

Psychological research has focused on the development of the three basic components of morality: the cognitive component, the behavioral component, and the emotional component, and the relationships between these three factors and their roles in the process of internalization. The cognitive factor involves the knowledge of ethical rules and the judgments of the "goodness" or "badness" of various acts. The behavioral factor has to do with actual behavior in a variety of situations involving ethical considerations. Most studies have investigated disapproved-of aspects of children's behaviors, such as cheating, lying, and the inability to delay gratification, resist temptation, or control aggression. However, recent studies of moral development have also included positive behaviors, often called *prosocial behaviors*, such as sharing, cooperation, altruism, and helping. Similarly, studies of the emotional dimension of morality have tended to be confined to negative aspects, such as feelings of guilt, often measured by confession or reparation following transgression, rather than feelings of satisfaction associated with prosocial acts. Again we find that different psychological theories have focused on different aspects of moral development. Cognitive theories have emphasized moral judgments; psychoanalytic theories have

(*Miss Peach* by Mell Lazarus. Courtesy of Mell Lazarus and Field Newspaper Syndicate.)

emphasized affective components of morality, particularly those of guilt and anxiety; and learning theories have emphasized ethical behavior. Both analytic and behavior theory have been greatly concerned with internalization, although they invoke different mechanisms to explain its development.

Freud believed moral behavior and the guilt experienced when violating moral standards were the result of the formation of the superego through identification, when children take in the ethical standards as they perceive them in their parents. Social learning theorists use the same learning principles of conditioning, the administration of rewards and punishments, and imitation as the foundation for the acquisition of all social behaviors including moral conduct and self-control.

Cognitive Theories of Moral Development

Alternative explanations for the acceptance and development of moral standards are presented by the cognitive theorists Jean Piaget and Lawrence Kohlberg. Piaget's theory of moral development involves many of the same principles and processes of cognitive growth that were encountered in the early presentation of his theory of intellectual development. In fact, the key thing to remember is that for these theorists the study of moral development is just an approach to the study of intellectual development as it bears on the specific topic of ethical cognition. Since intellectual growth proceeds through a specific sequence of stages, moral judgments will also advance in stages related to the changes in the child's general cognitive development.

Jean Piaget's Cognitive Theory of Moral Development

Piaget proposes a cognitive developmental theory of moral development in which the moral concepts of the child evolve in an unvarying sequence from an early stage, which is often called the *stage of moral realism*, to a more mature stage, referred to as the *morality of reciprocity*, or *autonomous morality*. No one could reach the stage of moral reciprocity without first having passed through the stage of moral realism. According to Piaget, mature morality includes both children's understanding and acceptance of social rules and their concern for equality and reciprocity in human relationships which is the basis of justice. He investigated changing moral judgments in two main ways. First, he investigated shifts with age in children's attitudes toward rules in such common children's games as marbles. Second, he studied children's judgments of the seriousness of transgressions by having children listen to stories and comment on why and to what extent the behaviors of the characters in the stories were wrong.

The preschool child shows little concern or awareness of rules. In children's games such as marbles the child does not try to play a systematic game with the intention of winning, but seems to gain satisfaction from the manipulation and multiple uses of the marbles. If two 3-year-olds are observed playing marbles, they may each be using different and idiosyncratic rules and thinking the point of the game is to enjoy themselves. At about age 5, however, the child begins to develop great concern and respect for rules. Rules are regarded as coming from external authority, usually the parents; rules are immutable, unchanging through time, and never to be questioned. What Piaget calls *moral absolutism* prevails. If a child of this age is asked if children in other countries could play marbles with different rules, she will assure the interviewer that they could not. This is reflected in the rigidty with which the child approaches social interactions, frequently falling back on a "my mommy says_____" ploy to solve disputes. In addition to rules being viewed as beyond the child's influence, any deviation from them is seen as inevitably resulting in punishment by *immanent justice*. Someone or something is going to get you one way or another! Such retribution might take the form of accidents or mishaps controlled by inanimate objects or by God. A child who has lied to his mother may later fall off his bike and skin his knees and will think, "That's what I get for lying to mother." In this stage, children also evaluate the seriousness of an act in terms of its consequences rather than according to the good or bad intentions of the actor. Behavior is assessed in terms of *objective responsibility* rather than intentionality. The two factors which contribute to young children's moral realism are the *egocentrism*, that is, their inability to subordinate their own experiences and perceive situations as others would, and their *realistic thinking*, which leads them to confuse external reality with their own thought processes and subjective experiences.

With older children at about ages 9 to 11, Piaget believes a *morality of reciprocity* begins to emerge. In contrast to the period of moral realism, moral judgments are now characterized by the recognition that social rules are arbitrary agreements which can be questioned and changed. Obedience to authority is neither necessary nor always desirable. Violations of rules are not always wrong, nor are they inevitably punished. The child considers the feelings and viewpoints of others in judging their behavior. When there is to be punishment, reciprocity in relating the punishment to the intentions of the wrongdoer and nature of the transgression should be considered; the punishment should be in the form of restitution that will make up for harm done or help teach the culprit to behave better if the situation should arise again. Finally there should be "equalitarianism" in the form of equal justice for all.

Some of these shifts in attitude from the stage of moral realism to that of moral reciprocity are vividly illustrated in the children's responses to stories reported by Piaget in his book *The Moral Judgement of the Child* (1932). Piaget would present the child with pairs of stories such as the following ones and ask the child if the children in each are equally guilty, and which child was the naughtiest and why.

Story I. A little boy who is called John is in his room. He is called to dinner. He goes into the dining room. But behind the door there was a chair, and on the chair there was a tray with 15 cups on it. John couldn't have known that there was all this behind the door. He goes in, the door knocks against the tray, "bang" to the 15 cups and they all get broken!

Story II. Once there was a little boy whose name was Henry. One day when his mother was out he tried to get some jam out of the cupboard. He climbed up on a chair and stretched out his arm. But the jam was too high up and he couldn't reach it and have any. But while he was trying to get it, he knocked over a cup. The cup fell down and broke. (Piaget, 1932, p. 122)

A characteristic response for a child in the stage of moral realism is given by a 6-year-old:

"Have you understood these stories?"
"Yes."
"What did the first boy do?"
"He broke 15 cups."
"And the second one?"
"He broke a cup by moving roughly."
"Why did the first one break the cups?"
"Because he was clumsy. When he was getting the jam the cup fell down."
"Is one of the boys naughtier than the other?"
"The first one is because he knocked over 15 cups."
"If you were the daddy, which one would you punish most?"
"The one who broke 15 cups."
"Why did he break them?"
"The door shut too hard and knocked them over. He didn't do it on purpose."
"And why did the other boy break a cup?"
"He wanted to get the jam. He moved too far. The cup got broken."
"Why did he want to get the jam?"
"Because he was all alone. Because his mother wasn't there." (Piaget, 1932, p. 129)

In spite of the fact that Henry was clumsy while trying to deceive his mother, John is regarded by the child in the stage of moral realism as behaving less ethically since he destroyed more cups, although it was unintentional. In contrast, Russ, a 10-year-old, shows advances to the stage of moral reciprocity when he responds that the one who wanted to take the jam was naughtiest. He is considering intentions. When asked if it makes any difference that the other child broke more cups, he replies: "No because the one who broke 15 cups didn't do it on purpose" (Piaget, 1932, p. 130).

Moral Judgments and Peer Interaction

It might be asked what factors facilitate this essential shift in moral judgments. In contrast to theories which emphasize the role of the parents in moral development, Piaget focuses on the contribution of peers. The movement away from moral absolutism, realism, and egocentrism can only occur in interpersonal relationships in which the child can contrast and question her point of view and those of others. Through cooperation and the making of shared decisions with peers, she becomes sensitive to the multiple roles, needs, and feelings she has in common with others. She realizes that the same act may be perceived in a variety of ways by different people and lead to different results.

This increased ability to make inferences about others is based on the cognitive development and improved intellectual ability of children to solve a variety of intellectual problems. It is also related to children's motivation to understand others and acquire social skills as they interact more with their peers. Children realize that it is useful to understand when someone is angry or hurt but is trying not to show it, when someone is pleased or displeased by their behavior, or when someone is tired and irritable.

As children become less dependent on adults, their increased feelings of control and participation in decision making and their growing ability to take on new roles enhance their respect for themselves and others. It frees them from the domination of external authorities and leads to a sympathy and concern with intentions in actions, which they would not be likely to attain if it were not for the agreement and cooperation inherent in interactions with people of equal status.

Piaget suggests that this mutual solidarity and respect, which is so critical in developing a sense of social justice, can only occur when children free themselves from relations of unilateral authority with adults, particularly with their parents. Although Piaget believes peer relations to be the greatest importance in the development of a mature morality, he does suggest that if parents moved from their traditional position of unilateral authority and attempted to establish a more egalitarian relationship with their children, they might thereby accelerate the acquisition of reciprocal morality. If adults were willing to conform to the same rules they impose on their children and to stress their own obligations and failures in their relationships with them, they might become a more positive force in ethical development.

Lawrence Kohlberg's Cognitive Theory of Moral Development

Kohlberg (1963a, 1963b, 1969) has extended, modified, and refined Piaget's theory, based on his analysis of interviews of 10- to 16-year-old boys who were confronted with a series of moral dilemmas in which they must choose between acts of obedience to rules and authority or the needs and welfare of others which conflicted with the regulations.

A representative dilemma is one in which a man needs a particular expensive drug to help his dying wife. The pharmacist who discovered and controls the supply of the drug has refused the husband's offer to give him all the money he now has, which would be about half the necessary sum, and to pay the rest later. The man must now decide whether or not to steal the drug to save his wife, that is, whether to obey the rules and laws of society or violate them to respond to the needs of his wife. What should the man do, and why?

Kohlberg formulated a series of three broad levels of moral development subdivided into six stages; each stage was based not only upon whether the boys chose an obedient or need-serving act, but also on the reasons and justification for their choices. Kohlberg believes that the order of the stages is fixed, but that stages do not occur at the same age in all people. Many people never attain the highest level of moral judgment, and some adults continue to think in immature preconventional terms of conforming only to avoid punishment and gain rewards.

Kohlberg would agree with Piaget in noting that the young child is oriented toward obedience, but for different reasons. Whereas Piaget regarded this early conformity as being based on the young child's dependency and respect for authority, in level 1, the *preconventional level*, Kohlberg regards it as based on the desire to avoid punishment and gain rewards. At level 1 there is no internalization of moral standards. At level 2, the *conventional level*, although the child identifies with his parents and conforms to what they regard as right and wrong, it is the motive to conform rather than ethical standards which have been internalized. It is only at level 3, the *postconventional level*, that moral judgment is rational and internalized and that conduct is controlled by an internalized ethical code and is relatively independent of the approval or castigation of others. At this level, moral conflict is resolved in terms of broad ethical principles and violating these principles results in guilt and self-condemnation.

The levels and stages of moral development as conceptualized by Kohlberg are as follows:

Level 1. Preconventional morality
Stage 1. Obedience and punishment orientation

This orientation involves deference to prestigious or powerful people, usually the parents, in order to avoid punishment. The morality of an act is defined in terms of its physical consequences.

Stage 2. Naive hedonistic and instrumental orientation

In this stage the child is conforming to gain rewards. Although there is evidence of reciprocity and sharing, it is a manipulative, self-serving reciprocity rather than one based on a true sense of justice, generosity, sympathy, or compassion. It is a kind of bartering: "I'll lend you my bike if I can play with your wagon," "I'll do my homework now if I can watch the late night movie."

Level 2. Conventional level: morality of conventional rules and conformity
Stage 3. Good boy morality

In this stage good behavior is that which maintains approval and good relations with others. Although the child is still basing his judgments of right and wrong on the responses of others, he is concerned with their approval and disapproval rather than their physical power. He is concerned about conforming to his friends and families' standards to maintain good-will. He is, however, starting to accept the social regulations of others and is judging the goodness or badness of behavior in terms of a person's intent to violate these rules.

Stage 4. Authority and social-order-maintaining morality

In this stage the individual blindly accepts social conventions and rules and believes that if society accepts the rules they should be maintained to avoid censure. It is no longer just conformity to other individuals' standards but conformity to the social order. This is the epitome of "law and order" morality involving unquestioning acceptance of social regulations. Behavior is judged as good in terms of its conformity to a rigid set of rules. It is unfortunate that most individuals in our culture do not pass beyond the conventional level of morality.

Level 3. Postconventional level: Morality of self-accepted moral principles
Stage 5. Morality of contract, individual rights, and democratically accepted law

There is a flexibility of moral beliefs in this stage that was lacking in earlier stages. Morality is based upon an agreement among individuals to conform to norms which appear necessary to maintain the social order and the rights of others. However, since it is a social contract, it can be modified when the people within society rationally discuss alternatives which might be more advantageous to a larger number of the members of the group.

Stage 6. Morality of individual principles and conscience

In this stage individuals conform both to social standards and to internalized ideals to avoid self-condemnation, rather than criticism by others. Decisions are based upon abstract principles involving justice, compassion, and equality. It is a morality based upon a respect for others. People who have attained this level of development will have highly individualistic moral beliefs which may at times conflict with the social order accepted by the majority. A greater number of nonviolent, activist students taking part in the anti-Vietnam war demonstrations had attained the postconventional level of morality than had nonactivist students.

Kohlberg, like Piaget, believes that stages of moral development are determined by the cognitive capabilities of the individuals. Like the orderly progression of Piaget's general cognitive theory of development with the attainments of one stage building on the achievements of earlier stages, moral development builds on the moral concepts in previous stages. Figure 16-1 presents the percent of moral statements of different types or stages of development at four ages (Kohlberg, 1963b). Although Kohlberg predicts no direct relation between age and moral maturity, it can be seen that more preconventional responses are made by young children and more postconventional responses by older children. The sequence should be invariant across cultures, although the ultimate level attained may vary among cultures and for individuals within the same society. Once an individual has attained a high level

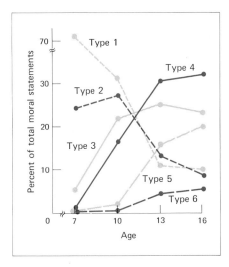

FIGURE 16-1 Use of six types of moral judgments at four ages. *(From Kohlberg, 1963 b.)*

of moral cognition, especially stage 6, she will not regress and go back to earlier stages of moral judgment.

Evaluation of Cognitive Theories of Moral Development

Studies of cognitive theories of moral development have focused on four main issues: first, the question of the invariance of the stages of moral development; second, the relation of moral development to other aspects of cognitive development; third, the effects of variations in social interactions with parents and peers on moral development; and fourth, the relationship between moral judgments and moral behavior.

Invariance of Stages of Moral Development   One of the central arguments of cognitive theories of moral development suggests that people progress from one level of moral judgment to another in a fixed and invariant sequence. In Piaget's theory, the general developmental progression from moral realism to moral reciprocity has been frequently replicated (Hogan & Emler, 1978; Lickona, 1976). In industrialized Western countries such as the United States, Great Britain, France, Switzerland, etc., across a wide range of populations and social classes and for both sexes there are regular age trends of development in moral judgment. In most Western countries there is a trend from moral realism to moral reciprocity with increasing age. However, the findings in cross-cultural studies are less consistent. A study by Havinghurst and Neugarten (1955) of ten American Indian tribes found developmental increase rather than the predicted decrease in belief in immanent justice in six tribes. Also, only two of the ten groups showed the expected shift in the conception of rules toward greater flexibility with age. It seems that cultural factors can alter the sequence of Piaget's moral judgments.

Although there is support for the general developmental sequence, recent research in moral development suggests that Piaget underestimated the cognitive capacities of young children. In judging the behavior of others, even 6-year-old children are able to consider other people's intentions when the situation is described in a way that they can comprehend. When the format of the moral stories is changed from a verbal presentation, which young children may have trouble processing, to videotaped presentations, 6-year-olds respond to the intentions of the actor as well as older children (Chandler, Greenspoon & Barenboim, 1973). As the authors note, "The medium is the message!" A further methodological shortcoming of Piaget's early studies may be another reason for the underestimation of the moral judgment abilities of young children. In the original Piaget stories, children always were required to judge whether a child who causes a small amount of damage in the service of bad intentions is any "worse" than one who causes a large amount of damage in the pursuit of good intentions. The intent of the child in the story was confounded with the consequences of his or her behavior. When stories are presented where good and bad intentions can be evaluated separately from good and bad outcomes, even 6-year-olds are able to use intentions as the basis for their judgments (Feldman, Klosson, Parsons, Rholes & Ruble, 1976).

There is general support for the assumptions that children proceed through Kohlberg's stages of moral judgment in a fixed and invariant fashion as well. Progress is generally toward higher stages than toward lower stages. Short-term longitudinal studies offer one course of supporting evidence. In one study, the moral judgments of 5- to 8-year-old children were initially assessed and then reassessed after six months and again after one year (Kuhn, 1976). Most of the children were at Kohlberg's stages 1 and 2. Using this short-term longitudinal approach, the investigator found that most of the children progressed toward the next higher stage over the one-year period. Progress was slow and gradual since there was no significant change over the shorter six-month intervals. Cross-cultural confirmation of this general pattern of upward stage movement has recently been found in a three-year longitudinal study of 8- to 17-year-old children in the Bahamas (White, Bushnell & Regnemer, 1978). Other studies have used role-playing and modeling techniques to determine whether moral judgments can be successfully modified. Although some studies report that shifts to less mature levels of moral judgment can be induced by modeling (Bandura & McDonald, 1963), the majority of studies indicate that it is generally easier to advance an individual's moral judgment to a higher stage than to shift it to a lower stage (Arbuthnot, 1975; Cowan, Langer, Heavenrich & Nathanson, 1969; Rest, 1976; Turiel, 1966). Moreover, subjects who are exposed to a model's reasoning about moral dilemmas at the stage above or a stage below their own stage of moral development preferred the more advanced to the less advanced stage (Rest, 1976). This short-term laboratory evidence is generally consistent with both Piaget's and Kohlberg's views that progress should be toward higher rather than lower stages.

Although children's moral judgments proceed in an upward direction, many children do not attain the higher stages outlined by Kohlberg. In cross-cultural studies conducted in Turkey, Taiwan, Yucatan, and Mexico, results found children in primitive tribal or village communities never reach the level of postconventional morality (Kohlberg, 1969). In recent studies of Bahamian children and adults, a similar picture emerges; most individuals reasoned at stages 3 or below (White et al., 1978; White, 1977). "Individuals in highly industralized settings seem to move through the lower stages at a more rapid rate and to achieve higher stages than do individuals in less industralized and less urban settings." (White et al., 1978, p. 59). Even within the United States, high-socioeconomic-status children pass through the sequence of moral stages more rapidly than those in poorer economic conditions; these wealthier children ultimately are more likely to attain postconventional levels of moral judgment. Cultural factors clearly seem to influence both the rate of development of moral judgments as well as the final level that will be achieved.

Relation of Moral Judgments to Other Cognitive Measures   It is not surprising that general cognitive maturity has been found to be related to moral maturity. Just as IQ was found to be associated with speed of development of concepts associated with sex-role typing, it is also associated with the attainment of both Piaget's and Kohlberg's stages of morality. A high level of abstract thinking is required in the development of evaluation of intent, generalized rational ethical standards, and sensitivity to the roles, perceptions, and feelings of others.

In one study, sixth-grade girls and college women were administered Kohlberg's moral dilemmas and a variety of cognitive measures (Tomlinson-Keasey & Keasey, 1974). All the females who reasoned at the postconventional level (stages 5 and 6) also showed formal operational thinking. However, not all who reasoned at the formal operations level reached the postconventional levels of moral development. Confirmation of this pattern comes from a more recent study (Kuhn, Kohlberg, Langer & Haan, 1977). Together, this evidence suggests that formal operations is a necessary but not sufficient condition for advanced levels of moral judgment.

In addition to general intellectual ability, the specific ability to take the role of others is emphasized as a key cognitive skill influencing moral responses. Both Kohlberg and Piaget have stressed the shift from egocentricity to consideration of the feelings and intentions of others as an important transition in moral development. Measures of role-taking skills do correlate with Kohlberg's levels of moral judgments, and shifts to higher levels of moral development are preceded by increases in role-taking ability (Damon, 1977; Selman, 1971a, 1971b, 1976).

Opportunities for role taking affect moral behavior as well. Children who are given the opportunity to play the role of disciplinary agent and enforce a rule on another child are more likely to subsequently follow the rule themselves (Bosserman & Parke, 1973).

Effects of Social Interactions on Moral Development In contrast to social learning theorists and psychoanalytic theorists, the cognitive theorists have not been as concerned with the effects of childrearing factors and parental influences on moral development. Piaget has emphasized the role of peers and Kohlberg that of social interactions involving role-taking opportunities in moral development.

There is evidence that social interactions with peers are important in moral development. Children who participate in more social activities are rated by their peers and teachers as more popular; as group leaders, these children have been found to be more mature in moral judgments (Keasey, 1971).

Some support for Kohlberg's emphasis on the importance of social role-taking experience in moral development is found in studies which show that restricted social environments, such as isolated communities, or large, impersonal, diffuse school environments where there is a lack of opportunity for intense and varied role-taking experiences, are related to undifferentiated, simplistic descriptions of social roles. This might be expected to restrict the role-taking abilities basic in moral judgment.

Although Kohlberg argues that parents do not play a crucial role in moral development, the cognitive structuring involved in parental discipline does affect both moral judgments and moral behavior. When parents use consistent disciplinary techniques involving reasoning and explanation (Aronfreed, 1961, 1976; Parke, 1974; 1977) or involving discussions of the feelings of others

(Hoffman & Saltzstein, 1967; Kohlberg, 1969), more mature moral judgments in addition to more self-controlled behavior occur. Moreover, recent evidence suggests that there is a positive relationship between parents' moral stages and the moral stages of their sons; no relationship between parents and daughters was found (Haan, Langer, & Kohlberg, 1976).

In contrast to sex-role typing, mothers seem to play a more important role than fathers in the moral development of children (Hoffman & Saltzstein, 1967; LaVoie, 1973). This may be because mothers seek information about their children's feelings and their interpretation of their transgressions before punishing the child, whereas fathers favor immediate punishment without discussion. There is more communication between mother and child about discipline (LaVoie, 1973). In addition to offering more verbal cognitive structuring of the moral contingencies in the situation, the mother may offer a more positive social model of sensitivities and concern with the perceptions and feelings of others.

Moral Judgments and Moral Behavior

Does knowledge of the maturity of a child's moral judgments help us predict how a child will actually behave when in a situation involving personal choices of ethically desirable or undesirable behavior? Generally not. Most evidence indicates that there is little relationship between moral judgments and moral behavior, such as cheating (Nelson, Grinder & Biaggio, 1969; Nakasato & Aoyamo, 1972; Podd, 1972). Much behavior is "impulsive" and not always guided by rational and deliberate thought. A child may have reached stage 3, the level of "good boy morality," where he is concerned with maintaining parental approval. However, when his younger brother breaks his favorite toy, he may kick him even if the parent is present and will disapprove of his action. The child may later even be able to offer mature reasoning that it was wrong to hit young children because they do not really know what they are doing. Thought, in short, does not always guide action (Aronfreed, 1976; Mischel & Mischel, 1976).

However, there is some suggestive evidence of closer relationships between moral judgments and moral behavior among older subjects. Experimental studies of cheating behavior of older subjects show that subjects who are in the two most advanced stages of Kohlberg's classifications of moral development (stage 5 of the morality of contract and stage 6 of the morality of individual principles and conscience) are less likely to cheat than those at earlier levels (Grim, Kohlberg, & White, 1968; Krebs, 1967; Lehrer, 1967). In a procedure used by Milgram (1963; 1974) in which adult subjects were asked to give increasingly painful electric shocks to another person who they believed had agreed to submit to the procedure, Kohlberg (1965) reports that most of the subjects at stage 6 in moral judgments refused to shock the other subject when he showed signs of pain. In contrast, the majority of subjects at lower levels complied.

Some relationship of cognitive level of moral development and behavior is also demonstrated in a study of college students' participation in the 1964 Berkeley free speech movement during disruptions at the University of California. Eighty percent of students at stage 6 participated in civil disobedience, whereas about 50 percent at stage 5 and only 10 percent at stages 3 and 4 were involved in activist protest (Haan, Smith, & Block, 1968). The authors assume that the orientation to their conscience as a directing agent of stage 6 students led them to protest the violation of ethical principles by this country's war activities.

Development studies across a wide age span would help determine when and how thought and action become more closely integrated as individuals develop.

It is clear that knowledge of moral judgments alone is insufficient to understand why people behave differently in various moral situations. Next, we turn to an examination of some of the other factors related to moral behavior.

The Behavioral Side of Moral Development: Which Children Cheat and When?

Situational factors play an important role in the performance of honest or dishonest behavior. The characteristics of the situation interact with the motives, values, past experiences, and attributes of the child to produce transgressions or resistance to temptation. Different children cheat in different situations for different reasons.

Children cheat in a variety of ways. (Photo (a) Brian E. Blauser, Black Star; photo (b) Rohn Engh, Photo Researchers, Inc.)

(a)   (b)

Sex Differences and Cheating

There are no consistent sex differences in honesty. Although teachers rate girls as being more self-controlled, trustworthy, and obedient than boys and although girls are less likely to admit cheating than are boys, the frequency of their cheating behavior tends to be similar (Burton, 1976; Krebs, 1969). Unfortunately, the frequency of cheating on examinations is high for both sexes, ranging from 50 to 80 percent in studies of elementary school, high school, and college students. Academic cheating does not seem to moderate with age. Girls are more likely to manifest antisocial behavior if they think there is little risk of being caught. Boys are more willing to take chances.

Intelligence and Cheating

A frequently reported finding is that bright students cheat less (Hartshorne & May, 1928; Hetherington & Feldman, 1964; Johnson & Gormley, 1972; Kanfer & Duerfeldt, 1968; Nelsen, et al., 1969). This is often explained by saying bright students have less need to cheat since on the basis of their past academic success they know they are likely to do well on tests. Some support is given this position by the finding that the correlation between IQ and cheating disappears when the task is a nonacademic game-type task, when risk of detection is minimized, or when an exam is particularly difficult (Hartshorne & May, 1928; Howells, 1938). When the situation is unfamiliar or the going gets tough, bright children cheat too.

Another possible explanation for the correlation between IQ and honesty is suggested by the results of studies which show that bright students are better able to judge the chances of being caught cheating or to figure out what an experimenter is up to, and that a deception procedure must be very subtle to trap them.

Motivation and Cheating

Motivational factors play an important role in honest or dishonest behavior. There is a complex interaction between the need to achieve, the extent of possible gains, fear of failure, and the possibility of detection. Children who have a high need to achieve and fear of failure are likely to cheat when they think they are not performing as well as their peers on a test (Gilligan, 1963; Shelton & Hill, 1969). It has been proposed that under these circumstances cheating is an attempt to avoid self-criticism and devaluation by peers (Hill & Kochendorfer, 1969; Shelton & Hill, 1969). When children think there is a high probability of being caught, they are less likely to cheat even when they are not doing well because this would result in a high loss of self-esteem and public regard.

When the gains involved in cheating are high, there is an increase in the frequency of cheating and a willingness to take greater risks. Students who are working their way through college cheat more than nonworking students (Parr, 1936). They have more to lose by failure. Similarly, as the pressure for academic and vocational success on males increases, there is an acceleration of cheating in the late high school and college years (Hetherington & Feldman, 1964; Feldman & Feldman, 1967). Students attribute much of the cheating in a university to the highly competitive atmosphere and the impact failure would have on future vocational opportunities and admissions to graduate schools (Smith, Ryan, & Diggins, 1972). The interaction between motivation and fear of failure is vividly illustrated in a study by Pearlin and his associates (Pearlin, 1971; Pearlin, Yarrow & Scarr, 1967). These investigators found that although parental pressure toward achievement is related to greater academic success in children, these pressures may also result in a greater motivation to cheat. If parents had high aspirations for their children and pressured them toward success, but were a low-income level, this resulted in the greatest cheating. The motivation to succeed was great but because of financial restrictions the possibilty of realizing the parents' goals was limited. It has also been found that if parents put great pressures on a child of limited intellectual ability to succeed, it will result in more dishonest behavior.

Group Membership and Cheating

Finally, the standards of the group with which the individual is involved and the behavior of those about him influence his moral behavior. There is a high correlation between the honesty of children and that of their siblings and parents (Hartshorne & May, 1928). Dishonesty and criminality in parents are also associated with delinquency in children (McCord, McCord, & Zola, 1959). This might be attributed to shared ethical standards within the family, to modeling of each other's behavior, or to exposure to the same childrearing and disciplinary factors.

Groups other than the family influence honesty. When students come together in a classroom or academic institution, they become more similar in their patterns of honesty. They modify their behavior according to the norms of the group, the behavior they see around them, and the verbalized standards of other members of the group. There is less cheating in schools which are on the honor system and where internalized control is expected than in schools where exams are closely monitored (Canning, 1956; Bonjean & McGee, 1965). In addition, within an academic institution there is less cheating within certain majors and living groups. There is greater cheating among fraternity and sorority members than among nonaffiliated members (Bonjean & McGee, 1965; Bowers, 1964; Hetherington & Feldman, 1964). Even within a classroom the student who happens to be assigned a seat among students who cheat is more likely to increase his dishonest behavior.

Moreover, the impact of the peer group on moral behavior is evident very early (Parke, 1974). Observations of nursery-school-age children revealed that 3- to 5-year-olds cheated less in a resistance to temptation situation, that is, in a room with forbidden toys, if they were told that the peer group had decided that no one should play with the toys. However, the child's relationship with the peer group is important: peer endorsement of rules produces the highest degree of self-control in children who are observed to be well-integrated into the peer group.

Consistency across Situations

Are children consistent in their moral behavior across situations? To answer this question, we turn to the most extensive investigation of moral behavior ever attempted. In their project, Hartshorne & May (1928) studied the responses of 11,000 school-age children who were given the opportunity to cheat, steal, and lie in a wide variety of situations: in athletics, social events, the school, the home, alone, or with peers. Burton (1963) took only the measures which were reliable from the original studies in deceit and found strong evidence for a general factor of moral behavior. Burton concludes that each child does have a different general predisposition to behave morally or immorally in a variety of situations. The more similar the situations, the greater the consistency in self-control; the less the situations resemble each other, the less generality of moral behavior is obtained. Measures of cheating on different achievement tests in the classroom are going to correlate more highly with each other than with measures of cheating on games in the home. Other studies have found positive correlations between a variety of tests of resistance to temptation in nursery school children (Sears, Rau, & Alpert, 1965) and between measures of dishonesty in classroom tests with adolescents (Barbu, 1951) and college students (Hetherington & Feldman, 1964). Such findings do not minimize the importance of situational variables such as fear of detection, peer support for deviant behavior, and the instigation of other powerful motivational factors, such as achievement needs in moral conduct. However, they do suggest that some children are more likely to yield to such demands than are others.

Parallel findings are obtained in the consistency of moral judgments across a variety of dimensions and situations. Although there is some modest consistency in level of moral maturity across the situations and dilemmas used to measure level of moral judgment, it varies according to the degree of shared factors in stories. Is the main issue in both stories the intentions of the person performing an act, or does one story involve intentionality and the other immanent justice? If both involve the same moral dimension, the correlation in level of moral maturity in judgments will be higher than if the dimensions differ (Johnson, 1962).

The Development of Altruism

Which Children Help and Share and When?

Although there has been a voluminous amount of research done on antisocial behavior, it has only been within the past decade that psychologists have become involved in the study of more positive, altruistic aspects of social behavior, such as cooperation, helping, and sharing. Therefore, much less is known about why and when prosocial behavior occurs.

Origins of Altruism

Altruism begins very early in life and is evident in a number of different ways. Some of the earliest instances of prosocial behavior can be seen in children's

Helping begins at an early age. (Suzanne Szasz)

pointing, playing, showing, and sharing. As we noted in our earlier discussion of communication (Chapter 8), children learn to "share" interesting sights and objects with others by pointing and gesturing even before the end of the first year. In a recent examination of early sharing, Rheingold and her colleagues (Rheingold, Hay, & West, 1976) have found that showing and giving toys to a variety of adults (mothers, fathers, and strangers) were very frequent behaviors among 18 month-old children. Moreover, these early sharing activities occurred without prompting, direction or praise. The authors "propose that the sharing behaviors, from the first holding up of an object for others to see, the first offering of an object to another . . . qualify as developmental milestones. That children so young share contradicts the egocentricity so often ascribed to them and reveals them instead as already able contributors to social life" (1976, p. 1157).

Other evidence from children's emotional reactions to others' distress is consistent with the view that altruism begins very early in life (Yarrow and Waxler, 1977). Even by the end of the first year, young children begin to show reactions to other's distress. Between 10 and 12 months, children become agitated or may cry in response to another child's distress, but there is little attempt to help. By 13 or 14 months, however, children often approach and comfort another in distress. Although these early approaches involve comforting, it is often general and not specific to the source of distress. By 1½ years, children not only approach a distressed person but offer specific kinds of help. Children

BOX 16-1
THE MOTHER'S ROLE IN LEARNING TO REACT TO OTHER'S DISTRESS

How do children learn to react in helpful ways when they have caused distress in another person or when they see another person suffering? To find out, Yarrow and Waxler (1978) devised a clever scheme: they trained mothers of 1½-year-olds to tape-record incidents of distress that occurred in the normal home situation that the child either caused or witnessed. The mothers recorded both their own reactions and the child's behavior over a nine-month period. In addition, observers visited the home for a few hours every three weeks in order to check on the accuracy of the mother's records. During the home visits, the mother simulated (that is, acted out) certain common distress situations, such as bumping her ankle and crying, as a further assessment of the mother's routine recordings. Mothers were found to be accurate and reliable reporters of their own and their children's reactions.

Even 1½-year-old children are active responders to another person's distress. On the average, children reacted in a helpful fashion about 30 percent of the time, either when they hurt someone else or when they merely witnessed another person's distress. However, children differed greatly in their responsiveness—some failed to respond at all, while others responded in the majority of distress situations (60 to 70 percent).

Mothers' reactions to both their own children's harmdoing and mothers' reactions when they witness another person's distress can influence their children's development of helpful behavior in distress situations. Mothers who frequently used explanations linking the child's behavior with its consequences for the victim had children who were more likely to respond in a helpful way when they caused harm to someone. These mothers might say, "Tom's crying because you pushed him"—a clear, but neutral explanation. Even more effective are explanations accompanied by strong emotional overtones such as, "You must never poke anyone's eyes" or "When you hurt me. I don't want to be near you. I am going away from you." Children of mothers who used these affective explanations were also more likely to intervene in bystander situations, where they did not cause any harm but saw that someone else was upset. Some maternal tactics such as physical restraint ("I just moved away from him"), physical punishment ("I swatted him a good one"), or unexplained prohibitions ("Stop that") were not effective and may even interfere with the development of altruism.

Altruism begins at an early age. Parents play an important role in facilitating the development of the child's emerging altruistic behaviors by helping children make connections between their own actions and other people's emotional states. Altruism appears to begin at home! ■

Source: Yarrow, M., & Waxler, C. Unpublished manuscript. National Institute of Mental Health, 1978.

with a broken toy may be offered another one to play with or a mother with a cut finger may be given a Band-Aid. Not all children help in situations of distress, nor do all children help to the same degree. To find out how mothers' childrearing practices contribute to children's reactions to distress in others was the aim of the study in Box 16-1.

The Stability of Prosocial Behavior	Does knowledge of children's early altruistic tendencies help predict children's helpful behavior at later ages? To find out children's nurturance and sympathy to their peers, thoughtfulness and understanding the viewpoints of other children were assessed in the nursery school and again in elementary school five or six years later. There was reasonable stability between the two age points ($r = .60$ for boys and $r = .36$ for girls); which suggests that there is some consistency across time in children's altruistic behavior (Baumrind, 1971; cited by Mussen & Eisenberg-Berg, 1977).

Next we turn to an examination of other ways that parents and other agents can influence the development of altruism in their children.

Preaching and Practicing Sharing	What kind of social values, family situation, and parental behaviors might lead to a lessening of self-concern and an interest in the feelings and welfare of others, which seems so basic in cooperative, helping, or sharing behaviors? Most parents advocate good conduct for their children. Only a deviant minority advocate selfishness or dishonesty.

However, many parents oozing virtuous platitudes seem to have self-centered children. Laboratory studies and naturalistic studies indicate that although both what adults say about altruism and their demonstrated altruistic behavior influence altruism in children, there is a tendency for the model's verbalizations to have more effect on what the child says, and the model's behavior more effect on what the child does. An interesting series of laboratory analogue studies was performed to investigate the "Don't do as I do, do as I say" conflict which confronts most children in listening to their parents' moralistic preachings while viewing their sometimes questionable ethical practices (Bryan & Walbek, 1970a, 1970b; Bryan & Schwartz, 1971). The effect of moral exhortation and the behavioral examples of filmed models on children's reactions in helping situations were investigated. Third- and fourth-grade children were exposed to an altruistic model (one who donated to the March of Dimes) or a greedy model (one who hoarded all his winnings in an experimental game). One-third of the children within each group heard the model exhort charitable actions (for example, "It's good to donate to poor children. Children should help other children."), one-third heard the model preach selfishness (for example, "No sir, why should we give any of our money to other people? It is not good to donate to the poor people."), and one-third heard neutral preachings (for example, "I hope I win some money today."). The hypocrisy conditions were those where the model's behavior and preaching were discrepant. Following the viewing of the model, the child was left alone to play a game and had the option of anonymously donating his or her winnings to poor children. After the game, the children were asked to evaluate the attractiveness of the model. Children were more likely to make self-sacrificing responses if the model had donated to the March of Dimes. Exhortations concerning charity failed to alter the altruistic behavior of the child. As is usually found, the filmed model's actions were a greater source of influence upon the observer's behavior than his words were. However, what the model said was an important influence on the child's judgment of the model's attraction. While the model's verbalizations of the virtues of giving did not change the child's behavior, such exhortations did play a significant role, as did the model's acts, in determining the model's attractivness. With young children the child regards either a generously talking or generously acting person positively; the discrepancy or hypocrisy involved in the selfish person mouthing altruistic platitudes does not mean he is a bad fellow. "The preacher of charity and practitioner of greed is not disparaged, his character is vindicated simply by his verbal allegiance to the norm of giving" (Bryan & Schwartz, 1971, p. 56).

However, with older children, particularly children above the age of 9, such hypocrisy is perceived negatively, and approval from "hypocrites" is aversive to children. When a selfish-acting, generous-sounding model praises a child for a charitable act, the child is likely to give less than she would with no social approval. She avoids doing what the hypocrite says (Midlarsky, Bryan, & Brickman, 1973). With age and increasing cognitive and interpersonal skills, children may be more able to perceive discrepancies and disapprove of the deviousness in hypocrisy.

The study presented in Box 16-2 of adults who were actively involved in the civil rights movement in the early 1960s suggests that parents' hypocrisy in preaching and practicing may have marked effects on the helping behavior of their children.

Responsibility Taking, Empathy, and Altruism

Does taking responsibility affect the development of altruism. Cross-cultural evidence of children from six cultures—Kenya, Mexico, Phillipines, Okinawa, India, and New England—suggests that "children who perform more domestic chores, help more with economic tasks and spend more time caring for their infant brothers, sisters and cousins, score high on the altruistic dimension" (Whiting & Whiting, 1975). Laboratory research confirms these findings. Some children were given responsibility for teaching other children to make puzzles for hospitalized children. Other children made puzzles but were not given any teaching responsibility. Children who had been assigned teaching responsibility were subsequently more willing to share their prizes with needy children and made more puzzles for hospitalized children than the boys and girls in the control condition (Staub, 1975).

Just as we saw in the case of moral development, role taking and empathy play an important role in altruism as well. Children who have well-developed role-taking skills were higher in kindness and helping than children who had less developed role-taking skills (Rubin & Schneider, 1973). In a more recent study, six-year-old children who received role-taking training were more likely to share with a needy child than children who did not receive this type of training (Iannotti, 1978). This direct experimental evidence clearly demonstrates that increasing role-taking can heighten altruistic behavior in children. It is assumed that children who are capable role takers are able to better appreciate another

BOX 16-2
HELPING IN THE CIVIL RIGHTS MOVEMENT

What kind of people were active in the civil rights movement of the late 1950s and early 1960s? Who marched, protested, and picketed? What kinds of parents produced these activists?

Rosenhan (1972) distinguished between two groups of actists: the fully committed and the partially committed. The *fully committed* had left their homes, jobs, and schools and had been immersed in the civil rights movement for over a year. In contrast, the *partially committed* had sacrificed little. They had participated in one or two marches but had not given up their other activities. The fully committed were guided by internalized moral standards involving a deep commitment to equality, what Rosenhan calls *autonomous altruism.* The partially committed were motivated by social conformity, or *normative altruism*; that is, they were concerned with approval from their group, the camaraderie of being involved in a common movement, and short-term personal rewards rather than altruistic motives.

What kind of parental characteristics might have led to these two different types of activism in their children? The fully committed had parents who had themselves been activists and had been concerned with the welfare of others; parents who had been involved in protesting Nazi atrocities, the Spanish Civil War, religious restrictions, etc. Their children spoke of the emotion they shared with their parents on these occasions. One subject described being carried on his father's shoulders during the Sacco-Vanzetti parades. In addition, these fully committed activists had always had a warm relationship with their parents

despite the fact that they sometimes had disagreements. Thus these young people had parents whom they loved, who served as warm, altruistic models.

In contrast, the partially committed had negative or ambivalent feelings toward their parents. They reported their relations while they had been in the home as hostile, and they were still rejecting and avoiding their parents. Rosenhan summarizes some of the feelings toward their parents of the partially committed as follows:

By contrast, the Partially Committed had parents who were at best mere verbal supporters of prosocial moralities and, at worst, hypocritical about those moralities. It was common for our Partially Committed to report that their parents preached one thing and practiced another. Moreover, the Partially Committed were so angered by the discrepancy between parental posture and action that we had reason to believe that our respondents had undergone a "crisis of hypocrisy" during their childhood which resulted in an inability to make enduring commitments to prosocial (as to other) matters later on. (1972, pp. 342–343)

These findings are in agreement with the laboratory studies. As children grow older, hypocrisy in adults leads to negative and adverse responses. Parents should practice what they preach. ■

Source: Rosenhan, D. L. Prosocial behavior of children. In W. W. Hartup (Ed.), *The young child* (Vol. 2). Washington, D.C.: National Association for the education of Young Children, 1972, pp. 340–359.

person's plight or distress. Of special importance is the child's empathy development, since knowing that another may be suffering is often not enough to motivate altruistic action; you may have to "feel" the same emotional state as the victim. Many assume that this capacity to "feel" the victim's emotions is an important determinant of altruistic behavior (Feshbach, 1974, 1978; Hoffman, 1975).

Cultural Factors, Cooperation, and Sharing

As was found in studies of honesty and resistance to temptation, cultural factors and group norms play an important role in positive social behavior. The Anglo-American culture, particularly the middle-class urban groups, is a highly competitive culture, and cross-cultural research has consistently demonstrated that the attitudes of Anglo-American children interfere with their ability to cooperate with others in problem solving, even when such cooperation would be to their advantage. Children raised in cultures which place less value on self-sufficiency and competition, such as Mexican or Canadian Indian families, are more able to work cooperatively together for common goals (Kagan & Madsen, 1971, 1972; Miller, 1973). Societies in which the norm of cooperation and orientation to the group goals is systematically inculcated in the educational system, such as in Russia or in the Israeli kibbutz, also show more cooperative behavior than do Anglo-Americans.

Values shift as children move away from traditional cultures. For example, Canadian Blackfoot Indian children who attend integrated schools are more competitive than those who remain in Indian schools. Influence can go both ways, as evidenced by the adoption of a more cooperative orientation by some of the white Canadian children in integrated schools (Miller, 1973).

The self-concern generated by a competitive orientation, along with focus on status needs and self-sufficiency, interferes with behaviors such as giving and sharing with others. In one study it was found that nursery-school-age boys who were highly competitive in games and were viewed as competitive in the classroom by their teachers were less likely to share candy with their two best friends than were less competitive children (Rutherford & Mussen, 1968). It has been proposed that any kind of self-concern will interfere with the individual's inclination to consider the needs and feelings of others (Berkowitz, 1972).

Cheating and altruism are not the only aspects of morality and self-control; there is another aspect, namely aggression, which is often prevalent among children. Next we focus our attention on this aspect of self-control.

The Development of Aggression

For parents, peers, and teachers, altruism is welcome; however, aggression is an unwelcome but common occurrence. For decades, psychologists have puzzled over the knotty problem of aggression. Why do some children attack others? How do these patterns change over age? What role do families, peers, and the mass media play in the development of aggression. Finally, how can aggression be reduced?

Developmental Changes in Aggression

A morning visit to a nursery school and an afternoon stopover at an elementary school playground reveal some striking differences in the form and frequency of aggressive behavior. The nursery school children not only display more aggression but are more likely to quarrel and fight over toys and possessions; in

Physical aggression is most common among young boys. (Al Lowry, Photo Researchers, Inc.)

other words, their aggression is *instrumental.* In contrast, the older children (six-to seven-years-olds) use more *person-oriented* or *hostile* aggression, such as criticism, ridicule, tattling, or verbal disapproval (Hartup, 1974). This shift from instrumental to hostile aggression may be due, in part, to the older child's ability to infer the intentions and motives of one's attacker. When a child recognizes that another person wants to hurt him or her, he or she is more likely to retaliate by a direct assault on the tormentor rather than by an indirect attack on the aggressor's possessions. Language and communication skills are also improving rapidly over this age span which increases the likelihood that aggression will be expressed verbally rather than physically. Finally, the rules change as children develop. Most parents and teachers become less tolerant of physical aggression as children mature, while they are more likely to ignore a "battle of words" even among older children.

One of the most striking aspects of these developmental trends is the markedly divergent courses followed by boys and girls: Nursery school boys more often instigate and are more often involved in aggressive incidents than are girls. These sex differences are primarily due to the higher incidence of hostile aggression among boys; children of both sexes display similar amounts of instrumental aggression (Hartup, 1974). Both the family and the mass media play an influential role in shaping the development of aggression. Next, we examine these two influence sources.

The Family as a Training Center for Aggression

Do parents contribute to their children's aggression? Although some parents may set out to deliberately teach aggression in order to "defend oneself" or "be a man," most parents do not view themselves as aggression trainers. The parents' typical control tactics, however, may contribute to their children's aggression. Whether with juvenile delinquents, or playground bullies, the answer is similar: Parents who use physical punishment, especially on an inconsistent and erratic basis, are likely to have aggressive, hostile children (Bandura & Walters, 1959; Lefkowitz, Eron, Walder & Huesmann, 1977; Patterson, 1976; 1979).

Patterson's (1976) work is of particular importance since his conclusions are based on actual observations of families of aggressive and nonaggressive children in their home environments. The aggressive children were referred to the Patterson project by schools and clinical agencies, for treatment of their excessive, antisocial aggressive behavior. The family environments of aggressive and nonaggressive children were strikingly different. Not only did the parents of aggressive boys punish more often, they punished more often even when the child was behaving appropriately!

Punishment has a very different impact on aggressive and nonaggressive children. Parental punishment has the anticipated suppressive effect when applied to nonaggressive children. In contrast, punishment does *not* suppress noxious and undesirable hostile behavior in aggressive boys; parental punishment serves to accelerate ongoing noxious behavior in these children. Problem children were twice as likely as normal children to persist in their behaviors when punished. Clearly punishment has a different meaning and a markedly different impact on aggressive and nonaggressive children.

As Patterson notes, however, children are not passive victims in this process but often actively elicit punitive reactions from their parents by their misbehavior. Clearly, a bidirectional model is most appropriate, which recognizes that both parent and child influence each other and both contribute to the development of aggressive behavior patterns.

Parents are not the only family members that contribute to the development of aggression. Children learn to behave aggressively in interaction with siblings, especially younger brothers and sisters who may provoke aggressive acts by their teasing, whining, or hitting. In turn, the older child learns to inhibit these aversive behaviors by retaliating aggressively (Patterson & Cobb, 1971; Patterson, 1976). Just as we saw in Chapter 13 that successful use of aggressive tactics in controlling peers can often reinforce and increase subsequent aggression, a similar process may operate in the family setting as well. To understand the development of aggression in the home, the family must be viewed as a social system in which all the interrelations among family members are recognized.

The Mass Media as a Contributor to Aggression

By the age of 16, the average child has spent more time watching TV than attending school and has witnessed 13,000 violent murders on TV (Waters & Malamud, 1975). As indicated throughout this book, exposure to aggressive models on TV can increase children's subsequent aggressive behavior (see Chapters 1 and 6). Moreover, heavy doses of TV violence can affect children's attitudes as well and lead them to view violence as an acceptable and effective way to solve interpersonal conflict (Dominick & Greenberg, 1972; Thomas & Drabman, 1977). Children learn a lesson from TV, that "violence works, for both the good guys and the bad guys; it gets things done" (Dominick & Greenberg, 1972, p. 331).

Moreover, there are other outcomes: heavy viewers show less emotional reaction when viewing aggression (Cline, Croft, & Courrier, 1973). As Box 16-3 shows, children who watch televised violence may become indifferent to real-life violence (Drabman & Thomas, 1975; 1976). However, exposure to TV violence affects children differently at different ages, due to shifts in children's cognitive abilities. Children who can distinguish fantasy and reality may react differently from those who are unable to make this distinction. Children who were told that a violent film clip was real (a newsreel of an actual riot) reacted more aggressively later than children who believed that the film was a Hollywood production (Feshbach, 1972). As children develop and are able to make this fantasy-reality distinction, many of the fictional TV programs may have less impact (Sawin, 1977).

Finally, as children's cognitive skills develop, they are better able to understand the relationships between action and consequence, and, in turn, may be less affected by TV viewing. Early studies of the effects of aggressive models indicated that punishing a model for his or her aggressive acts decreased viewer imitation (Bandura, 1965, see Chapter 6). However, TV plots are often complex and involve considerable separation of the action and the subsequent punishment, which may make it more difficult for young viewers to make the link between crime and punishment. To evaluate this hypothesis, third-, sixth-, and tenth-grade children watched an aggressive sequence which was followed by punishment either immediately before *or* immediately after a commercial (Collins, 1973). When the commercial was inserted between the crime and the punishment, the third-grade children indicated that they would behave more aggressively than when they saw the violent sequence followed by the punishment without a break. For sixth and tenth graders, the insertion of the

BOX 16-3
DOES TV VIOLENCE BREED INDIFFERENCE TO REAL-LIFE VIOLENCE?

Defenders of TV violence often note that exposure to violence may make us more sensitive and aware of others' suffering and plight. To find out, Drabman and Thomas exposed third-grade children to a violent TV detective program, while other children watched a baseball game. Next they assessed whether exposure to TV violence affected children's reactions to real-life aggression. The children were given responsibility for "baby-sitting" some younger children in a nearby trailer by watching them over a TV monitor. The third graders were told to seek adult help if the children got into trouble. Here is a description of the behavior of the younger children that the third-graders saw:

Each began criticizing the block structures that the other had built. After increased criticism the

boy knocked over one of the girl's buildings. This led to increased taunting, pushing, shoving and crying. The fight got progressively worse until it appeared that the camera was destroyed. (Drabman & Thomas, 1975, p. 87)

The third graders who had previously watched the violent TV program took longer to seek appropriate adult help than the children who saw the nonviolent film. Exposure to TV violence can breed indifference to another individual's plight! ■

Source: Drabman, R. S., & Thomas, M. H. Does watching violence on television cause apathy? *Pediatrics*, 1976, **52**, 329–331; and Drabman, R. S., & Thomas, M. H. Does TV violence breed indifference? *Journal of Communication*, 1975, **25**, 86–89.

commercial did not affect their subsequent aggression. This inability of young children to make links between actions and outcomes in regular TV programming may contribute to the heightened effect of TV on young viewers.

Control of Aggression

How can aggression be controlled? A variety of solutions have been offered, but few as often as the recommendation that children be offered safe outlets for their aggression. Let us examine this alternative first.

The Catharsis Myth   One of the most persistent beliefs about aggression is that opportunities for acting aggressively will reduce hostile and aggressive tendencies. The commonly accepted term for this process is *catharsis*. The catharsis doctrine asserts that aggressive urges build up in an organism and unless the reservoir of aggressive energies is drained, a violent outburst will occur. The implications are clear: provide people with a safe opportunity to behave aggressively and the likelihood of antisocial aggression will be lessened. This dictum is expressed popularly as "blowing off steam." Also there is widespread belief in catharsis in clinical circles. People are often encouraged to express aggression in group-therapy sessions. There are punching bags on many wards in mental hospitals, and Bobo dolls, pounding boards, toy guns, and knives in many play-therapy rooms.

In her popular advice column, Ann Landers has propagated a similar view, as illustrated in her suggestion for dealing with a 3-year-old child's temper tantrums:

Hostile feelings must be released. If children could be taught to vent their anger against furniture and not other people, they would grow up to be healthier and happier adults and we could close some of our reform schools and penitentiaries.

Ann Landers, February 24, 1969
Wisconsin *State Journal*

In spite of its apparent popularity, the research evidence in favor of this position is neither voluminous nor convincing. The findings from most studies have indicated that aggressive experiences may promote rather than "drain off" aggressive behaviors.

Notwithstanding, the proponents of catharsis theory maintained that their position had not received an adequate test from early studies. Catharsis, it was argued, will result only when the subject is initially angered and then has an opportunity to reduce the aggression through some safe aggressive outlet. Since subjects in the early studies were not aroused prior to their free-play session, these studies may not, in fact, have been a fair test. Here is one study that provides an adequate test of the catharsis issue (Mallick & McCandless, 1966). Half of a group of third-grade children were frustrated by a peer confederate who interfered with the subjects' task of building a block house in a short time and thereby caused them to lose a cash prize. The remaining boys were treated in a neutral fashion by the experimenter's accomplice. The boys then engaged in one of the following activities before being given the opportunity to aggress against the peer partner; (1) shooting a play gun at animated targets of a boy, a man, a woman, a dog, or a cat, (2) shooting at a bull's-eye target, or (3) solving arithmetic problems. As expected, the frustration manipulation proved effective; angered subjects more frequently administered uncomfortable shocks to the tormentor than the nonangered children did. In reality, no shocks were actually received by the other boy. However, contrary to catharsis theory, the type of intervening activity made little difference. Target shooting did not lower the aggressive behavior of the angered children any more than a passive session of arithmetic problems had. In contrast, a noncathartic technique *was* found to be effective in reducing hostility. Subjects who were provided with a reinterpretation of the frustrator's actions (for example, "he was sleepy and upset") subsequently directed less aggression toward him. It appears, then, that aggressive retaliation can often be avoided if the angered protagonist understands the reasons for his frustrator's thwarting behavior. Merely acting out aggressively toward an alternative target appears to be insufficient.

Given these and similar findings (Bandura, 1973; Baron, 1978), it is not surprising that public faith in catharsis theory is on the wane. Witness a reader's reaction to Ann Lander's "catharsis" advice:

DEAR ANN: I was shocked at your advice to the mother whose 3 year old had temper tantrums. You suggested that the child be taught to kick the furniture and get the anger out of his system. I always thought you were a little cuckoo. Now I'm sure.

My younger brother used to kick the furniture when he got mad. Mother called it, letting off steam. Well, he's 32 years old now and still kicking the furniture—what's left of it, that is. He is also kicking his wife, the cat, the kids, and anything else that gets in his way. Last October, he threw the T.V. set out the window when his favorite football team failed to score and lost the game. (The window was closed at the time.)

Why don't you tell mothers that children must be taught to control their anger? This is what separates civilized human beings from savages, Dummy.

—Star Witness
Ann Landers, April 8, 1969
Wisconsin *State Journal*

Clearly, having the opportunity to behave aggressively is unlikely to lower hostile tendencies.

Encouragement of Alternative Behaviors

The encouragement of alternative responses that are incompatible with the expression of aggression, such as cooperative behaviors, is an effective technique for controlling aggression. This was well illustrated by the Brown and Elliot (1965) study reviewed in Chapter 6 in which nursery school teachers decreased aggression by ignoring aggression and rewarding cooperative and peaceful behaviors.

Eliciting incompatible responses may be accomplished in other ways and not simply through direct reinforcement. Many years ago, Chittenden (1942) demonstrated that aggressive, domineering behavior could be successfully modified by exposing nursery school children to a series of puppet shows in which aggressive solutions to conflicts were associated with negative outcomes, while cooperation was encouraged. In combination with discussion and practice of the positive prosocial activities, aggression in the nursery school was markedly reduced. More recently, similar success has been achieved in reducing aggression by a verbal coaching strategy, in which teachers both note the negative consequences of aggression and at the same time teach the children alternative conflict-solving strategies (Zahavi & Asher, 1978).

Another approach to aggression control is to make someone laugh. Humor, of course, is a reaction that is quite incompatible with aggression. Watching a humorous cartoon can decrease aggression in angered college students (Baron & Ball, 1974; Mueller & Donnerstein, 1977).

Increasing Awareness of Harmful Effects of Aggression

Another technique for controlling aggression involves increasing the attacker's awareness of the harmful consequences of his or her aggression for the victim. Baron (1971) found that adults who heard expressions of pain and anguish from their victim were less aggressive than subjects not exposed to this type of feedback. Similar kinds of effects have been found in film studies, where the anguish of the victim is graphically displayed. For example Goranson (1969) showed college students a boxing film in which the loser of the match dies as a result of his injury. In a comparison group, the victim in the fight was not fatally injured. Subjects were then given the opportunity to administer electric shock to another student. Subjects who saw the film in which aggression had harmful consequences behaved less aggressively than the subjects who saw the other film.

The development of the capacity for empathy at six or seven years of age is probably responsible for these effects (Feshbach, 1974; 1978). Conversely, young children who are unable to respond empathetically to their victim's suffering do not show inhibition in response to victim pain but, as we saw earlier, may even increase their aggression (Patterson, Littman, and Bricker, 1967).

However, socialization is not always successful—as a glance at any daily newspaper will show. Some individuals seem to take great pleasure in other people's suffering, and many street crimes—such as purse snatchings—are often accompanied by much higher levels of violence than is necessary to successfully steal a purse. Seeing the anguish and pain of their victims seems to be the only motive behind these crimes of unnecessary violence. There is no doubt that pain cues increase rather than inhibit aggression in some individuals. Juvenile delinquents, for example, who see a film emphasizing the victim's pain and suffering reacted with more, not less, aggression (Hartmann, 1969). It is not just delinquents that appear to relish the suffering of their victims; even normal youngsters who are rated as aggressive by their peers appear to enjoy making others suffer.

This is dramatically demonstrated in a study of 12-year-old aggressive boys (Perry & Perry, 1974). Using a "rigged" procedure in which the boys thought that they were administering loud noxious noises to another child, the victim's reaction was varied. The victim signaled that either the noise "hurt a lot" or denied he was in any discomfort. When the victim denied that an aggressive attack caused any pain, high-aggressive boys escalated the intensity of their attacks. In the case of the low-aggressive boys, this denial of suffering did not increase the level of aggression. For the aggressive child, signs of pain and suffering are an indication that the aggression is successful. Moreover, aggressive individuals often show little or no remorse after behaving aggressively, while low-aggressive boys show self-disapproval after harming another person (Perry & Busey, 1977).

Possibly, highly aggressive children have never learned to be aware of other people's feelings. As Box 16-4 illustrates, training adolescents to be more aware and sensitive to the views and feelings of other individuals can be an effective way of controlling aggression. Empathy clearly plays an important role in the development of morality and self-control—whether altruism, aggression, or moral behavior.

Summary

The socialization of moral beliefs and behavior is one of the main tasks in all cultures. Different theorists have focused on different aspects of moral development. Psychoanalytic theorists have focused relatively more on affective compo-

BOX 16-4
"SEEING IT YOUR WAY": A NOVEL
ROUTE TO AGGRESSION CONTROL

Appropriate social behavior requires the development of perspective-taking skills which permit a child to understand other individual's feelings, thoughts, and viewpoints. Aggressive, delinquent adolescents have often failed to develop these skills, which may, in part, account for their continuing antisocial behavior. What effect does improving children's perspective-taking skills have on their social behavior? To answer this question, Michael Chandler (1973) enrolled a group of 11- to 13-year-old delinquents in an experimental program which employed drama and the making of video films as vehicles for helping them to see themselves from the perspective of others and for providing remedial training in deficient role-taking skills. For 3 hours a week over a 10-week period the boys developed skits, acted out various parts, consistently shifted roles in the plays, and watched replays of the video recordings of their skits. All these features were designed to improve role-taking and perspective-taking skills. A second group made color cartoons and documentaries but had no opportunities to see themselves from the perspectives of others, nor did they receive special training in role-taking skills. A third group served as a nontreatment control. The special training was effective in improving the role-taking abilities of the boys, while the boys in the other two groups did not change. Of special interest is the impact on their subsequent aggressive delinquent behavior. The number of delinquent offenses committed in the 18-month period for the intervention group was significantly less than for the nonintervention groups. Modification of role-taking skills effectively improved the social behavior of these adolescents. Aggressive, antisocial behavior may be reduced through role-playing training just as altruism and moral reasoning can be enhanced by this approach. ■

Source: Chandler, M. J. Egocentricism and antisocial behavior: The assessment and training of social perspective taking skills. *Developmental Psychology*, 1973, **9**, 326–332.

nents of morality, such as guilt and remorse; social learning theorists on moral conduct; and cognitive theorists on moral judgments.

Jean Piaget and Lawrence Kohlberg have both proposed theories involving invariant sequences of stages of moral development related to the increasing cognitive complexity of the child and the ability to perceive and respond to the intentions and feelings of others.

Piaget has emphasized the role of peers and Kohlberg the importance of varied opportunities for role taking in the development of moral judgments. Both have tended to minimize the influence of parents in the development of moral judgments. However, there is considerable evidence that consistent discipline involving reasoning and explanation and concern with the feelings of others leads to both more mature moral judgments and more self-control.

Cheating is related to motivational factors, such as the need to achieve, the extent of possible gains, and fear of failure and detection. In addition, group norms and the behavior of others around the child are related to honest or dishonest behavior.

It would be inaccurate to speak of honest or dishonest or moral and immoral people. The moral judgments, behaviors, and expressions of remorse which are all aspects of moral development are strongly influenced by situational factors. Some people are honest in certain situations. However, the evidence suggests that as the elements of situations and type of behavior assessed become more similar, more consistency of moral judgments and conduct occurs. More consistency among various dimensions of moral development also occurs with increasing age.

Altruistic behavior, contrary to earlier theories, begins very early, and helping, sharing, and exhibiting emotional reactions to others' distress occur in the second year of life. Parents influence the emergence of altruistic behavior both by their direct teaching in "distress" situations and by their example. In studies involving the modeling of adults' behavior, children's altruistic behavior is most affected by the conduct of the adult, and their imitative verbalizations are most influenced by what the adult says. Opportunities for responsibility taking appear to lead to increased altruistic behavior. Similarly, role playing and empathy both contribute to the development of altruism and helping. Altruistic behavior is influenced by cultural values. An emphasis on competition interferes with the development of altruistic behavior.

Aggression undergoes important developmental shifts; younger children show more instrumental aggression, while older children display more hostile or person-oriented aggression.

Parental disciplinary practices, particularly the use of physical punishment, may contribute to aggression. Violence in mass media also contributes to children's aggressive attitudes and behavior. Viewing violence may make children more tolerant of real-life aggression.

Catharsis, the belief that aggression can be reduced by behaving aggressively against a safe target, is not an effective control tactic. Encouraging alternative prosocial behaviors, presenting humorous material, and increasing a child's awareness of the harmful effects of aggression are more effective control techniques.

References

Arbuthnot, J. Modification of moral judgment through role playing. *Developmental Psychology*, 1975, **11,** 319–324.

Aronfreed, J. Moral development from the standpoint of a general psychological theory. In T. Lickona (Ed.), *Moral development and behavior.* New York: Holt, 1976.

Bandura, A. *Aggression: A social learning analysis.* Englewood Cliffs, N.J.: Prentice Hall, 1973.

Bandura, A. Influence of model's reinforcement contingencies on the acquisition of imitative responses. *Journal of Personality and Social Psychology*, 1965, **1,** 589–595.

Bandura, A., & MacDonald, F. J. Influence of social reinforcement and the behavior of models in shaping children's moral judgments. *Journal of Abnormal and Social Psychology*, 1963, **67,** 274–281.

Bandura, A., & Walters, R. H. *Adolescent aggression.* New York: Ronald, 1959.

Barbu, Z. Studies in children's honesty. *Quarterly Bulletin British Psychological Society*, 1951, **2**, 53–57.

Baron, R. A. Aggression as a function of magnitude of victim's pain cues, level of prior anger arousal, and aggressor-victim similarity. *Journal of Personality and Social Psychology*, 1971, **18**, 48–54.

Baron, R. A. *Human aggression.* New York: Plenum, 1978.

Baron, R. A., & Ball, R. L. The aggression-inhibiting influence of nonhostile humor. *Journal of Experimental Social Psychology*, 1974, **10**, 23–33.

Baumrind, D. Current patterns of parental authority. *Developmental Psychology Monographs*, 1971, **1**, 1–103.

Berkowitz, L. Social norms, feelings and other factors affecting helping and altruism. In L. Berkowitz (Ed.), *Advances in experimental social psychology.* New York: Academic, 1972, pp. 63–108.

Bonjean, C. M., & McGee, R. Scholastic dishonesty among undergraduates in differing systems of social control. *Sociology of Education*, 1965, **38**, 127–137.

Bosserman, R., & Parke, R. D. The effect of assuming the role of rule enforcer on subsequent self-control. Paper presented at the meeting of the Society for Research in Child Development, Philadelphia, 1973.

Bowers, W. J. *Student dishonesty and its control in college.* New York: Columbia University Bureau of Applied Social Research, 1964.

Brown, P., & Elliot, R. Control of aggression in a nursery school class. *Journal of Experimental Child Psychology*, 1965, **2**, 103–107.

Bryan, J. H., & Schwartz, T. H. The effects of film material upon children's behavior. *Psychological Bulletin*, 1971, **75**, 50–59.

Bryan, J. J., & Walbek, N. H. Preaching and practicing generosity: Children's action and reactions. *Child Development*, 1970, **41**, 329–353. (a)

Bryan, J. H., & Walbek, N. H. The impact of words and deeds concerning altruism upon children. *Child Development*, 1970, **41**, 747–757. (b)

Burton, R. V. The generality of honesty reconsidered. *Psychological Review*, 1963, **70**, 481–499.

Burton, R. V. Honesty and dishonesty. In T. Lickona (Ed.), *Moral development and behavior.* New York: Holt, 1976.

Canning, R. Does an honor system reduce classroom cheating? An experimental answer. *Journal of Experimental Education*, 1956, **24**, 291–296.

Chandler, M. J. Egocentricism and antisocial behavior: The assessment and training of social perspective taking skills. *Developmental Psychology*, 1973, **9**, 326–332.

Chandler, M. J., Greenspan, S., & Barenboim, C. Judgments of intentionality in response to videotaped and verbally presented moral dilemmas: The medium is the message. *Child Development*, 1973, **44**, 315–320.

Chittenden, G. E. An experimental study in measuring and modifying assertive behavior in young children. *Monographs of the Society for Research in Child Development*, 1942, **1** (Serial No. 31).

Cline, V. B., Croft, R. G., & Courrier, S. Desensitization of children to television violence. *Journal of Personality and Social Psychology*, 1973, **27**, 360–365.

Collins, W. A. Effect of temporal separation between motivation, aggression and consequences: A developmental study. *Developmental Psychology*, 1973, **8**, 215–221.

Cowan, P. A., Langer, J., Heavenrich, J., & Nathanson, M. Social learning and Piaget's cognitive theory of moral development. *Journal of Personality and Social Psychology*, 1969, **11**, 261–274.

Damon, W. *The social world of the child.* San Francisco: Jossey-Bass, 1977.

Dominick, J. R., & Greenberg, B. S. Attitudes toward violence: The interaction of television exposure, family attitudes, and social class. In G. A. Comstock & E. A. Rubinstein (Eds.), *Television and social behavior: Television and adoles-*

cent aggressiveness (Vol. III). Washington, D.C.: U.S. Government Printing Office, 1972, pp. 314–335.

Drabman, R. S., & Thomas, M. H. Does TV violence breed indifference? *Journal of Communication*, 1975, **25**, 86–89.

Drabman, R. S., & Thomas, M. H. Does watching violence on television cause apathy? *Pediatrics*, 1976, **52**, 329–331.

Feldman, S. E., & Feldman, M. T. Transition of sex differences in cheating. *Psychological Reports*, 1967, **20**, 957–958.

Feldman, N. S., Klosson, E. C., Parsons, J. E., Rholes, W. S., & Ruble, D. N. Order of information presentation and children's moral judgments. *Child Development*, 1976, **47**, 556–559.

Feshbach, N. The relationship of child-rearing factors to children's aggression, empathy and related positive and negative behaviors. In J. deWit and W. W. Hartup (Eds.), *Determinants and origins of aggression*. The Hague: Mouton, 1974.

Feshbach, N. Studies of the development of children's empathy. In B. Maher (Ed.), *Progress in experimental personality research*. New York: Academic, 1978.

Feshbach, S. Reality and fantasy in filmed violence. In J. P. Murray, E. A. Rubinstein, & G. A. Comstock (Eds.), *Television and social behavior: Television and social learning* (Vol. 2). Washington, D.C.: U.S. Government Printing Office, 1972, pp. 318–345.

Flavell, J., Botkin, P., Fry, C., Wright, J., & Jarvis, P. E. *The development of role-taking and communication skills in children.* New York: Wiley, 1968.

Gilligan, C. F. Responses to temptation: An analysis of motives. Unpublished doctoral dissertation. Harvard University, 1963.

Goranson, R. E. Observed violence and aggressive behavior: The effects of negative outcomes to observed violence. Unpublished doctoral dissertation, University of Wisconsin, 1969.

Grim, P., Kohlberg, L., & White S. Some relationships between conscience and attentional processes. *Journal of Personality and Social Psychology*, 1968, **8**, 239–253.

Haan, N., Langer, J., & Kohlberg, L. Family patterns of moral reasoning. *Child Development*, 1976, **47**, 1204–1206.

Haan, N., Smith, M. B., & Block, J. The moral reasoning of young adults: Political-social behavior, family background and personality correlation. *Journal of Personality and Social Psychology*, 1968, **10**, 183–201.

Hartmann, D. Influence of symbolically modeled instrumental aggression and pain cues on aggressive behavior. *Journal of Personality and Social Psychology*, 1969, **11**, 280–288.

Hartshorne, H., & May, M. S. *Moral studies in the nature of character: Studies in deceit* (Vol. 1); *Studies in self-control* (Vol. 2); *Studies in the organization of character* (Vol. 3). New York: Macmillan, 1928–1930.

Hartup, W. W. Aggression in childhood: Developmental perspectives. *American Psychologist*, 1974, **29**, 336–341.

Havinghurst, R. J., & Neugarten, B. L. *American Indian and white children. Chicago: University of Chicago Press, 1955.*

Hetherington, E. M., & Feldman, S. E. College cheating as a function of subject and situational variables. *Journal of Educational Psychology*, 1964, **55**, 212–218.

Hill, J. P., & Kochendorfer, P. A. Knowledge of achievement anxiety and knowledge of peer performance. *Developmental Psychology*, 1969, **1**, 449–455.

Hoffman, M. L. Moral development. In P. H. Mussen (Ed.), *Carmichael's manual of child psychology* (Vol. 2). New York: Wiley, 1970, pp. 261–330.

Hoffman, M. L. Altruistic behavior and the parent-child relationship. *Journal of Personality and Social Psychology*, **31,** 1975, 937–943.

Hoffman, M. L., & Saltzstein, H. D. Parent discipline and the child's moral development. *Journal of Personality and Social Psychology*, 1967, **5,** 45–57.

Hogan, R., & Emler, N. P. Moral development. In M. E. Lamb (Ed.), *Social and personality development.* New York: Holt, 1978.

Howells, T. H. Factors influencing honesty. *Journal of Social Psychology*, 1938, **9,** 97–102.

Iannotti, R. J. Effect of role taking experiences on role taking, empathy, altruism and aggression. *Developmental Psychology*, 1978, **14,** 119–124.

Johnson, C. D., & Gormley, J. Academic cheating: The contribution of sex, personality and situational variables. *Developmental Psychology*, 1972, **6,** 320–325.

Johnson, R. C. A study of children's moral judgments. *Child Development*, 1962, **33,** 327–354.

Kagan, J., & Moss, H. A. *Birth to maturity: A study in psychological development.* New York: Wiley, 1962.

Kagan, S., & Madsen, M. C. Cooperation and competition of Mexican, Mexican-American, and Anglo-American children of two ages under four instructional sets. *Developmental Psychology*, 1971, **5,** 32–39.

Kagan, S., & Madsen, M. C. Experimental analyses of cooperation and competition of Anglo-American and Mexican children. *Developmental Psychology*, 1972, **6,** 49–59.

Kanfer, F. H., & Duerfeldt, P. H. Age, class standing, and commitment as determinants of cheating in children. *Child Development*, 1968, **39,** 545–557.

Keasey, C. B. Social participation as a factor in the moral development of preadolescents. *Developmental Psychology*, 1971, **5,** 216–220.

Kohlberg, L. Moral development and identification. In H. W. Stevenson (Ed.), *Child psychology. 62nd Yearbook of the National Society for the Study of Education.* Chicago: University of Chicago Press, 1963. (a)

Kohlberg, L. The development of children's orientations towards a moral order. 1. Sequence in the development of moral thought. *Vita Humana*, 1963, **6,** 11–33. (b)

Kohlberg, L. Development of moral character and ideology. In M. L. Hoffman & L. W. Hoffman (Eds.), *Review of child development research* (Vol. 1). New York: Russell Sage, 1964.

Kohlberg, L. Relationships between the development of moral judgment and moral conduct. Paper presented at the meeting of the Society for Research In Child Development, Minneapolis, March, 1965.

Kohlberg, L. *Stages in the development of moral thought and action.* New York: Holt, 1969.

Krebs, R. L. Some relationships between moral judgment, attention and resistance to temptation. Unpublished doctoral dissertation, University of Chicago, 1967.

Krebs, R. L. Teacher perceptions of children's moral behavior. *Psychology in the Schools*, 1969, **6,** 394–395.

Kuhn, D. Short-term longitudinal evidence for the sequentiality of Kohlberg's early stages of moral development. *Development Psychology*, 1976, **12,** 162–166.

Kuhn, D., Kohlberg, L., Langer, J., & Haan, N. The development of formal operations in logical and moral judgment. *Genetic Psychology Monographs*, 1977.

LaVoie, J. C. Punishment and adolescent self control. *Developmental Psychology*, 1973, **8,** 16–24.

Lefkowitz, M. M., Eron, L. D., Walder, L. O., & Huesmann, L. R. *Growing up to be violent.* New York: Pergamon, 1977.

Lehrer, L. Sex differences in moral behavior and attitudes. Unpublished doctoral dissertation. University of Chicago, 1967.

Lickona, T. Research on Piaget's theory of moral development. In T. Lickona (Ed.), *Moral development and behavior.* New York: Holt, 1976, pp. 219–240.

Mallick, S. K., & McCandless, B. R. A study of catharsis of aggression. *Journal of Personality and Social Psychology*, 1966, **4,** 591–596.

McCord, W., McCord, J., & Zola, K. *Origins of crime.* New York: Columbia University Press, 1959.

Midlarsky, E., Bryan, J. H., & Brickman, P. Aversive approval: Interactive effects of modeling and reinforcement on altruistic behavior. *Child Development*, 1973, **44,** 321–328.

Milgram, S. Behavioral study of obedience. *Journal of Abnormal and Social Psychology*, 1963, **67,** 371–378.

Milgram, S. *Obedience to authority: An experimental view.* New York: Harper & Row, 1974.

Miller, A. G. Integration and acculturation of cooperative behavior among Blackfoot Indian and non-Indian Canadian children. *Journal of Cross-Cultural Psychology*, 1973, **4,** 374–380.

Mischel, W., & Mischel, H. A cognitive social learning approach to morality and self-regulation. In T. Lickona (Ed.), *Moral development and behavior.* New York: Holt, 1976.

Mueller, C., & Donnerstein, E. The effects of humor-induced arousal upon aggressive behavior. *Journal of Research in Personality*, 1977, **11,** 73–82.

Mussen, P., & Eisenberg-Berg, N. *Roots of caring, sharing and helping.* San Francisco: Freeman, 1977.

Nakasato, Y., & Aoyama, Y. Some relations between children's resistance to temptation and their moral judgment. *Reports of the National Research Institute of Police Science: Research on prevention of crime and delinquency*, 1972, **13,** 62–70.

Nelsen, E. A., Grinder, R. E., & Biaggio, A. M. Relationships among behavioral cognitive-developmental and self report measures of morality and personality. *Multivariate Behavioral Research*, 1969, **4,** 483–500.

Parke, R. D. Rules, roles and resistance to deviation in children. In A. Pick (Ed.), *Minnesota symposia on child psychology* (Vol. 8). Minneapolis: University of Minnesota Press, 1974, pp. 111–144.

Parke, R. D. Punishment in children: Effects, side effects and alternative strategies. In H. Hom & P. Robinson, *Psychological processes in early education.* New York: Academic, 1977, pp. 71–97.

Parr, F. W. The problem of student honesty. *Journal of Higher Education*, 1936, **7,** 318–326.

Patterson, G. R. The aggressive child: Victim and architect of a coercive system. In E. J. Mash, L. A. Hamerlynck, & L. C. Handy (Eds.), *Behavior modification and families.* New York: Brunner/Mazel, 1976.

Patterson, G. R. A performance theory for coercive family interaction. In R. B. Cairns (Ed.), *Social interaction: Analysis and illustrations.* Hillsdale, N.J.: Lawrence Erlbaum, 1979.

Patterson, G. R., & Cobb, J. A dyadic analysis of aggressive behaviors. In J. P. Hill (Ed.), *Minnesota symposia on child psychology* (Vol. 5). Minneapolis: University of Minnesota Press, 1971.

Patterson, G. R., Littman, R. A., & Bricker, W. Assertive behavior in children: A step toward a theory of aggression. *Monographs of the Society for Research in Child Development*, 1967, **32** (Whole No. 113).

Pearlin, L. I. *Class context and family relations: Cross national study.* Boston: Little, Brown, 1971.

Pearlin, L. I., Yarrow, M. R., & Scarr, H. A. Unintended effects of parental aspirations: The case of children's cheating. *American Journal of Sociology,* 1967, **73,** 73–83.

Perry, D. G., & Bussey, K. Self-reinforcement in high- and low-aggressive boys following acts of aggression. *Child Development,* 1977, **48,** 653–657.

Perry, D. G., & Perry, L. C. Denial of suffering in the victim as a stimulus to violence in aggressive boys. *Child Development,* 1974, **45,** 55–62.

Piaget, J. *The moral judgment of the child.* New York: Harcourt, Brace, 1932.

Podd, M. H. Ego identity status and morality: The relationship between two developmental constructs. *Developmental Psychology,* 1972, **6,** 497–507.

Rest, J. New approaches in the assessment of moral development. In T. Lickona (Ed.), *Moral development and behavior.* New York: Holt, 1976.

Rheingold, H. L., Hay, D. F., & West, M. J. Sharing in the second year of life. *Child Development,* 1976, **47,** 1148–1158.

Rosenhan, D. L. Prosocial behavior of children. In W. W. Hartup (Ed.), *The young child* (Vol. 2). Washington, D.C.: National Association for the Education of Young Children, 1972, pp. 340–359.

Rubin, K. H., & Schneider, F. W. The relationship between moral judgment, egocentrism and altruistic behavior. *Child Development,* 1973, **44,** 661–665.

Rutherford, E., & Mussen, P. H. Generosity in nursery school boys. *Child Development,* 1968, **39,** 755–765.

Sawin, D. B. The fantasy-reality distinction in televised violence: Modifying influences on children's aggression. Paper presented at the annual meeting of the American Psychological Association, San Francisco, August 1977.

Selman, R. L. Taking another's perspective: Role taking development in early childhood. *Child Development,* 1971, **42,** 1721–1734. (a)

Selman, R. L. The relation of role-taking ability to the development of moral judgment in children. *Child Development,* 1971, **42,** 79–91. (b)

Selman, R. L. Stages of role taking and moral judgment as guides to social intervention. In T. Lickona (Ed.), *Moral development and behavior.* New York: Holt, 1976.

Shelton, J., & Hill, J. P. Effects on cheating of achievement anxiety and knowledge of peer performance. *Developmental Psychology,* 1969, **1,** 449–455.

Smith, C. P., Ryan, E. R., & Diggins, D. R. Moral decision making: Cheating on examinations. *Journal of Personality,* 1972, **40,** 640–660.

Staub, E. To rear a prosocial child. In D. J. DePalma & J. M. Foley (Eds.), *Moral development, current theory and research.* Hillsdale, N.J.: Lawrence Erlbaum, 1975.

Thomas, M. H., & Drabman, R. S. Effects of television violence on expectations of others' aggression. Paper presented at the annual meeting of the American Psychological Association, San Francisco, August 1977.

Tomlinson-Keasey, C., & Keasey, C. B. The mediating role of cognitive development in moral judgment. *Child Development,* 1974, **45,** 291–298.

Turiel, E. An experimental test of the sequentiality of developmental stages in the child's moral judgments. *Journal of Personality and Social Psychology,* 1966, **3,** 611–618.

Waters, H. F., & Malamud, P. "Drop that gun, Captain Video." *Newsweek,* 1975, **85** (10), 81–82.

White, C. B. Moral reasoning in older adults: A cross-national comparison of aged Bahamians and rural Americans. Unpublished paper, University of Texas Health Science Center at Dallas, 1977.

White, C. B., Bushnell, N., & Regnemer, J. L. Moral development in Bahamian school children: a 3 year examination of Kohlberg's stages of moral development. *Developmental Psychology*, 1978, **14,** 58–65.

Whiting, B. B., & Whiting, J. W. M. *Children of six cultures: A psychocultural analysis.* Cambridge, Mass.: Harvard University Press, 1975.

Yarrow, M. R., & Waxler, C. Paper presented at the Biennial meeting of the Society for Research in Child Development, New Orleans, March 1977.

Yarrow, M. R., & Waxler, C. Unpublished manuscript, National Institute of Mental Health, 1978.

Zahavi, S., & Asher, S. R. The effect of verbal instructions on preschool children's aggressive behavior. *Journal of School Psychology*, 1978, **16,** 146–153.

17

Epilogue

Throughout this volume we have reviewed the results of many studies of
children's development. A variety of
theories have been offered to explain
and interpret this complex and often
only partially understood array of details
about development. Neither the data
nor the theories are final answers in our
continuing attempt to unravel some of the puzzles of development. As in any field of science, our information about child
development is constantly expanding and changing. Many
findings and facts that we highlighted in our first edition of this
book were replaced in this edition; others were retained or
elaborated. In spite of the temporary nature of many of the
"facts," we can identify some broad themes that characterize
our general views about development and the process of
research in child development. In closing this volume, we
hope that briefly reviewing these themes which are presented
in Table 17-1 will be helpful.

TABLE 17-1 THEMES OF DEVELOPMENT

1 The child is an active and competent organism.
2 The child's behavior is organized.
3 The child's behavior has multiple causes.
4 The child influences the responses of other people.
5 The child's behavior is influenced by social systems.
6 The child's behavior is culture-bound.
7 The child's behavior is situation-bound.
8 The child's behavior is time-bound.
9 Multiple research methods are necessary.
10 Multiple theories of child development are necessary.
11 Child development research influences and is influenced by social policy.

1 *The child is an active and competent organism.* In recent years a dramatic change has occurred in our view of the child. The child is not viewed as a passive participant in development, but as an active and influential partner in promoting his or her own growth and development. Even infants are no longer thought of as passive creatures with limited sensory, perceptual, and social capacities, awaiting the imprint of the adult world. Instead we recognize that infants possess a wide range of perceptual, cognitive, and social capacities.

2 *The child's behavior is organized.* The child's behavior is not just a disorganized bundle of responses, reflexes, and reactions. Instead, organization is evident in the child's behavior: even infant responses such as sucking, looking, and sleeping are highly structured response patterns.

3 *The child's behavior has multiple causes.* Current views stress that biological-genetic factors as well as situational-environmental factors play an important role in shaping the course of development. This interplay between biology and environment is evident in a host of ways including the role of nutrition in cognitive development, the effects of drugs on children's learning, and the influence of hormones on sex-role development.

4 *The child influences the responses of other people.* The early unidirectional view of development under which adults influence children but children do not alter adult behavior is no longer considered valid. Children play an active role in modifying and altering adult behavior even in infancy. A bidirectional view of child development is now widely accepted, with children playing an influential part in their own social and cognitive development.

5 *The child's behavior is influenced by social systems.* It may be more accurate to think of development as being a multidirectional, rather than a

bidirectional, process. The child is embedded in a variety of social systems and settings in which the members shape each other's behavior. These range from smaller immediate settings and systems, such as the family or peer group in which the child has considerable influence, to larger or more remote systems, such as the school, community, or greater society over which the child has less control. The nature of the interactions, stresses, and supports encountered in these systems will influence development.

6 *The child's behavior is culture-bound.* No single picture of development is accurate for all cultures, social classes, or racial and ethnic groups. Children develop different skills and competencies in different cultural milieus. Consequently no sweeping generalizations concerning children's development can be made without careful specification of a child's cultural background.

7 *The child's behavior is situation-bound.* The same child may behave in a very different manner in different situations or with different people—in the home, the laboratory, the school, or the peer play group. Thus children should be studied in mutliple settings, and caution should be exercised in making generalizations about children's behavior from one situation to another.

8 *The child's behavior is time-bound.* Knowledge about children is time-bound: as social conditions shift, children and families undergo changes that alter their behavior. Families' processes in the Depression differed from those in the more affluent seventies; changing sex roles are having an impact on the family; legal demands for integration are markedly altering the school experience for many children. One of the aims of child psychology is constantly to monitor these changes in order to show how these shifts affect children's behavior and to update our information about children.

9 *Multiple research methods are necessary.* No single research method is sufficient to understand child development. A wide variety of methods including naturalistic observations of children, experiments, self-reports, clinical studies, and standardized tests contribute different types of information about child development. Information from different methods, sources, and situations presents a more accurate multifaceted view of the complexity of human development.

10 *Multiple theories of child development are necessary.* Just as there are multiple methods, there are multiple theories. Although there are grand theoretical schemes that attempt to provide a full and comprehensive account of development, such as those of Piaget and Freud, child psychologists are becoming more modest and restricted in the scope of their theories. As the complex and multidetermined nature of development becomes apparent, minitheories that aim to explain smaller pieces of the developmental puzzle are becoming more popular. Separate theories of sex

typing, memory, aggression, and grammar development are more likely to be advanced by contemporary psychologists than elaborate theories aimed at explaining all of social or cognitive development.

11 *Child development research influences and is influenced by social policy.* A final theme of contemporary child psychology is the close link between basic research and the application of research findings. Just as basic research concerning the importance of the early environment for the child's development stimulated government programs such as Head Start and day-care programs, so in turn child psychologists have been more actively involved in issues of concern to society and government, such as problems of poverty, divorce, and school intergration. During the past decade there has been an increasing interdependence of child development as a basic research discipline and child development as an applied discipline.

Glossary

Accommodation A process that involves the adjustment of an individual's schemata to meet environmental demands.

Action zone of a classroom The areas in the front and down the central columns of desks of a classroom.

Active sentence A sentence in which the actor in the sentence precedes the predicate.

Activity A personality characteristic that might be conceived of as another form of stimulus seeking.

Adaptability Ability to modify attentional strategies to the demands of specific tasks or situations.

Adaptation The second functional principle involving the processes of assimilation and accommodation.

Adoption of roles The sociological term for the acquisition of behaviors, attitudes, and values appropriate for social roles in a culture.

Affect hunger   A behavior pattern characterized by a seemingly insatiable desire for individual social attention and affection.

Age of viability   The point at which the physical systems of the fetus are sufficiently advanced so that if born, the child may survive. This time for humans is 28 weeks after conception.

Alert inactivity   A state in which the infant's eyes are open and have a bright and shining quality; the infant can pursue moving objects and make conjugate eye movements in the horizontal and vertical plane. The infant is relatively inactive. The face is relaxed, with no grimace.

Allele   An alternate form of a specific gene at a particular locus.

Altruism   Prosocial behavior such as helping, cooperating, sharing, etc.

Amniocentesis   A procedure by which cells are removed from the amniotic sac in order to examine the cells of the fetus for the presence of certain chromosomal and metabolic disorders.

Amniotic sac   A membrane that contains the amniotic fluid, a watery liquid in which the developing embryo floats and which serves as a protective buffer against physical shocks and temperature changes.

Androgen   A male hormone.

Androgynous individuals   Those who possess both masculine and feminine psychological characteristics.

Animism   The attribution of life to inanimate objects.

Anoxia   The lack of sufficient oxygen to the brain, causing neurological damage or death.

Apnea   A condition involving short interruptions in an infant's breathing patterns that may ultimately cause brain damage.

Assimilation   A process by which an individual perceives and modifies an experience in accordance with the individual's existing schemata.

Associative intelligence (Level I)   A term used by Arthur Jensen in referring to skills of short-term memory, rote learning, and attention. Level I intelligence is not highly correlated with school success and tends not to be measured by standard tests of intelligence.

Attachment   The development of specific behaviors whereby an infant seeks to be near certain people.

Attention over time   The ability to modify attentional focusing as the information received changes or as feedback is acquired.

Authoritarian control   A method of discipline in which hostile, restrictive, power-assertive practices predominate.

Authoritative control   A method of discipline in which parents are not intrusive and do permit considerable freedom within reasonable limits, but are willing to impose restrictions in areas where they have greater knowledge or insight.

Autonomic nervous system   A body system related to emotional arousal and responsiveness.

Autonomous morality   (*See* Morality of reciprocity.)

Autosome   A chromosome that is possessed equally by males and females.

Autostimulation theory   A theory that REM activity in infancy may stimulate the development of the central nervous system.

Background noise level   A measure of the amount and variety of noise from sources such as TV, radio, appliances, and traffic.

Bidirectional view of development   A viewpoint stressing that adult behavior not only influences a child's behavior but in turn is influenced by the child's behavior.

Black English   A dialect that differs from other dialects in regular and rule-governed ways.

Canalization   The limiting of phenotypes to one or a few developmental outcomes. The stronger the canalization, the fewer alternative paths there are from genotype to phenotype.

Catharsis   A process by which aggression is thought to be reduced through the display of aggressive tendencies and hostilities.

Center-based intervention program   A program that focuses on exposing children to an educationally stimulating environment outside the home in attempts to facilitate the development of intellectual and sound competence.

Central memory score   The number of correct responses for objects the child has been asked to remember.

Centration   The focusing on one dimension of an object when several must be considered to solve a problem correctly.

Cerebral lateralization   The specialization of function of the brain in one or the other cerebral hemispheres.

Chromosome   A threadlike entity in the nuclei of cells. Beaded along the length of the chromosomes are genes.

Classical conditioning   A procedure that enables a previously ineffective or neutral stimulus (the CS) to elicit a response (the CR) because of repeated pairings of that stimulus with another stimulus (the US), which could already elicit a highly similar response (the UCR).

Climate   A characteristic of environments such as a classroom referring to the nature of the social and emotional experiences provided by persons in that environment.

Coercive cycle   A conflicted interaction between divorced parent and children in which the behavior of the parent becomes gradually more coercive in order to control the gradually more adversive behavior of his or her children.

Cognitive intelligence (Level II)   A term used by Arthur Jensen to refer to intellectual skills that include abstract thinking, symbolic processes, conceptual learning, and the use of language in problem solving. Level II intelligence is correlated with school performance and is measured by tests of intelligence.

Cognitive style   A relatively consistent way in which an individual processes, perceives, remembers, or uses information.

Complementary interactive stage   The third stage of infant interaction; children are engaging in complex social interchanges including imitation, reciprocal role relationships, and both positive and negative affect.

Concordance rate   A measure of the percent of cases in which a particular trait or disorder is present in both members of a twin pair if it is present in at least one member of the pair.

Concrete operational period   Piaget's third stage of intellectual development. It is characterized by logical reasoning, but consideration in thought is limited to things actually present.

Conditioned response (CR)   A response, closely resembling an unconditioned response, that is evoked by a conditioned stimulus after conditioning has occurred.

Conditioned stimulus (CS)   A stimulus that, by being consistently paired with an unconditioned stimulus, comes to elicit a response.

Conservation   The permanence of certain attributes of objects or situations in spite of superficial changes.

Content words   The most important meaningful words in a sentence.

Continuity   A basic dimension of self-identity that is the sense of being the same person over time.

Continuum of caretaking casualty   The range of adverse factors in environmental and family situations.

Continuum of reproductive casualty   The range of variations in reproductive complications that result in abnormalities in the child.

Control The ability to sustain attention, to attend to relevant and ignore irrelevant information in the environment.

Conventional level The second level of moral judgment according to Kohlberg. Morality is a matter of conformity.

Conversational rules Turn-taking, knowing when one is being addressed, and clues concerning the right words for the right situations.

Correlational strategy A research strategy in which the investigator observes if and how two factors are associated with one another, but does not systematically change characteristics in the child's environment. From research using a correlational strategy one cannot infer causal relationships.

Correlation coefficient A numeric index of how closely two variables are associated with one another. The absolute value of the correlation coefficient indicates the strength of the association, whereas the sign of the correlation coefficient indicates the form of the association.

Counterconditioning A method for reducing fear in which the fearful stimuli that typically evoke emotional reactions are presented in conjunction with pleasant activities.

Crossing-over A process in which genetic material is exchanged between pairs of chromosomes.

Cross-sectional method A method of studying the development of children in which the ages to be compared are represented by different groups of children.

Cross-sectional/short-term longitudinal method A method of studying child development that combines characteristics of the short-term longitudinal method and the cross-sectional method. In this method two or more short-term longitudinal studies are undertaken simultaneously, with the oldest age at which measurements will be taken in one group being the youngest age at which measurements are taken in a second group.

Crying A state in which the individual has crying vocalizations associated with vigorous diffuse motor activity.

Cytoplasm The material that constitutes the cell other than the nucleus.

Deoxyribonucleic acid or *DNA* A substance that contains the genetic code that directs the functioning of RNA. DNA is composed of phosphate, sugar, and the base pairs cytosine and guanine and thymine and adenine.

Dependent variable That measure of behavior the experimenter anticipates will be affected by the change in the environment that is introduced during the experimental procedure. For example, one group of children is fed a nutritious breakfast and no food is provided for a second group, after which all the children's performances on a reading test are measured, in anticipation that eating breakfast will affect reading test performance. Reading test performance is the dependent variable in this experiment.

Depth perception The ability to perceive distance, usually in a downward direction.

DES (diethylstilbestrol) A synthetic hormone, prescribed to prevent miscarriages, associated with vaginal abnormalities and cervical cancer in adolescent female offspring of mothers who took the drug during pregnancy.

Desensitization A method for reducing fear in which a child is taught to relax in the presence of successively more fearful stimuli until there is no anxiety even with the most fearful events.

Deviation IQ An index of intelligence that indicates how far above or below the mean the individual's intelligence test score lies relative to children the same age in the standardization group. The deviation IQ score was first used in tests designed by David Wechsler but more recently has been adopted by the Stanford Binet Scale of Intelligence as well. For all groups the average deviation IQ score is 100.

Differentiation theory   A theory that proposes that perception develops as an individual learns to attend to, identify, and discriminate features in the complex sensory input available to him or her.

Dimension checking   Systematically checking all dimensions in a discrimination learning task.

Discrimination   The detection of differences in stimulus situations so that a learned response is exhibited only to some stimuli.

Dizygotic twins or *fraternal twins*   Two individuals, born at the same time to the same mother, who are no more genetically alike than siblings because they came from separate zygotes.

Dominant allele   An allele that is more likely to be expressed phenotypically than another allele that is less powerful.

Down's syndrome or *trisomy 21*   A disorder characterized by physical and mental retardation and a rather typical appearance and attributable to either translocation or nondisjunction of chromosome 21. In the most common cases individuals have 47 instead of 46 chromosomes, with 3 rather than 2 chromosomes of the twenty-first set.

Dream sleep or *REM sleep*   A period of sleep characterized by rapid eye movements as well as fluctuations in heart rate and blood pressure. In adults dreaming occurs in this period.

Drowsiness   A state in which the individual is relatively inactive; the eyes open and close intermittently; respirations are regular, though faster in regular sleep; when the eyes are open, they have a dull or glazed quality.

Echoing   A technique for facilitating a child's verbal response that includes imitating part of the child's utterance but replacing unintelligible parts with one of the "wh" question-producing words of English.

Ecological psychology (Environmental psychology)   The subfield of child development that examines the impact of the child's daily social and physical environment on the child's development (for example, the impact of air pollution on development or the effect of school size on children's learning).

Ectoderm   The outer layer of the inner mass of the zygote, which gives rise to the hair, nails, and part of the teeth; the outer layer of the skin and skin glands; and the sensory cells and the nervous system.

Ectomorph   A body type that is thin with poor muscular development.

Egocentrism   The inability of the child to perceive situations from the perspective of others.

Eidetic imagery   The ability to visualize for several seconds or minutes things seen only for a short period of time.

Electromyographic recording   A sensitive recording of muscle movements.

Empathic stage   The third stage of expectations about friends, which emerges at about grades 6 and 7 and in which self-disclosure, understanding, and shared interests occur: "chumship."

Endoderm   The inner layer of the inner mass of the zygote, which gives rise to the gastrointestinal tract, trachea, bronchi, eustachian tubes, glands, and vital organs such as the lungs, pancreas, and liver.

Endomorph   A body type characterized by a softness and spherical appearance and the underdevelopment of muscle and bone.

Enrichment theory   A theory that proposes that each time an individual perceives an object, the individual learns a little more about the object and elaborates his or her schemata.

Erythroblastosis   A result of Rh blood incompatibility between mother and fetus, which results in the destruction of the red corpuscles and in an inadequate oxygen supply to the fetus.

Estrogen   female hormones.

Expansion   A language interaction in which an adult imitates and expands or adds to the child's statement.

Experimental strategy A research strategy in which the experimenter introduces a change into the child's environment and then measures the effects of that change on the child's subsequent behavior. The experimental strategy allows for the inference of causal relationships.

Exploratory drive A need for new experiences and information, and a curiosity about objects and events.

Exposure to a fearless model A method for reducing fear in which a child watches a model act fearlessly, thereby reducing fear in the child.

Extinction A procedure for decreasing the frequency of a behavior. In classical conditioning, the CS is presented alone; in operant conditioning, the anticipated reinforcer is withheld.

Factor analysis A statistical procedure that groups together test items or tests that are highly related to each other and that are relatively independent from other groups of test items or tests.

Feedback Responses to pupils' performance by a teacher to reward right answers or to correct errors.

Fetal Alcohol Syndrome A group of associated malformations in children born to alcoholic mothers including facial, heart, and limb defects, small stature, mental retardation, and behavioral abnormalities such as irritability, hyperactivity, distractibility, and stereotyped motor behaviors.

Field experiment An experimental strategy in which the investigator deliberately introduces a change in a naturalistic setting rather than in the laboratory.

Focusing The narrowing down of alternatives by logically eliminating all disconfirmed attributes in discrimination learning tasks.

Free verbalization A subject's description of a model's actions in the subject's own words.

Functional value An aspect of an object that makes it relevant to the attainment of an individual's goals.

Galumphing Fanciful, exaggerated roughhousing or dramatic play.

General activity level A measure derived from general activity including gross and fine motor movements.

General rules Rules for forming inflections on words that can be applied to novel material.

Gene A segment of DNA that forms the genetic code that will participate in directing an individual's development.

Genotype The material, inherited from an individual's ancestors, that makes the individual genetically unique.

Gestures Nonverbal signals used in communication with or without words.

Giving affection and personal acceptance A type of positive social reinforcement characterized by physical and verbal affection.

Giving positive attention and approval A type of positive social reinforcement characterized by attending, offering praise and approval, offering help, smiling, informing someone of another child's needs, and conversing with the child.

Gradient of generalization The principle that states that the greater the similarity between the original situation and the generalization situation, the greater the probability that the same behavior will be exhibited in the two situations.

Habituation The decrease in responsiveness over trials as a result of repeated presentation of a stimulus.

Heterozygous alleles Two differing alleles in an individual at a particular locus.

Home-based intervention program A program that takes place in the home and that focuses attention on the parent-child relationship and on improving the natural support systems of the family in order to facilitate the development of intellectual performance.

Homozygous alleles Two identical alleles in an individual at a particular locus.

Horizontal decalage Inability to solve some problems even though other similar problems requiring the same mental operations can be solved.

Hormone A powerful and highly specialized chemical substance that interacts with cells capable of receiving the hormonal message and responding to it.

Humanity A basic dimension of self-identity that is the sense of having capacities and experiences found only in humans.

Hypothesis checking Checking each possible attribute one at a time in a discrimination learning task.

Identification The Freudian term for the acquisition of the behavior and values of a model.

Identification with the aggressor or defensive identification A term used by Freudians to explain a child's acquisition of the characteristics of a threatening parent or individual.

Imagery A strategy for remembering that involves visualizing objects and combining the stimuli in unique ways.

Imitation or *modeling* The learning-theory term for the acquisition of behaviors done first by a model.

Immanent justice The child's belief that punishment and other adversities are the direct result of transgressions.

Impulsive A cognitive style characterized by rapid, inaccurate responding.

Incidental memory score The number of correct responses for objects the child had not originally been asked to remember.

Independent variable The characteristic that is changed by an experimenter in order to assess its effect on a second measured behavior. For example, if one group of children is fed breakfast and no food is provided for a second group, with the hope of discovering the impact of breakfast eating on reading performance, breakfast eating would be the independent variable.

Index of autonomic stability A composite measure of autonomic functioning.

Individuality A basic dimension of self-identity that is the sense of being a unique person, that there is no one else like oneself.

Induced verbalization A subject's description of a model's actions in the experimenter's words.

Inflections Variations in words which express different grammatical relations.

Innate releasing stimulus An environmental event that evokes a complex response having an inherited species-specific structure.

Input The amount of teaching in a classroom.

Instrumental aggression A form of aggression where the aggressive behavior is used as a means for attaining a goal.

Intelligence quotient (IQ) An index of an individual's performance on a standardized test of intelligence relative to the performance of others his or her age. The original intelligence quotient was calculated as follows:

$$\frac{\text{Mental age}}{\text{Chronological age}} \times 100$$

In many cases this formula has since been replaced by the use of the deviation IQ score.

Interagent inconsistency The inconsistency that arises when one adult punishes a behavior while another adult either ignores or encourages the same behavior.

Internalization　The process by which the basis of moral behavior shifts from external factors to personal feelings and ethical beliefs and which results in self-control.

Intersexuality or *hermaphroditism*　The presence of some of the sexual characteristics or reproductive systems of both sexes in the same individual.

Intraagent inconsistency　The inconsistency that arises when one person treats the same behavior differently from one time to another.

Intuitive period　A period of development lasting from 4 to 7 years of age, marked by the apperance of certain mental "operations" to solve problems; yet the child is not aware of the principles used in these operations.

Invariants　Characteristics of objects, or relationships among objects, that do not change under different conditions.

Irregular sleep　A state in which the eyes are closed; the body engages in variable gentle limb movements, writhing, and stirring; grimaces and other facial expressions are frequent; respirations are irregular and faster than in regular sleep; and there are interspersed and recurrent rapid eye movements.

Irreversibility　A characteristic of preoperational reasoning in which an individual fails to see that every logical operation is reversible, that is, can be returned to its original state.

Klinefelter's syndrome　A sex chromosome abnormality in which an extra chromosome is present in every cell. These Y individuals are males, but they are sterile and have feminine breasts and hips.

Lability　The frequency of spontaneous fluctuations in the autonomic nervous system.

Locus　The position of a gene on a chromosome.

Longitudinal method　A method for studying child development in which the same child or children are repeatedly observed at different ages.

Long-term memory　Knowledge of the world and memory for past events and experiences.

Mainstreaming　An educational practice whereby special children are integrated into regular classrooms.

Mediational deficiency　The inability to use verbal labels to assist remembering.

Mental age　An index of the child's absolute performance on a test of intelligence. If a child's performance is the same as that of an average 4-year-old, he or she is said to have a mental age of 4 years.

Mesoderm　The middle layer of the inner mass of the zygote, which gives rise to the muscles, skeleton, excretory and circulatory systems, and inner skin layer.

Mesomorph　A type of body build that is athletic and characteristically muscular, broad-shouldered, and large-boned.

Metalinguistic awareness　The knowledge that one knows language and can reflect, think, and talk about language.

Metamemory　Knowledge about memory including awareness of the limits of one's own memory ability, of what things are difficult or easy to remember, and of when a task or situation needs special strategies to aid memory.

Minimal brain dysfunction　A diagnostic label applied to children who exhibit behaviors similar to those found in children with known organic damage, but who do not show organic abnormalities detectable by present neurological tests.

Modifier gene　A gene that influences the action or phenotypical expression of other genes.

Monozygotic twins or *identical twins*　Two individuals, born at the same time to the same mother, who are genetically alike because they come from the same zygote.

Moral absolutism   The child's complete acceptance of rules imposed by others. Rules are seen as unchanging and to be followed without question.

Moral development   The gradual process by which the child internalizes society's standards of right and wrong.

Morality of reciprocity   The second stage of Piaget's cognitive-developmental theory of moral development. This mature stage of morality includes the child's understanding and acceptance of social rules and his or her concern for equality and reciprocity.

Moral judgment   Making decisions about right and wrong behavior.

Moro reflex   A reflex in which the arms are thrown out in extension and then brought toward each other in a convulsive manner; hands are fanned out at first and then clenched tightly. This reflex is in response to a loud sound or jarring or to a sudden head or body drop of a few inches.

Mutator gene   A gene that controls the rate of mutation in other genes.

Myelination   The development around nerves of an insulating fatty sheath that facilitates the speed of transmission of neural impulses.

Natural experiment   An experimental strategy in which the investigator capitalizes on a change in the world that occurs naturally rather than deliberately causing the change to happen (for example, a court decision to bus children or a power failure).

Normative stage   The second stage of expectations about friends, which occurs about grades 4 and 5 and in which similar values and attitudes toward rules and sanctions appear.

Norms   A statistical description of how a large group of people perform on a test that can be used to compare an individual's performance with that of people from the normative groups.

Object-centered stage   The first stage of infant social interaction; the children are interacting, but they are usually directing most of their attention toward a toy or object rather than toward each other.

Objective responsibility   The child's concern with a specific behavior and its consequence rather than with its intent.

Object permanence   A recognition that objects continue to exist even when they are no longer perceived.

Observational learning   The acquisition of new responses or the elicitation of old responses as a result of viewing the behavior of another individual (who is called the model).

Operant conditioning   A procedure for changing the probability that a certain response will be exhibited because of following the response with a consequence.

Operation   The internalized mental equivalent of a behavioral schema.

Organization   The predisposition to integrate and coordinate physical or psychological structures into more complex systems.

Overall measure of background stimulation   A composite measure consisting of noise level, general activity level, the presence of distinctive versus overlapping sounds, and frequency of sudden unexpected sounds.

Overregularization   The application of a rule to form regularities in cases where the adult form is irregular and does not follow the rule; for example, "goed" for "went."

Ovum   The female gamete or egg cell; a special cell that carries the genetic material of the mother.

Partial isolation   A condition in which monkeys were deprived of mothering, fathering, and the opportunities for physical interaction with peers, but were allowed to see and hear other young monkeys.

Passive sentence   A sentence in which the object of the predicate precedes the predicate and the actor follows the predicate.

Peers   Social equals who are similar on characteristics such as age or developmental level.

Period of formal operations   Piaget's fourth stage of intellectual development, characterized by flexible, abstract thought, complex reasoning, the consideration of multiple alternatives, and hypothesis testing.

Period of the embryo   The period of development during which differentiation of the most important organs and systems occurs. In human organisms it extends from the beginning of the third week to the end of the eighth week after conception.

Period of the fetus   The period of development marked more by the growth of existing systems rather than by the establishment of new systems. In humans it extends from the eighth week after conception until birth.

Period of the ovum   The period of development of the fertilized ovum or zygote between fertilization and implantation.

Permissiveness   A parental practice in which few or no restrictions are placed on children.

Person-oriented or *hostile aggression*   A form of aggression usually directed toward others, involving behaviors such as criticism, ridicule, tattling, or verbal disapproval. This form of aggression is used most frequently by older children.

Phenotype   The way an individual's genotype is expressed in observable or measurable characteristics.

Phenylketonuria   A disorder, caused by a recessive gene, that leads to the absence of an enzyme necessary to convert phenylalanine into tyrosine. This leads to an accumulation of phenylpyruvic acid, which has a damaging effect on the developing nervous system of a child.

Phocomelia   An anomaly associated with thalidomide; limbs are missing, and the feet and hands are attached to the torsolike flippers.

Phoneme   The shortest speech unit in which a change produces a change in meaning.

Phonology   The system of sounds for a language, that is, how the basic sound units (phonemes) are put together to form words and how the intonation patterns of phrases and sentences are determined.

Placenta   A fleshy disc attached to the uterus through which food and waste products are exchanged between the maternal and infant systems.

Plane of action   The level of cognition dominated by sensorimotor experiences.

Plane of thought   The level of cognition dominated by mental operations.

Planfulness   The ability to process certain selected types of useful information in accord with a plan or strategy.

Play   A nonserious and self-contained activity engaged in for the sheer satisfaction it brings.

Postconventional level   The third or highest level of moral judgment according to Kohlberg. Morality is based on self-chosen ethical principles. This level is generally occupied by mature individuals.

Pragmatics   The rules governing the use of language in context by real speakers and listeners in real situations.

Preconceptual period   A period of development lasting from 2 to 4 years of age, in which systems of representation appear.

Preconventional level   The first or lowest level of moral judgment according to Kohlberg. Morality is based on the consequences of behaviors. This level is generally occupied by young children.

Prematurity   Birth occurring before full term with accompanying low birth weight and biological immaturity.

Preoperational period Piaget's second stage of intellectual development, characterized by the beginning of the use of the symbolic function and thought processes limited by such things as irreversibility, centration, and egocentrism.

Prepared responses Certain response systems that infants are biologically prepared to exhibit efficiently very early in life. In humans, these are typically associated with feeding.

Production deficiency The lack of production of verbal labels that would assist remembering.

Progesterone A female hormone.

Prompting A technique for facilitating verbal response that includes rephrasing statements to make them easier to understand.

Prosocial behavior Positive behavior such as helping, sharing, cooperation, and altruism.

Punishment The technique of pairing a noxious stimulus with a particular response, with the result that the response is less likely to occur.

Range of reactivity Genetically based variations of an individual's responsiveness to environments.

Realistic thinking Distortion in logical thinking. The child's belief that his or her perspective prevails.

Recessive allele An allele that will not be expressed phenotypically when combined with a dominant allele. Recessive alleles are expressed when they are homozygous.

Reciprocal imitation A behavior pattern in which individuals imitate each other.

Reflective A cognitive style characterized by slow, accurate responding.

Reflective organism An individual whose thought processes include symbolic thought.

Reflex An involuntary response of the body to an external stimulus.

Reflexive organism An individual whose behavior is dominated by inherited perceptual and motor patterns.

Regular sleep A state in which the eyes are closed and the body is completely still; respirations are slow and regular; the face is relaxed, with no grimace, and the eyelids are still.

Rehearsal A strategy for remembering that involves repeating words subvocally or aloud.

Representational process The process of storing and later retrieving verbal or symbolic images of the model's actions.

Response generalization The substitution of different but related responses to the same stimulus.

Reward-cost stage The first stage of expectations about friends; it emerges at about grades 2 or 3 and is characterized by similar expectations, common activities, and propinquity (nearness).

Rh factor One aspect of blood type that can result in fetal erythroblastosis when the child is Rh-positive and the mother Rh-negative in type.

Ribonucleic acid or RNA The messenger carrying the DNA-originated directions from the nucleus of a cell to its cytoplasm. These directions lead to the synthesis of proteins, which make up the body.

Rooting response A reflex in which the head is turned toward a finger touched lightly to an infant's cheek. The infant opens her mouth and tries to suck the finger.

Round The total pattern of alternating turns forming a rhythmic ritual in play.

Rubella Also known as German measles; a common disease that generally is not serious in children or adults, but that can cause blindness and mental retardation in children born to mothers who contract the disease during the first three months of pregnancy.

Schema   A mental representation of an external event.

Schemata (sing.: schema)   The cognitive structures underlying organized patterns of behavior.

Schizophrenia   A severe mental disorder in which emotional and cognitive disorders occur often, resulting in bizarre behavior and beliefs.

Selective attention   The focusing of attention on only certain parts or selected aspects of experience.

Self-concept or *self-identity*   The complex network of cognitions, emotions, motives, values, and behaviors that is unique to each person.

Semantic generalization   A type of stimulus generalization that arises when two situations share the same meaning or conceptualization, or when two situations belong to the same class or linguistic group.

Semantic integration   The extension or reinterpretation of information on the basis of reasoning or meaning.

Semantics   The study of the meaning of words and of sentences.

Sensorimotor period   Piaget's first stage of intellectual development, characterized by intelligent motor and perceptual acts beginning with reflexes and gradually becoming more flexible and extending to a variety of situations. The culmination of this period is the emergence of symbolic thought.

Sex chromosome   A chromosome that is responsible for sex-related characteristics in individuals. Females have two X chromosomes, and males have an X chromosome and a Y chromosome.

Sexuality   A basic dimension of self-identity that is the awareness of femaleness or maleness.

Shaping   A procedure for teaching a response by reinforcing closer and closer approximations to the desired response.

Short-term longitudinal method   A method for studying child development that is identical to the longitudinal method in that the same child or children are observed repeatedly at different ages; but the span of age over which the observations are made is limited to a few months or years rather than the decades often required in a long-term longitudinal study.

Short-term memory   The process by which people remember over a brief period of time.

Sickle-cell anemia   A severe, chronic, often fatal form of anemia caused by recessive genes.

Sickle-cell trait or *sicklemia*   A condition in which individuals are heterozygotes who carry one recessive gene for sickle-cell anemia and a dominant gene for normal blood cells.

Simple interactive stage   The second stage of infant interaction; children respond to the behavior of peers and often try to regulate the behavior of the other child.

Size constancy   The tendency of an object to retain its size in our perception regardless of changes in viewing distance, even though the size of the retinal image changes.

Sociability or *introversion-extraversion*   The range of behavior from inhibited, apprehensive, and withdrawn behavior to outgoing, self-confident, and gregarious behavior.

Social cognition   The ability to understand the viewpoints, emotions, thoughts, and intentions of oneself and of others, and the ability to think about social relations and institutions.

Socialization   The process whereby an individual's standards, skills, motives, attitudes, and behaviors are shaped to conform to those regarded as desirable and appropriate for the individual's present and future role in society.

Social misfits   Individuals with depressed social initiative and motor control, high levels of fearfulness, and misdirected hostility.

Special children   Children who either are physically handicapped or learn more slowly or quickly than average children.

Sperm cell   The male gamete; a special cell that carries the genetic material of the father.

Stage of coordination of secondary schemata   A period of development lasting from 8 to 12 months of age, in which a child uses or combines previously acquired schemata as a means of attaining goals.

Stage of moral realism   The first or earliest stage of Piaget's cognitive developmental theory of moral development. This early stage reflects a simplistic, conforming approach to morality.

Stage of primary circular reaction   A period of development lasting from 1 to 4 months of age, in which an infant repeats and modifies the basic motoric functions of her own body.

Stage of reflex activity   A period of development lasting from birth until the end of the first month of life, in which infants refine their innate responses.

Stage of secondary circular reactions   A period of development lasting from 4 to 8 months of age, in which an infant's attention becomes centered on the manipulation of objects rather than focused on his body.

Stage of tertiary circular reactions   A period of development lasting from 12 to 18 months of age, in which a child actively experiments with objects in order to learn more about his environment.

Stage of the invention of new means through mental combination   A period of development lasting from 18 months of age onward, in which mental combinations replace the overt explorations and manipulations of the previous period.

State   A point along the continuum of alertness or consciousness ranging from vigorous activity to regular sleep.

Stimulus-augmenter   An individual who subjectively experiences a stimulus as more stimulating than does the stimulus-reducer.

Stimulus barrier   A group of responses, similar to those found in deep sleep, which serves to shut out unwanted stimulation.

Stimulus generalization   The process of transferring previously acquired responses from one stimulus situation to a new context.

Stimulus preference   The selection of the same attribute even when that attribute is not correct.

Stimulus-reducer   An individual who subjectively experiences a stimulus as less stimulating than does the stimulus-augmenter.

Submission   Passive acceptance, imitation, sharing, accepting another's idea or help, allowing another child to play, compromise, following an order or request with pleasure and cooperation.

Sucking   A highly organized response pattern, ready to operate at birth, which is both the principal means of feeding and a distress-reducing activity.

Sudden Infant Death Syndrome or *crib death*   An as yet unexplained phenomenon in which infants die in their sleep without a known cause.

Symbolic function   The appearance of systems of representation such as language.

Syntax   The structure of a language; the underlying rules that specify the order and the function of words in a sentence.

Telegraphic speech   Utterances made up of content words, such as in a telegram.

Teratogen   An agent that raises the incidence of deviations or produces malformations in the course of prenatal development.

Testosterone   A specific male hormone.

Test reliability   An indication of whether the test performance of individuals is consistent and stable; that is, if the test were to be taken on two separate occasions by the same person under identical circumstances, would that person's performance remain constant.

Test validity An indication of whether a test measures what it claims to measure.

Thalidomide A sedative and antinausea drug that, if taken by the mother early in pregnancy, is associated with a number of anomalies, the most characteristic of which is phocomelia.

Total isolation Deprivation of all contact with other living creatures. For monkeys placed in this condition, there was no contact even with caretakers.

Transformation The process by which a change occurs.

Turn Each child's verbal or nonverbal contribution in a social exchange.

Turner's syndrome A sex chromosome abnormality in which only an X chromosome is present in each cell (XO). These females are small and have a characteristic appearance.

Umbilical cord A soft tube composed of blood vessels carrying blood to and from the infant and the placenta.

Unconditioned response (UCR) The particular response elicited by the unconditioned stimulus.

Unconditioned stimulus (US) A stimulus that can elicit reliably a particular response (the UCR) without any prior learning.

Unidirectional view of development A viewpoint stressing the influence that adults, particularly parents, have on the behavior of children while ignoring the potential impact that children may exert on the behavior of adults.

Visual cliff An elevated glass platform divided into two sections. One section is a "shallow" side with a textured surface immediately below the glass; the other section is a "deep" side with a surface several feet below the glass.

Waking activity A state in which the individual frequently engages in diffuse motor activity involving the whole body; the eyes are open, but not alert, and respirations are grossly irregular.

Zygote The fertilized ovum formed by a sperm cell penetrating and uniting with the ovum at conception.

Name Index

Subject Index